Contemporary
Arab
Thought

Contemporary Arab Thought

Cultural Critique in Comparative Perspective

Elizabeth Suzanne Kassab

Columbia University Press
New York

Columbia University Press
Publishers Since 1893
New York   Chichester, West Sussex

Library of Congress Cataloging-in-Publication Data

Kassab, Elizabeth Suzanne.
   Contemporary Arab thought : cultural critique in comparative perspective / Elizabeth
Suzanne Kassab.
      p.   cm.
   Includes bibliographical references and index.
   ISBN 978-0-231-14488-9 (cloth : alk. paper) — ISBN 978-0-231-14489-6 (pbk.: alk.
paper) — ISBN 978-0-231-51617-4 (e-book)
   1. Civilization, Arab—20th century.   2. Criticism (Philosophy)   3. Criticism—Arab
countries.   I. Title.
   DS36.8.K356   2009
   909'.0974927082—dc22

                                                                            2009024406

Columbia University Press books are printed on permanent and durable acid-free paper.
This book is printed on paper with recycled content.
Printed in the United States of America

p   10 9 8 7 6 5 4 3 2
c   10 9 8 7 6 5 4 3 2 1

References to Internet Web sites (URLs) were accurate at the time of writing. Neither the
author nor Columbia University Press is responsible for URLs that may have expired or
changed since the manuscript was prepared.

COVER & INTERIOR DESIGN BY **MARTIN N, HINZE**

Certains, parmi nous, se sont écroulés et sont tombés dans la servitude du jour; d'autres continuent à maintenir, coûte que coûte, la tâche politique militante, si nécessaire, dans le cadre d'un parti, d'un syndicat ou d'une organisation plus ou moins secrète. D'autres sont morts ou continuent de survivre à la torture infligée. Mais qui, parmi nous—groupes et individus—a pris en charge le travail effectivement décolonisateur dans sa portée globale et déconstructive de l'image que nous nous faisons de notre domination, exogène et endogène? Nous sommes encore à l'aube de la pensée mondiale. Mais nous avons grandi dans la souffrance qui appelle sa force de parole et de révolte. Si je te disais qui que tu sois, que ce travail a déjà commencé et que tu ne peux m'entendre que comme survivant, peut-être écouteras-tu alors la lente et progressive marche de tous les humiliés et de tous les survivants.

—ABDELKEBIR KHATIBI,
"Pensée-autre," in *Maghreb pluriel* (1983)

Some among us collapsed and submitted to the servitude of the day; others continue to maintain at all costs the politically militant task, so necessary, within the framework of a party, trade union or more or less secret organization. Others have died or continue to survive the torture inflicted upon them. But who among us—groups or individuals alike—has undertaken the real decolonizing work in its global reach of deconstructing the image that we have created of our domination, both exogenous and endogenous? We are still at the dawn of global thinking. But we have grown up in the suffering that calls upon us to use the might of the word and revolt. If I were to tell you, whoever you are, that this work has already started and that you cannot hear me only as survivor, maybe you will then listen to the slow and progressive march of all the humiliated and all the survivors.

—translation by
HARRY HAGOPIAN

Contents

Preface

Growing up in Lebanon in the second half of the twentieth century, I could not imagine the Arab world without anguished debates on culture. The Arab mind was for me invariably associated with questions of cultural crisis, the need for and the impediments to cultural renewal, the necessity of cultural affirmation and preservation, the dangers of Western cultural invasion, the cultural glory of the past and its centrality as a source of inspiration and pride, and the lamentable cultural decline of the present, as well as questions of Islam, modernity, authenticity, tradition, and progress. For me, being Arab was synonymous with being preoccupied with these issues—with having an unhappy consciousness of the self and the world. It was difficult for me not to think that there was something "Arab" to this state of mind and almost unimaginable that people other than Arabs could have such preoccupations. This view led me to suspect that it was something in us—in our tradition, our religion, our "character"—that gave rise to this predicament, this unhappy state of mind. It also produced in me and fellow Arabs around me an overwhelming sense of solitude, of people overburdened with problems, who think they are the only ones to have them and who feel embarrassed for not being able to overcome them. For more than two centuries, our sole interlocutor has been the West, to which we have tried to measure up, from which we have tried to learn, and against which we have defended ourselves in often fruitless polemics and apologetics—a sterile fixation that has reinforced the sense of solitude as well as the sense of a threatened, defeated, and impotent self.

These Arab debates were for a long time on the fringes of my awareness. My education, typical of the Lebanese system, taught me next to nothing about them. But this neglect is not a Lebanese peculiarity alone. It applies to almost any student graduating in the Arab world, whether from high school or university. In the best cases, he or she would know something about the medieval Arab literary or theological heritage and perhaps something about modern Western intellectual history, but next to nothing about the modern and contemporary Arab intellectual debates, which, although ubiquitous in the media and often part of the political discourse, are nowhere taught in a serious and systematic manner, not even in the quite rare liberal humanities programs. It was after completing my graduate studies in philosophy in Europe and my return to Beirut for teaching that I developed a keen curiosity for local discussions. It was only then that I started to explore actively the region's cultural debates.

My training in continental European philosophy and my prolonged stay in Europe introduced me to the Western debates on culture and showed me the link between much of European philosophical debates and the cultural, social, and political history of Europe. It was quite a surprise for me to discover that those "rich and happy" people, Westerners, also had debates about cultural crisis and cultural identity. It is with great interest that I read the writings on *Kulturphilosophie* and examined the discourses of numerous European thinkers on the "Idea" and identity of Europe. I was fascinated by the whole phenomenon of identity construction. I was equally surprised by the U.S. discourses on cultural identity, especially by their attempts at affirming a distinct character and an intellectual maturity with respect to Europe. On the whole, I envied Westerners for having the freedom to examine in considerable depth the pressing questions impacting their societies and histories. What were Arabs' questions, though? Who was raising them and discussing them? In which publications, in which fora? I decided to undertake a personal investigative search, and this book is to a large extent the fruit of this investigation. It aims in the first place at identifying those questions in a systematic and comparative manner. A rigorous philosophical reflection on them would have to be elaborated and pursued after the questions are identified, for how can one engage in a philosophical activity if one has not determined one's questions first? Isn't philosophy first and foremost the art of articulating and pursuing questions? For an established philosophy department in the region (and such departments are not numerous) to adopt such a project as a truly philosophical project is a challenge in itself. To bring philosophy to serve the cause of thought, in the sense of an elaboration of one's questions, outside the mainstream tracks of Western or medieval Islamic philosophy necessitates a battle of its own. The standard objection that "this is not philosophy" is facile. The uses and abuses of philosophy as an established discipline are also many in our part of the world.

The comparative examination of the Western and Arab debates could not completely break the isolation of the Arab discourse, however. It was rather the discovery of a whole set of non-Western debates that finally opened up for me the way to unsuspected connectedness and exchange. From the African American debates to the African, Caribbean, South Pacific, Native American, Latin American, and Indian ones, a whole universe of discourse so familiar to an Arab in its issues, approaches, and challenges unfurled itself before me. Here were people who were not Mediterranean or Arab or Muslim, yet who raised questions not very different from ours and who struggled with challenges not dissimilar to ours. This discovery was for me momentous. It showed me that obsessive concern with cultural issues had nothing "Arab" about it and that we were not the only ones on earth to have been arrested by them. It obviously indicated that the raising of those issues had something to do with conditions that went beyond Arab givens. What are the similarities that cut across regions, religions, cultures, languages, ethnicities, and races? What new understanding of our own Arab concerns can they offer? What new light can they shed on the very nature, motivations, functions, and patterns of the discussions on cultural malaise and cultural critique in the non-Western postcolonial world? Finally, what Arab specificities can be identified in such a comparative reading?

In presenting the results of this exploratory journey, I discuss the main thinkers, publications, conferences, and themes of contemporary Arab cultural critique. I then place them in a comparative perspective by looking at European, U.S. American, Latin American, and African debates on cultural critique. My hope is that this preliminary study will serve as a groundwork for future analyses focused on specific notions and issues in a broad comparative framework.

Over the years, I have channeled my research into a wide range of courses that I have designed and taught at different universities in Lebanon and abroad. Class discussions, whether at the American University of Beirut and the University of Balamand in Lebanon or at Columbia and Yale in the United States, contributed substantively to the development of this project. To all students who participated in these classes, I am much indebted. I also benefited from several research stays in Europe and the United States. Professor Oswald Schwemmer, chair of philosophical anthropology and philosophy of culture at the Institute of Philosophy of Humboldt University in Berlin, hosted me in the summer of 2001 with a grant from the German Academic Exchange Program. In New York, Professor Richard Bernstein invited me as a Fulbright scholar to the philosophy department of the New School University in the fall semesters of 1999 and 2000. Between 2001 and 2004, I was visiting scholar at the Middle East and Asian Languages and Cultures Department of Columbia University. I thank Professors Hamid Dabashi and George Saliba for offering me the opportunity to teach courses in modern Arab thought in the department. I was happy to return to Columbia in the spring of 2008 as the Arcapita Visiting Professor of Modern Arab Studies at the Middle East Institute of the School of International and Public Affairs, headed then by Professor Rashid Khalidi. I also had a very productive academic year in 2006–2007 at the Macmillan Center for International and Area Studies of Yale University; I was a visiting professor in the Middle East Council, chaired at the time by Professor Ellen Lust-Okar and had been recommended to the council by Professor Hala Nassar from the Yale Department for Near Eastern Languages and Civilizations. Ari Ariel, my former student and Ph.D. candidate at Columbia read the entire manuscript and made numerous helpful suggestions. In Beirut, Marie-Thérèse, Abboudi, and Marwan Abou Jaoudé, owners and managers of al-Furat bookstore, over the years provided me with books and contacts that were not always easy to obtain otherwise. Copy editor Annie Barva transformed my Lebanese English into readable prose and helped me tidy up a mammoth manuscript that was written over a whole decade. My editor, Wendy Lorchner, supported the publication process of this book with enthusiasm and patience. I owe all these people as well as many other colleagues and associates my deep and sincere gratitude.

Contemporary
Arab
Thought

Introduction

Cultural Malaise and Cultural Identity in Twentieth-Century Western, Postcolonial, and Arab Debates

A rab thinkers, artists, and activists have been engaged for almost two centuries now in intensive debates about cultural identity, cultural decline, and cultural renewal. Questions of the cultural self have dominated conferences, publications, and political gatherings. From one turn of the century to the other, questions of cultural anguish have persisted: How are we to define ourselves? Are we Arabs or Muslims in the first place? What does Arabhood mean? How is Islam to be understood? Why have we lagged behind while others in the world have progressed? How can we change and modernize without becoming westernized and losing our souls? How can we recuperate our past glory, our dignity, our pride, and our previous political, military, scientific, economic, and cultural might? Is religion the cause of our decline? Should it be the source of our renaissance? Is secularism what we need? What kind of secularism? Has political oppression been the cause of our cultural crisis, or has our culture produced consecutive despotic regimes? Why haven't we been able to establish Arab unity? Why have we been incapable of instituting democracy? Why haven't we been able to vindicate our cause in Palestine?

These questions have been constant preoccupations of Arab debates on culture and politics. In spite of their apparent redundancy, they have solicited different approaches and changing attitudes in the course of the past century. Most Arab thinkers agree that the defeat by Israel in 1967 was a turning point in Arab popular and intellectual consciousness. It was a political and intellectual crisis that called for a reassessment and a revisiting of the modes of thinking that had prevailed as well as of the political and intellectual struggles that had hitherto been adopted. It necessitated an urgent reflection on the liberation and decolonization movements that had failed to achieve their goals. It led to the radicalization and polarization of two major trends: on the one hand, the search for totalizing doctrines, especially religious doctrines after the demise of the Left and of secular nationalism, and, on the other hand, the radicalization of critique. The first trend was the result of a deep yearning for a holistic vision that could offer an indigenous, nonalienating worldview and mobilize the necessary forces toward a way out of the humiliation and the oppression. The second was the outcome of a painful confrontation with the limitations and dangers of holistic views as well as of the growing realization of the vital need for critique in the face of multiple forms of oppression. Although numerous studies have been devoted to the rise of the ideological doctrines, especially the Islamist ones, very little has been written on the less noisy and less spectacular, but important growth of critique.[1] Yet the latter is as much part of the Arab social and intellectual scene as the former, and this book aims at redressing the balance by devoting due attention to it.

Like in any other society, whether in the West or elsewhere, this critical trend in Arab society represents a vulnerable but no less significant minority trend, especially in the region's volatile political and economic conditions. It is at the heart of the self-reflective turn of contemporary Arab thought. Unfortunately, it has not been sufficiently recognized by Arabs themselves, who often seem to be raising questions of culture from scratch, with nothing to build on. Many Arab thinkers have complained about this lack of continuity and accumulation in transgenerational intellectual work. This book takes stock of this recent critical effort and assesses its strengths and weaknesses, challenges and promises.

The twentieth century witnessed the collapse of the Ottoman Empire, which ruled over the area for about four centuries, and the first attempts at replacing it with a united Arab state. The Western powers, mainly Great Britain and France, animated by vested interests in the fall of the Ottoman Empire, supported these attempts, albeit ambiguously. They promised to support the creation of a united Arab state but did not keep their promise. Their intervention resulted in the division of the region into British and French mandates and in the thwarting of a united Arab state project. These mandates' official aim was to "help" their populations reach maturity and then independence. A wave of national struggles eventually achieved at least formal independence in the 1940s, 1950s, and 1960s. These independent states were ruled first by the old established notables and monarchs. In the aftermath of the creation of the state of Israel in 1948 and especially after the 1967 defeat of the Arab armies by this state, the 1960s and 1970s saw these established rulers replaced by revolutionary, often secular regimes that promised to adopt a more dedicated patriotic line. Most of these regimes turned out to be repressive ones, however. Those in power played the two oppositional forces, the Left and the Islamists, against one another, causing the collapse of the Left and effecting an intense power struggle with the Islamists. Finally, the last three decades of the twentieth century witnessed the increase of neocolonial and neoliberal pressures on the area, culminating in the two Persian Gulf wars and the U.S. invasion of Iraq.

It is against this sociopolitical and historical background that critical Arab thinkers have been reflecting on their societies' major concerns. This background is far from being homogeneous across the Arab world. In fact, the Arab east, North Africa, and the Persian Gulf—constituting what is designated as the "Arab world"—are very different from each other. Within every subregion, the socioeconomic, political, historical, and cultural givens differ from one country to another and from one society to another; moreover, many of these societies are multiethnic and multireligious. Nevertheless, the debates taking place in these diverse countries and societies show basic connections that affirm their belonging to a common, general universe of discourse.

Questions of cultural malaise, cultural critique, and cultural identity have not been the concerns of Arabs alone. In fact, they have been central themes of preoccupation for other postcolonials as well. They have also been major topics of discussion for Europeans and U.S. Americans in the course of the twentieth century. They have become prominent at particular historical junctures and have embodied a whole array of moral, political, and epistemological concerns. Discourses on cultural selfhood have expressed complex motivations, preoccupations, and intentions. They have often been confusing mixtures of descriptive and normative statements about what one "ought" to be on the basis of what one in essence "is" and "has always been." They have been founded on selective constructions of history that have often been presented as "natural givens" of history or metaphysics or both. They have invariably been shaped by power elements that determine who enunciates these discourses in a given community, at what given point in time, under what circumstances, through which mechanisms, and for what purposes. Exercises of cultural self-identification have acquired particular significance in times of crises and in times of ominous threats and changes, both in Europe and outside Europe.

In Europe, discourses on "Europe" held by European thinkers proliferated with the growing malaise of the turn of the twentieth century, then with the shock of World War I, the unrest of the 1920s and 1930s, the rise of fascism between the two world wars, the devastations of World War II, and more recently the formation of the European Union. Thinkers such as Friedrich Nietzsche, Max Weber, Ernst Troeltsch, Georg Simmel, Edmund Husserl, Martin Heidegger, Max Scheler, Karl Jaspers, Albert Schweitzer, Paul Valéry, Denis de Rougemont, Emmanuel Lévinas, and Jacques Derrida—to name but a few—offered conceptions of and reflections on European culture. Their discourses presented analyses of the specificities of European culture and often at the same time exhorted their societies to return to their foundational cultural values. In the 1990s, Derrida deconstructed the prevalent pattern of "thinking Europe" among these thinkers, calling it the "semantico-archeo-teleological" scheme of thinking Europe. He critically analyzed the assumptions made about a clearly "given" entity called "Europe," about the original *arche* serving as its foundations (Greek philosophy, Roman law, Judeo-Christian legacy) and about the *telos* toward which this Europe is believed to be inexorably progressing (enlightenment, reason, progress).[2] On the whole, these twentieth-century European discourses on Europe are self-referential; that is, their authors address what they consider to be their own culture in terms of that same culture, even when contrasting it with other cultures, such as the "Oriental," the "primitive," or the U.S. American culture. In places dominated at some point or other by Europe—that is, much of the rest of the world—discourses on cultural matters have had Europe at the center of their elaborations, both as addressee and as reference. Given Europe's overwhelming impact on these societies, colonial, anticolonial, and postcolonial discourses on culture have been fixated to a great extent on political and cultural Europe.

By *postcolonial*, I mean the time following the end of official colonialism and formal independence—a time, as we know, not free from unofficial or even official forms of external hegemony and occupation, whether political, military, or economic. By *official colonialism*, I mean both the occupation of lands and the subjugation of peoples by regular armed forces and official administrations in Africa, India, and the Middle East, as well as the colonizers' settling of lands and the enslavement of the indigenous and transferred peoples in the Americas, the Caribbean, and the South Pacific. In the carefully elaborated essay "Notes on the 'Post-colonial,'" Ella Shohat critically examines the many connotations of the term *postcolonial* and raises questions about its ambiguities, its "ahistorical and universalizing deployments," and its "potentially depoliticizing implications."[3] I adopt her cautionary remarks and use the term *postcolonial* here to mean the "post-anti-colonial critique" that she defines in the following way:

> *The term "post-colonial" would be more precise . . . if articulated as "post-First/Third Worlds theory," or "post-anti-colonial critique," as a movement beyond a relatively binaristic, fixed and stable mapping of power relations between "colonizer/colonized" and "center/periphery." Such rearticulations suggest a more nuanced discourse, which allows for movement, mobility and fluidity. Here, the prefix "post" would make sense less as "after" than as following, going beyond and commenting upon a certain intellectual movement—third worldlist anti-colonial critique—rather than beyond a certain point in history—colonialism; for here "neo-colonialism" would be a less passive form of addressing the situation of neo-colonized countries, and a politically more active mode of engagement.[4]*

The United States, like postcolonial countries in Latin America, Africa, India, the Middle East, and elsewhere, has striven since independence to assert a cultural identity of its own, inevitably related to, yet distinct from that of its former colonial power. This search has taken on a special relevance at particular junctures of its history, such as the turn of the twentieth century and the accumulation of industrial and financial wealth, World War II and the fracture of the cultural authority of Europe, the rise of multicultural and multiracial voices in the second half of the century, and finally the post–Cold War confrontation with terrorism. Interestingly, World War II more than World War I seems to have had a significant impact on the discussions about culture in both the United States and Latin America: European

culture, which had for so long shaped the culture of these two regions, imposing itself as the ultimate standard for authentic culture, was severely shaken
by a brutal inner European war that was later to involve other powers, including the United States. Philosophers from the United States and Latin America
set up an Inter-American Congress of Philosophy, first in Haiti in 1944 and
then in New York City in 1947 at Columbia University, to discuss the following questions: Had the time come to speak of U.S. and Latin American cultures that are independent and distinct from European culture? What place
would philosophy have in the constitution of this distinct character? It is interesting to note that whereas for the Latin Americans the question was
whether a country could develop an independent philosophy and a distinct
culture under conditions of economic and political weakness, for the U.S.
Americans the question was whether wealth and power could allow for genuine culture to emerge. Almost four decades later, at the eleventh meeting of
this same Inter-American Congress of Philosophy, held in 1985 in Guadalajara, Mexico, and devoted to "America and its philosophical expression,"
U.S. cultural imperialism had become the major issue of contention between
North and South American philosophers even in such a supposedly abstract
discipline as philosophy.[5] Indeed, in the decades following World War II,
"Euro-American" culture had become the hegemonic "Western civilization"
with which much of the rest of the world had to wrestle.

   Within the U.S. American postcolonial search for cultural selfhood, a
clear awareness of political, military, and economic might has remained
a constant factor. This awareness has been absent in most of the other postcolonial searches. Some of the persisting U.S. concerns throughout the
past century have been: What kind of culture can and should wealth
produce—a culture for the elite or a culture for the masses? Can mass culture be genuine culture? How is culture to be made relevant to American
realities? How is U.S. American identity to be defined? How is U.S. culture
to relate to and be demarcated from European culture? What is to be done
about the country's alleged anti-intellectualism? Can high culture and democracy coexist? Is the melting pot to produce a uniform culture? If yes,
which one? If no, how are cultural diversity and unity to be reconciled? Are
race and ethnicity relevant in defining U.S. culture? Can patriotism and
critique be compatible? Is it possible to reconcile the country's defensiveness vis-à-vis the Soviet Union and now Islamic terrorism with freedom of
thought, dissent, and pluralism?

   For much of the rest of the postcolonial world, the search for a sense of
cultural self has accompanied the struggle against European colonialism

and then U.S. neocolonialism in general under conditions of political, military, and economic weakness. This struggle has aimed at liberating lands from foreign occupation and exploitative hegemony, but also at recovering an empowering sense of self after having been defined, denigrated, and defeated by others. This quest for an affirmative sense of self has proven to be arduous. It has involved a sustained effort at intellectual and cultural decolonization under adverse conditions of economic underdevelopment, political subjugation, intellectual confusion, and psychological pain, and it has led to the following questions: How is one to regain dignity and pride without falling into self-glorification? How is one to recover from self-hatred and overcome despair? What does it mean to have a culture of one's own and a thought of one's own? What is the link between having an identity of one's own and having a philosophy of one's own? How does one establish such an identity or philosophy? What are the pitfalls and temptations of cultural authenticity and cultural essentialism? How does one reappropriate one's own history after it has been told and made by others? How does one recuperate one's own legacy after it has been denigrated and abused by others? How can one re-create a living relationship with one's history and heritage after one has been estranged from them by colonial alienation? Which history? Which heritage? Who is to decide and on what basis? How are history and heritage to be revived when modernization seems to be the urgent need of the day? Is it possible to traditionalize and modernize at the same time? Is it possible to modernize without becoming westernized? Which intellectual tools are appropriate for the creation of viable and coherent postcolonial meaning references? How is the sense of gap between ideas and realities in postcolonial settings to be understood, analyzed, and remedied? What are the importance and limits of contextualizing and historicizing ideas? What does intellectual decolonization imply? What is the role of language in intellectual emancipation? What are the possibilities and challenges of making cultural decolonization into a project of modernity and enlightenment? What is enlightenment for postcolonial societies? What does critique entail in a postcolonial situation? How does the gendering of critique contribute to the search for an empowering sense of cultural self? And finally, how does one affirm oneself and exercise critique at the same time?

The colonial legacy, the neocolonial constraints, and the disenchanting experiences of postcolonial independent states compound greatly the complexities of dealing with these questions. They multiply the pressures under which the issues of cultural selfhood are perceived and approached.

Such pressures include, first, the need to defend and restore a positive sense of self: an urgent and defensive need that leaves little room for raising questions, but that necessitates instead a robust sense of a solid, determinately and often deterministically fixed self, calling in all sorts of essentialized and naturalized notions of the self. It is also a need that favors recourse to apology and polemics, in which the essentialized definition of self given by the colonial Other is very often simply reversed and given a positive valence instead of the colonial, negative one. Second, there is the pressure to catch up with the West economically, politically, socially, and culturally, which precipitates the search for quick analyses, readily given models of explanation, and available ideologies that are imported at a time when autonomous intellectual agency is emphatically necessary for a sense of self. These quick solutions are typically adopted by postindependence voluntaristic and coercive states that want to implement fast policies of modernization and development with little or no tolerance for open debates on matters of public concern, often under new conditions of economic and political dependence.

Neither of these pressures leaves much room for raising questions of one's own, for taking the time to understand and analyze one's own particular situation, for developing an intellectual honesty in confronting realities, for expressing one's views and discussing them with other members of the community, or for imagining possible solutions to the given problems. All of these activities are already daunting given the complexity of the problems and the human tendency for complacency, facility, avoidance, and passive victimhood. In other words, these pressures cripple the already exigent faculty of thinking. Yet, as numerous postcolonial thinkers have come to realize with increasing clarity in the course of the past century, only genuine critical thinking can lead the way out of all the damage and the multiple forms of servitude. The greatest challenge for post- and neocolonial peoples is to restore for themselves this alienated capacity to think critically, especially at a time when they feel most tempted by totalistic visions and ideologies. In *Portrait du colonisé, précédé du portrait du colonisateur (The Colonizer and the Colonized)*, Albert Memmi describes well this colonial/postcolonial predicament:

> *The colonized's self-assertion, born out of protest, continues to define itself in relation to it. In the midst of revolt, the colonized continues to think, feel and live against and, therefore, in relation to the colonizer and colonization. . . .*

So goes the drama of the man who is a product and victim of coloniza-
tion. He almost never succeeds in corresponding with himself. . . .

Before and during the revolt, the colonized always considers the
colonizer as a model or as an antithesis. He continues to struggle
against him. He was torn between what he was and what he wanted
to be, and now he is torn between what he wanted and what he is
making of himself. Nonetheless, the painful discord with himself
continues.[6]

This "corresponding with oneself" is the authentic sense of self sought by postcolonial thinkers. Memmi summarizes the challenges of this quest: "It is obvious that he [the colonized person] is reclaiming a people that is suffering deficiencies in its body and spirit, in its responses. He is restored to a not very glorious history pierced through with frightful holes, to a moribund culture which he had planned to abandon, to frozen traditions, to a rusted tongue. The heritage which he eventually accepts bears the burden of a liability which would discourage anyone."[7]

In a much later book on the topic, *Portrait du décolonisé Arabo-musulman et de quelques autres (Decolonization and the Decolonized)*, Memmi offers a typology of the "new citizen" of the decolonized states and of the "immigrant" in Europe who comes from the decolonized countries, with a focus on the Arab Muslim. He wants to understand why decolonization so rarely succeeded. Unfortunately, this work does not help us move toward such an understanding. His description of the failures of the postcolonial state and society is often accurate, and his reluctance to put them all on the account of colonialism is well taken, but his claim about the absence of self-reflective critical thinking in decolonized societies in general and in the Arab Muslim world in particular is unfounded. In his introduction, he says: "This examination should have been undertaken by the elites in the countries under discussion, but for reasons that also required explanation, they seem to have been overcome by a strange inability to think or act, so that, through their own acquiescence, they have given free rein to the most backward among them."[8] Memmi seems to be unaware of the whole corpus of critical thinking that had accumulated since his earlier work on the topic in the late 1960s. The close examination of this corpus undertaken here dissipates much of the "strangeness" of this "inability" and shows the typicality of the challenges in thinking and reaching a healthy sense of self across the regions, religions, cultures, and languages of the colonized world.

In the struggle for cultural decolonization, the former colonial power or the present neocolonial power, meaning the West in general, has been the main addressee and reference, even when it is being attacked. The exchange has often taken the form of the polemical, apologetic, and rhetorical debate "us versus them." Both the actors in this struggle and the scholars studying it have directed their efforts at a one-to-one confrontation between the given society and the West in isolation from other comparable struggles in other societies of the postcolonial world. Although this isolationist approach is understandable, at least insofar as the actors are concerned given the West's overwhelming impact on their real and intellectual lives, it has had detrimental effects on both actors and observers. It has accentuated the misunderstanding of these various cultural struggles and facilitated their reduction to some essentialist element or other, be it race, religion, ethnic origin, tradition, or language. In some instances, it has supplied false arguments for an unfounded exceptionalism. This isolationist approach has also prevented an exchange from taking place between peoples of comparable experiences and strivings, thus leaving a whole potential of sharing and learning untapped. Furthermore, it has averted attention from these debates' decolonization context.

Only a comparative reading of postcolonial discussions about culture can lay bare their postcolonial conditions and enable us to explore their systemic nature across regions and cultures. The many commonalities found in the cultural debates carried out in linguistically, religiously, culturally, and racially different regions clearly indicate that their issues and problems cannot be due—at least not solely and not deterministically—to the specific language, religion, culture, or race of a given region. Rather, the economic, political, and historical conditions of colonialism and neocolonialism have had and continue to have a most crucial role in producing them and shaping them. Moreover, the comparative perspective enables us to see the particular forms that debates surrounding cultural decolonization take in each region given the region's particular historical, economic, social, political, and cultural characteristics. It helps clarify the specificities and particular challenges of each setting. Consequently, it can be a powerful tool against the various forms of culturalism, essentialism, and misplaced exceptionalism. Furthermore, bringing together several postcolonial debates can allow for a conversation to emerge between postcolonial thinkers and thus for a cross-pollination to occur among related concerns and kindred projects. By the same token, it can lead postcolonial actors engaged in cultural decolonization to have a wider perspective on their problematics and to grasp better the systemic nature of these problems. As a result, it can help them relinquish an often exclusive and essentialist fixation on the religion, race, and tradition of each of their societies and address the more fundamental nature of the cultural malaise found in the postcolonial predicament.

More than any other regional debate, the Arab one has remained relatively unknown, misrepresented, isolated, and stigmatized with exceptionalism. It has generally been approached in an essentialist way that reduces its discourses to a certain literate Islamic heritage, with little attention paid to the context and historicity both of the discourses and of the heritage. This essentialist approach has confined the understanding of these discourses to an immanent, ahistorical tradition and has isolated them from other regional discourses. Yet the reading of Arab debates in conjunction with other debates such as the African, the Latin American, the South Asian, the Caribbean, the African American, and the Native American reveals important commonalities and shows that the concerns and patterns of these debates go beyond immanent traditions. Among these commonalities are the search for a thought of one's own, which implies the search for ways of defining such a thought as well as the need to link ideas to concrete local realities and histories; the importance of contextualizing Western thought and of determining the parameters of the universal and the particular; the unveiling of the role of expanding capitalism and conquest in what is presented as "universal" thought; the importance of distinguishing fake Eurocentric universalism from the principles of universal reason; the concern with the pitfalls of self-affirmation manifested in chauvinism, parochialism, and the cult of difference; the caution against a culturalist-idealist understanding of the cultural malaise, oblivious of the global political and economic aspects of the dependency problematic; the challenges of traditionalization and modernization in the project of cultural decolonization; the need to ponder the place of gender in these questions of postcolonial cultural malaise and the call to rethink authenticity, cultural loyalty, and the nationalist community from a gender perspective; the necessity of double critique in the struggle against both external and regional hegemonic forces, on the one hand, and the internal repression and authoritarianism in postcolonial states, on the other; and, finally, the indispensable need for democracy as well as individual and civil liberties. In all these debates, the quest for a liberated, empowered, and distinct sense of self dominates, checked by a whole array of intellectual, cultural, economic, political, and often military challenges. This book examines contemporary Arab debates on culture from this broad perspective, bene-fiting from the wider, comparative understanding of the nature of these debates. The comparative reading sheds new light on the motivations, purposes, structures, and challenges of these postcolonial discussions of culture.

This work is not a comprehensive intellectual history of the post-1967 era, but an examination of its cultural debates. It breaks new ground in the understanding of contemporary Arab intellectual life by viewing it from three original perspectives: first, it focuses on the self-reflective critical turn at a time when attention has almost exclusively been devoted to the ideological side of this intellectual life, whether Islamist or nationalist; second, it recognizes and examines the political understanding of the cultural malaise among critical thinkers, an understanding that has been systematically overshadowed by both actors' and observers' culturalist reading of the malaise; and third, it breaks the isolation in which the production and study of the Arab debates on culture have been hitherto confined, mainly by putting them in a comparative postcolonial perspective.

Hence, the main questions the book explores are:

How has contemporary Arab critique approached questions of cultural malaise? Which issues has it addressed, and what shape has this critique taken?

To what extent and in what sense have Arab critical thinkers of the post-1967 era seen the cultural crisis as a political one? How old is this political perception of cultural problems in modern Arab thought, and what are its implications for the democratic struggle in the Arab world?

How do the concerns expressed and approaches adopted in these Arab debates compare with debates in other postcolonial regions of the world, such as Africa and Latin America? What patterns of thought does such a comparison reveal across regions, cultures, religions, and races? What does it tell us about the postcolonial nature of the Arab debates, and what relevance does this telling have for our understanding of contemporary Arab thought?

I selected the thinkers presented throughout the book on the basis of the significance of their contribution to the debates of concern here, irrespective of their geographic location and the language of their publications. More than half of them live and work in the Arab world and publish in Arabic. Some of them live abroad and publish in European languages (French, English, and German). Their works are sometimes translated into Arabic and discussed in Arab intellectual circles. Others publish both in European languages and in Arabic, visit the Arab world regularly, and participate in public and academic events there.

Chapter 1 initiates the discussion with a brief survey of the mid-nineteenth-century to mid-twentieth-century Arab cultural renaissance, known in Arabic as the Nahda (meaning "rise"), and focuses on the main issues of cultural malaise, cultural decline, and cultural renewal addressed by the leading figures of this period. The need for such a survey is twofold: first, the Nahda forms the historical background of the contemporary debates; second, it constitutes one of the main preoccupations of these debates. The concern regarding the failure or success of this early renaissance, the question of the effectiveness of its legacy, and the continuity of many of its themes and issues has occupied a central place in discussions of the late twentieth century and beyond.

Chapter 2 presents the ideas of five leading figures of the post-1967 era who expressed most emphatically the need to radicalize critique in the wake of the dramatic events of the 1967 defeat. It examines the arguments of their major works: Saadallah Wannous's in drama and culture, Qustantin Zurayq's in history and civilizational theory, Sadeq Jalal al-Azm's in philosophy and enlightenment, Abdallah Laroui's in history and ideology, and Nawal el-Saadawi's in gender and sexuality. Despite their differences in discipline and temperament, all five thinkers focus on the necessity of reclaiming people's critical faculties as citizens and as human beings. They urgently call for sobriety in the midst of a crisis that invites totalistic, escapist, and compensatory ideologies. They also call for self-criticism, a reexamination of certain prevailing modes of thinking, and a reassessment of the Nahda legacy. They set the tone of post-1967 Arab critique.

Chapter 3 looks at the wider discussions about culture in three major pan-Arab conferences—the 1971 Cairo conference, the 1974 Kuwait conference, and the 1984 Cairo conference. It also examines the critique that was made of these conferences and of the issues raised in them from Marxist, epistemological, and psychological points of view. Cultural modernity, cultural heritage, and cultural authenticity were these conferences' central themes, and they were approached from different angles and with different levels of critical acuity and consistency. Tradition and the past occupied a major place in the conferences, and there seemed to be a great need for self-affirmation and a strong urge to compensate present weaknesses with past achievements. Moreover, culture seemed to serve as a self-explanatory phenomenon. For Mahdi Amil, these tendencies showed an inclination to intellectualize the cultural malaise and to neglect its socioeconomic roots. For Muhammad Abed al-Jabiri, they were indicative of a certain making of the "Arab mind." And for Georges Tarabichi, they were an expression of a form of collective neurosis affecting most Arab intellectuals, caused by the unresolved trauma of the defeat.

The next two chapters pursue the lines of critique in theological and secular thought respectively. Chapter 4, on critical Islamic theology, examines the efforts made to introduce a new understanding of revelation and scriptural interpretation, to suggest new or renewed methods of contextualization and historicization in exegetical reading, and to add a comparative perspective that draws on both the classical Islamic legacy and recent findings in the humanities. It presents critical theologians' insistence on the human reception and transmission of the divine message. It discusses the feminists' unveiling of the gender and class biases in the making of the classical religious tradition, hitherto assumed to be neutral and objective and hence unquestionable. It shows these critics' concerns about the ideological mobilization of religion. Moreover, it looks at some attempts at developing a theology of revolution and a theology of liberation in Islam, but also in Christianity, particularly by Christian Palestinian theologians. The secular critics discussed in chapter 5, however, reflect on the difference between the secular discourse of the recent fin de siècle and the discourse of the previous fin de siècle, on the greater challenges facing the present discourse, but also on the importance of maintaining it because of these challenges. For these critics, maintaining this discourse means continuing public debates on a human—that is, nonabsolutist—level. It also means paying attention to historical realities instead of confining discussions about culture to an abstract level distorted by essentialist assumptions about history, heritage, identity, and Islam. It necessitates for these critics the problematization of the notion of the "indigenous" and shows the importance of a "double critique," internal and external. Moreover, it entails a reconsideration of the religious conception of what is called "Islamic civilization" and a sharp critique of the whole conciliatory pattern of thinking about Islam and modernity.

Chapter 6 locates these Arab debates in the broader Western and postcolonial contexts by looking at debates on cultural malaise in late-nineteenth-century and early-twentieth-century Europe, United States, Latin America, and Africa. It starts by presenting briefly the leitmotivs of the turn-of-the-century German *Kulturphilosophie*, related to the social, political, cultural, and social-scientific crisis of the time. It connects these leitmotivs to the wider European malaise articulated with particular intensity around World Wars I and II. Then it presents some of the major themes debated at about the same time in the United States, themes that are already postcolonial in nature in that they aim at affirming or questioning the existence, value, and viability of a distinctly and authentically U.S. culture with respect to that of old Europe. These U.S. postcolonial concerns are in turn compared and contrasted to those of its southern neighbors, the Latin Americans, who were raising similar questions about their own culture, but from a clearly poorer economic and political position. To the Latin American survey is added the African one, with its own themes and concerns. The focus on the Latin American and African cases stems from the desire to compare and contrast the Arab debates with non-Asian, non-Islamic, and non-Arab ones. In looking at the similarities and differences between all these debates, the chapter spells out certain common patterns of questioning and thinking in postcolonial concerns. Moreover, it sheds light on the shifting priorities of these debates in the latter part of the twentieth century, from issues of identity to issues of democracy, from essence to agency, and from ideology to critical thinking. The commonalities as well as the specificities of each region, especially the Arab one, are articulated.

Finally, the conclusion looks at how present Arab thinkers evaluate the second Nahda in some of their most recent statements, four decades after the dramatic defeat of 1967, at a time of unprecedented military, political, economic, and cultural turmoil in the Arab world.

In sum, the book offers reflections on the challenges of cultural decolonization in the Arab world in particular, but also around the globe in general—on the difficulties of thinking from a damaged self caught between a colonial past and a neocolonial present, between an external dependency and an internal social and political oppression. It ponders the trials faced in creating a healthy and empowering sense of cultural self under the most adverse circumstances. It measures the challenge of thinking from a disrupted sense of history, a distorted sense of reality, and a disturbed sense of self across regions, religions, cultures, languages, and traditions in postcolonial settings.

One
The First Modern Arab Cultural Renaissance, or Nahda

From the Mid–Nineteenth Century to the Mid–Twentieth Century

The modern Arab debates on culture date back roughly to the mid–nineteenth century, a time when most Arab lands had been under Ottoman rule for three hundred years, since the sixteenth century. The waning Ottoman Empire had started to lose control over some of its territories to breakaway nationalist movements: Greece in the early 1820s and the Balkans in the 1870s. It had suffered military defeats at the hands of one of its major rivals, Russia, in consecutive battles in 1806–1812, 1828–1829, 1853–1856, and 1877–1878. It was also facing growing financial and economic difficulties. For many Ottoman officials, economic, administrative, technological, and even political modernization had become necessary for the empire's survival. The extent and modality of the needed changes gave rise to a wide range of discussions and the formation of various political currents advocating reform. The mounting challenges of the empire also invited a growing intervention by European powers who were eager to benefit from the weakening Ottoman state. These trends resulted in the 1839–1876 Tanzimat reforms, a set of new laws that were to transform Ottoman subjects into equal citizens, irrespective of their religious and ethnic affiliation. It led to the establishment of a modern constitution and to the creation of a representative parliament in which Arab delegates were included. Provisions were also made to guarantee commercial privileges for Europeans. The principles of the reforms were declared in 1839 and 1856 in official statements known as the Gülhane decree and the Hatt-i-Humayun, respectively. These Tanzimat reforms were met with resistance by the sultans, who did not want to see their power being restricted by a fundamental law, as well as by the military and administrative classes, which had likewise much to lose. The new laws were eventually passed, but the Constitution was suspended in 1876 by Sultan Abdulhamid (ruled 1876–1909) soon after it was established, then reinstituted by the revolutionary Young Turks in 1908, and then suspended again in 1912.[1]

The empire's cosmopolitan center was not the only site of such momentous transformations. Their echoes and effects reached regional centers such as Tunis and Cairo. These places had to deal with their own local needs for change as well as with growing European interventions: the Napoleonic invasion of Egypt (1798–1801), the French colonial occupation of Algeria (1830–1962), the imposition of a French Protectorate over Tunis (1881–1956) and Morocco (1912–1956), and the British occupation of Egypt (1882–1952). Since then, the constant political players in most Arab lands have been the diverse local populations with their communal politics; the local rulers, sometimes foreigners imposed upon the people by outside forces; the regional power brokers; and the international interventionist powers. The actors working for change have constantly had to play these players against one another in making their way through a complex landscape of conflicting interests and agendas.[2]

Over the course of the nineteenth century, Cairo developed into a center of Arab modernization and eventually became the seat of what was to be called the Arab Renaissance, or the Nahda. Muhammad Ali Pasha, of Albanian origin, ruled Egypt for the Ottoman sultan from 1805 to 1849.[3] He was eager to modernize and strengthen Egypt, primarily the army and the administration, in order to maximize his autonomy vis-à-vis the Ottoman state. He initiated a number of economic projects and sent groups of young men to study abroad, mainly to Paris, creating a stimulating circulation of new ideas that eventually gave rise to unprecedented intellectual debates and movements. All these socioeconomic, administrative, military, political, and cultural factors on the local, regional, and external levels contributed to the intensification of cultural and intellectual activities in the last decades of the nineteenth century and the early decades of the twentieth century. This intensification was expressed in literary and media productions, educational reforms, an important translation movement, the formation of intellectual salons and political secret societies, and the development of protonationalist and protofeminist movements.[4] The margin of freedom that Cairo enjoyed compared to other places in the empire, which came under the growing censorship of the Ottoman ruler, facilitated the proliferation of these activities. The fall of the Ottoman Empire in the aftermath of World War I pushed Arabs to redefine themselves outside of the Ottoman parameters and to articulate post-Ottoman visions for themselves. Pan-Arab, pan-Islamic, and more regional (Syrian, Lebanese, and so on) projects were elaborated and debated. The British and the French soon divided the area into spheres of influence among themselves, however, and imposed mandates on a fragmented Arab homeland. It took these newly created Arab entities a couple of decades to achieve at least formal independence. In the meantime, the struggle in Palestine was raging, and the founding of the state of Israel in 1948 was to become one of the most, if not the most, significant events of the century, engendering a whole set of political, military, socioeconomic, cultural, and human problems—all of which remain unsolved to our day. In sum, the Ottoman reform projects, the post-Ottoman political struggles, and the colonial encounters with Europe stimulated a range of debates within and about Arab societies that came to be known as the Nahda debates.

The consecutive defeats by Israel (1948, 1956, 1967) were followed by military coups in Egypt (1952), Iraq (1958), Syria (1963), and Libya (1969), with promises of a more successful vindication of national and Arab rights. These promises became the convenient pretext for the development of militarized and police states that repressed their populations without achieving any significant victory against Israel. These states prevented the democratic processes of intranational, political, ethnic, and religious conflict resolution. They disenfranchised people and suspended political life by perpetuating emergency laws. They cracked down on all forms of independent and oppositional voices, be they secular or religious. They monopolized power and put in place an elaborate system of corruption. They instituted harsh censorship, repressing freedom of thought and freedom of speech that eventually led to a deterioration of the whole educational system. It is against these repressive regimes that popular movements in recent years have tried to revolt, demanding the cessation of emergency laws, the reinstitution of civil rights, and the reform of the state in Egypt, Syria, Morocco, and elsewhere. But these reform movements, like those of the preindependence period, have to navigate through the multiple agendas of regional and international forces that continue to influence the Arab world.

Despite these adverse and oppressive conditions and under the impact of the shock of the 1967 defeat, a critical intellectual movement emerged in the few remaining pockets of freedom. Some of its leaders, such as Moroccan historian Abdallah Laroui, called this movement the "second Nahda." The movement's efforts consisted of radicalizing critique and reexamining the past endeavors for enlightenment and liberation. The circumstances of this second Nahda were obviously more somber than those of the first: it was clouded by a century of disillusionments, disappointments, humiliations, and defeats; it had a narrower margin of freedom owing to the more established systems of state repression and rising religious oppression; it had to deal with a greater cultural defensiveness that developed in reaction to the growing aggressions and defeats; and, finally, it had to face a despair that the first Nahda had not known. The gap between the two periods and moods is perceived to be so large that many post-1967 critics wonder where the legacy of the first Nahda went and why its hopeful promises and liberal impulses were aborted. In fact, reclaiming that legacy and understanding the reasons for the discontinuity with it became one of the central preoccupations of the second Nahda.

Despite this discontinuity, many of the first Nahda themes reappeared in the second one. Their persistence preoccupied contemporary thinkers. Some found in this continuity of themes an additional reason for despair, seeing it as a sign of intellectual stagnation and a manifestation of an incapacity for cumulative learning, whereas others tried to understand the reasons for this persistence. Given this double concern with the continuity and discontinuity between the two Nahdas, it is important here to state briefly the first Nahda's major themes—briefly because a full rendering of the complex set of phenomena and trends is impossible here. Albert Hourani's *Arabic Thought in the Liberal Age, 1798–1939*, still remains the main reference on the subject.[5]

The major first Nahda figures had basically five main preoccupations:

1.   *The rise and fall of civilizations.* Much of the Nahda writings turned around the causes of the rise and fall of civilizations, based on a comparative awareness of European and local Egyptian-Arab-Muslim realities

of the time. The intensifying contacts with Europe during the nineteenth century shaped a certain perception of this continent that accompanied analyses of the region. This perception changed as the type of contact changed, especially when European powers became colonial occupiers. On the whole, Nahda thinkers were eager to grasp the secrets of progress, to understand what lay behind Europe's advancement and superiority in the hope of adopting it to their own societies. For some, the interest was more focused on acquiring the means of power from Europe in order to use it against its colonial expansion. There was also the need to define oneself vis-à-vis this spreading culture and vis-à-vis the modernity that it brought with it: How was one to define Egyptian, Arab, or Muslim culture with respect to European culture? Were they related? Could one find some common origins, facets, constituents to them? Or were they incommensurable? The various answers emphasized political justice, science, religion, and gender in different ways.

2. *Political justice.* For a majority of Nahda thinkers, political justice was the basis of European advancement and the primary condition for the Arab Renaissance. The rule of law and the accountability of rulers were seen as necessary requirements for development. Criticism of despotism was a Nahda leitmotiv. Justice had always been a central notion in classical Islamic political thought. What is notable here is that it is identified as the cornerstone of progress in the perception of European civilization.

3. *Science.* Some regarded science as another cornerstone of European superiority. Some looked at it as a constitutive element of modern culture, rational thinking, and a new worldview. Others considered it mainly as an instrumental key to power that led to the production of technology and strategic know-how. The call for education was another dominant theme of the Nahda. The Arab press that was created and developed during this epoch disseminated nonreligious and modern knowledge, scientific discoveries, and world news. New schools were opened, and old ones were reorganized. Translations into Arabic were made, and students were sent abroad to acquire European training.

4. *Religion.* Religion was a major Nahda concern for many reasons. Comparisons with Europe raised questions about the link between religion and progress and about the difference in the links between Christianity-progress and Islam-progress. Was Christianity more conducive to progress, explaining the development of European civilization? Or was Europe's success due to the marginalization of religion? How did Christianity and Islam compare with respect to modernity?

5. *Gender.* Finally, gender behavior was a significant part of the comparative cultural evaluation and a domain in which the gaze of the colonial European Other played an important role. According to the colonial discourse, Islamic cultures were inferior to European culture and in need of colonial improvement because they advocated discriminatory treatment of women and tolerated male homosexuality. Feminist doctrines and conservative sexual ideas were used to justify colonial interference. Nahda thinkers, both men and women, had to react to these judgments and to define their positions regarding these questions. Modernity, feminism, sexual mores, colonialism, and civilizational worth were thus intricately entangled.

The first and most famous account of modern European civilization from this comparative perspective was Rifa'a Rafi' al-Tahtawi's (1801–1873) Paris diary. Published in Cairo in Arabic (*Takhlis al-Ibriz fi Talkhis Bariz*) in 1834, it was quickly translated into Turkish to serve as a didactic introduction to European modernity.[6] It became the landmark publication of the early-nineteenth-century Nahda. Its author, a Sheikh trained at al-Azhar,[7] had been sent to Paris to supervise a group of students between 1826 and 1831. Al-Tahtawi wrote down his observations and experiences of the French capital and upon his return founded a school of languages, from which he launched an important movement of translation. He subsequently wrote a number of books promoting modern education for girls and boys alike and urging the clergy to integrate secular modern disciplines in the training of its members.[8] His Paris diary, recently translated into English,[9] shows a wide interest in the life of the Parisians, ranging from the social and cultural to the economic and political. It presents neither an unbiased nor an unapologetic view of Paris, but rather a relatively candid and uninhibited perception of a foreign culture.[10] The author seeks to grasp the secrets of that city's progress in the hope of adopting them for his homeland, which, in his opinion, clearly lagged behind on many levels. Most of the time he is fascinated by what he sees, without feeling threatened in his Islamic-Egyptian identity. He does present justifications here and there for seeking principles of progress in a non-Muslim country and in nonreligious achievements. He asserts that his faith encourages Muslims to seek knowledge and wisdom wherever they can be found, that this European civilization is not totally foreign to Muslims because it is based on Islamic sciences imported into Europe in the Middle Ages, and that the achievements to be learned from were the product of human effort and not the product of Christianity per se—justifications that have become standard arguments in defense of foreign borrowing since then. However, on the whole, his tone is not defensive, and his general attitude is not judgmental. Al-Tahtawi writes with great curiosity about a wide range of aspects of Parisian life—social mores and customs, gender roles, the architecture and interior design of houses, the nature of indoor and outdoor entertainments; he describes shops, restaurants, coffee houses, ballrooms, theaters, and museums; he talks about the transportation system, the mail service, and taxes; he reports on hospitals, schools, and universities; he speaks about the press, economic institutions, and factories; and he gives a detailed account of the 1830 Paris uprising.

Among the things that impress him most are the general valorization of knowledge beyond the confines of religion as well as the spread of literacy, even among women. He is amazed by the passion for learning, whether through newspapers, journals, books, or traveling. He appreciates people's encouragement of change, innovation, and creativity, as well as their allegiance to their country. He notes the use of human reason as the ultimate criterion of judgment as well as the general attitude of religious tolerance. For al-Tahtawi, however, what constitutes the solid foundation of civilizational progress in Paris is political justice—that is, a system of government that is not arbitrary, but determined by a fundamental law that clearly sets the rights and duties of both the ruler and the ruled. He translates the French Constitution article by article, for even though, as he says, its contents do not come from revelation or the sacred tradition, they contain valuable human wisdom. He emphasizes the importance of holding the ruler accountable through representative bodies that decide on the laws of governance. Certainly, al-Tahtawi does not advocate the adoption of the French Constitution in Egypt, nor does he promote liberal democracy. His boss, Muhammad Ali, whom he praises for his support of learning and modernization, would not tolerate such proposals. But al-Tahtawi does emphatically assert that the abuse of power by and the ignorance of political and religious rulers are among the major causes of civilizational decline. Political justice is, for him, the necessary condition for subjects' well-being, for prosperity, and for the advancement of knowledge—in sum, the necessary condition for progress. He prefaces his translation of the French Constitution with the following statement: "We should like to include this book—even though most of what is in it cannot be found in the Book of the Almighty God, nor in the *sunna* of the Prophet—May God bless him and grant him salvation!—so that you may see how their intellect has decided that justice (*'adl*) and equity (*insaf*) are the causes for the civilization of kingdoms, the well-being of subjects, and how rulers and their subjects were led by this, to the extent that their country has prospered, their knowledge increased, their wealth accumulated and their hearts satisfied."[11]

The centrality of political accountability, the rule of law, and the importance of political representation in Nahda thought is not acknowledged enough, yet these principles are among its leitmotivs. Indeed, the critique of despotism in general and in connection with questions of culture malaise in particular permeates much of the Nahda writings. This political critique runs throughout twentieth-century Arab thought, but at times it is overshadowed by a culturalist bent and becomes dominated by an obsessive concern with cultural authenticity, especially in the 1970s and 1980s, for a number of reasons that I explore later. This bent has given both contemporary Arabs and others the prevailing and false impression that Arab thinkers have always been predominantly preoccupied with the cultural and religious aspects of their civilizational and societal problems. The fact is that the critique of political despotism has been a consistent object of grievance in modern Arab thought, and a political understanding of cultural crises has persisted across generations of thinkers. The proposed remedies have differed from one thinker to another, ranging from religious repentance and piety to theocracy, populist nationalism, liberal or socialist nationalism, and full-fledged democracy. Al-Tahtawi's rendering of the secret of European civilizational progress is among the first expressions of this political critique. Subsequent landmark works that formulated this critique most pointedly are, as we will see, Abdel Rahman al-Kawakibi's description of the facets and effects of political despotism drawn from his experience with the Hamidian Ottoman rule toward the end of the nineteenth century, Saadallah Wannous's denunciation of the Syrian Baathist despotic regime since the late 1960s, and more recently the growing prison literature across the Arab world, reflecting on the dictatorships that govern so many of its states.[12]

According to al-Tahtawi, the principles on which European progress was based had their equivalents in Islamic culture: justice was a core value of Islam, French patriotism corresponded to Islamic solidarity, and reason used in Western science was applied even in the most traditional of Islamic disciplines—jurisprudence. He was clearly concerned with pushing for these principles, while giving them an indigenous character and even a universal character. He seems to have believed in the possible adoption of these principles in the near future; he must have considered change and improvement to be possibilities within reach. The equivalences he established were conceptually and epistemologically questionable, to say the least, but the purpose behind them was clear and hopeful. Some late-twentieth-century critics found the lack of conceptual and epistemological sharpness to be one of the causes of this first Nahda's failure. I examine their claims later on.

The France that al-Tahtawi experienced in Paris became, together with Britain, an occupying power in the Arab region in the second half of the nineteenth century. This momentous change obviously impacted Arab perceptions of Europe, which was no longer seen primarily as the seat of civilizational progress, but as a concrete military, political, economic, social, and cultural threat. Its civilizational advantage continued to be acknowledged, but it was now perceived as a power advantage in a dangerous conflict. The search for the secrets of progress was transformed into a search for the means of power. Henceforth, the concern with power and the power struggle as well as with the perception of Europe as a threatening force would overshadow Arab reflections on culture, politics, and the West. There would be the technological Europe, the cultural Europe, and the political Europe: the first to be imitated for instrumental reasons, the second to be rejected for identity-preservation reasons, and the third to be resisted for sovereignty reasons. For some, such a differentiation misses the essential link between these facets, especially the first two—namely, the cognitive and the wider cultural, humanistic, and democratic facets— all the dialectics of Enlightenment and modernity notwithstanding. For them, the differentiation thwarts a truly empowering modernization and consequently perpetuates the status of backwardness and dependency. A coherent and constructive perception of the West through the complex prism of all these considerations obviously becomes increasingly difficult.

The weight of the European interferences was already present in the thought of Khaireddin al-Tunisi (1822–1890), the Tunisian politician and reformer born a generation after al-Tahtawi. With a similar exposure to European civilization during a stay in Paris, al-Tunisi, like al-Tahtawi, was convinced that the principles of progress and prosperity were freedom and justice, and, also like him, he tried to convince his compatriots that these principles were not Christian per se, but the modern equivalent of those found in the spirit of the shariʿa, the Islamic canon law. He articulated his ideas in a book he published in Tunis in 1867–1868, *Aqwam al-Masalik fi Maʿrifat Ahwal al-Mamalik* (The Straightest Path in Knowing the States of Kingdoms), and later reissued in Constantinople. In it, he refers to al-Tahtawi's

Parisian diary.[13] More than al-Tahtawi, al-Tunisi was actively involved in politics: he became minister and prime minister in Tunis and later grand vizier in Istanbul. In his political career, he tried to apply the principle of justice in both Tunis and Istanbul mainly by strengthening the ministers' power to limit the ruler's power—an effort that the rulers in question resented and defeated. At the end of his career, he was discouraged and disillusioned, realizing that reform and modernization necessitated willing rulers and understanding populations. He also realized that countries such as Tunis, which were the target of European (French, British, and Italian) ambitions, on the one hand, and of the Ottoman Empire's hegemonic influences, on the other, had a very difficult if not impossible balancing effort to make in order to survive and undertake the much-needed reforms, especially in the midst of severe financial problems. Such international, regional, and local constraints unfortunately still challenge reform endeavors in the region today.

The transformations in the perception of the West become even more pronounced in the writings of Jamal al-Din al-Afghani (1838–1897), another influential figure of the first Nahda, but of the latter half of the nineteenth century. He moved between India, Afghanistan, Istanbul, Cairo, Paris, and London, and worked as a thinker and political activist for the mobilization against the growing European imperialism.[14] For him, this resistance required power instruments on the one hand and solidarity among people on the other. The source of the first was science, and the foundation of the second was Islam. Hence, science was to be adopted no matter where it happened to be developed at the time, especially because, according to him, it was a universal good that had no cultural and national specificity. The Muslims had developed science in the past, and the Europeans were its leaders at the present. Moreover, Muslims had in the past creatively employed the principle upon which it was based, rationality, and simply needed to reactivate it in themselves. As to solidarity, no stronger bond than that of religion could provide a solid base for it. Al-Afghani did admit in his writings that the two requirements, science and religion, could work in contradictory ways—that Islam, like all religions, would inevitably impede the freedom of thought so necessary for science. He stated this reservation in his famous exchange with the French Orientalist Ernest Renan, who claimed that Islam was inherently inimical to rational and scientific thought. Al-Afghani retorted by saying that all religions, including Christianity, were inimical to free thinking.[15]

Al-Afghani was not much of a systematic intellectual, and conceptual coherence was not his priority. His aim was to mobilize and empower his

Muslim contemporaries against European imperialism. He was critical of Muslim political and religious leaders. For him, good leaders were those who were willing to be guided by his visions. Unfortunately, none of those he approached in the many countries where he stayed were ready to be persuaded or submit to his will. However, he did become vastly influential and inspired a number of thinkers who became prominent in their own right, among them the Islamic modernist Muhammad Abduh (1849–1905).

Whereas al-Tahtawi had sought to introduce some basic principles of modernity and civilizational progress into a relatively unshaken Islamic Egyptian world, Abduh strove to secure a place for Islam in that rapidly changing world. For this purpose, it was imperative to reconsider the out-moded aspects of Islamic theology and jurisprudence, and so to reopen the door for new doctrinal and legal interpretations that were more in tune with changing realities and demands. It is he who formulated most clearly the famous "conciliatory" or "middle" path of Islam: the path that concili-ates the basic tenets of Islamic faith and jurisprudence with the fundamen-tal principles of modernity—reason, science, and civilizational progress.[16] Abduh claimed that Islam, more than any other religion and certainly more than Christianity, was akin to modernity because it naturally incor-porated reason, justice, equality, and freedom in its creed. In fact, he went so far as to claim that modern Europe was Muslim in its modernity with-out realizing it.

The "middle" path Abduh advocated was a constructive alternative to the blind imitation of a rigid and outmoded Islamic tradition as well as to the blind imitation of European civilization. He admired the achievements of European modernity, but he did not believe they could be transplanted into Islamic Egyptian society. In legal matters, people needed laws based on their own tradition, a tradition that needed reform and that contained in itself the principles of that reform. Among the principles he recalled were the Islamic medieval distinction between the fixed dogmas of the Islamic creed and the contingent aspects of practical applications, which needed to be adapted to ever-changing realities, and the idea of the general welfare of the community of believers according to which rules and sometimes doc-trines could and needed to be adjusted. In the early centuries of Islam, knowledgeable and wise scholars had constantly undertaken such adapta-tions. However, this trend had slowed down and disappeared with time due to the general civilizational decline. The causes of this decline, accord-ing to Abduh, went back to ignorant and corrupt ulemas who had been neither willing nor capable of enlightening the people and to the despotic

Ottoman rulers who had encouraged and exploited the slavish acceptance of authority.

Against this obscurantist leadership, Abduh actively militated for a reform of the clergy, especially of its education. In 1899, he became mufti, or head of the religious-legal system, of Egypt. In this position, he was able to introduce some changes in the Azhar program and to unify, systematize, and modernize the religious law to some extent. Politically, he leaned toward a form of constitutional monarchy, and at times he favored the idea of a just despot who would lead the country into rapid necessary reforms. He was critical of the British occupation, but at the same time wary of Egyptians' unpreparedness to govern themselves, believing that a gradual emancipation through education and reform would be more secure. He was in general against arbitrary rule and thought that people should hold rulers accountable:

> *There is still another matter of which I have been an advocate. People in general are blind to it and far from understanding it, although it is the pillar of their social life, and weakness and humiliation would not have come upon them had they not neglected it. This is, the distinction between the obedience which the people owe the government, and the just dealing which the government owes the people. I was one of those who called the Egyptian nation to know their rights vis-à-vis their ruler, although this nation has never had an idea of it for more than twenty centuries. We summoned it to believe that the ruler, even it if owes him obedience, is still human, liable to err and to be overcome by passion, and nothing can divert him from error or resist the domination of his passions except the advice of the people in word and deed.[17]*

Muhammad Abduh remains a towering figure of the first Arab Nahda, associated with the middle-path strategy, premised on the possibility of combining Islam with modernity, but without distorting either of the two terms in any significant way. For many, this solution was ideal in that it promised the best of both traditions: it opened the way for the much-needed modernization of Islam *and* allowed for a critical appropriation of modernity not based on blind and superficial imitation. For some, however, this conciliation that conveniently shunned clear positions and avoided painful choices could not but twist each of the conciliation terms. In the final analysis, according to them, it failed to address the real and difficult questions of the lived present reality. Many critics during the second

Nahda would consider this prevailing middle strategy to be one of the major causes behind the first Nahda's failure, as discussed in chapter 5.

Muhammad Abduh believed in and worked for modernization, but he conceived of it within religious parameters. His project was one of Islamic modernization. Some of the thinkers who came under his influence, such as Ahmad Lutfi al-Sayyid (1872–1963), Qasim Amin (1865–1908), and Ali Abdel Raziq (1888–1966), emphasized the modernization aspect of the project and were eager to give increasing importance to secular human experience. Others, such as Lebanese Islamic cleric and scholar Rashid Rida (1865–1935), leaned more than Abduh on the sacred tradition and on the early Islamic period as the model and inspiration for modernization and renewal.[18]

Among Abduh's followers was the Lebanese diplomat, writer, and translator Shakib Arslan (1869–1946). Arslan traveled widely in the West (Europe, the Americas, and the former Soviet Union) and defended the Arab cause as a delegate of the Syrian-Palestinian congress. At the League of Nations, he advocated the termination of the French and British mandates over Syria and Palestine. He was also a close collaborator of Rashid Rida, who had moved to Egypt to work for Abduh. Rida established a journal called *al-Manar* and dedicated it to the cause of Islamic reform and Islamic modernism. It is to this journal that an Islamic cleric from Java forwarded the following question: "Why did the Muslims fall behind? And why did others progress?"[19] Arslan obliged the questioner with an essay putting his question in the title. The journal published the essay in 1930 as the booklet *Limadha Ta'akhkhara al-Muslimun wa Limadha Taqaddama Ghayruhum?* (Why Did Muslims Fall Behind and Why Did Others Progress?)[20] It was widely distributed, and Muslims and Arabs received it with great interest at the time even though the French colonial authorities in Algeria banned it. Reprinted several times since then, it is still read and referred to today in the Arab world.

In this booklet, Arslan starts by agreeing with the questioner regarding Muslims' miserable state of weakness and decline and sets out to search for the causes of this downfall, comparing it on the one hand to earlier times of Islamic history and on the other to the prosperity and power of the modern Western (North American and European) and Japanese nations. For him, the factor that had propelled the Muslims into a glorious civilization beyond the confines of the Arab Peninsula was, without doubt, Islam. It is clear, then, that the explanation of their decline should start from the quality of contemporary Muslims' commitment to their faith. But the elaboration of the explanation does not limit itself to an exhortation for religious revival or to a reflection on the adaptability of Islam to modernity. On the contrary, it contains a strong rejection of all forms of Islamic exceptionalism. Arslan clearly emphasizes that religion alone cannot be seen as the determining factor in the cultural rise and fall of any people: "I do not deny that religion has a relation to civilization and power over it. But it cannot be said that religion is always the final determinant of the tendencies of civilization, because the power and influence of religion over nations sometimes weakens, they slip out of its control. Degeneration then overtakes them and disintegration creeps into their social fabric. Degeneration of the national character is the true cause of a nation's decadence and religion cannot be held responsible for it."[21] Christian, Buddhist, pagan, and Islamic nations equally have known times of civilizational growth as well as times of civilizational collapse. He corroborates this point with examples from Greek, Roman, European, Japanese, and Arab histories.

This general trend proves for him that factors other than the religious—namely, the political, the economic, and the moral—are at work in the rise and fall of civilizations. It is on the moral civilizational virtues that he focuses his exhortation. The most important among them are self-confidence, seriousness in thought, thoroughness in knowledge, resolution in commitment, and readiness to sacrifice in the various domains of thought and action. He sees in defeatism and despair the biggest dangers to cultural and political empowerment. Thinking of foreign and in particular Western superiority—based on superior knowledge, superior wealth, and superior armament—as insuperable is doomed to be a self-fulfilling prophecy. For him, this superiority comes from a deep commitment to knowledge and to communal solidarity. Wealth, science, technology, and military power are the outcomes of such a commitment, not its premises. This relationship applies to all religious and national communities.

To blame Islam for Muslims' cultural, material, and political poverty is to misunderstand the nature of civilizational development and to misjudge the nature of Western modernity, Arslan argues. The West, in his opinion, is no less religious and no less attached to its traditions than the rest of the world. He enumerates a long list of European and other peoples, including the Zionists, who pride themselves on cultivating their traditions and customs. But curiously, he adds, it is the Muslims who are branded with the accusation of being "traditionalists." He then describes the Western powers' zeal in converting conquered and colonized peoples to Christianity—a zeal that is never characterized as fanatic, whereas Muslim piety constantly is. So instead of discussing the Muslim cultural malaise in terms of some alleged Islamic exceptionalism, he attacks the double standards with which Islam is judged by others; and instead of calling for a defensive Islamic cultural purity, advocated by Muslim conservatives, he calls for a moral empowerment through resolve and serious striving. He criticizes the Muslim conservatives who through their dogmatism transform Islam into a hindrance to cultural progress. He also attacks the "superficial ultramoderns," as he calls them, who advocate the total banning of religion from the civilizational project, falsely assuming that the West has achieved progress mainly by discarding religion. Rather than rejecting their religion, Arslan says, Muslims need to develop their will and their resolve in overcoming their misery and to remember that their holy book professes those virtues. Contrary to widespread prejudices, he adds, the Qur'an does not condone fatalism and passivity. It exhorts Muslims to help themselves in improving their worldly and spiritual situation in order to deserve God's help and blessing. Arslan quotes numerous verses from the Qur'an to prove his point. In the final analysis, the keys to this improvement, he says, are resolve and serious striving, loyalty and willingness to pay the necessary price for the needed empowerment, as well as faith in one's self and in God. It is interesting to note that Arslan's diagnosis of and remedy for the civilizational retardation were secular—that is, independent of religion in its essence. However, he did not advocate secularism. In fact, he had pan-Islamist leanings.

A number of Arab Christians advocated more pronounced secularism. Indeed, Christian Lebanese thinkers from the mid–nineteenth century onward offered nonreligious, though not antireligious (but sometimes anticlerical) and certainly not anti-Islamic, views of progress and identity. Their early exposure to Western modernity through contacts with Europe and through missionary schools and their Christian sociocultural backgrounds gave them a specific position in this cultural problematic, one with particular advantages and distinct inconveniences. Among the advantages were the greater familiarity with Western ideas and languages and the greater ease in dealing with them, given the lesser need for religious defensiveness. Among the inconveniences for them were their minority status in a Muslim majority that set limits for possible critique and their being neither Eastern Muslims nor Western Christians, but Eastern Christians, aware of their native Christian identity and keen on their Eastern allegiance that distinguished them from the Western missionaries and the Western powers. Some of them translated their alienation from the majority into a strong identification with Europe and a total estrangement from their own environment, whereas others denied all differences and their minority situation. Obviously, theirs was (and still is) a sensitive location, typical of all minorities.[22]

The early pioneers such as Nasif al-Yaziji (1800–1871), Ahmed Faris al-Shidyaq (1804–1887), and Butrus al-Bustani (1819–1883) advocated a vision of identity based on the Arabic literary heritage and common Arab history, as well as a solidarity around this identity across religious divisions, albeit within the Ottoman boundaries. They made significant contributions to the modernization of the Arabic language through translation (especially of the Bible under the auspices of the American missionaries) and creative writing, and to the compilation of modern knowledge, for instance through the Bustani encyclopaedia.[23] In 1870, al-Bustani founded *al-Jinan*, a periodical in which he advocated political justice as the basis for prosperity and civilizational progress. He insisted that political participation was necessary for good government, that politics had to be separated from religion and the judiciary from the executive, that taxation had to be properly assessed, and that education had to be compulsory. *Al-Jinan* was shut down in 1886 with the increasing Ottoman censorship. At about this same time, most of the emerging Arabic press relocated to Cairo, where the margin of freedom was larger. Among the most important periodicals were *al-Ahram*, *al-Muqtataf*, *al-Hilal*, *al-Jami'a*, *al-Jawa'ib*, *al-Muqattam*, *al-Jarida*, and *al-Fatah*, the first women's journal in the Arab world, founded by Syrian Hind Nawfal (1860–1920) in 1892 in Cairo. This next generation, including thinkers such as Francis Marrash (1836–1873), Shibli Shumayyil (1850–1917), Jurji Zaydan (1861–1914), and Farah Antun (1874–1922) played a leading role in establishing an Arab press, including both political newspapers and literary and scientific periodicals. Through this press and through their books, they disseminated modern knowledge and modern ideas in a refreshed Arabic. These thinkers' emphasis was on science, freedom, and political justice. They all criticized despotism. Shummayil introduced the ideas of Darwin as well as the ideas of socialism. He attacked theocracies of all sorts and rejected despotism. Antun argued for separating religion from politics and believed that modern society was to be based on science, not religion. This position led to a heated controversy with Muhammad Abduh, who regarded it as an attack on Islam.[24] There was clearly a limit to which Christian thinkers could express themselves without risking misunderstanding and suspicion on the part of the Muslim majority. But Muslim thinkers, too, were attacked when the ideas they propounded displeased the majority's beliefs: for example, Qasim Amin's protofeminist views and Ali Abdel Raziq's secular political theory.[25]

Amin's *Tahrir al-Mar'a* (The Liberation of Women) (1899) and *Al-Mar'a al-jadida* (The New Woman) (1900) are among the major publications of the first Nahda.[26] The first book gave rise to an important controversy and was attacked in conservative quarters, including the Azhar.[27] The second book came in response to these attacks and confirmed even more strongly the first book's theses. Amin was a prominent judge in Cairo, trained in Cairo and Montpellier (France). His social and professional standing lent a significant weight to his statements. In his writings, he pushed further al-Tahtawi and Abduh's progressive stands regarding the education and rights of women.[28]

A comparative awareness dominates Amin's thought: he sees, on the one hand, the backward, unhappy state of Egyptian society and, on the other, the advanced and happy state of European societies. He finds it important to identify with intellectual honesty the causes of each state and to work for the improvement of his own society by learning from others' successful experiences and by relying on historical evidence. The woman and family questions are for him at the core of the societal and civilizational problems, and they are, he admits, delicate and difficult questions that need to be addressed courageously. For him, it is obvious that women's situation in his society needs to be improved by allowing them to have more physical mobility and social contact, secluding them less, protecting them better with marriage and divorce laws, and giving them access to education. In *The Liberation of Women*, he says that his purpose is not to imitate the West blindly or to oppose shari'a, but to militate for the progress and happiness of his people. Although wanting to preserve the social structure of Egyptian society, he sees the need to address its negative aspects, and the oppression of women for him is certainly one of those aspects. Interestingly, he relates this oppression to the government's political oppression: political despotism creates, according to him, a whole system of injustice in which the strong oppress the weak, whether in the state, the society, or the family. Women are deliberately maintained in a state of weakness by being deprived of education, social contact, and active life. Contrary to the prevailing belief, he says, their weakness is not "natural," but the consequence of all those forms of deprivation, which produce ignorant mothers, inept companions to husbands, unhealthy families, and hence ailing societies. The prevailing belief stems from old and well-entrenched customs and mores that are based on habit and ignorance. Yet even running a household requires a certain know-how, he adds. Some form of education is necessary, even if limited only to elementary education.

In addition to these rather instrumentalist justifications, Amin states that women should be able to have an understanding of their own and a will of their own, and that for this purpose freedom and education are indispensable. They are also indispensable for women's mental and physical well-being. For him, the liberation of women is good for the family and for the nation, but it is also good for them as persons: it is life affirming. It enhances life and happiness (Europe, for him, is the evidence of this assertion), provided women are prepared for it through a wide education that is not limited to book learning. Contrary to what many believe, he affirms, their education and liberation will not jeopardize their chastity, for freedom is the basis of virtue, responsibility, and self-respect. Rather, it is despotism, whether in the state or in the family, that corrupts morals and destroys virtue. Moreover, he thinks that real chastity should be more internal and autonomous than external and heteronomous, forced upon women by the control of their movement and clothing. Besides, it should also be men's burden and involve their own behavior and inner virtue. Hence, strict veiling and seclusion cannot be the right measures for ensuring virtue and chastity in society.

Like most thinkers of the Nahda, Amin needed to account for the causes of decline in his society, manifested in this case in the oppression of women, and to explain the causes of progress in Europe. Islam is clearly not the cause of decline for him, although he sees decline spreading throughout the Muslim lands in different ways. On the contrary, he thinks that Islam recognizes women as having rights and being equal to men. Moreover, it never justifies conformism and traditionalism. It offers an important impulse toward progress and civilization. Human customs and mores, ignorance and despotism, thwarted this impulse and dragged Islamic societies into a state of backwardness and traditionalism. European societies, in contrast, offer a credible model of success that challenges and threatens Eastern societies. This challenge and threat have to be met with the determination to change and improve Eastern societies in the direction of that success, instead of sinking deeper into weakness and passively suffering the Europeans' judgmental gaze.

In *The New Woman*, Amin praises the success of the European model more emphatically and criticizes the shortcomings of Islamic civilization even more severely, even though he had defended the exact opposite view a few years earlier in a polemical piece responding to the negative depiction of Egyptians by the Duc d'Harcourt.[29] In his new book, he says that it is not the admission of inferiority that has harmed Islamic societies, but the inferiority itself. To the claim that attempts at changing gender traditions constitutes a foreign plot against Islamic societies, he responds that the greatest plot would be to leave them as they are. He strongly argues against idealizing the Islamic civilization of the past and against attributing to it the character of unmatchable perfection. Perfection, he insists, lies in the future, not in the past. It is surely not achievable in this world, not even by the Europeans, but one ought to aspire to it by understanding the nature of civilizational rise and decline. It is true, he says, that Islam as a religion united the Arab tribes and provided the basis for a unified rule that eventually led to an important Islamic civilization. This rise was made possible by the incorporation of numerous achievements of other civilizations, but religion remained the dominant factor in Islamic civilization because at the time science had not been developed enough to prevail in it, as it has in the European civilization.[30] Moreover, unlike Greek and Roman civilizations, this old Islamic civilization never knew real political representation. As to the views concerning women, they were transmitted to Islam by the Arab warrior-tribal culture, based on war spoils and patriarchal values. None of these aspects, he asserts, made this past civilization a model for our future. Our common sense of general welfare should help us discern those elements that we need to reject and those that we need to preserve. By contrast, modern European civilization shows scientific and moral virtues, for the two are related: morality benefits from cognitive progress. The claim about the East's moral superiority versus the West's material superiority is a poor compensatory pretense reinforced by a superficial knowledge of the West. Finally, Amin emphasizes again the link between state and family despotism. The same pretext given to justify the repression of political liberties, he concludes, is given for the repression of women's personal liberties (leaving out for the time being a discussion of women's public liberties)— namely, the possibility that these liberties will be abused.

Two years after the publication of Amin's books, a number of articles on despotism and Arab reform appeared in the journal *al-Manar* and other Egyptian periodicals, written by Syrian thinker Abdel Rahman al-Kawakibi (1848–1902). The author collected them in two booklets that became landmark publications of the Nahda: *Umm al-Qura* (literally "The Mother of Villages," which was one of the designations of Mecca) and *Tabai' al-Istibdad wa Masari' al-Isti'bad* (The Characteristics of Despotism and the Deaths of Enslavement).[31] Al-Kawakibi was a Syrian official and journalist as well as a strong opponent of Sultan Abdulhamid, one of the most tyrannical rulers of the Ottoman Empire. In the 1870s, he founded and edited a number of Arabic newspapers in Aleppo, his hometown, in which he criticized oppression and called for reform and freedom. The Ottoman authorities closed down his newspapers and arrested him. He eventually left Aleppo, traveled through North Africa, Arabia, and India, and settled in Cairo in 1898, where he frequented the circle of Muhammad Abduh. He died there a few years later in 1902, allegedly poisoned by Ottoman agents.

Like Amin, al-Kawakibi believed that pervasive despotism was the main cause of decline, but unlike Amin he thought that the Arab component of Islamic societies was the depository of an important potential of reform. The Bedouin characteristics of pride, solidarity, and freedom were for him solid defenses against despotism. Moreover, the special linguistic, cultural, and historical association of Arabs with Islam conferred upon them the natural responsibility of taking charge of its religious affairs, which were in need of much reform in his opinion. For the Ottomans, he contended, Islam was mainly a means for power. Their interest in it was instrumental, so they could not be a nurturing force; under their leadership Islam could not but become a stagnation factor leading to a generalized deterioration in matters of doctrine, jurisprudence, and practice. Political power, he thought, was to remain in the hands of the Ottomans, but the caliphate as a primarily religious function with some limited local temporal power had to be reclaimed by the Arabs, and its seat had to be relocated to Mecca for a number of considerations: it was geographically at the center of the Islamic world between Africa and the Far East, it was far from foreign hegemony, it had a unique historical and symbolic significance, and it was the home of an old Arab population.[32] For al-Kawakibi, such a caliphate would launch an Islamic renewal; it would also rekindle Arab awareness of a special linguistic, cultural, and historical bond, a common heritage, and a glorious past upon which a common and promising future could be built. In this regard, he is considered to be one of the early proponents of a pan-Arabism stemming from a pan-Islamism.[33] Different senses of collective identity were already emerging among the different ethnic and religious groups of the Ottoman Empire, but they gained importance after its collapse as visions of alternative political entities based on alternative definitions of identities became urgent. Various definitions, from the pan-Islamic to the pan-Arab and the more regional (Lebanese, Syrian, Egyptian, etc.), competed to offer new national and political conceptions of the region. Questions were raised about the compatibility and legitimacy of each definition. In response, theories were elaborated about the history, the destiny, and the making of the region. Some were modeled after

European conceptions of nationalism and were affected by the experiences of European colonialism in the mandate period. At the time, Al-Kawakibi did not advocate a full-fledged Arab nationalism that would imply a total separation of the Arab lands from the Ottoman Empire. He wanted to affirm an Arab specificity within the empire, characterized by the roles and values mentioned earlier. He believed that the actualization of those roles and values would open the way to reform and progress in the East. The sine qua non for any move forward, however, was for him the abolishment of despotism.

Al-Kawakibi addresses his booklet to Easterners in general and to the youth in particular so that they will understand the nature and effects of despotism and before it is too late—that is, before despotism annihilates the last remnants of vitality in them—mobilize their forces against it instead of blaming fate, Islam, or others. The health that the East lacks, he declares, is that of political freedom. He starts his introduction with the cautionary remark that his observations are not drawn from a particular government or a particular ruler, but from the nature of the phenomenon in general—probably to protect himself from direct reprisals.

The question of government is, he says, the oldest and most important problem of humanity. It entails a whole set of related questions such as, What should be the functions of government? What should be the mechanisms of controlling them? What should be the extent of governmental intervention in religious, cultural, and educational matters? What role should the government play in supporting learning? Should it have the right to control people's acts and ideas? Or do people have basic liberties that the government should respect as long as they do not disturb the social order? What are personal rights, and what are public rights? Finally, does governing mean possessing power and its benefits or being entrusted with public interests? For al-Kawakibi, one thing is clear: good governance is indispensable for progress and prosperity—the same unambiguous conclusion that al-Tahtawi had reached more than half a century earlier and that critical Arab thinkers a century after al-Kawakibi would reach after the painful experiences of the despotic postcolonial Arab regimes.

Al-Kawakibi starts his reflections on despotism with some definitions and moves on to discuss it in connection with religion, science, glory, wealth, morality, education, and progress. Despotism, he says, is unaccountable, unlimited, arbitrary, self-serving, and exclusive rule. It is served by the coercive military power of the ruler and the incapacitating ignorance of the ruled. Many, he adds, blame Islam for it. Their accusation is understandable given the corrupt behavior of many Muslims who project onto rulers the awe they are expected to have for God and hence find themselves incapable and unwilling to hold their rulers accountable; it is also understandable given the Muslim rulers who have claimed to rule in the name of God. Such abuses, according to him, have taken place in both the East and the West. The Protestant Reformation was a revolt against them. It might be believed, he adds, that reforming religion is easier than reforming politics. The ancient Greeks and Romans, for instance, used polytheism to legitimize political pluralism, but this allowed anyone to claim divine attributes; moreover, polytheism, being wrong in principle, could not serve as a real solution to the problem of power. In Christianity, the clergy was given divine rights and attributes. Islam and the early rule of the four Rightly Guided Caliphs established a just rule (al-Kawakibi, like many others, obviously idealized this early period). Islam, he says, advocated justice, equality, and a governance based on consultation. It denied absolute authority over matters outside religion. But despotic rulers distorted this message, and their tyranny emasculated the people's faculty to question the self and the Other, including the ruler; it damaged their sense of right and wrong and killed all courage in them, which in turn reinforced the rulers' tyranny. Despotic rulers also suppressed the light of knowledge, whether in science or in the holy book, especially the fact that the latter teaches not to worship anyone but God. The Qur'an, says al-Kawakibi, contains the fundamentals of the scientific knowledge later gained by Western scientists, thus further validating the value of the sacred book—a thesis that still has currency today, but that is also strongly contested by many critical Arab thinkers. The people's ignorance, he says, feeds into their fear and submissiveness to the point that they find their enslavement to be normal and even good. The same mechanisms apply to the lesser despots, big and small clergymen, ignorant fathers, stupid husbands, and heads of associations.

Despotism, for al-Kawakibi, is the source of all corruption: it corrupts the mind, religion, education, science, and morals. It is the source of injustice, humiliation, ignorance, poverty, unemployment, and ruin. Some claim that despotism softens the character, teaches obedience, trains people to have respect for leaders, diminishes depravity, and decreases crime. In reality, he rejoins, people become "soft" as a result of losing their pride rather than their brutality; they become obedient out of cowardice and fear, not by choice; they become respectful of the strong out of hatred, not out of love; depravity diminishes due to incapacity, not due to moral purity or faith; and crime diminishes in the sense that it is hidden rather than prevented. Morality, he asserts, requires freedom of thought and expression. The wise have agreed that it is extremely difficult to cure nations of moral corruption. Prophets have tried to save nations from it by liberating their minds from worshipping anyone other than God, by strengthening their faith, by encouraging them to reown their will and to think and to act freely, and finally by introducing them to humane laws (a process that sounds much like that of the modern Enlightenment). Ancient wise men, according to him, followed the prophets in this path of liberation, from religion to the liberation of the conscience and to reasonable education. The Western modernizers opted for another path, moving out of the sphere of religion and into the sphere of natural education, believing that religion and despotism were associated. But Easterners are different from Westerners, who are inclined to be materialistic. Arab Muslims have shown that knowledge and religion can go together. What Easterners need is a religious renewal combined with a general reform, especially in education, which, he says, prepares the mind for discernment, for sound reasoning and understanding, as well as for perseverance and good habit formation. The absence of such an education is the East's greatest calamity, and it cannot be remedied under despotism. Sadly, this is exactly what present Arab thinkers have to say about the reality they find themselves in a hundred years after al-Kawakibi. Their foremost concern is the destruction of education and society caused by the despotic regimes of the postcolonial era.[34]

In order to liberate the East from the calamity of despotism, al-Kawakibi calls upon Muslims to heed their Prophet and their enlightening religion; he calls upon non-Muslim Arabs to step over the wounds and grievances that they might have suffered at the hands of their Muslim brothers, to go beyond religious and confessional divisions, and to let religion deal with the afterlife but human brotherhood with this world; he even calls on Westerners to help Easterners get rid of the shackles of enslavement. Resistance to despotism, he thinks, should be gradual and gentle. An alternative to despotic rule must be created, which requires long-term preparation through mass education that aims at reaching clarity of purpose rather than a will to revenge. Otherwise, he says, the change will lead to replacing one despotism with another. The co-opted clergy and the forces of terrorism, money, and habituation are all powerful instruments of despotism that cannot be challenged by an occasional outburst, but only by a gradual popular transformation. Interestingly, survivors of the late-twentieth-century Arab tyrannies propound this same kind of resistance. For many of them, the first necessary task is to reconstruct the nation's social fabric and to rehabilitate the basic human capacities with modest, piecemeal societal goals rather than with the quick and frontal defiance of total revolutions.[35]

The question of government was raised anew some two decades after al-Kawakibi, this time in connection with the abolishment of the caliphate by Kemal Atatürk in 1924. This act gave rise to a heated discussion about the necessity for the Arabs to reclaim the caliphate and relocate it to Arab territory. Ali Abdel Raziq, an Egyptian thinker trained at the Azhar and Oxford, entered the fray in 1925 with the book *Al-Islam wa Usul al-Hukm* (Islam and the Principles of Governing), in which he argues that Islam does not advocate a specific form of government and that it is up to Muslims to decide on the best form that will suit their needs in the present age, on the basis of human experience in various parts of the world: "There is nothing in religion which prohibits Muslims from rivalling other nations in all the political and social sciences. Muslims are free to demolish this worn-out system (of the caliphate) before which they have debased and humiliated themselves. They are free to establish the bases of their kingdom and the organization of their state according to more recent conceptions of the human spirit and according to the principles of government whose excellence and firmness have been consecrated by the experience of the nations."[36]

According to Abdel Raziq, the belief that Islam advocates the caliphate as a legal and political commandment is based on a confused perception of the Prophet's early succession. The Prophet, he claims, passed away without specifying a form of government that the community of believers would have to follow after him because he understood his mission to be primarily spiritual, not political. The fact that the first rulers to head the community after his death were both pious and responsible for its worldly affairs gave the impression that the community's leadership was to be, as a matter of principle and doctrine, both religious and political, thus creating the phenomenon and the notion of the caliphate. Later rulers manipulated the established tradition for their mundane self-interests and prevented the development of independent political thought: "Such was the crime that kings in their tyranny committed against Muslims. They concealed aspects of the truth from them and made them swerve from the right path. In the name of religion they barred their way from the paths of light, treated them arbitrarily, humiliated them and prohibited them from studying political science. Also, in the name of religion they betrayed them and snuffed out their intelligence in such a way that they could find no recourse other than religion even in questions of simple administration and pure politics."[37]

The book was fiercely attacked and its author prevented from holding any public office. He was accused of introducing an alien, Christian distinction between the spiritual and the political. It was argued that Islam, contrary to Christianity, was not only a spiritual message, but also a law, the application of which required political power. Denying this aspect of Islam amounted therefore to the emasculation of its power to the benefit of the West. Moreover, Abdel Raziq's individual reasoning deviated from the consensus of past and present scholars, who had solidly founded the notion of the caliphate on the sacred book and the sacred tradition. According to Abdel Raziq, this Islamic caliphate was to be understood as being democratic and free, based on consultation, deriving its legitimacy from the community of believers and not from God independently from this community. It is interesting to note here how the idea of democracy, obviously drawn from the West, had become the criterion of evaluation, even for those claiming to distinguish themselves and Islam from this West. It is also interesting to note this explicit concern with power in connection with Islam as a religion, a legacy, and a political foundation. Abdel Raziq was a student of Muhammad Abduh, and his views on the caliphate and on the existence of a concrete governmental doctrine in Islam as a creed were based on the latter's reformist impulses. Ironically, these views were in total opposition to those of another of Abduh's devoted students, Rashid Rida, who, based on the same reformist impulses, advocated the caliphate as an Islamic commandment and necessity.[38] Rida obviously opted for the Salafi orientation in Islamic reform. These two orientations illustrate the opposite potentials of Abduh's reconciliatory strategy for reform and modernization.

A year after Abdel Raziq's book came out, another book published in Cairo attracted the conservative establishment's wrath: Taha Husayn's (1889–1973) book on pre-Islamic poetry, *Fi al-Shi'r al-Jahili* (On Jahili Poetry).[39] In it, Husayn raises questions about the existence of pre-Islamic poetry as it was traditionally presented, even in the Qur'an. His aim, as he puts it, is not to question the credibility of the holy book, but to examine the claims made about pre-Islamic poetry, using the Cartesian method of doubt. He concludes that pre-Islamic poetry was constructed a posteriori in order to serve as a precedent to Islamic literature and in order to demarcate the Islamic from the pre-Islamic. He was accused of casting doubt on traditional and religious beliefs, and the book was banned. He was dismissed from his position as dean of the Faculty of Arts at Cairo University, but was later rehabilitated under the next, more sympathetic government. However, the book remained censored until 1995, when its full version appeared in Arabic for the first time.[40]

Throughout the first half of the twentieth century, debates about identity, progress, and liberation continued and proliferated. In 1936, as the

Anglo-Egyptian treaty was signed, ending the official British presence in Egypt, Taha Husayn wrote his famous *Mustaqbal al-Thaqafa fi Misr* (*The Future of Culture in Egypt*); it was first published in 1938.[41] He addressed it to Egypt's university youth and presented in it his views on culture and education for the newly independent Egypt. He was later to implement some of his ideas as an advisor to the Ministry of Education from 1942 to 1944 and then as the minister of education from 1950 to 1952.

Husayn's main purpose in the book is to present the guiding principles for the cultural and educational policies that are to buttress Egypt's independence on the economic, political, and cultural levels. He bases these principles on a certain understanding of the cultural identity of Egypt. They consist in a wide-reaching Europeanization of the country through the adoption of European knowledge and politics:

> *In order to become equal partners in civilization with the Europeans, we must literally and forthrightly do everything that they do; we must share with them the present civilization, with all its pleasant and unpleasant sides, and not content ourselves with words or mere gestures. Whoever advises any other course of action is either a deceiver or is himself deceived. Strangely enough we imitate the West in our everyday lives, yet hypocritically deny the fact in our words. If we really detest European life, what is to hinder us from rejecting it completely? And if we genuinely respect the Europeans, as we certainly seem to do by our wholesale adoption of their practices, why do we not reconcile our words with our actions? Hypocrisy ill becomes those who are proud and anxious to overcome their defects.[42]*

Only science and democracy, he believes, can empower the newly independent nation. Such an extensive borrowing from Europe cannot, according to him, endanger the nation's personality because Europe and Egypt are not really foreign to one another. Their religions, Christianity and Islam, have common roots in the Near East, and their intellectual traditions have been formed by these religions' encounter with the same Greek philosophical legacy. Much of European thought, he adds, is grounded in medieval Islamic philosophy. In the past, Islamic culture itself had developed by incorporating many foreign cultural elements. Moreover, having no clergy, Islam, in contrast to European Christian culture, does not need to go through the process of secularization and can directly appropriate the fruits of that secularization. Husayn refutes the stereotypical conceptions of Europe as being material and evil and of Islam as being spiritual and good. Islam, he adds, could not have radically changed ancient Egypt, just as Christianity could not have thoroughly changed Europe. Future Egypt needs to be rooted in that ancient Egypt, which maintained from very early times close ties with the European continent across the Mediterranean through trade, conquest, and culture. Alexandria, he reminds the reader, was a center of Greek and Hellenic culture for a long time. The present gap between Egypt and Europe is due to contingent historical factors, the most important of which is the long and detrimental Ottoman dominion over Egypt.

Given all these commonalities, Husayn suggests that Egypt be viewed more as a Western, European cultural nation rather than as an Eastern one. However, in spite of wanting to blur the Europe/Islam binary, he builds his arguments on an essentialist view of the West and the East, beginning his essay with the questions, "Is Egypt from the West or the East?" and "Is the Egyptian mind Western or Eastern?" (the East referring here to China, Japan, and India, and the West referring mainly to Europe and the United States): "At the outset we must answer this fundamental question: Is Egypt of the East or of the West? Naturally, I mean East or West in the cultural, not the geographical sense. It seems to me that there are two distinctly different and bitterly antagonistic cultures on the earth. Both have existed since time immemorial, the one in Europe, the other in the Far East." And he answers firmly: "We Egyptians must not assume the existence of intellectual differences, weak or strong, between the Europeans and ourselves or infer that the East mentioned by Kipling in his famous verse 'East is East and West is West, and never the twain shall meet' applies to us or our country . . . since our country has always been a part of Europe as far as intellectual and cultural life is concerned, in all its forms and branches."[43]

If Japan, in his opinion, could succeed in adopting European science and technology while keeping its cultural heritage, Egypt should surely be able do so as well, especially because Egypt has always had much closer ties with Europe. It is interesting to note that this construction and definition of Egypt's cultural identity aimed at providing a basis for the set of policies that Husayn wanted to advocate, especially in education. For him, it was the state's responsibility to ensure universal literacy by building a wide network of schools across the country and to strengthen the learning of the Arabic language in order to allow people to have access to Western modern knowledge, which would have to be made available through massive translation. Moreover, religious instruction, both Islamic and Coptic, had to be supervised by and subordinated to the state.

By assigning these tasks to the state, Husayn voiced the demand for centralization and homogenization that postindependence states were expected to undertake in the modernization process. This definition of Egypt's cultural identity became quickly controversial, but the need for modern education and science remained, and many states did build comprehensive school systems, which raised levels of literacy. These systems, however, suffered from the mismanagement and vicissitudes common among postindependence and postcolonial states. Moreover, the voluntaristic intent of such a state project was to lead to a coercive statism and an emasculation of various associative social forces so typical of these states. Finally, Husayn envisioned a leading role for such a modernized and educated Egypt in the cultural and political life of the Arab world and suggested various kinds of cultural and educational services Egypt could offer. This leadership role would become an object of severe contention in the power struggle among Arab countries in the problematic attempts to establish Arab unity. The founding of the state of Israel and its defeat of the Arab armies in 1948 brought the charismatic Egyptian leader Gamal Abdel Nasser (1918–1970) to power in Egypt. Abdel Nasser metamorphosed into an Arab and even a Third World leader, for a while galvanizing high hopes for a united and victorious Arab nation-state with principles of equality, justice, and socialism. However, he developed into an authoritarian ruler who did not tolerate dissent and critique. Taha Husayn was marginalized, and so were the proponents of the liberal school. But it was the Islamists who were the target of the fiercest repression, among them Sayyid Qutb (1906–1966), one of the main theoreticians of the Muslim Brotherhood.

Like Taha Husayn, Qutb served at the Egyptian Ministry of Education in the mid-1940s, but quickly found himself drawn to the Islamic opposition. Critical of the monarchy and opposed to the prevailing feudal system in the country, Qutb became increasingly convinced that Islam was the way to genuine social justice and to moral and political virtue. When the ministry sponsored him to go to the United States for studies in education, he earned a master's degree from the University of Northern Colorado, but decided to return to Egypt before starting a doctorate program. During this time, between 1948 and 1951, important events took place in the region: the establishment of the state of Israel, its defeat of the Arab armed forces, and the assassination in 1949 of Hassan al-Banna (1906–1949), who founded the Muslim Brotherhood in Egypt in 1928.[44] In 1952, the monarchy was overthrown in a coup led by army officers (the Free Officers coup) who held

the monarchy responsible for the 1948 debacle in Palestine and for collaboration with the former colonial powers. For a short period after the coup,
the Muslim Brotherhood cooperated with the officers' government. Soon,
however, disagreements surfaced when the government tried to co-opt the
Brotherhood, but refused to implement their Islamic policies in the country. A fierce struggle for power ensued from this tension. In 1954, Qutb
became the editor-in-chief of the Brotherhood's official journal, *al-Ikhwan
al-Muslimun*, which was soon banned. The Brotherhood strongly criticized
the 1954 treaty signed by Egypt and Great Britain that gave the latter certain military and economic privileges in the former. Many members were
jailed, among them Qutb. He was to remain in jail until his death in 1966,
when he was hanged by order of Abdel Nasser on charges of conspiracy
against the state. These alternating government policies of cooperation, co-
optation, and repression toward the Muslim activists were to become typical of most postindependence Arab states.

It is under such circumstances that Sayyid Qutb developed and published
his ideas, which were to become increasingly radicalized. They provided the
Muslim Brotherhood and other Islamists with the ideological framework for
their activism.[45] For Qutb, Islam needed a cultural renewal that was to satisfy the needs of the times, but that was to be founded on the fundamentals
of Islam, which he saw as an integral way of life. The renewal involved two
tasks: first, the establishment of a just social system based on the principles of
Islam and, second, the nurturing of the inner beliefs and convictions that
would support such a social system. The latter required the strengthening of
religious faith and the formation of a new Islamic culture on the basis of a
total and reformed educational vision. The problem for Qutb was that many
of the leading methods for educational reform had been founded in Western
culture, a culture that he thought was inimical to Islam and suffered from
many weaknesses, primarily materialism. Isolationism was not an option for
him, however, because influences across cultures were, he thought, an undeniable and unavoidable reality. So the renewal in question necessitated an
extremely cautious and critical selective borrowing:

Islam, then, enunciates for men a complete theory of life. . . .

*No renaissance of Islamic life can be effected purely by law or statute,
or by the establishment of a social system on the basis of the Islamic
philosophy. Such a step is only one of the two pillars on which Islam*

*must always stand in its construction of life. The other is the produc-
tion of a state of mind imbued with the Islamic theory of life, to act as
an inner motivation for establishing this form of life and to give coherence to all the social, religious, and civil legislation. . . .*

*But how can we possibly induce Islamic theory by a culture, educa-
tional methods, and modes of thought that are essentially Western and
essentially inimical to the Islamic philosophy itself; first, because they
stand on materialistic basis, which is contrary to the Islamic theory of
life; and second, because opposition to Islam is a fundamental part of
their nature, no matter whether such opposition is manifest or concealed in various forms?*

*As we have already maintained, we shall proclaim our defeat in the
first round whenever we adopt a Western theory of life as the means
for reviving our Islamic theory. So, primarily, we must rid ourselves of
the ways of the Western thought and choose the ways of native Islamic
thought in order to ensure pure results, rather than hybrid.*[46]

According to Qutb, all domains of knowledge, including the natural
and applied sciences, are rooted in the worldviews of the cultures in which
they were developed, so no borrowing can be safe. Natural sciences as well
as pedagogy, psychology, and education were marked by the pragmatism
that dominated Western culture. He referred to these disciplines in the
United States and to the work of pragmatists such as Charles Peirce and
John Dewey. This pragmatism focused on the technical aspects of things,
discouraged theoretical thinking, and served the materialist approach to
human issues. History, he believed, should be written and taught in a way
that did not privilege the West as its center. Similarly, students should be
made acquainted with their own literature before reading those of others.
In philosophy, Western thinkers might be introduced to students only after
they had mastered Islamic thought. Islamic thought itself needed a new definition, different from the one used by the Azhar University: thinkers such as
Ibn Sina (980–1037) and Ibn Rush (1126–1198), for instance, who developed
their philosophies with the use of Greek philosophy, could not be regarded
as Islamic thinkers, according to Qutb. Curricula had to ensure that students
were trained in their own traditions before they were cautiously exposed to
other, primarily Western, bodies of knowledge and belief. Only this kind of
education could give Muslims an empowered and renewed sense of their

own religious, moral, and cognitive self. Clearly, his was a pronounced cultural protectionist position that was to become more appealing to a growing number of people in the second half of the twentieth century.

———

This quick survey of ideas presented and discussed by Arab thinkers from the mid–nineteenth century to the mid–twentieth century offers a general view of the concerns that preoccupied them. The importance of these ideas does not lie primarily in their depth, originality, or consistency, but in their place in the Arab public debates of the time, whether in the daily press, the periodicals, the pamphlets, or the books. Some of them led to heated controversies, some provoked public condemnations, and some others inspired great enthusiasm. A number of their proponents occupied prominent official positions and managed to apply them in public policies. These thinkers—despite the diversity of their inclinations, ranging from the liberal to the conservative, secular, religious, conciliatory, protectionist, and Salafist—were concerned with the core cultural and political issues mentioned in this chapter: identity (perceptions of the self and the other), religion, education, women, and government. Mid-twentieth-century events—the establishment of the postcolonial Arab states, the founding of the state of Israel, and the consolidation of the Cold War power struggle in the region—exacerbated the urgency of these issues. The consecutive defeats by Israel, the hardening of state repression, the rise of Islamic fundamentalism, the effects of oil politics and economy, as well as the increase of Western intervention in the last decades of the twentieth century aggravated the conditions of the debate. Compared to the oppressive atmosphere of the present, the first Nahda seems to many contemporary Arab thinkers to have been a much more hopeful time, more confident in its liberating impulses and more optimistic in its reform projects. It also seems a very distant time, a remote epoch from which the present is disconnected and estranged. What caused this severance? What happened to the first Nahda legacy? Was any renewal, any liberation, any reform really attained? If yes, where were the effects of those achievements? If not, what prevented their realization? Moreover, how could Arabs be raising the same questions for more than fifteen decades, but start from scratch every time, with nothing to build upon? Were all the efforts of the past two centuries a sad Sisyphean exercise? These anguished questions regarding the first Nahda are, as we will see in chapter 2, an integral part of the second Nahda's concerns.

Two
Critique
After
the 1967
Defeat

*The Existential Dramatization of Critique the Day After the Defeat:
Saadallah Wannous's Theatrical Oeuvre*

An Entertainment Evening for June 5

Saadallah Wannous's 1967–1968 play *Haflat Samar min Ajl Khamseh Hu-zairan* (An Entertainment Evening for June 5) is about the opening night of a play called *Safir al-Arwah* (The Whistle of the Souls) that never actually gets started.[1] The opening takes place in a state theater in the aftermath of the June 1967 war. Official personalities as well as common people and refugees are invited. They have settled down in their seats waiting for the play to start. Both the stage and the spectator hall are lit, the curtain is up, and a blackboard on the stage reads: "At exactly quarter to nine in the morning of June 5, 1967, the state of Israel, representing the fiercest and most dangerous forms of world imperialism, launched a stupefying attack on the Arab countries. It defeated them and occupied a new part of their land. While this attack showed clearly the brutality and dangers of imperialism, it showed even more clearly our need to see ourselves, to look into our mirrors and ask: Who are we? And why?"[2]

After waiting for some time, the spectators become impatient and start shouting their anger at the delay, making mocking remarks such as "Is this an imperialist conspiracy?" "Have actors lost their roles?" "Is there a backstage crisis?" Finally, the director of the play appears on stage and addresses the public. The director, adds Wannous in his introductory remarks, is, as is customary in "our" country (meaning Syria, but also any other Arab country), also the director of the theater as well as the director of all the plays presented in it, alluding to the pattern of cumulating and monopolizing power. The director apologizes to the public and proposes to explain the reason for the delay and the confusion. He says that he wanted to produce an artistic event that would honor the dramatic circumstances the country was experiencing, that he first thought of a poetry evening, but then realized that people did not like poetry anymore. He then decided to offer a play, but having failed to find a suitable play in the available repertoire, he commissioned a writer to compose one for him that would express the scenes he envisioned. After they had come to mutual agreement on the text, the writer had at the very last minute, just before this evening's show, refused to allow the representation of his piece to take place—hence the delay and the confusion. The director starts to narrate his initial meeting with the writer as well as the three main scenes he had suggested. His narration is accompanied by the live representations of the meeting and of the scenes. For the first representation, the writer joins him on stage, commenting sarcastically on the flow of the narration. The spectators also make comments on the unfolding of the evening and on the opinions of the director, who wanted a dramatic representation of history on stage.

He tells the story of the three scenes: the first one is set on a city street, the second one on a battlefront, and the third in a front-line village square. In the first scene, people are seen panicking at the sound of sirens, raiding planes, and radio announcements broadcasting the news of the war: children are crying, and people seem to be totally disoriented. In response to the description of this scene, a spectator comments that this was not how things had happened, to which the director answers that what counts for him is not the scene's veracity, but the emotional buildup to the next scene at the battlefront. With the growing sound of explosions and whistling shells and bullets, four soldiers appear on stage showing a heroic confrontation with danger and death, making lyrical statements about their epic defense of their country. But the soldiers playing these roles also speak about the lack of adequate command and communication in their troops, the superiority of the enemy weaponry, their fears and more mundane concerns, their letters to their families, their conflicts with their parents concerning their love relationships, and so on. Although the director finds these concerns futile and unbecoming of the heroic situation in which soldiers are to stand for the patriotic defense of the country, the writer reminds him of the soldiers' humannesss. Uninterested in such considerations, the director moves on to his third scene, which portrays people in a front-line village faced with a dramatic dilemma—having to choose between fleeing from the approaching enemy and abandoning their lands or staying on their lands and dying in defense of their rights and properties. The set on stage is immediately changed at this point, and a village square is set up; two groups of villagers are shown in a heated debate about the pros and cons of each option. Finally, one group decides to leave, and the other chooses to stay. The men of the latter group kill their womenfolk and children in order to be able to face the enemy without fear of shame and dishonor. The scene is to end, the director says, with the crescendo of dramatic music and with the curtain falling slowly. "This was my idea of this evening's show," he adds.

Then, in almost simultaneous but parallel monologues, the director and the writer give their versions of the development of the project. Abandoning his sarcasm, the writer explains in a sad tone how he first got carried away in this project, despite his doubts and hesitations. He says how amazed he was that things continued to look the same after the war, how words continued to be used in the same way, how people wrote, read, and behaved as if nothing had happened. At first, he thought that his own malaise with words after the war might have been unjustified, so he went along with the director's project and wrote the play for him until he realized how rotten and inadequate the words in it were and how impossible it was for him to let them be spoken on stage. To the director, who commented that the war and its heroism had surely invigorated the writer's talent and filled him with inspiration, he says that the defeat had in truth crippled his imagination and impoverished his words. The director, in contrast, relates the promising cooperation he at first had with the writer and the bitter disappointment he experienced when the latter betrayed his commitment at the last minute. He concludes by announcing that in compensation for the thwarted evening, a folkloric dance would be presented. The dance, performed in the village setting of the last scene, is meant to fill everybody with the nostalgia of old rural feasts and to celebrate the glory of heroic deeds.

As the musicians and the dancers prepare to start, an old man in traditional village clothes rises from the back rows and heads toward the director, asking him candidly what the name of the village he represented was. The director explains to him condescendingly and impatiently that it is not a real village, but a symbolic village, standing for all of the country's villages, that the story is not a real one, but a symbolic representation of what the war stands for. "So," the old man asks, surprised, "you don't know the village you are talking about?" The director cannot be bothered by this man's remarks; he is anxious to have the dance begin. But the man persists, recalling his memories. In simple and humble terms, contrasting with the lyrical and emphatic terms of the director's narration, he says how vividly the village scene brought back to him the experiences of his own village: how they fled in panic, not understanding what was happening to them. They were unprepared, unguided, and abandoned, just like the soldiers they met as they fled. As the old man continues his story, the director attempts to silence him, finding no relevance in his utterances, but some spectators and the writer insist that he pursue his story. To a fellow villager, the old man says that people do not want to listen to them because they are strangers and because they own nothing, that people do not want to hear the complaint of their humiliation as refugees living in tents because they had not lived in palaces before the war anyway. Yes, he objects, they had not lived in palaces, but they had lived in dignity in their own modest houses and villages, led wars against other villages in forms that were familiar to them, unlike this war that they could not understand and could not participate in. As the old man returns to his seat, silenced by the growing sound of the music, another spectator surprises everybody by addressing the villager in anger, asking him why they fled and did not stay on their lands. More and more spectators leave their seats and move toward the stage, participating in the debate that becomes increasingly animated, despite the director's continuous objections as he loses control over his own stage and theater.

The old man is surprised that he can be asked such a question. Someone in the audience objects to the question, but another thinks that it is an essential question. When the director asks them to go and raise their questions elsewhere, people tell him to take his folkloric group to countries where there were no problems and no refugee tents, that in this country there were people who had left their villages and that people needed to understand why. They also tell him that his anger is due to the fact that he himself had never been a spectator and that he had become accustomed to silent and passive audiences that he controlled. The question is asked once again: "Why did you leave your villages?" The old man answers candidly:

> War was waged, how could we stay? Nobody explained anything to us, nobody ever talked to us or visited us. We heard the radio, but did not understand what was being said. Poor people like us are not visited by anyone, except by policemen and tax collectors. The teachers who are sent to our villages do not like us and do everything to be moved elsewhere. Only one day did a real man visit us. He carried a gun, but was not a soldier. He was a peasant like us, dispossessed of his land by enemies who had come from overseas. He told us how he was prevented by his own rulers from seeking justice and reclaiming his rights. He explained to us how our leaders kept us poor, ignorant, and humiliated so that we remain helpless. He spoke in terms that we understood. He moved on in his struggle, and we never saw him again.

The questioner adds, "But I know poor peasants who were able to stand in the face of a major aggression." Somebody in the audience says, "He is talking about the Vietnamese." The old villager answers, "We don't hear about far away countries." Different spectators interject, and one of them remarks, "Those Vietnamese are able to struggle because they are not strangers in their own country, because they don't live marginalized and neglected, because they have an identity, and because they know they have an identity; their leaders are not tanks, their palace windows are not canons, and their balconies are not information posts; they learn how to move around, and they learn how the world around them moves; their teachers are not crooks, their radios do not broadcast lies, and their newspapers are not futile."

At this point, a spectator erupts in anger and says that the villagers' flight was also everyone's, that all were responsible for it, that if he looked in the mirror, he could see the shame of that flight within himself. A number of spectators welcome the idea of exploring their images in a mirror and insist on the importance of examining themselves before assigning blame to others. One of them says that what he sees is a defeated people. Another says that one needs to look deeper, beneath the defeat, into the very being of the people, and that on that deep level what one would see is nothingness, erased pictures, mere shadows without features: "That is what we are," he adds, "images that have been erased in the name of national interest. Year after year we have lost our tongues, our ears, our eyes to what was claimed to be our national interest. Year after year questioning, seeing, and thinking were regarded as punishable crimes in the face of a national interest that was defended in dark dungeons. What is left in a picture in which the tongue, the eyes, and the ears are erased? We have become pale shadows. The world moves around us like bad dreams, blurred and obscure. Our history is a burden and our land slips away from under our feet."

"Still," somebody in the audience protests, "even if we had no features left in ourselves, we were still able to sense the coming dangers, like animals in the forest. We did sense the danger, and we did want to do something to face it and to bear responsibility." "But what good is it to want to act," someone else asks, "if we have no faculties left in us, no contours, no identity? What good is our will if our character is considered to be a conspiracy by those in power?" Others recall the day the attack was broadcast: how people took to the streets, how women and men offered what they had to stand in the face of the aggression. They were sent back home and told that the war was none of their business. "Our mistake," says another, "was to ask for weapons to fight, not for our eyes, not for our tongues, not for our right to think, not for our right to exist with identifiable features. Erased pictures we remained, incapacitated and defeated." At this point, an official from the front row gives orders to a number of his men to lock the exits and arrest those who had spoken and even those who had not.

What Wannous puts on stage here is the profound malaise of a majority of Arabs in the aftermath of the 1967 war: people overwhelmed by humiliation, disappointment, anger, and fear. With his inimitable honesty and lucidity, he depicts a malaise caused primarily, in his opinion, by state repression and manifested in military defeat, but also in cultural mediocrity, intellectual futility, and personal despair. As he saw the situation, cultural malaise, as a symptom of political repression, can be overcome only by a cultural critique that slowly and gradually paves the way for a democratic struggle. He regarded theater as an important milieu of cultural and political critique and so developed his notion of "politicizing theater."

Politicizing Theater
Oppression, violent subjugation, exploitation, mendacity, deception, demagogy, and empty lyricism are the persisting concerns of Saadallah Wannous's

(1941–1997) dramatic oeuvre, which consists of some two dozen plays. Many have been translated into foreign languages, including French, English, Spanish, Italian, German, Russian, and Polish. For more than three decades, the prominent Syrian playwright denounced these abuses of power and fought for the empowerment and liberation of his fellow Arabs. He studied journalism in Cairo and visited France, Germany, and Russia to study theater and participate in directing some of his plays. His plays were presented all over the Arab world, often provoking very heated debates about both their content and their form. He worked as a journalist and critic in Damascus and Beirut and wrote on both Arab and foreign theater and culture.

In the early 1970s, he wrote "Bayanat li Masrah ʿArabi Jadid" (Manifestos for a New Arab Theater),[3] in which he articulated his conception of the role and nature of the new theater he wanted to create. For Wannous, theater is primarily a relational phenomenon—a living dialogue and a live interaction between actors and spectators. It is the privileged space in which both parties share a moment of critical reflection on the sociopolitical and historical realities of their lives. The main questions that a serious theater should raise, according to him, are: Who is the public that the theater is addressing? What does the theater want to convey to this public? And how does it want to convey these things? The answers to these questions are to be searched for continuously and are bound to change with changing historical situations. The purpose of this theatrical relationship is to offer the public an opportunity to contemplate the realities of its environment, to develop a critical awareness of its main issues, and to help mobilize its energies toward changing those realities. The primary public Wannous has in mind is the common people, not the elite, and the change he wants to advocate is a progressive one—a change toward democracy and social justice. This is his understanding of the "politicizing" theater that he defends in "Manifestos," and it is not to be confused, he insists, with "political" theater that simply has politics as its topic. Politicizing theater is not to transmit a ready-made awareness. The aim is not to exchange one ideology with another, but to create an opportunity for people to form their own critical view of the most pressing sociopolitical issues. He admits that he may not always meet this standard in his own plays, but he affirms that it remains his main aspiration. The purpose is to shake up mentalities and encourage change.

More than any other artistic and intellectual activity, theater is first and foremost a public social event, says Wannous. It is not a mere text that can be smuggled. Therefore, it is particularly sensitive to the absence of liberties.

Democracy and freedom of thought are necessary for the public critique and dialogue that is theater. According to him, the blatant absence of democracy in the Arab world is one of the major factors causing the crisis of Arab theater, manifested in its lack of audacity in addressing pressing issues, the weakness of its intellectual and aesthetic forms, and its general mediocrity of production. Another factor, he adds, is the acceleration of real drama in the Arab world—that is, the intense succession of dramatic events throughout the second half of the twentieth century. The rapidity of these events has not left much time or opportunity to grasp them and to ponder their effects and implications. Still another problematic factor, he points out, is the quality of the media culture that Arab governments have been propagating in order to numb people's taste and critical faculties. It is against such formidable obstacles, he says, that a politicizing theater is to be created as an art that is liberating in its intellectual depth and honesty, its political progressive commitment, its innovative aesthetics, and its effectiveness in engaging a specific public about real issues.

This effectiveness is what makes a theater authentic, not the origin of its text. Creating an authentic Arab theater does not necessarily mean drawing texts from the transmitted heritage, the *turath*. Although Wannous often drew the plots and subjects of his plays from this heritage, he did not do so in order to make of this heritage reference an end in itself. More than the text itself, what counted for him is the way issues are addressed and dealt with. Moreover, texts are constantly open to new readings in light of the circumstances in which they are understood and presented. In this sense, adaptation from foreign plays is not necessarily an obstacle to an authentic theater. Most repertoires in the world, he says in "Manifestos," include a certain number of adaptations. Rather than confining itself to an isolated *turath*, Arab theater should open itself to world theater and culture. Authentic theater has to be local, but not exclusively or necessarily in a geographical sense. What counts is not the story of a play. The ancient Greeks, he adds, did not watch their famous plays to find out about the fate of Achilles or Agamemnon. That fate was already known to them. With every new enactment of those stories, they watched to contemplate the relevance of these stories to their own lives. It is futile to oppose Arab theater to European theater, he says, for there is no one monolithic European theater, but a whole array of different currents and traditions that belong to specific sociocultural histories. The authenticity of Arab theater can only come from the authenticity of the issues it addresses and the effectiveness of the forms it uses in engaging its public. In this respect, Arab theater can only be experimental, he adds—not in the European sense of going beyond the limits of classical, bourgeois theater, but in the sense of involving a constant search for means of effective interaction with the public, which can often be found in the habits of the people themselves.

This was the idea behind the setting of *Entertainment Evening for June 5*: a setting in which people interject, comment, and participate, like they do in entertainment evenings (*samar*) in which chatting and singing are mixed. The play was banned for a while, then performed in the Sudan (1970), Lebanon (1970), Syria (1971), Iraq (1972), and Algeria (1972). It was well received, but Wannous was disappointed that it did not produce the political effect he thought it should. People left it like they would from any other play, not at all mobilized in the way he had hoped they would be. Many years later, in the concluding piece of the section of his analytic writing devoted to theater, "Al-Hulm Yatada'a" (The Dream Collapses),[4] he states that he came to accept that a play can only be a play, not a revolution, and that words can only be words. After the 1967 defeat, he wondered what relevance writing could still have; he wanted to hold on to the belief in a deed-word, in a deed-theater, in an effective art that could create changes by addressing realities with honesty and depth. In 1971, with Syrian film-maker Omar Amiralay he made the film *Al-Hayat al-Yawmiyya fi Qarya Suriyya* (Daily Life in a Syrian Village). It depicts, as the title says, the ordinary life of people in a village in northeastern Syria. The Syrian authorities immediately banned it.

"I Am the Deceased and the Mourner"

Wannous's disappointments were to grow regarding both the effectiveness of his art and the political realities of the Arab world. They reached their climax in 1978 with the Camp David Agreement.[5] He perceived it as the ultimate betrayal of the Arab cause by a corrupt and dictatorial Arab regime, a regime that had contributed to the further fragmentation and division of the Arab world, more underdevelopment, more poverty, and more humiliation. In the same year, he wrote a piece in the Lebanese daily *al-Safir* entitled "Ana al-Janaza wa al-Mushayyi'un" (I Am the Deceased and the Mourner):

> *My life has neared its end and I still dream of saying "No." I wanted, and I want to say "No" to the "Yes" citizen, to the prison-homeland, to the modernization of the methods of torture and domestication, to the official discourse, to the visas for Arab countries, to the fragmen-*

*tation and the division, to the referenda of 99.99 percent, to the bal-
loon celebrations, to the wars that strengthen the police, to the victo-
ries which offer the leadership of the Arabs to the oil princes, that
increase the gains of the businessmen, and lead to the agreements of
Camp David. . . .*

*I wanted and I want to say "No." And I search for my tongue but find
only a foam of blood and fear.*

*From my severed tongue the defeat started, and the funeral procession
set out. . . . From my suppressed "No" the enemy got through, as well
as the separation, the poverty, the hunger, the prison, the torturer, and
the contemporary Arab collapse. . . .*

*Briefly, if it weren't for my suppressed "No," half of me wouldn't be in
the coffin and the other half dragging itself behind it. And my deprivation from my "No" made me not only into the victim and the spectator, the dead and the mourner, but also into a conspirator. . . .*

*. . . [T]he "No" citizen is, for the Arab thrones, a bigger danger than
the Israeli danger, and a conspiracy worse than the imperialist
conspiracies. . . .*

*. . . And until I recuperate my suppressed "No," the funeral procession
will continue, with us dragging our tails behind it.[6]*

After this, he produced little for a number of years. His silence lasted till
the mid-1980s. In the 1997 interview Omar Amiralay filmed as Wannous
was in the hospital for the final stages of the cancer treatment he had un-
dergone for many years before his death that year, the ailing playwright
related in sober and sincere words how he had contemplated suicide during
those years of his life following the Camp David Agreement (the early
1980s) as he saw all his dreams and projects collapse.[7] Ten years earlier, in a
1986 interview, he had explained how this severe crisis had led him eventually to deepen his self-examination and to resume, with more modesty but
more determinacy, the struggle for truthfulness and liberty.[8] This struggle
may seem less ambitious, he added, than working to establish the unity of
the Arab world, creating a modern state, liberating Palestine, and achieving
socialism, but it is in the long run more urgent and more fundamental: it is

the struggle for enlightenment. The place of culture in society needs to be reconsidered. Culture needs to be liberated from narrow politics, without becoming a futile entertainment for the elite or a mediocre activity for the masses. Culture is to be the privileged domain of enlightenment and critical thinking. In 1996, he was asked to write the speech for World Theater Day, organized since 1962 by UNESCO's International Theater Institute. He called it "Al-Juʿ ila al-Hiwar" (The Hunger for Dialogue).[9] In this speech, he pleaded, as he had done throughout the past three decades, for dialogue among individuals and groups, and he insisted once more on the need for democracy and pluralism. Dialogue, he said, can start from theater, where it can take place on numerous levels: between the actors and the spectators, between the theater and the city, and between the spectators themselves. But Wannous was always afraid that the people, himself included, having been subjected all their lives to dictatorships, had become small dictators, seeking approval and applause, intolerant and deaf to others. He emphasized the importance of being aware of and overcoming this internalized tendency to authoritarian monologuing. "We are condemned to hope," he said; "this cannot be the end of history."

Revisiting the Nahda

The struggle against despair and resignation increasingly became Wannous's most urgent existential and political task. The intellectual core of this struggle was the need to make enlightenment possible and sustainable despite the sociopolitical obstacles and in the midst of an extremely difficult historical situation. Significant efforts toward enlightenment had been deployed for almost a whole century since the first Nahda. None of that momentum seemed left in the late twentieth century, however. What had severed the last decades of the twentieth century from this legacy of critical thinking? What had prevented the legacy's fruition? Why had modern Arab thought found itself in a hopeless redundancy, raising the same questions it had raised at the beginning of the Nahda, but with less liberty and less clarity? Why do contemporary Arab thinkers feel unable to rely on that legacy and to build on it? Why do they have the impression of always having to start from scratch in the total absence of a cumulative critical heritage? From the mid-1980s onward, Wannous focused much of his writing on these questions. In 1990, together with Abde al-Rahman Munif, Faysal al-Darraj, and Gaber Asfour, he launched a periodical devoted to the renewed study of that Nahda, *Qadaya wa Shahadat* (Causes and Testimonies).[10] Its purpose, as he put it in the introduction of the first issue, was not to cover the present intellectual bankruptcy with a few symbolic figures of that period or to indulge in compensatory nostalgia, but to reconnect with an intellectual legacy that had become more relevant than ever. The periodical was to engage in a reflective dialogue about this relevance and in a search for the reasons for the rupture that prevented the continuation of its impetus, but it was discontinued after the seventh issue because of the deterioration of Wannous's health in the mid-1990s.

In the journal, Wannous wrote on Rifaʿa al-Tahtawi, Khaireddin al-Tunisi, Taha Husayn, and Sayyid Qutb, and analyzed the power structure of the postindependence governments that in his opinion had wasted the fruition of their legacy. What he underlines in al-Tahtawi's thought is its focus on change and progress inspired from the French model he saw during his stay in Paris from 1826 to 1831 as head of the student mission sent by Muhammad Ali, governor of Egypt at the time. His mind, says Wannous, was free from polemics and apologetics. He was eager to understand the basic principles that had led to the cultural, socioeconomic, and political progress of Europe in general and of France in particular. Al-Tahtawi was fascinated by the principles of law, reason, freedom, and patriotism that gave rise to a homeland that ensured rights and protected liberties. He saw the linkage between the epistemological and the political systems of that homeland and understood the need to borrow both. He was well aware of the conservative reaction in his native Egypt and addressed their concerns without spending his whole energy arguing with them. Al-Tahtawi, a sheikh himself, says Wannous, read the sacred text in light of the progressive models he experienced abroad and made the theological notions fit into these models rather than the other way around. He advocated education for all, including young girls and women, laypeople as well as clerics and scholars of religion. In a modern state, he thought, religious education is not enough to enlighten citizens because the laws of such a state cannot all be based on religious jurisprudence. He saw the importance of education in changing society and in leading to a modern representative political system. What strikes Wannous is the serenity with which al-Tahtawi perceived the foreign advanced model and the freedom with which he reasoned and pleaded for change—characteristics that fade with time as we near the postindependence era. Wannous sees three reasons for al-Tahtawi's confident attitude: (1) his affiliation with the leadership of Muhammad Ali, who was adamant about modernizing Egypt, primarily in the administrative and military sectors—a modernization process that inevitably produced changes in the other sectors, including the cultural; (2) the fact that

Muhammad Ali had subdued the conservative religious groups and institutions by confiscating their properties and marginalizing their power;
and (3) the fact that European colonial aggression had not yet expanded in
the region and thus had not yet created, according to Wannous, great confusion and skepticism regarding the validity and legitimacy of the modernization project.

In the work of the Tunisian reformer of the 1860s, Khaireddin al-Tunisi,
Wannous appreciates the early and clear warning against separating the
Europe of reason, science, and industry from the Europe of goods consumption. Already then, al-Tunisi had seen the danger of rejecting the first
in the name of identity and religion and accepting the latter in view of
modernizing the external aspects of life.[11] Doing either would create, according to him, the worst kind of dependency and underdevelopment: it
would lead to an economic state of subservience and deprive the region of
the principles of reason and freedom indispensable for progress because of
an erroneous defensive logic of cultural particularity. Sadly, adds Wannous, al-Tunisi's fears were increasingly justified, especially under the
postindependence governments. Both al-Tahtawi and al-Tunisi, he says,
understood that the principles of European modernity did not clash with
Arab identities, but rather with the interests of the ruling elites. These
elites compensated for their popular illegitimacy and political ineptitude
with a political and economic subservience to foreign powers; and they
covered themselves by propagating an ideology of national and religious
authenticity. Salafi thought itself, by insisting on a selective borrowing
from the West based on the distinction between an acceptable technological transfer and a cultural exchange prohibited in the name of a return to
the purity of religious origins, has provided a most dangerous justification
for economic dependence and political oppression.

For Wannous, what is also remarkable in al-Tahtawi and al-Tunisi's
thoughts is their rootedness in the historical realities of their times. Their
ideas encompassed the cultural as well as the political, the intellectual as
well as the historical. As intellectuals, these thinkers were integrated in
their societies and were not marginalized like the intellectuals of the late
twentieth century. The same could be said about the Nahda pioneers of
Arab theater, such as Marun Naqqash (1816–1817 to 1954–1955) and Ya'qub
Sannu' (1839–1912). Their plays, according to Wannous, had a greater impact
on their audiences, in spite of a literacy rate lower than in our times, because they were clearer in addressing their societies' concerns. They are today criticized for having made loose adaptations and even distorting pieces

of the world repertoire by taking too many liberties and using them for their own purposes.[12] And yet, for Wannous, their theater was more effective because it was not a detached intellectual or even academic activity, but a social and political activity in the first place.

Attempts at explaining the failure of the Nahda enlightenment project usually point out its lack of radicality, its Europeanized estrangement from its environment, its weak cognitive basis, and its confinement to a certain upper social class. Rather than restricting the matter exclusively to the intellectual sphere, asserts Wannous, we should seek answers in the interface among the political, economic, and social spheres. After the death of Muhammad Ali and the rise of Abdulhamid to the Ottoman throne, the modernization process came to a halt in Egypt. The country drowned in huge external debts, and the Salafis regained power and influence. More important, colonialism began to tear apart not only the region's social and economic structures, but also the knowledge and awareness of the Nahda thinkers. Colonial aggression resulted in prejudice regarding the European model of enlightenment and created ambiguities and suspicions with respect to the whole Nahda project. Both secularists and enlightened Islamic thinkers found their proposals caught in the double standards of a Europe that both championed supposedly universal enlightenment principles and at the same time led colonial wars. This confusion contributed to the strengthening of the conservative reaction. The colonial aggression blurred the Nahda problematic further by setting the terms of the confrontation, the Christian Europe versus the Muslim Orient, at a time when Christianity was definitely not the primary motive of this colonial Europe. The Arabs themselves, especially the Salafis, adapted these colonial terms, which were then used to redefine the Nahda problematic in terms of the old and the new, the pious and the irreligious.

Despite this confusion, some thinkers pursued the Nahda project. For Wannous, Taha Husayn's work is among the most radical enlightenment accomplishments. He summarizes the main features of Husayn's achievement in five points. First, by critically studying the literary tradition and deconstructing some of the most established beliefs about it, Husayn desacralized *turath* and moved it from the metaphysicotheological domain to the historical one. By unveiling the untenable arguments supporting the existence of pre-Islamic poetry as it had come to be assumed until then, he questioned the sacred and relativized the absolute, noting especially that many of the arguments he was deconstructing were found in the Qur'an. For him, all the inherited legacy, including the sacred book, was open to the free investigation of the critical mind and subject to open debate. No one today, says Wannous, would have the freedom and audacity to undertake publicly such a critique. Second, Husayn faced the religious institutions and their conservatism. He criticized the Azhar's outmoded and narrow educational system as well as the traditional Islamic scholars' intolerant ignorance. He believed that religion had become a tool of terror in the hands of power, and he clearly advocated the separation of state from religion. Third, he believed in the unity of human culture, a unity that does not deny the specificities of individual cultures. He recognized the Greek and Roman influences on Egyptian and Arab cultures. He believed in the unity of human reason, and the Europe he wanted to adopt was the Europe of the Enlightenment. Fourth, he saw that his enlightenment project required a sociopolitical ground without which it could not be carried out. For him, it was clear that there could be no reason and no science without freedom, no freedom without secularism, and no secularism without a modern state, public education, and democracy. And fifth, Husayn practiced what he believed in and carried out his project as much as he could as the head of the Education Ministry and in all the positions he came to hold during his lifetime.

It is not a surprise, adds Wannous, that this man could not accept the July revolution of 1952 that brought Gamal Abdel Nasser to power in Egypt. From then on, Husayn was marginalized, and, instead of flourishing, his project was brought to a halt. The conservatives of the time depicted him as an intellectual feudal, and the progressive thinkers did not embrace his project, preferring the contentment provided by the ready answers of superficial ideology. In spite of the 1952 revolution's achievements, Wannous thinks it paved the way for the failures that followed by disenfranchising the people, confiscating political work, and adopting a conciliatory thought that shunned any real and radical confrontation with ideology.

The Nahda thinkers, according to Wannous, may not have left us final and complete answers, but their courage in raising fundamental questions, their freedom in searching for answers, and the rootedness of their intellectual work in the sociopolitical realities of their times should remain for us valuable sources of inspiration. If colonialism was the phenomenon that thwarted enlightenment efforts at the turn of the twentieth century, the postindependence state was the factor that crushed these same efforts even more forcefully in the second half of the twentieth century. It is important, says Wannous, to analyze the power structure of the petty bourgeoisie governments of this epoch because it is this structure that severed the line of

earlier enlightenment activity and strangled critical thinking through political oppression. The postindependence state failed to modernize in any
real way, failed to defend successfully the national causes, failed to promote healthy and fair prosperity, failed to ensure its citizens' freedom and
dignity. It instrumentalized cultural issues to the benefit of its power needs
by creating fake problematics, like that of "authenticity versus contemporaneity." It championed an ideological and superficial authenticity even
while it indulged in economic dependence on the West.

In addition to all these failures and not unrelated to them were the
many military and political defeats of the second half of the twentieth century, the many revolutions crushed by colonial, neocolonial, and Zionist
pressures. In view of so many defeats, escape from reality, whether in the
form of an illusory attachment to an idealized golden past or the confident
expectation of a predetermined glorious future, is a great temptation, but
also an ultimate defeat, according to Wannous. And it is this ultimate defeat that he calls upon thinkers of the late twentieth century to prevent: the
awareness of the defeat should not deteriorate into a defeated awareness, as
Syrian Marxist thinker Yassin Hafez (1930–1978) might put it.[13] Even if the
struggle is Sisyphean because of the present circumstances, intellectuals
have to carry on the task of reflecting critically on reality and thinking
from within history. Historical awareness and historical thinking are for
Wannous one of the most important forms of critical thinking necessary
for enlightenment—hence, his admiration for the work of Qustantin Zurayq
and Abdallah Laroui, which I examine later in this chapter.

The scope of despair and humiliation is such, Wannous says, that it is
not easy to resist the recourse to *turath* used as an incantation or to withstand the lure of an inexorably glorious Islam, untouched by the vicissitudes of concrete history. It is on this desperate need to escape reality that
Islamist thinking feeds. The thought of Sayyid Qutb is a good illustration
of such ahistorical thinking, according to Wannous. In its cyclical view of
history, Islam is bound to regain power in order to patronize humanity
and to lay the ground for divine governance. By turning Islam into an abstract, ahistorical ideology, this view produces spiritual poverty, nurtures
religious and confessional conflicts, provides a logic of power and oppression, puts reason on the decline, and imposes "absolute truth" instead of
opening possibilities of dialogue and tolerance. This assessment was confirmed by the behavior of Islamist groups in the 1980s and 1990s, thinks
Wannous. The rise of such groups is surely a complex phenomenon that
needs to be analyzed from many angles, but one thing is clear: they are as

oppressive as the oppressive regimes they want to replace. They are in many ways a reaction and a product of these despotic regimes, but what they have to offer is just another form of oppression, this time in the name of God. Given a choice between an oppressive earthly god and a merciful heavenly God, people, in their despair, might be tempted to opt for the latter, especially after having been for a long time conditioned to obey. This militant Islamism hides the real problems of society, however, and paves the way for more dependency: first, by widening further the gap between the internal cultural and religious authenticity, on the one hand, and the external westernization of consumption and transfer of technology, on the other; and second, by prioritizing as its initial task the conversion and reform of fellow Muslims—a priority that suits the exploiting foreign powers well. As a result, this Islamist revolution can only solidify the power structure of the regimes it wants to fight and replace because what it has to offer is in reality more oppression, more dependency, and more parochialism. The mistake, says Wannous, is to think that this type of reactionary thinking will wither away by itself by becoming obsolete and that the manifestations of the petty bourgeois power structure will be temporary deviations and aberrations. Today, more than ever, this type of thinking and this mode of exercising power need to be squarely confronted.

Against this reactionary Islamist thinking, Wannous underlines his belief that the future cannot be found in the past and that Arabs have to reaffiliate themselves with the rest of humanity, with universal history and universal culture. In his reading of the second half of the twentieth century, Wannous concludes that the problem of enlightenment in the Arab world is not cultural, but political. The cultural component is one aspect of a more general national problem caused by political oppression—an oppression that erases faces and people, as he articulated in his 1967 play. Throughout his life, he insisted with growing emphasis on the importance of recognizing political oppression as the fundamental problem of Arab societies, so he increasingly called for a struggle for democracy as a necessary basis for enlightenment. This understanding of the root of the malaise as a political problem due to oppression began, as we saw, with the early-modern reflections on backwardness and progress, on decline and renewal. With the colonial invasion of the region and then the establishment of the newly independent nation-states, the focus on local political justice seems to have been replaced with an urge to affirm a cultural authenticity and an urgency to form a state and a nation with a heavy authoritarian and voluntaristic hand. When disillusionment regarding the postindependence states and governments set in, the concern for political justice and democracy once again came to the fore with increasing strength and determination. Whereas the 1970s and 1980s were dominated by culturalist concerns for heritage and authenticity, the 1990s were witnessing a growing preoccupation with the political.

It is indeed important to note that for about two centuries, thinkers in the Arab world have perceived and advocated with more or less urgency the centrality of political freedom for the multifaceted empowerment of their societies. In the postcolonial era, many Arab thinkers have tried to understand the way in which postindependence power structures confiscated this freedom. Their struggle, often under life-threatening conditions, has been to regain that freedom for themselves and for their fellow Arabs. This shift of emphasis from cultural identity to democracy appears in the works and debates I examine in this book. The 1967 defeat seems to have been the traumatic experience that laid bare the political realities of postindependence governments, a trauma exacerbated by the increasing sense of frustration in the face of growing Western hegemonies, ruthless forms of local repression, and the radicalization of militant fundamentalism. For many, the primary condition for any way out of the doom is the empowerment of the people through the recovery of civil and political liberties. Wannous's oeuvre offers a rich canvas of the main themes and issues of the growing Arab critique in the second half of the twentieth century that addressed the need for a renewed enlightenment, a rethinking of authenticity, an opening to the world, a revisiting of the Nahda, a recentering of attention on political oppression, and resistance of despair. The four thinkers I discuss next articulated this struggle differently in their different disciplines and with their different temperaments.

Humanistic Nationalism and Critical Reason: Qustantin Zurayq

The Battle for Culture

Qustantin Zurayq (1909–2000) is among the most prominent thinkers who reflected critically on the intricate aspects of composing a cultural identity. His work, spanning the second half of the twentieth century, aimed at formulating a conception of Arab nationalism that was enlightened and humanistic rather than chauvinistic and defensive like the many pan-Arab, pan-Islamic, and regional nationalist ideologies of his time. His views inspired the Arab nationalist movement and constituted a distinctive body of ideas and ideals that still represent today an alternative to those ideologies. Zurayq was respected and honored till the end of his life for both his intellectual probity and his moral integrity.[14]

Born in Damascus in 1909, Zurayq received an undergraduate training in mathematics at the American University of Beirut and a doctorate degree in history from the University of Chicago. He became a distinguished professor of history at the American University of Beirut and was its acting president for many years. He was also the rector of the Syrian University in the early 1950s and the president of the International Association of Universities from 1965 to 1970. He was a founding member of the Institute for Palestinian Studies based in Beirut until 1982.[15] He served as the plenipotentiary Syrian minister in Washington, D.C., and as the Syrian delegate to the United Nations General Assembly and Security Council from 1946 to 1947. However, he saw himself primarily as an educator and considered his main contribution to Arab nationalism to be in the field of academia. His published works, often with multiple reprints, cover a period of sixty years. His first book, *Al-wa'y al-Qawmi* (On National Awakening), appeared in 1939, and his last book, *Ma al-'Amal?* (What to Do?), was published in 1998. His collected works were published in Beirut by the Center for Arab Unity Studies in four volumes in 1994.[16] To my knowledge, very few of his works have been translated into European or other languages, although the collected works contain some articles and speeches written in English by Zurayq himself.[17] His writings include reflections on some of the major events of the times in the Arab world, such as the *nakba,* or the disaster, referring to the establishment of the state of Israel in 1948, which involved the dispossession of the Palestinians, and Israel's defeat of the Arab armies in 1967.[18] They also include comments on the various intellectual debates of the epoch. Here, I focus on his two major treatises: one on culture, *Fi Ma'rakat al-Hadara* (In the Battle for Culture, 1964), and one on history, *Nahnu Wa al-Tarikh* (We and History, 1959), because much of his conception of Arab nationalism rested on elaborate reflections on culture and history.

But before I discuss these reflections, it is important to note the traits that characterized Zurayq's thought and writing in a general way. Zurayq succeeded in combining a sense of reality, based on a relentless concern for facts and givens, with a sense of hope, based on a belief in people's capacity to confront and transform realities. In his work, sober, modest, and courageous intellectual honesty accompanied a deep sense of compassion and commitment. His tone was invariably modest and moderate. His theorizing addressed rather than evaded the moods of pain, despair, and disquietude or anxiety (*qalaq*) that prevailed among his fellow Arabs. Transforming disquietude from a paralyzing anxiety into a mobilizing force for reflection and action was a challenge he attempted to meet throughout his intellectual career. His last book, addressed to the new generation, focuses precisely on this challenge. He was a caring and loving thinker who called for tolerance and openness, but who could not tolerate quietism, escapism, fanaticism, and mediocrity. Ever vigilant against all forms of simplistic reductionism, absolutism, and determinism, he constantly reminded his reader of the complexity of human phenomena. His thought was based on a solid faith in the capacity of the human being and in the capacity of the Arab as a human being to make history and to make culture using the assets at hand. All these traits constitute in themselves a most valuable moral and intellectual legacy to thinking culture.

For Zurayq, Arab nationalism was primarily a civilizational project rather than a defensive obsession with identity boundaries in need of protection. For this project, the civilizational powers of Arab individuals and collectivities had to be set free for the sake of liberation, progress, and abundant life. *Fi Ma'rakat al-Hadara* (In the Battle for Culture) is not about a battle *between* cultures, but about a battle *for* culture—not a culture given for consumption or glorification, but a culture to be earned and created by human effort. Zurayq did not tire of emphasizing the decisive role of human agency or of attacking all forms of cultural and historical determinism:

> *The main factors in civilizational changes are in our view acquired volitional human factors. . . . We doubt all analyses that deny human freedom—whether in the individual or in the collectivity—that neglect its effect and that consider human behavior to be determined. Natural or environmental factors, such as race and heredity, geographic situation, economic system, and social, intellectual, and moral conditions, are all possibilities or bonds. And possibilities and bonds do not make life, nor do they give rise to cultures. It is the human being who becomes aware of these bonds and strives to overcome them, and who realizes the possibilities and works to fulfill them, who is the maker. It is with this awareness and this striving that civilizations rise and fall.[19]*

The complexity of cultures, analogous to the complexity of life itself, cannot be reduced to one factor, be it natural or metaphysical. Here, Zurayq rejects the various doctrines of determinism and monism that prevail in theories of culture: destiny in ancient Greek thought; progressive reason in European Enlightenment thinking; evolutionary progress in the positivism of Darwin, Spencer, and Comte; the will of God in monotheism; and the "absolute *Geist*" or "Idea of freedom" in Hegel. Such doctrines, according to him, are superimposed on human history rather than derived from its concrete givens. He equally rejects deterministic forms of cultural pluralism, such as Spengler's romantic essentialist relativism.[20] Human history, says Zurayq, shows a variety of human cultures that have distinct characteristics, but also at the same time common features due to the universality of the human powers that give rise to them. It is only by being studied in connection to one another and within the universal human perspective that cultures can be understood and appreciated. All his comments on Arab culture are made within this wide humanistic framework. Distinct cultures, such as the Chinese, the Arab, the Indian, or the European, can be viewed as identifiable entities only insofar as we can distinguish them from one another and refer to them individually, but not in the sense of rigidly closed and defined units. Each society's unifying characteristic (*mayyiza*) is to be understood as a "personality" (*shakhsiyya*), a "spirit" (*ruh*), or a "general ambience" (*jaww ʿamm*) prevailing over the various domains of life at a given time. He immediately adds that this unifying characteristic is difficult to define: Where would one look for it? What kind of data would enable us to recognize it and grasp it with certainty? Far from conceiving "general ambience" as some kind of a given essence, we should loosely define it and use it with great caution. It is the closest that we get to the idea of identity in his four-hundred-page essay on the topic. The notion of identity itself, *huwiyya*, never appears in it.

The Revolution of Reason and the Distinction Between the Prescriptive and the Descriptive

Cultures or civilizations,[21] for Zurayq, are the whole set of material and spiritual elements that prevail in a given society at a given point in history: technological inventions and devices designed primarily to control the environment, customs and folklore, religion and value systems, laws and norms of *savoir-vivre*, forms of government and economy, language and writing, literature and arts, science and philosophy, as well as outstanding personalities. These elements display the complexity and interconnectedness of life and serve as important multifaceted approaches to the study of human societies at a time of increased specialization and fragmentation of knowledge.

Zurayq is among the rare theoreticians of human culture who explicitly distinguish between a descriptive review of cultures and a normative critical evaluation of the Arab world and beyond,[22] not because he thinks that these two aspects can be neatly and absolutely separated, but because he believes that they need to be accounted for in different and nuanced ways. He explicitly affirms his greater interest in the evaluative reflection on cultures and underlines the importance of bringing to consciousness, as much as possible, the motivations, foundations, and purposes behind such a reflection. Values, in terms of which the evaluation is to be conducted, need to be made explicit, accounted for, and recognized as moral and ethical preferences so that a clear debate can be engaged about them. These values for Zurayq are not to be superimposed as abstract and perennial givens, but to be drawn from an understanding of cultural phenomena, their constitutive elements, their different manifestations, their different functions, their patterns of change, and the human powers that bring them forth. This is what he proposes to do in *Fi Maʿrakat al-Hadara*, with the purpose of better understanding the pressing issues of the contemporary Arab world. In order to distinguish these two different aspects of thinking culture, he explicitly chooses to use the term *hadara*, "culture," to designate the descriptive givenness of a culture, and the term *tahaddur*, "the process of becoming civilized," to refer to the evaluative criteria in terms of which cultures are to be critically assessed.

The human powers that make culture are for him the civilizational powers of human reason in its critical, creative, cognitive, moral, and aesthetic functions. Faith in these powers and work toward their realization are the founding acts of human cultures. These powers call upon a whole set of values that make up the important requirements for human agency and creativity—namely, respect for truth, intellectual honesty, hard work, perseverance, seriousness, sense of commitment, responsibility, and freedom. They allow humans to acquire scientific knowledge, to nurture a conscience, and to develop a sense of beauty and justice. Their function is to serve the liberation and dignity of the human being. Through science, people are empowered to control their environment and their natural resources, and thus to liberate themselves as much as possible from the natural elements as well as from superstition, dependence, and magical-wishful thinking. Through their conscience, people are enabled to work toward a just and moral society and to liberate themselves from oppression. They are reminded that the final purpose of any empowerment is to serve the freedom and dignity of human beings as individuals and communities. The real progress that civilizational powers achieve is in the more abundant lives that humans can have through the realization of these powers. The Arab culture's current state of weakness and decline is caused by the atrophy of these powers among Arabs due to a number of historical circumstances. Only a relentless effort to reactivate them can show Arabs the way out of their predicament. This reactivation requires a sober confrontation with their past and present realities and an honest examination of themselves. It requires what Zurayq calls a "revolution of reason":

> *This revolution of reason is, in our view, the guarantee for any other revolution and the necessary condition for its solidity and success. It is, for us, the need that gathers in it all the needs of the Arab peoples in this crucial period of their lives and in the fierce cultural struggle they are engaged in. . . . It is with rationalism that these peoples realize that their first problem is cultural underdevelopment, and with it that they come to examine themselves and long for the process of civilization; it is with rationalism that they believe in truth and in reason, that they envisage the future, that they open up for the good wherever it comes from, that their productive forces emerge, that they realize their human potentials and master their political, economic, and social revolutions.*[23]

This revolution of reason, he says, is the authentic revolution that can lead the Arab peoples toward development and solidarity. It is the only revolution that can bring about an Arab national unity based on a secular democracy in which diverse individuals and communities can fulfill themselves in a framework of tolerance and mutual respect. Such a revolution can be undertaken only with a sense of self that is well rooted in both the past and the present, but also that is sharply critical of them, confident in its ability to achieve change and liberation. Critical history writing is indispensable for the formation of such a sense of self. Here we see the dialectical connection between critique and a certain understanding of self: an understanding of the self that is not deterministically defined by history, nature, or metaphysics makes room for agency, choice, deliberation, responsibility, and critical thinking; critical thinking implies in turn a notion of the self that is capable of reflecting on itself, of distancing itself from itself, and of refashioning itself. Unfortunately, the pressures of a postcolonial and voluntaristic state push rather for a defensive notion of the self that is "massively solid"; they push for a defensive and repressive evasion of critical thinking and questioning.

The Writing and the Making of History

Zurayq's essay on history, *Nahnu Wa al-Tarikh* (We and History), is devoted to the formulation of guidelines for writing critical history. Its topic is the making of historiography and the making of history. For both, one needs an interest in and a respect for truth. History writing is not to serve the temptation to mystify the past or escape the present. It is to give a clear awareness of one's embeddedness in a concrete history, of one's historicity in thought and action, and at the same time of one's capacity and duty to have a critical view of the past, thanks again to the critical powers of reason. It is these powers that can prevent the past from becoming a dead and paralyzing burden and that can serve instead as the foundation for creating a progressive future on the basis of a solid sense of rootedness in the individual and the community. These powers can enable the historian to reflect critically on his or her motivations, models of analysis, and criteria of judgment. Of course, no historian can totally detach himself or herself from his or her own historicity, but a critical reflection about it can enhance a valuable awareness of his or her position in and toward this history. Again, Zurayq rejects all forms of historical determinism and all forms of dogmatic ideological reading of history, whether chauvinist, theological, or Marxist. He also rejects narrow views of Arab history that reduce it to Islamic history or to a regionalist, factional history. Arab history for him needs to be understood in the widest sense possible and to be explored in connection with other ancient and recent civilizations of the area. The authenticity of our national historical rootedness, he says, is to be accompanied by the authenticity of our rootedness in human history at large.

History is to be judged with a mind free of dogma as much as is humanly possible. But history in a different sense also judges us in the way we meet our present challenges and in the kind of questions we raise about the past. It judges us on our seriousness and on the level of our awareness. It judges us on our ability to question:

And history judges on the quality of questions that we ask about it. We may question, but not question ourselves. We may direct our questions to our natural and human environment. Our questions may be right or wrong, deep or superficial, wide or narrow, serious or futile. We may ask to get a quick and easy answer because we get satisfied

with the near and the easy and because we do not yearn for the diffi-
cult. And if we turn from the exterior to ourselves, we may fulfill the
requirements of questioning or not, we may possess the necessary
courage to examine and criticize ourselves or not, and we may have
the needed intellectual and moral probity to do that well or not.[24]

This ability to question, with all the virtues it requires, is for Zurayq the decisive characteristic of an authentically empowered culture. The battle for nationalism is a battle for culture, which is in turn a battle for critical reason. This call for reason may be taken for a naive belief in an Enlightenment ideology or a blind imitation of the West. For Zurayq, critical reason is neither a Western essence nor a Western property. Westernization does not appear as an issue or a concern in his works. Rather, he sees critical reason more as the dominating characteristic of modernity, with all its achievements and weaknesses. He does admit that critical reason has greatly empowered Western cultures, but differently in different domains. He thinks that the West's critical reason has achieved more in science than in morality, that it has been used more to produce instruments than to ponder final ends. He is well aware of the Western power politics, of the gap between the advanced and the underdeveloped countries, and of the colonial and neocolonial impact of this Western modernity on the rest of the world, in particular the Arab world. To face this impact, he argues, Arabs have to grasp the fundamental workings of this modernity that is increasingly spreading around the globe. For their own advancement, they also need to take the principles of enlightened modernity, argued throughout his theories on culture and history, as empowering principles in themselves. For Zurayq, this task of critical reason remains an ideal goal to be approximated by constant effort. Like enlightenment through critical reason, Arab unity is for him a goal that has to be worked for. This unity has preoccupied many Arab thinkers throughout the twentieth century. It has been the central issue of debate in numerous Arab conferences and studies in which the nature, requirements, chances, purposes, setbacks, and failures of Arab unity have been repeatedly analyzed. Zurayq's approach is distinguished by an ethical concern for unity's ends and means. This unity, for him, is not the telos of an inexorable ethnic or religious destiny, but a form of solidarity for mutual empowerment by democratic means aimed at serving both individuals' and communities' dignity and freedom.

In many ways, this call for reason is obviously a call for the Enlightenment values—values that in the course of the twentieth century came under

attack by many Western thinkers, who disclosed their repressive components (Horkheimer, Adorno, Foucault) as well as their unfounded claim on
the nature of human understanding (Gadamer, McIntyre). The complex
debates that took place in the West on the critique of the Enlightenment and
the critique of modernity belong to a Western history in which many of the
achievements of the Enlightenment were realized, such as democracy, rule
of law, and basic liberties. These achievements are rarely questioned, even
by the strongest critics of the Enlightenment. The absence of these achievements in the postcolonial world gives to Enlightenment values a different
priority and a different urgency there—hence, the dismay that many non-
Western thinkers experience when anti- and post-Enlightenment critique is
imported into the postcolonial world. The main critique that these thinkers
direct against modernity and its Enlightenment ideals centers on the colonialism that accompanied those ideals, referring to it as the "underside of
modernity." For them, the racism and the double standard that characterized the European Enlightenment are the most problematic aspects of
modernity. Most Western critics of modernity in general ignore these two
aspects.[25]

In the course of his intellectual career, Zurayq saw in the most painful
events of the region valuable occasions to raise fundamental questions
about the self and about the ways these events are confronted. His essays
on the 1948 and 1967 dramatic events are exercises in such a questioning
that call for a cultural change through critical reason, a battle for cultural
development, and a battle for critical reason in dealing with those events.
Indeed, after 1967, many voices would join his in insisting on the need to
turn the critical gaze inward. Egyptian social thinker Anouar Abdel-Malek
summarizes this turn in the introduction to his anthology of Arab political
thought published first in Paris as *La pensée arabe contemporaine* and then
in a modified English version as *Contemporary Arab Political Thought*:

*The axis of that analysis has now shifted dramatically. The other—
imperialism—is no longer set up as the sole or even the main problem.
Determinant factors endogenous to socially and historically specific
contemporary Arab societies are now the main focus for analysis.
True, even before 1967, both levels were considered, especially by Arab
Marxists, ever-attentive to issues of class struggle. But the primacy of
the united national front against imperialism meant that endogenous
criticism had to be relegated to the background—or at least that was
the prevailing sentiment at the time. The June 1967 war broke that*

reticence completely. Since then, the Arab masses and the Arab intel-ligentsia have critically scrutinized the structure of national life in its entirety, from the economic to the ideological, and not excluding the apparatus of state, the centrepiece of any society, whatever cabinet may be in power. That scrutiny was like a blade turned in the wound, and orientated the Arab people towards a revolution lying beyond the national liberation which would have to be won through political armed struggle.[26]

The Critique of Religious-Metaphysical Thought: Sadeq Jalal al-Azm

The Thunderbolt of 1967, the Nahda's Fragility, and Self-criticism

In a 1997 interview, Syrian philosopher Sadeq Jalal al-Azm, born in Damascus and trained at Yale University, described the impact of the 1967 defeat on the Arab intellectuals as follows: "Naturally, the defeat of June 1967 interrupted all plans and revealed the fragility of the modern Arab intellectual renaissance on which the Arab liberation movement based its hopes. Most of these hopes revolved around the concept of the inspired leader, and when the leader [Abdel Nasser] fell everything crashed with him, leaving nothing behind but emptiness, loss, and confusion. I would not be exaggerating when I say that the defeat hit us like a lightening bolt." Further he says: "The 1967 defeat was an exceptional event in every sense of the word, a terrifying explosion which destroyed the foundations of the Arab liberation movement."[27] The liberation movement, especially in its socialist trend under the leadership of Abdel Nasser, had, in al-Azm's opinion, undertaken a number of transformations on the economic and political levels by overthrowing the monarchy and seizing power and by redistributing land and abolishing the feudal system. But it had not really challenged the "superstructure" of Arab society—that is, the systems of thought, value, and belief. It had tried to conveniently shun a real confrontation with these systems. The 1967 debacle showed for al-Azm that no real revolutionary transformation could be accomplished without such a radical confrontation. For him, it was certain conservative ways of thinking and behaving that were largely responsible for what had happened. His book *Al-Naqd al-Dhati ba'd al-Hazima* (Self-Criticism after the Defeat), published in Beirut in 1969 (and reprinted three times by the following year) addressed precisely these conservative ways.[28] In the 1997 interview, Al-Azm added:

I and others like myself fell victim to the prevailing belief that the changes we were witnessing had surpassed all the issues brought forward by the Arab Nahda *(Renaissance) of the late 19th and early 20th Centuries. In other words, we fell victim to the erroneous idea that history had already decided all the issues raised by the* Nahda *in favor of progress, genuine modernization, modern science, secularism, socialism, and national liberation. We also felt that retreat from all this had become impossible and that duty dictated the need to continue the struggle at all levels in order to deepen these values in our contemporary lives. Based on this, I used to criticize some intellectuals of the period who were in the habit of marshaling the ghosts of Muhammad Abduh and al-Afghani in support of their views, as though nothing had transpired since the beginning of the Twentieth Century. As intellectuals and thinkers, we used to view ourselves as part of a new reality which had overtaken the* Nahda *phase. We used to think that we represented a movement which had, at least in principle, transcended the issues raised by Muhammad Abduh, al-Afghani, and the rest of the luminaries of* al-Nahda. *But today we find ourselves defending the accomplishments of* al-Nahda *against Salafi and other obscurantist attacks. Our mistake was to believe that the period in question, namely the 1960s, had historically superseded the* Nahda.[29]

It was at this point that he and his companions, he says, realized the need for a radicalization of critique for the sake of a genuinely progressive and revolutionary future. For this purpose, scientific thinking was to replace metaphysical-religious thinking. He undertook this task in his 1970 book *Naqd al-Fikr al-Dini* (Critique of Religious Thought).[30] The book caused a scandal, and al-Azm was brought to trial in Beirut on charges of provoking religious troubles, but was acquitted. At the time, he was a professor of philosophy at the American University of Beirut. Soon after the publication of the book, the department declined to renew his contract, most probably because of his Marxist positions. Al-Azm then worked for the Research Center of the Palestinian Liberation Organization in Beirut but was dismissed for his unflinching and uncompromising critical positions. For the same reasons, he also became persona non grata in Syria. After long years of exile in the West (with some of that time in the United

States), he returned to Damascus in 1990 and became chair of the philosophy department at the University of Damascus and professor of modern
European philosophy, all the while upholding his advocacy for secular critique. In the 1997 interview, he explained how the dramatic events of the
1960s had pushed him to abandon the aloofness of a philosopher and to
begin to comment on political, economic, and even military issues.[31]

In *Self-Criticism After the Defeat*, he raises a number of questions reminiscent of Zurayq's preoccupations. In his introduction, he hopes that Arab
thought has matured enough not to mistake his critique for calumny, but
instead to receive it as a harsh but constructive analysis of the recent dramatic experiences. He starts this analysis by comparing the 1967 Israeli-
Arab war with the Japanese-Russian war of 1904: in both cases, a small
country defeated a much larger nation, contrary to all expectations. But
whereas the defeat of 1904, according to him, provoked in Russia a severe
questioning of established attitudes and institutions, leading to the revolution of 1905 and eventually to that of 1917, the Arab defeat did not seem
to lead to self-examination. Instead, the evasion of responsibility was the
dominant trait of the Arab reaction to the defeat, a reaction that was for
him as troubling as the defeat itself. His analysis suggests that both phenomena, the defeat and the reaction to it, were indicative of a certain
prevailing mentality among the Arabs of the time. They blamed the defeat on a number of external factors: God's punishment for their lack of
religious commitment, the trickery of the Israeli armed forces, their brutality, the support given to Israel by Western forces as a result of the
world Zionist hegemony, colonialism and imperialism, the contingent
circumstances of the battle itself, and so on. The use of the term *nakba*
(disaster) itself to refer to the defeat, he points out, suggests that what
happened was some kind of a natural phenomenon over which Arabs had
no control whatsoever.

According to al-Azm, all of these approaches lack accurate factual foundations and elude the Arab share of responsibility in the course of events.
For him, theological explanations clearly have no place in what happened.
The Israeli army's behavior should not have surprised peoples and states
that regarded Israel as a dangerous enemy and viewed the confrontation
with it as an existential one. Its acts should instead have been anticipated
and prepared for. Similarly, colonial and imperialistic factors were well
known to the Arabs while they were consciously preparing for the battle. As
for the power of Israel, he says, Arabs had either trivialized it or inflated it
instead of facing it in realistic terms: on the one hand, with an exaggerated

sense of their own omnipotence they presented the march on Israel as a "stroll"; and, on the other hand, they presented Israel and the Zionist world hegemony as omnipotent and invincible. For al-Azm, both attitudes lacked a respect for truth and a concern with reality. He sketches briefly the economic situation of the Jews in the United States and their relative power in a country that is ruled by WASP money and by a white racist supremacy that is applied to Jews as well as to blacks, Native Americans, and other minorities. The idea of a Zionist manipulation of "innocent" Western powers blurs the fact that these powers have their own imperialistic economic and political interests in the area and that it is in their interest to crush liberation movements that stand in their way.

Easy, quick, simplistic, and ill-informed analyses cannot, in al-Azm's opinion, be the answer to the Arab predicament. They are the product of a prevailing mentality typical of the *fahlawi* personality, the "smart" or con man, in Arab societies—a typification elaborated by Arab sociologist Hamid Ammar in a study published in 1964.[32] This character seeks success with the least possible effort and in the shortest possible way; he is not concerned with failure as such, but rather with the embarrassment and the shame that it brings; he is not interested in confronting realities, avoids sacrifice, and cannot sustain long-term commitment; he has no work ethic, no perseverance, no seriousness; his excitement for revolution is superficial; he is in reality a rather conservative character who has no sense of initiative, no individual interest or ability to bear responsibility, no creativity; he is basically subservient to authority. Whether among students, civil servants, or officers, this prevailing character, according to al-Azm, is largely responsible for how things are handled in the Arab world: with a lack of seriousness, a lack of perseverance, and a lack of creativity. It is the character of a weak individual, subjected to the pressures of a patriarchal, traditionalist society that has failed to modernize itself. And one of the manifestations of this failure is the political and military defeat of 1967. Clearly, al-Azm uses a sharp tradition/modernity binary in which modernity is associated with reason, science, analysis, and democracy (and the West) and tradition is associated with myth, religion, rhetoric, and hierarchical authority. In this binary, no attention is paid to the myths carried by modernity, such as those of progress and total emancipation, and no account is made of the critical components that tradition might contain. For al-Azm, what is most pertinent here is modernity's principle of questioning authority and tradition—in other words, modernity as critique and as an indispensable tool for liberation and agency.

It is interesting to note that the book *Self-criticism After the Defeat* was recently reedited and published in Damascus.[33] Reflecting on this reissue in 2007, almost four decades after the book's first appearance and forty years after the defeat, Palestinian literary critic Faysal al-Darraj explains the book's continuing relevance by pointing to the persisting state of defeat in the Arab world since 1969.[34] At the time, its author, says al-Darraj, believed in the possibility of overcoming the crisis and the defeat. Arab regimes had not yet sunk into deep inertia and impotence in all matters except holding on to power and repressing their people; and Arab societies had not yet immured themselves in populist religious doctrines. Underdevelopment and defeat remain for him the two conspicuous ills of much of the Arab world and the state of impotence its dominating sense. The notion of impotence, *al-ʿajz* is indeed the recurring notion in fin de siècle Arab discourses. Moreover, for al-Darraj, the book's continuing relevance resides in its honest spirit of critique, which is needed more than ever, and in its attempt at explaining the human disappointments caused by 1967 in human terms, without reference to occult factors.

Oppositional Syrian intellectual Yassin al-Haj Saleh, imprisoned in 1980 at age nineteen for his affiliation with a Marxist student association and released sixteen years later in 1996, has some interesting thoughts on the continuing contemporaneity of the June 1967 defeat. He thinks that the Arab nationalist discourse has made it into a founding event, a kind of original sin, in terms of which everything is to be understood. Only a deconstruction of this narrative, he says, will show the 1967 defeat, although painful and humiliating, to be merely the historical event that it was. For him, the events that followed, such as the repression in Syria between 1979 and 1982, and the wars waged by Saddam Hussein, were much bigger disasters for Arab peoples than the Six Day War of 1967. But no such deconstruction has taken place so far, and no new narrative has come to replace the nationalist one. al-Haj Saleh believes that the power and knowledge structures of 1967 persist, and with them the myth of the founding event.[35]

The Call for Enlightenment and the Attack on Metaphysical Thinking

Al-Azm relates the defeat of 1967 to the failure of radical modernization. Arabs, he says, were not defeated because of the lack of weapons, but because of the lack of human power trained to use modern weapons and modern warfare. They need to understand the importance of science in empowering themselves militarily, politically, socially, and culturally. No socialist revolution can be successfully undertaken without a scientific approach to matters. The defeat showed the need to radicalize revolution in the face of rising reactionary forces in the wake of the defeat, forces that often hide behind the claim of respecting traditions and customs. Half measures, based on the fear of taking clear positions, cannot lead to satisfactory results. The idea of the Arab nation or Islam as a "middle" nation, not aligned with any camp and equidistant from all ideologies, indicates a lack of commitment to changes that are necessary.[36] Among the needed social changes is the emancipation of women as a goal in itself and as an indispensable contribution to the socialist revolution. But the most important change is to be made in the overall mode of thinking—namely, from the mythical-metaphysical thinking of religion to the rational-material thinking of science. In the 1997 interview, al-Azm said that even before 1967 he had seen the importance of applying critical philosophical thinking to certain contemporary cultural questions, such as reading the sacred texts critically. He noted that in *Critique of Religious Thought* he mentioned his rereading of the story of Iblis (Satan) from an existentialist-Marxist point of view. After 1967, however, it became even clearer to him that what was needed was a more fundamental attack on the reactionary modes of thinking that prevailed at the time even among those who understood themselves to be revolutionary. He saw his critical work as a work of enlightenment:

> We viewed ourselves within the context of the Arab liberation movement as forces of enlightenment in the classic sense of the term. If we go back to the European Enlightenment of the Eighteenth Century, we find that this movement was the direct result of the scientific revolution of the Seventeenth century. The Enlightenment meant codifying the new knowledge which resulted from the scientific revolution and then disseminating it throughout society, making it available not only to all who wanted it, but also to the centers of power and authority in state and society. The idea was to make this new knowledge the basis for organizing production, administering society and the state, and rearranging intellectual, educational, and political life, instead of basing all of these on theology and customary practice. This new knowledge meant also the development of an advanced and critical consciousness based on the new sciences and new social and class developments in the more advanced European countries of the time.

This is why we emphasized Hegelian leftism which gave rise to an enlightened and critical approach to the intellectual life of Germany during the Nineteenth Century instead of emphasizing the Eighteenth Century.[37]

It is in this enlightenment spirit that he launched his attack on the religious and metaphysical modes of thinking in *Critique of Religious Thought*. This attack was also directed against the superficial and untenable conciliatory position that the liberation movement had hitherto adopted toward the cultural tradition and that had resulted in the protection of backward institutions and mentalities. In the book, al-Azm opposes science to religion and refutes the claim that Islam does not conflict with science. The whole system of belief formation, he says, is different from one realm to the other: in religion it is based on the authority of sacred texts and established references, whereas in science it is based on doubt, the challenge of established beliefs, and the search for yet unknown but knowable matters. As long as the religious mode of belief formation dominates, no new knowledge can be acquired. According to him, a number of untenable strategies have been adopted to meet the challenge posed by science to religion: concordism, which holds that all claims of science are found in one way or another in the holy book—a ridiculous position that cannot be taken seriously; the rejection of science altogether, which can only produce intellectual suicide; and the distinction between the temporal and the eternal, which cannot really be held because the two modes of thinking cannot coexist in a society. For al-Azm, the only solution is to direct the emotions and the energies operative in religiosity toward art and nonreligious political activism. In using this sharp binary (religion/tradition versus science/modernity), he seems oblivious to the possibility that religion can serve as the ground for mobilization for change and revolution, as in the case of the church in the African American struggle for civil rights in the United States, in the Polish and East German struggles against Communist rule, and in the Latin American liberation movement.[38]

In Defense of Arab Dissidence
In the decades following *Critique of Religious Thought*, al-Azm remained consistent in his defense of critical thinking and a sharp opponent of the Islamic fundamentalist movements that became dominant in the last quarter of the twentieth century. In the long article "The Importance of Being

Earnest About Salman Rushdie," he compares Rushdie's *Satanic Verses* to the dissident-sacrilegious works of Rabelais, James Joyce, and Jean Genet. He criticizes the Western reaction to the death sentence decreed for Rushdie by Khomeini because instead of embracing Rushdie as an Islamic dissident as had been done with Soviet dissidents, the reaction more or less blamed him for provoking prevailing Islamic powers. The assumption behind the reaction is that such intolerance befitted the world of Islam: "Perhaps the deep-seated and silent assumption in the West remains that Muslims are simply not worthy of serious dissidents, do not deserve them, and are ultimately incapable of producing them; for, in the final analysis, it is the theocracy of the Ayatollahs that becomes them."[39]

In the article, Al-Azm recalls the long tradition of dissidence in the history of Islamic thought and all the works that were banned and the authors who were condemned in more recent history for transgressing established beliefs, including his own *Critique of Religious Thought*, Taha Husayn's *Fi al-Shi'r al-Jahili* (On Jahili Poetry), Ali Abdel Raziq's *Al-Islam wa Usul al-Hukm* (Islam and the Principles of Governing), and many others. He sees in these recurring incidents a persistent need for questioning traditional conceptions and a sustained vitality in critical thinking amidst momentous sociocultural transformations: "Why do these Rushdie-type cases and incidents keep coming up with such striking regularity? Why all these Rushdies? Could it be that Muslim societies in general and Arab societies in particular are so positioned in the modern world, so integrated into the main drift of contemporary history, so racked by transforming oppositions and tensions as to make the production of more and more Rushdies a virtual inevitability?"[40]

He notes that the majority of the signatories to Rushdie's defense and the freedom of speech in the Muslim world were Arabs. He adds: "Rushdie's carnivalesque manner of calling things by their names without mental reservations and/or resort to euphemisms is already a contribution to greater contemporary Muslim self-awareness and critical self-examination. More specifically, his work will eventually find its place in the mainstream efforts of millions of living educated Muslims searching to make sense out of the deplorable conditions of historical irrelevance that their cultures and societies unquestionably suffer in the modern world." But, he adds, there is nothing predestined about the frustration and depression of Muslims living in the modern world. What they need is "Reason and Revolution, rather than mere good old Submission."[41]

The Critique of Ideology and Historicization: Abdallah Laroui

Contextualizing Ideas

According to Moroccan historian Abdallah Laroui, the need for self-examination radicalized by the defeat of 1967 started with the establishment of a postindependence petite bourgeoisie type of sociopolitical structure in a number of Arab countries in the 1960s. Change seemed to be stalled, and traditionalism appeared to be as anchored as ever. His work searches for the sociocultural reasons behind this predicament.

Trained as a historian at the Sorbonne in Paris and then serving as a professor of history at Rabat University in Morocco, Laroui published his first book in 1967 in French, *L'idéologie arabe contemporaine* (Contemporary Arab Ideology). It was immediately translated into Arabic and had a powerful impact on the Arab intellectual scene. It was followed in 1974 by *La crise des intellectuels arabes: Traditionalisme ou historicisme?* which was translated into Arabic and English in 1976.[42] What Abdallah Laroui calls the "contemporary Arab ideology" is the set of models of explanation or action that Arab intellectuals have used since the nineteenth century for their identity, their past, and their society. *L'idéologie arabe contemporaine* is an exercise in self-reflection devoted to a critical examination of the tools of thinking that have dominated the Arab mind since the Nahda in order to achieve an awareness of the nature, function, origin, and adequacy of these tools and models. For him, these models and tools do not exist outside space and time as abstract and disembedded universals, but are the product of specific sociohistorical realities. Only such an effort in contextualization can save Arab thinking from the pitfalls of anachronism and ideological delusion. This effort at examining the link between models of explanation or action and sociohistorical realities is what Laroui calls *historicism*.[43] He considers it to be an indispensable critical tool for Arab self-reflection. Based in part on a number of public lectures delivered in Rabat, Algiers, Tunis, and Beirut, his second book, translated into English as *The Crisis of the Arab Intellectual: Traditionalism or Historicism?* develops this investigation further. In the preface, he states his main concern:

> What are the definitive achievements of the Nahda, the shortcomings of the traditional political parties, the causes of the relative failures of Nasserism and of Baathism, the reasons for the failure of Arab Marxism? What interested my listeners was not so much the positive results as the

failures of these movements; for the question they were asking, given the situation around 1970, was this: Why, in spite of all our efforts, are we facing the same difficulties as our parents and grandparents faced?

The central thesis of this book is that the concept of history—a concept playing a capital role in "modern" thought—is in fact peripheral to all the ideologies that have dominated the Arab world till now.[44]

Critiquing Ideological and Ahistorical Thinking

For Laroui, ahistorical thinking amounts to a failure to see the real and so to an inability to effect any intellectual and political change in reality.[45] Ahistorical thinking is a way of escaping an overwhelming reality and of taking refuge in hypostatized absolutes, such as an atemporal past, an essentialist self, and a static tradition. The task of the Arab intellectual is therefore to demystify these absolutes and to reconnect ideas and actions to historical reality. Throughout the decades after the publication of *Crisis,* Laroui will emphasize the centrality of history and historicity for Arab thought and action. He explains in *Crisis* that although the readiness to reflect on these modes of thinking was present in the post–World War II era, the circumstances were not favorable to it:

Prior to the Second World War, Arab ideologists believed in the evidence of their thought and were scarcely concerned with understanding the nature of their thought processes. . . .

It was after their obtaining of political independence, the coming to power of a provincial petite bourgeoisie, the appearance of an "unattached" Arab intelligentsia of Palestinian origin whose literary production, published in Beirut, were disseminated throughout the Arab world, that the conditions were realized for the emergence of a "second degree" awareness; that is, the Arabs became aware of their thinking as ideological thinking. A general frame of reference was achieved that at once struck a fatal blow at provincialism, the objective basis of first-degree thinking.[46]

Yet *Crisis* does not end on an optimistic note, and much of it is devoted to exploring the factors that keep obstructing the growth of self-reflective, critical thought in the Arab world.

Laroui bases his analysis on what he regards as two undeniable facts. The first is the political, economic, social, scientific, and cultural retardation in which the Arab world has found itself in its modern encounter with the West. This retardation, he says, is the primary experiential fact that has shaped the Arab intellectual mode of thinking the self in the recent past. The urgency of catching up with the West has pushed Arabs to borrow ready-made models of explanation and action before looking at them in a critical and thorough fashion. The second fact is the intricate connection with the West that resulted from the colonial encounter. The West is omnipresent in Arab reality and Arab thinking, he says. Every Arab definition of the self contains a certain idea of the West and certain Western ideas about history, economy, society, and so on. This interpenetration of ideas and ideologies is not to be wished away. It is a fact that can only be dealt with critically—that is, by an awareness of the context of these ideas and of their historicity, which is attainable only through a close examination of the West's history.[47] In the absence of a historical knowledge of Western realities and Western ideas, the misuse of theories has often misguided Arab thinkers regarding themselves and the West. In the context of this interpenetration, Orientalism has had a confusing effect, presenting the "Orient," or the Arab world, as a field of symbols and ultimate meanings in the absence of serious positive historiography.[48] Laroui never tired of showing the correlation between Western Orientalism and colonial/imperial aggression, on the one hand, and Arab traditionalism, on the other.

According to Laroui, the holistic and essentialist approach to the Arab world is also found in an anthropology that reduces history to culture, culture to ideology, and ideology to theology—a reduction also adopted by Arab traditionalists. In this sense, he views his work as a cultural investigation, but not a culturalist one, meaning that the set of ideas and values he studies are not static superstructures or static objective spirits, but tools of understanding and action in a particular situation of striving and struggle, determined by a set of socioeconomic and political factors.[49] Again here a historical approach seems to him to be indispensable.

Laroui sketches three ideal types of interpreting and dealing with the retardation: the religious, the political, and the technophile. He follows their influences in the three forms of states that have dominated the Arab world in modern history: the colonial state, the liberal state, and the nationalist state. It is in the latter that he finds a growing concern with authenticity, both among rulers and in the opposing intelligentsia. He explains this concern as a reaction to the failure to catch up with the West and to a desolate present that seems to be hopelessly out of control.[50] The quest for authenticity seems to be closely associated with an interest in tradition:

> In the preceding chapters, it was already easy to see that if in Arab ideology self-consciousness was first a consciousness of the West, it was also consciousness of the past. To define oneself is for the Arabs mostly to determine a permanence throughout history. But this is only true at the end of the process; it is when the self cannot be grasped anymore that one resorts to the past to guarantee one's identity; it is when authenticity is but a nostalgic quest that it is identified with a postulated continuity.

> What is to be described is this long movement of Arab consciousness toward a stage where history becomes the essential element of the debate and at the same time loses its fluidity to become a protecting myth.[51]

Moreover, "The search for the past thus follows that for the self, so it is not surprising that one notices a perfect parallelism between the destinies of these two notions of authenticity and historical continuity."[52] This continuity is sought in religious dogma, in culture, especially the literary, and in language. But the history of religious dogma, Laroui observes, shows a clear diversity and change in the various periods of time. Its continuity is constructed and postulated. Literary culture is even more rooted in specific sociocultural realities, and when it is not, it becomes a dead weight. As to language, he says it is the most desperate attempt at establishing some sense of self:

> Until the historical material becomes malleable, that economy ceases to weigh as a fate, that nationalization and arabization do not seem contradictory, that linguistic pragmatism regains its rights, an intelligentsia, traditional or modern, lonely and abandoned, makes of this vision its exalted ideology: the past gets rid of a too resistant present and gets concentrated in a language, beautiful in itself—not for us, at a moment of our life. As a condensed image of the past, language becomes a fetish that one implores to guarantee an increasingly problematic authenticity and an increasingly illusory continuity.[53]

Laroui reminds us that other peoples have also known this kind of des-peration and have resorted to language and history to locate their self-identity and pride, as the Germans and the Russians did at certain points of their history.[54]

In this state of desperation and hopeless incapacity to catch up with the West, two contradictory modes of reasoning (translated as "reasons" in the text) with two contradictory logics seem to tear apart Arab consciousness—a technological mode that seeks salvation in technological progress and a mode that emphasizes authenticity as a certain intuitive sentiment of existence:

> To this question "What to do?" and to the one that flows from it "What method to follow?" the national state answers with two different voices. The technophile, having defined the West by technology, thinks that the method sought is given in technological Reason. The champion of au-thenticity, showing that this Reason does not account for his rejection and his revolt, raises against it the banner of another Reason, that of the instinct, of sentiment, of a certain tonality of existence.

> But neither gives a general validity to their choice or follows the re-spective logic till the end. The technophile realizes that his own situ-ation escapes any thought that is limited to positive Reason and refuses to acknowledge in theory what he practices in reality. The champion of authenticity, in contrast, never goes so far as to doubt the necessity of industrial and scientific development, founded on this same Reason that he despises continuously.[55]

For Laroui, the only way out of this impasse is to adopt the critical-historical approach: historical in the sense of engaging in a "positive"—honest and sound—history writing that puts the present in a real continu-ity and so allows us to examine it and to deal with it as a reality;[56] and historical also in the sense of contextualizing ideas and theories, especially those coming from the West, on the basis of a serious and nonfragmentary study of its history—a study that would enable Arabs to appropriate criti-cally and hence fruitfully the theories that they would deem useful, includ-ing Marxism, which Laroui himself adopted.[57] Only such a historicist con-textualization and critical appropriation would allow Arabs to become real contemporaries of their thoughts and their realities. In this connection, it is interesting to note the quotation he uses as an epigraph to the chapter "Historicism and the Arab Intelligentsia" in *Crisis*, from Marx's *Toward a*

Critique of Hegel's Philosophy of Right: "We are philosophical contemporaries of the present without being its historical contemporaries."[58]

Demystifying the Absolutes of Language, Heritage, and History

This need to make ideas and theories correspond to the reality at hand—in other words, the need to think the real—is the focus of Laroui's quest for authenticity. Authenticity should be the center of one's thought,[59] not by denying the Other, but by having a strong and critical awareness of one's self and the Other. Moreover, the approach is to be critical in the sense that it resists utopianism, exclusivism, and romanticism[60] and does not give in to the illusory worship of absolutes such as language, culture, and the past:

> *For all objective observers, the true alienation is this loss of self in the absolutes of language, culture, and the saga of the past. The Arab intellectual blithely plunges into them, hoping thus to prove his perfect freedom and to express his deepest personality. Here, then, are found the inward chains binding him to a present he yet claims to repudiate. Historical consciousness alone will allow him to free himself of them. Then he will see reality, perhaps for the first time. He will see that the absolutes he worships are alien to him, for they may be internalized only through intellectual analysis and synthesis, that is, through voluntary effort—never through inward understanding and intuition.[61]*

In other words, it is important to realize that language, culture, and the past are not givens to be taken for granted, but phenomena that need to be seriously explored and investigated in order to be appropriated in concrete living situations. Otherwise, one will continue to pursue the hopeless delusion of finding in them magical answers to difficult and real problems. Similarly, only serious effort will enable Arabs to resist the temptation of the double alienation of medievalization and westernization.[62] Finally, only a critical vigilance can protect them from empty sentimentalism and sterile rhetoric, from repression, and from the abuse of human rights:

> *All too long has the Arab intellectual hesitated to make radical criticisms of culture, language, and tradition. Too long has he drawn back from criticizing the aims of local national policy, the result of which is a stifling of democracy and a generalized dualism. He must condemn*

superficial economism, which would modernize the country and rationalize society by constructing factories with another's money, another's technology, another's administration. When it comes to the problems of minorities and local democracy, he must cease from censoring himself for fear of imperiling an apparent national unity. The Arab revolutionary intellectual has too long applauded the call to Arab unity, the while accepting and sometimes justifying the fragmentation that is reality.

Everyone subscribes to a unity founded on feeling; a unity founded on economy is condemned as being too slow to transpire. There are those who prefer to panegyrize Arab unity rather than bring it about. Only an historical critique can put an end to such seductions.[63]

Indeed, Laroui insists on the important link between a historicist, contextual view of things and democracy and science: namely, through thought that is open to falsification, discussion, modification, and relativization instead of absolutization:

In order that history may become the domain of well-defined, serious thought, it is necessary to regard becoming as the absolute. When you describe a given fact and wish to give it its true weight, you must not be at all certain of its value or that it possesses an absolute meaning or that it must be forever deprived of such a meaning; rather, you should believe that its meaning will slowly take shape, day after day, event after event, without ever attaining complete realization. All historical action is always in suspense, every sentence is under consideration. This principle is at once the foundation of historicism, democracy, and modern science. The democratic principle means that no one in society possesses political truth, that this truth will only gradually take shape through the procedures of discussion and successive elections—a process that should ideally cause truth to emerge, a truth that the body politic will be able momentarily to agree upon. Similarly, in order that there may be scientific activity, nature must be neither altogether unknowable nor susceptible of immediate knowledge by mystical illumination.[64]

Moreover, given the basic fact of interpenetration between the Arab world and the West, between Arab ideologies and Western ideologies, both Arabs and Westerners should make this critical effort. Each should get to know the critical face of the other. It is on this critical terrain that a true dialogue and understanding can be achieved, and it is through such a dialogue that critique can be enhanced further. The dilemma of technological reason versus the concern with authenticity and the need for a wholesome human being have also been preoccupying the West for the past century: "Once again the West is at the heart of the debate, and in the polemic opposing technophilia and concern for authenticity, one recognizes with no doubt the opposition, constant in the West for a century, between technological Reason and the exigencies of the total Man."[65]

The yearning for an integrative sense of the self, for reconciling instrumental reason with a sociohistorical, linguistic, cultural, emotional, and corporeal embeddedness, is a Western yearning as much as it is an Arab quest. It is thus a common aspiration that can liberate us from essentialist and reductionist views of our cultures and multiple reasons: "The West opposed to us is an opaque West, confident in its parks, roads, canons, that believes it can do without the acquiescence of the human. But the critical West that, without renouncing this beautified and comfortable frame, reminds everybody of the hope, expressed in the past in scattered legends, of a unified and reconciled human, and that beyond itself and us addresses the future—that West should be heard if we want to go beyond the inarticulate sounds of an impotent furor."[66]

Having argued for the necessity of critical thinking for developing an empowering sense of self, Laroui measures the almost forbidding obstacles that stand in the way of growth. Which sector of petty bourgeois Arab society is to support critical thinking: The army? The dominating party? The bureaucracy? The working class? The intellectual class? In the prevailing sociopolitical system, he says, none of these sectors has an interest in bringing forth any fundamental change. This inertia is further reinforced by a generalized defensiveness in response to the Zionist aggression, particularly after the 1967 defeat. In the face of all these hurdles, Arab intellectuals must continue their task against all odds and radicalize critique with all their strength.

Since the publication of *L'idéologie arabe contemporaine* in 1967, Laroui has remained consistent in his fierce attack on the apologetic and polemic uses of the notion of authenticity. He has continued to criticize ideological and superficial approaches to Western and Arab histories of ideas and events. He has relentlessly emphasized the universal yearning for an integral view of the human being and remained faithful to his commitment to the importance of critique in understanding authenticity. For him, today's Islamist is just another champion of authenticity, tempted by the same seductions he has described, but with the increased violence caused by an even deeper state of desolation and despair.[67]

Critique of the Medieval Concept of Absolute Reason

In the past two decades, Laroui has focused his Arabic writings on specific concepts—history, liberty, reason, ideology, and the state—devoting a volume to each. In all of these studies, he has continued to examine the flaws of reasoning and the problematic assumptions made in understanding them.

In his study on the state, he points out the great divide between state and society in Morocco and the Arab world in general.[68] He describes the lingering sultanate model of government in the minds of the rulers and the ruled alike, as well as the normative values of obedience and despotism that go with this model. In his study on reason, he examines the prevailing conciliatory mode of thinking articulated by Muhammad Abduh during the first Nahda and dominant in Arab thought since then.[69] The basic premise of this conciliatory mode of thinking, as Laroui sees it, is that there should be no contradiction between Islam and modernity because Islam, as Abduh claimed, is the religion of reason, and reason is the dominating principle of modernity. The paradox that Abduh noted was that although this was the nature of Islam, Muslim societies lived in a state of backwardness and obscurity, whereas Western-Christian societies lived in a state of enlightenment and progress even though Christianity is in many respects inimical to reason—for instance, by upholding the existence of miracles and by viewing faith as independent of reason. He concluded that Muslims' backwardness could only be a transient phenomenon, that it resulted from a misunderstanding of Islam due to prolonged foreign Ottoman rule. Christian societies, in contrast, had progressed because they had moved away from their religious beliefs. Laroui notes that Abduh was not the only thinker to have made the link between the religious doctrine of a society and its socioeconomic and cultural conditions. Max Weber, for instance, as is well known, offered such a link for European societies. The problem with Abduh, Laroui says, is that he confined his reflection on the matter to the doctrinal level and did not pay attention to the historical circumstances that affected those conditions. Moreover, he did not recognize the change that modernity had brought to the very nature and concept of reason. The reason Abduh referred to was that of the medieval theological discourse: an absolute and textual reason. This reason was overcome by modernity, something that, according to Laroui, Abduh failed to realize. Therefore, all attempts at reconciling the two different concepts of reason are doomed to fail, and the claim that "Islam is the religion of reason" and hence the religion of modernity and civilization cannot serve as the foundation for modernizing Muslim societies, as Abduh and many Muslim thinkers after him wished to think. Only a serious break with the medieval notion of reason and with the heritage shaped by it can open the way for real change and progress. Hence, a genuine resolve to make an honest choice is needed. Reform in the sense of a renewal of the old has to be abandoned. Productive renewal will have to be more creative than imitative. For Laroui, this prescription applies even to the luminaries of the past, considered to be carriers of reason and science, such as Ibn Khaldun (to whom he devotes the second half of his book on reason).[70] These luminaries cannot be taken as models for all times and places. They have to be situated in their own historical contexts and regarded as limited by the assumptions and concepts of their times. (Chapter 5 looks more at this criticism of the conciliatory strategy in the works of Muhammad Jaber al-Ansari and Nadeem Naimy.)

Egyptian sociologist Anouar Abdel-Malek spoke of the Arab of the 1960s as a person of *ressentiment* who was seeking dignity and striving to restore a sense of self. He expected this Arab to be angry and negative toward the Other until his autonomy was found and his political self-determination ensured. Then he expected this Arab to emerge from that *ressentiment* and engage in a more positive and authentic exchange with the Other.[71] More than three decades later, however, the humiliation and the despair have grown deeper than ever, and the *ressentiment* has become only more bitter. For Laroui, the only antidote to fundamentalist traditionalism is "hope, the vision of an unobstructed future."[72] The future in the Arab world has never been unobstructed, however. The dramatic events shaking the Arab world since the first Gulf War have amplified the vulnerability of this burgeoning self-critique, exposing it to the turmoil of inner anger, desperation, and violence as well as to external aggression, terror, and power politics.

Gendering Critique: Nawal el-Saadawi and the Late-Twentieth-Century Arab Feminists

To this early post-1967 intellectual ambience belongs the towering voice of the renowned Egyptian feminist Nawal el-Saadawi. Trained as a physician and psychiatrist in Egypt, she started to practice medicine in the mid-1950s in the Egyptian countryside and later in Cairo. She rose to become Egypt's director of public health, the assistant general secretary of the Medical Association, and the chief editor of a health journal. Upon the publication of her first nonfiction book, *al-Mar'a wa al-Jins* (Woman and Sex) in 1972, however, she was dismissed from her post in the Ministry of Health and forced to relinquish the rest of her official positions. She then moved to Addis Ababa, Ethiopia, to work for the United Nations program for women in Africa and later to Beirut to serve as an advisor to the Economic Commission for West Asia. She returned to Egypt in 1980 and resumed her activities as a militant and a writer, criticizing Anwar Sadat's regime for its neoliberal measures, its attack on Nasserites, socialists, and leftists in general, and its encouragement of Islamic fundamentalism. As a result of her critique, she was imprisoned for three months along with a large number of left-wing critics.[73] Upon her release in 1982, she founded an Arab nongovernmental association called the Arab Women's Solidarity Association and devoted herself to advocating democracy and women's rights. Pressured by the government and threatened by Islamic fundamentalists, she started dividing her time between Egypt, the United States, and elsewhere, lecturing and teaching around the world and pursuing her militant writing. El-Saadawi is today a world figure who identifies herself as an Arab, Muslim, and African feminist from the South. She has influenced generations of Arab men and women and contributed significantly to the gendering of cultural critique in the Arab world. She has also been a highly controversial figure for both conservatives and progressive critics.

By directly addressing issues of sexuality in Egyptian society in simple and accessible Arabic, el-Saadawi provoked the wrath of the political and religious establishments in Egypt in the 1970s. In five successive nonfiction books,[74] she raised questions of sexual pleasure and sexual fulfillment, presented the basics of human anatomy, and tackled the issue of virginity and the tragic stories related to it—all based on her clinical work in rural and urban Egypt. She also reflected on the social and economic context in which relations between men and women are situated, critiquing the relational ethics that govern them. This reflection led her to address prevailing conceptions of marriage and gender roles as well as forms of oppression and injustice. It became increasingly clear to her that various forms of misery were linked to one another: that disease was closely connected to poverty and ignorance, and that sexual oppression was connected to social, economic, and political oppression. It is the perception of these linkages that made her realize that the struggle against these ills had to be conducted on the political level by initiating public debates about them through writing, whether in novels, nonfiction books, or newspaper and journal articles, and by attacking all forces of oppression, be they local or foreign. The 1967 debacle added to this conviction and increased her determination to fight for social, economic, and political justice, both inside the Arab world and in the face of foreign pressures, all the while keeping women's issues at the forefront of the battle. In the introduction to a collection of her work, *The Nawal el Saadawi Reader*, she summarizes her journey:

> [A]fter a few years I realized that the diseases of the peasants could only be cured by curing poverty. From this point on, I realized that writing was a stronger weapon than medicine in the fight against poverty and ignorance.
>
> I started by writing poetry. Then I wrote short stories, novels and plays. Writing was a release for my anger. What angered me most was oppression: oppression of women and oppression of the poor. I used to write about love. Love that was nonexistent in the relations between men and women. I used to praise freedom and justice, without which life would have no value.
>
> Then I discovered the relation between love and politics. Between poverty and politics. Between sex and politics. I realized that the political regime imposed the will of men upon women and imposed poverty and slavery upon the poor and the destitute. Later I discovered the relationship between the local rulers and the international rulers. And I understood what constitutes global imperialism, class exploitation, and patriarchal oppression of the family.
>
> I realized the connection between the liberation of women and the liberation of the country from subordination or occupation by any form of new or old colonialism. I understood the connections between sex, politics, economics, history, religion and morality. This might be why my writings led me to the loss of my position in the government and to prison, to the confiscation of my books and to my being black-listed.[75]

The themes listed here have indeed been to date the leitmotivs of el-Saadawi's prolific and active career.[76] She has criticized the Western, in particular the U.S., domination of world aid agencies, which are instrumentalized to serve the capitalist interests of the North, transforming development into a neocolonial project. She has also taken to task the programs for the eradication of poverty that fail to address the northern roots of the southern problems, and that end up threatening the very existence of the poor. She has called for bridging the gap between the North and the South through constructive dialogue and collaboration between the progressive militants of both sides that would contribute to the establishment of a real universal democracy based on global economic justice instead of a disguised Western capitalist hegemony. Such a hegemony also prevails, she argues, in global feminist fora, where white Western feminists claim to speak in the name of all women, especially nonwhite and non-Western women. For her, the rise of traditionalism and fundamentalism are reactions to the oppressive West. However, she finds that these reactions reinforce the local patriarchal oppression and practice their own forms of oppression. They are not specific to the Arab or Islamic world, but are universal phenomena that need to be resisted with antipatriarchal and anticapitalist struggles informed by the linkages between the different forms of oppression: local and foreign, economic, political, military, cultural, and sexual. It is for such struggles, she says, that she founded the Arab Women's Solidarity Association in 1982. One of its main objectives was to raise awareness about these global phenomena and in this sense to "unveil the mind," to clarify the true nature of the problems at hand, and on the basis of such a clarity to build networks of solidarity and resistance. For her, these struggles define the "authentic" identity of Arab Muslim women:

> We Arab and Muslim women know that our authentic identity is based on unveiling our minds and not on veiling our faces. We are human beings and not just bodies to be covered (under religious slogans) or to be naked (for consumerism and Western commercial goods). We know that veiling women is the other side of the coin of nakedness or displaying the body. Both consider women as sex objects.

> One of our slogans in the Arab Women's Solidarity Association is "unveil the mind." We speak and write in Arabic. We join all struggles of liberation for ourselves and our countries. We study our history, and try to redefine Islam in intellectual terms. We question the dominating Islamic tradition defined by men. There is nothing in Islam that prevents women from participating fully in all political or religious activities.

The authentic identity of the Arab women is not a straitjacket or dress, or veil. It is an active, living, changing process which demands a rereading of our history, and a reshaping of ourselves and our societies in the light of present challenges and future goals. Arab women employ Islam, history, culture and heritage for the sake of greater freedom and justice for themselves. . . .

Islam and other religions in their early revolutionary eras loosened the chains of slavery and declared that no man or woman should kneel except before God. Faith in God as a symbol of justice and freedom can add fuel to revolutionary fervour against all types of exploitation and injustices. Islam in our region can be a spiritual force in the struggle against foreign penetration. But this must not blind us to the fact that "God" in the eyes of the oppressed is different from "God" in the eyes of the oppressors. Under the name of "God" as a symbol of absolute power our oppressors try to justify dictatorship.[77]

A younger feminist from Palestine, Amal Amireh, has studied the reception of el-Saadawi's work in Arab and Western settings. She shows the significance of the context of this reception and examines the transformations of el-Saadawi's discourse as it traveled from the Arab world to the global scene and the Western book market in particular. In her carefully nuanced study, Amireh describes first the powerful impact of el-Saadawi's ideas on Arab men and women, and reviews the Arab critiques of her work on both the literary and the analytic levels.[78] On the literary level, in some foreign circles her writing was generally thought to be weak and unduly taken to be representative of contemporary Arab literature. On the analytic level, it was controversial, rejected not only by conservatives for its feminist and sexual content, but also by some rather progressive thinkers, such as the Paris-based Syrian critic and Freud translator Georges Tarabichi (to whose own work I turn in chapter 3). Tarabichi found her feminist thought elitist, individualistic, and subjective, but acknowledged the legitimacy and importance of her themes.[79]

Amireh shows how in the Western scene el-Saadawi's work has been translated and marketed to fit into preestablished stereotypes about Arab Muslim women as victims. A good example is the translation of *Al Wajh al-'Ari li al-Mar'a al-'Arabiyya* as *The Hidden Face of Eve* even though it literally means "The Naked Face of the Arab Woman."[80] Moreover, certain chapters and passages are omitted from the English translation, such as those that criticize capitalism and refute the claims of Arab exceptionalism in oppressing women, whereas others are expanded, such as those related to clitoridectomy. Amireh examines also el-Saadawi's own ambiguity and sometimes complicity in presenting her cultural and political positions in the international fora, especially regarding complex phenomena such as the Iranian Revolution.

Amireh's critical evaluation of el-Saadawi's work is not the only exercise in assessing feminist views. The beginning of the twenty-first century witnessed several efforts in reconsidering Arab feminists' century-old struggle. *Al-Raida*, a quarterly published since 1976 by the Institute for Women's Studies in the Arab World of the Lebanese American University in Beirut, devoted its centenary issue of winter 2003 to a retrospective on Arab women's movements. Its guest editor, Rosemary Sayigh, explains that the retrospective aims at making a contribution to the historical and evaluative reflection on both feminist and nonfeminist Arab women's movements—a reflection, she adds, that was still in its initial stage.[81] The issue first presents essays on the state and history of these movements in different parts of the Arab world, then interviews with a number of Arab women thinkers and activists based on a set questionnaire, and finally a gender-sensitive profile of each of the twenty-two countries constituting the Arab League. The first two parts address the range of subjects that preoccupy much of contemporary Arab writing on women's issues—the impact of Orientalism and colonialism on the study of Arab women, the effects of nationalism and postindependence state building on Arab feminism, the repercussions of the rise of Islamism, the role of women in Arab democratic movements, women's struggles through nongovernmental organizations and the question of foreign funding, as well as the questions of employment, health, education, literacy, pluralism, minorities, conflict, and violence. These two parts tackle the intricate interface among cultural overdetermination, cultural embeddedness, authenticity, and feminist critique, and question the ubiquitous binaries of modernization/westernization and tradition/identity. They underline the importance of exchanging thoughts with women struggling in other parts of the South and the East and discuss the tensions with Western feminism. Finally, they propose a new history of women's presence in Arab cultural and political struggles, especially those of the earlier Nahda times, which has been largely unacknowledged to date. Most of these topics are common to other postcolonial women's writings, and I examine these commonalities in chapter 6.

Also in 2003, the Lebanese Association of Women Researchers published the proceedings of a conference it organized in Beirut in 2001 on Arab women of the 1920s. In the introduction, the editors explain that the association had focused on this particular decade because of the dearth of knowledge about the lives and activities of Arab women in years that witnessed significant changes in the region after World War I.[82] Indeed, after the collapse of the Ottoman Empire and the imposition of the French and British mandates despite the 1916 and 1919 Arab revolts, the newly created Arab entities in the Levant had their first modern constitutions, the Balfour Declaration began to have its effects in Palestine, socioeconomic processes of modernization continued to transform Arab societies, and the discovery of oil in the Persian Gulf region started a radically new era for the region. According to one of the conference participants, Lebanese historian Wajih Kawtharani, the 1920s witnessed, on the one hand, the fruition of the Nahda efforts in the adoption of constitutional rule and in the openness to westernization, and, on the other hand, the rise of the conservative authoritarian reaction to these trends—a reaction that was eventually to jeopardize the Nahda project in its basic orientations and to hinder the development of an active Arab civil society. The conference aimed at shedding light on women's ill-known presence and struggle amid these tensions and transformations. Scholars from different Arab countries explored biographies, oral histories, legal records, publications, literary salons, public debates, associational and artistic movements, as well as women's participation in political, professional, and educational institutions in order to document, analyze, and evaluate the 1920s from the perspective of the women involved in these institutions.

Some of the most significant findings were in the legal and conceptual realms. Studies of the legal records of the time,[83] especially those related to family law (marriage, inheritance, property ownership), showed that the changes introduced by the Western occupation or mandate powers were not beneficial to women and that this Western legal modernization worsened in some respects their rights in divorce and property management. In fact, as Afaf Lutfi Sayyid Marsot concludes, Western patriarchal notions came to reinforce and add to local patriarchal views. Moreover, the dominating Western authorities applied laws that were in general more reactionary and more conservative than native laws.[84] Moreover, research on the biographies, oral histories, writings, and achievements of women who were ignored or marginalized in official histories of the epoch showed that some of these women were committed to cultural change, but at the same time critical of blind and total westernization, and that already then voices were raised to criticize the patriarchal views of feminism advocated by its male proponents.[85] According to these views, women's education, mobility, and legal rights needed to be improved simply to show to Westerners that Egyptian or Arab or Muslim culture was not intrinsically bad with respect to women and hence that it was not unworthy of respect as a culture, especially compared to Western culture. Furthermore, these improvements were regarded as necessary for the production of mothers capable of raising good citizens. The conference findings put in question the binaries that have prevailed in the dominant discourses since the Nahda—specifically the East/West binary associated respectively with tradition and modernity, backwardness and progress. They also show women's alertness to the complexity of cultural critique under foreign gaze and hegemony because of their position inside their own culture and in the face of a massively interfering foreign culture.

The conference was organized in cooperation with the Women and Memory Forum founded in 1995 in Cairo by a group of Egyptian women researchers interested in contesting the prevailing Egyptian cultural history that has marginalized or ignored the place of women and minorities in it.[86] By tapping into alternative sources such as oral histories and unpublished or forgotten writings, the forum aims to produce and disseminate missing facets of history and so to question the gender assumptions in the official narratives. It seeks to lay bare the negative representations and perceptions of Arab women in the cultural realm and to integrate gender as a category of analysis in the study and interpretation of Arab cultural history. This gender critique is intended to have an impact both on the practical life of contemporary women and society, as in marriage law, and on the presentation of popular culture in the rewriting and telling of popular stories. Thus, the forum regards its work to be both intellectual and political. This feminist project of reconsidering national cultural histories is similar to feminist cultural contestations elsewhere in the postcolonial world, for instance in India. In her seminal book *Dislocating Cultures: Identities, Traditions, and Third-World Feminism*, Indian philosopher Uma Narayan sharply articulates the importance and challenges of such contestations. In the first chapter of the book, "Contesting Cultures: 'Westernization,' Respect for Cultures, and Third-World Feminists," she writes:

> *Just as daughters seldom recount their mothers' stories in the same terms as their mothers tell them, feminist daughters often have accounts of*

their mother-cultures that differ in significant ways from the culture's own dominant accounts of itself. . . . Re-telling the story of a mother-culture in feminist terms . . . is a political enterprise. It is an attempt to, publicly and in concert with others, challenge and revise an account that is neither the account of an individual nor an account "of the culture as a whole," but an account of some who have power within the culture. It is a political challenge to other political accounts that distort, misrepresent, and often intentionally fail to account for the problems and contributions of many inhabitants of the context. It is a political attempt to tell a counter-story that contests dominant narratives that would claim the entire edifice of "our Culture" and "our Nation" for themselves, converting them into a peculiar form of property, and excluding the voices, concerns, and contributions of many who are members of the national and political community.[87]

Among the Women and Memory Forum's projects are an oral library and documentation center as well as a workshop for storytelling. Through conferences and publications, it sheds light on a number of women writers and activists from the late nineteenth century and the early twentieth century, such as Malak Hifni Nassif (1886–1918) and Nabawiyya Moosa (1886–1951), thus offering a new picture of the Nahda period.[88]

One of the forum's founding members and leading figures is Hoda Elsadda, trained in English and comparative literature, for many years professor of English at Cairo University. Her initial work on gender started with a revision of the common marriage contract in Egypt. Together with feminist Egyptian writer Salwa Bakr, she launched a series of six periodicals under the title *Hagar* between 1993 and 1998. In the meantime, she cofounded the forum.[89] In the first *Hagar* (1993), she examines the ideas of Qasim Amin, one of the Nahda pioneers and the most prominent advocate of women's liberation of that time, in "Al-Mar'a: Mantiqat Muharramat: Qira'a fi A'mal Qasim Amin" (Woman: Realm of Taboos: A Reading in the Works of Qasim Amin).[90] Elsadda's aim is to lay bare the implicit assumptions of this advocacy that might have led to the failure of the projects of liberation and the Nahda. At the time she was writing, she says, the Egyptian Parliament was discussing the judiciousness of women's work outside their home (at the height of the employment crisis caused by the government's neoliberal policies): for her, a clear indication of a regression to a pre-Nahda conservatism. According to her analysis, the failure lay in having locked the issues of liberation and renaissance in fixed and absoluticized binaries, abstracted from history and lived realities—the Western model and the local tradition—and in having ignored the agency of women themselves. During the Nahda, the question of women, she says, was invariably raised in connection with the wider questions of cultural decline and renewal, in which Orientalists and colonial actors had an important role and presence. Many ideas related to these questions were formulated in response to and under the gaze of such Westerners. In the case of Qasim Amin, this connection is manifest in the exchange he had with the Duc d'Harcourt. Amin wrote *Les Egyptiens* as a response to the latter's criticism of Egyptian and Muslim culture and of the treatment of women in them. Amin rejected d'Harcourt's negative views and presented a defense of Egyptian and Islamic traditions and customs, including divorce, polygamy, and seclusion, justifying some of them by pointing to Egyptian women's own supposed weaknesses (commenting even on their ugliness). A few years later, however, Amin was to revolt against the limitations imposed on women and to call for their advancement through education, some mobility, some unveiling, and some margin of activity outside the home.

Elsadda finds three major flaws in Amin's position. First, its androcentrism: he decided what was good and useful for women from his male perspective and in view of the benefits that such a limited liberation could bring to Muslim society and culture. For her, his liberational project clearly remained confined to the patriarchal understanding of the family, which he defended by referring to the Western patriarchal model. Second, Amin adopted the Western principle of progress without questioning the colonial hegemonic ideology that accompanies it and without cautioning himself and his readers against the judgmental scale of civilizations that it presupposes. She adds that Amin did not recognize the place of power in this comparative perception of cultures: the dominating power position that the Duc d'Harcourt, as a Westerner, held with respect to him and the dominating power position that he, Amin, held with respect to the women of his own society. And third, Amin stopped short of engaging any truly innovative change in tradition. His liberational project did not lead him to a new reading of the founding religious texts, be they the sacred text or the traditional corpus produced around it, nor did it call for a revisiting of the notion of chastity, the question of veiling, or the wider principle of patriarchal domination. The latter topics remained for him untouched/untouchable taboos. In the absence of a new historicization and contextualization of the sacred tradition, Amin's project, as well as the Nahda project in general, failed to produce any genuine breakthrough. The ahistorical nondialectical

approach to both tradition and the West made of the enlightenment project an impossible mission: "Not only does Qasim Amin constrain his
project by positing a constant in the past but he makes things worse by
positing a constant in the present, namely the Western model that he adu-
lates as the absolutely most advanced stage of human evolution. So his
enlightenment project becomes an impossible mission consisting in ele-
vating a fixed past to a fixed present."[91]

In "Malak Hifni Nassif: Halaqa Mafquda min Ta'rikh al-Nahda" (Malak
Hifni Nassif: A Missing Chain in the Historiography of the Nahda) in the
second *Hagar* volume (1994), Elsadda examines the ideas of a woman of the
same epoch who engaged some of the leading male figures of the Nahda on
the question of women's liberation and whose work has been ignored in the
established Nahda narratives: Malak Hifni Nassif (1886–1918).[92] Nassif's father was a student of Jamal al-Din al-Afghani and a friend of Muhammad
Abduh. She was the first girl in Egypt to graduate from elementary school
and was an avid reader of her father's library. She wrote for *al-Jarida* newspaper, which was edited by the liberal nationalist Ahmed Lutfi al-Sayyid,
founded a number of women's associations for social work, and died prematurely at age thirty-three. In her writing, Nassif, in contrast to al-Sayyid and
Amin, emphasized the importance of women's agency. She believed that
women were to be given the opportunity of education and then the freedom
to design their own path to liberation. In this effort toward liberation and
again in contrast to her male counterparts, the veil was of minor relevance.
Appearances were not to be confused with more fundamental issues; more
important, they were to be left to women's discretion. For her, neither veiling
nor unveiling could be automatically equated with chastity or modernity,
respectively. The issue of polygamy for her was one of the more fundamental
issues from which she herself suffered. Indeed, she discovered after her
marriage that her husband already had a wife. Minimizing the importance
of unveiling made her suspicious in reformers' eyes, and for conservatives
her criticism of polygamy raised questions about her loyalty to Islam and
tradition.

Nassif rejected the patronizing, utilitarian attitude of the Nahda spokesmen. Interestingly, unlike most of her contemporary male modernists, she
found an inspiring model in the Turkish woman rather than in the Western woman. In a 1909 public lecture addressing women at the Umma Party
Club, she said: "The imprisonment in the home of the Egyptian woman of
the past is detrimental while the current freedom of the Europeans is excessive. I cannot find a better model of today's Turkish woman. She falls

between the two extremes and does not violate what Islam prescribes. She is a good example of decorum and modesty."[93]

Unlike her male counterparts, Nassif celebrated Egyptian women's beauty and clothing and refused to go by the Western criteria of beauty dictated by the Westerners' power position. Moreover, she strongly rejected both the prevailing inclination to blame Egyptian women for the backwardness of Egyptian society and the common idealization of the "modernized" Egyptian man who had to "suffer" an underdeveloped environment and the company of inadequate Egyptian women. These men, in her eyes, bore a considerable responsibility for the way things were in their society. She saw gender roles and gender characteristics as products of historical conditions rather than as natural tendencies. She accused Egyptian men of holding double standards: of showing respect and admiration for Western women and contempt and resentment for Egyptian women. Western women, according to her, needed to be demystified without being vilified. She believed that the blind infatuation with the West, the lack of awareness of the role of power in the valorization of cultures, and the absence of a more honest and balanced appreciation of Egyptian lived realities could not but lead to a fake *nahda*.

A century later many of these flawed assumptions and uncritical binaries still dominate the discourse on Arab women, says Elsadda. For her, the conference organized by the Egyptian government's Supreme Council of Culture in 1999 to celebrate the hundredth anniversary of Qasim Amin's 1899 *Tahrir al-Mar'a* (Liberation of Woman) in Cairo is a good case in point.[94] Women are still given the task of incarnating and representing the nation's progress and identity. "Real authenticity" is opposed to "real modernity" without a critical deconstruction of the terms of this persisting binary. Elsadda argues that these issues would benefit from the postcolonial reflection that has been growing in different parts of the world.

Two further contemporary critiques of Qasim Amin are worth adding here, those of Georges Tarabichi and Leila Ahmed. Tarabichi sees in Amin's views on the condition of Muslim Egyptian women a typical expression of the narcissistic wound experienced by Arabs in their encounter with the West in modern times.[95] This expression has, according to him, two typical facets: a reaction of denial regarding the existence of the wound and a reaction of apology justifying its existence later on. The first reaction is formulated in Amin's response to the Duc d'Harcourt, in which he denies the existence of anything reproachable in the condition of women in Arab civilization and Islamic shari'a and allows only a limited criticism of women's situation in his Egyptian society. He presents an idealized and glorified image of the self and mounts a strong defense of the traditional norms of polygamy, divorce, veiling, and seclusion. The second reaction is found in two books Amin wrote a few years later on the liberation of women, in which he launches an attack on these same norms, blaming them for the backward condition of women in Egypt and blaming the backwardness of women for the backwardness of the whole nation. This attack develops into a harsh criticism of Islamic tradition that ultimately comes close to d'Harcourt's denigration of this tradition. Thus, for Tarabichi, Amin ends up adopting his aggressor's views and starts calling for the total Europeanization of his country. In the final analysis, he ends up acknowledging the authority of European views of Islamic societies and cultures. This glorification of the Other and deprecation of the self is counterproductive, says Tarabichi, because it reinforces the self-defense mechanisms that it wanted to dismantle in the first place.

By going through these successive phases of apology, self-criticism, and total acceptance of the Other's judgments, Amin displays, according to Tarabichi, the whole spectrum of reactions that the Nahda thinkers had in their time:

1. *With the staunch Salafists, he asks in his first book: How can we not change and remain ourselves?*

2. *With the modernizers, he asks in his second book: How can we change but remain ourselves?*

3. *And with the advocates of total change, he asks in his third book: How can we change and not remain ourselves?*[96]

Tarabichi argues that these inconsistent responses were not caused primarily by the Nahda thinkers' mental inaptitude, but rather are the inevitable outcome of the colonial situation in which one is forced to affirm one's identity and change at the same time—a situation that is in itself a schizophrenic state. Western colonialism transformed colonized cultures and societies into tributaries. And what is the narcissist wound if not the condition of both becoming a tributary and losing control over its course?

Egyptian feminist Leila Ahmed examines this overdetermining and confusing interface between culture and gender in the third part of her 1992 book *Women and Gender in Islam*. She shows how the cultural malaise

experienced under the gaze of the Westerner dominates the woman question and subjects it to its own purposes. According to her, Qasim Amin's
calls for the "liberation" of women are subordinated to his civilizational
angst. They are ultimately based on the acceptance of the colonial thesis,
which claims that an inherent connection exists between Muslim Egyptian
culture and the oppression of women: they "presented strident criticism of
Muslim, particularly Egyptian, culture and society. In calling for women's
liberation the thoroughly patriarchal Amin was in fact calling for the
transformation of Muslim society along the lines of the Western model
and for the substitution of the garb of Islamic-style male dominance for
that of Western-style male dominance. Under the guise of a plea for the
'liberation' of woman, then, he conducted an attack that in its fundamentals reproduced the colonizer's attack on native culture and society." The
numerous reactions to Amin's calls (more than thirty books and articles)
were also governed by the same priorities, especially the concern with the
cultural: "Opponents with a nationalist perspective were therefore not necessarily any more antifeminist than Amin was feminist."[97]

In this reasoning, the need to change or preserve the native culture
supersedes the issue of women's liberation and inevitably leads to one of
two necessary conclusions: either to reject the culture and replace it with
that of the Westerners if one is to change women's condition or to mini-
mize or oppose such a change for the sake of affirming, defending, and
preserving one's own culture—alternatives that are equally absurd. Indeed, Western feminists would not have considered rejecting their own
culture and espousing that of others in order to vindicate their rights. For
non-Westerners, however, the matter was presented in just this way because of the colonial association between women's issues and cultural issues. Colonialists, who were otherwise staunch antifeminists at home,
pushed selective feminist agendas to discredit the colonized cultures and
to justify their colonial endeavors. The positions held by Lord Cromer,
British consul general in Egypt between 1883 and 1907, are for Ahmed a
glaring example of this typical pattern. Even while fixating his "liberational" mission on the question of the veil, he restricted the education of
women in Egypt and opposed the feminist demands in his own society:
"This champion of the unveiling of Egyptian women was, in England,
founding member and sometime president of the Men's League for Opposing Women's Suffrage. Feminism on the home front and feminism directed against white men was to be resisted and suppressed; but taken
abroad and directed against the cultures of colonized peoples, it could be

promoted in ways that admirably served and furthered the project of the dominance of the white man."[98]

Ahmed eloquently summarizes this colonial manipulation of feminism:

> *Even as the Victorian male establishment devised theories to contest the claims of feminism, and derided and rejected the ideas of feminism and the notion of men's oppressing women with respect to itself, it captured the language of feminism and redirected it, in the service of colonialism, toward Other men and the cultures of Other men. It was here and in the combining of the languages of colonialism and feminism that the fusion between the issues of women and culture was created. More exactly, what was created was the fusion between the issues of women, their oppression, and the cultures of Other men. The idea that Other men, men in colonized societies or societies beyond the borders of the civilized West, oppressed women was to be used, in the rhetoric of colonialism, to render morally justifiable its project of undermining or eradicating the cultures of colonized peoples.*[99]

Throughout the spectrum of positions, from the extreme conservative ones to the most liberal ones, this colonialist conflation of cultural and feminist issues set the parameters of much of the subsequent Arab debates, trapping feminist struggles in cultural struggles, often creating mirror images of the colonial discourse that affirmed the local culture and tied women's rights to issues of cultural betrayal and loyalty. The challenge of Arab Muslim feminism, according to Ahmed, is to break this association and to approach the question of women from within the Arab Muslim culture, drawing on its ethical-liberational components, liberated from the culturalist determination of that colonial conflation.[100]

Algerian sociologist Marnia Lazreg examines a similar manipulation of women's issues by the French in their colonial control of Algeria. She recalls the famous scene of May 16, 1958, that epitomizes this manipulation, when French generals gathered a few Algerians bused from their villages to witness the dramatic unveiling of a few Algerian women by French women. She comments:

> *In reality the event of May 16, 1958 did lasting harm to Algerian women. It brought into the limelight the politicization of women's bodies and their symbolic appropriation by colonial authorities. It brought home to Algerian women their vulnerability, at a time when*

many of them thought they were making history and imposing them-
selves on men's consciousness as more than mere sex symbols. Their
sexed body was suddenly laid bare before a crowd of vociferous colo-
nists who, in an orgy of chants and cries of "Long Live French Alge-
ria," claimed victory over all Algerian women. Much has been said,
and rightly so, about the generals' manipulation of the veil as a politi-
cal symbol separating the colonizers from the colonized, or its mean-
ing as native men's last bastion of resistance to the French, guarantee-
ing a safe haven of personal power in an otherwise dominated society.
Little has been written about its meaning for women.[101]

Lazreg's book *The Eloquence of Silence: Algerian Women in Question* attempts to retrieve the women's reactions, which most actors of the time ignored: "The 'Ulama, colonial administrators and writers, F.L.N. [Front de
Libération National] leaders and intellectuals, including Fanon, all held conceptions of women that were at odds with women's lived and felt reality."[102]

Even present-day scholars, she comments, especially the Westerners
among them, continue to silence the lived experiences of Algerian women
by applying the reductionist interpretive key of "Islam" in trying to understand their issues, including the issue of their failure to reach gender equality after liberation.[103] The war of liberation, she says, aimed at freeing the
country from colonial occupation, and it succeeded in achieving this goal.
This priority could not have accommodated other concomitant struggles.
She underlines the FLN's ambiguity regarding gender issues during the
war and thinks that the legacy of women's involvement in it belonged to
a later struggle that was to be undertaken after the war: "Consciousness of
difference between women and men as an instance of *social* inequality, instead of the expression of biological difference ordained by a divine force,
is not the automatic outcome of militancy in a decolonization movement.
It is the product of a historical struggle marked by setbacks as well as suc-
cesses, depending on the conjuncture."[104]

Joseph Massad analyzes the conflation of culture and gender issues by
examining its internalization in modern Arab discourses on sexual desires, especially same-sex desires. He shows how under the Western colonial gaze, Arab thinkers of the modern era deal with the civilizational
worth of their culture, past and present, in terms of the practices and expressions of certain forms of sexual desires. The normative judgment of
these practices and expressions remain central to their evaluative representations: "While the premodern West attacked the world of Islam's al-

leged sexual licentiousness, the modern West attacks its alleged repression of sexual freedoms." Concerning the Nahda historiography, he adds: "In the course of writing classical and medieval Arab history, these modern historians encountered an ancient Arab society with different sexual mores and practices that were difficult to assimilate into a modern Arab nationalist project informed by European notions of progress and modernization and a Victorian sexual ethic."[105]

In undertaking a wide archival work, Massad has produced an intellectual history of Arab representations of sexuality that are often constructions and reconstructions of a literary and cultural tradition influenced by Orientalist, imperialist, and nationalist agendas:

> *The project of researching and writing about the past was a project of re-membering it, of piecing it together from extant material, and of evaluating it critically with the aid of modern methods in order to make it the basis for modern Arab civilization, indeed to invent it as a civilization. The varied authors seemed interested not only in reproducing how the Arabs of the past considered their own desires and sexual practices, but also, and more centrally, how modern Arabs were to assess these epochs and their desires and practices. The resulting corpus varied from reproducing accounts provided by medieval historians whose work survived the "age of decadence" of the Ottoman period and those excavated by European Orientalists, to evaluating that corpus and framing it within modern criteria of ethical and moral judgments that were alternately nationalist, religious, liberal, Marxist, psychoanalytic, secular, and feminist.[106]*

By compiling and critiquing this corpus of Arab representations, Massad makes a valuable contribution to modern Arab intellectual history. He succeeds in showing the ever-present epistemic and axiological influence of Western views, but he sometimes seems in the process to reduce the Arab positions solely to this influence. It is true that the purpose of his book is to show this influence, which justifies to a great extent the focus on it, but one may still ask whether the conservatism regarding sexual mores during the Nahda period and since then was a product of Orientalist influence only. Massad does recognize the judgmental attitudes among Arabs regarding sexuality, but his main concern remains concentrated on the Western discourses and their internalized Arab versions, which posit allegedly universal ontological categories that confuse subjects with practices: "This is not to say that societal forces, Islamist and secular, have not been severely judgmental in some cases of same-sex (and different-sex) practices, but simply, that it is an ontological and a logical error (not to speak of an anachronism) to collapse subjects with practices or to conflate sexual desires with identities."[107] Unfortunately, Massad does not provide non-Orientalist accounts of the workings of those societal forces and does not elaborate on the non-Western, Arab views on sexual desires, practices, and subjects and their possible variations through time, space, class, and so on.

The culturalist-reductionist approach to Arab societies has had a detrimental effect on the scholarship produced about them in general and on gender issues in them in particular. For the past three decades, critiques of this approach have been voiced, and a valuable learning process has taken place regarding the use of set categories, habitual assumptions, and expected conclusions. Janet Abu-Lughod's 1980 article "Decolonizing the Women of Islam" welcomes the emergence of a scholarly trend that starts to pose women's issues independently of the East–West debate.[108] In the 1981 article "Roles and Functions of Arab Women: A Reappraisal," Rosemary Sayigh examines the impact of Orientalism on the study of Arab women by looking at the Algerian and Egyptian cases.[109] She articulates three damaging aspects of this impact. First, a huge amount of energy has been expended on the Arab side to defend Islam against Orientalist claims in controversies that have proven to be more polemical than informative. This defense has led to an idealization of the religious-legal status of Arab Muslim women and a neglect of their real situation as well as to a focus on the past rather than on the present, but without expanding Arabs' knowledge of the past in any substantial way. Second, women have become the site of the polarized East–West cultural conflict initiated and sustained by Orientalists and then internalized by Arabs. The divide has polarized positions regarding women's issues between an irreconcilable progressive camp and a reactionary camp, and has reduced the image of women to undifferentiated and sweeping characterizations. Third, the unquestioned belief in the beneficial consequences of modernization for women's conditions has prevented a concrete study of these consequences on the various sectors of Arab societies, from the urban to the rural, from the rich to the poor, and so on. Sayigh recognizes and welcomes a scholarship that is rebelling against these assumptions and divides: women social scientists' rebellion against male neglect of women's perspectives and Arab scholars' rebellion against the domination of Western interests and approaches in the fields of Arab studies.[110] In a brief historical survey of scholarship on women in the

Middle East and the Arab world, Cynthia Nelson identifies the rise of an indigenous quest on the part of Arab women scholars to produce such scholarship.[111]

Lazreg's indigenous quest concerns the possibility of self-knowledge for Algerian women. An Algerian sociologist herself, she explains how certain colonial views and assumptions about the Middle East and Arab societies still linger in Western academia, even as it becomes self-reflective about its own social scientific and feminist disciplines. Reviewing the Western literature produced on women, she shows how "Islam," whether as religion or culture, continues to serve as the main explanatory paradigm of radical difference for these societies, thus disregarding their historical realities. She examines this silencing effect in the study of Algerian women: "How, then, can an Algerian woman write about women in Algeria when her space has already been defined, her history dissolved, her subjects objectified, her language chosen for her? How can she speak without saying the same things? . . . To study women from a phenomenological perspective is different from merely interviewing them to elicit from them information about their lives that *confirms our* conceptions of *them*."[112] It is such a phenomenology that she offers in her book *The Eloquence of Silence*.[113]

Independence from colonial rule (at least formal independence, given the interferences and dependencies that continued to affect the region) did not set women free from being the site of nationalist agendas. Their bodies, rights, and roles were to serve postindependence nation building conceived through a persisting patriarchal lens. Patriarchy continued to prevail, not only among conservatives and Islamists, as is often believed, but also among secularists and leftists, as Egyptian political scientist Mervat Hatem has shown.[114] Many Arab states to a large extent co-opted feminist movements and demands and manipulated them to serve their own interests. This co-optation granted women some rights but made these rights dependent on the state's expediency considerations.[115] The state also repressed independent feminist voices, as most postindependence Arab regimes repressed most independent voices. In "Toward the Development of Post-Islamist and Post-nationalist Feminist Discourses in the Middle East," Hatem examines the rise of independent and semi-independent women's groups in the Arab world in the 1980s, looking at the factors behind this proliferation of women's associative activities and analyzing critically the discourses that accompanied them.[116] Her overall assessment is that women's new discourses remain to some extent captive of mainstream discourses of modernism, nationalism, and dependency theory. The factors behind the emergence of

men's groups were, according to her, the demise of state femi-
_.i was discredited along with the postrevolutionary regimes; the
United Nations' Decade for Women, which generated interest in and support for women's concerns; the rise of Islamism and the fears it provoked
among women opposed to its conservative values and restrictive gender
views; and the establishment of women researchers in the field of the social
sciences and the publication of scholarly journals devoted to women's issues
and disseminating a new form of gender awareness. Hatem thinks, however, that these efforts have not led to a real break from the established patriarchal discourses on women's issues. She identifies three types of patriarchal discourses.

First, the modernist-nationalist discourse advocates a limited and ambiguous amount of change in women's rights and roles while preserving
male leadership in the family, workplace, and political system, thus leaving
patriarchy unchallenged. Islam here is to be modernized, but to remain the
main reference for society. Despite the limits in the proposed changes
and despite a focus on urban-middle-class women, this discourse claims
to advocate full liberation. Conservative nationalists and conservative
middle-class women find its propositions to be an assault on Islam. This
discourse, Hatem thinks, does address some women's issues, but only in
limited scope. Second, the national liberation discourse couples the struggle for liberation with the imperative of cultural preservation. It puts contradictory demands on women: both to take on new public roles and to
maintain the traditional value system. The issue of inequality is postponed,
and the benefits to women are very limited. And third, the dependency
discourse addresses gender inequality but relates it and subordinates it to
the larger socioeconomic dependency of the nation. It shifts attention to
the foreign, often Western, culprits behind the inequality and takes it away
from the local patriarchal system.

What is needed, according to Hatem, is a deeper reflection on the local
workings of patriarchy, an analysis of the manifestations of inequality in
women's personal and family lives, and a rethinking of the notions of liberation, change, and culture. She recognizes in the new women's discourses
the same difficulties that challenge Arab societies in general: "The present
ideological struggles between the discredited modernists (who failed to
deliver development to younger generations of men and women and the
lower middle classes) and the ascendant Islamists (who claim that there is
an Islamic solution to these problems) make it difficult to develop an independent discourse. The political and the ideological choices that this strug-

gle offers are old and tired concepts and roles that cannot be expected to deliver new solutions. In this sense, the crisis of Arab feminist discourses is a reflection of the real crisis facing Arab societies."[117]

Among the most daring voices to question official cultural histories is that of Ella Habiba Shohat, an "Iraqi Jewish Israeli American."[118] Hers is directed against the Zionist version of Jewish cultural history presented and defended by the state of Israel. In this version, Jewish cultural history is reduced to its Western component, and its values and projects are given an exclusively Eurocentric character. Arab Jews have found themselves outside this official history—their cultures, languages, and memories omitted or vilified as backward, poor, inferior, and valueless. They have seen themselves transformed into the despised and embarrassing Ostjuden of the old European Jewry, the "Orientals" or the "blacks" of Israel, who cannot but be colonized by the Western enlightened Jews. In her groundbreaking essay "Taboo Memories and Diasporic Visions: Columbus, Palestine, and Arab-Jews," Shohat describes this phenomenon of cultural discrimination:

> *The strong cultural and historical links that Middle Eastern Jews have shared with the Arab Muslim world, stronger in many respects than those they shared with the European Jews, threatened the conception of a homogeneous nation on which European nationalist movements were based. As an integral part of the topography, language, culture, and history of the Middle East, Sephardim have also threatened the Euro-Israeli self-image, which sees itself as a prolongation of Europe, "in" the Middle East but not "of" it. Fearing an encroachment from the East upon the West, the Israeli establishment attempted to repress the Middle Easternness of Sephardic Jews as part of an effort to westernise the Israeli nation and to mark clear borders of identity between Jews as Westerners and Arabs as Easterners. Arabness and Orientalness have been consistently stigmatised as evils to be uprooted, creating a situation where Arab Jews were urged to see Judaism and Zionism as synonyms, and Jewishness and Arabness as antonyms. . . . Israel has taken it upon itself to "cleanse" Arab-Jews of their Arabness and redeem them from their "primal sin" of belonging to the Orient. . . . The Ostjuden, perennially marginalized by Europe, realized their desire of becoming Europe, ironically, in the Middle East, this time on the back of their own Ostjuden, the Eastern Jews. The Israeli establishment, therefore, has made systematic efforts to suppress Sephardi-Mizrahi cultural identity. . . . Despite its obvious shifts since the partition of*

Palestine, however, Sephardi popular culture has clearly manifested its vibrant inter-textual dialogue with Arab, Turkish, Iraninian, and Indian popular cultures.[119]

For her, the political significance of this ideologization of cultural history cannot be overstated: "This conceptualisation of East and West has important implications in this age of the 'peace process,' because it avoids the issue of the majority of the population within Israel being from the Middle East—Palestinian citizens of Israel as well as Mizrahi-Sephardi Jews; for peace as it is defined now does not entail a true democracy in terms of adequate representation of these populations, nor in terms of changing the education, cultural, and political orientation within the state of Israel."[120]

Equally significant, therefore, is the contestation of this conceptualization. A nonmystifying recognition of this common Arab culture and history to Jews, Muslims, and Christians can and should serve, Shohat believes, as a solid ground for a promising search for peace in a region that has been severely damaged by ideological divides nourishing violent policies and endless wars. She describes her own intellectual and political involvement with this contestation:

In a first-of-its-kind meeting between Mizrahim and Palestine Liberation Organization representatives held at the symbolic site of Toledo, Spain, in 1989, we insisted that a comprehensive peace would mean more than settling political borders, and would require the erasure of the East/West cultural borders between Israel and Palestine, and thus the remapping of national and ethnic-racial identities against the deep scars of colonizing partitions. A critical examination of national histories may thus open a cultural space for working against taboo memories and fostering diasporic visions.[121]

The Arab world continues to be caught in fierce intrastate and interstate power struggles. Exclusionary, totalizing, and hegemonic cultural ideologies and narratives are becoming increasingly polarizing. But dissident voices still resist these trends, if only by way of challenging some of the prevailing narratives. A reflective learning process has been growing despite all the mental and existential havoc. A certain wisdom has been born from the bitter experiences. It might not be able to initiate much on the ground for the time being, but it can certainly serve as an anchor of some lucidity amidst so much fury and despair. The feminist contribution to this wisdom consists in an increased awareness of the politics of modernity, authenticity, and tradition. As women have been the site of identity, progress, and civilizational measure, the examination of their lives, conditions, and agencies in the past two centuries can add layers of complexity to the stories of modernity, nationalism, and Islamism in the region. It can shed light on the emancipatory promises as well as the regulatory constraints of modernity, on the public and private margins of liberty made possible by modernization, but also on the forms of domesticity introduced by the modernizing agendas of nationalism. It can reveal the selectivity of borrowings from the modern West, even among contemporary Islamists.[122] Arab feminist critique offers a valuable rethinking of all these notions that dominate not only gender politics, but nation and community politics as well.

The Radicalization of Critique and the Call for Democracy: Reclaiming the Individual's Critical Faculties

The work of the thinkers discussed in this chapter clearly indicates a coming of age, the engagement in a work of critique turned inward toward modes of thinking and acting in the postcolonial era rather than on the colonial Other, as was the case during the anticolonial struggle. The decades after independence witnessed revolutions against the ruling old guard, the affirmation of national identity, efforts at establishing a national economy, projects for securing national cohesion and justice, and endeavors to create modern institutions, spread literacy, and ensure universal education, as well as attempts at unification ventured for the sake of Arab unity. However, the continued Western intervention and influence, driven by geopolitical and economic interests, and the creation of the state of Israel, surely added greatly to the difficulty of these tasks. The need to face the adverse effects of these factors and the urgency to build the new nation-state imposed certain priorities, such as the military and security, at the expense of civil liberties. It also favored the strengthening of a defensive nationalism that does not tolerate dissent. These elements inevitably increased the chances of power abuse.

The shock of the 1967 defeat provoked the bitter realization that fundamental mistakes were made in carrying out these postcolonial projects. Some Arabs continued to view their governments and fellow nationals as faultless victims, but for many a fundamental questioning of ideas and policies had become necessary. The reactions took various forms. In some cases, radicalized revolutionary forces seized power—for instance, the Free Officers in Egypt and the Baath Party in Syria and Iraq. Unfortunately, these forces proved to be more repressive than the regimes they replaced. In other circles, the 1967 defeat reinforced the Islamist option as an alternative to secular and westernized regimes. For a number of intellectuals, however, the only fruitful response was the critical examination of hitherto prevailing thoughts and practices, including their own, their fellow citizens', and their rulers'. Romantic nationalism, essentialist identity, ideological and ahistorical thinking, mystified authenticity, and political despotism were the center of this critical reconsideration, as shown in this chapter.

The self-reflective examination was not limited to these issues, however; it extended to the preindependence era and the Nahda's renewal movement. It became important to understand why the Nahda had failed to deliver on its promises and to know what had stood in the way of completing its enlightenment project. It became equally important to reconnect with it after a long break, to reclaim it as a founding moment of modern Arab thought, to own its legacy, and to work for its continuity. In the late twentieth century, as the margins of liberty dwindled, it was necessary to seek inspiration in those initial impulses of free questioning and debate: contemporary critique could build on past endeavors of enlightenment with the aim of working toward their fruition—a formidable but unavoidable challenge in the midst of great humiliation, oppression, and pain. These post-1967 thinkers' most pressing demand was clearly the restoration of people's critical faculties in view of a long-term struggle for enlightenment on both the cultural and the political levels. The malaise was in the first place political, caused mainly by repression and the lack of democracy. For these thinkers, culture was a vital milieu for critique and public debate, an enabling platform for political agency. Critical thinking of one's own and the critical reappropriation of the past as well as of the West were seen as necessary for overcoming the malaise.

The demand for critique was not limited to these thinkers. It dominated a wide spectrum of the post-1967 Arab intellectual scene. Its concerns were the subject of numerous conferences and publications, where they were approached from different angles, with varying levels of sharpness and consistency. The next chapter examines three major conferences organized in 1971, 1974, and 1984 to discuss the cultural crisis of the period in its historical, conceptual, political, religious, and economic dimensions. It also looks at critical evaluations of these debates from different perspectives. A survey of these discussions shows the persistence of the ideology of absolutes described by Laroui. In fact, the notions of tradition (*turath*), authenticity (*asala*), and contemporaneity (*mu'asara*) dominate much of the 1970s and 1980s, eclipsing to a great extent the political aspect of the malaise and privileging identity issues over questions of critique. The discussions lay bare the persistence of that ideology and the challenges of critique.

Three

Marxist, Epistemological, and Psychological Readings of Major Conferences on Cultural Decline, Renewal, and Authenticity

The cultural concerns that preoccupied the prominent thinkers of the second half of the twentieth century were the subject of major pan-Arab conferences of this period. The three most important conferences were the Cairo conference of 1971, "Al-Asala wa al-Tajdid fi al-Thaqafa al-ʿArabiyya al-Muʿassira" (Authenticity and Renewal in Contemporary Arab Culture); the Kuwait conference of 1974, "Azamat al-Tatawwur al-Hadari fi al-Watan al-ʿArabi" (The Crisis of Civilizational Development in the Arab Homeland); and the Cairo conference of 1984, "Al-Turath wa Tahaddiyyat al-ʿAsr fi al-Watan al-ʿArabi" (Heritage and the Challenges of the Age in the Arab Homeland: Authenticity and Contemporaneity). Clearly, the dominating issues were authenticity, specificity, identity, heritage and contemporaneity, cultural renewal, openness, crisis, progress and underdevelopment, and the role of religion, politics, and colonialism in these matters. Major thinkers contributed to these conferences as participants or commentators or both. In their comments, they reflected on the ways in which these issues were formulated, the angles from which they were approached, and the modes of thinking through which they were apprehended.

The Cairo Conference of 1971: "Authenticity and Renewal in Contemporary Arab Culture"

The 1971 Cairo conference "Al-Asala wa al-Tajdid fi al-Thaqafa al-ʿArabiyya al-Muʿassira" (Authenticity and Renewal in Contemporary Arab Culture) was organized by the Arab League Educational, Cultural, and Scientific Organization (ALECSO), established in 1970. The leading literary journal of the time, *al-Adab*, reported on it and presented the twofold aim that the organizers set for the conference:[1] first, to identify those elements through which the Arab can still feel that he or she belongs to a particular nation with a particular spirit and a particular character; and second, to discuss how these elements may or should interact with the culture of the age and what issues this encounter might or does create. *Al-Adab*'s reporter listed the topics that the organizing committee had chosen for the conference: authenticity and renewal, the specificities of Arab culture, the position of this Arab culture in the present age, as well as authenticity and renewal in Arab poetry, fiction, theater, essay, critique, travelogue literature, and language—an ambitious program that was poorly and hastily prepared by Arab League bureaucrats, who, according to the reporter, failed to attract contributions that would have allowed the conference to do justice to the anticipated topics.[2]

All in all, eight papers were presented, some of a very poor quality. Six were published in *al-Adab*.[3] The program was particularly disappointing, added the reporter, given the importance of these topics for the contemporary Arab intellectual in particular and for the Arab citizen in general. For the past seventy years, he said, the questions of authenticity and renewal had been frequently discussed; they had acquired an additional significance since the defeat of 1967, which had forced Arabs to search for a sense of themselves, for their place in this world, caught as they were in the revolt against all that led to the defeat and in the tensions of belonging that it exacerbated. The issue of authenticity and renewal had thus become one of the main concerns of Arab culture. Another factor leading to the increased preoccupation with authenticity, he added, was the multitude of shifts Arab thinkers made from one intellectual trend to another: from positivism to existentialism, from conservatism to liberalism and radicalism, from traditionalism to Marxism, and so on.[4] Such shifts raised questions: Is there a core to our self? Is this core changing in its appearance and fixed in its essence? What is the nature of our relation to our past? What is our relation to other cultures? Who are we and why? Sentimental phrases could not provide satisfactory answers to these pressing questions, he said. They needed to be addressed seriously, but this conference unfortunately fell short of doing so. Indeed, some of the papers were quite poor, but others managed to make some interesting points, which I discuss briefly here.

Shukry Ayad: Authenticity as the Search for a Sense of Self Between One's Own Heritage and the Present Age

In "Mafhouf al-Asala wa al-Tajdid wa al-Thaqafa al-Mu'assira" (The Concept of Authenticity and Renewal and Contemporary Arab Culture), Egyptian literary critic Shukry Ayad explains that the concept of authenticity started to become prominent in the mid-1950s.[5] Earlier generations, those in the 1920s and 1930s especially, had rather thought in terms of the old and the new, tradition and innovation. What these concepts and authenticity conveyed, he says, was a sense of selfhood (*dhatiyya*), both on the individual level and on the national level. The challenge was to combine the two levels. Writers sought to express themselves as individuals, but at the same time they also felt that in the face of an invading Western culture, they needed to anchor themselves in an established heritage of their own, especially considering that the Western culture of the age did not favor the growth of individuality. The concept of authenticity expressed this search for selfhood. The writers of the 1920s and 1930s had adopted a conciliatory position between the old and the new by returning critically to the heritage and by selecting from the present age those elements that enhanced their own expressivity. "Honesty" is what they aimed at. With the proliferation of radical trends on the Western literary scene, however, it became increasingly difficult to maintain this position because the elements of the age were so multiple and contradictory. From the proliferation of different trends came the need to set a certain standard of authenticity: hence, the emergence of the term *authenticity* in the mid-1950s. But, states Ayad, whether the focus of the present age is on tradition and innovation or on authenticity and renewal, all are seeking a certain sense of self in the current conditions, marked by the influence of the Western cultural trends.

Mohammad Mazali: Authenticity as the Creative Return to the Self and the Basis for Opening Up to the World and Its Challenges

For Tunisian scholar Mohammad Mazali, the time had come, after the struggle against colonial occupation, to ask ourselves about our identity and our future: Who are we exactly, what do we want to become, and what should our role in the world be? His paper "Al-Asala wa al-Tafattuh" (Authenticity and Opening Up) provides the following answers.[6] We are a people whose religion is Islam and whose language is Arabic, a people who view in a dynamic way a future of dignity, justice, peace, and brotherhood. In this big Arab homeland, concentrated on the Mediterranean coast, we face the threat of imperialism and Zionism, and we find ourselves in a world threatened by nuclear war and multiple forms of pollution. We have to make up our minds: either to retreat in despair, defeat, and spite or to face our world with honesty and justice, drawing on our moral and spiritual values and seeking inspiration in our religious and intellectual heritage—a heritage that we need to mobilize in a creative spirit, as our ancestors did in the past. Authenticity, for him, is this critical and creative return to the self in order to build on the strength of those values a confident sense of self that can serve as a base for openness. Authenticity is also an intelligent listening to the spirit of the age as well as an awareness of its givens in view of a fruitful interaction with it, without surrender or the development of an inferiority complex. Authenticity, he adds, is a preservation of the essence of identity, a harmonization with life, and an openness to a future that can be bright if we know how to strive in unity toward what al-Farabi called the "Virtuous City." Some, he says, tell us that ours is no longer the age of nationalisms, that what counts nowadays is development, that from a Marxist point of view nationalism is a reactionary ideology, and that in this scientific age national identities make no sense. These considerations, according to him, do not apply to societies that have experienced economic, political, military, and cultural aggression through colonialism. However, the reaction to this aggression has often taken the form of a stagnating refuge in the past. Such a reaction has only aggravated the state of defeat and produced a false meaning of authenticity. A reaction of self-affirmation is needed instead, but in the form of a creative and dynamic opening up to the world of the present age.

Zaki Naguib Mahmud: The Necessity of Adopting Rational Western Culture

Finally, in "Mawqif al-Thaqafa al-'Arabiyya al-Haditha fi Muwajahat al-'Asr" (The Position of Modern Arab Culture in the Face of the Present Age), Egyptian philosopher Zaki Naguib Mahmud, trained at the University of London, identifies Arab culture's main difficulties with the prevailing (Western) culture.[7] At the core of Arab culture, both old and new, is a sharp distinction between God and His creatures, the Absolute Idea and the changing world, eternal truth and historical events, reality and appearance. The changing world, the corporeal, are taken to be appearances or signs for another, everlasting world. It is this divide, according to Mahmud, that has determined the attitude toward reason throughout Arab cultural history. Reason has been limited to an instrumental role in the realization of ultimate goals that are grasped through intuition or faith. Worldly human reason cannot determine these goals; they are given as part of everlasting truth. Twice in its history, Arab culture had to deal with an incoming rational culture: first, Greek philosophical culture in the first few centuries of Islam and then Western scientific culture beginning in the nineteenth century. Mahmud says that although the two epochs cannot be taken to be identical (without explaining why and how), they show two similar typical reactions to the incoming rational culture: either to embrace it and accord it with Arab culture, as the philosophers of the classical age or the thinkers of the Nahda did, or to antagonize and reject it in a defensive way. The first reaction has in both cases been limited to a small number of intellectuals, whereas the second reaction has spread and become the attitude of the masses. The latter has recently manifested itself in a widespread rejection of the principles of the Western scientific culture—namely, the natural view of the human being, human values, and human reason. The rejection has not been complete, however, and there has been a partial adoption of the culture of the age, mainly in the consumption of its technological products. Those who have rejected the whole structure with its divide have failed to have any general impact. Mahmud elaborates on this analysis in his book *Tajdid al-Fikr al-'Arabi* (The Renewal of Arab Thought),[8] published the same year as the conference in Cairo. In both the conference paper and the book, he seems to reduce what he calls "Arab culture" to religion—that is, to Islam—and the confrontation between Arab culture and Greek philosophy or Western culture to a confrontation between religion and reason. He in the end calls for a wide-ranging westernization.

The Kuwait Conference of 1974: "The Crisis of Civilizational Development in the Arab Homeland"

The second conference I focus on in this chapter, "Azamat al-Tatawwur al-Hadari fi al-Watan al-ʿArabi" (The Crisis of Civilizational Development in the Arab Homeland), was organized by Kuwait University and its alumni association in 1974. It was held six months after the 1973 October war in which Egypt scored a partial victory against Israel. It is also during this time that an Arab oil embargo on Western countries succeeded in putting pressure on their foreign policies in the Middle East. This conference was more successful than the previous Cairo one in that it gathered a wider number of Arab thinkers (all men), who offered qualitatively better contributions, twenty-four in all, including papers and commentaries. All were published partly in the May 1974 issue of *al-Adab* and partly in the June 1974 issue of *al-Maʿrifah*.[9] Lebanese Marxist philosopher Hassan Hamdan (alias Mahdi Amil) critically reviewed and analyzed them in a book published a few months after the conference, *Azamat al-Hadara al-ʿArabiyya am Azamat al-Burjwaziyya al-ʿArabiyya?* (The Crisis of Arab Civilization or the Crisis of Arab Bourgeoisie?).[10] The papers connected the crisis of Arab civilization to history, colonialism, religion, politics, family structures, education, and social values. They devoted special attention to intellectual retardation in the civilizational crisis, the notions of specificity and authenticity, as well as the notions of progress and retardation in general.[11] In all of these themes, the dominating concerns were the contemporary Arab fixation on the past and the Arab alienation from the present age. I examine the main points made in the seven most pertinent papers, the conference's final declaration, as well as a general review of the meeting published in the 1974 June issue of *al-Adab*.

Zaki Naguib Mahmud: The Call for Westernization

In this conference, we encounter the same Zaki Naguib Mahmud of the 1971 Cairo meeting, this time presenting a paper entitled "Al-Hadara wa Qadiyyat al-Taqaddum wa al-Takhalluf" (Civilization and the Issue of Progress and Retardation).[12] Mahmud starts by underlining the need for a definition of the term *civilization*. Due to the difficulties of reaching a satisfactory definition, he proposes instead that four instances of high civilization be considered: Pericles' Athens of the fifth century BC, Maʾmun's Baghdad of the ninth century AD, Renaissance Florence of the fifteen century, and Paris of the Enlightenment in the eighteenth century. Common to all these civilizations, he notes, is the recourse to reason in the various fields of thought and action. The recourse to reason manifests itself in the reliance on the means-end relationship, the priority given to the long term over the short term, the explanation of phenomena through natural causes, and the realistic and objective view of things. Civilizational progress, then, according to Mahmud, should be measured according to this criterion of reason. This criterion does not apply to art, literature, or the emotions: there can be no progress in matters of love, art, or fiction as there can be in science, technology, and moral utilitarianism. The latter determine the level of progress in a given civilization, and, he says, Arab civilization surely suffers from a serious delay in progress in these fields. In our age, according to Mahmud, Europe and the United States represent advanced civilizations. Arabs should take them as models of progress in science, rational planning, productivity, and social and political liberties. Arabs find themselves in a civilizational crisis because they have superficially and nominally accepted these principles of progress. They have claimed that their heritage has championed rationality, but on the deep level they have not really made these principles theirs.

Suheil Idriss, founder and editor of *al-Adab*, states in his comments on Mahmud's paper that taking Europe and the United States as the models of advanced civilization overlooks their noncivilized features, such as racism and their support for Zionism. It also leaves out other civilizational models such as East Europe and the Far East. Idriss finds problematic Mahmud's separation of reason from art, literature, and emotions, and disagrees with the inapplicability of progress to belles lettres. Finally, he finds Mahmud's proposal to be a confirmation and perpetuation of the Arab status quo of dependency. Egyptian education scholar Abdallah Abdel Da'im asks whether rationalism was the cause of advanced civilizations or the effect of their progress. He also wonders if instrumental reason can be taken as the dominating principle of the first three models mentioned by Mahmud.

Shaker Mustafa: The Weight of the Past and the Need for a Historical Investigation

In his paper, Shaker Mustafa proposes to examine "the historical dimensions of the development crisis of Arab civilization" (from the title of his paper "Al-Abʿad al-Tarikhiyya li Azamat al-Tatawwur al-Hadari al-ʿArabi").[13] He starts by noting that in contrast to other nations, such as China, Russia, and Japan, the Arab nation has tried to adapt to the present age with great difficulty and without much success. He quickly adds that although underdevelopment is not limited to the Arab nation and applies to many of the world's populations, it is important to understand the specificities of the Arab challenges. One of the main problems he sees in the Arab case is a nonhistorical view of present phenomena because of a failure to recognize the historical factors that led to the present situation, especially to the present estrangement from the epoch. Arabs seem to have a problem with time, he says, overwhelmed as they are by a weighty history rich in political, religious, scientific, artistic, and literary achievements. They seem to live in the past more than in the present. They tend to cultivate a romantic, religious, and mostly nonscientific view of this past. The political and military defeats by Israel and the technological and economic defeats by Western imperialism have forced them to admit their retardation, to reconsider their heritage (*turath*), and to engage in a second *nahda* in educational, developmental, and social reforms. But they themselves have also reinforced the use of the past as a refuge and made a compensatory ideological use of this legacy, sometimes religious and sometimes nationalist.

Mustafa thinks that it is extremely important to overcome these ideological temptations and to develop a truly historical view of this past in order to have a real understanding of the present situation. For him, such a historical investigation has to be carried out in four fields: in the economy and the forms of material production; in politics and the structures of power; in social relations, including family, tribalism, confessionalism, women, sexuality, and moral values; and finally in the intellectual sphere, including language and ideologies. All these factors are interrelated, he says, and their separation is only for analytic purposes.

In the economic field, the means of production, especially in agriculture, have remained traditional. Trade, which made the Arab fortunes in earlier times, waned with the age of discoveries in the sixteenth century, becoming more local and less prosperous. The twentieth century witnessed the rise of a petty bourgeoisie still caught in the old ways of thinking and acting, with no new future vision. Its economic, political, ideological, and intellectual leadership, secured through military coups and repressive regimes, proved to be catastrophic for the Arab region. On the political level, for the past ten centuries society was divided into three classes: a foreign military class, local families of notables, and the rest of the population. The first two classes provided each other protection and legitimacy, often with the support of religious clerics. They formed a repressive, exploitive system that ruled in the name of Islam, but had nothing of the Islamic principles of justice. The system alienated the people from the rulers: contempt, neglect, and hostility from the latter were faced with suspicion, hatred, and noncooperation from the former. Governments came to be regarded as enemies, and local loyalties were reinforced to the detriment of wider solidarities. The colonial system replaced the old military rulers with a capitalist class with which it associated itself. This class, in contrast to its European counterpart, appeared to be westernized, but at the same time fulfilled the same oppressive function as the former military class. Moreover, the colonial system imposed the division and fragmentation of the region into separate states. This political oppression went hand in hand with social, patriarchal, and sexual oppression. The social oppression produced an attitude of passivity and fatalism, a sense of helplessness, dependency, and social deception.

Finally, on the intellectual level, for long centuries the achievements of the classical age have been passively and repetitively transmitted without creativity. These achievements are presented as already established and final truths to be learned and accepted. To this presentation is added the view of the sacred character of the early period of Islam, the most perfect of all times from which there can only be a decline. This view is strengthened by the compensatory use of this "perfect" epoch as a point of comparison to the poor present. An educational and linguistic system that does not aim at encouraging original and innovative thinking transmits this lack of creativity and intellectual productivity, and the system alienates people from the lived and the thought. The result is an alienation both from the present age and from the cultural heritage. Only a work of historicization, according to Mustafa, can deconstruct the state of siege in which Arabs have been living for the past ten centuries. He does not say more on the modalities of this liberation, nor does he rely on concrete historical studies to corroborate his claims regarding ten centuries of Arab history.

Ibrahim Abu-Lughod: The Impact of Colonialism on the Cultural Crisis

In "Al-Isti'mar wa Azamat al-Tatawwur fi al-Watan al-'Arabi" (Colonialism and the Crisis of Development in the Arab Homeland), Palestinian historian Ibrahim Abu-Lughod offers his thoughts on the effect of colonialism as a historical event on the development of the Arab world.[14] The idea of the linear progression of civilization, he says, comes from Darwin via Spencer. As is well known in the Third World and even in Europe and the United States, he adds, this idea was used to justify colonialism, whether in the form of indirect colonialism through political and economic hegemony or in the form of direct colonialism or settlement colonialism as in Algeria, Libya, and Palestine. Advanced Western civilization was to lead backward societies that, unlike Western societies, were still under the domination of religion and irrationalism toward the path of civilizational progress.

In contrast to the prevalent Orientalist claim, Abu-Lughod affirms that the Arab region had not been stagnant since the Middle Ages, frozen under political despotism. Efforts for change and reform were being deployed well before the Western intervention—for instance in Tunis, Egypt, and Syria. Unfortunately, he does not offer more precise information or references to support this claim.[15] According to Abu-Lughod, these sociopolitical and intellectual movements were thwarted by the colonial intervention, contrary to the prevailing belief that it was the intervention itself that triggered the Arab Renaissance (Nahda). They drew on the Arab Islamic tradition (although, again, he does not offer references). Colonialism added new sources of inspiration, but it also changed the vision of the future. Arab thinkers started to take the Western visions to be the true visions of progress. Colonialism brought with it institutional models imported from the West—creating double models, for instance in education. This shift gave rise to a westernized minority that despised the people and its traditions. It created an intellectual tension that was to become the source of a civilizational crisis. Attempts were made to harmonize the two poles of inspiration, the Western and the Islamic traditions, by the leaders of the Nahda, such as al-Afghani, Abduh, Abdel Raziq, al-Bustani, and Husayn. But the polarization remained because the sociopolitical realities of the Arab world in the twentieth century did not allow the fruition of these attempts. Instead of nurturing a dialogue between the advocates of the two poles, these realities favored a dialogue with the West. Although supposedly addressing the people, political thinkers and actors addressed Western thinkers, trying to gain their approval and acceptance. Western views were welcomed, and efforts were made to indigenize them.

Most of the military and political liberation movements accepted the retardation/progress scheme, believing that they could achieve progress better than the colonial forces had. They also accepted the region's fragmented reality and gave up on the precolonial era's pan-Islamic and pan-Arab ideologies. No inter-Arab dialogue was really engaged. In order to overcome the colonial view of things, says Abu-Lughod, Arabs need to write their history from their own point of view and to produce their own analyses of their socioeconomic and cultural realities. The challenges are momentous. Many

Arabs have internalized the bigotry against their own culture, and conservatives and Salafis have used the struggle against colonialism to repress intellectual freedom. The 1967 defeat, he adds, has led the radicals to become more revolutionary and the Salafis to become more Islamic. Those who at this time (early 1970s) fear for the future of Arab civilization think that the settlement policies in Palestine will eventually lead to a total confrontation between the radical and the Salafi trends, and ultimately to the triumph of the Salafi view, producing a total intellectual bankruptcy (a prediction that was sadly confirmed in the decades after 1974). Abu-Lughod ends his paper with a plea for the establishment of an Arab academy of scientific and historical research that will guarantee Arab scholars the means and the freedom to conduct and publish research that will pave the way for an authentically Arab thought based on Arab heritage and current research. Such an academy would also offer new educational visions that might replace the ones prevailing since the previous century.

Fouad Zakariyya: The Ahistorical Exaggeration of the Past
The relation to history is also the focus of the two papers on the intellectual aspect of retardation in Arab civilization—the first by Egyptian philosopher Fouad Zakariyya, for many years professor of philosophy at the University of Kuwait; and the second by Ali Ahmad Sa'id, alias "Adonis," the Syrian poet and literary critic, and one of the leading figures of the contemporary Arab literary scene. The main thesis of Zakariyya's paper, "Al-Takhalluf al-Fikri wa Ab'aduhu al-Hadariyya" (Intellectual Retardation and Its Civilizational Dimensions), is that this sense of retardation, decline, and weakening has emerged in the minds of contemporary Arabs as a result of the comparison of the present Arab situation with the past, when Arabs were the makers of a leading civilization.[16] Today's Arabs, he says, look back at this glorious past with intense nostalgia and feel deep bitterness regarding their present weakness and dependency. The past, he says, stands as an independent and rival force to the present instead of being integrated into the present as part of its historical constitutive element. In the final analysis, this nonhistorical view of the past handicaps thinking and produces the ubiquitous problem of "authenticity and contemporaneity," in which authenticity is associated with the civilizational legacy of this past, or *turath*, in a conflictual link with the present age. Zakariyya examines both the negative and positive attitudes toward this *turath*.

The negative critics of *turath* underline in the Arab civilizational legacy the element of irrationality, the mythical mode of thinking, and the repression of liberties. These aspects also surely existed, he says, in the European traditions, yet they did not prevent progress from taking place in Europe. They were incorporated in the history of the development of European modernity and scientific progress, and were recognized as stages of this evolution that were eventually overcome. Unlike Arabs, the Europeans are not fixated on their legacies. Contemporary Arabs seem to blame their cultural legacy both for having created the problems of their present and for preventing solutions to them. Defenders of *turath*, in contrast, blame the present civilizational decline on the turning away from tradition. For Zakariyya, Arabs seem to be unique in this passionate defense of tradition. In one of the extreme forms of this defense, it is claimed that tradition contains all that one needs—that all scientific discoveries, for instance, are already found in the Qur'an. Even if for the sake of argument one were to agree with this claim, he adds, it would still mean that discoveries would have to be made first and then "identified" as already stated in some form or other in the sacred book. But most champions of *turath* reject this exaggerated claim, refusing to reduce the Qur'an to a book of science. Many of them regard the Arab medieval intellectual production to have surpassed all subsequent achievement, especially Western, believing in the superiority of the Arab accomplishments for all times. But paradoxically, adds Zakariyya, this reasoning implicitly recognizes the Western achievements as the standard of measurement. This self-glorification is based on a comparison with others, mainly the West, that maintains these others as the real challenge.

As in the case of the negative critics of *turath*, the problem here is in the misunderstanding of the function of tradition: tradition is seen as the source of both the problems and the present solutions, but a source that is outside the present, disconnected from it. What makes tradition into this central and yet external agent, according to Zakariyya, is the lack of continuity between past and present. Tradition has not become part of contemporary Arabs' living mind. A tradition that is really a living heritage does not need to be "revived," he adds, but *turath* is a heritage that has died because it is only a disconnected and reified legacy. For a heritage to be truly living, it needs to be critically appropriated and overcome. He proposes the following lesson from the European Renaissance: tradition and in the first place Aristotelian thought were critically rejected, but then they were put in their historical context and no longer maintained as an object of either attack or glorification. An Arab renaissance will necessarily be different from the European one, given the different histories, but it will have to be based on a critical consideration of tradition. Struggles and debates about tradition, says Zakariyya, are in reality struggles and debates about the present—a present that fails to own its past and address its current issues properly.

In his comment on Zakariyya's paper, Qustantin Zurayq disagrees with Zakariyya, stating that the wrong view of *turath* is a manifestation rather than the cause of the intellectual retardation in question. He thinks that it is important to understand the factors that caused that the discontinuity between the past and the present and the reasons for the halt in cultural growth. According to him, one should speak of a civilizational rather than a cultural decline because this decline happened on many levels, including the political, the economic, and the social. Such declines happen in all civilizations, he adds, so one cannot speak of an Arab specificity in this regard, but it remains important to understand the circumstances of the Arab decline. He offers a number of hypotheses for it without suggesting a definite answer: Did it occur because the Arab state was fragmented due to the domination of local loyalties? Was it due to the foreign, non-Arab elements in the state? Was there a decline in Arab zeal and commitment after the period of conquest? Was the downfall due to the weaknesses and shortcomings of the civilization that the Arabs produced? Or is civilizational decline the pattern of history in all civilizations? Was the decline due to all these factors or to some other ones? It is important, says Zurayq, to understand the multifaceted causes of this decline and the discontinuity with the past. Finally, he adds, although the European Renaissance rejected the Aristotelian scholastic tradition, it revived the Greek tradition: hence, the importance of knowing well one's tradition in order to make use of it positively and negatively—a knowledge that he considers lacking in the Arab present in spite of all the fixation on and obsession with tradition.

Adonis: Theological Idealism as the Major Hindrance to Creativity, Modernity, and Authenticity

For Syrian poet and literary critic Adonis, traditional forms of thinking are at the root of the cultural decline. His paper articulates, as its title says, "some thoughts on the manifestations of intellectual retardation in Arab society" ("Khawatir Hawl Madhahir al-Takhalluf al-Fikri al-ʿArabi").[17] The basic problem, according to him, is the subjugation of reason, thought, and politics to religion, to the sacred text (the Qurʾan), and to the religious tradition (the sunna). This subjugation is illustrated in the thought of the medieval philosopher Abu Hamid Muhammad ibn Muhammad al-Ghazali

(1058–1111) and is still prevalent today in Arab society. This mode of thinking is characterized by a number of traits. In the theological view of things, worldly logic and historical logic are marginalized by the logic of revelation. This view presents an idealism of origin (Arabs are the best nation created by God) and an idealism of end (the Arab nation is destined for heavenly paradise), both of which transcend the vicissitudes of history. This religious tradition is consolidated by a pre-Islamic patriarchal system that is authoritarian and repressive. The state is the political image of this patriarchal system. Unity is upheld in the form of a denial of societal conflict, struggle, and need for revolution. Progress is seen as the conservation of the ideal origin. It is the work of a heavenly God and not a human achievement. This view considers tradition as the measure for all things, implying a reverence for what is known and a deep suspicion of what is new and different. To this trait is added the privileging of the letter to the content, the preference for oration over writing. Pre-Islamic poetry is taken to be the reference for all good poetry. All of these traits discourage creativity and determine the way modernity is accepted—at least, in its most superficial aspects. Islam, Adonis adds, distinguishes sharply between God, on the one hand, and the world and humans, on the other. The ruler alone is free; he rules in the name of God in a system that mixes religion with politics. Any deviation from the majority of the community is regarded as an unacceptable deviance. No room is left for individual freedom, creativity, and imagination. Yet to be human is to be creative. What is needed is a break from this traditional system of thinking and a rejection of all forms of *salafiyya* (absolute reverence for the fathers of tradition) as well as of all forms of subjugation to a sacralized past.

Adonis expands on these views in other works. In the preface to the new 1998 edition of his 1980 book *Fatiha li Nihayat al-Qarn* (Overture to the Century's Endings), he draws the following somber balance sheet:

Thirty years: everything is getting worse.

The space of freedom has shrunk, and the repression has increased. Our chances for building a democracy and a civil society, for making room for pluralism and diversity, have decreased, and the foundations for violence and oppression have grown stronger.

And we have today less religiosity and less tolerance and more confessionalism and more fanaticism. We are less united and more fragmented. We are less open, accept less the different Other, and are more closed and enwrapped in darkness.

So we are today poorer and weaker.

And what we call homeland is becoming a military barrack, a confessional hamlet, a tribal camp.[18]

The book is a collection of papers and essays Adonis wrote between 1967 and 1979 on various issues such as the 1967 defeat, the relation between culture and politics, and the relation between theater and modernity. The 1998 edition contains comments on these individual texts written some two decades later. Here, I am concerned mainly with the last three pieces in the book: the "Bayan al-Hadatha" (Modernity Manifesto) written in 1979, the comment on this text written thirteen years later in 1992 under the title "Al-Hadatha wa al-Tamazzuq al-Maʿrifi" (Modernity and the Cognitive Rupture), and finally the text added six years later in 1998, "Al-Huwwiyya wa Asʾilat al-Hadatha" (Identity and the Questions of Modernity).

As a poet and literary critic, Adonis was among the first contributors to the revolutionary modernist movement and to its journal *al-Shiʿr*, founded in 1957 by leading Lebanese literary figure Youssef el-Khal (1917–1987)[19] and published between 1957 and 1964 and then between 1967 and 1970. It is regarded as one of the most important expressions of Arab literary and intellectual modernism. It was the main platform for Arab avant-garde poetry that broke the traditional rhyme rule of classical poetry and opened the way for a more liberated, experimental, and existential Arab poetry. El-Khal was influenced by U.S. American poetry during the years he spent in New York as a member of the Lebanese delegation to the United Nations in the late 1940s and early 1950s.[20]

Adonis's primary interest is in poetic modernity, but for him its link with cultural modernity in general is evident. First, he thinks that many misconceptions among Arabs about poetic modernity need to be corrected: modernity in Arab poetry cannot be reduced to a form, like that of breaking away from the traditional poetic meter, or to the sheer evocation of contemporary topics. Moreover, modernity's main characteristic does not lie in a simple opposition to traditional Arab poetry or in a straightforward copying from modern Western poetry. More than a phenomenon of a certain age, place, or culture, modernity is for Adonis an attitude and an energy: the attitude of questioning the self and the other, the world and tradition; the energy of creating new visions, immersed in the *génie* and the mastery of the language and hence in tradition, and at the same time inspired by the lived experiences of the present reality. Poetic modernity in this sense and modernity in general, he argues, cannot but be authentic. Genuine modernity and genuine authenticity can only emerge from a root-edness both in tradition and in lived reality, from free creativity. It is because such a creativity has been prevented from developing in the Arab world that neither modernity nor authenticity have been possible there. Modernity and authenticity did emerge and blossom in the past, and they gave rise to the achievements of the classical Arab culture. The obstacles to their renewal are, according to Adonis,

1. *The textual referentiality that dominates Arab social and intellectual life.* The canonical texts, mostly in the literal sense, are taken as the main references of understanding and interpretation. They are given priority over concrete reality. Knowledge thus is reduced to an exercise of jurisprudential hermeneutics instead of being in the first place an exploration of the nature of things experienced in concrete reality. Knowledge becomes a textual interpretation and inevitably a reproduction of the same old ways of looking at the world and at the self. This way reason is paralyzed, and the Arab person herself or himself is marginalized, together with her or his lived experiences.

2. *The conception of identity as something already given and formed once and for all, an original to which all descendents should conform.* Such a conception of the self makes all genuine questioning, searching, and creating superfluous, if not forbidden. It unavoidably leads to an absence of creativity, to an absence of thought, and hence to an absence of modernity. Identity is a dynamic, historical phenomenon that is constantly in the making through questioning the self in its concrete reality and questioning the other as a dimension of the possibility of the self.

3. *And finally, the monistic view of truth, power, tradition, and community.* The concept of the abstract and metaphysical One has not left room for pluralism, difference, or diversity. The consequence of such a concept and such a view is the denial of knowledge and of the human individual. It is, however, not the "nation" that creates, he argues, but the individual. The nation is the collection of individuals, and the individual has primacy over it. The identity of the nation cannot but be plural, and its political organization cannot but be democratic. This configuration necessitates a separation between power and knowledge as well as between power and

religion. The mission of political power is to be understood in civil, not religious terms. Religion has become an instrument of control and power instead of being a field of meditation. Adonis adds ironically and bitterly: if God has died in the West, He is the only one alive in our part of the world; here, it is the human being who has died.

Unless these obstacles are overcome, says Adonis, no genuine modernity and no genuine authenticity can emerge. Authenticity is not a state of being in the past to which the Arab needs to return, but a free and creative movement forward. Without creativity and without real thought, understood as a real interaction with the concrete given, the Arab is bound to remain absent from her own reality, approaching the latter through the tools of absence, either those of some imagined past or those borrowed from another. In this absence, in her own reality the Arab remains caught in the cage of a presumed fixed self, living with the mind, the taste, and the instruments of another. The Nahda failed to sustain the creative energy and the genuine questioning necessary for a real revival of Arab culture. Adonis does not discuss the socioeconomic and political factors that may have contributed to this failure, however.

In spite of this dynamic conception of identity, Adonis himself falls into essentialist views of the self and the other. In his first major study of the Arab literary legacy, the four-volume work *Al-Thabit wa al-Mutahawwil: Bahth fi al-Ibdaʿ wa al-Itibaʿ ʿInda al-ʿArab* (The Constant and the Changing: A Study in Creativity and Imitation Among Arabs), published in Beirut in 1973, he wanted to discover "the" main characteristics of this legacy and to understand how "the" Arab Muslim mind worked, what its inner world was, who "the" Arab was. He also insisted that his approach was not historical, for his interest was in these general characteristics. In the 1980 preface to the 1994 edition of these volumes, he says that his aim is to discover the following: "What is the Arab Muslim? How has he thought and how does he think? What is his inner world? What is his will? What is poetry? What is language? Does the human being in his consciousness have an agency, is he a creative individual or just a delegated being?"[21] His answer to the first essentialist questions is that the Arab-Muslim is ruled by theologism, conformity to the past, conformity to language, and resistance to doubt, experimentation, and change. But to what extent are these characteristics specific to Arab culture alone, and to what extent can they be predicated to fourteen centuries of cultural, social, and political life?

More surprising are his views on the East and the West formulated in 1979 in the "Modernity Manifesto." In a strikingly inconsistent sequence of statements, Adonis swings between blunt, essentialist categorizations of the East and the West and humanist, universalist claims. On the one hand, he sees the East/West divide as a circumstantial, colonial divide, and on the other he sees it as an essential divide. The West is reason, technology, materialism, whereas the East is the heart, the metaphysical, inspiration, creativity, poetry. For him, this essential difference does not lead to a clash of civilizations, but rather to a relation of complementarity. All poetic creativity in the West is inspired from the East: religion, philosophy, poetry, and art in general are Eastern phenomena; whenever the West engages in them, it orientalizes itself. Thought in both parts of the world has resigned: the West is dominated by the devil of technology, and the East has submitted to despotism. For him, Baudelaire is an Eastern mystic, Novalis a Sufi, and Rimbaud a rebel against the West with an Eastern voice. Among the "Eastern Westerners" are painters such as Kandinsky, Klee, and Picasso. More generally, Western culture is a reaction to medieval Islamic culture. On the universalist side, however, he says, there is no such thing as an East/West divide, and, in fact, what we have is a global human culture, a human joint venture at the origin of which is a questioning and searching human being. Modernity itself, he says, is a global phenomenon, and the difference between the West and the East is a difference in degree. Islam itself is a universal call, neither Western nor Eastern.

It is precisely this kind of essentialism that Sadeq Jalal al-Azm calls "counter-Orientalism" or "Orientalism in reverse" and attacks in his essay "Al-Istishraq wa al-Istishraq al-Maʿkus" (Orientalism and Orientalism in Reverse).[22] In it he criticizes both the critique of Orientalism by Edward Said and the adoption of much of the essentialism of Western Orientalism by contemporary Arab ideologists. In Said's deconstructive effort, which al-Azm commends and supports otherwise, he finds a certain essentialism that reduces Western attitudes toward the East throughout the ages to a number of recurring patterns and marginalizes the nonliterary aspects of these attitudes:

In an act of retrospective historical projection we find Said tracing the origins of Orientalism all the way back to Homer, Aeschylus, Euripides and Dante. In other words, Orientalism is not really a thoroughly modern phenomenon, as we thought earlier, but is the natural product of an ancient and almost irresistible European bent of mind to mis-represent the realities of other cultures, peoples, and their languages, in favour of Occidental self-affirmation, domination and ascendency. Here the author seems to be saying that the "European mind," from Homer to Karl Marx and A. H. R. Gibb, is inherently bent on distort-ing all human realities other than its own and for the sake of its own aggrandizement.

It seems to me that this manner of construing the origins of Oriental-ism simply lends strength to the essentialistic categories of "Orient" and "Occident," representing the ineradicable distinction between East and West, which Edward's book is ostensibly set on demolishing. Similarly, it lends the ontological distinction of Europe versus Asia, so characteristic of Orientalism, the kind of credibility and respectability normally associated with continuity, persistence, pervasiveness and distant historical roots. This sort of credibility and respectability is, of course, misplaced and undeserved. For Orientalism, like so many other characteristically modern European phenomena and move-ments (notably nationalism), is a genuinely recent creation—the prod-uct of modern European history—seeking to acquire legitimacy, cred-ibility and support by claiming ancient roots and classical origins for itself. . . .

If Academic Orientalism transmutes the reality of the Orient into the stuff of texts (as he [Said] says on page 86), then it would seem that Said sublimates the earthly realities of the Occident's interaction with the Orient into the ethereal stuff of the spirit.[23]

But it is al-Azm's critique of what he calls counter-Orientalism that is really scathing. Whether in secular nationalism or in the recent Islamic revivalism, one finds, according to him, the same essentialism and reduc-tionism found in Western Orientalism, especially in the aftermath of the Iranian Revolution, thus showing many Arab intellectuals' disarray:

Their central thesis may be summarised as follows: The national sal-vation so eagerly sought by the Arabs since the Napoleonic occupation of Egypt is to be found neither in secular nationalism (be it radical, conservative or liberal) nor in revolutionary communism, socialism or what have you, but in a return to the authenticity of what they call "popular political Islam." For purposes of distinctness I shall refer to this novel approach as the Islamanic trend.

I do not wish to dispute the above thesis of the Islamanics in this presentation. Instead, I would like to point out that the analyses, beliefs and ideas produced by the Islamanic trend in defense of its central thesis simply reproduce the whole discredited apparatus of classical Orientalist doctrine concerning the difference between East and West, Islam and Europe. This reiteration occurs at both the ontological and epistemological levels, only reversed to favour Islam and the East in its implicit and explicit value judgements.[24]

To illustrate his point, al-Azm takes issue with Adonis's claims, particularly those made in his "Modernity Manifesto." This critique gave rise to a fierce controversy between the two authors, Adonis defending himself and al-Azm reacting to his defense in a series of essays and counteressays published in Arabic journals in 1981 and 1982, both restating the arguments I have presented here. The texts were then collected and published by al-Azm in *Dhahniyyat al-Tahrim: Salman Rushdi wa Haqiqat al-Adab* (The Mental Taboo: Salman Rushdie and the Truth Within Literature).

Anouar Abdel-Malek: Arab Specificity and Authenticity

In the paper "Al-Khususiyya wa al-Asala" (Specificity and Authenticity) for the 1974 conference, the Marxist Egyptian sociologist Anouar Abdel-Malek reflects on the "authenticity/contemporaneity" problematic.[25] He was research professor at the Centre national de la recherche scientifique in Paris, and then coordinator of the United Nations University's Project on Sociocultural Development Alternatives in a Changing World in Tokyo. He has published widely in Arabic and French, and his writings have been translated into English, Spanish, Italian, Portuguese, Turkish, and Japanese. According to him, Orientalists and their local Arab culturalist agents have represented the world in terms of national and cultural units, and they have decided to consider every myth-minded culture to be "authentic"— worth studying and preserving. In North Africa, two opposite educational systems and cultures have been artificially created: a "fundamentalist," Azhar-based education and a Western, "modern" education, leading to the false association of Arab heritage with reactionary thought and the association of anything Western with modernity. Instead of this polarizing East/West schematic dichotomy, Abdel-Malek proposes that the specificity of every society be explored by investigating its persisting features in the course of history. More specifically, he proposes that the structures of the production of material life, the patterns of the reproduction of life, the systems of state and power, and the sets of religious beliefs be looked into together; he also recommends that the dialectical relation between the elements of change and those of continuity in a given society be examined. The interaction of all these aspects produces, according to him, a certain specificity for each nation. A grasp of this specificity would show how to modernize it in the most efficient way without falling into westernization and dependency. The proper modernization of this specificity would produce authentic contemporaneity. What is specific to Egypt, according to Abdel-Malek, is the persistence of a centralized state and army as well as the persistence of a set of religious beliefs in the form of a lasting monotheism. In this search for the specificity of national characteristics, however, he does not succeed in avoiding East/West essentialistic categorizations. On the contrary, in a series of articles and interviews given between 1973 and 1983 he emphasizes Egypt's "Easternness" and the civilizational link that connects the countries lying between Japan and Morocco.[26] He expresses his enthusiasm for the wind of change carried by the liberation movements in the region since the 1955 Bandung meeting and the Egyptian victory over Israel in the 1973 October War, supported by the Arab oil embargo.

Egyptian Marxist thinker Mahmud Amin al-Alim (1922–2009), a prolific critical writer and editor of several journals, among them *Qadaya Fikriyya*, comments critically on the two main points of Abdel-Malek's paper: the authenticity/contemporaneity issue and the specificity issue. On the first point, al-Alim says that instead of overcoming the authenticity/contemporaneity dichotomy, Abdel-Malek deepens it by associating it with the local/Western dichotomy, by regarding all Western thought as Orientalist, colonialist, and hegemonic, and finally by considering the issue as one of ideas only. Abdel-Malek does not examine ideas in relation to lived realities. Is the authenticity/contemporaneity opposition a purely intellectual contradiction in Arab thinkers' minds? Or is it a contradiction that they find in their lives and that gets reflected in their thought? Is it a result of their adoption of Western thought, as Abdel-Malek claims?

Al-Alim answers these questions by tracing back the intellectual dichotomy to the uneven development of Arab societies and to the uneven distribution of goods and modern services in them. These disparities and real contradictions can only be dealt with through a real commitment to change within liberation movements. Change can happen only if Arab societies critically appropriate rather than copy ideas from abroad. Western or foreign thought in general is not a monolithic whole. Some of it, such as Marxism, is genuinely universal and scientific. It is important for al-Alim to distinguish between colonial thought and scientific thought. Marxism makes room for local specificities. It might be useful for revolutionary struggles when properly appropriated. For him, Abdel-Malek's rejection of Western thought is ideological and contributes thus to the further polarization of the schematic dichotomy.

Abdel-Malek's approach to specificity is no less problematic, according to al-Alim. His characterization of this notion, especially in the case of Egypt, is based on sweeping judgments and absolute generalizations. It ignores the particularities of different epochs, the turns and the changes in the course of time. Yet these particularities are the important specificities to discover, not in order to be perpetuated, but to be overcome and changed. The nonchanging features are not the object of the critical sociohistorical science advocated by Marx, from whose work Abdel-Malek claims to borrow, especially in his book on Egypt.[27] Marx, states al-Alim, spoke of the specificity of social functions in specific periods of history, not of constant specificities throughout history. In the case of Egypt, Abdel-Malek looks at the prevalence of the centralized state (which al-Alim does not see as unique to Egypt), but he does not pay attention to the peasants' revolt movements against this state at different points in time. Neither does he notice that his own notion of specificity can be used to perpetuate that same centralized and repressive state, even though that is not his objective. Abdel-Malek expects that state to conduct the revolution toward the rightly understood concept of modern authenticity, as he has defined it, but can such an expectation be justified? Change, according to al-Alim, can come only from a popular democratic struggle against a state that supports a dependent and uneven development. Only from such a struggle can a healthy sense of social and national self emerge and a truly modern authenticity develop. Two directions have been suggested for a modern authenticity: a utilitarian eclecticism that borrows a little from tradition and a great deal from Western thought (suggested by Zaki Naguib Mahmud) or an adapted Western Marxism, but as a theoretical ideology rather than a scientific method, not leaving much room for real material dialectic (suggested by Abdallah Laroui). Neither of these directions can be fruitful, according to al-Alim, because of their weaknesses.

Al-Alim offers a number of alternatives. Rather than paying so much attention to authenticity, Arabs should deploy efforts to raise awareness about their history and their present situation in the form of concrete and specific studies. Arabs, like other peoples, do not need to affirm their specificity or authenticity. They have their own characteristics shaped by the accumulated and sedimented experiences of history, just as other peoples have theirs. Moreover, ideologies have value only if they are associated with analyses and visions that are rooted in lived realities, concrete struggles, and the particular needs of nations. Furthermore, the attitude toward tradition should be neither that of rejection and contempt nor that of sacralization and glorification, nor even that of eclecticism. Tradition should be assimilated, socially and historically contextualized, and critically appropriated in its totality. It should include popular as well as written heritage, and it should be used as a source for critical and creative inspiration. Finally, the same critical-historical approach should be adopted for understanding the present age. Only such an approach can lead to both modernization and authenticity, provided the struggle is carried out democratically by all the people. This call for a shift of emphasis from identity affirmation to a nonelitist democratic struggle is one of the main features of the Arab cultural critique in the late twentieth century. Al-Alim states it very clearly in his critique of Abdel-Malek's paper for the 1974 Kuwait conference:

> Our battle for modernization won't be carried out by a cultural elite, and it won't be realized by a centralized state that monopolizes political, military, economic, and intellectual power with no clear social reference. But it will be a struggle of the masses based on a revolutionary conceptual awareness of our realities and of the realities of our epoch for the sake of establishing a democratic, progressive government that can overcome economic and social underdevelopment and national division, and that can ensure the possibility of the largest democratic participation for the Arab masses in organizing and developing their lives. This would be our real contemporaneity. It is not the contemporaneity of an ideological awareness, no matter how revolutionary, or the contemporaneity of equipments and institutions, no matter how scientific. Neither is this contemporaneity a matter of rejecting salafism or adopting rationalism in general, but it is the historical revolutionary act of masses armed with revolutionary ideas. Not only would this be our contemporaneity, but it would also be the way to achieve our specificity and our authenticity. Contemporaneity and authenticity are the two sides of the same coin. . . . Our position

vis-à-vis European thought, or what is called Western thought, is not that of sacralization or denigration or absolute rejection or eclecticism. But we arm ourselves with the fruits of human science, applying their products critically and creatively to our specific reality.[28]

Muhammad Nuwaihi: The Inflation of Reactionary Religious Authority as the Major Obstacle to Cultural Development and Religious Modernization

The last paper I examine from the 1974 conference is by Muhammad Nuwaihi (1917–1980), an Egyptian literary critic and head of Arab studies at the American University of Cairo between 1973 and 1980. His paper offers, as he says, further elaborations on thoughts about religion that he had started to formulate in "Nahwa Thawra fi al-Fikr al-Dini" (Toward a Revolution in Religious Thought), which was published in a special issue of *al-Adab* (May 1970) devoted to revolution in Arab culture.[29] In the latter paper, Nuwaihi deals with the hegemony of religion in Arab cultural life:

Religious objections are always the first to be raised against any new idea, whether the idea deals with problems of religion itself, or with ethics, politics, the system of government, economics, the system of production and distribution of wealth, the traditions, customs, and practices of society, science, philosophy, art, language and literature. For in our Arab countries, religious considerations continue to outweigh all other considerations in the minds of the people. And it is still from the religious point of view that they first consider any new opinion that is announced to them, or any new school of thought which claims their support. They do not ask themselves: Is this opinion right or wrong in itself, or is this school of thought useful or harmful in itself? Instead, they ask themselves: is it in conformity with religion or contrary to it?[30]

This inflation of religious authority is to be blamed, according to him, not on Islam as such, but on the men of religion, the ulemas, who have appointed themselves as the only legitimate interpreters of Islam, a religion that does not advocate priesthood. They have become de facto guardians of reactionary public values because of their vested interest in the power they have accumulated over time and because of their ignorance in both matters of the world and matters of religion. Not only do they lack an adequate understanding of the present world, but they also have a poor knowledge of the religious traditions they claim to represent.[31] These traditions were formed throughout the centuries in a dynamic process of responding with vitality, flexibility, and broadmindedness to the demands of changing times. The Qur'an, with its fundamental doctrines and general beliefs, demands that each generation of believers understand those doctrines and beliefs anew and apply them according to the givens of their times. Instead of continuing this creative process of renewed interpretation and practice, the inept religious leadership has failed to keep up with the changes introduced by the state in many of the legal, social, and political sectors of life. As a result, average Muslims find themselves torn between traditional religious beliefs that the ulemas have not revised and sociopolitical and legal realities that do not match these beliefs. This inner contradiction gives rise to torment, resentment, and fragmentation. What is needed, according to Nuwaihi, is a modernization of the religious views and a new understanding of the place of religion in human society that leaves room for independent judgment.

In his 1974 Kuwait conference paper "Al-Din wa Azamat al-Tatawwur fi al-Watan al-'Arabi" (Religion and the Crisis of Development in the Arab Homeland), Nuwaihi seeks a way of making of religion a developmental force rather than a hindrance to progress, a way that comes from a broad perspective that involves religions in general, not just Islam.[32] He points out that Islam is in the line of monotheistic religions and not a religion that is entirely foreign to all other religions—thus precluding the exceptionalism that is often attributed to it. Within this broad perspective, Nuwaihi raises the question of religion's place in the present age. Those who hold that religion no longer has a place, he says, present three categories of arguments: intellectual, moral, and practical. According to the intellectual argument, religion belongs to mythical thinking, which was good for a certain phase, but was no longer tenable after the rise of rational thought. The success of science and the way it was often fought by clerics discredited religion in the modern age, and the struggle against clerical institutions became a struggle against religion. This intellectual opposition soon became a moral opposition due to the repression that men of religion exercised against scientists and free thinkers in general. On the practical ground, great prejudice arose toward religion when clerics gave support to social and economic injustice, often allying themselves with the rich and the powerful and dissuading rebellion instead of supporting it (be it in the case of slavery or in the case of women, for instance).

Many believe that these well-taken points do not apply to Islam because it never had a clerical institution. In response, Nuwaihi comments that although the absence of a clerical institution may be true theoretically, de facto Islamic clerics have always exercised tremendous power and authority. Thus, Muslims can learn a great deal from the experience of others in adapting religion to the modern age. Four developments contributed, according to him, to the preservation of the essence of faith in the modern West: first, the distinction made between religion and those who speak in its name as the official interpreters of religion; second, the clear admission that clerics may have not only intellectual flaws, but also moral flaws; third, based on the previous two points, the elaboration of new and alternative readings of the sacred texts that correspond better to the present age, benefiting from the margins of metaphorical interpretations that these texts offer; and fourth, in connection with the third point, the understanding of the historicity of the sacred texts, without putting in question the divine origin of revelation—that is, the understanding of the human languages and cultures through which divine messages are and need to be transmitted. It may once again be claimed, he says, that the first two points do not concern Islam because it does not uphold a clergy; nevertheless, we need to stay vigilant about the real power of clerics, even in Islam.

The Arab world has strongly fought the fourth development, especially in recent times. Taha Husayn's attempt at critically studying the text of the Qur'an in connection with what is taken to be pre-Islamic poetry was and still is fiercely rejected. Such resistance to this development would be even stronger in our day, adds Nuwaihi.[33] But what might be emphasized and expanded is the third development, especially because updated readings have been an accepted practice in Islam since the early times. The symbolic and metaphorical interpretation of the Qur'an and the constant adaptation of the religious rules and practices to the needs of changing times were the pillars of Islamic jurisprudence. This adaptation did not contradict the eternal character of the message of Islam in its basics. It is only in recent centuries that people have come to regard past interpretations and past legislations to be completed and sacred dogmas. People forget that these interpretations were the fruits of human efforts and that Islam encouraged the constant renewal of these efforts.

This arrest in adaptation is, according to Nuwaihi, one of the most important impediments to cultural progress in the contemporary Arab world. In a sense, he adds, it is understandable that people resist change in general, particularly in matters that are considered holy and divine, but this natural reluctance to change should not be sanctioned by a traditionalist dogmatic justification that not only prevents progress and adaptability, but also distorts the nature of religious interpretation and legislation as they were practiced in the very tradition of Islam. During the first five centuries or so of Islam, he says, interpreters and legislators called upon a wide array of human principles and considerations to help them in the complex process of understanding the will of God in ever-changing circumstances. Among them was the principle of opinion (ra'i), which included the principle of consensus (ijma'), requiring the agreement of the majority of interpreters, and the principle of analogy (qias), connecting new interpretations with significant precedent cases. Another principle was that of interest (maslaha), according to which certain laws and rules could be bent under certain circumstances when the community's interest was at stake. The Prophet himself encouraged believers to be in charge of worldly matters, saying that they were more knowledgeable in them than he was. All these elements prove the existence of a considerable margin for creativity and innovation in traditional exegesis and jurisprudence, as the leaders of Islamic modernism in the early twentieth century, such as Muhammad Abduh and his students, emphasized. This margin needs to be used again for the community's interest. A secular approach to most worldly things needs to be adopted, and not at all in a spirit of opposition to religion, but on the contrary in line with the traditional practice of the founding figures of Islamic jurisprudence and hermeneutics.

The comments on Nuwaihi's conference paper came in the form of an apology for Islam, praising its superiority over all other religions and its completed perfection as it stands. Yes, some new interpretation might be needed, it was argued, but secular thought can never provide the criteria with which such an interpretation can be done. What is needed is a moral revival.

The Final Declaration

The final declaration of the conference, "Al-Bayan al-Khitami," emphasized the importance of going beyond the tradition/Western dichotomy in dealing with the issue of civilizational retardation.[34] It affirmed that tradition was inevitably part of Arab civilization, but that the past could not own the future and that conflating turath with authenticity was a dangerous amalgam that prevented progress. Real turath revival meant the critical assimilation of its history. An open discussion of the role of religion in society was needed, and room was to be made for modernizing Islam while preserving the essence of its creed. The declaration stated that the Arab world's political problems were the lack of democracy, the absence of unity, and the weakness of planning. Politicians and intellectuals' purpose ought to be the political and intellectual emancipation of their fellow Arabs. Arab thought ought to be free from intellectual terror, committed to Arab causes and morally tuned to the feelings of the Arab masses. Science and rational thinking were to be strengthened and put to the service of socioeconomic development. Arab self-critique was important in the struggle against colonialism. Finally, the understanding of the historicity of the various factors delaying Arab civilizational progress was a good ground for working on these factors in view of changing them.

In the June 1974 issue of *al-Adab* (the issue following the one that included some of the conference papers), François Bassili, an Egyptian thinker based in New York, published a commentary on the final declaration, "Ihtifa' bi al-Mu'tamar al-Hadari: Thalath Nadharat Naqdiyya" (Celebrating the Civilization Conference: Three Critical Views), centered around three main points.[35] First, Bassili wonders how thought can be free and at the same time in tune with the feelings and morals of the masses, committed to the causes of the community. He raises a number of questions: Haven't we learned from long and bitter experience that such requirements always produce ready-made, automatic judgments that repress all critical thinking that does not conform to official discourses? And what does it mean for thought to be moral? Whose morals? Has progress ever taken place anywhere without challenging prevailing morals? Finally, who decides what the interest of the masses is? Arabs still suffer from the lack of critique and the lack of accountability, he points out, and they are still unable to deal with dissent. Thought, he affirms, needs to be free, free from the "interest of the masses" and free from "national security," notions that have been both abused and used to justify despotism and repression. According to him, the total freedom of thought should have been the recommendation of the final declaration.

Second, he finds the declaration to be too conservative in its positions regarding religion, more timid than some of the suggestions made in the conference. It should have clearly asked for the separation of religion from state. And third, he notes that the theme of sexuality was totally absent from the conference debates, as were women, as both participants and a topic of discussion, even though sexual repression is a major aspect of the Arab civilizational crisis. Sexual deprivation and consequently sexual obsession are severe problems for Arabs, with serious repercussions for the mental health of their societies and with psychological and economic ram-ifications on both the individual level and the collective level. Bassili writes of a sexual famine and a sexual tragedy that needs to be addressed: no Arab revolution can succeed, he said, without a sexual revolution.

Mahdi Amil's Marxist Reading of the 1974 Conference Propositions

A few months after the publication of the conference proceedings, a thor-ough study of their main theses was presented in a book published in Beirut by Lebanese Marxist philosopher Hassan Hamdan, also known as Mahdi Amil (1936–1987).[36] In this book, Amil attacks the very logic that underlay the thinking of most, if not all, of the participants' ideas, with the exception of those presented by the leftist Mahmoud Amin al-Alim. Ac-cording to Amil, that logic is idealist, metaphysical, and essentialist, pre-senting civilizational issues as intellectual issues, unconnected to material, socioeconomic, and political factors, governed by some essence of "the Arab heritage" or of "the Arab mind" going back to the dawn of time in a holistically viewed history. Due to this metaphysical, idealist approach, civilization is analyzed as a transhistorical phenomenon with a core iden-tity that remains the same throughout the ages. To this idealist, essentialist logic Amil opposes a Marxist-Leninist logic that recognizes the strong link between intellectual and cultural manifestations, on the one hand, and socioeconomic and political interests and realities, on the other. Moreover, this logic, in contrast to the former, does not assume history to be a conti-nuity of the same, but a dialectical process of opposite forces and interests. For him, the idealist, essentialist view is that of the bourgeois, capitalist class, including the Arab bourgeois class. Many Arab thinkers who are critical of the bourgeois viewpoint remain caught in it nonetheless, repro-duce its concepts and assumptions, and thus fail to propose a genuinely different view. The Kuwait conference, he states, is a good illustration of this phenomenon.

Even in Zaki Naguib Mahmud's positivist approach, Amil sees an ide-alist understanding of civilization. Among the four examples Mahmud gives, it is rationality—an intellectual trait—that he takes to be the charac-terizing element of civilization, thus assuming rationality to be a universal, ahistorical characteristic. Even if, for the sake of argument, one were to ac-cept this characterization of civilizations, says Amil, one would still have to admit that rationality is a historical phenomenon that is understood dif-ferently in different places and at different times depending on the definer's interests. Instrumental reason, which focuses on consciously formulated calculations and leaves out the not-so-conscious class interests, and the reason of the modern Euro-American civilization, which Mahmud takes as the model to adopt, are components of a historically defined reason, namely that of modern capitalism. This historical definition is universalized in Mahmud's reasoning, and so he presents what is historical as being natural. In this process, the Arab capitalist bourgeoisie is proffered as the tragic champion of scientific rationality, whose efforts continuously fail because of the flawed "Arab mind" and "Arab heritage." Yet a thirteenth-century son of this same heritage, Ibn Khaldun, had well understood and explained the interconnections between culture, economy, and politics, expressed in his concepts 'imran and hadara. The other major mistake in Mahmud's reasoning—one that is often made in Arab debates on culture—is, according to Amil, the assumption that the Arab bourgeoisie can and ought to play the role that was played by the Western bourgeoisies. This assumption ignores the crucial colonial difference. For him, the imperialist condition imposed on the Arab region in the past two centuries has made of the Arab bourgeoisie a dependent socioeconomic, political class that cannot be compared to the Euro-American bourgeoisies either on the socioeconomic level or on the political level or for that matter on the intellectual-cultural level. Instead of considering the implications of this imperialist-colonial reality, Arab thinkers have the tendency to focus their thoughts on their "mind," their "heritage," their "religion," the "essence" of their civilization, and their "faulty" identity. Rather than seeing the fundamental problem in the advocated "model" that produces a dependent and distorted bourgeoisie, they search for the root of the crisis in their supposedly defective self, which does not seem capable of emulating this model. They do not see that the structural reality of imperialism makes such an emulation impossible. They do not examine the sociohistorical and ideological conditions of colonial dependency that prevent the development of a scientific, productive, and creative thought among Arabs.

Equally problematic for Amil is the way Arab thinkers such as Mahmud, Mustafa, Abdel-Malek, Zakariyya, and Adonis conduct historicization. They trace the causes of the present crisis back to "old tribal" structures, to perennial power systems, to unchanging mental patterns, or to invariable features of a monolithic tradition, dating from the early Umayyad or Abbasid periods or even earlier, instead of tracing it back to the more immediate historical background of the past two centuries dominated by the reality of colonialism. For Amil, this recent history has a much more important relevance to Arab societies' present situation than some holistic history reaching back to the dawn of time.

Amil next turns his attention to the way Adonis and Zakariyya address the intellectual aspect of the "civilizational retardation." He attacks Adonis's blatant essentialism, which posits the existence of an Arab mind that one can find exemplified in a representative figure such as al-Ghazali. Even if for the sake of argument one agrees that some similar way of thinking can be found in both the past and the present, says Amil, this way of thinking nevertheless cannot be the same because of the inevitable change in the historical givens in the past and the present. The problem, he says, is not in the representativity of the chosen figure, but in the idea that a single and unique mode of thinking can prevail throughout the centuries. Moreover, Adonis's focus and attack on religion, he adds, places the problem again on the intellectual level, reminding us of Feuerbach and Bauer in the early idealist critique. What is useful instead, says Amil, is to see how the bourgeoisie manipulates religion for its own interests. Also troublesome for Amil is Adonis's insistence on the individual's opposition to the repressive collectivity because that insistence does not acknowledge the bourgeois collectivity as the real problem. Finally, Amil wonders how Adonis can hope to overcome this civilizational crisis, as he depicts it, through individual creativity: By which mechanism should or can the individual break from those essential patterns Adonis describes? The solution he seems to advocate is intellectual, consisting of a creative revolt, based on the assumption that thought operates on its own independently of its surrounding realities.

Zakariyya, like Adonis, has an idealist approach to the issue, contends Amil. Amil agrees with Zurayq's critique of Zakariyya's claims and adds a further critique concerning the circularity of the latter's reasoning. Zakariyya, he says, offers a number of interesting insights concerning the present Arab fixation on the past, but he falls into the essentialist fallacy by attributing this fixation to some inherent trait of the "Arab mind": Arab thought is backward because it has an ahistorical view of the past, and it has an ahistorical view of the past because it is a backward thought. Furthermore, Zakariyya emphasizes the lack of historical continuity between the Arab past and the Arab present, claiming that the cultural severance from the Arab past is the cause of the halt in the growth of the Arab mind and in turn the cause of the cultural retardation; and at the same time the cultural severance itself is regarded to be a form of cultural retardation. Zakariyya also obviously assumes that history evolves in a continuous line, not in struggles, conflicts, and discontinuities. According to Amil, Zakari-yya claims that the arrested growth in Arab culture and the "Arab mind" is the manifestation of a diseased mind that cannot resume its growth unless it ceases to be itself and becomes the healthy, "Other" mind that is the mind of the age—that is, the Western mind. Again, Amil insists that instead of thinking in terms of "Arab" and "Western" minds, one ought to ask about the sociohistorical factors that lead to certain cultural and intellectual de-velopments rather than to others. Similarly, instead of conducting com-parisons between the European and the Arab "renaissances," one ought to examine their historical circumstances: this examination would be a truly historical mode of thinking.

Coming to the issue of the so-called Arab Renaissance, or Nahda, Amil says that many impute its failure to the making of the "Arab mind" or to the persistence of the problematic features of "Arab tradition." They do not realize that the Nahda was bound to fail because it was carried out by a dependent bourgeoisie that came to power under colonial conditions and not through a real break with old local socioeconomic and cultural struc-tures. This bourgeoisie, because of its dependency, could not really produce a new thought. Its ideology could not become an authentic Arab thought. For similar reasons, a second *nahda*, which some had predicted for the last decades of the twentieth century, cannot take place. Only a realization of the colonial reality of the present and the rise of a working class in opposi-tion to this dependent bourgeoisie can bring about a new formulation of the current crisis, no longer in terms of progress and retardation, but in terms of dependency and liberation; only then can a new culture emerge. Here, one may wonder, along with Laroui, which sector of society will be carrying out this oppositional work. Amil assumes that a working class has been developing in the Arab world. To what extent is this assumption justified? What is real is the growth of discontent in large sectors of Arab populations regarding their rulers' bad governance. This discontent has expressed itself in oppositional fundamentalist groups, but also in the struggle for the defense of people's political rights through democracy. Both types of struggle against repressive regimes characterized the Arab political scene of the last decades of the twentieth century.

Civilizational progress and retardation, adds Amil, were introduced through imperialist domination, which was prepared for and accompanied by the Orientalist discourse on civilizations. This discourse affirmed the West's role in leading backward civilizations to progress and modernity, as defined by the West and for the West. Only a Marxist-Leninist analysis of these historical processes can unveil the reality and ideology of these power struggles. For Amil, this assessment is true not only for the Arab world, but also for the other continents that experienced colonialism, primarily Asia, Latin America, and Africa. Unlike Zurayq, who claims that civilizational rise and decline happen in all civilizations, and unlike Abdel-Malek, who thinks that the Arab specificity in centralized state and army power is the impediment to progress, Amil affirms that the civilizational crises in the colonial world do not happen for "cultural" reasons, but because of real hegemonic interventions in civilizations' histories. Hence, according to him, the search should not be made into the structure of Arab civilization in order to locate the essence that permeates its past and present or into the flawed nature of the Arab mind, but into the socioeconomic and political structures of societies dominated by a dependent colonial bourgeoisie.

The critique of idealism and the critique of essentialism are invaluable contributions to the debates on cultural malaise in the postcolonial world. They are increasingly emphasized (as I discuss in chapter 6) and recognized as important cautions against an exclusive and misleading focus on the cultural self, whether in its self-glorifying version or its self-denigrating version. Connecting culture and thought to their economic and political contexts and historicizing the past, whether cultural or political, instead of viewing it as a monolithic, unchanging whole, governed by a core of essences, are crucial requirements for a broader and healthier understanding of cultural issues. In the last decades of the twentieth century, postcolonial thinkers, including Arabs, have underlined the urgency of these demands. Many of them have come from a leftist, socialist, or Communist background and have relentlessly drawn attention to the political and economic problems underlying cultural questions. They have been the victims of persecution in their countries, sometimes because of their ideologies and most of the time because of their oppositional critical voices. Mahdi Amil was gunned down in Beirut in broad daylight, presumably by Islamist militants. The killers were never caught, and no one claimed responsibility for his assassination. He had just been elected as a member of the executive council of the Lebanese Communist Party. A few months later a fellow council member, the Communist thinker and writer Hussayn Muruwwah, was also shot dead in Beirut.

These assassinations occurred in 1987, the time of the rise of the Islamists in Lebanon, which witnessed the liquidation of leftist activists and thinkers in one of those long episodes of struggle between the two main oppositional forces in the Arab world in the second half of the twentieth century. Indeed, with the fundamentalists' prominence in the last two decades of the twentieth century, it is difficult to imagine and remember that the Marxists enjoyed the same prominence in the 1960s and 1970s. Many of them, such as Abdallah Laroui, Mahdi Amil, Samir Amin, and Mahmoud Amin al-Alim, worked toward a critical and independent appropriation of Marxism in the Arab context. The demise of Marxism in the Arab world was due not only to the discredit brought to it by Communist regimes led by the Soviet Union, but also and in the first place to the persecution of its adherents by Arab governments, whether in Egypt, Iraq, or Syria. Their legacy is yet to be recovered and assessed.[37]

Another leftist thinker who has been drawing attention to the economic realities underlying the cultural issues for decades now is Egyptian economist Samir Amin. Trained in Paris, he has been for many years the director of the United Nations African Institute for Planning, the cofounder and director of the Third World Forum based in Dakar, Senegal, and the cofounder of the World Forum for Alternatives. He is the author of numerous works in Arabic and French, some of which have been translated into English and published mostly by the Monthly Review Press in New York and Zed Books in London.

Amin shares with Amil the critique of the civilizational and capitalist ideologies.[38] He believes that these ideologies, internalized by many Arab and Third World thinkers, present a false diagnosis of the difficulties of the so-called developing world. Common to these ideologies is the belief that the European model of economic and political development is the only way to development and that all countries should imitate this model in order to catch up with its achievements—specifically in the application of the scientific spirit, rationality, and efficient organization, in the adoption of tolerance, and in the concern for equality and the respect for human rights and democracy. This expectation was expressed in the humanist universalism of the European Enlightenment. The failure to imitate or catch up was explained in terms of factors internal to those non-European societies: outmoded tribal, religious, ideological, and cultural dogmatisms that prevented them from progressing. As a result, the early universalism gave way to a twofold "cultural involution," as Amin calls it: a European provincialism and a confirmation of European exceptionalism, on the one hand, and a reactionary Third World provincialist fundamentalism, on the other, affirming a total cultural otherness vis-à-vis Europe.

For Amin, this reading of the West/Third World divide is not adequate. He thinks that an economic analysis of the problem sheds a better light on this divide. The worldwide expansive direction inherent to capitalism cannot but aim at a homogenization of the world that it cannot really achieve—hence, the ideological impasse and the move to the two forms of provincialism and exceptionalism. The dream of progress within this capitalist economy is impossible, adds Amin. It is an economy that cannot be generalized to the entire planet, for two reasons: first, it is based on a center with peripheries that are required to remain peripheral and hence not to catch up; and second, it wouldn't be realistically feasible for them to become centers for ecological reasons. The planet would not survive a Western pattern of consumption spread to the whole world. The only way out of the impasse, he says, is to delink Third World economies from Western capitalism and to open the way to a new polycentric world economy.[39]

As far as the Arab world in concerned, Amin thinks that the Nahda reforms were timid and ambiguous. They did not achieve the break with the old metaphysics necessary for modernization, and for engaging in a real religious reform. This failure led to a confused debate on cultural malaise that contrasts cultural identity with modernization, falsely understood as westernization. It was the failure of a peripheral liberal bourgeoisie that falsely thought it could imitate Western bourgeoisies.

The Cairo Conference of 1984: "Heritage and the Challenges of the Age in the Arab Homeland: Authenticity and Contemporaneity"

The Center for Arab Unity Studies

The Center for Arab Unity Studies, which organized and published the proceedings of the third conference under discussion here, was established in Beirut in 1975 by a number of independent scholars and intellectuals.[40] It is committed, as its name indicates, to the project of Arab unity, an aspiration dear to many generations of Arabs since the beginning of the twentieth century. It presents itself as an independent institution dedicated to promoting the cause of Arab unity by sponsoring studies and translations and by organizing conferences on the various pressing issues of the Arab world. The idea for such a center emerged in the aftermath of the 1967 Arab debacle. It was to be a nonpoliticized, nonpartisan research center, welcoming Arab thinkers from all over the Arab world irrespective of their ideological, intellectual, national, or political affiliations. It set its agenda on six major issues: unity, democracy, social justice, independent development, national independence, and cultural revival. And, indeed, during the thirty-five years of its existence the center has organized a large number of conferences in various Arab countries, sponsored numerous publications and studies, and thus become an important forum of Arab discussions, respecting freedom of speech and opinion, welcoming a great variety of Arab thinkers, and addressing some of the most burning issues of the Arab world. For most of the conferences, an elaborate problematic is formulated, and speakers are invited to prepare papers on specific topics related to it. The papers are made available to a number of discussants, who then prepare commentaries on them. A general discussion involving the wider audience of participants usually follows. The papers, the commentaries, and the discussions are then published in a detailed volume. These publications are a valuable source of insight into the various Arab debates.[41]

The 1984 Cairo conference, "Al-Turath wa Tahaddiyyat al-ʿAsr fi al-Watan al-ʿArabi" (Heritage and the Challenges of the Age in the Arab Homeland: Authenticity and Contemporaneity), gathered a considerable number of prominent Arab thinkers (the proceedings volume lists one hundred participants, only six of whom were women, none of them commissioned to present a paper). They came from various Arab countries, different scientific disciplines, different intellectual trends, and different generations. The conference was organized around three major sets of questions: the different concepts involved in the problematic of authenticity and contemporaneity in a comparative context; the main dimensions of the problematic, including the principles and aspects of modernization in relation to Western thought, culture, and institutions; and the position of the various Arab trends vis-à-vis modernization and authenticity as well as vis-à-vis the main challenges that modernization will present to the Arab world in the future.

The conference proceedings present a general panorama of the Arab concerns and intellectual trends of the time as well as certain general characteristics that are interesting to note:

1. The growing awareness of the weight of the colonial and postcolonial condition on the modalities of dealing with various problems; more precisely, the growing realization of the extent to which the colonial situation gave rise to a defensive "authenticity thought" that prevented the emergence of an authentic response to colonialism—that

is, a response capable of genuinely addressing it in an autonomous and efficient way.

2. The concern with fact finding and the interest in social scientific data motivated by an urgent need for problem solving. This pragmatic and empirical emphasis on dealing with the problems at hand is relatively new and indicates an approach to issues different from the hitherto rather rhetorical approach. It is accompanied by a concern with empowerment and with overcoming the state of generalized helplessness.

3. The recurring attack on ideologies and ideological thinking as being sterile, uninformed by reality, and rigid.

4. A repeated call to attend to reality and lived experience, to relate words, concepts, analyses, and theories to the concrete, particular experiences of the region's people and communities. Indeed, the categories of "life" and "reality" recur frequently in the various conference papers.

5. The realization that freedom and democracy are necessary conditions for making this rapport to reality possible; the insistence on freedom as a sine qua non condition for real thinking—in other words, questioning, addressing facts, examining authority, and imagining alternatives. Many thinkers see free dialogue as an indispensable condition for pragmatic, intellectual, cultural, and political progress.

6. The need to turn the gaze to the self and not remain captive to the constant challenge by the Other; and the need for self-critique to be serious, sober, and intellectually honest, free from apology and from polemics with the West.

7. Reactions of defensiveness, apology, and self-glorification as well as tendencies to seek refuge in the past, to flee from reality, and to retreat into an essentialized self—present sometimes even in the words of participants with critical intent.

In some instances, such reactions and tendencies provoked heated debate in the conference. In his paper, Moroccan writer and professor of literature Mohammad Berrada, for instance, attacks the ideological approach to *turath*, saying that such an approach fails to enrich the heritage cognitively and to create a genuinely living relation with that heritage, for this relation would require a questioning of *turath* from the present point of view, and such a questioning is an in-depth activity. He says that ideological thinking, by its very nature, cannot undertake, but on the contrary can only obstruct. Revisiting *turath* from the living reality of the present would break the static representation of both authenticity and modernization, sever the opposition between them, restore their dynamic nature, and put them back in the fluid course of history and change. For Berrada, the "authenticity versus modernization" problematic is the result of the failure to break both from Western colonization and from dependency on the past. This break can come only from critical thinking.[42] For the late Moroccan thinker and writer Abdelkebir al-Khatibi (1938–2009), Arabs have become traditionalists because they have forgotten tradition, and they have become a people of dogmas and ideologies because they have forgotten existential thinking. This forgetfulness, he says, is nurtured by metaphysical thinking, by a hatred for life transformed into a theology of evil, and by the same double dependency vis-à-vis the West and a dead past.[43]

In his comment on the conference, Lebanese political scientist Ghassan Salamé notes that most of the papers and discussions were devoted to the past and *turath*, but very few to the challenges of the age, which were supposed to be the other conference focus, thus demonstrating a persisting preoccupation with the past. He also notes that *turath* still needs to be defined: Is it to include popular culture or remain limited to the written classical culture? Is it to be reduced to religion, and if yes, to Islam alone? Lebanese professor of Arabic literature Muhammad Najm raises the same questions, remarking that it would have been more honest to call this conference "Religion or Islam and Modernization" because it ended up revolving around *turath* as Islam. How can one speak of this *turath* as given and known when half a million manuscripts lie unexamined, when most of the attention has so far gone to the literary and religious in this legacy, and when hardly any attention has been devoted to the social and the scientific in it? Who defines this *turath* and how?

Finally, for the first time a section of a conference was devoted to a comparative perspective, with papers presented on the Japanese and the Indian views of the authenticity and modernity issue. These papers, presented respectively by a professor from Hawai'i University and a professor from Jawaharlal University, are linear narratives of economic and political changes in twentieth-century Japan and India; they do not touch in any depth on the questions of cultural malaise. It is important to note that modernization in South Asia, in Japan in particular, has fascinated Arab thinkers since the time of the Nahda. Japan recurs very often in Arab discourses as the happy model to be followed, as the example of successful technological modernization and cultural conservation. This fascination has not necessarily been based on any substantial knowledge of South Asia, however. In fact, it is only now that some serious studies of Japan have started to appear in the Arab world.[44]

Muhammad Abed al-Jabiri: A Critique of the Marxist, Liberal, and Fundamentalist Readings of Tradition

Well-known and prolific Moroccan philosopher Muhammad Abed al-Jabiri presented the opening paper of the conference, "Ishkaliyyat al-Asala wa al-Muʿasara fi al-Fikr al-ʿArabi al-Hadith wa al-Muʿasir: Siraʿ Tabaqi am Mushkil Thaqafi?" (The Problematic of Authenticity and Contemporaneity in Contemporary and Modern Arab Thought: A Class Conflict or a Cultural Problem?).[45] It deals with many of the issues addressed by Mahdi Amil, but with positions and conclusions contrary to his. The paper is not a direct answer to Amil's thoughts (at no point does al-Jabiri refer to them as such), but in response, as he says in his introductory remarks, to the task he was given by the organizers: to elaborate on the class and ideological conflicts surrounding the authenticity/contemporaneity issue in the Arab world. Al-Jabiri says he was unable to make such elaborations because of his belief that the relevant issue is not class-related, but rather strictly intellectual and cultural. This is not to deny the intricate links between societies and ideas; these links do exist, although not in the simple mirror fashion that is often assumed. However, in spite of or in addition to these links, certain intellectual issues have an existence of their own, independent of the circumstances that give rise to them. On the one hand, he gives the example of abstract bodies of knowledge such as mathematics, physics, and logic; and on the other, he points to intellectual issues that last beyond the social and historical contexts in which they originally emerged. For him, such an independence applies to the Arab authenticity/contemporaneity issue. Although he recalls the historical circumstances that brought about the issue, he insists that the latter should be treated as a strictly intellectual matter. For Amil, those circumstances have to do with the colonial phenomenon. For al-Jabiri, this phenomenon created the question for every Arab and not for a specific class of Arabs. But he, unlike Amil, does not examine the repercussions of the colonial phenomenon on Arab countries' internal power and social structures, nor does he link the ideas of the cultural malaise to those structures. Rather, he analyzes such links in the early developments of the Arab heritage, especially in the ninth century, but not in the modern period, and even while analyzing those links, he maintains the independent status of the intellectual questions raised.

Colonialism imposed the authenticity/contemporaneity issue on Arabs, he states. It brought into the Arab world a new culture and a new system that put Arabs in the presence of two cultures and two systems, the local and the colonial. In the face of this double system, three positions were adopted: traditionalization, westernization, and eclecticism. They were expressed on the intellectual and theoretical level through the authenticity/ contemporaneity problematic, on the ideological level through the liberal-socialist problematic, and on the political level through the regionalist-nationalist problematic. Colonial change and modernization, he says, created in the Arab world, like elsewhere in the colonial world, a double social reality: modern and traditional. People dealt with this duality in a dual fashion: they accepted the modern for their material life and the traditional for their cultural, spiritual life. To this duality was added the dual perception of the Western Other both as a model and as an aggressor. All of these dualities created in the Arab mind, regardless of social class, a tense confusion and division. Specific to the Arab case was the clear intellectual and emotional awareness of a massive Arab literate heritage that one could easily uphold as an ideological defense in the face of these challenges. But to this awareness also belonged the painful realization of the wide gap between this imposing heritage and the demands of the present age: hence, the central question of the Nahda, asking why others progressed, but Muslims lagged behind, and the tension between a heritage of one's own and a modernity made by others. Here is the locus of the authenticity/contemporaneity problematic. But, al-Jabiri observes, not all times of change have been thought in terms of such a problematic. He takes as contrasting examples the first Islamic Revolution and the European Renaissance.

Revolutions, according to al-Jabiri, typically reach out to distant pasts in order to legitimize their rejection of more recent pasts. European Renaissance thinkers used Greek and Roman antiquity, for instance, to legitimize their critique of medieval Europe; Protestant Reformers regarded the primitive church as a legitimate basis for their rejection of the established clerical institution. Similarly, the first Muslims took the Abrahamic origin and tradition as the legitimate basis for rejection of the prevailing pagan religions and traditions around Quraysh in the Arab Peninsula. In none of these cases was the new regime presented in opposition to tradition. Instead, it was legitimized by reference to a better, more authentic tradition.

Modernization or change was not opposed to authenticity. By contrast, in the first Nahda of the turn of the twentieth century and throughout that century, modernization was constantly thought of in opposition to authenticity. Why has that been so? asks al-Jabiri. Because, he answers, in the other cases the change came from within tradition itself, without the interference of a threatening Other, whereas in the case of the more recent Arab history change was dominated by the presence of the colonial and neocolonial West. This presence, he says, triggered a defense mechanism that transformed the past into a fixed bastion of identity and a base for self-affirmation rather than a springboard for immanent processes of change and modernization. Under such conditions, no immanent change could be undertaken without putting at risk the very identity of the cultural self, which was so urgently needed for resistance against the invading Other. What made things more complicated, he adds, was the fact that this invading West was recognized at the same time to be the carrier, at least to some extent, of the principles of development and progress needed for that same resistance. How was it possible to adopt these principles without further jeopardizing cultural identity and national independence? Hence the dilemma between modernization and authenticity.

Three typical attitudes were adopted: the conservative and traditionalist attitude, which argued that development can be achieved only by a return to tradition and a total rejection of the West; the modernist attitude, which advocated total westernization; and, finally, the eclectic attitude, which proposed to pick and choose from the two spheres whatever elements were deemed useful. Obviously, observes al-Jabiri, none of the attitudes was fruitful. They trapped Arabs in a sterile and passive double dependency, one vis-à-vis the West and one vis-à-vis tradition, both poorly researched and poorly understood. Only the critical appropriation of both Arab tradition and Western tradition, al-Jabiri proposes, can help Arabs move beyond this dilemma and open more fruitful ways of being themselves and engaging in modernization. The Muslims of the early centuries of the Islamic Empire felt free to borrow from the various available cultures and traditions and to use them to produce a rich culture of their own. What contemporary Arabs need, according to him, is that same courage and will for critical appropriation. Al-Jabiri does not take into consideration the difference in the Arabs' power position in the two historical epochs, however, nor does he acknowledge the implications of this difference for the way cultural issues are apprehended. More precisely, although recognizing this factor of power, he still insists that the fundamental problem and the fundamental solution are of an intellectual nature, and in the final analysis he presents the matter as a lack of courage and will for critical appropriation among contemporary Arabs.

Al-Jabiri continues his comparison between the European and the Arab views of tradition and modernity as well as of the past, present, and future. For the Europeans, he says, the break with tradition took place within the tradition itself and hence did not raise questions about its authenticity. Descartes's break with tradition did not raise questions about cultural authenticity with respect to the tradition he was breaking from. The same applies to Bacon's break, al-Jabiri says. In Europe, discontinuity has taken place immanently—that is, within the same tradition. The latter changes from within, so to speak, without traumatic foreign interference. This sense of continuity, he adds, is further enhanced by an ongoing construction of European cultural history throughout the centuries, a constant writing and rewriting of history that constructs the past into an intelligible chain of events and trends to which the present can relate in a meaningful way: what he calls the historicization of tradition and cultural legacy and their rationalization. In the Arab world and in Arab consciousness, however, he says, there is an unbridged gap between the present and the past. The available cultural histories are old histories, written by people from past times, with different preoccupations and different givens. He thinks Arabs need to reconstruct their cultural history so that they can reappropriate it for themselves. They need to appropriate this past critically through historicization and question it from their present horizon. Only such a rewriting of the Arab intellectual legacy can offer a modern view of tradition and an indigenous ground for modernization and critique.[46]

In contrast to the fundamentalist, liberal, and Marxist readings of tradition, al-Jabiri wants to offer a scientific reading. For the fundamentalist reading, the intellectual legacy is an end in itself, and whereas the liberal looks at this legacy from a Western-Orientalist vantage point, the Marxist finds himself caught in the vicious circle of revolution and tradition, as al-Jabiri puts it.[47] The "scientific" reading that he wants to propose instead is a critical, rational, and objective reading, which is what makes it, for him, a modern reading of tradition; and it is this modern reading that can allow for an authentic modernization process to get started.[48] For him, an objective reading of texts from tradition requires a "disjunctive method"—that is, a heuristic dissociation between the reader and the text that will allow each one to speak for himself or itself.[49] Al-Jabiri thinks that the first Nahda failed to lead to such an appropriation because of a lack of autonomous thinking and because of the use of ready-made solutions owing to a certain structure in Arab reason, a certain way of thinking entrenched in the Arab mind, which resulted in an inadequate reading of the past and the cultural tradition. This criticism applies not only to the turn-of-the-twentieth-century Nahda, but also to the contemporary attempts at cultural revival and cultural revolution:

> *The entirety of modern and contemporary Arab thought is character-*
> *ized by a lack of historical perspective and objectivity. And that is why*
> *it was never able to offer from tradition anything but a fundamental-*
> *ist reading that treats the past as transcendental and sacral while*
> *seeking to extract from it ready-made solutions to the problems of the*
> *present and the future. If such a remark perfectly applies to the Isla-*
> *mists, it is no less applicable to the other schools of thought[,] all of*
> *which claim their own founding fathers with whom they can find "sal-*
> *vation." All the schools of Arab thought seem to borrow their prospect*
> *for renewal from a past-related (or past-based) model: the Arab-Islamic*
> *past, the European "past-present," the Russian experience, the Chinese*
> *one . . . and one could extend the list. When facing a new problem, this*
> *kind of thought resorts to the mechanical mental exercise of seeking*
> *ready-made solutions, relying on a rather poor "foundation."*
>
> *But this mental exercise is part of a whole, even if it is an essential*
> *part of it. This whole is the structure of the Arab reason. It is therefore*
> *this reason that we ought to submit to careful analysis and to rigorous*
> *critique, before proposing its renewal and its modernization. The Arab*
> *reason can only be renewed through a serious questioning of the old*
> *and through a global and in-depth critique, to which I hope to have*
> *made a modest contribution with my work:* Naqd al-ʿaql al-ʿArabi
> *[Critique of Arab Reason].*[50]

Indeed, in a series of monographs published since the 1980s, al-Jabiri has produced analyses of the "constitution," "structure," and "making" of "Arab reason"; studies of contemporary Arab discourses; and "new" readings of the Arab intellectual legacy.[51] His main claim is that certain problematics, approaches, and modes of thinking emerged in the process of constituting the bodies of knowledge that came to form the bulk of what is recognized as the Arab heritage. This process took place under concrete historical circumstances, shaped by a set of political, economic, social, and ideological factors. In his analyses, he offers, as he puts it, an "archeological" exploration of these circumstances and processes that ultimately produced that body of heritage, and he insists on the importance of understanding the historicity of these intellectual developments. According to him, these developments brought forth modes of thinking and sets of questions that lasted way beyond those historical circumstances and became the persisting features of "Arab reason." His work, as he sees it, is an exploration of the way "Arab reason" was constituted in historical and intellectual processes and how this reason was in a dialectical fashion instrumental in producing this tradition. He combines on the one hand a strong historicist approach to thought, both in its constituting and constituted nature, and on the other an equally strong structural approach that is rather ahistorical and essentialist. What reconciles the two positions for him is the belief that intellectual and cultural problematics have a time of their own that is independent of the historical time: "The relative—but nevertheless very often real—independence of this thought vis-à-vis these factors compels us to resort to those components that are inherent to the thought itself in order to grasp its historical field. What we mean here by 'historical field' of a thought system corresponds in fact to the 'duration of the life of a problematic,' or to its 'era': it is a period during which the same problematics persists in the history of a given thought."[52] Even if one were to accept this belief for the sake of argument, one would have to wonder with Mahdi Amil whether that same problematic can remain the same in inevitably changing circumstances.

In the first volume of his critique of Arab reason, titled *Takween al-'Aql al-'Arabi* (The Constitution of Arab Reason), al-Jabiri affirms that what he means by "Arab reason" is not some occult quality to be praised or denigrated in some Orientalist fashion, but the instrument of thought that both produced and was produced by Arab culture. This culture can be defined in different ways, he says, and it can be given different beginnings, provided one accounts for one's choice explicitly. It can include the Summerian, Pharaonic, Syriac Phoenician, Amazighi, or Yemeni beginnings and legacies. He argues for an inclusive and plural understanding of Arab culture that recognizes all of these legacies and influences, but insists at the same time on the importance of Arabic language as a unifying element.[53] He defines Arab culture, however, in terms of the legacy that is effective today in the minds and hearts of contemporary Arabs—namely, the Arab Islamic culture. The formative period of this culture is roughly the period from the mid–eighth century to the mid–tenth century. It was a formative period because during this time much of what came to constitute Arab heritage was written down and recorded. It is referred to as the "age of recording" (*'asr al-tadween*). In those years, much of what was orally transmitted about the Prophet, his life, his sayings, and his acts, the theological interpretations and debates, the criteria of exegesis and jurisprudence, but also the rules of grammar, linguistics, and philology were articulated and established in the form of foundations, principles, and disciplines. Also basic and comprehensive historical compilations were produced. It is during this time that the state administration was arabized (from the Persian and Greek) and that numerous works of translation and adaptation were made. Finally, it is the time of rise in nonreligious treatises, debates, and controversies. Al-Jabiri shows the intricate connections between these intellectual developments and the socioracial, political, and religious sectarian struggles for power in this epoch.

An examination of his historical analyses of these connections falls obviously outside the scope of my framework here, but the conclusions he draws from these studies for his critique of Arab reason are relevant. Among his main findings is that the central divide in this epoch seems to have been between a Sunni caliphate state defending a rational ideology with a conservative social outlook and a Shiʿa oppositional movement holding an irrational ideology with a revolutionary, progressive social outlook. For al-Jabiri, the defeat of reason at the hand of irrational mysticism is one of the most important and lasting legacies of this formative period, a legacy very detrimental to cultural progress. Three "epistemological systems," as he calls them, were produced during this epoch: *(a)* the system of explication based on the analogical mode of thinking that explains the unknown in terms of the known, using a past model—widely utilized in disciplines such as grammar, rhetoric, philology, lexicography, Qurʾanic exegesis, theology, Islamic law, and legal theory; *(b)* the system of illumination or gnosticism used in mystical disciplines, Sufism, Shiʿi thought, alchemy, astrology, magic, numerology, and so on; and *(c)* the system of demonstration or inferential evidence used in the natural sciences, logic, mathematics, and metaphysics. The first two systems by their very nature could produce only limited intellectual results, and the third one could not fully flourish in the Arab world as it did in the West because it had to face the constant pressure of gnosticism and irrationalism. Facing this pressure was thus the main function of Arab Islamic philosophy throughout its history. It is this function and not the now obsolete cognitive content of this philosophy that can and ought to be revived.

If one were to accept al-Jabiri's assessment of the nature and function of Arab Islamic philosophy, the question would still be: What would give this philosophy's struggle against gnosticism and irrationalism more chances of success today than it had in the past? And isn't this mode of reasoning tantamount to seeking a model in the past, an approach that al-Jabiri seems to condemn strongly? To what extent are these "epistemological systems" specifically Arab, and to what extent is the description of their destinies in Arab history founded on a serious and objective historiography? If, for the sake of the argument, one accepts the existence of these entrenched modes of thinking, what would be the sociopolitical and historical reasons for their persistence in time? Al-Jabiri spends too much time examining the similarities in the modes of thinking and in the problematics and does not show enough sensibility to the changes that might have occurred over the period of a millennium. Finally, his analyses, although rich in historical contextualization and historicization, at least for what he calls the formative period, remains permeated with essentialist tendencies. He speaks, for instance, of "the Arab mind" in comparison with "the Greek" and "the Western" minds: for the first, the world is explained in terms of "man" and "God," nature being the instrumental real for discovering God, whereas for the two other cases God is used to ground the correspondence between human reason and the laws of nature. His historicizing work is replete with such sweeping generalizations.

What al-Jabiri proposes is a new "age of recording," in which works of critical appropriation would be undertaken on the basis of an epistemological break with past and unfruitful modes of thinking. He also advocates a reemergence of rationality and demonstrative thinking through the revival of the legacy of Averroes, or Ibn Rushd (1126–1198). This prominent twelfth-century Aristotelian philosopher who lived in Andalusia claimed that philosophy and religion could not contradict each other because both led to truth and that truth was one, so truth could not be opposed to truth. Well-known Islamic philosopher al-Ghazali, who lived in the Arab East earlier in the eleventh-twelfth century (1058–1111), argued, in contrast, that human reason erred when it crossed the borders of possible experience and when it claimed to deny the existence of anything outside the boundaries of its understanding; in other words, he had argued that a realm of faith lay beyond the realm of human understanding.[54] Al-Jabiri sees in Averroes the champion of rationality who struggled against the "Oriental" philosophies of al-Ghazali, Avicenna, Shi'ism, and Sunni Sufism. Only an epistemological break from Arab Oriental irrationalism, according to al-Jabiri, can permit the creation of a new rationalist movement in Arab Islamic culture. He sees the Maghreb as the heir of the legacy of rationality and the Mashreq as the heir of the legacy of irrationality, thus ironically adding to the flaws of his reasoning an "internal Orientalism" directed from the Arab West against the Arab East. On the occasion of the eight hundredth anniversary of Averroes's death, the Center for Arab Unity Studies launched the project of a new edition of his writings under the direction of al-Jabiri.[55]

Syrian thinker Georges Tarabichi devoted a whole monograph to denouncing al-Jabiri's claims in detail and called it *Naqd Naqd al-ʿAql al-ʿArabi: Nadhariat al-ʿAql* (Critique of the Critique of Arab Reason: The Theory of Reason).[56] Its publication in 1996 gave rise to a fierce controversy that reached the Arab daily press.[57] Tarabichi accused al-Jabiri of a poor and even dishonest use of sources as well as of three forms of partiality: an epistemological bias against all forms of reason different from demonstrative reason, a sectarian Sunni (orthodox) bias against Shiʿism, and finally a West Arab bias against the Arab East. More important, he accused al-Jabiri of completely failing to produce a genuine critique or to become aware of and overcome the narrow determining historicity of his own mind. The controversy is still going on.[58]

Mahmud Amin al-Alim also criticizes al-Jabiri for his lack of historical perspective, despite his contextualizing efforts.[59] Al-Alim thinks that al-Jabiri focuses exclusively on the official history of the dominating trends and that he does not pay enough attention to the marginal and rebellious trends. Moreover, he finds him to be too centered on the fixed and constants elements of what he calls "Arab reason." In fact, by being so centered, he stretches the past into the present and falsely assumes that certain notions of the past remain as dominant as they were in the past. For instance, in his book on Arab political reason, al-Jabiri thinks these notions to be those of the tribe, the spoils, and the doctrine. Moreover, by paying too much attention to concepts, he loses sight of the contemporary economic, political, and neocolonial realities that shape to a great extent the current political scene in the Arab world. In his book on the structure of Arab reason, al-Jabiri advocates the revival of the Averroes-rationalist trend. In his book on Arab political reason, he advocates the revival of the early Mohammedan politics for its democratic virtues, with a religious authority as its reference. Al-Alim asks, Can such a dual advocacy be consistent? Can it be the way to a genuine revival? He is not convinced that it can.

Al-Jabiri is not the only Arab thinker to have turned to Averroes for a new Arab enlightenment project. He belongs to a group of contemporary

Arab intellectuals who find in the medieval philosopher the achievements and potentials of an indigenous rationalist thought. The modern revival of interest in his work began in the late nineteenth century with the work of a number of Orientalists, especially Ernest Renan, whose book *Averroès et l'averroisme: Essai historique* (1852) influenced a number of Arab thinkers of the Nahda period, the most famous among them being Farah Antun and Muhammad Abduh. One of its main theses was that Averroes's attempts at developing a rationalist philosophy in Islamic culture failed and was bound to fail because of the Semitic race's incompatibility with rational thinking. Semites, he affirmed, were made for poetry and religion, whereas Aryans were made for rationality and science. So it was no surprise to him that Islamic culture could not assimilate Averroes's rationalist philosophy and that it would instead adopt al-Ghazali's antiphilosophical school of thought and let religion dominate its various fields. Although Arab thinkers did not accept Renan's racism,[60] they adopted his broad view of the history of Arab Islamic culture—namely, the view that sees in the triumph of al-Ghazali's supposedly antirationalist thought one of the main causes for the decline of Arab Islamic culture since the twelfth century. This view still prevails today. It informs, for instance, the 1996 film *al-Massir* on the life of Averroes, directed by Egyptian filmmaker Youssef Chahine. According to most contemporary Arab intellectuals, Averroes's philosophy was positively received in Europe and contributed to the development of the European Renaissance and Enlightenment, but was fought and neglected in the Arab world itself. This difference was seen as one of the answers to the question, Why did others progress while Muslims declined? Thus, the revalorization and revival of Averroes became significant in changing the course of Arab Islamic culture.

In a thoroughly researched and carefully argued study, German scholar of Islamic studies Anke von Kügelgen examines the reception of Averroes's work in contemporary Arab thought, a reception that grew significantly after the 1967 defeat.[61] She identifies two main trends in this reception. First, the medieval philosopher's importance is seen not so much in his contributions to Aristotelian philosophy or in the concrete contents of his various works, but in the fundamental critical orientations of his general oeuvre that eventually led to the European Renaissance and Enlightenment. Averroes is seen as the prototype of the philosopher and scientist, the defender of tolerance and openness, the advocate of the freedom of worship and the freedom of thought, the supporter of the separation of religion from philosophy, and the spokesman for the supremacy of philosophy and rationality. To this trend belong Farah Antun, Tayyeb Tizini, and Muhammad Abed al-Jabiri. In the second trend, the focus is on the Islamic character of Averroes's rationalism, a rationalism developed in Islamic jurisprudence rather than in hellenized Islamic philosophy; in other words, this trend emphasizes the rational nature of Islam and Islamic sciences. To this trend belong Muhammad Abduh, Muhammad Amara, and Hassan Hanafi. Both trends valorize rationality as championed by an indigenous leading intellectual figure from the classical heritage and attack irrationalism, fatalism, and superstitious thinking indiscriminately conflated with mysticism.

Also common to both trends is the consideration of the European Enlightenment as the important standard for evaluating the importance of Averroes's thought and the view of Western rational culture as the right direction to be followed. Von Kügelgen's detailed analysis further shows that this political and ideological "back to Averroes" movement does not favor a serious study of his legacy; rather, it twists his work to fit present interests. In many respects, the real contents of his philosophy do not correspond to the modern concerns. For instance, she says, Averroes did not always advocate the separation of religion from philosophy, nor did he stand for absolute tolerance or defend the equality of all people. The urgency of putting his legacy to immediate use has prevented a scholarly consideration of his legacy—a criticism, von Kügelgen says, that applies to most contemporary Arab thinkers involved in the Averroes revival, including al-Jabiri. However, she thinks that this revival has made some important positive contributions: first, it blurs, if not erases, the established picture of a spiritual Orient and a rational West by shedding light on the rationalist work of a prominent figure of Arab Islamic heritage; second, by recalling Averroes's openness to Greek philosophy, it encourages an openness to Western culture in a way that does not view the latter as either a model or an enemy, but as a culture with equivalent components; third, and by the same token, it offers a new self-understanding of Islamic culture; and finally, it draws attention to Averroes's place in Arab Islamic culture after it had been neglected in favor of his place in Western medieval and Renaissance thought, especially among Western scholars.

For Saadallah Wannous, not only the work of Averroes, but the entire cultural heritage is dealt with in this ideological manner, showing a "defeated awareness" that shuns reality, both past and present. For him, the 1984 Cairo conference was another manifestation of this avoidance of reality and of the unhealthy gap between thought and reality in Arab debates.

In the opening essay of the *Qadaya wa Shahadat* issue devoted to *al-thaqafa al-wataniyya* (national culture), entitled "Al-Thaqafa al-Wataniyya wa al-Wa'y al-Tarikhi" (On National Culture and Historical Awareness),[62] Wannous addresses this feature of Arab thought and devotes half of the text to the 1984 conference. He notes that although al-Jabiri recognizes the impact of colonialism on Arab issues and on the authenticity/contemporaneity problematic in particular, he rapidly moves the subject to the strictly intellectual, ideal level with a questioning of "Arab reason." In the conference paper on the problem of development in the Arab world, says Wannous, it is suggested that the solution should be sought in Arab heritage and not in Western views of development. In the paper on the political dimensions of the cultural crisis, he points out, it is claimed that all the Western liberal political concepts are already found in Islam and that what is needed is an exploration of the Islamic heritage. The contribution on the legal aspects of the cultural malaise proposes a return to Islamic traditional law. *Heritage* and *tradition*, or *turath*, Wannous says, recur as words of incantation that hold in them the magical solutions to all Arab problems. The actual, real problems of development are not presented or analyzed, nor are the real legal problems. The whole history of abuse and injustice, even under Islamic rule and law, is neglected. Instead, a scholastic, futile debate is conducted on the nature of this ubiquitous heritage. Many reject Mohammad Arkoun's effort to study and define this heritage systematically as a condescending Orientalist proposal and rebuff Qustantin Zurayq's sober analysis of modernity as an invitation to westernization. Neither heritage nor the present age get to be seriously presented and described. Both are assumed to be already known, but they are not.

The transposing of real present and past problems into abstract cultural questions, Wannous says, is the evasion of reality by a defeated thought. This evasion perfectly suits the rulers, who would not tolerate a discussion of reality—that is, a discussion of the unfair distribution of wealth, the abuse of human and civil rights, and the disrespect of law. It also fits the interests of imperialist powers, which would rather see locals busy themselves with abstract, scholastic debates than struggle for their real national interests. Social, economic, and political problems are made into abstract, intellectual problems, and so historical awareness that would lead to debate and controversy is avoided at the price of depriving Arabs of a treasure of experience and knowledge. This intellectualization of problems leads to the evasion of the present reality that may open up questions, depriving people of an awareness of the causes of the problems and of the possibilities of searching for solutions. By isolating Arabs in cultural difference, it denies them the chance of cultural interaction and openness, confining them to a cult of difference that the imperialists encourage. Deprived thus of all means of judgment and knowledge, Arabs have become susceptible to the magic of ideology that promises them the illusion of being on the right and pure path, confident of a divine mission to patronize humanity, after a supposedly short interval of decadence. Broken in their spirit and agency by despotism and oppression, they have given in to utopian views that ignore both history and reality.

In the wake of the 1967 defeat, recalls Wannous, Syrian Communist thinker Yassin Hafez[63] warned against slipping from an awareness of the defeat to a defeated awareness that loses sight of reality. One should, says Wannous, look into the psychology of the oppressed and the defeated to understand this symptomatic gap between thought and reality, but one should also overcome the defeated awareness by sustaining the courage to look into the real problems: the despotism and ruthless repression that shatter people's souls and pushes them to focus their energies on "smuggling" their lives through the systems of injustice and abuse—exactly as his characters in *An Entertainment Evening for June 5* were trying to do a quarter century later. The only option left to genuine intellectuals is to resist the defeat of awareness, even if their efforts are doomed to be Sisyphean in the face of forbidding obstacles. They have to accept their marginal status, but they need to persist in their struggle for freedom and liberation, both on the intellectual level and the political level. They have to persevere in their work of witnessing, of crying in the wilderness, of being a leaven for hope in the midst of despair. Wannous wrote this essay in 1990. Almost two decades later, the repression and terror inside Arab regimes, in the Islamist oppositional movements, as well as in the Middle East policies of Western governments have grown much larger. The difficulty and necessity of resisting the defeated awareness on so many fronts simultaneously are more formidable than ever.

Georges Tarabichi: The Psychological Reading of the Authenticity/Modernization Problematic

Georges Tarabichi analyzes the authenticity/modernization problematic that dominated the Cairo conference and much of post-1967 writings in the Arab world. Tarabichi resides in Paris and writes extensively on contemporary Arab thought. He has translated several of Freud's works into Arabic, and the psychoanalytical approach is an important part of his analytic apparatus. In *Al-Muthaqqafun al-ʿArab wa al-Turath: Al-Tahlil al-Nafsi li ʿIsab Jamaʿi* (Arab Intellectuals and Tradition: A Psychological Analysis of a Collective Neurosis), published in 1991, he examines from a psychoanalytic point of view Arab intellectuals' contemporary fixation on the Arab cultural legacy, or *turath*.[64] In the first chapter, "Al-Radda wa al-Nukus" (The Trauma and the Regression), he argues that the authenticity/modernization problematic is not a cultural problematic, but a psychological one. The obsessive resort to *turath* is a phenomenon proper to the last decades of the twentieth century. Never before had Arabs turned so emphatically to the past cultural legacy as they did after the 1967 defeat by Israel. In this turn, contemporary thought distances itself from the modern Arab thought of the Nahda. Tarabichi disagrees strongly with al-Jabiri, who sees no significant difference between the two periods and regards both intellectual productions, the modern and the contemporary, as instances of the pathological functioning of Arab reason. Tarabichi views this diagnosis as ahistorical and faulty. Contemporary Arab thought, he says, did inherit some of the tensions of modern Arab thought, such as the tension between self-glorification and the need for compensation vis-à-vis the superiority of the West, on the one hand, and critique and the need to improve the self, on the other. It also maintained the tendency toward ideological inflation and revolutionary thinking due to the need for rapid change. However, he argues that this tendency was aggravated by the successive events of the century and most of all by the defeat of 1967. Although the 1967 war was neither the only war of the century nor the only defeat, it was a turning point in Arab consciousness. Whereas al-Jabiri thinks that treating this loss as a trauma was the work of unhealthy Arab reason, Tarabichi regards the event as a real trauma for Arabs in general and for Arab intellectuals in particular. It was a trauma because it was an irremediable defeat in the following senses: *(a)* The defeat was totally unexpected because it was preceded by a time of great self-confidence and optimism. *(b)* It was felt not only as a military defeat, but also as a blow to the whole socioeconomic, technological, and cultural foundations of the Arab nation, and the narcissistic wound it caused was accompanied by a severe damage to the foundations of self. *(c)* It was a defeat that could not be overcome and transformed into a memory in subsequent years by any achievement that might have made up for it. *(d)* On the subconscious level, it was lived as the shameful loss by and of the father, personified in the Egyptian, Arab, and Third World leader Gamal Abdel Nasser. Indeed, after leading a socialist revolution in Egypt and nationalizing the Suez Canal, Abdel Nasser had become an idolized hero who with his policies and charisma inspired in the whole Arab nation a great sense of confidence and pride. His defeat in 1967 and then his death in 1970 were felt as a deep humiliation and a tremendous loss. An orphaned nation had to mourn a humiliated and castrated father.

For all these reasons, the 1967 defeat was definitely a trauma, according to Tarabichi. It released a powerful feeling of guilt that was channeled against the very idea of the Nahda and the revolutionary ideologies that it had advocated, including that of Abdel Nasser; the Nahda was now seen as a betrayal of tradition, Islam, and authenticity. The defeat was seen as the punishment for the betrayal. The (Islamic) Ottoman rule, which was hitherto considered responsible for much of the Arab underdevelopment, was now celebrated in a regressive nostalgia. The past legacy, the *turath*, was now the ersatz father that was resorted to in a state of traumatic regression, and this father was now expected to have the magical powers of restoring pride and self-confidence and of providing solutions to the insurmountable problems at hand.

According to Tarabichi, this traumatic regression has manifested itself in the following ways:

1.   A refusal to grow and a rejection of the world, industrialization, and modernity; an escape from reality and the avoidance of interacting with it. Challenges—an omnipresent notion, Tarabichi says, as in the title of the 1984 Cairo conference, "Heritage and the Challenges of the Epoch"—are perceived as aggressions to be fought and resisted rather than opportunities to be seized productively.

2.   The denial of personal agency in history and the understanding of history in terms of impersonal forces such as *turath*, Arabic language, Arab race, Islam, and such collective aggregates.

3.   "The family reflex," in the sense of a defensive particularism, and various forms of chauvinism, producing a tension between the universality of Islam and the particularity of the Arab nation.

4.   The use of sexual terminology and symbolization in the description of political and military events, as in the "rape" of Palestine.

5.   A systematically contrarian reaction, especially vis-à-vis the West.

6.   A turning against and away from the Nahda.[65] Whereas the Nahda distinguished between the imperial West and Western culture in general and within this culture distinguished the spiritual from the material, the regressive contemporary thought refuses to make these distinctions; it rejects the West as a whole and positions itself against it in an essentialistic,

totalizing antagonism. Whereas the Nahda called for openness in various degrees and worked toward closing the gap between the Arab world and the West, regressive contemporary thought insists on keeping the two worlds apart. And finally, whereas the Nahda fought against Western military invasion and the revolutionaries in the 1950s fought against Western economic hegemony, contemporary thinkers want to fight Western cultural invasion and hegemony, seeking disalienation against them in a passionate identification with the "authentic *turath*."

7.   The reinforcement of ego-centrality as a compensation for the narcissistic wound, which was already present in the Nahda, but is now amplified with the successive defeats and the overwhelming problems of the present; and the consideration of Oriental or Islamic centrism as superior, but also as victimized (i.e., even as victims, Arabs want to consider themselves the center of victimhood in general).

8.   The childish need to reject the other, not to owe anything to anybody, and to find everybody owing to oneself (e.g., Islam as the basis and ultimate destination of all civilization, especially the Western)—in other words, the view of the Other as a source of impurity.

For Tarabichi, *turath* as ersatz father does not have the magical powers for a true disalienation; the solution can be found only by facing reality, by growing and activating the forces of agency. Whether one agrees with Tarabichi's psychoanalytical reading of contemporary Arab consciousness (or subconsciousness) or not, the fact remains that most Arab critical thinkers agree that *turath* and the idea of authenticity associated with it are the last desperate resort for pride and hope after a century of disasters and in the face of an unbearable present. This choice has often led to an ideologization of *turath* and an ideologization of Islam as a religion and a religious tradition.

An example of an Islamocentrist view is that of Tunisian historian and philosopher Hisham Djaît in *L'Europe et l'Islam* (*Europe and Islam*). In it, he says, "Modern Europe was the last moment, and perhaps for that reason the most crucial moment, of an extremely fertile era in the history of humanity, an era inaugurated by the birth and expansion of Islam. Why Islam? Because analysis shows it to be the axis around which the world system would turn."[66] Another attempt at replacing Eurocentrism with Islamocentrism is manifested in the work of the Egyptian philosopher Hassan Hanafi, one of the leading theoreticians of the "Islamic Left," both a movement and a journal that aim at combining revolutionary ethos with the values of Islam for the purposes of mobilizing the vital forces of the region toward autonomy, rationality, and social justice. Hanafi sets out to produce a critical reconstruction of Islamic and Western intellectual history. In his book *Muqaddima fi 'Ilm al-Istighrab* (Introduction to the Science of Occidentalism), published in Egypt in 1991 and then in Beirut in 1992, he elaborates on what he calls a "science of the West."[67] This science aims at historicizing and provincializing Europe and the West in general. It purports to make of the West an object of knowledge rather than exclusively a source of knowledge, as it has been. In contrast to Western Orientalism, this science of the West should be objective and free from ideological intentions. He wants it to be scientific, not polemic. Unfortunately, the book is replete with essentialist, ideological, and polemical tones, making use of vengeful, militaristic language to formulate this science. One of the book's main theses is the coming downfall of Western culture and the rise (again) of Eastern culture because the latter is much more rooted in history and much more humane. The center of civilization is now returning to the Orient after an interval of displacement in the West. Tarabichi directs a scathing attack against the book in *Arab Intellectuals and Tradition*, applying the Freudian psychoanalytic method to Hanafi's thought.[68] He sees in Hanafi's work one of the clearest expressions of many Arab thinkers' neurotic regression to tradition viewed as their Islamic heritage. According to Tarabichi, Hanafi's attempt at articulating a science of Occidentalism illustrates this regression very well. It is motivated by a vengeful reaction to a narcissistic wound whereby the Other, in this case Western civilization, is expected to wane and to be replaced by a triumphant Islamic civilization. The revenge is in the coming of an Islamocentric world, not of a plural world. This "science" is full of contradictions, which Tarabichi shows one after the other by juxtaposing contradictory quotations from Hanafi's text. For instance, Western civilization is considered to be totally "other," but at the same time to be a product of the old Islamic civilization, especially as far as the European Renaissance and the Enlightenment are concerned. Its principles of reason are to be found in classical Islamic theology of the Mu'tazilite trend.[69]

Mahmud Amin al-Alim agrees with Tarabichi that Hanafi's views of Western and Islamic civilizations are seriously flawed.[70] He finds Hanafi to be essentialist in these views and thinks that he uses a deterministic understanding of history as well as a static, Aristotelian concept of identity. Moreover, he thinks that Hanafi's presentation of the history of Western ideas lacks method and is too fixated on the religious interpretation of intellectual trends. For al-Alim, the project of an Islamocentric world cannot be but another form of alienation from the world that would only aggravate Arabs' dependency and backwardness. Having said this, he thinks that Tarabichi is at times too hard on Hanafi and that he sometimes takes quotes out of context. Furthermore, he believes that Tarabichi's characterization of all post-1967 Arab thought as neurotic and regressive ignores the radical critique that came in the aftermath of 1967, for instance in the work of Laroui and al-Azm. He also finds Tarabichi's exclusively psychological reading of Arab thought and its focus on the subconscious to be reductionist and neglectful of other important factors, such as the economic and the political.

Critique in These Conferences: The Fixation on Tradition and the Intellectualization of the Malaise

The participants in these conferences, like the thinkers discussed in the previous chapter, are engaged in self-reflection and critique regarding both the self and the other. They are reflecting on the modes of thinking with which cultural malaise has been approached so far and examining the kind of questions that have been raised about it, such as the question of the tension between authenticity and contemporaneity. Finally, they too are searching for a balance between self-affirmation and critique. In this wider circle of debates, however, especially in the mid-1980s, the tendency is to assert identity, specificity, and authenticity, and to associate these elements with heritage, Islam, and the past. It is useful here to recall the titles of these conferences: "Authenticity and Renewal in Contemporary Arab Culture," "The Crisis of Civilization Development in the Arab Homeland," and "Heritage and the Challenges of the Age in the Arab Homeland: Authenticity and Contemporaneity." The keywords are *renewal, development, crisis, heritage, authenticity,* and *contemporaneity.* Although the conference papers were to connect these notions to one another and to offer a vision of a new, authentic, and modern Arab culture, they centered on heritage as the basis for such a vision. The legacy of the past and the past itself were constantly referred to as representing the core of the self, opposed to a contemporary age that is not of its making. These discussions show the difficulties of decentering and demystifying the past, identified to a great extent with Islam and seen as a source of identity, pride, and power. The calls for historicizing the past and critically reestablishing a continuity with it are many, but the consistent and satisfactory responses to these calls are few.

Another phenomenon apparent in these debates is the tendency to focus on the cultural rather than the political aspects of the malaise, despite the recurring calls for democracy. Moreover, the cultural is often approached in an idealist, intellectualist manner that isolates it from its historical, colonial, and socioeconomical conditions. All of these tendencies constitute some of the major challenges to the historicizing, demystifying, and deconstructive work of critique. Finally, the traumatic effect of the 1967 defeat and its aftermath is recognized as the significant context within which this work is carried out. Chapters 4 and 5 examine the critical efforts made in both the religious, theological sphere and the secular sphere in spite of these challenges.

Four
Critique
in
Islamic
Theology

Already during the Nahda, as we have seen so far, Islamic theology was a pivotal domain of reform and modernization under the leadership of clerics such as Muhammad Abduh, Ali Abdel Raziq, and Muhammad Ahmad Khalafallah. Their ideas were met with conservatism and traditionalism by the official religious establishment headed by al-Azhar as well as by leading Islamists such as Hassan al-Banna, the founder of the Muslim Brotherhood, and Sayyid Qutb, its theoretician. But the calls for theological critique and modernization continued, for instance in the ideas of Muhammad Nuwaihi. Nuwaihi mentioned four ways in which religions in general have adapted to modernity: first, by distinguishing between religion and official speakers of religion; second, by recognizing the possible intellectual and moral flaws of these speakers; third, by developing the metaphorical interpretation of sacred texts; and finally, by historicizing revelation. Recalling Muslim authorities' and the public's resistance to the fourth way, he pleaded for the expansion of the third way to renew Islam as a religion and a culture.

It is, however, the fourth way that some critical Islamic thinkers of the second half of the twentieth century adopted as a major project of theological and cultural reform. The most prominent among them are Mohammad Arkoun and Nasr Hamid Abu Zayd. For both, the opening of new ways of understanding Islam as a divine message and as a tradition and culture starts with the historicizing of revelation. This historicization implies the examination of the human context of revelation and transmission, including the historical, cultural, linguistic, and gender prisms through which they take place. A number of feminist critics analyze the gender aspect of theology. Moreover, religion in the Arab world, like elsewhere, has been mobilized to advocate for social, economic, and political justice: Islamic and Christian liberation theologies have been articulated to relate faith to the trying circumstances of Arab realities and to let the liberating message of the sacred texts be heard in the dark times of oppression and despair. In this chapter, I look at the strengths, weaknesses, and specificities of these theologies and consider their contribution to Arab cultural critique in general. Finally, I examine the critical function that traditional religious institutions may perform in the Arab Islamic context.

From the Unthought and the Unthinkable to the Thinkable: Mohammad Arkoun

Mohammad Arkoun is an Algerian professor of Islamic studies at the Sorbonne in Paris, where he was also trained. Since the early 1960s, he has been writing on questions of theory and method in Islamic studies as well as on various topics of Islamic theology. His writings have been mainly in French, but some are in Arabic and lately in English as well. His main project has been to rethink Islam by using the recent findings in the humanities and the social sciences in order to shed new light on the sacred texts and traditions of Islam and by so doing to explore the historicity of revelation in Islam, as has been done in other monotheistic religions. Indeed, one of Arkoun's major concerns throughout his career has been to put Islam and its studies in a comparative perspective on religion, encompassing Judaism and Christianity. Finally, like many other thinkers of the second half of the twentieth century and beyond, he has been preoccupied with the modes of thinking in modern and contemporary Arab thought, especially with the tension between ideology and critique.

In a number of texts, Arkoun makes a cogent presentation of the genesis and goal of his endeavor. I refer to two of these texts (both in English): the 1985–1986 Annual Distinguished Lecture in Arab Studies, which he gave at the Center for Contemporary Arab Studies of Georgetown University, published as *Rethinking Islam Today*, and his introduction to his book *The Unthought in Contemporary Islamic Thought*.[1] In both texts, he explains how growing up in the midst of the anticolonial struggle in the 1950s in Algeria impacted and shaped his intellectual interests. In this struggle, he says, an Arab Muslim personality was opposed to a French colonial power that claimed to be the representative of universal modern civilization. He recalls the intellectual poverty with which Islam was taught at the University of Algiers in those days. It is this personal "existential experience," as he calls it, that pushed him to examine the French colonial authorities' claim and at the same time to search for a better understanding of Islam. The study of Islam needed to be fundamentally reconsidered not in yet another reform attempt, but in a thorough rethinking of its theoretical and epistemological premises. This reconsideration meant subjecting Islamic studies to a radical critique in a social and cultural space dominated by the militant ideologies of the anticolonial and the postcolonial struggles—a challenging but necessary undertaking, according to him. It had two ultimate goals: first, to develop a new epistemology for the understanding of religion as a universal dimension of human existence and, second, to articulate a theory for the comparative study of cultures, especially those with a tradition of revealed religions.

The elaboration of such an epistemology implies, for Arkoun, a number of tasks:

1. The deconstruction of the logocentrism of the traditional Islamic studies, whether produced by Western or Muslim scholars, and the rehabilitation of the mythical and prophetic dimensions of the phenomenon of religion.
2. The integration of the modern humanities and social sciences—such as linguistics, semiotics, anthropology, and history—into these studies, which are to be understood as an anthropology of the past rather than as a mere compilation of events, genealogies, and records and are to be undertaken for the purpose of understanding the historicity of revelation.

3. The widening of the scope of tradition to include orthodoxy as well as unorthodoxy and the examination of the elements of power and ideology that go into the definition of these categories.

4. The uncovering of the regimes of truth and the regimes of power that define what is thinkable and what is unthinkable in the study of religion—Islam in particular—in a given period of history.

Islamic studies, according to Arkoun, have been dominated from early on by the primacy of Logos over mythos, which has marginalized, if not eliminated, religion's existential, symbolic, and prophetic dimensions. The same can be said, he adds, about Judaism and Christianity, especially in the Middle Ages under the impact of Greek philosophy. The integration of the latter into the elaboration of the theologies and religious laws of these monotheistic religions led to the privileging of deductive reasoning over imagination, of defined categories and concepts over more fluid notions, and of the written over the oral. The stable essences and substances of classical metaphysics imposed strict boundaries within which religious phenomena can be explored. This logocentrism has produced a constraining "regime of truth": "In my attempt to identify a logocentrist attitude in classical Arab thought, I wanted to demonstrate that the axiomatic propositions, the postulates, the categories, the forms of demonstration used in Medieval thought expressed in the Syriac, Hebrew, Arabic, Persian, Greek, and Latin languages, were in fact shared and common to the Medieval mental space. And this strongly logocentrist frame of thinking imposed an epistemic *regime of truth* different from the other discursive frame represented by what I call the *prophetic discourse*."[2]

Here, the term *prophetic discourse* refers to the whole mythological dimension of religious practice and interpretation, not in the pejorative sense of myth as "primitive," but of myth as the realm of the imaginary, the symbolic, the metaphorical. The imagination and, in this connection, the collective imagination (which he calls the *imaginaire social*, borrowing from French thinker Manuel Castoriadis) draw on processes of meaning formation and layers of sedimented meaning that go beyond the strict limits of revealed religions and shape their interpretation and practice in significant ways. For Arkoun, any adequate theory of religion needs to account for the realm of the imaginary:

Traditional theological thought has not used the concept of social imaginaire and the related notions of myth, symbol, sign, or metaphor in the new meanings already mentioned. It refers constantly to reason as the faculty of true knowledge, differentiated from knowledge based on the representations of the imagination. The methodology elaborated and used by jurists-theologians shares with the Aristotelian tradition the same postulate of rationality as founding the true knowledge and excluding the constructions of the imagination. In fact, an analysis of the discourse produced by both trends of thinking—the theological and the philosophical—reveals a simultaneous use of reason and imagination. Beliefs and convictions are often used as "arguments" to "demonstrate" propositions of knowledge. In this stage of thinking, metaphor is understood and used as a rhetorical device to add an aesthetic emotion to the real content of the words: it was not perceived in its creative force as a semantic innovation or in its power to shift the discourse to a global metaphorical organization requiring the full participation of a coherent imagination.[3]

This logocentrism continues in contemporary Western culture in what Arkoun calls the "tele-techno-scientific reason";[4] and postmodern critique, he adds, has remained largely Eurocentric. What is needed is the development of a critical epistemology that integrates both new disciplines that allow the exploration of that *imaginaire* and believers' religious experiences. He understands this enterprise to be in line with what previous theologians in the classical age had done, such as al-Ghazali in *Ihya' 'ulum al-din* and Shafi'i in *Risala*.[5] At the same time, he is certain that the modern version will be different from the classical because of the epistemic discontinuities between the two epochs. Thinkers of the early period shared certain conceptual and metaphysical assumptions even when they differed in their intellectual positions; these assumptions are no longer accepted today. He gives as examples the two major antithetical figures of the classical age, al-Ghazali and Averroes: in spite of their sharp theological and philosophical differences, they both mixed juridical reasoning with philosophical reasoning and mixed religious convictions and legal norms with philosophical representations and methodology; moreover, they both ignored historicity.

The disciplines Arkoun has in mind for his modern critical project are modern semiotics and linguistics (which are bound to be different from what they were the classical age) as well as anthropology. Through a critical Islamic study informed by these disciplines, the historicity of revelation can come to the fore. By "historicity of revelation," he means the unavoidably human and worldly forms of God's revelation to humanity, which implies their embeddedness in history, culture, and language. Hence, acknowledging and understanding this embeddedness without discrediting the absolute character of the divine message become essential to any proper study of revelation. The mechanisms through which the worldly, the specific, the contingent, and the relative lead to the transcendental, the absolute, and the eternal in religious language deserve special attention. Such an approach denies the existence of a "perfect" time in which all truth was revealed and completed, a time that most reformist and revivalist movements call for a return to. This call to a "perfect" time in the past, Arkoun argues, misunderstands both the historicity of revelation and the historicity of the reception of the revealed message. The latter, however, for Arkoun, remains a topic to be explored in an interdisciplinary, cross-religious, and cross-cultural approach:

> *All semiotic productions of a human being in the process of his social and cultural emergence are subject to historical change which I call* historicity. *As a semiotic articulation of meaning for social and cultural uses, the Qur'an is subject to historicity. This means that* there is no access to the absolute *outside the phenomenal world of our terrestrial, historical existence. The various expressions given to the ontology, the first being the truth and the transcendence by theological and metaphysical reason, have neglected historicity as a dimension of the truth. Changing tools, concepts, definitions, and postulates are used to shape the truth.*[6]

Both the uncreated status of the Qur'an and its final compiled form are examples of beliefs that were produced by certain regimes of truth combined with a certain regime of power:

> *Islam is presented and lived as a definite system of beliefs and non-beliefs which cannot be submitted to any critical inquiry. Thus, it divides the space of thinking into two parts: the unthinkable and the thinkable. Both concepts are historical and not, at first, philosophical. The respective domain of each of them changes through history and varies from one social group to another. Before the systemization by Shafi'i of the concept of* sunna *and the* usuli *use of it, many aspects of Islamic thought were still thinkable. They became unthinkable after the triumph of Shafi'i theory and also the elaboration of authentic*

"collections," as mentioned earlier. Similarly, the problems related to the historical process of collecting the Qur'an in an official mushaf *became more and more unthinkable under the official pressure of the caliphate because the Qur'an has been used since the beginning of the Islamic state to legitimize political power and to unify the* umma.[7]

Hence, for Arkoun, both epistemological systems and power systems play a crucial role in drawing the boundaries around what he calls a given "logosphere"—a horizon of givens constituted by a language and a culture. These systems present preferences as necessary truths and use power to impose ideological limits to the activity of thought, producing a whole realm of the unthought. Changing the unthinkable into a thinkable is the task of critique:

When the field of the unthinkable is expanded and maintained for centuries in a particular tradition of thought, the intellectual horizons of reason are diminished and its critical functions narrowed and weakened because the sphere of the unthought becomes more determinate and there is little space left for the thinkable. The unthought is made up of the accumulated issues declared unthinkable in a given logosphere. A logosphere is the linguistic mental space shared by all those who use the same language with which to articulate their thoughts, their representations, their collective memory, and their knowledge according to the fundamental principles and values claimed as a unifying weltanschaaung. *I use this concept to introduce the important dimension of the linguistic constraints of each language on the activities of thought.*[8]

The elaboration of a new critical epistemology[9] that would take into account the historicity of both revelation and religious traditions, that would make room for myth and the imaginary, that would pay attention to language and meaning systems, that would include the unorthodox, the oral, and the minority, and that would reject logocentrism and Eurocentrism is the task of a critique of Islamic reason, which is also the title of a book Arkoun published in 1984, the same year that Muhammad al-Jabiri published the first volume of his critique of Arab reason.[10] Whereas Arkoun intends to rehabilitate the imaginary and the prophetic in view of acknowledging the human creation and interpretation of meaning in what is believed to be a divine message, al-Jabiri intends to reestablish the primacy of demonstrative reasoning in view of rehabilitating what he believes to be the rationalist trend in the Islamic tradition. Given the rhetorical, demagogical, sentimentalist, manipulative, and apologetic abuses of beliefs in public debates in the Arab world, especially in those pertaining to sensitive issues such as religion, tradition, and identity, it is understandable that many contemporary critical thinkers insist on upholding rationality and demonstrative reasoning. On the one hand, this insistence often unfortunately leads to an exclusive valorization of this kind of reasoning and to the marginalization of all other forms of thinking and experiencing. On the other hand, the negative perception of mysticism as a trend that encourages irrationalism and hence at least partly responsible for the Arab decline in the arts and sciences has bred a certain suspicion toward the prophetic and spiritual dimensions of Islam. Again, this suspicion has been to the detriment of the experiential aspect of faith. Arkoun stands out as a critic who tries to reincorporate these dimensions in his new theology. In any case, compared to al-Jabiri, he remains more consistent in his historicist view of tradition and shows no proclivity to an essentialist conception of the "reason" in question. Furthermore, for Arkoun, the critique of Orientalism does not in and of itself create such a critical epistemology. The latter is to be undertaken in addition to the critique of Orientalism, a critique to which he contributed in 1964 with a sharp analysis of the articles of Gustav von Grunebaum. In a polite but firm attack, Arkoun criticizes von Grunebaum's essentialist, sweeping judgments.[11] He quotes a passage from von Grunebaum that is worth reproducing here in connection with the main focus of our study—namely, the issue of reflection and critique in modern Arab thought:

> *It is essential to realize that Muslim civilization is a cultural entity that does not share our primary aspirations. It is not vitally interested in analytical self-understanding, and it is even less interested in the structural study of other cultures, either as an end in itself or as a means toward clearer understanding of its own character and history. If this observation were to be valid merely for contemporary Islam, one might be inclined to connect it with the profoundly disturbed state of Islam, which does not permit to look beyond itself unless forced to do so. But as it is valid for the past as well, one may perhaps seek to connect it with the basic antihumanism of this civilization, that is, the determined refusal to accept man to any extent whatever as the arbiter or the measure of things, and the tendency to be satisfied with*

truth as the description of mental structures, or, in other words, with psychological truth.[12]

As Arkoun shows in his critical review, he is aware of the great difficulty of being critical in a situation of struggle, internal or external. He ends his Georgetown lecture with the following statement: "I learned through the Algerian war of liberation how all revolutionary movements need to be backed by a struggle for meaning, and I discovered how meaning is manipulated by forces devoted to the conquest of power. The conflict between meaning and power has been, is, and will be the permanent condition through which man tries to emerge as a thinking being."[13] Arkoun's Egyptian counterpart, Nasr Hamid Abu Zayd, to whose work I turn in the next section, was to pay a high price for denouncing this link between power interests and hermeneutic preferences.

In his classic overview of Arab thought, *La pensée arabe*, published in Paris in 1975,[14] Arkoun reflects on the particularly difficult task for Arab thinkers to create empowering structures of meaning, caught as they are between the need for critical thinking and the pressure of ideological struggles. After the Nahda intellectual movements of the nineteenth and early twentieth centuries, the post-1950 era, according to him, came to be known as the period of the *thawra*, revolution, under the impact of the Algerian anticolonial revolution, the Egyptian Free Officers revolution, and the Palestinian revolution led by the Palestine Liberation Organization. The voluntaristic, one-party rule that characterized the postcolonial epoch rested on ideological struggles and established authoritarian states. The struggle against continuing Western imperialistic intervention mobilized socialist ideas and, at a later stage, Islamist ideologies of resistance. Crises in socioeconomic developmental offered fertile ground for protest ideologies. None of these factors and ideologies, says Arkoun, favored the development of serious critical work for overcoming the intelligibility limits of the prevailing intellectual traditions and articulating a critical analysis of the formal Western humanism that accompanied imperialism. Repression, self-censorship, and pressures toward conformism on the part of state regimes and revolutionary groups damaged severely the growth of critical thinking. The unthought and the unthinkable remained unchallenged and kept growing, especially with regard to anything pertaining to theology, sexuality, and women. Religious institutions put under state control were transformed into institutions of charity and conservative social mores, and they ceased to produce innovative work. Religious movements stopped being interested in theological, spiritual issues even though they have been and are for him liberation and protest movements based on religious ideologies. Negative aggressive attacks against these movements, such as al-Azm's in the 1970s, are not helpful reactions to them, he argues.

Arkoun often complains in his writings about the poor reception of his ideas. They are little known to Arab intellectuals, perhaps because he writes in French and is based in Paris—although he has been publishing in Arabic quite regularly since the late 1970s—or they are rejected as inadequate, if not blasphemous, to Islam. In his introduction to *The Unthought in Contemporary Islamic Thought*, he writes:

> *When I try to explain the methodological necessity to suspend—not to ignore totally—all theological interference with a linguistic analysis of the Qur'anic discourse, Muslims—ordinary believers as well as cultivated "intellectuals"—would ask immediately "how can you carry on a linguistic discourse analysis on a divine word expressed in Arabic which is itself elected as a divine language?" Or "what you consider as a text is actually an indivisible part of the uncreated Qur'an collected in the Mushaf." Not only do these questions reveal the intellectual impossibility of grasping a very simple methodological rule, but they stop the proposed exercise with naive so-called theological objections betraying a total ignorance of the rich theoretical debates generated in classical theology on the issue of God's created speech. This is clearly what I call the unthinkable and the unthought in contemporary Islamic thought.[15]*

Indeed, this is the kind of reaction his ideas received when he presented them at the 1984 Cairo conference (discussed in chapter 3). Abu Zayd reports the very same reactions to his own work, which in important respects is similar to Arkoun's.[16] But if Arkoun's ideas have not draw much attention from the Arab intellectual scene, his Egyptian colleague's did in an excessive and negative way. By developing a similar critical theology, Abu Zayd attracted the wrath of Egyptian Islamists for theological and political reasons. He had to flee his country and find refuge in the Netherlands. The two thinkers seem to have developed their ideas independently of one another. More recently, they have started to interact in meetings and writings. In April 2004, they met, along with a number of other Arab intellectuals from different countries, at a conference to launch the Arab Institute for the Modernizing of Thought.[17] It was legally founded in 2002 in Geneva, initiated and funded by Libyan businessman Mohammed Abdel Muttalib al-Hawni, and aimed at supporting translations, studies, and publications in the various fields of the social sciences, humanities, media, and education in the Arab world. Its overall purpose was to revive the Nahda project by providing financial and institutional support to free and enlightened intellectual debates that would contribute to critical Arab self-reflection. The launching event included a press conference and a scholarly conference, "Modernity and Arab Modernity," which gathered a number of prominent Arab thinkers, such as Sadeq Jalal al-Azm, Aziz al-Azmeh, Kamal Abdel Latif, Fahmy Jedaane, and the Saudi woman writer Raja' bin Salameh. The conference proceedings, a statement of the institute's goals, and a list of its founding members were published in Beirut in 2005.[18] By the time the volume came out, however, the institute had unfortunately already ceased to exist. The head of its council, Nasr Hamid Abu Zayd, and its secretary, Georges Tarabichi, declared that it was dissolved due to a lack of funds: although registered in Geneva and thus considered a European institution, it could not benefit from European funds because its realm of action fell outside the boundaries of Europe. And Arab potential donors, they said, were suspicious of its critical, modernizing, and secular goals. All it could present in the thirty months of its existence were seven original monographs and eight translations.

The Historicity of Revelation and the Struggle for Thought in the Time of Anathema: Nasr Hamid Abu Zayd

In 1993, Nasr Hamid Abu Zayd was denied promotion at Cairo University and then accused of apostasy. A religious court asked him to divorce his wife, Ebtehal Yunes, an associate professor of French civilization in the same faculty, under the pretext that as an infidel he could no longer remain married to a Muslim woman. He tried to challenge the verdict through the Egyptian civil courts, but in 1994 the religious courts confirmed the verdict of his apostasy, and his marriage was annulled. Under the pressure of death threats, he left Egypt in 1995 with his wife for the Netherlands, where he was offered the chair of Islamic studies at Leiden. The death threats were to be taken seriously because in 1992 Islamists had gunned down a secularist thinker, Farag Fowda, in broad day light in Cairo, and the assassins were never brought to trial.

Abu Zayd had studied Arabic literature at Cairo University and become an assistant teacher in the Arabic department in 1972. The department and the faculty had pressured him to do his graduate work in Islamic studies in order to fill the chair of Islamic studies that had remained vacant since 1954. Abu Zayd was reluctant at first to comply with the department's recommendation, knowing how the chair had become vacant and what had happened to the previous student who had ventured into the field. Indeed some two decades earlier Muhammad Ahmad Khalafallah had submitted a thesis, "Al-Fann al-Qasasi fi al-Qur'an al-Karim" (The Art of Narration in the Qur'an), written under the direction of Amin al-Khuli, then chair of Islamic studies. It was devoted to the study of the Qur'an with a critical-literary methodology.[19] The thesis was rejected, Khalafallah was transferred to a nonteaching position in the Ministry of Education, and al-Khuli was forbidden to teach or direct Islamic studies and was forced into retirement by the Free Officers' government.

Abu Zayd eventually agreed to go into Islamic studies and wrote his master's thesis on the different methods of interpretation applied historically to the Qur'an. His doctoral dissertation was on the hermeneutics of the Qur'an from a Sufi point of view; it was devoted to the work of the great Andalusian Sufi Ibn Arabi. After completing these two theses, Abu Zayd published the main findings of his research in *Mafhum al-Nass: Dirasah fi 'Ulum al-Qur'an* (The Concept of the Text: A Study in the Sciences of the Qur'an) in Cairo in 1990.[20] Among his main findings was the ubiquitous influence of sociopolitical factors in the politics of interpreting the sacred text. He had himself witnessed this influence in his own time, when the Qur'an was presented in the 1960s as supporting socialist and anti-Zionist orientations and then in the 1970s as advocating liberalism and private property. More recently, Islamist militant groups and their religious discourse had magnified this phenomenon, which pushed him to write *Naqd al-Khitab al-Dini* (The Critique of Religious Discourse), published in Cairo in 1992.[21] In the introduction to this book, Abu Zayd denounced the hypocrisy and corruption of some Islamist activities, such as Islamic investment companies that had abused the people's trust and embezzled their investments. It so happened, however, that one of the members of his promotion committee was involved with one of these banks.[22] Once again, a nexus of religious, political, and economic factors weighed in on the course of an academic career and an intellectual debate. In this book, Abu Zayd described what he calls the five "mechanisms and postulates of the Islamist discourse":[23]

1. *The conflation of religion with religious thought—that is, the sacred text with the various theological, exegetical, and legal traditions dealing with it.* The Islamists, he says, speak in the name of God and pretend to know His intentions and His will. They claim to be the only ones, like ulemas and men of religion, to hold this truth. But they also pride themselves on the absence of a clerical institution in Islam and declare secularism to be an imminent danger. By making these claims, they confuse their own reading and understanding of the sacred text with the supposed truth of the text itself. They reduce the Islamic religious tradition to a monolithic, ahistorical corpus of absolute and homogeneous truths that are to govern Muslims' lives in detail. They attribute to religion a totalistic function of ruling life, even though from the very beginning of Islam a distinction was made between the domains of application of the religious text and the domains of reason and human experience. Here, Abu Zayd recalls the Prophet's oft-quoted statement that his Companions and people in general were more knowledgeable than himself in matters of the world. Islamists deny this distinction.

2. *The reduction of all phenomena to a single cause, a unique principle, namely God the Creator, in such a way as to negate the world and human agency.* Turath is also used as a sole authority, produced independently of human efforts. This mode of thinking, according to Abu Zayd, leads to viewing things from within a global determinism that offers a convenient ideological cover for social and political despotism.

3. *The opportunistic use of both Islamic tradition and European tradition.* The first is reduced to a number of schools of thought, eclectically selected according to preferences and needs that are then presented and imposed as the authentic tradition. The second is either totally rejected or partially accepted, especially in its scientific achievements, which Islamists see as the fruition of the Islamic *génie*, transmitted to Europe in the Middle Ages and during the European Renaissance. Like Saadallah Wannous, Mahdi Amil, and others, Abu Zayd believes that this distinction between European science and technology, on the one hand, and European liberal values, on the other, reinforces the situation of dependency and weakness that Islamists wish to overcome.

4. *The imposition of a culture of certitudes, starting from the certitude of faith and spreading to certainties across all domains of life.*

5. *Finally, ignoring history, on the one hand, and praising the realism and pragmatism of Islam, on the other, that distinguish Islam from other monotheistic religions and make it superior to them.*[24]

According to Abu Zayd, these misleading forms of reasoning in the Islamist discourse cannot but lead to mistaken conclusions. Because these conclusions and arguments are made in the name of God, however, anyone who opposes or challenges them is constantly threatened with accusations of apostasy, blasphemy, and with excommunication. Conflict and disagreement between people is thus transformed into a conflict between people and God, and these mechanisms of thought are made into formidable weapons of intellectual terrorism. Although they are sometimes used in good faith in the search for solid ground in the struggle for dignity, meaning, and justice, adds Abu Zayd, they are most often used to control people and to seize social and political power.

In addition to these mechanisms of thought, the Islamist discourse assumes two closely related postulates: sovereignty (*hakimiyya*) and the text (*nass*). The principle of *hakimiyya* is that of taking God's word in God's book as the sole arbiter in human affairs. It is the principle of relying on the sovereign judgment of God and in this sense the principle of applying the rule of God as the only legitimate rule over people. The notion of *hakimiyya* refers to the battle of Siffin, which took place in 657 between two claimants to the leadership of Muslims after the Prophet's death—his son-in-law, Ali bin Abi Taleb, designated by the Companions as the fourth legitimate successor of the Prophet at the head of the community, and Mu'awiya, his cousin. It is the latter who in the middle of the battle called on his troops to brandish the holy book on their swords as a call to let the word of God arbitrate the conflict. Many, including historians of the classical age, such as Tabari, have seen this act as a trick to win the battle. Indeed, Mu'awiya was victorious, and Ali bin Abi Taleb and his grandsons were killed, provoking the first and most important schism in the Muslim community, the Sunni/Shi'i divide.

According to Abu Zayd, the recourse to the book of God assumes that its content is clear and evident to all, an assumption that is untenable given the numerous controversies and debates that started shortly after the compilation of the sacred text and the recording of the Prophet's sayings and acts (the hadith). The hadith is regarded as the main source of inspiration for the Muslim to reach an understanding of the Qur'an and apply its commandments; it is also referred to as the sunna, or the right path. The complexities, ambiguities, and sometimes contradictions of these texts have given rise to heated discussions and a whole corpus of scholarly disciplines aimed at establishing criteria and rules according to which the issues raised can and should be settled. Arkoun, Abu Zayd, and many others believe that the dominant sociopolitical classes more or less imposed the "right" understanding, the "valid" interpretations, and the "orthodox" rules; in other words, there always was a politics of interpretation. Even within traditionally established schools of thought, the notion of "text," strictly speaking, was used to refer to those passages in the sacred book that were unambiguous. The Islamists, according to Abu Zayd, misuse this notion by stretching it to the totality of the text. It is important to recall, he adds, that the discussion as to which passages should be regarded as absolutely clear (*muhkam*) and which as ambiguous (*mutashabih*) remains unresolved. Moreover, the discussion about the need and legitimacy of a metaphorical versus a literal reading of the sacred text has been an important and integral part of the classical theological and exegetical tradition in Islam.

Abu Zayd contends that by falsely assuming a plain and completed clarity of meaning in the text, the principle of *hakimiyya* opens the way for an absolute authoritarianism of the text. It transforms social and political issues into textual issues. If the idea was to prevent the rule by people over people by letting the word of God rule, the principle ends up justifying a totalitarianism of the text, exercised by people who claim to be its sole spokesmen. The principle of the absolute sovereignty of God is perverted into the subjugation and servitude of people to a group ruling in the name of God. The principle also divides people between those who know the will of God and understand its wisdom and those who do not. Thus, the ground is laid for the disenfranchisement of people. Those who dare to oppose are obviously guilty of impiety and blasphemy. In the recent history of Egypt, recalls Abu Zayd, the Muslim Brotherhood used the notion of *hakimiyya* against the Free Officers, who fiercely repressed them as well as other opposing groups. After the death of Abdel Nasser, Anouar el-Sadat gave his rule an Islamic face in order to pass unpopular, neoliberal, socioeconomic policies and ultimately an unpopular peace agreement with Israel.[25] At the beginning of his administration, he encouraged the Islamists to fight and intimidate the Nasserites, socialists, and Communists. The Islamists benefited from these measures until they turned against his foreign policy regarding Israel and assassinated him in 1979. In this process, the state covered up both its lack of popular legitimacy and the Islamist challenge to the authenticity of its Islamic character with an Islamization of public life and discourse through its media.[26] In the 1980s and 1990s, a distinction was created between an "extremist" and a "moderate" form of Islamism; the first designation was used to label militant and opposing groups, and the second one to characterize the state and the official religious establishment headed by the Azhar, which was under state control. Abu Zayd strongly rejects this distinction and insists on the commonalities between the two camps in the basic modes of thinking, describing their differences as differences in degree and tactic only. For him, their discourses, whether designated "extremist" or "moderate," belong to the same "religious discourse," which is characterized by the mechanisms and postulates described earlier. Both employ religious ideology to disenfranchise people and control power, and both distort traditional theological concepts to serve their interests.

Fundamental to the concept of *hakimiyya* is the concept of text, which the Islamists understand to be the statement of God's will and judgment—hence, the centrality of this concept in Abu Zayd's refutation of such religious discourse and in his stand against the ideological manipulation of religious texts. In *Mafhum al-Nass* (The Concept of the Text), he says that Islam is a civilization of the text, but built upon an ongoing dialogue with the text. All attempts at detaching the text and its readings from their sociohistorical and cultural background distort the nature of the sacred text as God's message to humans. The divine origin of the text does not prevent a cultural reading of it; on the contrary, it is through its cultural, historical, and human components—which are bound to be relative, contingent, and specific—that this message can be communicated to and received by humans. These contingent elements open the text to human preoccupations in the course of history. Without them, the sacred text would be an abstract metaphysical thing, at best a divine soliloquy that would miss the whole purpose of revelation—to communicate a message from the Enunciator to the receiver. After all, in the Prophet's mind the message takes on the human characteristics of language, understood in its broad cultural embeddedness. Abu Zayd draws here on Ferdinand de Saussure's distinction between *langue* and *parole*, with *langue* defined strictly as a sign system and *parole* defined as the living use of this system by humans in a specific culture with various psychological and meaningful associations and connotations. Abstracted from its human formulation and reading, the sacred text becomes a fetish, an object of idolatry. The loss of the human dimension in the phenomenon of revelation and its transmission allows the dominant groups to occult that dimension and to present themselves as the spokesmen of the absolute and the divine. "Religious or profane, texts are governed by unchanging rules," Abu Zayd points out in *Naqd al-Khitab al-Dini* (The Critique of Religious Discourse). "The fact that they are revealed does not change anything to the matter, since as soon as they get inscribed in language and in history, and address humans in a given historical context, they become human texts. They are governed by the dialectic of the immutable and the changing: immutable in their materiality, and changing in their meaning." Moreover, "[t]he Qur'an is a religious text immutable in its wording. Approached by human reason, it loses this immutable character and becomes a dynamic concept with multiple meanings. The immutability is one of the attributes of the absolute and the sacred, while the human is relative and changing. The Qur'an as a sacred text in its wording, becomes comprehensible thanks to what is relative and changing—that is to say, the human—becoming thus a 'human' or a 'humanized' text."[27]

People, says Abu Zayd, mistake the contextualization of statements with the limitedness of their meanings to specific contexts; in other words, they confuse historicity (*tarikhiyya*) with temporality (*zamaniyya*). In this connection, he introduces the notion of "witness values," values or meanings that belong to a specific context and that through their specific belonging convey meanings that go beyond the context. Only such a contextualization and historicization of the sacred text can allow the sacred text to speak to people and have a renewed significance for them, away from the manipulation of pressure groups. Moreover, he insists that the historicization he is proposing is different from the traditional Qur'anic sciences of the circumstances of revelation and the circumstances of abrogation: the first one refers to the whole Qur'anic discipline that examines the context within which specific verses were revealed in order to better capture their meaning, keeping in mind that the revelation of the Qur'an stretched over a period of twenty years; and the second refers to the circumstances in which the Prophet abrogated certain verses after they were revealed, verses that were generally imputed to the malicious work of the devil.

Abu Zayd wants to examine the Qur'an as a cultural, linguistic product. He is of course not the first one to undertake such an endeavor: Amin al-Khuli, Ahmad Khalafallah, and Taha Husayn had elaborated similar approaches before him. All were condemned by the religious establishment. According to Abu Zayd, the suppression of this approach to the sacred book is one of the main reasons for the Nahda's failure. This failure is usually and rightly attributed to the fragility of the middle class, to its lack of socioeconomic autonomy, and so to its political dependency, but, for him, it was also due to the fact that the partisans of enlightenment did not break the traditional epistemological horizons of religious studies and kept within the boundaries drawn by the traditionalists, refraining from opening wide the linguistic, cultural, and historicist approaches to religious texts. The ahistorical view of the sacred text as well as of the whole religious tradition prevented the Nahda thinkers from forming a real enlightenment movement. Muhammad Abduh himself, the most important Nahda reformist, gave up on his historicizing approach under pressure from the conservatives. The objection against this approach—whether in the case of Abduh, Husayn, Khalafallah, or al-Khuli—is based on the idea that the sacred text of God cannot be reduced to a cultural, historical text. And yet, he says, it is the great figures of the interpretive school of the classical age, the likes of Jurjani and Zamakhshari, who through their linguistic and critical study of the sacred text showed the wonders of the Qur'an. Those who object to this approach misunderstand the nature of revelation as a communication to humans in a human language in a historical context.

The question then is, What is the sacred book's status? This question, as is well known, was the object of a theological controversy in the ninth and tenth centuries, involving linguistic and exegetical theories, and opposing the Mu'tazilites to the conservative Ahl al-Hadith. The former held that the word of God was an act and not an attribute of God, and that as an act it bore characteristics common to God and the world; hence, for them, the Qur'an was created, eternity being an attribute of the essence of God, not of His acts. The latter believed that the Qur'an and its language (Arabic) were, as attributes of God, uncreated and eternal. The theological controversy was associated, as is often the case, with political struggles between the adherents of the two schools of thought. At first, the Mu'tazilite view was supported by Caliph Ma'mun (813–833 AD). After him, Caliph Mutawakkil (847–861 AD) settled the controversy by imposing the conservative view, claiming that the Qur'an had two aspects: an uncreated, essentially divine aspect and another more worldly aspect that is an imitation of the first one. By political fiat, therefore, this view was transformed into a creed, a dogma. Although Abu Zayd sees the importance of remembering the history of this debate, he believes that what is needed is not a return to the Mu'tazilite views, but their further development with the use of modern textual sciences that pay attention to the unsaid and the implicit in texts. Without such a new epistemological break, religious discourse will remain confined to the regurgitation of a frozen heritage, incapable of giving birth to a lively heritage that is capable of transformation and adaptation. It will lead to the unfruitful project of Islamicizing the present age instead of modernizing Islam. The latter project, according to Abu Zayd, requires not only intellectual innovation and courage, but also vigilance vis-à-vis an extended and massive legacy that can always present ready and familiar answers.

The all too human input is obvious in texts recorded centuries after the death of the Prophet, relating the life, statements, and deeds of the Prophet and his Companions—the hadith. These texts, says Abu Zayd, were inevitably shaped by their writers' epistemological, cognitive, and social conditions as well as by the intellectual and sociohistorical givens of the scholars who later developed a huge corpus of disciplines to examine the authentic and the inauthentic in the reported stories about the Prophet and his Companions. Only the recognition of the human side in the composition of the hadith can make them dynamic texts that speak to present readers, and this recognition can come only from a free and critical examination of them.

Obviously, in the climate that has prevailed in the Arab world and in Abu Zayd's home country Egypt since the 1950s, freedom and critique have been severely challenged. Abu Zayd's life and intellectual career have born the brunt of these challenges, and much of his work has been devoted to analyzing and confronting them. The phrase "thinking in the time of anathema," from the title of his 1995 book, captures the gist of his journey. The challenges to critical thinking, as most critical thinkers of this period have noted, are epistemological, psychological, and political. On the one hand, this period has been dominated by voluntaristic and authoritarian governments more concerned with staying in power than with ensuring popular legitimacy, accepting accountability, respecting opposition, and tolerating dissent. These governments have sometimes had to compensate for the lack of internal legitimacy with foreign support, thus reinforcing dependency and serving foreign-interest priorities. Consecutive governments have practiced various forms of intimidation, imprisonment, torture, and killing; instrumentalized religion whenever expedient; and co-opted mainstream religious establishments to cover governmental policies and outbid Islamist opposition claims. This opposition, in turn, has ironically not been less intolerant and authoritarian in its own methods and proposals, which it presents as an alternative to the current governments' unjust and impious rule. It too has not hesitated to use intimidation and violence. Together, governments and militant Islamists have silenced the secular and democratic forces.[28] The marginalization of these forces has left people with a choice between unjust, repressive government and religious authoritarian rule: under such circumstances, it is difficult to believe in democracy as a viable alternative, especially with the fears that it might bring to power the only organized oppositional force left on the ground, the Islamists. In the midst of the accusation campaign against him in 1993, Abu Zayd affirmed in an interview his commitment to democracy, but not without somber resignation:

> All of us defend democracy, but we place an implicit condition: that it not increase the power of anyone else. A lot has been said about the blood that might flow if the Islamists were to come to power, and therefore we should get rid of democracy before the Islamists do. That's part of the structure of closed thinking—that "we" know the truth and give ourselves the authority to predict and preempt the future. There was no democracy in Algeria, and Algeria has paid in blood for its absence. If the mechanisms of the political system bring one's opponent to victory, one does not stop resisting. Conceding victory doesn't mean surrendering. We are mixing two issues here: what it means to concede to others their rights, and what it means to surrender. The struggle for advancement won't ever be decided in the Arab world until it tries Islam—the Islam which the Islamists have in mind. Of course I'm scared. If they come to power, I'll be left out in the cold. No doubt about it. But my fears about my own personal safety should not outweigh my fears about the future of the umma [Islamic community]. Defending our opponents, the Islamists, as intellectuals is like defending ourselves as individuals. I don't mean to defend their interests, but I can't support freedom and say "except the Islamists." Some will tell you that when the Islamists talk about freedom, they mean freedom only for themselves. That's true. But that doesn't mean we should make the same mistake.[29]

Whether this scenario is the only one left for the Arab world and whether it is the only way to defend democracy and freedom in this context are difficult and decisive questions for Arabs today. The fact remains that the predicament described by Abu Zayd reflects the exacerbation of the crisis of freedom in Arab societies in the postindependence era.

To these stern political challenges are added the psychological problems caused by the decades of developmental failures, economic crises, and military defeats in a highly volatile region. Like most Arab intellectuals,

Abu Zayd notes the impact of the 1967 defeat on everyone, theorists and nontheorists alike. Anger, humiliation, and helplessness have pushed them to take refuge in a glorious past, in an authentic specificity that no vicissitude of history can alter, and of course in religion as a last resort of strength, hope, and sense of self. His book *Dawa'ir al-Khawf: Qira'a fi Khitab al-Mar'a* (The Circles of Fear: A Reading in the Discourse on Women), published in 2000, addresses the consequences of this frustration, manifested in increased intolerance and aggression toward the most vulnerable in society—primarily free thinkers, women, and minorities.[30] He notes how in the mid-1970s, at the time of the neoliberal policies (and the Camp David Agreement), attacks on Egyptian Christian Copts coincided with legislation sending working women back home, supposedly for their own good, for the good of their (and the nation's) children, and for the sake of solving the growing unemployment problem, caused in part by those policies. He reports how governmental media ridiculed women's professional ambitions and played on society's entrenched patriarchal reflexes, exposing women and their hard-won social rights to public disrespect, and how the media ultimately referred to the sacred book for justification—all this, of course, in tune with Islamists' reactionary positions regarding women. Women working outside the home were blamed for the thwarted development and the failed economic policies. Social problems, says Abu Zayd, were once again covered up with religious issues, and religious issues were reduced to textual certainties. Both critics and defenders of Islam soon fell into the trap of arguing with textual references disconnected from their contexts and historicity: for the critics, all ills are caused by Islam, and for the defenders, all solutions are found in Islam, and in both cases Islam is perceived ahistorically. Associated with gender essentialism and biological determinism, this textualism was and continues to be used to repress women, without coming in any way closer to solving socioeconomic and political problems. Not only is it risky to denounce these injustices and distortions in an atmosphere of intolerance and intellectual terror that can reach the level of physical aggression and elimination, it is also extremely delicate given the sensitivity of each issue, be it religion, women, or the nation. Like most critical thinkers discussed in this book, Abu Zayd finds himself torn between his solidarity with a people in pain, wounded in their dignity and identity, and his commitment to the sober analysis of the wounds that is necessary to any solution. Time and again he expresses both his outrage at obscurantist groups' manipulation of this despair and his irritation at having to prove good faith and good will with every critical statement. But to what extent is critique possible in this position between solidarity and critique? He raises this question about himself and about Arkoun in an article on the debate ensuing from the latter's analysis of the "wonderful" in his book *Lectures du Coran* (Readings of the Qu'ran).[31]

Abu Zayd salutes Arkoun's courage and freedom in tackling questions related to the reading of the sacred texts. He also appreciates Arkoun's position of solidarity, which Abu Zayd distinguishes from the Orientalists' pseudo-neutral position and the Islamist militants' opportunistic manipulative position. But Abu Zayd wonders to what extent this position of solidarity imposes on Arkoun's work certain concessions with regard to his critical project. This project, according to Abu Zayd, consists in reading the sacred texts independently from a theological commitment—that is, by suspending faith and theological creed. Yet the approach that Arkoun wants to adopt at the same time is that of a global reading that brings to the text the whole set of ritual and spiritual experiences of the text in the community of believers. To what extent can this approach be consistent with the historicization that Arkoun wants to conduct? Arkoun also aims at developing a linguistics that captures the mechanisms that transform the specific and the relative into the transcendental and the absolute, and through which religious language opens the reader to the experience of the spiritual, the "wonderful." Doesn't this approach amount to tying linguistics again to theology? asks Abu Zayd. In the article on Arkoun, he notes Arkoun's awareness that no reading can be innocent; he recognizes the latter's openness to self-critique if ideological elements are to be found in his own analysis of the sacred text. But Abu Zayd wonders to what extent his own thought might be inflected in turn by his position and his commitment. Some of this inflection is perceptible in his introduction to *The Circles of Fear*. In it, he reiterates the statement he made at the eve of the verdict that condemned him as an apostate and annulled his marriage: "I think, therefore I am Muslim."[32] He, like many liberal Muslim thinkers, recalls that the hadith promises a reward for efforts deployed to understanding the word of God, even those with a wrong result, and a double reward for efforts leading to a right result. He reaffirms the importance the Qur'an gives to the use of reason and asserts that an Islam sure of itself can and should afford free discussions and open debates. The problem is that Islam in this politically, militarily, economically, and culturally tormented Arab region is far from being sure and comfortable with itself.

Feminist Historicization of Religious Traditions:
Nazira Zain al-Din, Fatima Mernissi,
and Leila Ahmed

Feminists have also undertaken the historicization of traditional religious references to expose the sexist biases that have produced the established understanding of Islam. This task involves the contextualization of the development of these references, the identification of the social groups and power structures that have influenced their formation, the uncovering of alternative developments that took place over the course of history but were marginalized, if not suppressed, and finally the recognition of the possibility of developing alternative religious interpretations.

Among the early-twentieth-century feminist pioneers was the Lebanese scholar Nazira Zain al-Din (1908–1976), who contested the validity of the arguments presented in support of veiling, secluding, and discriminating against women. She presented her views in 1928 in *Al-Sufur wa al-Hijab* (Unveiling and Veiling). She was barely twenty years old. The book raised a heated discussion in the press among clerics and intellectuals. Zain al-Din collected their reactions and addressed them the following year in *Al-Fatat wa al-Shuyukh* (The Girl and the Sheikhs).[33] Trained in foreign schools in Lebanon, she was also familiar with Islamic religious sciences thanks to her father, who supported and encouraged her intellectual endeavors. He was the first president of the High Court of Appeals in Lebanon and a scholar in Islamic religion and jurisprudence. In his house, she met learned men, including religious scholars, with whom she debated with remarkable audacity and intelligence. The first book was prompted when Muslim clerics successfully pressured the Syrian government in 1927 to forbid women to circulate unveiled. She disputed the clerics' right to intervene in civil law and asked political authorities to legislate and apply laws that protected the freedom of individuals. She viewed the nation as an areligious community, composed of Christians and Muslims. She could not understand how a nation that demanded liberation from colonialism could oppress a sector of its own society.

Through her writings, Zain al-Din contested the authenticity of misogynistic hadith sayings, such as the one stating that women are inferior in reason and faith. She reclaimed for herself the right accorded to her by Islam to read religious texts, using her own free mind and independent will. She criticized those traditional clerics who accepted the misogynistic hadith stories without questioning and doubted those stories that valorized women. She attacked traditionalism in general and emphasized the importance of reason and individual judgment, both of which Islam encourages. According to her, judgment ought to be used in discerning the right from the wrong in the legacy handed down to us by the ancients. She recontextualized those verses of the Qur'an that lent themselves to a misogynistic reading and explained the lack of total egalitarianism in the holy book by saying that there must have been a limit to how much the new religion could challenge the mores of the time. As to religious legislation, she said that its sexist bias was due to the fact that exclusively men had produced it, whereas women would have been (and should be) more competent to legislate those aspects pertaining specifically to themselves. Faith, piety, chastity, and honor, she believed, could not be reduced to external appearances and certainly not to a piece of cloth such as a veil. The holy book, she thought, did not command veiling, nor did it stipulate the segregation of sexes. Veiling was not only an insult to women, but also to men because it portrayed men as being invariably traitors, aggressors, and violators of honor. She denounced the fact that men measured piety by the veiling of women even while disregarding their own immoral behavior. The failures and weaknesses of men and of clerics in particular, she concluded, distorted the liberating and empowering message of Islam. The discrimination against women was an aspect of those failures and weaknesses. Addressing her male critics, she wrote: "You have not developed with time. Time has folded your flags and you have squandered your ancestors' heritage. Do you want, now, to unfurl your flags over your women's faces, taking your women as a substitute kingdom for the kingdoms you have lost?"[34]

In the late 1980s, well-known Moroccan sociologist Fatima Mernissi published *Le harem politique* (translated as *The Veil and the Male Elite*), in which she examines the sayings attributed to the Prophet as well as the verses of the Qur'an used to justify misogynistic positions in Islam.[35] Like her predecessor, Mernissi claims the right as a Muslim to read and examine the tradition that has been transmitted to her as "the" authentic Islam on the basis of a whole corpus of sciences established in the few centuries following the Prophet's death: the *tafsir*, or commentaries on the Qur'an; the *asbab al-nuzul*, or the treatises on the situational causes of the revelations; the *nasikh* and the *mansukh*, or the treatises on the Qur'anic verses that, according to some experts, were nullified by later contradictory revelations; the hadith, or stories reported about the Prophet and his Companions; the *sira*, or biographies of the Prophet and the Companions, including the prominent women who were part of his life; and the legal schools of thought based on these explanations and interpretations—indeed, a voluminous body of scholarly work elaborated by generations of remarkable men of science and competence. Since then, this corpus has served as the firm foundation for the practice and understanding of Islam, but it is also a well-guarded tradition, says Mernissi, that has been used to exercise moral and political power: "It is not just the present that the imams and politicians want to manage to assure our well-being as Muslims, but above all the past that is being strictly supervised and completely managed for all of us, men and women. What is being supervised and managed, in fact, is memory and history. But up until now no one has ever really succeeded in banning access to memory and recollection." Further she adds: "Let us lift the veils with which our contemporaries disguise the past in order to dim our present."[36]

Given the significance of religion to Muslims' social and political life since the early times of Islam, this body of knowledge, according to her, has often been manipulated to serve the sexual and political interests of those in power—that is, the male elite—to such an extent that even at the earliest moment a way of distinguishing false from authentic stories about the Prophet had to be established using a wide range of knowledge concerning the chain of transmission, hence the sciences of *isnad* (attribution) and hadith. The men who developed these sciences were doubtless men of great intellectual and moral integrity who mastered an amazing range of encyclopedic knowledge. The most famous among them, such as Tabari and Bukhari, refused to yield to political or financial pressures, admits Mernissi: "If at the time of al-Bukhari—that is, less than two centuries after the death of the Prophet—there were already 596,725 false Hadith in circulation . . . it is easy to imagine how many there are today. The most astonishing thing is that the skepticism that guided the work of the founders of religious scholarship has disappeared today."[37] Hence, there is a need to reread and reassess this scholarship. Such a rereading shows, according to Mernissi, that even those solid scholars could not be infallible. Even they could make mistakes, and even they had their own personal, social, and historical biases. In *Le harem politique*, she undertakes the task of checking some of the misogynistic hadiths validated by reference to a serious source, such as Bukhari. One states that "those who entrust their affairs to a woman will never know prosperity," thus disenfranchising women in the political sphere; according to a second one, "the Prophet said that the dog, the ass, and woman interrupt prayer if they pass in front of the believer, interposing themselves between him and the *qibla*,"[38] thus affirming women's religious impurity and inferiority. She also analyzes verse 33 of sura 33 in the Qur'an, which is used to justify the veiling and seclusion of women. Finally, she discusses the issues of physical violence against women as well as slavery. Following the methods of the religious sciences, she refutes the validity of these sayings and exegetic interpretations, examining the chain of transmission and drawing on the circumstances of the ten years of the *hijra* in Medina,[39] where the Prophet was under great military and social pressure both from his enemies and from some of his followers. Her main conclusion is that the Prophet was far more respectful and loving toward women than were the later leaders of the community, such as Umar ibn al-Khattab.[40] Evaluating her findings and conclusions lies outside the scope of this study, but her critical historicizing and contextualizing of the established religious sciences are relevant for my purposes here. According to this approach, empirical cases of the Prophet's epoch need to be hermeneutically transposed to our times. In Abu Zayd's terminology, one would say they have to be used as "witness instances" instead of being taken literally, as has often been the case, especially in issues regarding women: "The imams," states Mernissi, "by remaining at the level of empirical cases, did not help Islam to develop a theory of the individual, of the sovereign, inviolable, changeless will that would not disappear in certain circumstances."[41]

It is interesting to note that Sudanese unorthodox reformer Mahmoud Mohamed Taha also takes up the distinction between the messages of Mecca and those of Medina as the basis for a new understanding of Islam.[42] According to him, the Meccan message was partly abrogated and partly modified by the Messenger in Medina to fit the circumstances of the time in view of coming back to it in the future, when people would become more susceptible to receiving it. He calls this Meccan message the Second Message of Islam, characterized by an egalitarian, democratic, socialist, and pacifist ethos. It is to become the basis for a new shari'a that will express true Islam, an Islam opposed to jihad as a violent means of propagating Islam as well as to slavery, capitalism, gender discrimination, discrimination against non-Muslims, polygamy, divorce, veiling, and the segregation of women from men. Again here I cannot discuss the tenability of Taha's hermeneutics, but I can add it to those attempts at reformulating Islam on the basis of an egalitarian and humane ethics.

In *Women and Gender in Islam: Historical Roots of a Modern Debate*, the U.S.-based Egyptian feminist Leila Ahmed puts Islamic gender issues in a comparative perspective, encompassing the cultures of Mesopotamia and the Mediterranean Middle East in order to dispel the exceptionalist approach so often taken in the field.[43] She then traces the development of gender views and practices under the influence of Islam in the course of history, from the rise and fall of the medieval Islamic Empire to the modern, colonial, and then independent Mediterranean states. Ahmed perceives in Islam two somewhat contradictory messages: a patriarchal hierarchy of the sexes, on the one hand, and an egalitarian ethics, on the other. The former, she says, has obviously found more resonance in the succeeding societies of Islamic history, especially among the rulers; like Mernissi, she thinks that the time of the Prophet was less misogynistic than the later periods—for instance, the time of Umar ibn al-Khattab—and far less misogynistic than the Abbasid period. This period witnessed the impressive growth of the Islamic Empire both in power and in wealth. The numerous conquests brought into the Islamic centers unprecedented riches, including slaves and concubines. Ahmed contends that this wealth led to the commodification and weakening of women in general. It accentuated the oppressive patriarchal way of life, and it is under such androcentric conditions that the foundational Islamic sciences were formulated, codified, and presented as the orthodox Islam. The interests of the powerful male elite that had shaped the Qur'anic sciences and the religious legislation were occulted. Even the compilation of the holy book itself, she thinks, could not have escaped the influence of those interests:

> *The role of interpretation in the preservation and inscription of the Quran is, however, suppressed in orthodox doctrine, and the belief that the text is precisely as Muhammad recited it is itself a tenet of orthodox faith. Similarly, to question whether the body of consecrated Islamic law does in fact represent the only possible legal interpretation of the Islamic vision is surrounded with awesome interdictions. That its central texts do embody acts of interpretation is precisely what orthodoxy is most concerned to conceal and erase from the consciousness of Muslims. This is understandable, because the authority and power of orthodox religion, whose interests were closely bound up in the Abbasid period with those of the ruling elite, and the state, depended on its claiming a monopoly of truth and on its declaring its versions of Islam to be absolute and all other interpretations heresies.[44]*

And yet alternative interpretations of the Qur'anic message did emerge, says Ahmed, among Kharijites, Sufis, and Qarmatians. Even in the orthodox legal schools, some divergences concerning marriage contracts and divorce laws indicate for her the possibility of other forms of religious laws. This margin of difference in the orthodox legislation "suggests that a reading by a less androcentric and less misogynist society, one that gave greater ear to the ethical voice of the Quran, could have resulted in—could someday result in—the elaboration of laws that dealt equitably with women."[45]

In the shedding of light on the interpretive and historical nature of the established religious tradition Ahmed sees the possibility of opening the horizon of religious understanding to new, more egalitarian, and more progressive versions of Islam:

> Both the more radical forms of Sufism and the Qarmatian movement diverged in their interpretation of Islam from orthodoxy in particular in that they emphasized the ethical, spiritual, and social teachings of Islam as its essential message and viewed the practices of Muhammad and the regulations that he put into effect as ephemeral aspects of Islam relevant primarily to a particular society at a certain stage in its history. Again, therefore, the issue is difference of interpretation, not in the sense of different understandings of particular words or passages but in a more radical, pretextual or supratextual sense of how to "read" Muhammad's acts and words and how to construe their relation to history. Was the import of the Islamic moment a specific set of ordinances or that it initiated an impulse toward a juster and more charitable society?[46]

An Islamic Theology of Liberation: The "Islamic Left" of Hassan Hanafi

That Islamic impulse toward a more charitable and just society is what Egyptian philosopher Hassan Hanafi, trained in phenomenology at the Sorbonne, wants to capture in his "Islamic Left" project. His aim is to mobilize the revolutionary forces of the Islamic heritage, sedimented in the hearts and minds of the masses, in order to fight local oppression and foreign hegemony and to struggle against the unjust distribution of wealth within the Islamic nation (the *umma*). The purpose of this Islamic Left is to fight the external dangers of Western imperialism and Zionist aggression and to confront the internal dangers of despotism, backwardness, and fanaticism. In combining leftist with Islamic orientations, Hanafi has opted for an uncomfortable position: the Islamists have suspected him of being a covert Marxist, and the secularists have suspected him of being in reality an Islamist. At least until 1989, he was forbidden entry to some Persian Gulf states, including Saudi Arabia, on the ground that he might be there to instigate an Islamic revolution. He was recently accused of blasphemy in Egypt.

In his early youth, Hanafi started as a member of the Muslim Brotherhood and moved toward a more leftist form of Islamism in the late 1970s. In 1967, he started a teaching career in Islamic and European philosophy at the University of Cairo. He translated Spinoza, Lessing, and Sartre, and devoted many studies to classical figures of Islamic thought. By 1981, he had completed the eight-volume work *Al-Din wa al-Thawra fi Misr (1952–1981)* (Religion and Revolution in Egypt [1952–1981]).[47] In the same year, he launched a periodical called *The Islamic Left*, which he devoted to his project. In its first issue, he explained the purposes, modalities, and motivations of such a project. He justified the need for it by the failure of the various projects of change in the Muslim world (of which the Arab world, according to him, was only a part, but a foundational part): the Islamic forces that came to power used Islam as a superficial cover for their alliance with the Western governments, local feudalism, and capitalism; many of the oppositional Islamic forces were dominated by fanaticism and Salafi orientations and were interested only in coming to power; the liberal movements were restricted to the upper classes and had adopted Western culture; westernized Marxist movements remained alien to the masses, found themselves caught in the power struggle of the foreign governments with which they were allied, and were increasingly concerned with their own survival; and finally, many of the revolutionary forces turned counterrevolutionary, and the rising middle classes started to be more interested in preserving the status quo than in revolutionary movements. The distinctive character of the Islamic Left, according to Hanafi, is on the one hand its connection to the culture of the masses, shaped to a great extent by an effective Islamic legacy, and on the other hand its serious commitment to opposing the current state of injustice and oppression—hence, the term *left*. He situates his project in continuity with those of Jamal al-Din al-Afghani and Muhammad Abduh and sees his periodical as the heir of theirs, *al-ʿUrwa al-Wuthqa* and *al-Manar*, respectively. He explains that instead of choosing what he calls a secular slogan—such as "Muslims of the world, unite!"—he adopted a Qurʾanic verse, thinking that it would resonate better with the masses: "And we desired to show favor unto those who were oppressed in the earth, and to make them examples and to make them the inheritors" (28:5). This is how he describes the association of religion with revolution: "The task of *The Islamic Left* is to uncover the revolutionary elements inherent in religion, or, if you wish, to show the common grounds of one and the other; that is, interpret religion as revolution. Religion is the gift of our heritage and revolution is the acquisition of this age. . . . This is not an external and forced reconciliation, for religion is in essence a revolution, and prophets were reformers, innovators and revolutionaries. . . . The historical record of prophethood in the Qur'an depicts it as a revolution against social and moral decay."[48]

Some Islamists, Hanafi adds, might say that in Islam there is no Left and Right. Yes, perhaps in principle it is so, he says, but in reality there are among Muslims the ruled and the rulers, the exploited and the exploiters. He often speaks of his work as a contribution toward a revolutionary theology similar to the Latin American theology of liberation. He is among the rare Arab thinkers, if not the only one, to show interest in this theology. In the collection of essays he published in 1976, *Fi Fikrina al-Mu'assir* (On Our Contemporary Thought),[49] he includes his long article "Religion and Revolution in Latin America: Camilio Torres, the Rebel Saint," in which he praises the courage and commitment of the militant priest Camilio Torres. However, his presentation does not offer reflections on the similarities and differences between this Latin American theology of liberation and his own Arab Muslim theology of revolution. Such a comparison would surely be a research project worth undertaking.

For Hanafi, the focus on the revolutionary elements of Islam is inspired by the many successful revolutions in recent and ancient history conducted in the name of Islam, such as the Iranian and Algerian revolutions and the much earlier one led against the Crusaders. As he explains in the first issue of *The Islamic Left*, he understands his Islamic revolution to be primarily civilizational rather than political:

> The Islamic *Left is not a political thesis, as may be inferred from the term "left," but a civilizational one as denoted by the term "Islam."* The Islamic Left *intends to highlight the points of advance in our heritage such as rationalism, naturalism, freedom and democracy which are what we need in this century. It uncovers two dimensions which we overlooked in our tradition and which caused the crisis ailing our modern awareness: Man and history. We wrapped Man and isolated*

him into a personified being or doctrinal law, and, as a result, we lived
at the margin of our world and lost ourselves and our lives.

The civilizational revolution of the Islamic Left is to be directed against
two fronts: the external front of Western imperialism and the internal
front of local despotism. On the first front, the task is to denounce the fake
"purity" and universalism of European civilization by showing its many
foreign components, the Islamic in the first place, and by pushing it back to
its own geographical and historical boundaries. It is to launch, as mentioned earlier, an "Occidentalism" in the sense of a science of the West that
makes Western civilization an object of study, while avoiding the biases
and distortions with which Westerners produced Orientalism. "*The Islamic Left* takes upon itself the task of pushing Western civilization back to
its natural boundaries and demonstrating its provinciality and growth according to its specific circumstances, its particular history, its religion and
the character of its peoples. This will enable us to break the siege under
which non-European nations are placed, to show the specificities of these
nations and assert their identities. Thus, the civilizational models will multiply and the ways of progress will diversify."[50] As indicated earlier, instead
of a future plural world of civilizations, Hanafi thinks in terms of an Islam-
centered and Islam-led world civilization to replace Eurocentrism. His
science of the Occident fails to fulfill its promise.

The civilizational revolution is also to be directed against the internal
problems of oppression, poverty, and backwardness, for the "best nation of
the earth" is not only defeated and humiliated by foreigners, but also impoverished and repressed by its own rulers:

No nation on earth is suffering from repression, oppression and tyr-
anny more than Muslim nations are. Thus, our life confirms what the
West said about us and called it "The autocracy of the East," wherein
only one individual, the president, is free and does as he wishes, and
everyone else, in Hegelian terms, is disempowered, oppressed and has
no freedom, as Hegel says. We have become the example of the lack of
democracy and public freedom, and the supremacy of customary and
extraordinary laws. Human rights committees are sent to us to inves-
tigate the conditions of our detainees, unions are dissolved, elections
are subjected to fraud, military coups are staged, one opinion domi-
nates, one party rules, and we kill each other. Those in power are pa-
triots, and those outside of it are traitors. After a coup d'état, however,

yesterday's hero becomes today's traitor and the traitor of today the hero of tomorrow. The criteria of patriotism and freedom have vanished, and he who holds power has become the exclusive patriot. The state controls everything and steers national awareness through the mass media so much that Muslim peoples are no longer able to express the other view, and opposition is erased and, whenever it emerged despite tyranny and oppression, is charged with treason, collaboration, heresy and atheism.

And to complete the picture of the wretched situation, he enumerates the people's three main concerns or obsessions, echoing the majority of critical Arab thinkers: "Backwardness is also evident in the retreat of reason in the face of the divinely prohibited and the sacred (taboos) we fear to come close to: Allah, the government and sex, even though we think of them night and day and experience them in our imagination to make up for our deprivation."

Moreover, the civilizational revolution is not to be a textual one. It is to be based on the realities of the Muslim world, on facts and statistics, as he says, raising questions about the distribution of wealth and issues of injustice rather than centered on detached preaching or rhetorical manipulation. And yet, despite a strongly articulated antitextual position, Hanafi himself focuses his work on the renewal of heritage by using elaborate studies of textual references. Instead of asking "Who owns what?" as he advocates, what he does in his actual work is to raise again the standard question: What went wrong in our culture, more particularly in our religious sciences? He seeks no social scientific, economic, geographical, historical, or legal data, but once more simply revisits and analyzes religious disciplines. Just before publishing *The Islamic Left*, he had presented his project of heritage renewal in *Al-Turath wa al-Tajdid* (Heritage and Renewal) in 1980, and in 1988 the entire project was published in five volumes under the title *Min al-ʿAqida ila al-Thawra: Muhawala fi Iʿadat Binaʾ ʿIlm Usul al-Din* (From Doctrine to Revolution: An Attempt at Rebuilding Fundamental Theology).[51] His justification for such an endeavor in the context of an Islamic Left is that in order to change reality, one needs to change the forms of awareness of reality, and Muslims' awareness is to a great extent shaped by the accumulated body of beliefs and worldviews in the transmitted legacy. This psychological reservoir (*al-makhzun al-nafsi*) of beliefs and thoughts needs to be addressed and reformed by revisiting the four religious disciplines that constitute the core of the Islamic legacy: theology, philosophy, jurisprudence, and Sufism. The reconstruction of this legacy should consist in (once again) recuperating the rational elements and discarding the nonrational ones. It is the loss of the rational elements that, according to him, has caused the decline of Islamic culture. Here, we are back to the culturalist-idealist approach to the crisis, despite all the intentions to draw attention to economic and political issues. The reconstruction project aims at highlighting the secular nature of Islam and at transforming the religious sciences into human sciences: theology and philosophy into a cultural anthropology, the doctrine of the imamate into political science, the debate about reason and tradition into an epistemology and methodology, the questions of free will into psychology, the old natural sciences into the modern ones, and metaphysics into social psychology or sociology of knowledge; the disciplines of jurisprudence are to be transformed into modern disciplines of law, politics, and economics; and finally, mysticism is to be transformed into psychology and ethics. Anke Von Kügelgen and Abu Zayd agree that this reconstruction sacrifices analytic accuracy, historical precision, and scholarly rigor for a preset ideological agenda.[52]

Indeed, Abu Zayd devotes a long chapter of his book *Naqd al-Khitab al-Dini* (The Critique of Religious Discourse) to Hassan Hanafi's Islamic Left. Contrary to the Salafi discourse, he says, Hanafi's project does not want to shape the present after the past. It shows an awareness of the historicity of transmitted legacies and in this sense offers better chances for an effective renewal. However, it does not draw the rigorous consequences of this historicity. It seems to understand history as a chain of events rather than as sets of economic and political power structures. It fails to examine carefully the sedimentation process through which tradition becomes a lived awareness, a "psychological reservoir," a *makhzun nafsi*, a process that involves complex forces and circumstances of selection and activation. Moreover, Abu Zayd points out, even with a certain historicist understanding of tradition, the past in Hanafi's thought remains omnipresent, and the focus on tradition remains its common point with the Salafi approach, despite their differences on other points. Both the Islamic Left and the Salafi conservative Islamism hold on to the centrality of tradition; it is for them the storehouse of problems and solutions: for the latter, Islam is the solution, and for the former, the renewal of *turath* is the solution. Furthermore, Hanafi presents his project as a conciliation between the two antagonistic movements of the nation, the secularist and the Salafist, although in reality they are not as opposed as he claims they are. Both use *turath*—the former as a support to its claims, and the latter as a frame of reference; their disagreement is on the use of *turath*. Hanafi's project suffers, according to Abu Zayd, from the tensions of this conciliatory position not only between secularism and conservatism, but also between the old and the new, and more so since it does not thoroughly examine the intricate elements of their dialectics. Finally, the Islamic Left fails to reach its goal: it does not account for the complexities of the dialectical tensions; it freezes the present in the past; its reconstruction of heritage amounts to an ideological coloring rather than an epistemological rebuilding; it does not consider seriously the consequences of the historicity of tradition; and it remains an idealist approach to culture and tradition. Yet despite these important weaknesses, Hanafi's project remains for Abu Zayd a more promising endeavor than the conservative Salafism.

Mahmud Amin al-Alim criticizes Hanafi along similar lines.[53] To want to revolutionize the present by revolutionizing tradition is, in al-Alim's opinion, anachronistic. It presupposes falsely that the present is shaped mainly by dominating concepts and that these concepts are the same as those of tradition, unaffected by the passage of time. Equally anachronistic is Hanafi's project of critiquing the old legacy from the viewpoint of today's needs and concerns. This legacy's questions and priorities are not ours. Hanafi's work, according to al-Alim, is a present-day engagement with tradition that does not become a renewal of that tradition. Rhetoric and polemics dominate this engagement. Heritage is reduced to the religious legacy, and the latter is reduced to the Islamic-Sunni tradition.

Egyptian secular critic Fouad Zakariyya, whose work I examine in the next chapter, offers a more condemning assessment of Hanafi's thoughts on religious mobilization and Islamic fundamentalism. In his 1988 collection of essays *Al-Haqiqa wa al-Khayal fi al-Haraka al-Islamiyya al-Mu'assira* (*Myth and Reality in the Contemporary Islamist Movement*),[54] Zakariyya devotes three chapters to Hanafi's work. He finds him incapable of self-reflection and accuses him of subjectivism regarding the Islamists. Hanafi lets his thoughts be carried away by his emotional support for them and fails to recognize their dangerous disrespect for democracy, their fixation on ritual religiosity and gender discrimination, their reactionary stand in theological matters, and their disinterest in the people's political and economic struggles. Zakariyya thinks that Hanafi himself remains inconsistent on questions of exegesis, theological innovation, and modernization: at times he seems to be praising literalist jurists of the medieval past as defenders of Islamic authenticity, but at other times he seems to be advocating change and progress. For Zakariyya, Hanafi's work suffers from lack of depth and critical rigor.

A Christian Arab Theology of Liberation: Naim
Ateek and Mitri Raheb in Palestine-Israel

A different liberation theology comes from Palestine through the work of Arab Christian theologians. It aims at connecting the Christian Gospel to the lived experiences of the people there, whether in the occupied territories or inside the state of Israel. It stems from the need to reconcile the belief in a God of justice, peace, and love with the harsh realities of occupation, dispossession, and discrimination. It attempts at rereading the sacred texts after their appropriation by Zionist endeavors, both Jewish and Christian. I focus here on the works of Naim Stifan Ateek and Mitri Raheb.[55] The first is canon of the Anglican St. George's Cathedral in Jerusalem and pastor of its Arabic-speaking congregation, trained at the San Francisco Theological Seminary, and the second is the pastor of the Evangelical Lutheran Christmas Church in Bethlehem, trained at Marburg University in Germany.[56]

Both theologians see the need to liberate their faith and contextualize it—that is, to let the word of God speak to the people in their concrete situation—because they believe in the importance of facing theologically and ecclesiastically the challenges their situation poses for the Christian message. They find it imperative to work toward a liberation theology that can make their faith meaningful to their own particular context, which is different from the Western one and which is deeply marked by the existence of the state of Israel. Both men are strongly committed to a nonviolent resolution of the conflict. Both believe in a two-state solution to the problem, and both acknowledge the centrality of the Jewish Holocaust in the making of the Jewish state and worldview. However, they think that a post-Auschwitz Christian theology should not be blinded to the Palestinians' suffering. For them, peace cannot be achieved without recognizing the wrong done to both people.

Interestingly, Ateek and Raheb begin their respective books, *Justice and Only Justice: A Palestinian Theology of Liberation* and *I Am a Palestinian Christian*, by presenting their complex identities as Arabs, Palestinians, and Christians of different denominations. Moreover, they have different relationships with Israel: Ateek is an Israeli citizen living in Jerusalem, and Raheb is a Palestinian resident from Bethlehem and so an inhabitant of the

occupied territories.[57] The two authors obviously see the need to inform
their readers about the ill-known realities of the Christians of the Holy
Land—ill known especially in the West, where people often automatically
equate "Arab" with "Muslim" and do not realize that the oldest churches
and the first Christian communities were in the Middle East. These communities did become minorities with time, after the rise of Islam, the establishment of the consecutive Islamic states in the region, and the socioeconomic difficulties facing their communities as a result of the Israeli
occupation of the West Bank. Raheb explains briefly the present realities
and challenges of these minority communities in Palestine-Israel and describes the implications that they have for the emergence of a liberation
theology and policy in their churches.[58] Ateek starts with an overview of
the Palestinian-Israeli conflict and shows how it continues to affect the
Christian communities. For him, the challenge of a liberation theology is,
among other things, to transmogrify this marginalized minority condition into one of dynamic witness.[59] However, the two men remain ecumenical in their Christian outlook, in their solidarity with their Muslim
compatriots, and in their search of a peaceful understanding with the
Israeli state. Both search for ways of remaining true to the Christian call
to love one's enemy in the midst of protracted repression, violence, and
injustice.

The call on the church as an institution to stand with the poor and the
weak against injustice and oppression and to cease its alignment with the
rich and powerful is common to all liberation theologies, whether in North
America (among the African Americans), Latin America, or South Africa.[60]
Equally common to them is the need for a new theology that is responsive to
the lived realities of the people in the different contexts. It is no surprise that
they have been met with some resistance from the established traditional
ecclesiastical institutions, especially from the older and more centralized
churches, which would perhaps not wish to politicize the message of the
Bible. What distinguishes the Palestinian problem from the problems on
other continents is that it is burdened with the existence of a "biblical" state,
justified on the basis of a biblical text. It inevitably puts the sacred text, its
message, and its inspirer in a particular light. Raheb expresses this dilemma
in the following way:

The Joshua and David so familiar to me suddenly became politicized,
somehow no longer seen in continuity with Jesus, as they used to be.
They were instead placed into a kinship with Menachem Begin and

Yitzhak Shamir. Their conquests were no longer for spiritual values but for land—my land in particular.

My Bible now showed an aspect previously unseen by me. The Bible I had heretofore considered to be "for us" had suddenly become "against us." It was no longer a consoling and encouraging message to me but a frightening word. My salvation and that of the world were not the issue in the Bible any longer. The issue was my land, which God had promised to Israel and in which I no longer had a right to live unless I was as a "stranger." The God I had known since my childhood as love had suddenly become a God who confiscated land, waged "holy wars," and destroyed whole peoples. I began to doubt this God. I started to hate this God and quietly became "indignant at God, if not with blasphemy at least with great grumbling."[61]

In a similar vein, Ateek writes:

Before the creation of the State, the Old Testament was considered to be an essential part of Christian Scripture, pointing and witnessing to Jesus. Since the creation of the State, some Jewish and Christian interpreters have read the Old Testament largely as a Zionist text to such an extent that it has become almost repugnant to Palestinian Christians. As a result, the Old Testament has generally fallen into disuse among both clergy and laity, and the Church has been unable to come to terms with its ambiguities, questions, and paradoxes—especially with its direct application to the twentieth-century events in Palestine. . . . What has been seriously questioned is the nature and character of God. What is God really like? What is God's relation to the new State of Israel? Is God partial only to the Jews? Is this a God of justice and peace? . . . The answer lies largely in the doing of theology.[62]

For Ateek, "the doing of theology" necessitates reclaiming the Bible in a spirit of love and peace. It requires de-Zionizing and demythologizing the sacred text through a hermeneutics that allows its reconciliatory and liberational message to be heard. Within the Jewish tradition, he recognizes three approaches to the Scriptures: a nationalist approach based on an exclusively ethnic relatedness to God; a Torah-oriented approach focused on the legal aspect of the religion; and a prophetic approach that emphasizes the ethical-universalist dimension of Judaism. According to him, the creation of the state of Israel empowered the Jewish people materially, but impoverished it spiritually by narrowing its scope to the exclusively ethnic horizon and by damaging its ethical integrity. Among the Jewish thinkers who critically reflect on this "empowerment versus ethics" problematic is Marc Ellis, with whom Ateek has been in dialogue for many years. The two men and Raheb refer to each other's work.[63] Ellis deplores the ethical prejudice that empowerment has brought to the Jews with the state of Israel. For him, genuine Jewish liberation can happen only through the serious pursuit of justice and peace, especially with the Palestinians, who became the first victims of their empowerment. True liberation, he argues, should preserve the memory of slavery and oppression lest it lead to forgetfulness and consequently to renewed oppression, this time at the hands of the former victims. However, perpetuating a constant sense of victimhood can itself lead to an unhealthy attitude. The challenge is to find a healthy balance between remembrance and forgetfulness.

Raheb, too, believes that some of the basic biblical notions—such as election, the promised land, and the exodus—need to be revisited. Election, he says, should be understood as a statement of faith, a promise, a call to service rather than as a claim, a privilege, or an ideology. The promise of the land, he feels, is meant by God as a call to obedience to His will and to justice. The exodus is also to be understood as a universal promise of liberation from oppression to a life of righteousness and not as an exclusive license given to the Jewish people to dispose of land and property.

Both Ateek and Raheb believe that the minority status of the Arab Christian communities has spared their churches the temptations of power, unlike the Jewish and Muslim communities and unlike the Western churches. Ateek says: "In contrast to both Judaism and Islam, Christianity in Israel-Palestine exists as a minority. Christians live their lives in a pre-Constantinian context. The object of much persecution, they have endured faithfully throughout the centuries, sustaining their faith tenaciously against great odds. Even now, when many Muslims and Jews are living in a spirit of militant triumphalism, the Church continues to live in the shadow of the cross."[64] And Raheb writes: "Arab Christians were sometimes made forcefully aware that their Western co-religionists cultivated a Christianity strange to them. Arab Christian existence was strongly linked to the sign of the cross from the very beginning. To them, the cross was the reality of a suffering church rather than the inheritance of a triumphant church. Western churches, on the other hand, related the sign of the cross to power, vested interests, and expansion."[65]

What is this theology of the cross that these Palestinian theologians are advocating? It is certainly not that of helpless victimhood, nor is it that of apocalyptic chastisement. It is rather a theology that calls for enduring suffering in the hope of redemption in peace and is sought through resisting injustice and working for reconciliation. Raheb reflects on the meaning of loving one's enemy in the Israeli-Palestinian context: "To love one's enemy means neither to cover up the conflict nor to downplay its seriousness, but rather to endure the tension inherent in that conflict without succumbing to hatred. One should love the persons but not the unjust acts they commit. To love one's enemy means, therefore, that despite the conflict one recognizes the enemy as a creature of God who has a right to live, to be forgiven, and to love—but not the right to commit an unjust act."[66] Ateek elaborates on the challenges of this endurance:

It took me all these years to accept the unacceptable: a Jewish state on part of "our" Palestine. As a boy, remembering my family's harsh exile from Beisan, and later, as a person of faith and a clergyman, my own struggles with hate, anger, and humiliation were not easy. But these feelings had to be challenged continuously by the demands of love and forgiveness. At the same time, I knew without a doubt that injustice is sinful and evil; that it is an outrage against God; and that it is my duty to cry out against it. It has taken me years to accept the establishment of the State of Israel and its need—although not its right—to exist. I now feel that I want it to stay, because I believe that the elimination of Israel would mean greater injustice to millions of innocent people who know no home except Israel. . . .

In other words, any proposed solution involving Israel should be an offer I would accept for my people, the Palestinians. Every proposal should be weighed carefully so that each side can recognize it as good and just to both. Otherwise, the proposal would have no credibility.[67]

These challenges are indeed trying, and the temptation to channel all this hate, anger, humiliation, and suffering into various forms of triumphalism is all too human. None of the three religions in question is immune to this temptation, especially when it can refer to a powerful state in the present, such as Israel, or to a mighty state of the past, such as the Islamic Empire. But these triumphalist reactions to pain inhibit the deeper and more constructive exploration of an ethical reaction that calls for the moral radicalization of the search for justice and peace. The challenges facing the Arab Muslim communities in the region are formidable, and the levels of anger and humiliation ever higher. Nevertheless, a Muslim prophetic liberation theology that can overcome the shortcomings of Hanafi's Islamic Left would be a valuable contribution to a more life-affirming orientation in the culture of the region.[68]

In these Christian and Muslim Arab communities, there is a sense of revolt against political and economic injustice, expressed, among other ways, in religious mobilization. In both communities, there is a search for means of empowerment in the face of so much oppression and helplessness—hence, the centrality of this notion of empowerment and the importance of reflecting on it critically. It may be the disguised blessing for Arab Christians to have a minority status that enhances their sensitivity to the prophetic vocation of their faith, especially when they manage to resist despair and emigration—knowing, of course, that even within this minority group, the prophetic voice would itself be a minority voice. Such a prophetic theology would be *une pensée autre*, a "different thought," to use a formulation coined by the Moroccan thinker Abdelkebir al-Khatibi, to whose work I turn in the next chapter. This "different thought," born of the margins, would be protected from the lethal temptation toward a monistic and totalizing self-sufficiency. But what are the chances that this prophetic voice will be heard in such a tense conflictual setting? What are the chances of Muslim and Jewish (and Arab Jewish) prophetic-liberational voices being heard in the region?

Egyptian feminist Leila Ahmed deplores the absence of the ethical and spiritual dimensions in the mobilization of Islam called to the cause of Islamist feminism and nationalism. Commenting on the autobiographical narrative of the Islamist feminist Zeinab al-Ghazali, she writes:

> As the testament of a religious revolutionary, al-Ghazali's account is striking in a number of ways. First, it is remarkable that a spiritual commitment to Islam seems to be absent. Islam figures as a path to empowerment, to glory, to a properly regulated society—but not as a spiritual path. Similarly, the qualities of a reflective consciousness, of an acuity of moral perception, which might be expected in someone with a religious mission, again seem to be absent. . . .
>
> Al-Ghazali's account is striking in the second place for the openness with which it links the need to restore Islam with the need to restore a

nation suffering from the humiliations of imperialism and for the openness with which it preaches that Islam is the path to power and glory. The call to Islam is not made to call souls to God or proclaim a fundamental truth but to restore to power and give "control [of] the whole world" to the nation of Islam.[69]

In the critical theology I reviewed in this chapter, I noted the search for a new hermeneutics: an effort to historicize sacred texts, whether the Qur'an or the Bible, without putting in question their divine character. Muslim theologians see the need to historicize the Qur'an against the ab-soluticization of allegedly atemporal readings and transmissions of it; and Christian theologians see the need to historicize the Bible against the Zionist readings of it, whether Christian or Jewish. Moreover, theologians of both Christian and Muslim Arab communities emphasize the importance of contextualizing their faiths—that is, of introducing in them the necessary changes that allow them to speak to the people in their present and local realities. In both cases, theology is to become more immanent, more lively, and more responsive, breaking the alleged fixity of religious traditions as well as adopting and initiating new modes of thinking and new modes of believing that cannot but have an impact on the culture in general.

On the Potential for Critique of Traditional Islam: Talal Asad's Analysis of the Public Criticism by Ulemas in Saudi Arabia

So far in this chapter, I have looked at attempts to open Islamic thought—that is, theology, exegesis, prophetic tradition, and jurisprudence—to new horizons of interpretation, by subjecting the texts these attempts produced in the course of time to a historicizing critique. By revealing the human context of the formation and transformations of this textual production, this critique has called for the elaboration of a new hermeneutic that responds to the needs and values of the present day. We also saw the attempt at mobilizing religion to fight economic and political injustice by transforming Islam into a theology of revolution. All these attempts have faced challenges and obstacles from the massive literary tradition, from the resistance to changing intellectual habits, from the concern with identity affirmation and defensiveness, as well as from state repression, patriarchal resistance, and intimidation, if not anathematization, by militant Islamists.

However, critique has also been practiced by traditional clerics who explicitly distance themselves from the rebellious ambitions of militant Islamist groups. The U.S.-based British anthropologist Talal Asad analyzes a powerful instance of this type of critique, namely an open letter written and signed by several hundred Saudi ulemas and addressed to the king of Saudi Arabia as the "Servant of the two noble Sanctuaries [Mecca and Medina], may God prosper him," and hence as the leader of the Saudi religious community. The letter was published in May 1991 in the aftermath of the Gulf War, which resulted in the stationing of U.S. troops on Saudi soil. It came out in the form of a leaflet that was distributed throughout the kingdom, but not publicized in the private and state Saudi media. It formulated the following demands, as quoted and translated by Asad: " 'The establishment of a consultative assembly to adjudicate on domestic and foreign affairs . . . with complete independence, . . . a just distribution of public wealth, . . . guarantee of the rights of the individual and of society,' and the removal of all infringements on the wishes and rights of people, including human dignity . . . , in accordance with legitimate . . . and recognized moral rules . . . as well as a complete and thorough review of all political, administrative, and economic organizations in the kingdom to ensure that they are run in accordance with the Islamic *shariʿa*."[70] Interestingly, Asad reports that shortly after the publication of this letter, another one with a more deferential tone was sent to the king (addressed as "king" and hence as a political leader), this time signed by a number of Western-educated Saudis asking for modernizing reforms.

The ulemas' demands clearly indicate a serious failing in the performance of the king and head of the community of believers on such fundamental matters as human dignity, individual and social rights, and domestic and foreign affairs, including the economic, the administrative, and the political. The ulemas based their criticism on the central notion of *nasiha* (advice) in Islamic moral theology: the exhortation to do good and avoid evil that every Muslim owes to his fellow Muslim by offering arguments to convince the other person, without the use of violence and in proper ways that reassure him or her of the good faith behind the advice. This morally corrective criticism is the obligation of good Muslims—including rulers, especially if they are unjust—to their community. It is based on the most important (and well-known) sayings of the Prophet reported in the hadith: "Whosoever of you sees an evil action, let him change it with his hand; and if he is unable to do so, then with his tongue; and if he is not able to do so, then with his heart—and that is the weakest part of faith"; and "If something is done with kindness and gentleness it is thereby beautified, and if it is done with force and violence it is thereby rendered ugly." The ulemas' *nasiha* is further based on the notable precedent of public criticism directed at a head of state by thirteenth-century jurist Ibn Taymiyya, who went to jail for publicly admonishing the prince for not doing what he ought to do. The ulemas' public criticism belongs to an orthodox discourse that has, according to Asad, its own requirements. It does not build on sheer authoritarianism, as some may tend to think. It is to offer a persuasive argument on the basis of tradition-guided reasoning and within the boundaries of a discursive coherence. Although tradition-bound, the ulemas' discourse in this criticism addresses a current situation and a new social space formed by modern institutions (administrative, economic, ideological) and modern social classes (Western-educated citizens): in this sense, Asad thinks that it is thus part of modernity rather than a reaction to it, as is often held.

The answer to the letter came not from the king, but from his Council of Senior Ulemas, who deplored its public character. Asad reports two arguments that the critical ulemas formulated in support of making their advice public, however: first, a moral argument pertaining to the public nature of the matter, namely the *umma*'s (Islamic community's) public good, of which both the people and the ruler need to be aware; and second, a tactical argument saying that all advice given to the king privately had been so far ignored and that the criticism would have more chances to be heard in a public forum.

Asad's purpose in focusing on this open letter is to refute the widespread claim that the practice of public criticism is alien to Islam and that Islamic states do not have room for it because of their absolutist character. He considers the rise of public criticism in Western absolutist states, in particular that of Kant under Frederick the Great. This criticism, too, had been bound by certain limits, as shown in Kant's unpublished letter to the king promising him not to attack religion in public. The limits set by the political power are also seen in Kant's distinction between the private and the public use of reason: in the first case, reason is to give precedence to the obedience of established laws and authorities in the realm of official and professional duties; in the second case, reason is to exercise its full critical powers in the intellectual realm, the public of readers and writers. The first limit is a political one, and the second is a sociological one, the restriction to a small circle of intellectuals. As Asad notes, some see in Kant's invitation to legal and political obedience a justification for state authoritarianism, but others detect in Kant's public critical reason the development of the liberating aspects of secular, bourgeois society. What Asad wants to draw attention to is the difference in the genealogies of these two types of public criticism, which are connected to different genealogies of state formation, instead of to the measurement of one type (the Islamic) according to the history of the other (the Western). In the Western case, the setting is that of the political authority of a strong state (eighteenth-century Prussia) in which religion is on the retreat and feared for its disrupting effect on social peace and stability. In the postindependence Islamic states, such as Saudi Arabia, religion in the context of a theocracy has the upper hand and shapes public criticism accordingly. Recalling the practice of criticism in traditional Islamic institutions also refutes those claims that hold religion and reason, and so religion and critique, to be natural opposites. Asad refers here to positions such as Sadeq Jalal al-Azm's.

This is not to say, adds Asad, that the ulemas' public criticism is not limited and limiting; he agrees here with many Saudis who think so. But the limitations are not due to religious thinkers' intrinsic incapacity to contemplate change or to the fundamental contradiction between religion and reason. They are rather due to the particular articulation of a discursive tradition at a certain point in time. For many, including numerous Saudis, the ulemas' criticism entails a system of divinely ordained norms as well as a controlled moral disciplining that may not be acceptable to all in a universal sense. Indeed, it assumes people to be members of a preestablished moral space rather than universal and autonomous individuals inhabiting the morally neutral, rational space of political liberalism. Here Asad contests the moral neutrality of modern political liberalism, which he sees as heavily shaped by secularized Christian values, and recalls the different conceptions of rationality that have prevailed in the course of Western intellectual history.[71] Further, he adds that secular ideologies have not been immune to tyranny, contending that what is decisive in matters of tyranny and freedom is not what justification is used to legitimize power, but rather the behavior that is adopted in this justification. For him, what makes Islamic public criticism seem so radically different is the fact that it is evaluated by a dominating Western discourse: "Finally: It is necessary to stress that I am not concerned with the truth or otherwise of Saudi religious beliefs but with the kind of critical reasoning involved in *nasiha*. I have tried to show that the Islamic tradition is the ground on which that reasoning takes place. And that is no more than may be said about political and moral reasoning within the modern liberal tradition—except that modern liberalism deploys powers that are immeasurably greater, including the flexible power to construct a 'universal, progressive history,' which the other tradition does not possess. That today is the main condition that limits religious criticism in the contemporary Middle East."[72]

Asad's attack on Islam's exceptional and intrinsic incapacity to allow public criticism is well taken, as is his contextualization of the emergence of such criticism in the state genealogies of the West and the Middle East. But as we saw throughout this chapter, the limits on religious criticism are not set only by the Eurocentric hegemonic discourse. Moreover, granted that Western liberalism is reasoned on the ground of a specific cultural and religious tradition, one would still have to admit that a secular, liberal state provides a significantly larger margin of freedom than a theocracy, especially in terms of the liberties of worship, thought, and expression. This distinction, of course, does not preclude the existence of a religious voice of critique, as a voice among others, within a secular, liberal state. Indeed, the co-optation of the traditional religious institutions by postindependent Arab states did result in the loss of an important critical, potentially oppositional voice, especially in societies in which religion plays a significant role. This co-optation was part of a state policy aimed at repressing all oppositional and independent forces of civil society. Furthermore, as some have indicated, one can also imagine the development of some Islamist movements into religion-inspired political parties, like the Christian Democrat Party in Germany for instance.

Islamic Critique and the Cultural Malaise

Religious modernization was among the prime Nahda projects. Consecutive Nahda figures from al-Tahtawi to al-Afghani to Abduh called for modernizing the education of the ulemas, the Muslim clerics who bore, according to them, a great deal of responsibility for the backward state of Muslim societies. Al-Afghani and Abduh thought that a modernizing reformation was more natural to Islam than it was to Christianity because of Islam's inherent inclination toward rationality and because of the absence of a clerical body (at least theoretically) in it. A close analysis of their conception of the European Reformation and a comparison between their own reform projects and those of the Christian reformers of sixteenth-century Europe still need to be made. Religion was central in the Nahda movement for a number of reasons. On the one hand, most of the early Nahda figures were clerics themselves because, as in most traditional societies, clerics were the ones to benefit from some form of education and thus to play the role of an intelligentsia. On the other hand, Arab societies were religious in general, the way traditional societies everywhere typically are, and so religion governed many sectors of social life, from education to law, morality, and social mores. Thus, any modernizing change in public life necessitated a change in religion, and the early Nahda figures were eager to introduce this change. Understandably, their calls and attempts were met with resistance on the part of the religious establishment, especially when they involved theological matters that touched on the sacred text and on the consecrated tradition. In the course of the twentieth century, however, the more Islam was mobilized to serve as a defensive identity ideology and the more it was politicized to face external and internal threats, the more difficult it became to approach it in critical and innovative ways.

Arkoun and Abu Zayd belong to this line of Nahda reformers; however, they come at a time when the mobilization and politicization of Islam is at its highest. But it is also a time when the work of critique is most needed in order to breathe new intellectual and even spiritual life into religion and to reclaim theology as a discipline of reflection that requires freedom of thought and freedom of expression and that necessitates a long-term commitment to genuine work free from the circumstantial manipulation of religious ideas. The emphasis on the human component in religious traditions—be it in the exegesis of religious texts, in the legislation of religious laws, or in the very constitution and transmission of tradition—is extremely important: it opens the way to an active and critical reappropriation of these traditions to those living today, and it breaks the rigid authoritarianism with which certain historical forms of understanding Islam have been imposed as "the" correct, objective, and unique way of understanding it. The historicity of revelation is in this respect one of the major issues of contemporary theological critique. Its proponents claim for themselves the critical spirit with which the early theologians of Islam operated. The humanization and historicization of Islamic theology obviously cannot but bear the fruits of critique on the wider cultural scene: hence the importance of sustaining such efforts in spite of violent rejection and marginalization. It is important here to appreciate the perseverance of these critical theologians, including the feminists among them, in the face of these reactions.

The inconsistencies of Hanafi's work, in contrast, show the challenges that surround this critical path and the ways in which critique can slide back into ideology, textualism, and revengeful claims of power—as indicated, for instance, in his wishful prediction that an Islam-centered world will replace a West-centered world. His project of mobilizing the people's Islam in the struggle for economic and political justice is interesting, but it lacks rigor and depth. A more radically critical reflection on issues of faith, empowerment, and liberation may produce more promising Islamic theologies of liberation. But such a radicalization of critique is wanting not only in Islamic theology, but also in Christian and Jewish theologies as well. They all need to address the following questions: What does it mean to seek empowerment in religion? Is it to identify oneself with politically, economically, and even in some cases militarily powerful institutions associated with religion, like the historical Islamic state, the present Jewish state, or the various Christian states and institutions? The identification with such institutions may provide disempowered people with a sense of an affirming might, but at what price? Can it really render human liberation, ethical integrity, and moral force? Or does it necessarily create new forms of bondage, such as sectarianism, jingoism, and nationalistic forms of servitude in which ethical integrity is heavily compromised? Given the realities of the Christian minorities in the Arab world and in Israel-Palestine in particular, Palestinian Christian theologies of liberation seem more successful than Islamic ones in mobilizing faith for the ethical and spiritual capacities of liberation and justice. Their attempts are worth pondering.

Finally, by recalling the religious establishment's critique function, Asad reminds us of the loss of one of the critical voices among others that resulted from the co-optation of religious institutions by the postindependence Arab regimes. These regimes were not the only intolerant forces of the era, however. The Islamist organizations opposing them were equally intolerant. The first victims of the bitter struggle between them were the secularists, who found themselves the target of both the regime and the Islamists in a public life that became increasingly Islamicized as a result of the rivalry between a state that wanted to prove its religious legitimacy (having no other ground of legitimacy) and a mounting Islamist opposition that proposed Islam as "the" solution to all the ills plaguing Arab societies. But the secularists have persisted: threatened, vulnerable, and marginalized, they still stand their ground. It is to them that I turn in the next chapter.

Five
Secular
Critique

S ince the time of the Nahda, secular critique has been a persistent component of Arab cultural critique. At the turn of the twentieth century, it was considered a prerequisite for modernization: on the political level, it meant the separation of religion from politics and the state; and on the intellectual level, it stipulated the replacement of a religious mode of thinking with a scientific one.[1] The issue took on a renewed prominence in the aftermath of the 1967 defeat. Some thinkers, such as Sadeq Jalal al-Azm, blamed the lingering religious-metaphysical mode of thinking for the way things were handled before, during, and after the debacle. Others saw themselves forced to take on the defense of political secularism in the face of the rising political Islam, which many people interpreted as a reaction to the 1967 defeat. Indeed, by the end of the twentieth century, the secularist discourse had become a defensive one in the face of an increasingly dominating fundamentalist discourse. Despite the growing pressures of fundamentalism, on the one hand, and the failures (defeats, repressive measures, and corrupt administrations) of the so-called secularist Arab regimes, on the other, the proponents of secular views in culture and politics stood their ground, sometimes at the cost of their lives.

Their secular critique touches on a number of issues and defends a whole array of principles. Their secular understanding of worldly issues aims at keeping public debates on the human level and at favoring tolerance and rational exchange in the face of intellectual terrorism and political disenfranchisement. It insists on basing the arguments of these debates on historical givens, not on dogmatic beliefs and wishful thoughts. It calls on a critical examination of assumptions made about identity and civilization in public discourse, warning against the pitfalls of an ahistorical, vitalistic, and essentialist views of cultural identity. It draws attention to the traps of superficial calls for the Islamicization of social science and knowledge in general and to the importance of problematizing the notion of "indigenization." It raises critical questions about intellectual decolonization and about the meaning of having a thought of one's own. It touches on the issue of cultural specificity, civilizational self-sufficiency, and universal openness. It addresses the strengths and weaknesses of the intellectual strategies that aim at conciliating Islam with modernity as well as the ambiguities involved in defining Islam. It ultimately puts the emphasis on the importance of maintaining public debates on the human level, shunning away from absolutes, and calling for democracy as the only human framework for peaceful and inclusive exchange and coexistence.

Critique of the Exclusive Monopoly Over "True" Islam: Farag Fouda

Farag Fouda (1945–1992) was an Egyptian agricultural economist who in the 1980s and early 1990s argued against the Islamists in books, articles, and public debates. He directed scathing criticisms against their bigotry, hypocrisy, and violence. He denounced their greed for power and their obsession with sex, often with sarcasm and humor, but always with an uncompromising firmness. As a founding member of the Egyptian Human Rights Organization, he denounced the Islamists' intolerance and their attacks on the sizable Christian Coptic minority. In 1990, his collection of articles *Nakun aw la Nakun* (To Be or Not to Be) was condemned by the Islamic Research Foundation of Al-Azhar University and withdrawn from circulation; and the State Security Services called Fouda in for interrogation.[2] At the Cairo Book Fair in February 1992 before an audience of fifteen thousand, he attacked the religious speakers for their unwarranted claims and their flawed scholarship.[3] In his last book, *Al-Haqiqa al-Gha'iba* (The Absent Truth),[4] he brought together his main arguments against his opponents, insisting from the beginning that the book was about Muslims, not about Islam. In fact, *The Absent Truth* was in particular a response to Abd al-Salam Faraj's *Al-Farida al-Gha'iba* (The Absent Duty),[5] which advocated a return to the literalist, conservative jurisprudence of medieval times.

In *The Absent Truth*, Fouda addresses the Islamists' call for the application of the religious shari'a law and for the establishment of the Islamic state as a solution to the decadence of Islamic societies in general and of Egyptian society in particular. He presents refutations of their claims and denounces their methods of intimidation and distortion. What Islamists portray as matters of doctrine and faith are in reality, according to Fouda, matters of power. What these people are seeking, he says, is political power, not paradise or spiritual salvation. Instead of answering their accusations of impiety and infidelity with counteraccusations, he proposes to offer reasoned arguments and proofs based on empirical, historical givens so that these important issues can be discussed in total freedom, rationality, and transparency. He invites his readers to consider the following two points of view: that of the Islamists and that of the non-Islamists (without being anti-Islamic). The Islamists claim that Egypt has become a pagan, pre-Islamic (Jahili) society or, in a more moderate formulation, a society that has strayed from true religion, and they therefore argue that this situation necessitates the society's immediate reform by the introduction of shari'a law, which alone can bring the solution to the society's many problems. The other point of view does not come from outside or in opposition to Islam, he says. It affirms, first, that Egyptian society is not a pagan society and that it has proven throughout its history, from the Pharaonic to the Christian and the Muslim eras, to be a religiously inclined society. Second, the call for applying shari'a law amounts to a political demand for an Islamic state, which requires from the advocates of this call a political program that explains to people how the application of shari'a in an Islamic state will solve the problems of housing, wages, inflation, external debt, productivity in the public sector, education, economy, and egalitarian citizenship, particularly with regard to women and religious minorities.

Clearly, he adds, it is easier to make accusations of heresy and apostasy than to come up with solutions to these critical national problems. Islamists have attacked and condemned those religious thinkers who have understood Islam in its core as a call for justice rather than as a set of outdated formal measures. Good governance, adds Fouda, cannot be founded only or primarily on the piety of the ruler or of the ruled because in the final analysis they are human, and as humans they are prone to temptations and mistakes. The whole history of Islamic rule, from its very beginning, shows that rulers and ruled have not been immune to faults and failures. Even the early period of the four Rightly Guided Caliphs, who were the Prophet's Companions and who ruled people who were the Prophet's contemporaries, had its share of violence and civil wars. Three of the four caliphs were assassinated by fellow Muslims, and strong disagreements plagued their appointment and rule. The periods that followed, the Umayyad (661–750) and the Abbasid (750–1258), were not any better. In three consecutive chapters devoted to these periods in *The Absent Truth*, Fouda demystifies this Islamic past, using classical historians of the time to reveal the all-too-human character of a past that the Islamists have idealized and presented as the true Islamic rule that must be restored. Throughout this history, says Fouda, the state has been a burden for religion.[6] The good governance of a state can be ensured only by mechanisms through which rulers can be held accountable. Of course, he adds, the conception and application of such mechanisms are much more difficult than forcing shari'a punishment or devoting attention to appearances, as in growing beards and not listening to music. Finally, he says, Islamists should be confronted with the tasks of real politics. The current Egyptian law does not allow them to form a political party because the Constitution does not permit the formation of religious political forces. But they exist de facto on the ground in organized networks, and they should be faced with the real challenges of politics. At least then one can meet them on the ground of worldly realities, and they would have to debate real social and political issues among themselves. Some fear that giving the Islamists greater political scope will also encourage the formation of Christian political parties, but this possible result is not a serious danger, he says, because Christians in Egypt, in their large majority, have always adopted the secularist option.

In the final analysis, concludes Fouda, what we (secularists) want to fight is not religious thought per se, but violence. Those who believe that Islam is both a religion and a state project have the right to exist, and we should fight for their liberty of thought and expression. We differ from them and think that Islam is a religion, not a political doctrine, but they

deserve our support because both they and we are threatened by the intolerant attacks of the violent Islamists, and they more directly than we. With
good intentions on both sides, the two groups should be able to meet each
other halfway: they by elaborating an enlightened hermeneutics adapted to
the present age, accepting the changing circumstances of time, adhering to
national unity, and respecting the law; and we by realizing that democracy
should make room for both them and us, accepting difference, practicing
tolerance, and agreeing with them that Islam is concerned with ultimate
goals, progress, and the community's interest. Thinking, he says, should
take precedence over anathematization, and tolerance should be able to
contain us all. We all are Egyptians and equal patriots, Muslims and Copts,
not a majority of rulers and conquerors versus a minority of ruled prisoners of war. As Muslims, we should not be terrorized by self-appointed
representatives of Islam. Islam does not give sanctity to anyone but the
Prophet. Fouda ends his introduction to *The Absent Truth* by saying that
violent Islamists should know that the "future can be made only with the
pen, not the sword, by work and not by retreat, by reason not by Darwish
life, by logic not by bullets, and most important they have to know the
truth that has escaped them, namely that they are not alone ... [in] the
community of Muslims."[7]

In June 1992, two members of the Islamic Jihad shot Farag Fouda dead
as he left his office with his fifteen-year-old son. He was forty-seven years
old. The killers were never apprehended.

The Importance of Keeping the Debate on the Human Level: Fouad Zakariyya

Egyptian philosopher Fouad Zakariyya addresses the same problems in
two of his books published in the 1980s: *Al-Haqiqa wa al-Wahm fi al-
Haraka al-Islamiyya al-Mu'assira* (The Truth and Illusion About the Contemporary Islamic Movement) and *Al-Sahwa al-Islamiyya fi Mizan al-'Aql*
(The Islamic Awakening in the Balance of Reason).[8] Zakariyya compares
the post-1967 secularist position with the position at the turn of the twentieth century. In that early phase, he says, the secularist discourse proposed
a vision for the modernization of Arab society based on the European
model in order to empower it and liberate it from the European colonial
domination, but at the beginning it did not have an elaborate theory to
support that vision. In the early decades of the twentieth century, explicit

theoretical debates were to take place, initiated by the writings of Farah Antun, Ali Abdel Raziq, and others. The context of the secularist discourse in the aftermath of the 1967 defeat is, according to Zakariyya, one of set-backs on all levels: a domestic context of increased repression and social injustice as well as a wider context of increased dependency due to a grow-ing imperialism. It is also a context marked by the resurgence of reaction-ary cultural and intellectual trends.[9]

In this post-1967 context, says Zakariyya, the secularist discourse has become a defensive discourse, concerned with refuting Islamist theses rather than with offering a positive social and political project. It seems to be supportive of the status quo, whereas the Islamists seem to be in favor of change. In reality, he asserts, the secularists are not against change, but they insist that the debate about change remain on the human level, with-out the involvement of "spokesmen of heaven" and with the acknowledg-ment that all points of view are human points of view. For the secularists, it is important to keep the struggle on the human level because the appeal to heaven conceals a secret desire to abrogate the conditions of this struggle, namely its humanness. Another misrepresentation is the Islamists' appear-ance as the persecuted group that is disadvantaged in the battle against the others. The Islamists were indeed persecuted at several points, says Zakari-yya, but at all times their struggle with the different governments has been a struggle over power; they have not been persecuted for their ideas and be-liefs. They have benefited at various points from governments' efforts to crush the Left and race to exhibit an Islamic face through the Islamicization of the media and of public life in general.[10] Moreover, he says, Arab govern-ments have never been really radically secular, contrary to the myth of the secular Nasserite period. They all have more or less been Islamic in their character. Furthermore, the Islamic heritage, especially the religious and the textual, mobilized by the Islamists is deeply rooted in the psyche and culture of the masses and is thus easier to appeal to than are secularist ideas.

All of these factors, says Zakariyya, give the Islamists a considerable advantage over the secularists and constitute the ground for an uneven battle between the two. In addition, the Islamists benefit from the general lack of critical thinking among people because of the authoritarian type of rule imposed on the people by consecutive repressive governments. This re-pression has facilitated the Islamists' use of rhetorical and unfounded argu-ments. Among the former is the claim that secularism equals atheism and materialism. The separation of politics from religion does not necessarily entail atheism, however, says Zakariyya, nor does it imply that anything that is not religious is materialist—that is, devoid of all ethical or moral component. In an internalization of Orientalist claims, the Islamists here associate materialism with science and place both of these arenas in opposition to the essence of the Muslim heritage, which is supposed to be inimical to science. They also present secularism as yet another form of conspiracy against the Muslim Arab world, a conspiracy meant to destroy its culture and confusedly imputed to Christian, imperialist, Jewish, Zionist, Masonic, and Orientalist forces.

Other arguments are less rhetorical. They include the well-known and oft-repeated argument regarding the cultural specificity of secularism: that it is the product of a Western Christian cultural history in which the church, as a religious institution, repressed science and freedom of thought. Because no such institution exists in the Muslim world, no mechanism to neutralize its power is needed. Zakariyya says that even without a juridical stipulation, Islam did and still does have institutional authorities, which persecuted free thinkers and scientists in the Middle Ages and continue to do so in recent times. He adds that the origin of an idea does not limit its validity to its place of origin. In fact, if the matter is that of intellectual dependency, the Islamists are the ones who manifest a lack of intellectual independence by relying excessively on the thought of the ancients, chosen selectively; they are the ones who fear independent thinking. Rather than a specific historical or cultural intellectual trend, says Zakariyya, secularism is a mode of thinking that replaces authority with critique. Authority-based thinking and critical thinking can exist and have existed both in the past and at present, in the West as well as in the Muslim East. Islamic heritage contains significant manifestations of rationalist, independent critique. This critique is thus not the exclusive property of some trends of Western culture. It is part and parcel of Islamic culture, and reviving it is the most urgent cultural imperative in the Arab world. Finally, he thinks that religion and politics cannot be mixed together. Politics is the changing realm par excellence; it is characterized by the plurality of forces and opinions, whereas religion is in its core the realm of the atemporal and the unified. Separating the religious from the political cannot render religion recreational, as the Islamists claim, because secularism does not conflict with faith. Furthermore, historical experience has shown that a nonreligious rule ensures more freedom for all, including minorities. In contrast, claims of infallibility, especially in the name of God, have led to repression and persecution. Arab Muslim Andalusian rule, he says, cannot be taken as a model, as the Islamists have suggested, because it was very loosely Muslim and not a real theocracy. But dominant discourses in the Arab world and the religious discourses in particular have not given much importance to historical experience. History as a learning process through which improved views of society and government can be gained is neglected in favor of a revealed system of values that has set once and for all the ideals of human existence.

According to Zakariyya, the human labor in adapting these ideals to the changing circumstances of life has once again been ignored, as has the human wisdom accumulated through historical experience, outside or in addition to revealed wisdom. Moreover, no effort is made to confront those revealed ideals with the reality of the actual practices in history and at the present time. The lack of historical thinking, the occultation of the human effort in envisioning the good life, and the subjection to tyranny have repressed the notions of secular humanism and human rights in the Arab person:

One can safely say that the suffering of the Arab nation as a whole, in the domain of freedom of thought in particular, exceeds that of most nations on earth at the present time. As for the more positive or social rights, such as the right to education, culture, suitable employment, and so on, these are always subservient to the demands of the regime. The regime's self-preservation comes first.

What is even more deplorable is that constant subjection to suppression has led the ordinary citizen to lose a sense of having inalienable rights. Gradually, violation of legal rights becomes something that belongs to the nature of things. In my view, this is the greatest danger that may threaten any society in the field of human rights because when man is defeated from within, he loses the ability to stand against oppression and even the awareness that he has been deprived of anything.[11]

Islam, says Zakariyya, shapes Arabs' worldview to a great extent. Although not all Arabs are Muslims (some are Christians and some are Jews), and not all Muslims are Arabs (in fact, only a minority of Muslims are Arabs), Islam nevertheless constitutes the cultural background of Arabs, and it is only normal that the notions of human rights are understood in terms of this prevailing culture.[12] But this understanding is characterized by an apologetic stance of comparison with the West, which remains the reference point of the comparison even when it is presented as inferior to the Muslim conception of human rights. Muslim superiority is claimed to come from its historical priority (shariʿa was written prior to the Declaration of Rights during the French Revolution) and more important from its divine and hence infallible origin. In this apology, no contribution from history or human experience is sought, says Zakariyya, and no attention is paid to the empirical realities of the application of these rights. The time since the elaboration of the Islamic rights starting with the Revelation is seen as a time of decline, not a history of experiences from which Muslims have to gather wisdom and develop further their understanding and application of those rights, and certainly not as a time of human experiences leading to a new or different conception of human rights. Religious and political authoritarianism, he says, have suppressed creative thinking and have nurtured obedience and submissiveness. Nasr Hamid Abu Zayd explains Muslims and Arabs' reluctance to embrace so-called universal human rights by pointing to the West's lack of moral and political credibility even though it supports and promotes these rights. The West continues to treat "the rest" with injustice, contempt, and racism, and is interested primarily in exploiting their riches and dominating their politics to the detriment of whatever democratic forces may exist in them. The problem, says Abu Zayd, is not religious or cultural, but political.[13]

Finally, Zakariyya wonders if an "Islamic awakening" is really under way. What the Islamists have proposed, after the failure of the liberals and the socialists who came to power in the Arab world, is not a real vision for an empowered future, but a set of formal changes in physical appearances (the veil and the beard), a focus on formal rituals, and an obsession with sex. This project does not seriously address the fundamental issues of injustice, however. By concentrating on what superficially makes a "good Muslim," it fails to address the social dimension of the many problems at hand. Some propose formal Islamic reform with progressive intentions, but many, he says, benefit from the pushing forward of reactionary and obscurantist ideas. His sense is that in reality an ideology of slumber and death is being propagated in the guise of an awakening.

Critique of the Essentialist and Romantic Conception of Identity: Aziz al-Azmeh

A major participant in the secularism debate is the Syrian historian Aziz al-Azmeh. He has held several teaching and research positions in Europe and the United States and is currently affiliated with the University

Humanistic Center of Central Europe in Budapest. He is a prolific writer and a widely read author, both in the West and in the Arab world. He has extensive publications in Arabic and English on topics pertaining to modern and classical Arab history, society, and thought. For my purposes here, I draw on three of his works, two in Arabic and one in English: the 1992 book *Al-'Ilmaniyya min Manzour Mukhtalif* (Secularism from a Different Perspective); the 1996 collection of articles and interviews *Dunia al-Din fi Hader al-'Arab* (The World of Religion in the Arabs' Present); and finally, the 1993 collection of lectures and essays delivered in European languages published under the title *Islams and Modernities*. [14]

The different perspective al-Azmeh proposes is one based on the modern historical reality of Arab societies, instead of the widespread theoretical and idealist perspective centered on the compatibility of Islam with secular ideas. The history he focuses on is that of the transformations in Arab societies generated by the reforms initiated in the Ottoman Empire in the course of the nineteenth century. If and when importance is given to nineteenth-century legal, administrative, and institutional reforms, says al-Azmeh, attention is usually exclusively turned to the reforms undertaken by Muhammad Ali, who governed Egypt from 1805 to 1849 after the Napoleonic invasion of the country in 1798; and this event is regarded as the main trigger of the modernization processes in the region. In fact, he adds, Muhammad Ali's reforms, which aimed at modernizing Egypt and strengthening its autonomy vis-à-vis the Ottoman Empire, coincided with similar reforms launched by the Ottoman state throughout the empire. These Ottoman reforms aimed initially at strengthening the empire in the face of its enemies, especially after the 1774 and 1792 defeats by Russia. They were met with resistance on the part of the religious institutions and authorities, but many of them were eventually imposed, notably the ones of the mid–nineteenth century known as the Tanzimat (1839–1871). The Tanzimat's purpose was to modernize both the state and the societies administered by it and to create an egalitarian form of citizenship irrespective of religion, race, or ethnicity in order to curb ethnic groups' nationalist ambitions and to maintain some level of political cohesion. The growing irredentist movements, the central state's weakened military and administrative capacities, and the financial and economic troubles had increased the European powers' interventions. The reforms included, for instance, the consideration of a non-Ottoman Muslim as a foreigner, the acceptance of the court testimony of a *dhimmi* (non-Muslim citizen in an Islamic state subject to a form of protection), the formation of civil courts, the appointment of some Christian judges in these courts (for instance, Copts in Egypt), and the cancellation of punishments that did not rely on a positive law. According to Erich Zürcher,

> *The canon law of Islam, the Şeriat, was never abrogated, but its scope was limited almost completely to family law (questions of ownership now also being brought under the sway of the secular law) and it was codified along European lines in 1865–88. The statesmen of the Tanzi-* mat *created new secular laws and institutions to replace the tradi- tional* kanuni *system, first and foremost where the changing position of the foreigners in the empire or the Ottoman Christians demanded it. In 1843 a new penal code was introduced which recognized equality of Muslims and non-Muslims. At the same time, mixed tribunals were introduced for commercial cases in which foreigners were in- volved. In 1844, the death penalty for apostasy from Islam, a provision of the Şeriat was abolished.*[15]

Al-Azmeh speaks of these legal and administrative reforms as a project of social engineering engaged in by the Ottoman state, but with unequal consequences. Some of the reforms remained incomplete or were not im- plemented successfully and consistently due to a number of factors. Zürcher mentions five: the lack of adequately trained and trustworthy personnel; the fact that the reforms were imposed from the top and not demanded by the people at large; the persistence of the patrimonial-clientalist system; the reforms' focus on creating new laws, new regulations, and new institu- tions rather than on abolishing the old ones; and, finally, the lack of suffi- cient economic and financial means. The reforms led to the 1876 Ottoman Constitution, which was later suspended by Sultan Abdulhamid and then reinstated following the 1908 Committee of Progress and Union revolu- tion. In spite of these reversals and failures, the reforms created, according to al-Azmeh, real societal changes and real historical discontinuities that had repercussions throughout the twentieth century. They diminished the influence of religious institutions and authorities, and brought into being a more secular intelligentsia, more secular social mores, and a more secular- ized conception of political government.

Contemporary thinkers often forget, neglect, or ignore these changes and discontinuities, says al-Azmeh, minimizing their impact and seeing the resurgence of Islamic forces as the natural return of the repressed, or the return of Arab societies to their "Islamic nature" after an insignificant episode of deviation from their "natural course." The historical causes of this resurgence—in other words, its historicity—is thereby denied. Yet these causes are real. They have to do with the retreat of the postindependence state from its social and economic functions, a retreat later aggravated by the neoliberal measures of structural adjustment programs;[16] they are connected to the crackdown of the Left in the Arab world; and they are related to the separation of the Arab world from the radical secularist experience of Kemalist Turkey after the collapse of the Ottoman Empire.

Ignoring this set of historical transformations and denying the secular realities of Arab societies that developed in the past two centuries, however incomplete and fragile, means a failure to approach the question of secularism realistically and rationally. The failure, according to al-Azmeh, is due to a certain mode of thinking about identity and history, which in turn is based on a number of unwarranted and distorted assumptions. Among these assumptions is the Islamic "nature" of Arab societies in a reductionist, essentialist, and ahistoricist sense. It is claimed that these societies are part of a homogeneous Islamic nation that functions as a monolithic living entity, governed by an atemporal spirit that remains unaffected by the events of time. In this core spirit lies the authenticity of the nation, which inexorably comes back to the fore after inconsequential periods of latent existence. For al-Azmeh, this view of identity is not specific to the Islamists. It is a pervasive conception that nationalists presupposed earlier and that Islamists now use in their turn. It is a romantic, vitalist, populist, and determinist conception of community that cancels out historical reality and rationality, and that produces a Jacobin view of politics based on homogeneity, voluntarism, and force. It is typical of populist movements in general, as experienced, for instance, in Russia, eastern Europe, Africa, and East Asia. In this romantic-populist view, authenticity comes to be understood in a certain way:

> Asala is the Arabic term for authenticity. Lexically, it indicates salutary moral qualities like loyalty, nobility, and a sense of commitment to a specific social group or a set of values. It also indicates a sense of sui generis originality; and in association with the senses previously mentioned, asala specifically refers to genealogical standing: noble or at least respectable descent for humans, and the status of equine aristocrats. Combined together and transferred to an attribute of historical collectivities, Arab, Muslim or other, asala becomes a central notion in a Romantic conception of history which calls forth features

*commonly associated with such a conception. Of primary importance
among these features is a vitalist concept of nationalism and of politics, replete with biological metaphor and, occasionally, a sentimentalist populism.*

*Ultimately, therefore, the notion of authenticity is predicated on the
notion of a historical subject which is at once self-sufficient and self-
evident. Its discourse is consequently an essentialist discourse.*[17]

This romantic view uses a discourse that exoticizes Islam and confers
upon it a specific and incommensurable culture and history. Al-Azmeh
traces these conceptions of identity and culture back to the Western romantic, anti-Enlightenment legacy and more particularly to German romanticism, and he often refers to Johann Gottfried Herder's work in this connection. However, a more differentiated view of romanticism would allow for a
more nuanced appreciation of this legacy. Al-Azmeh's imputation applies
more to the later romanticism of Johann Gottlieb Fichte, the Schlegel
brothers, and Ernst Arndt, all of whom held reactionary political views
with collectivist, medievalist, and totalizing conceptions of nationalism.
But it does not apply to the early romantics such as Johann Georg Hamann,
Friedrich Heinrich Jacobi, Friedrich Schiller, and Herder, who were trying
to serve the cause of the Enlightenment rather than attack it and to limit its
hubris rather than abandon it. Herder is a pivotal figure in this respect.
Throughout his work, he tried to reconcile the universal humanism of the
Enlightenment with the particularism of specific collectivities, the fundamental common anthropological characteristics of all humans with the
uniqueness of every culture, without ever falling into the solipsism of incommensurable cultures. Whether he succeeded in resolving these tensions is a question that lies outside the scope of this study.[18] Suffice it here
to say that it would be unfair to accuse him of advocating absolute particularism and essentialism. On the contrary, his critique of European colonialism, his suspicion of European universalism as a disguised ethnocen-
trism, and his attack on the overvaluation of reason and abstract thought
are of amazing relevance to our present world, two hundred years after
they were formulated.

Of significance here is the fact that in its first phase Arab nationalism
was inspired by the French conception of nationalism, based on adherence
to a set of laws and values. It wasn't until after World War I and the establishment of the French and British mandates on the Arab lands that Arab

nationalists turned to the German conception of nationalism based on language, culture, blood, and soil and formed by the late romantics such as Arndt. Obviously, the mandate experience was not a positive experience of French political culture—a culture that many Arab reformers had hitherto admired. Moreover, several Arab thinkers found in the Germany of the romantic era a similar absence of a unified state around which people could be called to rally. Bassam Tibi, a Syrian political scientist based in Germany, has examined closely the development and transformations of Arab nationalism, including the growing influence of German romanticism on thinkers such as Sati' al-Husri (1879–1968),[19] as the region came under the colonial rule of the French and British mandates. Tibi describes the impact of this colonial experience on Arab intellectual history, particularly the move from one conception of nationalism to another.[20] I turn shortly to Tibi's own secular critique of Islamic fundamentalism.

In order to refute the Islamists' claim to a specificity in history and thought, al-Azmeh compares the history of medieval Islamic rule with that of Byzantine Christianity and connects the recent rise of Islamic fundamentalism with the rise of culturalism and irrationalism around the world. The ideology of authenticity is for him but one facet of a more general reactionary trend represented in the global and Western ideologies of culturalism.[21] Some of these ideologies advocate "postmodern," anti-Enlightenment, anti-Cartesian views that challenge the hegemony of Logos in favor of the different, the nonrational, and the nonuniversal: "This position, with its legion of representatives, is linked to more than anti-imperialist revindication. It embodies what is perceived, and not for the first time, as a crisis in the supposed excess of Cartesian reason, and encompasses a correlative shift from the innocent naturalness of reason to reclaiming an innocent naturalness of desire, need, locality, fragmentariness. . . . [N]otions of a return to natural innocence, to the recovery of immediacy and of subjectivity, and disenchantment with abstraction in thought have always come together as a bundle."[22]

Al-Azmeh is not the only Arab postcolonial thinker to be critical of this antirationalist trend and to argue for its inapplicability in postcolonial contexts, where noncritical forms of thought and discourse are dominant and tempting. The late Palestinian historian of ideas Hisham Sharabi (whose work I discuss later in this chapter) and the U.S.-based Algerian feminist sociologist Marnia Lazreg also emphasize the dangers of the postmodern critique of rationalism and humanism. In the preface to his 1988 book *Neopatriarchy: Theory of Distorted Change in Arab Society*, Sharabi writes: "My feeling is that while the intellectual world of late capitalism perhaps can accommodate without much damage the aestheticism and skepticism of a Foucault or a Derrida, the intellectuals of the post-colonial periphery, including the Arab world, can ill afford the risk of philosophical and anti-theoretical skepticism; and even were they to take this risk, it would—probably—only lead them to political paralysis."[23] Lazreg in turn strongly attacks the self-referential antihumanism of postmodern thought and its cult of difference:

> *Antihumanism has not provided any authority higher than itself that could monitor its excesses. Old-style humanism, in contrast, and despite its shortcomings, makes itself vulnerable to criticism by appealing to its unfulfilled promise of a more reasonable rationalism or a more egalitarian universalism. Indeed, the universalistic claim to a supracultural human entity embodied in reason provided colonized societies with the tool necessary to regain their freedom. Colonized women and men were willing to give up their lives in order to capture their share of humanity celebrated but denied by colonial powers. But what does antihumanism offer "different" peoples? On what grounds (moral or otherwise) can powerless people struggle against their relegation to the prison house of race, color, and nationality into which antihumanism locks them? . . . As it now stands, difference is seen as mere division. The danger of this undeveloped view lies in its verging on* indifference.[24]

Al-Azmeh connects the Western and the "Oriental" versions of this antirationalism. He points out the similarities between what he considers to be the postmodern ideologies of difference and the postcolonial ideologies of authenticity, seeing in them mirror images of the same culturalism: "in this way, orientals, most particularly those who describe themselves as post-colonial, re-orientalize themselves radically when they speak of regaining their authenticity and singularity. Thus arises a traffic in mirror images between re-orientalized orientals speaking for authenticity and postmodernists speaking for Difference." He describes the complicity between these various manifestations of the culturalist rhetoric, including both those that are sympathetic to difference and those that are not, as "Western xenophobia, postmodernist xenophilia and xenophobic, retrograde nationalisms and para-nationalisms in Eastern Europe and countries of the South, in which I include political Islamism and Hindu communalism. This is an objective complicity between exoticism and the rhetoric of identity and authenticity. By objective complicity I refer not only to their contemporaneity, their intersection at a given point in time, but also to a conceptual concordance."[25]

Al-Azmeh also sees the repercussions of these culturalist and antirationalist assumptions about the self for the conception of knowledge of both the self and the other. Knowledge of the self is understood to be self-evident and immediate, and knowledge of the other to be a matter of sympathy rather than a discursive activity: "Reason thus becomes multiple, and knowledge of the self, which constitutes self-expression—of the social self, the historical self or whatever other definition of subjective identity is proffered—is reduced to a solipsism. Trans-cultural communication becomes problematized as one requiring an act of sympathy which alone, according to this conception, allows access to a meaning that is, ultimately and in principle, inaccessible, it being the sense apprehended by an irreducible subject. And, of course, this is only to be expected when using the organismic, vitalist metaphor of organic self-possession and self-enclosure."[26] Furthermore, the door is therewith opened for a local, specific knowledge of the self and of the world and hence for the call for an "Islamicization" of knowledge. (I look at Bassam Tibi's critique of this conception of knowledge later in the chapter.)

Although such a harsh critique of the ideology of authenticity may be understandable and to a great extent justified and even necessary, one should be careful not to throw the baby out with the bath water given the dangers of the assumptions this ideology makes—namely, essentialism, the incommensurability of cultures, and the marginalization of discursive reason and agency. If the ideology of authenticity is to be condemned for all these dangers, the quest for authenticity as a search for an empowered sense of self that seeks acknowledgment for one's identity and history cannot and should not be ignored, especially in a postcolonial context. Rather than condemning the concern with authenticity, attention should be paid to how identity and history are understood. Moreover, the critique of Enlightenment values should be contextualized: although this critique is needed and justified, the wholesale rejection of these ideals —implying the rejection of discursive reason, individual liberties, and democracy—is dangerous, particularly in postcolonial societies, where they have hardly been institutionalized. The devastating consequences of their absence are the painful experience of those living in and reflecting upon these societies. Many thinkers are thus exasperated regarding the postmodern "playful" totalizing attacks on the Enlightenment launched by those blessed with many of its achievements.

Al-Azmeh pursues his denunciation of the metaphysical and essentialist view of identity. One of the further aspects of this view is the constant attempt at conciliating the essence of identity—however defined—with the current ideologies or trendy values, but at the price of twisting the two sides of the conciliatory operation. By a sleight of hand, he says, Islam is successively or simultaneously presented as advocating nationalism, socialism, capitalism, and human rights. Al-Azmeh takes the example of the human rights issue. Islam, like most religions, discriminates between believers and infidels as well as between men and women. It cannot as such fit into the egalitarian principles set by the human rights outlook. Most religions, as shown in European and Arab histories, become tolerant only when obliged to by nonreligious forces coming from the state or civil society.

In the secularist reforms of the past two centuries, says al-Azmeh, the approach to religious authorities and institutions has always been conciliatory. These reforms have come from outside religion, not against it. But the tendency to accommodate religion has increased with the rise of Islamism in the past few decades. Like Zakariyya, al-Azmeh thinks that the secularist position has become increasingly defensive, justifying itself in the face of what is presented as the "natural Islamic position" of Arab societies. Islamism has imposed a symbolic realm in which others, including secularists, are pushed to compete. It has also aggravated the obsession with indigenizing all acceptable concepts through the religious legacy. Those who defend Abu Zayd by saying that he is a good Muslim really end up strengthening his opponents' position. Instead, he ought to be defended in the name of such liberties as freedom of speech, freedom of thought, freedom of worship, and freedom of expression. The Islamists' recent success has reinforced the false impression of the "natural" Islamic core of Arab societies and has blurred the circumstantial and rather recent character of this success.

Secularism, concludes al-Azmeh, is not a ready prescription or a total solution to Arab problems, but it is the direction in which world history is moving, and Islamists cannot convincingly claim to offer a viable alternative direction. Their androcentric, patronizing, and obscurantist views cannot promise a desirable future in a world engaged in an irreversible, universal modernity. Only the recognition of the complex realities of Arab societies and an understanding of the incomplete and plural aspects of universal modernity can open the way for a constructive vision of an Arab future.

Al-Azmeh's book *Al-'Ilmaniyya min Manzour Mukhtalif* (Secularism from a Different Perspective) was discussed in a roundtable organized by the Center for Arab Unity Studies, and the proceedings were published in his book *Dunia al-Din fi Hader al-'Arab* (The World of Religion in the Arabs' Present). Wajih Kawtharani and Ridwan al-Sayyid formulated the most important critiques of his approach. Kawtharani is a Lebanese historian specializing in the Ottoman history of the Arab East. His work is one of al-Azmeh's main sources in the historical analysis of secularism.[27] Kawtharani agrees with al-Azmeh that Arab societies have been secularized in many respects, not only in their recent past, but even in their earlier history, when they were officially under "Islamic" rule. He also shares with him the secular stance regarding the present and the future. However, he disproves of the harshness of al-Azmeh's judgments. He thinks that because al-Azmeh is caught up in a tense polemic with the Islamists, he is unable to remain true to his commitment to a realist, historical, and constructive approach. He finds him dogmatic in his secularist view: more secularist (*laîciste*) than secular (*laîc*) and deterministic in his view of the secularist direction of history. These polemic, dogmatic, and deterministic tendencies prevent him from putting more effort and sympathy into understanding the causes of the rise of Islamism, which have made many in Arab societies receptive of the Islamist call. How can the Islamists mobilize this much popular support if their claims are so disconnected from reality, as al-Azmeh claims they are? His opposition to them seems to limit his exploration of the historical, including the colonial and socioeconomic burdens that have stripped these societies of their productive means and have left them with nothing but their past and their God. Al-Azmeh's opposition also prevents him from appreciating some of the positive aspects of the conciliatory approach he attacks so fiercely, namely the possibility of assimilating new or renewed ideas into the prevailing culture.

Ridwan al-Sayyid, a Lebanese scholar of Islamic studies,[28] also criticizes al-Azmeh for his secularist dogmatism, historical determinism, and totalistic rationalism that mirrors his opponents' totalistic fundamentalism. Al-Azmeh speaks in the name of history, says al-Sayyid, like they speak in the name of the holy text. His dogmatism is reminiscent of that of the Marxist-Leninists in the 1970s, to whom al-Azmeh belonged in his youth. In his zeal to counter the metaphysical specificity claimed by the Islamists, he erases all specificity: his comparison between the medieval Islamic state and the Christian Byzantine state does not hold. Among the significant differences he misses is that religion was added in the latter at a later stage, but was a constitutive element in the former. Al-Azmeh, says al-Sayyid, conceives of Islam as being totally irrational and consistently in the service of power, even though in reality it has often played the role of the censor of power. The only solution to the political mobilization of Islam that al-Azmeh suggests is the desacralization of its holy texts, according to al-Sayyid. Al-Azmeh's animosity toward religion does not allow him to understand why Islam became a "state," then a "solution": Can these phenomena be explained solely on the basis of the backwardness and irrationality of religious institutions? Finally, al-Sayyid thinks that al-Azmeh fails to appreciate the reformists' efforts and contributions. His overall tone, he adds, is not democratic.

Al-Azmeh responds to his critics by admitting the oppositional drive behind his arguments, which was provoked, as he puts it, by the aggressive inflation of the Islamist claims. He says that the Islamic reforms of the past are not satisfactory anymore and that new reforms need to be engaged. He insists on the importance of distinguishing between a Muslim as a believer or a person from a Muslim family and an Islamist. He goes back to denouncing the Islamists' voluntaristic effort to create an Islamist society within Arab society and to warning against essentialist conceptions of identity.

Critique of the Islamicization of Knowledge and the Quest for an Indigenous Social Science: Bassam Tibi, Abdelkebir Khatibi, and Hisham Sharabi

After Bassam Tibi, Syrian social thinker and professor of International Relations at the University of Göttingen in Germany, completed his work on Arab nationalism, he wrote a number of works on Islamic fundamentalism in German, English, and Arabic, many of which were translated into other languages as well. Among these many studies, I refer to three books in English: *The Crisis of Modern Islam: A Pre-industrial Culture in the Scientific-Technological Age*, *The Challenge of Fundamentalism: Political Islam and the New World Disorder*, and *Islam Between Culture and Politics*.[29] In particular, I examine his analysis of the fundamentalists' call for the "Islamicization" of knowledge in the journal article "Culture and Knowledge: The Politics of Islamicization of Knowledge as a Postmodern Project? The Fundamentalist Claim to De-Westernization."[30] In these studies, Tibi proposes a multilevel approach to the rise of Islamic fundamentalism, relating it to both local and global factors and analyzing it on the sociopolitical and cultural levels.

One of the major causes behind the rise of Islamic fundamentalism, according to Tibi, is the primary failures of postindependent nation-states in the Arab world: their failure to ensure socioeconomic development and failure to institutionalize secular principles of law, justice, and citizenship, which as a result could not send down solid roots in Arab societies. These failures were magnified by the 1967 defeat; they pushed people to disavow those principles and to regard them as well as the political and intellectual elites who upheld them as foreign and imported: "Secular nationalism gained ground and superseded Islam politically in the aftermath of the dissolution of the Ottoman Empire in 1924. Until the Arab defeat in 1967 in the Six Day War secular nationalism was the prevailing ideology. The 1967 defeat marked the failure of the secular model and resulted in a crisis of the secular nation-state. The Islamic revival has been a result of this crisis."[31]

Elsewhere he adds that this secular ideology never really struck roots in people's minds, nor was it translated into tangible transformations:

> We need to remind ourselves of the rise of nominally secular nation-states in most Islamic countries in the twentieth century which institutionally underlies these secular outlooks. Those nation-states, however, continue to be nominal in that they lack the needed structural roots. It follows that a substantial secularization in the sense of a structural process of functional differentiation of society had not yet taken place. Thus, secularism in dar al-Islam was more or less simply an ideology based on normative claims set by Westernized intellectuals. It was not related to social processes of secularization. Secular orientation has been a product of Western education and does not reflect existing realities.[32]

This secularization in name only led to what Tibi calls a "crisis of meaning"—that is, an absence of credible meaning structures with which people could accommodate to a rapidly changing and increasingly interconnected world.[33] It allowed a greater receptivity for Islamist ideologies, which had the advantage of resonating better with familiar, local, and traditional ideas. For Tibi, the rise of Islamic fundamentalism was both the expression of political frustration with the disappointing nation-state and the answer to a sense of cultural and ideological disarray. However, having recognized the political and historical circumstances of the emergence of the Islamist

omenon, he seems to drift toward a culturalist interpretation of it,
laining it as a cultural-intellectual difficulty or a reluctance to grasp
.d accept what he calls cultural modernity.

Islamic fundamentalism, he adds, offered an appealing alternative to
bankrupt secular ideologies and initiated a process of "desecularization."
The sense of political and cultural crisis was not restricted to the local
scene; it touched on the status of Arab societies in the world, especially
vis-à-vis the West: it was a status of weakness, defeat, backwardness, which
caused humiliation and dismay for a people defined by their own sacred
book as the finest community in all of humanity (Qur'an: Surat 'Imran,
3:110). According to the Islamist ideology, Islam offered not only a political
philosophy, but also a cultural strategy to face the Western hegemony and
to replace it. According to Tibi, this strategy does not aim at combating
cultural hegemony, but rather at replacing one cultural hegemony with
another, and as such cannot be acceptable:

> *The leaders of Islamic movements criticize Western dominance from
> a civilisational rather than a political viewpoint. Their contention is
> not based on an assumption of egalitarian and pluralist definitions of
> cultures and civilizations. Islamists want, rather, to reverse the hege-
> monic power situation in favour of Islam. They envisage a reversal
> leading to the emergence of structures that shift the center of power in
> decentring the West to pave the way for a global dominance of Islam.
> My unbreakable commitment to religious and cultural pluralism
> leads to an unequivocal rejection of the Islamists' claim to dominance.
> This claim is both anachronistic and lacks intercultural open-
> mindedness. To be sure, cultural pluralism is not relativism. I do share
> the criticism on Western hegemony, but reject the drive to substitute
> one hegemonic structure with another, albeit an Islamic one.*[34]

Echoing al-Azm and al-Azmeh, he says: "No other civilization in the world
feels so bitterly that the European expansion has taken place at its expense."[35]

With this hegemonic claim, Islamists challenge and oppose the West
politically and culturally, in contrast to earlier generations of Arab Muslims (and Christians and Jews) at the time of the Nahda, both secularists
and religious reformers, who tried to learn and benefit from the West in
order to empower Arab societies. Today's Islamists look at these thinkers,
people such as Rifa'a al-Tahtawi and Muhammad Abduh, as alienated
westernizers:

Still, in the earlier colonial and even postcolonial periods, non-Western peoples, the Muslims among them, were at pains to emulate the West, despite these humiliations. They even employed such Western concepts as the right to sovereignty and self-rule in their struggle against colonialism. But after a few decades of living in nominal nation-states that failed to meet the challenge of modernization, and failed, as well, to devise a beneficial strategy for emulating the West, the non-Western peoples rediscovered an awareness of their own civilizations, a need to search for other alternatives, basically to grow from one's own heritage. Religious fundamentalism has been the salient progeny of these processes.[36]

Indeed, this shift in attitude from a constructive curiosity to a negative defensiveness toward Western cultural modernity is important to underline at a time when the cultural defensiveness appears falsely as having been Arabs' perennial attitude vis-à-vis the West.

By drawing on the local religious heritage, the Islamists, according to Tibi, are not traditionalists. They are semimodernists, holders of an "Islamic dream of semimodernity." This dream (already deplored by Saadallah Wannous and Khaireddin al-Tunisi before him, as we saw) consists in accepting the instrumental-technical achievements of European modernity, but rejecting its cultural aspect. And yet, says Tibi, cultural modernity alone, in its universal principles, can ensure the freedom of individuals, the democracy of societies, the production of knowledge, and the possibility of true tolerance. Among these principles are the freedom and ability to subject traditions to critical reasoning, the autonomy of individual action, a human-centered and rational view of the world, a sense of *Könnenbewusstsein* (an awareness of capability, but now dramatically vanishing amidst so much incapacitation, as discussed in the conclusion), and the political culture of pluralism, private religiosity, individual human rights, and secular democracy. The failure to institutionalize these values in Arab countries is the result of both Western colonialism and postindependence Arab administrations:

The Muslims, just as peoples of other civilizations, did not gather, in their encounter with the West, the fruits of the Enlightenment, did not partake of the cultural dimensions of modernity. Rather, they were confronted by the ugly face of institutional modernity manifested in military superiority and political domination. It is true that in their separate histories these non-Western civilizations did not pursue the processes of building a democratic civil society and ensuring individual freedoms that led Europe ultimately to the establishment of a basic code of human rights. And the West did little to aid the introduction of democracy into the Islamic world. It is wrong, however, to blame only the West for this failure of democratization, for Western policies are the one constraint, local preconditions and predispositions the other.[37]

Not only did democracy fail, but so did radical rational critique. For Tibi, the subjection of ideas and beliefs to reason should not be regarded as a cultural treason because Islamic civilization has had a rationalist tradition. The problem for him, as it was for al-Azmeh and others, is the conciliatory position usually adopted by religious reformers such as Muhammad Abduh:

Orthodox and even reformist Muslims stand strongly against the subjection of any aspect of Islamic revelation to human reasoning. In this regard, Muhammed Abduh restricted his reform in an effort to reconcile revelation and reason. The result is a continuance of the existing great tensions. This is the background to the major predicament of contemporary Islam with modernity. Islamic modernism and Islamic reform of the late nineteenth century failed to go beyond the described duality and thus were unable to cope with the ensuing ever-growing tension. The islamist resolution of this perennial conflict is the deadlock of the proposed "Islamicization of knowledge." This "resolution" leads to nothing more than a new, but even greater impasse.[38]

On an exacerbated note, Tibi adds that what is needed is not atheism, but the assertion of the human capability to build knowledge and organize communal life: "Even Descartes acknowledges that man is created by God but that man is able to create knowledge on his own, by his own means. Why are Muslims unable to share this view? Why always use the fact of colonial rule to dismiss cultural modernity? Why involve the belief in Allah to disregard the ability of man?"[39]

What the Islamic fundamentalists are offering, according to Tibi, is a neoabsolutist, desecularization project aimed at reversing the "disenchantment of the world" with a defensive-assertive cultural strategy. This project is not emancipatory, however, he says, because it cannot ensure liberties, establish democracy, and secure human rights. Nor can it be the basis for the production of modern knowledge. He affirms that his critique of Islamic fundamentalism is based on the principles of cultural modernity, which he regards to be universal. He distinguishes between the universality of these principles and knowledge, on the one hand, and universalism and globalism as hegemonic projects and realities, on the other. Moreover, like al-Azmeh and Lazreg, he strongly rejects the suggestion made by some Western scholars and Islamists that Islamic fundamentalism should be considered a postmodern phenomenon. This fundamentalism, like all forms of fundamentalisms is not postmodern; it is premodern with a "dream of semimodernity": "Universality of knowledge is desirable, in contrast to universalism which is an ideology that I dismiss, as much as I dismiss postmodern fashions and globalism."[40]

Also like his two colleagues, he regards postmodern relativism, both cognitive and cultural, to be in reality a form of indifference to what is "other" and a convenient justification used by religious fundamentalisms, including the Islamic: "Is relativism, as currently displayed by Western intellectuals, an attitude of tolerance? Or is it not rather related to moral indifference and thus virtually a setback to ways behind the rationalism of the Enlightenment and behind objective knowledge?"[41] Tibi insists that his commitment to modern knowledge, rationality, and Enlightenment values is neither naive nor blind. He shows clear awareness of the Western critique of modern science, rationality, and modernity in general. His concern, he says, is the fundamentalist animosity toward human reason and its emancipatory yearnings.

An important part of the Islamist cultural project is the Islamicization of knowledge, in particular the Islamicization of the social sciences, in the sense of subjecting it to the dictates of Islamic revelation. Tibi quotes one of the major proponents of this epistemological Islamicization, the Egyptian Adel Hussain: "'Current Western sociological theories are not only ignorant about our environment and about its historical background. They are, moreover, inimical theories which, in the best cases, look down to us. The worst we can do is to adopt them, which would be tantamount to subjecting ourselves to the disdain these theories treat us with.'"[42] The alternative social science Hussain proposes is elaborated within the framework of Islamic faith, based on the belief that the holy Qur'an contains all the premises of valid and authentic knowledge. In this statement, Hussain indicates that Western social science fails in two respects: first, on the methodological level by lacking the necessary knowledge of the environment and history of the Arab world; and second, on the political level by being biased against this world.

What is important here is, again, not to throw the baby out with the bath water. The concern for a social knowledge of one's own is not unjustified. Such knowledge is important for forming a self-reflective awareness and for elaborating informed policies for development. However, its framework need not be that of a holy book. In fact, Islamists have not been the only ones to call for an indigenous social science. The postindependence era witnessed the concern with such a science as part of the intellectual, cultural, and even political decolonization process across the board. Secular modernists had this concern as much as traditionalists and religious thinkers did. But even the secularist demand for an indigenous social science had to face the challenges of intellectual decolonization. The 1991 article "Anthropology and the Call for Indigenization of Social Science in the Arab World"—authored by four women social scientists with a twenty-five year experience in anthropology, three of them Arab and one of them non-Arab—examines these challenges.[43] The authors start with a look at the historical context of the quest for social scientific indigenization that came to maturity in the 1970s: according to them, the quest corresponds to the crisis of the social sciences in the West as a result of the anti-imperialist critique both within the West and outside it in the form of the national liberation movements of the Third World. This critique led to the questioning of the taken-for-granted universality of Western social science. It also showed the pressing need for a local social science that would be relevant to the region and serve its interests.

The authors identify two trends in this quest: a radical one and a neotraditional one. Both connect the quest to the crisis of the intellectual in the postindependence Arab countries. In the radical trend, the link is made between these countries' socioeconomic dependency and their scholars' intellectual dependency, which led to the latter's alienation and marginalization. The production of a social science of little relevance to their environment is seen as a consequence of this multilayered dependency. Radicals think that the change in the scientific field cannot wait for a change in the politicoeconomic field. In fact, they believe that an intellectual change can contribute to the political change. The change is to be sought not in a total rejection of the existing and to a great extent Western body of knowledge, but in the search for a science that will account for the region's specificities. They emphasize the need for a democratic political system in which scholars can work freely, without being censored, but also without being co-opted by the government to justify the status quo. The authors think that the advocates of indigenization in this radical trend present an accurate description of the crisis, but that they do not offer concrete ways of transcending it. These advocates assert their need to be intellectually independent, but do not elaborate methodological and theoretical means to realize that independence. The neotraditionalists, in contrast, reject the existing body of social science in toto and call for an exclusively local and generally Islamic science. They reproduce therewith the "Us versus Them" essentialist dichotomy, in which each group is seen as uniform and totally different from the other. Advocates of indigenization in this trend falsely assume, according to the authors, that they are and can remain unaffected by global influences in their social and scholarly milieus, in their thought patterns, and in the standards that validate their scientific work in the final analysis. They do not take into consideration the extent to which the availability of funding and the possibilities of training depend on outside and in most cases Western institutions. Moreover, they do not admit that it is on the basis of global criteria that they demonstrate the value of local traditional thinkers or bodies of knowledge.

The authors are not against the need for a more relevant social science for the area, in the work of Western as well as non-Western scholars. What they draw attention to is the importance of problematizing the concept of indigenization,[44] of not reducing it to the nationality of the scholars involved. They see the importance of taking into consideration the dependency context within which "indigenous" knowledge is to be produced and of avoiding the "Us versus Them" essentialist divide, which would imply that only Arabs can understand and study Arab societies. Engaging others in the act of inquiry remains necessary, provided the ways and methods of that engagement are devised. The authors recognize the centrality of certain conditions for the production of excellence in social science—namely, the existence of independent and well-organized local scientific communities that are protected and supported politically to nurture scientific creativity and critical thinking. Furthermore, the quest for scientific indigenization raises for them important questions of pedagogy: What knowledge is to be taught? How and to what end? What indigenous curricula are to be devised for Arab institutions of higher learning for the purpose of serving such a quest? Finally, the authors believe that the introduction of the gender element in this quest would enrich it and further the process of decolonizing the mind:

If "a new wind of cultural decolonization is blowing through the Arab Middle East," which is having a profound impact on the lives of women, then we should expect a new scholarship to emerge in order to grasp and understand it. Those scholars who are attempting to understand and explain this very phenomenon (some are committed to changing it as well), are also confronting their own cultural identities and modes of knowing in ways that never previously were considered to be part of the research "problematique." It is in this context of the challenge of authenticity and relevance of one's own research to the broader political struggle of decolonizing the mind that the scholarship on women in the Arab Middle East of the 1980s must be examined.[45]

Moroccan psychologist and writer Tahar Ben Jelloun, now an award-winning author established in Paris, addresses the question of political support for critical thinking. In an article originally written for *Le Monde* in 1974, "Décolonisation de la sociologie au Maghreb: Utilité et risques d'une fonction critique," later translated into English as "Decolonizing Sociology in the Maghreb: Usefulness and Risks of a Critical Function," he reviews the state of social scientific research in the political context of postindependence Maghreb (i.e., the Arab West or North Africa).[46] Most of his remarks sadly remain valid to our day. He recalls how sociology was used for colonial penetration and control, and he notes how the decolonization of sociology and the break with the colonial ethnographic tradition became afterwards an essential part of cultural and political decolonization. He presents briefly the various research centers set up by the postcolonial states inside and outside main universities to produce locally relevant social science, to analyze what had been unanalyzed, and to contribute to the development of the countries in question. He also explains how these same states quickly co-opted these centers to preserve their own stability and consolidate their legitimacy. He tells the readers how some were shut down and how the rest was asked to remain "neutral" and to adopt a functionalist approach that would not challenge the status quo, but at most explain it. The postindependence states sometimes preferred foreign researchers over native researchers for their political neutrality. Clearly, the governments did not want a sociology that challenged them or that escaped their control. Under these conditions, real questions and innovative methodologies could only be elaborated outside these official centers. Drawing on the assessments of major social scientists of the Maghreb, Abdelkebir al-Khatibi from Morocco, Mostefa Lacheraf from Algeria, and

Abdelkader Zghal and Hachmi Karoui from Tunisia, he shows how critical governments' willingness to accept critique is for the development of a real indigenous social science—in other words, how central the freedom of thought and expression is for such a science. He finally warns against the narrow nationalistic ideological constraints over knowledge: "The appropriation of knowledge is first of all the fact (the *act*) of rethinking history and ideas spawned by the West and which occupy our consciousness too much. To this dominating and possessive knowledge we must oppose critical theory building, capable of making us subjects conscious both of our creative possibilities and of the fragility of any purely nationalist discourse."[47]

In 1973, Zghal and Karoui had published a report in English on social scientific production in Tunisia, "Decolonization and Social Science Research: The Case of Tunisia."[48] In it, the authors draw attention to the selective way in which modernists involved in postcolonial state building apprehended social reality and how they ignored whatever did not fit in their modernist perspective, a selectivity that prevented a proper understanding of the real difficulties that stood in the way of modernization. Zghal and Karoui also insist on the importance of studying the postcolonial modernization processes in a wide comparative framework involving other Third World countries. Emphasizing the importance of adequate political conditions, they state: "Finally, we cannot conclude this note without mentioning a problem which goes beyond the academic framework but which conditions the conduct of social science research: the capacity of societies or more exactly of political regimes of third world countries to tolerate criticism. Without a modicum of tolerance, no true research is possible, even if there are scholars whose scientific competence is beyond dispute. Unfortunately even such a minimum level of tolerance is not found in the majority of the countries of third world who are now going through a critical phase in their structural changes."[49]

Moroccan sociologist and renowned writer Abdelkebir al-Khatibi addresses the issue of intellectual decolonization in two essays written in French in 1981: "Pensée autre" and "Double critique." Some of the main ideas formulated in them are gathered in an article in English called "Double Criticism: The Decolonization of Arab Sociology."[50] Contrary to what Franz Fanon declared shortly before his death—that Europe was now over—Europe, says al-Khatibi, persists in our (Arabs') intimate being as a tormenting and dominating power. This fact, he thinks, needs to be addressed by thorough work on ourselves and a reconsideration of Europe, rather than by dealing with it with dismay, despair, and *ressentiment*. Claiming our right to difference in a naive fashion cannot resolve that torment. What is needed, he says, is a double radical critique: the critique both of Arab and the European traditions and of the metaphysical bases on which they are founded. Insofar as Europe is concerned, a dialogue should be engaged with the thinkers who have put into question its metaphysical foundations, thinkers such as Nietzsche, Heidegger, Blanchot, and Derrida. It is no coincidence, al-Khatibi thinks, that Derrida's deconstructive work has developed together with the concerns of decolonization. A parallel deconstructive work should be undertaken on the Arab side—specifically, the deconstruction of a tradition that remains patriarchal and theological. For al-Khatibi, Arab traditionalism is metaphysics reduced to theology with a secret desire to replace God; Salafism is this metaphysics made doctrine, destined to become violent and cruel. Rationalism is metaphysics made technique with a strong will to power. Salafism intends to use this rationalism for its own purposes. Speaking, according to him, is the critical transformation of life, death, and survival, whereas metaphysical thinking is a system of cruelty that has domesticated us into a servile morality. From a clearly antireligious position, al-Khatibi states that what hurts the Arab being is the survival of God and that authenticity is but another poison of theology.[51]

The Maghrebi generation of the 1960s, he says, has been caught between Third World nationalism, more precisely the theological ideology of Arab nationalism, and dogmatic French Marxism. It has remained captive of both ideologies' destructive metaphysics.[52] It is on the margins of Western metaphysics and Islamic theology that Arab thinkers, according to him, have the chance of developing a genuinely emancipatory, decolonizing thought—*une pensée autre*, an "other thought," an alternative thought. This alternative thought is to take Europe as a difference that inhabits us, as an encounter with alterity that offers us the chance of a dialogue with the world. Moreover, this alternative thought cannot be the return to the inertia of the foundations of our being, of the religion and theology of the Maghreb (i.e., the Arab West), which are now disguised in various revolutionary ideologies. This no-return is bound to shake the Maghreb, but it is at the same time unavoidable for opening it to the big questions of the contemporary world. There can be no going back to the self, but only critical transformations. "Arab," he says, is the name of a "done" civilization in its founding metaphysical element—not in the sense of a really dead civilization, but in the sense of a civilization incapable of renewing itself as thought except through the insurrection of an alternative thought that is in dialogue with world transformations. "Arab," he adds, should also indicate a plurality, a diversity. The idea of an *umma*, a community of believers—a unity that denies the existence of differences, the existence of Copts, Berbers, Kurds, and so on, and the existence of the feminine in the margin of the margin—is a thing of the past.[53] Theocracy, as an idea of power and the power of an idea, is a thought of the past. Its persistence in the imaginary should be analyzed. It is interesting to note here that al-Khatibi's younger Moroccan colleague Mohammed Bennis, poet and literary critic, also attacks this notion of unity magnified in Islamic theology. According to Bennis, the theological notion of the One inspired by Islamic monotheism permeates the various domains of Arab culture and supports a monistic, centralized, and authoritarian modality of thought and action that does not make room for plurality and difference. In a strongly essentializing statement, he says:

> *This unique entity [the One defined by Islamic theology], whose essence is immutable, annihilates all that eclipses its own name or evokes its numerical character. It escapes history and replaces it with the absolute.*

> *This theological vision of the subject acting in history and civilization is anchored in our consciousness and in our unconscious. We see this subject spreading its rays across the totality of the Arab world. It is personified socially in the father, politically in the tribe, and culturally in the echo of the latter and in its extensions. It is even seen disguised under new terms such as unity, socialism, liberty, democracy, terms that are thus transformed, on the basis of the sociocultural givens of the present Arab world, into simple metaphors of the One, because the One does not submit to plurality, change, or difference.*[54]

For Bennis, any project of cultural renewal and cultural critique has to address this monism, whatever difficulties may arise in dealing with such a theologically inspired concept.

The nostalgia of a totalizing unity and a founding origin has to be given up, says al-Khatibi. On the world scene, Arabs are more or less marginal, dominated, underdeveloped, a minority; this position is precisely their protection against any form of complacency, he thinks, because a thought that is not inspired by poverty, according to him, is always destined to dominate and humiliate. A thought that is not marginal, fragmentary, and unfinished is invariably a thought of ethnocide. Such a view is not an exaltation of poverty as such, he adds, but the call for a plural thought that will not be based on self-sufficiency.[55] I return to these important reflections on power, postcolonial thought, and cultural critique in the comparative remarks in chapter 6.

The Maghreb, says Khatibi, by its very location between the Orient, the Occident, and Africa, has the chance of developing such a plural thought culturally, linguistically, and politically. However, the "outside" has to be rethought as well, decentered, subverted, and derouted from its domineering determinations. Only such a modified "outside" can push us away from our nostalgia for a father and uproot our yearning from its metaphysical soil.[56] Such a plural thought would be a thought in languages and not a thought in Arabic. Given the bilingual reality of the Maghreb, to think in languages would offer the invaluable chance for its thinkers to nurture a plural thought that would be a genuinely decolonized thought. The latter would break the constraints of a self-sufficient identity and break the silence of colonized societies, producing an archaeology of silence, the unsaid, and the unexplored. For him, a decolonized sociology would be a part of such a plural thought.[57]

The late Hisham Sharabi (1927–2005), professor of European intellectual history and Omar al-Mukhtar Professor of Arab Culture at Georgetown University as well as chairman of the Washington-based Center for Policy Analysis on Palestine until his death, also recognized a chance in linguistic plurality—namely, the possibility for Arab thinkers to immerse themselves in Western intellectual discourses, which would allow them to grasp these discourses from within.[58] Such a grasp would lead to a critical stand vis-à-vis these discourses as well as vis-à-vis Arab sociocultural realities. It would create a healthy, critical distance from which these realities can be viewed—that is, neither from the viewpoint of an alien other nor from the viewpoint of a defensive self. According to Sharabi, critical Arab thinkers have since the 1970s and 1980s increasingly been moving in this direction, especially those in the expatriate communities. But they have not yet developed an original, coherent theory to conceptualize their societies' cultural phenomena. They have been more concerned with problematizing than with theorizing, and they have often imported Western concepts and foreign jargons without integrating them into their writing in the form of clarified notions in plain language. He applies his criticism to the work of al-Khatibi: "their tone is rhetorical and they are more concerned to insert borrowed concepts and methods in their discourse than to explain and ground this discourse in intelligible 'Arab' terms. Thus, for example, Jabiri's Foucaultian archeology, Khatibi's Barthesian semiotics and Benniss's Derridan deconstruction tend to be inserted directly into the new language without proper 'translation'—a fact which has tended to narrow this critical circle and encourage trendy Western forms of thought and interpretation."[59]

For Sharabi, this tendency illustrates some of the linguistic and paradigmatic difficulties involved in working with foreign intellectual traditions and theories. Without a solid grasp of the latter, one might think that these traditions and theories, like consumer goods, can be transferred from one sociocultural and historical sphere to another, without an awareness of the contextual constituents and implications. The so-called traditionalists, in contrast, want to develop a totally antagonistic approach completely ignorant of Western traditions. This reaction to the Western origin of the humanities and the social sciences is understandable but unfruitful:

> First, the scholarly disciplines in the humanities and social sciences are all initially products of Western experience and thought. Second, the kind of knowledge that the Other, the object of Western knowledge—in this case Arab society and culture—has of itself is therefore essentially Western knowledge even when it is locally produced. Modern Third World scholarship is basically derivative scholarship, producing and re-producing a Western knowledge. This latter fact sheds strong light on one of the major impulses of fundamentalist Islam and its insistence on the need for a total break with the West and return to Islamic values and categories—that is to say, to independent interpretation and scholarship.
>
> Against this background the current movement of secular cultural criticism in the Arab world presents itself not as a synthesis or a compromise binding Western-type modernity to Arab and Islamic modes of thought, but rather as an oppositional discourse seeking to transcend both Western hegemony and fundamentalist resistance through systematic critique.[60]

Indeed, Sharabi was among the first scholars of modern Arab thought to draw attention to this Arab secular critique of the past few decades and to predict the growing tension between the religious conservative and the secular radical trends on both the epistemological level and the political level. In 1988, he wrote: "the struggle in the next decade . . . will be primarily a cultural struggle, with decisive social and political consequences, between the forces of religious conservatism and the forces of secular critical modernity."[61] These forces, according to him, have emerged from the postcolonial reality of Arab societies, which Sharabi calls "neopatriarchy": "It can be fairly said that neopatriarchal society was the outcome of modern Europe's colonization of the patriarchal Arab world, of the marriage of imperialism and patriarchy."[62] This society is characterized by external dependency and internal heteronomy, which together produce a distorted modernity, a modernized patriarchy that is neither modern nor "authentic"/traditional.[63] It is not really modern because it is still governed by authoritarianism and tribalism; and it is no more a traditional patriarchy because of a limited, formal, and superficially imitative modernization of society. Sharabi summarizes this neopatriarchal society's attributes:

1. Social fragmentation—i.e., the family, clan, religion, or ethnic group (rather than the nation or civil society) constitute the basis of social relations and corresponding social organization.

2. Authoritarian organization—i.e., domination, coercion, and paternalism (rather than cooperation, mutual recognition, and equality) govern all relations from the microstructure of the family to the macrostructures of the state.

3. Absolutist paradigms—i.e., a closed, absolutist consciousness (in theoretical practice, in politics, and everyday life) grounded in transcendence, metaphysics, revelation, and closure (rather than in difference, plurality, diffusion, openness, etc.).

4. Ritualistic practice —i.e., behavior governed by ceremony, custom, and ritual (rather than by spontaneity, creativity, and innovation). And so on.[64]

Sharabi's contrast between tradition and modernity is at times too schematic and uncritical, and the opposition he draws between the elements constituting each pole, such as reason/myth and science/religion is too sharp. His belief is that this lack of genuine modernity and creative productivity cannot be countered by grand revolutionary doctrines of liberation or by a "classical revolutionary seizure of power," which may very well produce new forms of authoritarianism and repression. Nor can Islamic fundamentalism be the effective liberating force from neopatriarchy, despite the receptive ground for it in the state and the population at large.[65] He argues:

> My contention is that though Islamic fundamentalism may be able to contain the anomic manifestations of neopatriarchal society, it can offer no cure for the structural disorders of that society, of which, at this terminal stage, anomie is the most pervasive symptom. Essentially idealistic, fundamentalism will address only symptoms, and its solutions will necessarily be authoritarian, based on absolutist doctrine and methods. Thus at the same time that fundamentalism may appear as a liberating force, it will inevitably be oppressive: as it violently brings down neopatriarchal society (or ineluctably decomposes it from within) it will inexorably retreat toward authoritarian patriarchy.[66]

As he sees things, only a secular, multifocal, and pervasive resistance to the various forms of oppression can open the way to real liberation.

Critique of the Conciliatory and Unitary Pattern of Thinking: Muhammad Jaber al-Ansari, Hisham Sharabi, and Nadeem Naimy

Muhammad Jaber al-Ansari

The heightened polarization between the secularist-liberal and religious-conservative positions as well as the attempts at reconciling them has been the object of an extensive study first presented as a doctoral dissertation in the Arabic department of the American University of Beirut in 1979, but not published until some two decades later, in 1996, because of the author's concerns about the possible reactions to what he saw as sensitive intellectual, religious, and political issues, as the publisher explains in the 1999 second edition.[67] The author is Bahraini intellectual and political activist Muhammad Jaber al-Ansari, who has held numerous academic positions and public offices in Bahraini administrations and continues to serve in these areas in various capacities in the Persian Gulf region. He writes extensively both in the academic field and in the press, mainly on matters pertaining to Arab thought and Arab politics. In his 668-page-long work, he closely examines the conciliatory pattern of thought (*al-tawfiqiyya*) that many contemporary thinkers—including Sharabi, al-Azmeh, Laroui, and al-Azm—have regarded as one of the main causes of the absence of a real liberating and changing force in modern Arab thought. He analyzes the strengths and weaknesses of this pattern and follows its developments since the rise of the Arab Islamic civilization in the seventh century.

Al-Ansari observes that this civilization was shaped by the absorption of a number of cultures that came under Islamic rule as a result of rapidly expanding conquests. The Islamic ruling forces assimilated these cultures— including the Near Eastern, Christian and non-Christian, Syriac, Greek, Hellenic, Roman, Persian, and Indian—as part of a new, original, and dynamic civilization. This civilization's theoreticians came to see it as a "middle" (*wasatiyya*) community (or nation), capable of absorbing foreign elements and destined to incorporate, reform, and complete the preceding monotheistic messages, namely Judaism and Christianity. At the same time, however, this emerging Arab Islamic civilization was based on a to- talistic system (*nizam shumuli*) that clearly demarcated itself from other worldviews and creeds; in other words, it was a system characterized by a distinct and comprehensive set of values, conceptions, and regulations for individual, social, and political life. The assimilation was accordingly strongly oriented toward a principle of unity that safeguarded that system—a princi- ple that Adonis, al-Khatibi, Bennis, Sharabi, and others have criticized, as noted earlier. It was meant to produce unified notions of God, community, creed, rule, state, and law, steering toward a unified, final, eternal, and fixed doctrine. Plurality and multiplicity were perceived as a threat, an intolerable blasphemy in the form of polytheism, a heresy or deviation from the right path regarding the doctrine, and a danger of civil war for the state and the community.

According to al-Ansari, this concern for unity and unification also de- termined which aspects of those foreign cultures were integrated. Persian Manicheanism, for instance, was rejected, whereas Aristotelian and Neo- platonic philosophies were welcomed. Aristotle's logical principle of non- contradiction as well as the Neoplatonic idea of emanation from the One clearly suited the Arab Islamic emphasis on unity in contrast to the dualist principle of Manicheanism. Speaking in Nietzschean terms, al-Ansari says that Arab Islamic civilization seemed to have adopted the Appolonian elements of Greek culture, but not the Dionysian ones that expressed the conflictual and tragic tensions of human existence.[68] This choice may be one reason why the Arab Islamic civilization did not produce drama as a literary genre that displays situations of struggle, doubt, and crisis, and instead privileged the conciliatory intellectual resolution of opposites and the establishment of certainties. In religious matters, attention was likewise directed toward intellectually conciliatory positions that avoided confrontation between opposites such as faith and reason, rather than toward inner spiritual journeys fraught with crises, anxieties, and uncertainties. This choice is perhaps why, he says, we do not find writings like St. Augustine's *Confessions* in Islam, except in marginalized and repressed corners, where such confessions are succinctly mentioned and the emphasis placed on the "happy end" of the journey and the certainty of faith. As an example, he recalls the crisis that al-Ghazali briefly mentions in his *Deliverance from Error*.[69]

According to al-Ansari, this prevailing demand for unification by a totalistic system has given rise to three patterns in Arab religious, intellectual, and political thought. First, what he calls the Salafi pattern of thought is based on a strictly conservative attitude that is culturally protectionist and religiously literalist. It advocates a purist defense of Islam as a totalistic system and rejects the introduction of foreign elements into it. It generally prevails in rural and remote regions not much exposed to foreign influences and characterized by simple socioeconomic structures. These social milieus are the bases of defense against foreign invasion and the reservoirs of conservative renewal energies. Here, al-Ansari leaves out urban conservative groups that also uphold Salafi modes of thinking.

Second, the "rejectionist" pattern of thought revolts against the system and adopts foreign ideas and beliefs to contest it. It is in general a minority phenomenon, found in peripheral pockets of rebellion, as in mountainous areas, and it is often associated with social revolts led by racial or religious minorities. The movements that apply it are usually persecuted and repressed. Among them are the Gnostics, the Batinis,[70] the materialists, and those who contest prophecy. Al-Ansari does not expect Arab mainstream milieus to harbor this rejectionist pattern.

Third, the "conciliatory" pattern is protective of the Islamic system, but with more flexibility and openness than the Salafi pattern. It upholds the system as a set of final and core values, but allows for the integration of certain foreign elements into it when they are deemed compatible with those values and after being Islamicized or indigenized. The integration process is generally accompanied by a whole range of apologetic justifications. This mode of thinking aims at reconciling a fixed core with various new elements; in other words, it invites change but always within the limits of a fixed system—hence, the inevitable tensions and ambiguities. Most, though not all, Islamic philosophers and Mu'tazilites of the classical period advocated such a "middle" position. Whereas rejectionists borrow in order to contest the system, proponents of conciliation borrow in order to defend the system and strengthen it. Urban and trade centers, open to foreign contacts and based on the circulation of people and goods, are the natural home of this "middle" pattern. It was thus the dominant pattern during the early centuries of Islam because much of the economy was based on trade and because of the cultural sophistication these centuries witnessed under the Arab and Persian rules in contrast to the subsequent Moghul, Seljuk, and Turkish rules. This conciliatory position was threatened and replaced by the more strictly defensive and conservative Salafi position at times of invasions, such as during the Crusades. In general, it is this conciliatory position that gave Islam an open and tolerant edge.

Al-Ansari warns his readers that this typification is to be taken cautiously as a broad generalization rather than a fixed categorization—a generalization that is meant to help clarify the history and nature of the conciliatory pattern of thinking in Arab Islamic civilization so that its present chances of success can be critically assessed. As mentioned earlier, many wonder whether a "middle" position will be able to absorb the polarization that has been growing between liberal secularists and religious conservatives in the Arab world since independence and especially since the 1967 defeat and Abdel Nasser's death. According to al-Ansari, the polarization has increased since the collapse of early-twentieth-century attempts at conciliation led by Islamic reformers such as Muhammad Abduh. In fact, al-Ansari connects the exacerbated polarization of the last third of the twentieth century to that of the first third, when the secularists seemed to be on the verge of imposing themselves on the Arab scene, as the fundamentalists are today. He revisits those early decades of the century to explain this connection.

The first reactions to the European interventions and to the weakening of the Ottoman centralized caliphate came from Salafi, conservative movements in the course of the nineteenth century: the Wahhabi in Arabia, the Jaza'iri in Algeria, the Mahdi in Sudan, and the Sanussi in Lybia. But it seems to have become increasingly evident, says al-Ansari, that the confrontation was not only political and military, but also civilizational and that cultural reforms were thus necessary to face the new challenges. This realization gave rise to the first conciliatory and reformist attempts of the modern times at the hands of Muhammad Abduh. But these reforms soon appeared to be inadequate to face the growing European invasion, with the British occupation of Egypt in 1882 and the imposition of the British and French mandates on a fragmented Arab region after the collapse of the Ottoman caliphate and the defeat of the Arab struggles for unity and independence by these same European powers. An imposing and imposed European modernity seemed to overwhelm the conciliatory attempts. Abduh himself may have realized that, says al-Ansari, referring to Albert Hourani's characterization of this change. According to Hourani,

> *Abduh's purpose, in all the acts of his later life as well as his writings, was to bridge the gulf within Islamic society, and in so doing to strengthen its moral roots. He thought this could only be done in one way. It could not be done by a return to the past, by stopping the process of change begun by Muhammad Ali. It could only be done by accepting the need for change, and by linking that change to the principles of Islam: by showing that the changes which were taking place were not only permitted by Islam, but were indeed its necessary implications if it was rightly understood, and that Islam could serve both as a principle of change and a salutary control over it. He was not concerned, as Khayr al-Din had been in a previous generation, to ask whether devout Muslims could accept the institutions and ideas of the modern world; they had come to stay, and so much the worse for anyone who did not accept them. He asked the opposite question, whether someone who lived in the modern world could still be a devout Muslim. His writings were directed not so much to convinced Muslims doubtful whether modern civilization was acceptable, as to men of modern culture and experience who doubted whether Islam, or indeed any revealed religion, was valid as a guide to life. It was this class which was the greatest danger to the* umma, *if it was won to metaphysical secularism; but equally it was from this class only that the leadership of a revived* umma *could be drawn.*[71]

Indeed, secularist views were increasingly defended between 1918 and 1930, and not only by Christian thinkers, as was the case before World War I,[72] but also now by Muslim thinkers and even by sheikhs such as Ali Abdel Raziq, who defended the nonpolitical nature of the Islamic message based on arguments drawn from Islam itself. Al-Ansari sees in the early Christian secularist efforts, which remained limited in their impact because of their minority setting, an important impulse to the subsequent Muslim endeavors.[73] Other influential factors were the secularist transformations in postwar Turkey with the abolition of the caliphate in 1924 and the institutional changes introduced by the colonial powers, such as the Parliament in Egypt introduced by the British. These secularist voices called for the comprehensive adoption of European cultural modernity, both in knowledge and in politics. Al-Ansari mentions a number of them.

In 1926, the Egyptian Ismail Mazhar (1891–1962) wrote in the modernist periodical *al-Muqtataf*, founded by the Lebanese Ya'qub Sarruf (1852–1927), and advocated a radical rationalist revolution. He attacked all forms of metaphysical thinking, including the traditional Islamic one that combined Islam with some type of science—a type of thinking that reformists such as al-Afghani wanted to revive. Against the revival of such a conciliatory strategy, Mazhar called for the adoption of the European scientific reasoning. After Sarruf's death in 1927, Mazhar started his own journal, *al-'Usur*, which continued the main line of *al-Muqtataf*, but with a bolder critique of religion and conciliatory thinkers, and even of some secularist thinkers such as Ali Abdel Raziq and Taha Husayn. *Al-'Usur*, which appeared between 1927 and 1930, contributed to the dissemination of liberal and secularist ideas. In 1926, Husayn published his critical analysis of religious stories and texts, *Fi al-Shi'r al-Jahili* (On Jahili Poetry), applying, as we saw in chapter 1, the Cartesian method of doubt. He examined the sources of knowledge concerning pre-Islamic poetry, including the Qur'an, and raised questions about the a posteriori construction of this poetry according to Islam's views and needs. The groundbreaking aspect of Husayn's work was the opening of sacred and traditional texts to scientific secular analyses. The book was banned, and its author was obliged to draw back his claims. Another Egyptian, Muhammad Hussein Haykal (1888–1956), propagated the positivist and evolutionary ideas of Auguste Comte. In 1922, he wrote a book on the life of Jean-Jacques Rousseau emphasizing the latter's notion of natural religion. He conceived of the identity of Egyptian literature and history as founded on the Pharaonic civilization.

The period between World War I and the mid-1930s also witnessed, according to al-Ansari, the development of a secularist nationalist thought in the work of thinkers such as the Egyptian Ahmad Lutfi al-Sayyid (discussed in chapter 1) and the Syrian Sati' al-Husri, who were the first to attack one of the pillars of Arab Islamic culture: the close association between the religion of Islam and communal identity. These thinkers advocated a secular nationalism, Egyptian for Sayyid and Arab for al-Husri. Finally, these years likewise saw the emergence of Arab Marxist writings and the formation of Communist parties in Lebanon, Syrian, Palestine, and Egypt by many Christians and some Muslims.

All this secularist intellectual and political activity came to a head, says al-Ansari, in the early 1930s and gave way to a comeback of the conciliatory school of thought, and then, with the latter's failure after a couple of decades, to a growing opposition between the secular and conservative poles, with the conservative religious tendency advancing this time. He offers a number of explanations for the aborted course of secularism after its brief ascent in the first decades of the twentieth century. First, many of those secularist thinkers realized how estranged their public was from their secularist ideas and how these ideas could not resonate with the still religious and tradition-minded masses. This realization pushed them to revise their calls, sometimes in ways that suggested a complete turn away from them: Husayn published 'Ala Hamish al-Sira (On the Margin of the Biography of the Prophet) in 1935,[74] about the beauty of the imaginary and the emotional aspects of traditional popular myths, rejecting the exclusive valorization of pure reason; and Muhammad Hussein Haykal wrote in 1935 about the life of the Prophet, after having written on the life of Rousseau. According to al-Ansari and in contrast to some other contemporary critics such as al-Azmeh,[75] these turns did not always constitute a total abandonment of the previous modernist positions, but rather a move toward conciliating them with romantic views of tradition, identity, and religion. The turns were sometimes dramatically expressed by those who experienced them, however. Al-Ansari refers to the introduction in Haykal's 1936 book Fi Manzil al-Wahi (In the House of Revelation),[76] which describes the crisis caused by this transformation. Haykal justifies his turn and attacks those who accuse him of betraying his earlier critical position and of shifting to a populist, traditionalist position. He states that he, too, for a long while believed that moral and spiritual European ideas were to be sown in his land in order to produce progress and salvation, until he realized that those seeds could not live in a soil that was not theirs, until he understood that what really moved and impregnated his people was their Islamic history. Islam offered a much wider scope of human brotherhood than the narrow nationalism for which he had enthused earlier, especially the Egyptian Pharaonic nationalism. For him, this change in view did not amount to abandoning critical and scientific thinking, but to recognizing and honoring the living Islamic identity and impulse of his people.

Among the factors behind the retreat of the secularist movement, al-Ansari also mentions the reality of colonialism as the other face of European cultural modernity and the discredit it threw on the whole secularist-modernist project. The secularist intellectuals, he adds, did not articulate a clear and strong critique of colonial Europe, expecting Europe to be true to its culture and thus letting themselves be associated with it in the people's eyes. Europe itself was going through severe political and cultural crises during this time, leading to the rise of fascist movements that diminished further the credibility of European democratic and secular principles. The fragmentation of the Arab region as a result of the French and British man-dates was an additional obstacle to the possibility of a comprehensive change. Moreover, the colonial powers rather than the people themselves made many of the modernist changes, such as the establishment of the Parliament in Egypt. The independence negotiations later on did not lead to genuine autonomy, but to new forms of dependence. In addition, the state of Israel was being projected in religious terms: the European powers, perceived to be Christian, were seen as being implicated in the creation of a Jewish home on Arab Muslim lands. Finally, the absence of an economy that could produce a solid middle class receptive of radical modernist ideas also played a role in the lack of popular support for these ideas. Colonial interests clearly did not encourage the development of a modernizing in-dustrialization process. Furthermore, the rise of a lower middle class to power in the postindependence era favored the adoption of the "middle" ideology. This class, says al-Ansari, saw its interests neither in total revolu-tion nor in total conservatism (as Sharabi notes in *Neopatriarchy*); it re-pressed Communists as well as fundamentalists.

For all these reasons, he concludes, this encounter with Europe did not bring about a solid Arab modernist movement that could embrace modern science with all its assumptions and implications and that could consign religion to the personal, inner realm. The radical attempts at moderniza-tion were associated with the old rejectionist movements that were tradi-tionally seen as deviant and threatening to the community. Al-Ansari also agrees with the widespread opinion that in contrast to the earlier encoun-ter with the Hellenic culture in the classical period, Muslims did not choose this encounter with Europe; rather, they experienced it from a position of weakness and defeat, and it was framed in the military and political con-text of colonialism.

As a result, secularist ideas, says al-Ansari, gave way by the mid-1930s to new conciliatory propositions in doctrinal as well as political matters. Conciliatory nationalist and revolutionary ideologies avoided abstract and purely rationalist orientations and incorporated romantic and religious elements, thus proposing mixed doctrines that combined secularism and modernism with romanticism and traditionalism. He examines the renewed attempts at reconciling philosophical thinking with Islam in the work of thinkers such as Mustapha Abdel Raziq (Ali Abdel Raziq's brother) and Muhammad Hussein Haykal. He then analyzes three ideologies in particular: the Baath ideology of the Syrian Michel Aflaq (1910–1989), the Syrian nationalist ideology of Antun Sa'adeh (1904–1949), and the revolutionary socialism of the Egyptian leader Gamal Abdel Nasser. He presents the conceptual construction of these conciliatory ideologies, underlining the unresolved tensions and contradictions they harbored. In addition, he follows the development of the tensions as these ideologies become the doctrine of ruling parties and leaders in the second half of the twentieth century. The leaders' repressive policies and their failure to fulfill developmental and liberational promises, as well as the circumstances of the 1967 defeat followed by the death of romantic-tragic, liberating, and despotic leader Abdel Nasser, did not allow for a real confrontation between the opposing elements to take place, run its course, and reach a mature resolution.

Having explored the reasons for the floundering of the radical secularist-liberal movement, having noted the failure of the early- and mid-twentieth-century conciliatory efforts, and witnessing the growing polarization between the secularist-liberal and religious-conservative positions in his own time, al-Ansari wonders if one can once again bet on the conciliatory strategy as a solution to the intellectual, social, and political tensions plaguing Arab societies today. This is the main question of his book and his purpose in examining closely the very nature of the Arab conciliatory approach to those tensions, an approach that consists, as he puts it, in avoiding real conflict and a clear settlement and in shunning a full-scale opposition. To what extent, says al-Ansari, can such an approach be a fruitful way of solving those tensions today? He probes the approach at a deeper level in order to expose its assumptions and to analyze the fundamental conceptions of the pertinent issues involved in it. For him, the main flaw of modern conciliatory thought is its failure to understand the nature of reason upon which modern Western culture is based. Arab modern thinkers do not realize that this new "Hellenic" culture they are trying to conciliate with traditional and even reformed Islam is drastically different from the culture their predecessors dealt with in the Middle Ages: its notions of reason and logic are no longer those of Aristotle, with their metaphysical and epistemological certainties, but rather those of the Cartesian doubt and the Kantian critique, of the Hegelian logic and dialectics; Aristotelian certain reason has been replaced with skeptical reason, and Aristotelian logic with Hegelian dialectical logic. Arab Muslim thinkers, observes al-Ansari, understand European cultural modernity as a revolt against traditional Christianity, but do not pay enough attention to the fact that the revolt was primarily a revolt against Aristotelian metaphysics, logic, and cosmology. They do not realize that they are now dealing with a postmetaphysical culture and a postmetaphysical reason, with a new conception of faith: faith as intuition for Descartes, as moral necessity for Kant, and as dialectical synthesis for Hegel. The relation of this modern reason to faith is a troubled one, compared to the harmonious and stable relationship found in Averroes or Aquinas.

Some Arab thinkers, he adds, see in contemporary Christian or spiritual philosophies—such as those of Bergson, Jaspers, and Berdaîev—the return of European reason to faith, but again without understanding the changes in the modern notions of reason and faith, and without recognizing the place of anxiety, tension, and finitude brought into them. This European culture is no longer the Aristotelian Hellenic culture that Muslim thinkers of the classical age adopted and conciliated with the system of Islam. The question to be raised now, for al-Ansari, is whether Muslim thinkers can make postmetaphysical reason and logic theirs in their endeavor to harmonize Islam with cultural modernity, whether Islam can accept the troubled, unstable, and dialectic nature of these new concepts. He thinks that without grasping these fundamental transformations of cultural modernity, conciliatory thought cannot possibly hope to succeed in offering adequate attempts at harmonization. Superficial views of this modernity can easily open the way to superficial, partial, and eclectic compositions of conciliation, but these compositions will crumble at the first challenge and produce only ruins (*rukam*); they cannot generate foundations upon which solid intellectual advances can be secured and through which some form of accumulation (*tarakum*) can take place.

Given the complexity of Islamic and European modern cultures, he says, it will always be tempting to try and make easy conciliations, but they will always be ruinous ones. Moreover, as long as real conflicts and challenges are shunned, no qualitative move forward can be achieved in any of the multiple dualisms that haunt Arab thought: secularism and Salafi conservatism, the modern and the ancient, the West and Islam, modernity and Islam, socialism and Islam, reason and faith, contemporaneity and heritage. Avoidance of full-fledged conflict will produce only dishonest solutions in which the opposing elements are emptied of their substance and twisted to fit forced resolutions. In Arab Islamic thought, notes al-Ansari, conflict is never limited to the two poles of these oppositions, but invariably encompasses a third, conciliatory pole. This characteristic makes resolution harder to achieve because of the constant need to find a "middle" way that prevents real confrontation, which alone can lead to a real resolution. The persistent preoccupation with the harmonious "middle" way—for him, an Arab Islamic specificity—transforms the inevitable tensions into secrets and faults instead of healthy and legitimate realities that need to be explored and pondered. This "middle" culture seems to lack the appropriate ways of channeling these tensions because the tensions are perceived as threats that question textual authority, challenge doctrinal certainty, and endanger communal unity. Beliefs, in particular religious ones, are presented as stable truths given from the outset, rather than as convictions reached after troubled journeys. Such journeys, as mentioned earlier, are not granted much room in the literature. Here, al-Ansari mentions, as a rare example of the genre, the text with which Abbas Mahmud al-Aqqad (1889–1964) introduces his book *'Abqariyyat Muhammad* (The Genius of Muhammad) and in which he describes his thirty-year existential journey of anxiety, disquietude, and search before reaching the certainty of faith.[77]

Al-Ansari detects in Arab contemporary thought certain impulses that he thinks may contribute to the acceptance of dialectic logic and the accommodation of troubled existential experiences. He sees these impulses in Arab Marxist thought and Arab existentialist writing, both of them marginal on the Arab intellectual scene and increasingly so under the pressure of fundamentalist ideologies, but still carrying for him the possibilities of a wider accommodation of the features of cultural modernity in Islamic culture and thought.[78] Marxist thought, he says, can show that dialectical opposition may lead to unity, albeit in more complex ways than with classical logic, and thus that it need not necessarily become nihilistic. And existentialist writings, such as those by Egyptian Qur'anic scholar A'isha Abdel Rahman, especially her 1967 book *Maqal fi al-Insan: Dirasa Qur'aniyya* (Essay on the Human: A Qur'anic Study),[79] can familiarize and conciliate Arab readers with the troubles of true inner journeys. Berdaiev's suggestion to create a new medieval age as a meeting platform for faith and reason, religion and socialism, and certainty and existential agony may be a fruitful proposition for a new Arab conciliatory thought, for in the final analysis the task is to open Islam to the dialectical nature of the modern age.

Al-Ansari appears to be supportive of Berdaiev's proposal and to defend the conciliatory mode of thinking, though in a modernized fashion, yet in the introduction to the second edition of his book he clearly rejects

such an understanding of his position. He says that his close analysis of the
workings of conciliatory thinking cannot warrant such an interpretation.
At no point in his book, however, does he state his rejection of it in an explicit manner, perhaps as a cautionary measure of self-protection in a
repressive Arab environment. Indeed, throughout the sections in which he
explains what a modernized form of conciliatory thinking should incorporate, his statements are conditional, suggesting that *if* this form of thinking
were to be upheld, it would need to change its assumptions in important
respects. The fact remains that his thorough and frank analysis of this prevailing mode of thinking offers a powerful critique of the entire conciliatory approach to the pressing issues of the modern Arab world, which has
failed to achieve a real breakthrough in any one of those conflictual issues.
Having said this, I should raise a question about the adequacy of applying
the Hegelian teleological model to our postmetaphysical world. For al-
Ansari, the issue is that of harmonizing the unitary nature of Islam with
the dialectical principle of the current age. A better characterization of this
age, in my opinion, is the differentiation of the various fields of life and
knowledge, faith and reason, morality and science suggested by Weber,
Luhmann, and others. Moreover, the existential inner experiences to be
verbalized and legitimized presuppose the existence and acceptance of individuals who are allowed to express their inner lived experiences. The
Arab world's socioeconomic and political conditions, both internal and
external, have not favored the emergence of such spheres of individual,
social, and intellectual life, as al-Ansari himself notes. On both counts, it
is not possible to harmonize with the modern age the totalistic nature of
an Islam understood as a unitary, comprehensive system. Hence, the
question becomes whether a differentiated Islamic culture is possible in
which no unitary principle is forced upon the various domains of life and
thought in a totalistic manner, but in which the different cultural forces,
old and new, nurture and interact with the dynamic elements of those
domains. Can this happen in a defeated and threatened Arab world? And
at the same time, can any defeat or threat be faced without the abandonment of a defensive, unitary, and totalistic system? This difficult predicament has plagued the Arab world since the Nahda and troubles it today
more than ever.

Hisham Sharabi and Nadeem Naimy

For Hisham Sharabi, the ambiguities and contradictions of the conciliatory attitude are to a great extent responsible for the failure of the first

Nahda. They plagued the positions of the three main groups of Nahda thinkers—the religious reformists, the Muslim secularists, and the westernizing Christians. The first two groups were too immersed in and defensive of their Islamic background, and the third was too marginal in the Islamic majority to effectuate radical and public breaks with the traditional and prevailing beliefs. In his book *Arab Intellectuals and the West: The Formative Years, 1875–1914*, Sharabi offers an insightful analysis of these groups' psychological, social, political, and intellectual characteristics. The impulse for reform originated to a great extent in the challenge posed by Europe to Muslim society, and so it took the form of a defensive reaction that aimed at reinstituting and strengthening Islamic truth rather than at exposing that truth to free criticism. Thus, it did not lead to thorough philosophical elaborations or to radical theological reconsiderations. Many of the reformists, such as Muhammad Abduh and Jamal al-Din al-Afghani, understood themselves as reformists similar to Martin Luther. In reality, says Sharabi, theirs was a neo-orthodox reform that called for a return to the original springs of Islam, but that never overstepped the conventional limits of traditional thinking. Consequently, a genuine critical consciousness failed to emerge. The religious reformists were more concerned, according to Sharabi, with practical success and power-oriented transformations vis-à-vis the West than with truth and critique. They saw the problem in Muslims and not in Islamic doctrines and notions, so they unwittingly enhanced the role of the Muslim clergy. In contrast to the religious conservatives who continued to assert the self-sufficiency of Islam and to deny the external challenge, the reformists deployed argumentative efforts to address this challenge, but never in a radical self-critical manner.

The Muslim secularists dealt with social and political matters independently from religion, but remained, according to Sharabi, socially and intellectually immersed in the prevailing Islamic culture and subject to societal pressure. They shunned religious questions and avoided frontal confrontations with deeply entrenched beliefs. Due to this position, their ideas lacked sharp doctrinal focus and remained in many ways ambiguous. Like the reformists, they perceived Europe as a fundamental "other," an agent of modernization but also a threat to their Islamic world. They never delved into serious studies of Europe and, like the reformists, were concerned primarily with the power contest with it.

The westernizing Christian thinkers, in contrast, were more inclined to free critical thinking and better equipped to grasp Europe because of their Europeanized education and their social position in the Arab Islamic world. As members of a religious minority, they were more interested in secular views of history and society and less focused on defensive arguments against Europe. Due to their social position, however, they could not push any of these orientations too far without risking a collision with the Islamic majority. They had to keep their statements vague and general, and they could not publicly assert sharp critical stands without being accused of betrayal and animosity against the majority religious culture. In all three cases, concludes Sharabi, the inability or unwillingness to take clear stands prevented the development of a full-fledged critique, essential for any genuine *nahda*.

Lebanese literary critic Nadeem Naimy, professor emeritus of Arab literature at the American University of Beirut, shares with al-Ansari the critique of conciliatory thinking.[80] Naimy explicitly regards this type of thinking to be a calamity for Arab intellectual life and to harbor a fundamental flaw in the understanding of the modern Arab problems of culture and modernity. This flaw consists not only in misunderstanding the post-metaphysical nature of modern reason, but more important in confusing religion and civilization in Islam. In a paper for a conference held in Beirut in 1998 on the liberal beginnings of modernity during the age of the Nahda, Naimy analyzes the conciliatory mode of thinking as it reached its paradigmatic form in the thought of Muhammad Abduh around the turn of the twentieth century. It became the dominant form of thinking thereafter.[81] One of its most explicit expressions is Abduh's famous statement about Islam's being the religion of reason, science, and civilization, in contrast to Christianity, which he saw as a religion of mysteries, miracles, and priesthood. For Abduh, this difference explains why cultural modernity necessitated a secularization process in the Christian West and why this modernity would increasingly move toward Islam. The Protestant Reformation is an example of such a move: it was Islamic in its structure and purpose.[82] The supreme evidence for Abduh's view is the great civilization that Islam gave rise to before it started to deviate from its true course. Within this view, signs of progress in cultural modernity are indigenized in some form or other—that is, are seen as being Islamic in nature—and signs of backwardness are regarded as alien to true Islam. Accordingly, those who adopt modernity need not distance themselves from Islam, and those who adhere to Islam need not shun or antagonize modernity.

A number of questions remain open in this kind of reasoning, says Naimy: What can guarantee that this deviation will not happen again? How can one explain the stunning development of the sciences in the non-

Muslim West? And how can one account for the significant contributions made to Islamic civilization by Eastern Christians? But the more fundamental problem for Naimy is the attempt to conciliate between, on the one hand, a religion, namely Islam, that like any other religion consists at its core of a fixed and absolute doctrine and, on the other hand, a culture, namely Western modern culture, that like any culture is by nature relative, unfinished, and changing. For him, this basic flaw has plagued much of modern Arab thought and has prevented it from producing solid, sustainable, and creative positions regarding questions of culture. Instead of confronting an Arab Islamic culture with a Western modern culture on the basis of concrete historical and objective studies, this flaw has placed a religion in opposition to a culture—a grave mistake in terms of conciliation that is bound to lead to untenable conclusions. Starting from this confusion, any proposition for change is fated to be perceived as an invitation to heresy, for the proposed change would be a change in a religious doctrine. Thus, no intellectual modernization can go far if started from this premise: it is bound to be condemned and rejected, or at best be marginalized and neglected. Naimy gives a number of examples of such failed attempts at the hands of prominent twentieth-century thinkers in theology, literary critique, and nationalist thought.

Ali Abdel Raziq's attempt at demonstrating from an Islamic religious point of view the absence of a prescribed form of government in Islam was refuted with great vigor by Rashid Rida from an equally Islamic point of view. Abdel Raziq's book was banned, and its author was forbidden to practice his religious and academic functions. He did not base his thoughts about the caliphate on an empirical study of the advantages and inconveniences of this form of government as found in the history of its existence, asserts Naimy, but on the doctrine of Islamic creed. In so doing, his project of separating a specific political system from the religion of Islam remained anchored in religion and provoked a stronger linking of the two in the reaction to his project. Taha Husayn wanted to liberate literary critique from religion and to apply Cartesian doubt to the religious stories and texts, such as the story of Abraham or of the construction of the Ka'aba. But these stories, according to Naimy, are not believed because they can withstand Cartesian examination, nor was Cartesian doubt destined for religious beliefs. The inevitable reaction came in the form of a condemnation and a stronger subjection of literary critique to religious control. Muhammad Hussein Haykal, who initially advocated a secular Pharaonic nationalism for Egypt, ended up turning to an Islamic Egyptian nationalism. His turn was mainly that of repentance because his first Pharaonic conception of nationalism was in many respects a religious conception. He too failed to liberate nationalism from religion. On the contrary, he eventually reinforced the bond between them. Finally, Abbas Mahmud al-Aqqad wanted to conciliate Darwinism with Islam, claiming that the Qur'an contains the principles of that scientific doctrine. Others after him, including Nasserites, would likewise claim to find scientific ideas as well as positivism and socialism in the Qur'an—all in an attempt to indigenize cultural and scientific ideas in the doctrine of a religion and its sacred texts. These attempts at indigenization aim at conciliating cultural and scientific views, which are by nature relative and falsifiable, with a religious doctrine that is by definition fixed and absolute. They are bound to distort at least one of the terms of the conciliation: either to render science fixed and absolute or to make religion falsifiable and relative. In either case, no credible conclusion can be reached, and no promising progress can be achieved. Furthermore, adds Naimy, this kind of reasoning invariably leaves it up to others, non-Muslims, to come up with scientific discoveries and novelties, which Muslims will then "Islamicize" with an unwavering sense of their own self-sufficiency and perfection. In this whole approach, he says, Islam is seen to contain and to have contained at all times all the answers to all matters past, present, and future. In this view, others' discoveries of novelties simply become occasions to unveil more of this perfection.

In his contribution to a conference on Arab cultural policies for development organized in Baghdad in 2000, Naimy closely examines this sense of self-sufficiency.[83] Two entities, "Islam" and "Western culture," are opposed, he says, as two total and separate formations in the absence of a comprehensive, universal human cultural context. The Arab Islamic heritage that could have helped greatly in inspiring creativity and in affirming identity in the face of colonialism has been turned into a factor for immobility and sterility. In many Arab Muslims' minds, he adds, what rendered the classical Islamic civilization great was Islam, which gathered the community of believers under its banner and raised it to power. Hence, for them, Islam's return to glory is a salvational return to faith and not a renewal of the numerous creative forces that produced this rich and complex civilization. It is also a return to a completed culture that can and ought to be taken as a completed identity: the statement of an "I am" from which any "I think" is to follow. In an unpublished manuscript,[84] Naimy argues that this inversion of one of the fundamental principles of modernity has doomed the vitality and creativity of Arab thought to the confines of a debilitating apology. This "completed" Arab Islamic culture, in its self-sufficiency, has obviously nothing to learn from others, nor anything new to give to others. According to Naimy, it condemns Arab culture and thought to a provincial and totalistic sterility. It is in this flawed under-standing of their own culture and heritage, he says, more than in the mis-understanding of other cultures, including the Western, that the main handicap of modern Arab thought lies. It is this perception of their own civilization and not the alleged weakness of institutional structures and material opportunities that challenge Arab cultural creativity in our times. Only an openness to world culture and a proper understanding of the complex historical range of the Arab Islamic heritage can enable a specifi-cally Arab contribution to be made on the local and universal scenes, as was the case in the work of the expatriate writers of the turn of the twenti-eth century—namely, Jubran Khalil Jubran, Ameen Rihani, and Mikhail Naimy. Cultural specificity can emerge only from a creative assimilation of both the universal and the local, and not from confinement to an allegedly completed and absolute civilization. Arabs, he concludes, complain about the hegemonic and leveling effect of cultural globalization, but do not real-ize the leveling impact on themselves of their own preset, totalizing, and unitary conception of their cultural identity. They do not see how from the outset such a conception stultifies the creativity, originality, and vitality of Arabs' plural community.

Secularism, Democracy, and Cultural Critique

This survey of secularist writings shows that what they primarily advocate is not a disenchantment of the world as much as a serious opposition to the sacralization of viewpoints, civilizational legacies, and cognitive disci-plines. What they object to is claims of monopoly over truth and attempts at imposing absolute truth on all. In the present Arab conjecture, the truth the authors of these writings have in mind is a religious truth, remember-ing that secularist ideologies also professed such monopolies in the recent past. However, under the current circumstances, the objection is to the sacralization that would transform human dissention into acts of blas-phemy or crimes of apostasy. Obviously, these writings are responding to rising Islamist claims to truth, cultural authenticity, political power, and moral righteousness.

For a number of Arab thinkers, the secularist demands are in reality demands for democracy. Al-Jabiri believes that secularism is a nonissue for Islamic societies because Islam does not have a "church" and because throughout history the Islamic rule has been political rather than theocratic. The demand, according to him, should be for democracy and rationality.[85] Against such recurrent remarks, critics retort that clerics, although not instituted by the Qur'an into an official hierarchical body, do have and do exercise an important measure of power and that the mundane character of historical Islamic rule has often been ambiguous and is presented by Islamists as religious whenever convenient.

Burhan Ghalyun, a Syrian political thinker based in Paris and professor of contemporary Arab studies at the Sorbonne, finds it more urgent at present to call for democracy than to call for secularism, especially considering that the latter has been instrumentalized and discredited by several Arab ruling parties in order to repress freedom and impose secular progressive ideologies. What is needed, according to him, is a democratic state instead of the nationalist one that has been advocated since independence. The democratic state would offer the neutral procedural institutional framework within which society would express and exercise its political projects. Only such a state would reconnect society to the state and bridge the gap that has grown under the nationalist state's rule. Ghalyun thinks that the latter has in fact ruled against society.[86]

Indeed, complaints about repressive state practices, the absence of representation, and the lack of governmental accountability have been a significant aspect of postindependence Arab malaise. For some Arab intellectuals, the crisis is more a crisis of democracy than a crisis of culture. One year before the conference "Heritage and the Challenges of the Present Age in the Arab Homeland" was held in Cairo in 1984 (discussed in chapter 3), another big conference was convened in Limasol, Cyprus,[87] by the same organizer, the Center for Arab Unity Studies, to discuss the crisis of democracy in the Arab world. As in the Cairo conference, some one hundred participants were gathered, this time to explore the concepts of democracy in general, Arab thought and democracy, democratic practices in the Arab world, case studies, and future challenges to democracy in the Arab region. Egyptian sociologist and head of the Ibn Khaldun Center for Development Studies,[88] Saad Eddin Ibrahim, begins his introduction to the published Limasol conference proceedings with the results of surveys that the Center for Arab Unity Studies conducted in the 1970s on Arab public opinion concerning a number of issues, including that of Arab unity, in order to set its own research and study agenda.[89] The center surveyed around eight thousand Arab citizens from ten different countries and from various walks of life. The findings showed that the absence of democracy was regarded as one of the major problems of the Arab world, together with underdevelopment, divisions in Arab region, the question of Palestine, foreign hegemony, and economic disparities. The absence of democracy—due to a number of causes, including the despotism of postindependence revolutionary regimes, their failure to prevail in the face of Israel, and the increasing economic inequalities that were accentuated by the oil wealth—continues to be a major concern for Arabs, he adds.

In his introduction to the collected volume *Democracy Without Democrats?* Ghassan Salamé, Lebanese political scientist and professor of international relations at the Institut d'etudes politiques in Paris, describes the postindependence state in the Middle East:

> *The abrupt introduction of that statist machine, whether Pahlavi, Kemalist or Arab, has marked a profound watershed in a development which might have favoured democracy more. Not only were the modern heirs to empires usually the military, not only did their "states" risk being nothing but complements to their armies; in imposing their authority they also disrupted a process of statist modernization and democratic evolution, slower and more endogenous, but also better adapted to local time schemes, which had begun in the nineteenth century. "Skipping stages" was only a way of taking a swift hold on societies, authoritatively defining their needs and aspirations and setting about the task of coming to their aid with a greater or lesser degree of success. Secularization too often meant the exclusion of those who, in the name of tradition, required this modern machine to be accountable. Nationalization was the reply to those who wanted to go on deriving some slight say from their comfortable economic situation. State nationalism meant the exclusion of all who were defined through sectoral identities, or who intended to oppose the state monopoly of contact with foreign countries and their powers and ideas. The modern state has thus generally been constructed on a series of exclusions and ostracisms, the combined effect of which was to multiply the number of political orphans and orphans of politics, for politics*

*henceforward was the state and nothing but the state. . . . Prison and
exile became the natural homes of all questioning of current policy,
which was worn right down by the state apparatus; to oppose was to
leave, to leave was to betray.*[90]

This situation obviously meant that no genuine representation was possible: "If nation-building was also, or even primarily, a wide operation of
exclusion, the question of representation, crucial to all democratic experience, was first practiced as the co-opting of forces and individuals, one of
its essential functions being to obscure the fact that the state sought first
and foremost to create a political desert around it; rump parliaments, sub-
missive syndicates, associations created by and for the state. Populism subsequently turned out to be an ideal complement to this political desert."[91]

From this political malaise emerged a set of writings devoted to the
study of state and society in the Arab world.[92] In the article "Sur la causalité d'un manque: Pourquoi le monde arabe n'est-il donc pas démocratique?" (On the Causality of a Lack: Why Is the Arab World Not Democratic?),[93] Salamé presents the strengths and the weaknesses of the religious,
cultural,[94] economic, and external explanations of the absence of democracy in the Arab world, privileging the historical approach that reveals the
circumstances of the ambiguous connection between the nationalist and
democratic projects. He looks at three phases of the projects in recent Arab
history that he characterizes as "liberal":

1. *The modernizing reform era of the Ottoman Empire (the Tanzimat).*
The reforms of this era, he says, were perceived in the Ottoman provinces
and certainly in the Arab provinces as a Turkish matter that did not engage
the Arabs seriously. They alienated Arabs from the imperial center. Moreover, Arabs were concerned by the minimizing of the Islamic character of
the empire that was implied by the introduction of the Western constitutional model. That Islamic character had given them a special status in the
empire. They also associated the parallel constitutional movement taking
place in Egypt with westernization, foreign debts, and foreign intervention.

2. *The national liberation era from the 1920s and through the 1960s* (in
Egypt between 1923 and 1952, in Iraq between 1924 and 1958, and in Syria
between 1920 and 1963). In Egypt, the highly popular Wafd Party failed to
impose its representativity on the Khedive and the British, showing thereby
the political elite's ineptitude. As a result, the most politicized sectors of the
population shifted their support to extraparliamentary forces, paving the way

for the 1952 military coup. In Iraq, the British prevented the establishment of a representative assembly until a king of their choosing was installed and a treaty with London was signed, thus undermining from the very beginning the independent working of constitutional institutions. These institutions were further weakened by the performance of a ruling political class that manipulated them for their personal and sectarian benefits. The country's wealth came to be divided between the urban notables and the rural big landowners. This parceling of wealth led to a growing alienation from democratic institutions and to preparing the ground for a military takeover. In Syria, after the fall of the Ottoman Empire and before the advent of the French mandate, a constitutional monarchy was established. In the successive decades, however, the constitutional institutions were devalorized as a result of their abuse and corrupt management. Again, the result was a series of military coups. Salamé concludes that the political elite's failure to respect the popular will that was entrusted to them and their indulgence in corruption led to the severe discrediting of constitutional politics and to a deep skepticism vis-à-vis democracy.

3. *The era of authoritarian regimes established after the thwarted democratic attempts.* These regimes claimed to be more dedicated to the national liberation cause, more committed to national unity (even at the price of a forced uniformity and the repression of minorities), and more devoted to economic development, social justice, and modernization. They were invariably authoritarian regimes, however, that increasingly disenfranchised people politically and impoverished the majority economically. In fact, they failed in all three tasks of national liberation, unification, and economic development. The police state they consolidated destructured the social fabric and made all organized opposition impossible, apart from the Islamist opposition when it was not violently eradicated or severely subdued. People have been left with the choice between the regime and chaos or the regime and the Islamists. The only limited liberalization measures being taken by these regimes have aimed at managing the severe economic impasses they themselves produced. These measures make room for some popular participation, but they remain controlled enough not to produce any real democratic transformations. In some cases, such as Lebanon, the plural consensual political system has allowed for some margin of democracy and freedom. However, the system remains vulnerable to various forms of foreign interference that might easily shake the delicate consensual balance, especially in an extremely volatile geopolitical environment. Even in times of relative stability, however, the question of individual

democratic freedom remains hostage to a constant tension between a communal hegemony and a state hegemony. Given all these factors, democratic liberalization in the Arab world remains for Salamé a hope for the future rather than a reality in the present. In the final analysis, Arab intellectuals, who in principle play an important in advocating democracy, do not seem to be seriously engaged in the democratic struggle.

Aziz al-Azmeh shares Salamé's pessimism. In "Populism Contra Democracy: Recent Democratist Discourse in the Arab World," he reflects on the ubiquity of the notion of democracy in contemporary Arab discourse. For him, it indicates a formal, talismanic, and instrumentalist use of the term rather than a real commitment to the values and principles embodied in it: "Democracy as propounded in much of current Arab political discourse is generally endowed with a virtually talismanic quality, as a protean force capable, when meaningfully put into practice, of solving all outstanding problems. It has become an ideological motif as ubiquitous today as Arab unity or Arab socialism once were in an Arab past which, though proximate, seems to have receded into the mists of time."[95] Democracy is used either by the state to describe what is in fact its limited opening to popular participation under acute economic pressures in order to implement painful economic policies or by oppositional groups that are no more democratic than the authoritarian states themselves. In the latter's oppositional contestation, democracy is expected to close the gap between state and society and to allow people to express their "true" and "natural" being through representation and participation. The problem, says al-Azmeh, is that given the prevailing vitalistic, naturalistic, and romantic view of identity, this contestation cannot but lead to nondemocratic populism:

The trajectory of the populist discourse on democracy is one which has its initial terminus in an unintended but telling concordance between the main critiques of state despotism by left-wing authors and islamist ideologues, who both claim the state to be alien to society. This reaches its final terminus in the islamist discourse on how best to remedy this situation, by bringing representation into correspondence with the supposedly islamic essence of the people. This critical line which underlines, with much pathos, the state of estrangement, diremption, non-correspondence between society and polity anchors its criticism on the romantic assumption of an original identity, whose restoration is to be sought by democracy.[96]

In the absence of robust, realistic, and historicizing approaches to the question of democracy, al-Azmeh is pessimistic about the prospects of democracy in the Arab world: "Arab democratic pluralist theory, beyond the terms of populism dominated by Islamism, is still a marginal phenomenon, without an ideological or political center. Its ahistorical perfectionism, its desire for full representativeness, causes it to veer, *volens nolens*, to populism which it cannot sustain politically. Thus adrift, contemporary Arab democratist discourse feeds the main political carrier of populism at present, which is the totalitarian plebiscitarianism of political Islam, for other forces had been almost eradicated by the Arab state as organized political forces—albeit not as very strong cultural, ideological, indeed, historical constants of modern Arab life."[97]

To the liberal elites' mismanagement of their political mandates, the revolutionary and monarchical rulers' authoritarianism, the populist character of the contemporary discourse on democracy, and Arab intellectuals' lack of serious democratic commitment are added economic and political factors, which American political scientist Lisa Anderson underlines in "Arab Democracy: Dismal Prospects."[98] In spite of the demand for democratic procedures and institutions by substantial numbers of Arabs, she says, Arab governments continue to resist democratic changes. According to her, this resistance is due to the nature of these governments and to the kind of economies established in the past few decades. The economies have a large informal sector that escape governmental control and taxation; they are largely sustained by foreign aid, debt relief, and a heavy reliance on internationally controlled market conditions, especially regarding oil; they carry the burden of a large nonproductive public sector that provides sustenance to a considerable mass of their populations who are incapable of earning a living independently from the state; the burden grows continually with a high rate of population growth and the constant deterioration of education and skill training, and with this burden grows governments' difficulty in satisfying the increasing needs. All these economic ailments create an increasing estrangement between Arab governments and their peoples.

These governments are also more sensitive to the international patrons who influence their finances and their economies than they are to their own people. The patrons in their turn behave according to their oil and security interests and show little concern for domestic issues of democracy and human rights. This estrangement is aggravated by the ruling elites' tenuous legitimacy, even the younger ones among them, who inherited power from their fathers not only in the monarchies but also in the republics, where ruling positions have become "hereditary." Despite some lip service to democracy, these young leaders, when solicited, are as focused on maintaining power as the older ones. Like the latter, they set their priority in managing the crises of their countries rather than in solving them. They use the radical Islamic threat and the Israeli-Palestinian conflict as a justification for their oppressive policies. As a result, both leaders and alienated populations seek moral and material support abroad, rendering their countries even more prone to foreign interference. The United States plays an important role in supporting nondemocratic regimes in return for economic and strategic benefits. Given these economic and political structures, Anderson argues, both change and the maintenance of the status quo promise to be undemocratic: "the next generation of leaders in the Arab world will be drawn from one of two groups: those within the state and its ruling circles, and those living at its margins. Neither are great proponents of liberal democracy. The elites appear to be modern but not democratic, often a dangerous combination, as the communist experiment showed, and the masses are angry."[99] Change, according to Anderson, would have implications for U.S. foreign policy:

Democratization would force wide-ranging, raucous, and possibly violent debates about the resolution of the Arab-Israeli conflict, the role of the United States in the region, and the pervasive view of inequity in the world, which the current rulers now suppress with America's perhaps reluctant but very real blessing.

Thus far, the United States has evinced no appetite for the inevitably awkward and painful discussion of its past and present role in the region that genuine democratisation would entail. It continues to collude with the regimes in power, permitting fixed elections and human rights fakery to provide a fig leaf that allow it and its client regimes to continue in the game. This will serve the interests of neither peace nor democracy in the region (nor regional development and prosperity for that matter), and it is not too early to confront the significant role that American policy will play in either facilitating or impeding democratisation in the Arab world.[100]

Anderson wrote this article in 2001. After the invasion of Iraq and the disastrous consequences that it had on the region, the prospects of democratization in the area have most likely become even more dismal.

If regimes have shown no intention, no interest, and no ability to initiate genuine democratic transformations, can such transformations be
instigated on the oppositional side? Azmi Bishara, Arab-Israeli thinker
trained in philosophy and former member of the Knesset, believes that the
impediments to democracy in the Arab world are the same as those that
obstruct Arab unity: this situation is what he calls the "Arab Question." He
elaborates his thesis in *Fi al-Mas'ala al-'Arabiyya: Muqaddima li Bayan
Dimuqrati 'Arabi* (On the Arab Question: Prolegomena to an Arab Democratic Manifesto).[101] For him, the absence of democracy due to poverty,
nondemocratic education, vast socioeconomic disparities, and the rural-
ization of the city is not unique to the Arab world. It is found in many regions of the Third World. What is specific to the Arab region is the recent
Islamicization of the political contestation.[102] He argues that the condition
for the possibility of both Arab unity and democracy is a revalidation of
the idea of Arab nationalism, which had been discredited under the revolutionary authoritarian regimes after 1967. This revalidation is to revive the
early ethical conception of Arab nationalism, articulated in the thoughts
of Qustantin Zurayq and Sati' al-Husri: a nationalism that, like all nationalisms in the world, has a romantic component, but that is constructed
around values of egalitarian, inclusive, plural, and democratic citizenship.
This conception had drawn on the moral stock of religion without becoming religious itself and without separating nationalism from the popular
cultural and religious base. Only such a nationalism can be the framework
for democracy in the Arab world. To renounce such a nationalism is to accept implicitly or affirm explicitly the sectarian fragmentation of Arabs
into warring communities, exacerbated by U.S. military intervention in
the region. Even at times of peace, communalism cannot lead to democracy, he says, unless the communities themselves are democratic, but they
cannot be so unless they open up to larger frames of belonging. The balance between nondemocratic forces cannot bring about democracy. Hence,
for him, the rule of communalism, as in Lebanon, can only be a deceptive
pseudodemocracy. Similarly, the balance of power among the authoritarian state, democratic modernists, and nondemocratic Islamists cannot
produce democracy. None of the adjustments made by the rulers under the
pressure of the economic impasses have led to democratic transformations.
The regimes have succeeded in keeping the opposition busy with side reforms, in mobilizing prenational loyalties, and in "offering" limited reforms
in so-called acts of generosity.

Bishara emphasizes that democracy cannot be created without a political will. It cannot be produced by revolutions, but only by a perseverant

commitment to its principles. The oppositional forces, especially the Islamists because they are the only organized opposition at the moment, should agree on democracy as the rule of the game. Only then will people cease to support the authoritarian state out of fear of the Islamists' nondemocratic orientations. What Bishara does not explain is what would guarantee such a pact and confer to it credibility in the eyes of the people.

The late Iliya Harik (1934–2007), Lebanese political scientist and professor emeritus of Indiana University, addresses the lack of credibility and trust in the Islamist oppositional movement with respect to democracy in his book *Al-Dimuqratiyya wa Tahaddiyat al-Hadatha Bayn al-Sharq wa al-Gharb* (Democracy and the Challenges of Modernity Between East and West).[103] Politically moderate people in the Arab world, he says, believe that Islamists are not democratic, even when the Islamists claim the opposite. Indeed, he adds, democrats in general and secular democrats in particular see in the Islamic awakening a serious threat to any potential democratic transformation. They wonder if Islamists mean it when they advocate democracy, if they do so out of political opportunism, and if their understanding of democracy is the same as democrats' understanding. Harik identifies a number of causes for this suspicion. He thinks that the lack of trust is due in part to the difference between the Islamists' words and their deeds. Their behavior—whether they are in the opposition, as in Egypt, Syria, Jordan, and Algeria, or in power, as in the Sudan, Iran, and Afghanistan—is definitely not democratic. The realities of their nondemocratic performances belie the professions of democracy made by prominent figures among them, such as Youssef al-Qaradawi, Mohammad Salim al-Awa, Muhammad Amara, Fahmi Huwaydi, Tariq Bishri, Hassan al-Turabi, and Rashid al-Ghannushi.[104]

The Islamists' statements are no less troubling than their behavior. They claim to uphold parliamentarianism, but their understanding of the role of parliament and legislation seems confused. They set limits to universal human legislation and restrict it to the clerics. Parliaments are expected to comply with the commandments of the Council of Clerics. Equally troubling for democrats is the Islamists' open intention to use state institutions to impose religious beliefs and to forbid expressions of thought that go against those beliefs, thus leaving to nonconformists the choice between dissimulation and punishment. By insisting that this approach will still amount to democracy, they empty the basic notions of democracy, such as human legislation and freedom of thought, of their content. Islamists, Harik adds, offer many general statements but little concrete policies and specific plans in matters of public concern. What is also a source of anxiety for non-Islamists is that in cases of power struggle between the moderates and the extremists among Islamists, the latter seem to prevail. The more moderate elites seem to give in to the extremist majority that is radicalized by increased socioeconomic and cultural marginalization. Instead of encouraging the moderates, Arab states persecute them as much as they persecute the extremists. Finally, the different Islamist movements do not distinguish themselves enough from one another to offer clarity about their precise individual positions and programs.

And yet, says Harik, an Islamic, faith-based democratic party is thinkable, a party that would draw on some of the central tenets of Islam, such as justice and the subjection of governors, and that is governed by the rule of law and according to the dictates of moral values. With their undemocratic behavior and discourse, however, Islamists are squandering an important moral capital that they might have mobilized for the cause of democracy. But this connection does not warrant unfounded polemical statements claiming that Islam *is* democracy or that Islam *has always been* democratic, even *avant la lettre*. The solution, adds Harik, is in the hands of Muslims, not in Islam, and democracy is not the solution as much as it is the more promising way of reaching the least evil solutions to the complex problems of human communal life. Its advantage lies in allowing people to express themselves and to convince others with peaceful means of projects they might have for the public good. In this sense, he says, democracy is conservative in that it relies on people's present convictions; however, it does not freeze the status quo and makes peaceful change possible, though slow. Harik warns against making democracy conditional on people's cognitive qualifications, their accomplished individualism, or their modernist persuasions. Championing democracy for such ultimate purposes, he says, undermines it. Democracy consists in respecting people's choices as they come, with the possibility of convincing them otherwise. Furthermore, democracy is in, the final analysis, a matter of normative preference, not a "scientific truth." Just as some may wish to be free, others may want to be taken in charge. In other words, democracy cannot be defended as an absolute true good, but as a relative good preferable over other options through its advantages over them. It is an aberration to want to impose it on people in the name of freedom, secularism, modernity, or nationalism. Harik concludes by emphasizing the need to articulate and engage in local discourses on democracy, grounded in local realities, by locals with genuine and clear democratic convictions.

Recentering the Historical, the Human, and the Partial: The Secular Call for Democracy and Human Rights

Just as the critical thinkers of the previous chapters regarded history to be central for demystifying heritage, the secularist thinkers here find history to be indispensable for demystifying the Islamic past; and just as the former found it necessary to recall the human component of tradition for making creative reappropriation of that heritage possible, the latter emphasize the importance of keeping the debate about Islam, culture, and politics on the human level in order to keep the dialogue going and to avoid intellectual terrorism.

History is important, first, to correct the misrepresentations of the early Islamic past, which is claimed to be the ideal model that society has to return to for spiritual and especially political salvation. History is also important to recognize the secularizing phenomena that have affected the region during the past two centuries. Finally, according to the secularist thinkers, rather than being perceived as an inexorable decline from a pristine glory, history is to be valued for itself as the reservoir of experiences and events from which one can and ought to learn in order to deal with the pressing moral and political questions of the present. For the secularists, the recognition of the reality of history aids in staying in touch with reality and in preserving a modicum of agency in shaping history, instead of being passively subjected to its alleged essences.

The critique of the Islamist conceptions of society, history, and identity reveals certain modes of thinking that are and have been operative not only among Islamists, but among nationalists and others as well: the essentialist view of identity, the conciliatory mode of thinking, and the notion of cultural self-sufficiency. The persisting attempt at reconciling Islam with the various ideas of modernity without having to make any radical changes in Islamic thought and without having to make clear moral choices and consistent ethical commitments has led to consecutive impasses, according to these thinkers. Equally sterile has been the confusion between Islam as a creed based on a revealed sacred book and Islam as a civilization brought forth by human creative powers under concrete historical circumstances. Finally, warnings are formulated against a totalistic view of culture that presents Arab or Islamic culture as a self-sufficient, unitary, and uniform culture. Secularist thinkers agree on the need for a thought of one's own and more particularly for a social science of one's own. But they emphasize the importance of problematizing the notion of indigenization and of distancing it from nationalist and Islamist chauvinistic views.

In this late-twentieth-century secularist discourse, recognized as a defensive discourse compared to that of the beginning of the century, the focus is not on refuting the religious worldview as such, but rather on securing basic liberties such as the freedom of thought and the freedom of expression and on rejecting intellectual terrorism. This discourse is concerned with denouncing exclusive claims to truth, virtue, and righteousness. It aims at meeting the Islamists' political propositions on the political level and at deconstructing their totalistic assertion that "Islam is the solution." The secularist thinkers' most fundamental concerns are, in the final analysis, the demand for democracy and the defense of human rights.

Six
Breaking the Postcolonial Solitude
Arab Motifs in Comparative Perspective

The Western Debates

European *Kulturphilosophie*

Cultural malaise and cultural critique as well as civilizational decline, collapse, and renewal were also dominant issues in recent European history, especially around the turn of the twentieth century. They gave rise to a whole range of intellectual, artistic, and political movements and to a set of new disciplines related to culture, such as the philosophy of culture (*Kulturphilosophie*), the science of culture (*Kulturwissenschaft*), the history of culture (*Kulturgeschichte*), and the sociology of culture (*Kultursoziologie*). As the names of these disciplines indicate, much of these intellectual and political reactions took place in Germany due to its special history in Europe.

The general malaise in Europe was caused by a number of socioeconomic, cultural, and political developments such as the continent's rapid industrialization (albeit at different paces in different countries); the mechanization of many sectors of life; the acceleration of urbanization; the formation of the masses; the unprecedented expansion of the various fields of knowledge, especially the natural and the historical; the waning of religious authority and the further "disenchantment of the world"; and the rise of social protest movements, including those of workers and feminists. In Germany, these trends were exacerbated by the unification of the country—which many perceived as its hegemonic prussification, giving rise to a growing cultural tension between the state-dominated Protestant culture and the minority Catholic culture (the famous *Kulturkampf*)—and by a relatively late but accelerated industrialization that led to a sharp social and political polarization, from which emerged what the conservatives came to call the socialist "red danger" (*Rote Gefahr*). Different shades of nationalism, from the liberal to the most conservative, came in conflict with one another. Finally, on the intellectual level a growing malaise developed from the rising relativism, skepticism, psychologism, positivism, and naturalism, as well as from the fragmentation and excessive specialization of knowledge.[1]

Thus, in contrast to the Arab case, the malaise in Europe was caused not by the lack of progress, but by its excess and one-sidedness in the technological and material realms, but less so in the moral-spiritual realm; it was not due to the poverty of knowledge, but to its overexpansion to the point that it was impossible to own, appropriate, and meaningfully link the growing knowledge to one's life; it did not stem from poverty in the means of power, but from their proliferation in the absence of secure and meaningful ultimate goals and values; finally, it was not caused by a modernity introduced in fragments by foreign colonial powers, but by a home-grown modernity that increasingly revealed itself to be a mixed blessing.

Much of the literature of the time is an attempt at diagnosing the ills of a civilization in crisis and at offering remedies for them. The two interrelated foci of the malaise were the link of culture to life and the link of culture to values. Two of the main philosophical currents of the epoch analyzed these foci: the philosophy of life (*Lebensphilosophie*), associated with the works of Friedrich Nietzsche, Wilhelm Dilthey, and Georg Simmel; and neo-Kantianism (*Neukantianismus*), associated with the works of Wilhelm Windelband, Heinrich Rickert, and Ernst Cassirer. According to

these analyses, the cultural products that are expressions or externaliza-
tions of life at some stage of development become alienated from the life
that gave rise to them in the first place. They become ends in themselves
and even convenient pretexts for avoiding the deeper questions of human
life. One translation of this conflict is in the German distinction between
Zivilisation and *Kultur*. The first is associated with material progress and
prosperity; with technology, mechanization, and material utility; with
metropolitan life, bourgeois spirit, and specialized knowledge (*Fachwis-
senschaft*); and interestingly at times also with French Enlightenment,
rationality, and skepticism. The second is associated with well-rounded
education (*Bildung*), religion, spirit (*Geist*), decorative art, vital drives and
instincts, passions, nature, and the human body, and it is often sought in
natural medicine, folklore, the cult of youth (*Jugendstil*), and even sometimes war as the outburst of elemental vital forces of rejuvenation.[2]

Friedrich Nietzsche (1844–1900) explains in his inimitable way how intellectual productions, when ill appropriated, can become irrelevant to the
basic questions of life. As he states in the 1873–1874 essay *The Use and Abuse
of History*, "The modern man carries inside him an enormous heap of indi-
gestible knowledge-stones that occasionally rattle together in his body, as
the fairy tale has it. . . . [I]t is not a real culture but a kind of knowledge
about culture, a complex of various thoughts and feelings about it, from
which no decision as to its direction can come." Further on, he says: " 'Give
me life, and I will soon make you a culture out of it'—will be the cry of every man in this generation, and they will all know each other by this cry.
But who will give them this life?"[3]

Banishing spirituality, instinct, emotions, and will from the relationship to cultural productions in the name of rationality and objectivity
strips the fundamental content and relevance of culture to life. Nietzsche
criticizes the abuses of the typical attitudes toward historical knowledge—
namely, the monumental aggrandizement of history to inspire pride but at
the cost of truth, the antiquarian attitude that reveres all things historical
at the expense of critical thinking, and the critical attitude, obviously the
more useful one for Nietzsche, that judges the past and ultimately condemns it. In order to be useful, any of these perceptions of the past, he says,
should serve life: "We need it [history] for life and action, not as a convenient way to avoid life and action, or excuse a selfish life and a cowardly or
base action. We would serve history only as it serves life; but to value its
study beyond a certain point mutilates and degrades life; and this is a fact
that certain marked symptoms of our time make it as necessary as it may

be painful to bring to the test of experience." Not only has knowledge lost its significance to life, but values have also ceased to offer guidance and meaning: "And the power of gradually losing all feelings of strangeness or astonishment, and finally being pleased at anything, is called the historical sense or historical culture. The crowd of influences streaming on the young soul is so great, the clods of barbarism and violence flung at him so strange and overwhelming, that an assumed stupidity is his only refuge. Where there is a subtler and stronger self-consciousness we find another emotion too—disgust. The young man has become homeless: he doubts all ideas, all moralities."[4]

Wilhelm Dilthey (1831–1911) describes the same sense of disorientedness in the 1898 essay "Present-Day Culture and Philosophy" (originally delivered as a lecture):

> *From this dissonance between the sovereignty of scientific thought and the inability of the spirit to understand itself and its significance in the universe springs the final and most characteristic feature in the spirit of the present age and its philosophy. . . . [A]ll yardsticks have gone, everything firm has become shaky; an unrestricted freedom to make assumptions, and playing with unlimited possibilities allow the spirit to enjoy its sovereignty and at the same time inflict the pain of a lack of content. This pain of emptiness, this consciousness of the anarchy in all deeper convictions, this uncertainty about the values and goals of life, have called forth the different attempts in poetry and fiction, to answer the questions about the value and goal of our existence.*[5]

For Dilthey, it is important for philosophy to address this existential anguish and to elaborate the foundations of an understanding of historical human life that can overcome relativism and skepticism by developing a theory of the human (*Geisteswissenschaften*). This elaboration is to be based on the examination of real, empirical human experience without limiting this experience to sense data. Kant had founded the natural sciences on the transcendental categories of the human mind, so the task now, according to Dilthey, was to provide the human sciences with categories of meaning derived from human historical life that could make sense of human experience and guide it at the same time:

> *Everything historical is relative; when we assemble it in our minds it seems to work towards dissolution, scepticism and impotent subjectivity.*

Thus this period poses a particular problem. What is relative must be related more profoundly with what is universally valid. . . . We must first become fully conscious of what the relativity of all historical reality implies. The study of all the conditions of man on this earth, the contacts between nations, religions and concepts, inevitably increased the chaos of historical facts. Only when we have grasped all the forms of human life, from primitive peoples to the present day, does it become possible to see the generally valid in the relative, a firm future in the past, greater esteem for the individual through historical consciousness and to recognize reality as the yardstick for progress into the future; this we can then link with clear goals for the future. Historical consciousness itself must contain rules and powers to help us confront the past and turn freely and independently towards a unitary goal of human culture.[6]

Dilthey's hermeneutic method was to establish a theory of meaning interpretation that can make the history of human culture intelligible.[7]

For Georg Simmel (1858–1918), cultural products' tendency to separate themselves from life is not incidental; it is inherent to culture as such. Culture, according to him, has two poles: subjective and objective. The subjective pole is the human psyche that expresses life by producing and appropriating cultural products; the objective pole is those products once they are shaped into items of the objective world. Culture consists in the active interaction between the psyche and the cultural products. In the process of culture, as he puts it, "the spirit creates a vessel for itself," an added value to life, leading to a richer and rounded personality. It is interesting to note that many cultural critics of this epoch express a nostalgia for Goethe as a representative of the ideal of a well-rounded personality—an ideal that became increasingly difficult to attain in turn-of-the-century Europe because of the profusion and fragmentation of cultural products. In his 1908 essay "The Style of Life,"[8] Simmel writes: "The preponderance of objective over subjective culture which came about during the nineteenth century is more or less summed up by the fact that the educational ideal of the eighteenth century was the cultivation of man as a personal inner value, whereas in the nineteenth century this was supplanted by the concept of cultivation in the sense of the sum total of objective knowledge and modes of behaviour. The gulf between the two conceptions appears to be steadily widening."[9]

Ernst Cassirer (1874–1945) did not share this tragic view of culture.[10] He disagreed with Simmel on the perception of cultural products. He believed that they are not fixed and finished products, but that their being is constantly shaped by humans' interaction with them. They continuously acquire new life and enrich the life of those who come into contact with them no matter how foreign to them. In "The Tragedy of Culture," he answers Simmel's arguments:

> For that consolidation which life undergoes in the various forms of culture—in language, religion, and art—is not the absolute antithesis to that which the I requires by its very nature; instead it is the very condition by virtue of which it discovers and comes to know its own being. . . . However significant, however substantial, however at rest in itself and in its own point of focus a work of culture may be, it is and remains only a point of passage. It is no 'absolute' touching the I, but the bridge which leads from one I-pole to another. In this there lies a real and most significant function. The living process of culture has its being in the very fact that it is inexhaustible in its creation of such mediation and transaction.[11]

Like a number of European thinkers in the early decades of the twentieth century, Cassirer believed that a proper understanding of human culture is necessary and that it requires an investigation into the mental structures that make culture possible, as Kant had done for the understanding of natural science. Working toward such an understanding prior to Cassirer were Dilthey from the philosophy of life current[12] as well as Wilhelm Windelband (1848–1915) and Heinrich Rickert (1863–1936)[13] from the neo-Kantian current. For Cassirer, the task was to identify the modes of thinking, representing, and imagining that are operative in the cultural phenomena of language, art, myth, religion, and science, and to determine the basic power that makes these phenomena possible in the first place. This creative power is that of symbolizing: it allows humans to step out of immediate factual reality and to move into a world of meanings and ideals. Hence, understanding human culture requires the study of symbolic forms, which he did in a four-volume work.[14] Moreover, freedom is essential for actualizing the creative power of symbolizing because it is essential for the creation of ideals and the possibility of ethics. The ethical questions of freedom and value are for Cassirer part and parcel of a genuine philosophy of culture. In his 1936 essay "Critical Idealism as a Philosophy of Culture," he writes:

> We cannot build up a philosophy of culture by mere formal and logical means. We have to face the fundamental ethical question that is contained in the very concept of culture. The philosophy of culture may be called a study of forms; but all these forms cannot be understood without relating them to a common goal. What does, in the end, this evolution of forms mean; what does, so to speak, this gallery of pictures mean as they are displayed in myth, in language, in art, in science? Does it mean nothing but a pastime which the human mind plays, as it were, with itself? Or has this play a general theme and a universal task?[15]

Such a critical philosophy of culture, Cassirer admits, cannot by itself protect culture from its demons or from the anxieties caused by them, but it can at least reveal the conditions for the very possibility and future of culture, as he explains in the 1939 article "Naturalistic and Humanistic Philosophies of Culture" in words much like Qustantin Zurayq's later that century:

> The continually erupting anxiety over the destiny and future of human civilization can hardly be prevented by a critical philosophy of culture. It, too, must recognize this barrier to historical determination or prediction. All that can be said on this score is that culture will advance just to the extent that the truly creative powers, which in the final analysis are only brought into play by our own efforts, are not forsaken or crippled. This one prediction we can make, and for ourselves, for our own action and decisions its certainty is of unique and supreme importance. To be sure, it does not give us unqualified certainty in advance that we will achieve specific goals; what it does show us is the necessity of our own subjective response in the face of these goals.[16]

Interestingly, Edmund Husserl (1859–1938) and Emmanuel Lévinas (1906–1995) shared this ethical concern about culture in reaction to the rise of fascism in Europe and specifically Germany in the mid-1930s. I refer here to Husserl's famous 1935 Vienna and Prague lectures "Philosophy and the Crisis of European Humanity" and "The Crisis of the Sciences as Expression of the Radical Life-Crisis of European Humanity"[17] and to Lévinas's less well-known 1934 essay "Quelques réflexions sur la philosophie de

l'hitlérisme" (Some Thoughts on the Philosophy of Hitlerism).[18] The purpose of all these lectures and essays, including Cassirer's, was the exhortation to uphold the values of reason, specifically truth and freedom, against
the growing temptations of irrationality, relativism, skepticism, sheer force,
and blind chauvinism. This exhortation was a cry in the wilderness in an
epoch torn between nationalist enthusiasm and cultural pessimism, as expressed in Oswald Spengler's *Decline of the West*,[19] a book that immediately
became a German and European best-seller. In contrast to Cassirer, Husserl, and Lévinas, Spengler (1880–1936) presented a deterministic and mo-
nadic view of cultures in which human agency was subordinate to forces
that shaped the fate of cultures. Cultures were organic, like natural beings,
and had a certain life span during which they were meant to fulfill some
kind of inherent entelechy. For Spengler, Western culture had exhausted its
energies and was heading toward its inexorable decline. Max Weber (1864–
1920) undertook a much more sober comparative examination of the forms
of rationalization in Europe and elsewhere in his famous but not uncontro-
versial 1904–1905 essay *Protestant Ethic and the Spirit of Capitalism*,[20] in
which he tries to account for the specificity of European modernity by analyzing the link between economy and certain forms of religiosity.

The ethical preoccupation with culture had already been voiced in the
wake of World War I, which Europeans, even those who had believed that
the war could contribute to the regeneration of culture, experienced as a
profound trauma. The trauma was expressed by writers such as Paul Valéry
(1871–1945) in his famous 1919 piece "La crise de l'esprit" (The Crisis of the
Mind), where he states, "We later civilizations . . . we too know now that we
are mortal";[21] and it was depicted most vividly by the visual representations of Otto Dix (1891–1969) and George Grosz (1893–1959). Among these
voices was that of Albert Schweitzer (1875–1965), to whom Cassirer refers
more than once in his writings. Schweitzer's two essays "The Decay and the
Restoration of Civilization" and "Civilization and Ethics" had been in the
making since 1900, says their author in the 1923 preface to his book *Kulturphilosophie*.[22] As their titles indicate, these essays address the European
cultural crisis and gather most of the leitmotivs of the time: the overorga-
nization of life in its external manifestations and the abdication of independent thinking under the influence of mass culture, propaganda, and
nationalistic fanaticism:

> *Thus we have entered on a new medieval period. The general determi-
> nation of society has put freedom of thought out of fashion, because*

*the majority renounce the privilege of thinking as free personalities,
and let themselves be guided in everything by those who belong to the
various groups and cliques.*

*. . . With independence of thought thrown overboard, we have, as was
inevitable, lost our faith in truth. Our spiritual life is disorganized, for
the over-organization of our external environment leads to the organization of our absence of thought.[23]*

These leitmotivs also include the loss of faith in the values of reason, such
as truth and solidly founded ethics, due to the partly justified romantic
critique of the Enlightenment:

*Our age has an almost artistic prejudice against a reflective theory
of the universe. We are still children of the Romantic movement to a
greater extent than we realize. What that movement produced in opposition to the Aufklärung [Enlightenment] and to rationalism seems
to us valid for all ages against any theory that would found itself solely
on thought. In such a theory of the universe we can see beforehand the
world dominated by a barren intellectualism, convictions governed by
mere utility, and a shallow optimism, which together rob mankind of
all human genius and enthusiasm.*

*In a great deal of opposition which it offered to rationalism the reac-
tion of the early nineteenth century was right. Nevertheless it remains
true that it despised and distorted what was, in spite of all its imper-
fections, the greatest and most valuable manifestation of the spiritual
life of man that the world has yet seen. Down through all circles of
cultured and uncultured alike there prevailed at that time a belief in
thought and a reverence for truth.[24]*

What is needed, states Schweitzer, is a philosophy of reason that is at the
service of life and a worldview that is life affirming. Civilization, in the final analysis, is for him a product of the reverence for life. Philosophy and
ethics in particular are to produce and defend such a worldview. Their failure is one of the main roots of the civilizational collapse, of which World
War I was a manifestation rather than a cause.

After the war, there were indeed attempts at creating transnational
bridges within Europe and at promoting cultural and intellectual ex-

changes for the sake of healing the wounds of intolerance, demoralization, and division, and of reviving the "old European values." Among these attempts was the Viennese cultural association Kulturbund, founded in 1922, together with its press organ the *Zeitgeist*. The group expanded into the Fédération des unions intellectuelles, which organized public lectures and symposia across Europe.[25] It operated until the German annexation of Austria in 1938. Such attempts to construct cultural bridges were undertaken even before World War I. In 1910, some of Windelband and Rickert's students in Freiburg founded the international journal *Logos: Internationale Zeitschrift für Philosophie der Kultur*.[26] A German-Russian venture, it was published until the takeover of power by the Nazis in 1933. Its main editors were Richard Kroner, Georg Mehlis, and Arnold Ruge on the German side and Nikolai von Bubnoff, Sergius Hessen, Fedor Stepun, and Boris Jakovenco on the Russian side. The plan for it was to reach out to other European and world partners and to appear in four or five European languages. An Italian version was prepared in 1914, but these ambitions were soon aborted by the outbreak of the war. *Logos*'s goal was to elaborate a new culture ("neue Kultur schaffen") that connected culture to reason in a neo-Kantian understanding. The idea for it had been formulated in the book *Vom Messias: Kulturphilosophische Essays* (On the Messiah: Essays in the Philosophy of Culture) by Kroner, Bubnoff, Mehlis, Hessen, and Stepun, published in Leipzig in 1909, shortly before the launching of the journal. In it, Kroner wrote:

> We all, who live at the beginning of the twentieth century find ourselves in a shaking world, with no substantial concepts, no ideals, no spiritual substance, no faith, and no conviction, in a world of sophistry, big words, and emptiness. Our heart, filled with intuitions and longing for high revelations and the realm of ideas, has been suppressed and could not grow in the air of cynical skepticism and blasé decadence, inherited from materialism. In this atmosphere all speculative thoughts that would lead us toward a divine world seem like a ludicrous conceptual poetry that is not to be taken seriously; our moral consciousness has become uncertain, it tries to understand itself in disguised egoism and humiliates itself in inherited instincts and thus becomes estranged from itself. The spirit of religion is also lost, and we try to make up for our spiritual poverty by pretending that we have matured and reached a rational view of the universe. . . . It is as if the ice-cold hand of death had run over all the creations of the

*mind, and here they stand meaningless, without a soul, shadowy like
wax figures, sheer machines.*

*[However,] a new life is awakening from under the ruins, and a new
desire flows through our heart asking for recognition from reason, an
intuition of the higher orders of being, waiting for a savior to bring
them to us. . . .*

*Thus matures the time for a deeper self-awareness and the soul discov-
ers again the original source of heavenly gifts. Inner life gains back
power and significance, and silences all pseudo-critiques of reason.
The human regains awareness of his or her creative being. The mind
comes of age. . . .*

But who will be the leader and spokesman of this new life? . . .

*We want a solid construct of well-founded and rooted truths, we want
a strong faith in values and ideas. . . . We desire not a table of new
values, but a new priest for the ancient, eternal values.[27]*

None of these attempts at creating transnational bridges protected Europe from its demons, however, and it fell prey twice to brutal, fratricidal
outbursts of violence. Nevertheless, throughout the first half of the twentieth century, reflections and debates on Europe's cultural ills as well as
exhortations to return to its alleged "nature" and "origins," such as Greek
philosophy and Roman law, and to its "goals," such as enlightenment and
freedom, persisted. There were also critical deconstructions of these discourses in the latter part of the century, for instance by Jacques Derrida
(1930–2004) and Joseph Fontana.[28] However, as this brief European survey shows, most of these discussions remained Eurocentric. The rest of
the world is rarely evoked in them. The fear that Europe would lose its
political, economic, and cultural preeminence in the world was voiced
here and there, including already in Valéry's "Crise de l'esprit." But some
voices were critical of colonialism and of Europe's double standards regarding what it considered to be its founding values of humanistic enlightenment, from Johann Gottfried Herder's (1744–1803) in the eighteenth century to Jean-Paul Sartre's (1905–1980) in the mid–twentieth
century.[29] Notwithstanding a distant and distancing presence of the
Other, European thinkers considered the main issues of cultural malaise

to be European modernity and, in the late twentieth century, late Western modernity and postmodernity. Rarely, if ever, was this modernity linked to anything outside the continent, however. Thinkers of the postcolonial world offer a very different picture when they make the link between modernity and colonialism, seeing the latter as the "underside of modernity," and "provincialize" Europe by uncovering its ambiguous claims to universality.

With the globalization of its big cities, partly or largely due to its colonial and neocolonial policies as well as to the later outbreak of global terrorism, the European continent has become more and more defensive in different ways: through the resurgence of conservative or even extreme right-wing movements and discourses or through the development of a postmodern cult of difference that is prone to a regressive parochialism. Europe sees itself increasingly torn between a consistent universalist outlook and an ethnocentric provincial reaction. Finally, it is interesting to note that the Arab travelers to Europe of the nineteenth and early twentieth centuries did not take notice, or at least did not address explicitly, Europeans' tribulations and anxieties, their ethical uncertainties and spiritual disorientation, or their experiences of an overwhelming cognitive inflation, technological hyperdevelopment, and accelerated urbanization. What impressed and interested the earlier travelers—among them al-Tahtawi, al-Tunisi, al-Shidyaq, and Marrash—was the overall general progress of European civilization in its socioeconomic and political advances as well as in its scientific achievements. It is not until later, in the early decades of the twentieth century, that the distinction between a materially advanced Europe to be learned from and a morally decadent and culturally invasive Europe to be resisted was underlined. Some Arabs, such as Qasim Amin and Taha Husayn, considered this distinction to be a mediocre apologetic stance, whereas Islamists such as Sayyid Qutb stressed its importance emphatically. In general, even in the later decades of the twentieth century, Europe's inner debates remained poorly known in the Arab world, at least on the scholarly level, despite some feeble attempts at European or Western studies in its schools.

The U.S. Postcolonial Debates on Culture

The gap between material growth and the abundance of means, on the one hand, and moral and spiritual disorientation and the uncertainty of ultimate ends, on the other, that characterized the European cultural malaise from the late nineteenth century to the mid–twentieth century migrated to the U.S. debates on culture in a magnified way. This "new" country was achieving unprecedented levels of material success in the form of industrial expansions, agricultural and urban developments, and financial growth. Tremendous material wealth and power were accumulating and giving to successful settlers and entrepreneurs a robust sense of self-confidence and empowerment. For some, however, this material success did not translate into an equal success in the cultural domain. The discrepancy tarnished for them the image of a new and successful American civilization. Not only was there a gap between the material and cultural achievements, but the latter were not even really "American." They were imported from the old continent, which, even when surpassed materially, remained the source of and the reference for respectable culture. Surmounting the gap between the imported culture and the local realities of the "new" continent was a major concern of U.S. thinkers. Here, the problem in the culture was not so much its moral and spiritual disorientation, as in Europe, but its estrangement from the distinct realities of the new environment—realities that needed to be identified and articulated.

In a renowned piece called "Sweetness and Light," English critic Mathew Arnold (1822–1888) criticized the exclusive valorization of "external," material things, such as industrial achievements, political and economic power, population growth, and physical vigor in both his own native England and the United States. He saw "faith in machinery" as the most important danger to human society. Greatness, he thought, is to be seen in increased spirituality and increased inwardness, and democracy is to serve the diffusion of this greatness. Culture is to introduce light (intelligence) and sweetness (beauty) to society and by so doing to serve the very humanity of human beings.[30] In the first half of the twentieth century, John Dewey (1859–1952) addressed the persisting if not growing domination of money and materialism, standardization, homogeneity of thought and emotion, intellectual and moral mediocrity, and lack of genuine interest in cultural matters—all traits he claimed characterized the "American mind." He pleaded for the instrumentalization of this industrial and financial infrastructure for educational and cultural purposes.[31]

As early as 1837, Ralph Waldo Emerson (1803–1882) formulated in his famous speech "The American Scholar" the yearning for a genuinely "American" thought that would express the new and independent "America" and not simply be imitative of Europe.[32] In the early decades of the twentieth century, George Santayana (1863–1952) emphasized the necessity of creating a culture that would address the lived and changing realities of the succeeding generations. In his well-known essay "The Genteel Tradition in American Philosophy,"[33] he criticizes the old culture of the fathers, characterized by its aloofness and disconnectedness from the changing realities of the country. He pleads for the creation of "real native philosophies" that would replace the old "genteel" intellectualism. And in "Americanism," he warns against the domination of experimental science and industrial invention in the new generation's reason. The danger, he thought, is for science to become a vehicle of power over matter and not a tool for enlightening the spirit. Waldo Frank (1889–1967) called this obsession with power "Americanism," but he traced it back to European modernity. The latter, he thought, emptied medieval European culture of its spiritual dimension and caused the downfall of this culture. It is this agonizing culture that arrived in America. Only the revival of that great spiritual tradition, according to him, with the help of the impulses of the New World, could save old European culture from the lethal temptations of greed and war.[34]

The issue of power in connection with the new country's self-understanding is a central theme of Reinhold Niebuhr's (1892–1971) work. In "The Innocent Nation in an Innocent World" of 1949,[35] he examines the country's self-image, originating in its founding myths, and the impact of this self-image on dealing with the country's growing power in the first half of the twentieth century. He focuses on the notions of innocence and virtue that permeate this self-understanding and traces them back to the main sources of U.S. culture: New England Calvinism, Virginian Deism, and Jeffersonianism. From the first viewpoint, the United States was a "separated nation," willed by God to be a new, "purer" church, the culmination of the Protestant Reformation. From the second viewpoint, it was a new political community, free from tyranny, prejudices, and social vices thanks to the country's abundance. According to Niebuhr, this self-understanding produced in the country a number of illusions: the illusion of the possibility of absolute new beginnings, the illusion of the innocence of a virtuous community, and the illusion of the harmlessness of self-interest. These illusions contrasted with the country's realities, especially in the aftermath of its involvement in World War I and World War II, and they prevented it from bearing its responsibilities in the face of its growing economic and political power.

At the beginning of the twentieth century, Randolph Bourne (1886–1918) was already calling into question the exclusively Anglo-Saxon definition of these founding myths and of the country's overall identity in his famous essay "Trans-national America."[36] The English Americans, he states, have kept a strong cultural link with their old country heritage, but blame all other immigrants for doing the same with their respective backgrounds. They have taken their particular heritage as the norm to be imposed on others for the making of the "common" American culture under the idea of the "melting pot." This ideal, according to Bourne, is in reality the project of assimilating all immigrants to the particular culture of the ruling class and not the project of creating a common culture by the consent of the governed. What he proposes instead is a "transnational America" that would be a federation of cultures, a cosmopolitan, international culture woven from the immigrants' various cultures. The native culture of America, for Bourne, lay in the future, not in the past. It was to be invented by the collaboration of all immigrants.[37]

These efforts at articulating the identity, specificity, and value of U.S. culture were dominated to a large extent by white Anglo-Saxon men who took for granted the white European character of this culture. Until the later decades of the twentieth century, this character was challenged only rarely by various other components of U.S. society from racial and multicultural points of view. An examination of this challenge, interesting and important as it is, lies outside the scope of my study.[38] Suffice it here to mention W. E. B. Du Bois's (1868–1963) famous writings at the turn of the twentieth century, asserting the presence of African Americans in the economic, political, and cultural reality of the country, and those of Vine Deloria in the early 1960s, which voiced loud and clear, with humor, wit, and determination, though not without pain, the Native Americans' presence and situation in the same reality.[39]

The positioning vis-à-vis Europe took a dramatic turn at the end of World War II. Indeed, the destruction of Europe in this war seems to have been a significant turning point for American thinkers in analyzing their relationship to Europe and their own country. The collapse of Europe politically, economically, and militarily raised questions about the survival of its cultural status in the world and in the United States in particular: Could it still be taken as *the* reference for culture and thought? If not, which culture might serve as an alternative reference to replace it? What implications would this change have for American cultural and intellectual orientations? Two midcentury debates voiced these American concerns most eloquently. One of them was initiated by the leading literary journal of the time, the *Partisan Review*. In 1952, it called U.S. thinkers to a symposium to discuss the following:

For more than a hundred years, America was culturally dependent on Europe; now Europe is economically dependent upon America. And America is no longer the raw and unformed land of promise from which men of superior gifts like James, Santayana, and Eliot departed, seeking in Europe what they found lacking in America. Europe is no longer regarded as a sanctuary; it no longer assures that rich experience of culture which inspired and justified a criticism of American life. The wheel has come full circle, and now America has become the protector of Western civilization, at least in a military and economic sense.[40]

The journal invited participants in the debate to reflect on four main questions:

1. To what extent have American intellectuals actually changed their attitude toward America and its institutions?

2. Must the American intellectual and writer adapt himself to mass culture? If he must, what forms can his adaptation take? Or, do you believe that a democratic society necessarily leads to a leveling of culture, to a mass culture which will overrun intellectual and aesthetic values traditional to Western civilization?

3. Where in American life can artists and intellectuals find the basis of strength, renewal, recognition, now that they can no longer depend fully on Europe as a cultural example and a source of vitality?

4. If a reaffirmation and rediscovery of America is under way, can the tradition of critical non-conformism (going back to Thoreau and Melville and embracing some of the major expressions of American intellectual history) be maintained as strongly as ever?[41]

Three major phenomena seem to have occasioned this set of questions: first, the collapse of Europe in World War II; second, the rise of the United States as an economic, political, and military power; and third, the rise of the Soviet Union as a threatening rival power. This period was the heyday of McCarthyism, during which the lines between dissent and betrayal and between patriotic loyalty and total conformism were blurred, to say the least. The wealthy and powerful United States had by then developed a mass culture of consumerism and information in a democratic system and had opened job opportunities in governmental and educational institutions to intellectuals. In this context, most participants agreed that there was indeed a change of attitude toward the country among intellectuals—a positive change compared to the attitude in earlier decades. They were less eager to desert it for want of culture, and they had more opportunities to find work in its institutions. Its democratic system had proven its solidity and had gained affirmation by the incoming of European intellectual refugees. But some were weary of the confusion between political allegiance to the country and total intellectual and cultural conformism. Concern was expressed about the hysterical reactions to the Communist threat, which endangered the right of dissent and the space for creativity. Some feared that affirming America would lead to living down to its "mindlessness"— in other words, its anti-intellectualism and the leveling effect of its democratic mass culture. They raised questions about the effectiveness of writing in such a culture. Others saw in the democratic institutions and the channels of mass culture opportunities to disseminate knowledge and culture. For some, however, Europe's political and economic collapse did not necessarily mean that its culture had become obsolete. For them, it was important to acknowledge the continuity between American and European cultures and to realize that the latter could still be a source of inspiration for the former. Finally, "America" as a holistic and totalizing notion was a problematic concept that as such did not make sense. One could not relate to such a huge set of phenomena and realities all at once.

The question of Europe's successor in intellectual leadership was posed even more dramatically two years after the end of World War II at the second Inter-American Congress of Philosophy. The first one had been held in 1944 in Port-au-Prince, Haiti,[42] and had paved the way for this second encounter, which was held in conjunction with the annual meeting of the American Philosophical Association at Columbia University in New York City in 1947.[43] The main topic of the Inter-American Congress was whether the Americas were ready to take over the responsibilities of culture and philosophy since Europe's "demise." What tasks did these responsibilities entail? How was such readiness to be measured? And what was the role of philosophy in promoting world peace?

The consensus was that such responsibilities necessitated an intellectual maturity, the mark of which was a distinct philosophy—that is, the ability to produce a systematic thought of one's own. Hence, the questions posed at the congress included: Is there a North American philosophy? Is there an Ibero-American philosophy? If yes, what constitutes their distinct characters? Moreover, in what sense can one speak of specific philosophies given the universal nature of philosophy? The rationale of these first inter-American meetings was that North and South America needed to address these serious questions together, and for this, they needed to get acquainted with one another. Up until then, each had engaged separately with Europe and did not show any interest in a dialogue with one another. The chairman of the congress organizing committee, Cornelius Krusé, then professor of philosophy at Wesleyan University, described the situation:

> It was the fall of France, more than any other single factor, that especially in Ibero-America constituted a clear call to a new duty. North American culture not having had, in general, Ibero-America's intimate contact with France, has, it is true, been more affected by what was happening in Britain. Both Americas, however, were becoming aware that whether they wished it or not, both political and cultural leadership were being thrust upon them. Out of this situation, a new one for our hemisphere, whose countries began their history as colonies of European mother countries, there grows the necessity of a continuous common consultation and common action. But, unfortunately, until quite recently the two Americas were almost completely unaware of each other culturally. Politically, geographic proximity, and a common colonial tradition with a somewhat parallel history of breaking away from mother countries, had provided brief contacts and mutual involvements. But culturally, Ibero-America and North America were, up until World War II, much closer to Europe than to each other.[44]

In this new cultural mission of the Americas, philosophy was to examine and clarify values and meanings, which inevitably involve meaning contexts and hence cultures. South Americans had more experience in this task, states Krusé, because of their multicultural composition. F. S. C. Northrop, professor of philosophy at Yale, contrasted Mexico with the United States in this regard and invited his compatriots to learn from the Mexican intellectual debates that had arisen from the plural nature of its society and from the existence of a variety of ideologies in it. He underlined the importance of reflecting on the connections between cultures and philosophy.[45] Moreover, affirming the existence of a distinct North American philosophy implied a definition of a North American specificity.

For Harvard professor of philosophy Ralph Barton Perry, North American philosophy is an expression of the American mind, which is characterized by self-confidence, resourcefulness, buoyancy, belief in success, the readiness to seize opportunities, and the pursuit of wealth. American culture is hospitable and eclectic. It has no interest in originality. Culture is imported and, if necessary, bought with no embarrassment. About his fellow Americans, he wrote: "If they do not make it they can buy it. This does not offend their pride, for they feel that they buy it with what they *have* made."[46]

One of Perry's fellow Americans had, as we know, a different perception of this confident American "buoyancy" and a different view of this celebrated European civilization. Indeed, W. E. B. Du Bois believed that the cause of the collapse lay in the greed and arrogance of Europeans who had no qualms about dehumanizing others for the sake of their enrichment and their empowerment. In the process, they had dehumanized themselves and marched to their own doom. All the Christian values of brotherhood and love as well as all the beliefs in human progress had not prevented them from enslaving others. In 1947 in *The World and Africa*, he wrote: "The dawn of the twentieth century found white Europe master of the world and the white peoples almost universally recognized as the rulers for whose benefit the rest of the world existed. Never before in the history of civilization had self-worship of a people's accomplishment attained the heights that the worship of white Europe by Europeans reached." Long before Europe committed the war crimes that ruined its own societies, he pointed out, it had committed the very same crimes against the people of color around the world: "There was no Nazi atrocity—concentration camps, wholesale maiming and murder, defilement of women or ghastly blasphemy of childhood—which the Christian civilization of Europe had not long been practicing against colored folk in all parts of the world in the name of and for the defense of a Superior Race born to rule the world." Yet he also addressed the fall of European civilization in World War II in the following way:

> *We are face to face with the greatest tragedy that has ever overtaken the world. The collapse of Europe is to us the more astounding because of the boundless faith which we have had in European civilization. We have long believed without argument or reflection that the cultural status of the people of Europe and of North America represented not only the best civilization which the world had ever known, but also a goal of human effort destined to go on from triumph to triumph until*

the perfect accomplishment was reached. Our present nervous break-down, nameless fear, and often despair, comes from the sudden facing of this faith with calamity. In such a case, what we need above all is calm appraisal of the situation, the application of cold common sense. What in reality is the nature of the catastrophe? To what pattern of human culture does it apply? And, finally, why did it happen?[47]

For the Latin American thinkers participating in the Inter-American Congress of Philosophy of 1947, one of the major concerns was how to strike the right balance between developing a philosophy that was rooted in the particular lived realities of the Latin American environment and preserving the discipline's abstract, universal nature. On the one hand, too much focus on the first aspect might transform philosophy into politics and ideology and might jeopardize the quality of philosophical work. On the other hand, regurgitating European philosophy with no critical appropriation and no critical thinking of one's own to address concerns of one's own would not amount to genuine philosophical thinking. Such a genuine Latin American philosophy, according to Venezuelan philosopher Risieri Frondizi, was still to be made:

Up to the present, Ibero-American philosophy is simply the rethinking of the European problems that have reached our shores. It is certain that European philosophic currents acquire, in this soil, characteristics of our own, and perhaps in this way there will be arrived at in the future a conception purely Ibero-American, but up to now the process of digestion necessary for the rise of such a conception of our own, has not been completed. . . . We wish to refer, nevertheless, to this stage, because no doing permits us to point out what is lacking in present-day thought which would enable us to speak of an Ibero-American philosophy, in the same way as we speak of German, English, or French philosophy.[48]

Mexican philosopher Leopoldo Zea also underlined the importance of developing a Latin American philosophy that would satisfy the requirements of universality and particularity. For him, the universal is to be found in the human commonality between people everywhere, and the particular is to derive from the reflection on the concrete realities of each. The specificity would come from the distinct preoccupations and the distinct approaches. While exploring these specificities, philosophers should explore that commonality by getting interested in other cultures, settings, and peoples. An inter-American encounter like this congress was, for him, an important step in this direction. North and South Americans, he said, need to discover one another and correct the distorted images they have constructed of each other so that they can recognize in each other a valid interlocutor: "Ibero-America, feeling herself impotent in the field of the material, sublimated her impotence by considering herself the maximum expression of spirit in America, while assigning to North America a purely material role. For her part, North America saw in Ibero-America nothing but a group of half-savage tumultuous peoples, worthy only of despotic government. Mutually, the two Americas denied one another's spiritual capacity, and absolute misunderstanding came to rule their necessary relations." On the basis of a true dialogue, an "American" thought can be developed:

> *The universal, to which all philosophy should aspire, must be achieved starting, as does all authentic philosophy, from our reality. For this reason, it is urgent that we define, clarify, make explicit, just what that reality is. It is necessary to abstract from that reality what we can call the idea of America, i.e., that which is common to our two Americas, of the North and of the South. In this Congress we have already asked ourselves if there exists an Ibero-American philosophy or a North American philosophy. Why not go on to question ourselves about the possibilities of an American philosophy? That is, why not question ourselves about the possibilities of a philosophy which respects what is private to each one of the Americas and can at the same time be valid for both?*[49]

Four decades later, in 1985, the eleventh Inter-American Congress of Philosophy was held in Guadalajara, Mexico, to discuss "America and its philosophical expression." The proceedings of this meeting show the extent of the failure of the dialogue attempted in 1947. Within those four decades, the two Americas seemed to have become more estranged from one another and the divide between them to have spread wider. The United States had continued to grow in power and self-confidence and had become part of the hegemonic Western culture against which Latin America was still struggling to position itself. U.S. philosophers showed no sensitivity to cultural imperialism within the discipline, as demonstrated in Richard Rorty's 1985 keynote address, which focused on the analytic and continental trends of Western philosophy and asserted that philosophy could develop only in enclaves of freedom and prosperity. Canadian and Latin American participants voiced protests, their discontent directed against the assumption made about the normativity and universality of Anglo-Eurocentric traditions of philosophy. Leopoldo Zea, also present at this meeting, argued that the history of Western philosophy itself showed that important philosophical ideas were developed in resistance to forces of oppression and injustice. Ofelia Schutte, a Cuban feminist philosopher based in the United States, described the meeting as the great "dis-encounter." She demanded a more inclusive choice of participants and speakers as well as the adoption of Spanish as an official conference language in addition to English.[50]

Although the search for a thought of one's own, distinct from Western thought, remained a persistent quest for Latin American, Arab, and African thinkers, it ceased to be one for the U.S. American thinkers as their country became one of the leading powers, if not the leading power, in Western culture. In the last decades of the twentieth century, the U.S. debates centered around the place of Anglo-Eurocentric tradition in the country: whereas some challenged the hegemony of this tradition and called for a more inclusive, racial, and multicultural understanding of culture and identity, others defended the Anglo-Eurocentric tradition against those challenges that they perceived as threats to "serious" culture and to the country's identity.[51] Renowned Mexican writer Octavio Paz (1914–1998) saw in these challenges the premises of a more dialogical United States. In a lecture delivered at the University of Texas at Austin in 1969 and commenting on his famous book published some twenty years earlier, *The Labyrinth of Solitude* (to which I return later), he said:

> *For the first time in the history of the United States (earlier, only a few poets and philosophers voiced it), there is a powerful current of opinion that places under judgment the very values and beliefs on which Anglo-American civilization has been built. Is that not unprecedented? This criticism of progress is a portent, a promise of other changes. If I asked myself, "Can the United States carry on a dialogue with us?" my answer would be yes—on condition that first they learn to speak with themselves, with their own otherness: their Blacks, their Chicanos, their young people. And something similar must be said to Latin Americans: criticism of others begins with criticism of oneself.[52]*

Indeed, self-critique, critique as the condition of the possibility of dialogue with others, and relations with the United States are important themes of twentieth-century Latin American debates on culture, in addition to the ubiquitous issues of imitation, domination, and liberation.[53]

The Non-Western Postcolonial Debates

The Latin American Debates

Beginning in the 1930s, issues of cultural identity and cultural malaise became prominent topics of public and intellectual debates in Latin America generally and in Mexico particularly. The Mexican Revolution, the Spanish Civil War and the inflow of Spanish refugees, including intellectuals, and the rise of fascism between the two wars in Europe animated the Mexican intellectual and artistic scene. They gave rise to a whole set of discussions about Latin America's relation to European culture, the existence of a distinct Latin American culture, racial mixity and identity, imitation and originality, inferiority and dependency, and nationalism and authenticity. These themes dominated Latin American debates on culture throughout the twentieth century. In my rapid survey, I focus on the central notions of imitation, domination, and liberation.

Mexican philosopher Samuel Ramos addresses the various aspects of the Mexican cultural malaise in his landmark book *Profile of Man and Culture in Mexico*, published in 1934.[54] He analyzes the malaise by looking at the Mexican psyche that embodied it and seeing in it a number of challenging tensions and disconnections caused by the givens in the country. There was, on the one hand, the divide between the Europeanized privileged classes and ruling elite on one side and the rest of the people on the other. The two revolutions that shaped modern Mexico—the 1810 revolt against Spanish rule and the 1910 revolt against the colonial type of government that had lingered after independence—had not succeeded in bringing these two components of Mexican society closer to one another. In both revolutions, the leadership had failed to forge a cohesive nation. The lack of political stability and security throughout the nineteenth century had hindered the construction of a national cultural project that could be sustainable. No substantial accumulative work was achieved. Instead, quick attempts were made here and there to propose short-lived and superficial projects. These failures and weaknesses created a deep sense of inferiority. The contrast between aspirations, often borrowed from European Ideals, and local realities nurtured a strong sense of self-denigration, which was compensated for by pronounced machismo and chauvinism.

In addition, the Spanish Conquest had brought into the country an antimodern Catholic theocracy, which, in Ramos's opinion, suited the natives but ultimately clashed with the modernist ambitions of the Creoles (Europeans of the colonized countries). The latter were neither American nor European, but people' with hybrid affiliations who were motivated by individualist interests in an economy geared toward the exterior, much of the wealth produced in the country being channeled to the old continent. The natives had no interest in change. They were "by nature," according to Ramos, rigidly attached to their conservative traditions: "We do not believe that the Indian's passivity is the result only of the enslavement which befell him at the time of the Conquest. Quite possibly he submitted to conquest because he was naturally inclined to passivity. Even before the Conquest natives were set against all forms of change and renovation. They stuck to their traditions and were routine and conservative by character. A will to the immutable was engraved on their style of culture."[55] He called this alleged immutability "indigenous Egyptianism."

In a word, history had lent Mexico a derivative culture that was based on an unhealthy imitation of Europe, a culture that did not correspond to the country's local realities. Ramos summarizes the Mexican malaise in the following terms:

> Mexicans have not lived naturally, their history has always lacked candor. That is why they now should quickly heed that voice, which demands a life of sincerity. We must have the courage to be ourselves and the humility to accept the life that fate bestowed upon us without being ashamed of its poverty. All the ills that have outlived us are due to our failure to practice these simple rules of austerity; we have chosen to feign a situation which is very superior to that in which we actually live. Many of our sufferings which now afflict us will disappear the day we cure ourselves of our vanity. As a consequence of living outside the reality of our being, we are lost in a chaotic world, in the midst of which we walk blindly and aimlessly, buffeted about by the four winds. . . . It is a consolation to note that for some years the Mexican conscience has steadfastly sought true national introspection. But unfortunately the examination of our conscience has not been undertaken with the rigor, depth, and objectivity that the case requires.[56]

The solution, however, cannot reside in a wholesale rejection of everything foreign and isolationism, nor can it be in some mystified form of

"Mexicanism": "We must not continue to practice a false Europeanism; but it is just as urgent to avoid another dangerous illusion, cherished by an equally false type of Mexicanism. . . . Just as 'Europeanism' was founded on the ideal of a culture which could exist apart from life, 'nationalism' was founded on the belief that Mexico was already complete in itself, with a definitive national physiognomy, and that its only need was to be drawn out into the light of day, like an unearthed idol."[57]

What Mexicans need, according to Ramos, is a true knowledge of self that is to be acquired through a scientific approach to the Mexican mind. The idea of a "Mexican science," he adds, does not make sense. Science is necessarily universal. It is the absence of such a truthful introspection that has made openness to European culture problematic. Once such a knowledge of self is secured, then selective appropriation from Europe can be made. Only then can damaging imitation be transformed into constructive assimilation. Of particular importance is the appropriation of science and technology, which are needed to shield the country against the U.S. hegemony and threat. Finally, such a conscious assimilation of European culture would ultimately produce a confident Mexican personality, endowed with a real culture connected to real Mexican life:

> In the future Mexico must have a Mexican culture, but we have no illusions about its being original or unique. By Mexican culture we mean universal culture made over into our own, the kind that can coexist with us and appropriately express our spirit. Curiously enough, the only way open to us—in order to shape this Mexican culture—is to continue learning about European culture. Our race is a brand of a European race. Our history has unfolded in a European manner. But we have not succeeded in forming our own culture, because we have separated culture and life. We no longer want an artificial culture that lives like a hothouse flower; we do not want a false Europeanism.[58]

Writing in the late 1940s, Octavio Paz noted that Europe, as a possible reservoir of assimilable culture, had been severely shaken and that the Latin American problem of producing genuine thought had become a world problem. The nakedness and solitude of humans had become universal:

> For the first time, Mexico does not have at her disposal a set of univer-sal ideas that can justify her situation. Europe, once a storehouse of ready-to-use ideas, now lives as we do, from day to day. Strictly speak-

ing, the modern world no longer possesses any ideas. Hence the Mexican must face reality in the same way as everyone else: alone. But in his nakedness he will discover his true universality, which previously was a mere adaptation of European thought. His philosophy will be Mexican only in its accent or emphasis or style, not in its content. Mexicanism will become a mask which, when taken off, reveals at last the genuine human being it disguised. Under the present circumstances, then, our need to develop a Mexican philosophy becomes a need to think out for ourselves certain problems which are no longer exclusively ours but pertain to all men. That is, Mexican philosophy, to be truly that, must be philosophy plain and simple.[59]

For Paz, this thinking for oneself would require a radicalization of critique. The Mexican Revolution, according to him, failed to realize its goals, namely that of reconnecting with the country's realities and establishing a free and inclusive society based on the exercise of critique. Artists did produce valuable paintings and novels in the spirit of the revolution, he says, but on the whole the Mexican intelligentsia bore a considerable responsibility in this failure: on the one hand, it lost its critical edge by getting involved in the power apparatus, and on the other, it proved incapable of composing a comprehensive vision for the country: "The Revolution began as a discovery of our own selves and a return to our origins; later it became a search and an abortive attempt at a synthesis; finally, since it was unable to assimilate our tradition and to offer us a new and workable plan, it became a compromise. The Revolution has not been capable of organizing its explosive values into a world view, and the Mexican intelligentsia has not been able to resolve the conflict between the insufficiencies of our tradition and our need and desire for universality." So the task now was to undertake genuine thinking: "Nothing can justify us now: we alone can answer the questions reality is asking us. Philosophical reflection thus becomes an urgent necessity. It is not enough to examine our intellectual past or describe our characteristic attitudes. What we desperately need is a concrete solution, one that will give meaning to our presence on earth."[60]

Like Ramos, Paz complained about the absence of an authentic sense of self: "Mexicanism is a way of not being ourselves, a way of life that is not our own." But unlike him, he saw the solution in a liberating critique rather than in a quest for a more appropriate form of cultural borrowing. Identity, always nominal and fleeting, though necessary, might be the key to an empowering sense of self:

Pronouns, like nouns, are masks, and there is no one behind them—except, perhaps, an instantaneous we which is a twinkling of an equally fleeting it. But while we live we can escape neither masks nor nouns and pronouns: we are inseparable from our fictions, our features. We are condemned to invent a mask and to discover afterward that the mask is our true visage. In The Labyrinth of Solitude *I tried hard (without wholly succeeding, of course) to avoid both the pitfalls of abstract humanism and the illusions of a philosophy of Mexican-ness: the mask that changes into a face, the petrified face that changes into a mask. In those days I was not interested in a definition of Mexican-ness but rather,* as now, *in criticism: that activity which consists not only in knowing ourselves but, just as much or more, in freeing ourselves. Criticism unfolds the possibility of freedom and is thus an invitation to action.*[61]

Leopoldo Zea, who was one of Ramos's students, described the Latin American cultural predicament by saying that Latin Americans did not relate to their region's autochthonous cultures and that the culture they related to was not theirs, no matter how much they wanted to identify with it.[62] In the 1942 essay "The Actual Function of Philosophy in Latin America," he states:

What belongs to us, what is properly Latin American, is not to be found in pre-Columbian culture. Is it to be found in European culture? Now, something strange happens to us in relation to European culture: we use it but we do not consider it ours; we feel imitators of it. Our way of thinking, our world view, is similar to the European. European culture has a meaning for us that we do not find in pre-Columbian culture. Still, we do not feel it to be our own. We feel as bastards who profit from goods to which they have no right. We feel as if we were wearing someone else's clothes: they are too big for our size. We assimilate their ideas but cannot live up to them. We feel that we should realize the ideals of European culture, but we also feel incapable of carrying out the task: we are content with admiring them and thinking that they are not made for us. This is the knot of our problem: we do not feel heirs of an autochthonous culture, because that culture has no meaning for us; and that which has meaning for us, like the European, does not feel as our own.[63]

This estrangement from the adopted culture translates itself into a gap be-
tween thought and reality. Latin American thought is not a reflection of
Latin American realities. Unless it becomes so, it will remain an immature
imitation of a foreign thought: "The malaise is that we want to adjust the
Latin American circumstance to a conception of the world inherited from
Europe, rather than adjusting that conception of the world to the Latin
American circumstance. Hence the divorce between ideas and reality." The
inability to apply European ideas and ideals is the source of much of the
sense of inferiority: "The malaise resides in that we perceive what is Latin
American, that is, what is ours, as something inferior. The Latin American
man's resistance to being like a European is felt as an incapacity."[64]

This sense of inferiority exists also vis-à-vis North America. The latter,
in turn, expresses its own sense of inferiority toward Europe by outdoing
European achievements in quantity without being able to be truly creative
in its own right:

*North America has strived to become a second Europe, a magnified
copy of it. Original creation does not matter, what matters is to achieve
the European models in a big way and with the greatest perfection.
Everything is reduced to numbers: so many dollars or so many meters.
In the end, the only thing that is sought with this is to hide a feeling of
inferiority. The North American tries to show that he is as capable as
the European. And the way to show it is by doing the same things that
Europeans have done, on a bigger scale and with greater technical
perfection. But this only demonstrates technical, not cultural ability,
because cultural ability is demonstrated in the solution one gives to
the problems of man's existence, and not in the technical imitation of
solutions that other men found for their own problems.*

*The Latin American man, however, feels inferior not only to the Euro-
pean, but also to the North American man. Not only does he no longer
try to hide his feeling of inferiority, but he also exhibits it through self-
denigration. The only thing that he has tried to do so far is to live
comfortably under the shadow of ideas he knows are not his own.*[65]

In taking up the challenge of articulating and dealing with one's own
problems lies the possibility of breaking away from the pattern of imitation.
A truly Latin American thought, according to Zea, would be the product of

a systematic reflection on the Latin American realities or "circumstances," a term borrowed from Spanish existentialist philosopher José Ortega y Gasset (1883–1955). Philosophy would have a serious contribution to make to such a reflection. It would be both rooted in the lived local realities—in this sense, historicized—and at the same universal because it would still address human issues, but from a Latin American perspective. The universal would then consist in the collection of such different perspectives. In the Latin American context, Zea argues, it should produce a humanist, inclusive, "mestizo" consciousness. Undertaking this task would replace the sense of inferiority with a sense of responsibility: "To be aware of our true relations with European culture eliminates our sense of inferiority and gives us instead a sense of responsibility. This is the feeling that animates the Latin American man today. He feels that he has 'come of age.' . . . The Latin American man knows himself to be the heir of Western culture and now demands a place in it. The place that he demands is that of collaborator." Unless Latin Americans undertake such a serious reflection, they will remain captive of ever-changing ideologies in the absence of a comprehensive national vision and a regional identity: "We are continually experimenting and projecting with always-changing ideologies. There is no single national plan because there is no sense of nation. And there is no sense of nation for the same reason that there is no sense of what is Latin America."[66]

For Peruvian philosopher Augusto Salazar Bondy, the malaise is not peculiar to Mexico or Peru. It is a general feature of Latin American thought and philosophy. Attempts have been made to explain the phenomenon by saying that Latin America is a young nation, that it is not inclined to theoretical thinking, that it has universal openness, and that its institutions do not provide good conditions for intellectual original production. In reality, says Bondy, what is taken to be universal openness is a limitless receptivity due to the state of dependency the region is in, like all other regions of the Third World, which suffer from underdevelopment and foreign economic and political hegemony. This state can produce only a nonauthentic thought geared toward a culture of domination: "The dominated countries live with a view to the outside, depending in their existence upon the decisions of the dominant powers, that cover all fields. This trait is not alien to the receptivity and the imitative character of the philosophy—and not only the philosophy—that is typical of Hispanic America. Likewise, these countries lack vigor and dynamism because of their depressed economy and because of the lack of cohesion in their society that underdevelopment creates."[67]

Philosophy, according to Bondy, can and ought to create an awareness of this dependency and lack of authenticity. The discrepancy between models of culture and conditions of existence produces a distorted self-consciousness. It is the lucid awareness of the dependency condition that can open the possibility of transcending it by dissipating the myths and illusions that have surrounded its realities. Philosophy as a critical and analytic discipline of thinking should shape a more truthful image of self and thus help overcome the generalized state of inauthenticity:

> *Hispanic philosophy . . . must be an awareness that cancels prejudice, myths, idols; an awareness that will awaken us to our subjection as peoples and our depression as men. . . . It must be . . . a critical and analytical awareness of the potentialities and demands of our affirmation as humanity. All of which requires a thought that from the beginning will cast aside every deceptive illusion and, delving into the historical substance of our community, will search for the qualities and values that could express it positively. These qualities and values must be precisely those capable of finding resonance in the entirety of Hispanic America, and, along with other convergent forces, unleashing a progressive movement that will eliminate underdevelopment and domination.[68]*

He recalls the history of ideas that deals with this Latin American cultural malaise, starting with the work of his fellow Peruvian José Carlos Mariategui (1894–1930)[69] in the 1920s and moving on to the work of Ramos, Zea, and others, and states that the effort has been focused so far on theoretical proposals. What is needed now is a revolutionary action based on these proposals, which would then liberate not only the dominated societies of the Third World, but the dominating societies of the First World as well:

> *When philosophy proposed to liberate itself historically, it did not even achieve the liberation of the philosopher, because no one can be liberated when he or she dominates someone else. So if we want to look at things truthfully, the only possibility of liberation is opened for the first time in history with the Third World, the world of the oppressed and underdeveloped, who are liberating themselves and at the same time liberating the other, the oppressor. Then, for the first time, there can be a philosophy of liberation. In the concrete struggle of*

classes, of groups, and of nations, there is another who oppresses me,
whom unfortunately I must displace from—the machinery of domi-
nation. Philosophy must be involved in this struggle, for otherwise it
[only] constructs an abstract thought, and then, on the pretext that we
are going to liberate ourselves as philosophers, we do not liberate any-
one, not even ourselves.[70]

Recent writings from the region show the persistence of the issues of imitation and identity in Latin American debates.[71] Two analyses from Brazil connect the questions of imitation and authenticity to the phenomena of modernity, nationalism, and colonialism. In the 1995 essay "National by Imitation," Brazilian literary critic Roberto Schwarz recognizes the problem of imitation in Brazilian cultural life, but criticizes the naive way in which it was hitherto approached.[72] According to him, the higher classes and the intelligentsia mistakenly identified themselves with European ideas and ideals and distanced themselves from their local experiences and their own compatriots. As their story is presented, they corrected the mistake intellectually by becoming more "native" and more patriotic. For some, overcoming the gap between an imported culture and national realities required the repudiation of all things foreign. This trend was strong until the 1960s, when populist nationalism started to come under attack and to be seen as being parochial and reactionary. To follow the trends of the transnational cultural industry was then the right thing to do. The philosophies of Michel Foucault (1926–1984) and Derrida offered in this respect an appealing critique of the original/copy hierarchy and seemed to solve for some the problem of imitation by dissolving the hierarchy altogether.

According to Schwarz, these philosophical theories do not erase the real problems of subordination or the givens of national history. The historical fact of the matter is, he says, that Brazil has been trying to conciliate slavery with republican bourgeois citizenship. The colonial economic structures based on exploited labor for the benefit of European (and later U.S.) industry have remained untouched since Brazil's independence in 1822. This neglect has led to the cultural separation and exclusion of the poor and the absence of a cohesive and integrated national society. The phenomenon of imitation has been the expression of this socioeconomic divide and, as such, the product of modernity in Brazil. For Schwarz, to become authentic it is not enough to stop copying from the metropolitan centers, nor is it a matter of intellectual taste or choice. What need to be addressed are the multiple exclusions and oppressions upon which modern Brazil was built.

Schwarz's fellow Brazilian critic Amos Nascimento elaborates on the ideologies that came with this modernity—colonialism, syncretism, and populism.[73] Syncretism and populism, he says, were supposed to be inclusive nation-building projects, but they were in reality Europeanist-assimilationist projects that excluded and oppressed the natives and the Africans. Countercultural projects were developed in enclaves to resist these hegemonic projects, such as the Jesuit mission of the Guaranis, the *quilimbos* (rural congregations of former slaves), and the *modernismo* movement of the 1920s that was critical of the westernizing modernity. These resistance enclaves opposed the colonial movement, whereas the colonial movement went along with humanism and Enlightenment in Europe. The enclaves are the postmodern expressions of Latin America in that they voiced the views and interests of those who were left out of the modernity project.

The association of modernity with colonialism, genocide, slavery, and expatriation has been a recurrent subject of Latin American thought. Argentinean philosopher Enrique Dussel, exiled in Mexico, describes these phenomena associated with modernity as the "underside of modernity."[74] According to him, modernity is a European phenomenon that is constituted in a dialectical relationship with a non-European alterity. It was made possible by the enslavement of the New World, and in this sense Latin America is, for him, the essential alterity of modernity. Modernity includes both a reason of emancipation and a reason of genocide. In a provocative formulation, he associates the Cartesian foundational statement "Ego cogito, ergo sum" with the brutality of modern Europe vis-à-vis the rest of the world: "From the 'I conquer' applied to the Aztec and Inca world and all America, from the 'I enslave' applied to Africans sold for the gold and silver acquired at the cost of the death of Amerindians working in the depths of the earth, from the 'I vanquish' of the wars of India and China to the shameful 'opium war'—from this 'I' appears the Cartesian *ego cogito*."[75] Against this modernity and this annihilating and subjugating reason, Dussel wants to affirm the "reason of the Other"—that of the poor, the slave, the Indian, the woman, the child, and the subalternized popular cultures—instead of the postmodern irrationalism and critique of reason. A philosophy of liberation is to be the elaboration of the "reason of the Other" by thinkers whose task it is to give voice to this Other. The latter is the face of alterity in the Lévinasian sense—that is, the face that represents the call of God that summons one to answer in ethical thought and action.

Dussel's philosophy of liberation has been the object of animated debates. Latin American feminists have criticized it for its conservative and mystifying tendencies. Ofelia Schutte thinks that Dussel combines radical rhetoric with traditional conservative moral values, especially with respect to women, marriage, and gender issues, and that his ideas remain in line with the Catholic Church's official magesterium.[76] In fact, she finds his philosophy of liberation to be less liberational and progressive than some of the tenets of the Latin American theology of liberation. She thinks that his attempt at reconciling Marxism with the Catholic faith is not convincing. Moreover, she expresses concern about the claim of speaking for the Other, the "people" or the "poor," fearing that it will become another way of paternalizing them. Finally, she worries about the total "othering" of those outside the "center," as he defines it, and about making them into the ethical face of God on earth. She shows strong reservations toward what she considers Dussel's emotional and mystical arguments.

Elina Vuola too asks, Who is to define the Other and to represent the face of the oppressed?[77] Claims of authorship here can easily turn into a form of authoritarianism, especially if certain elements of ethical, religious, and—inevitably—political absolutism are mixed with it. "People," she says, would be transformed from an empirical reality into a normatively constructed ideal. Moreover, she notes that gender does not appear in the articulation of this entity. She thinks that although Dussel was the first male Latin American intellectual to take up the issue of women, his elaborations of it suffer from his conservative and not always consistent philosophical choices. Like the Catholic Church, he takes for granted the natural givenness of sexual difference. Moreover, his dealing with women's issues remains abstract and remote from the realities of everyday life. Vuola prefers to his approach the more pragmatic approach of activists who are more involved in dealing with concrete problems than busy with theological issues.[78] She refers here to the Gebara nuns who provide help to women in abortion crises and fight the conditions of an "abortive" society, as she puts it, instead of fighting "abortion" in an absolute manner. She believes that no true liberation philosophy or theology can develop without a comprehensive revisiting of the fundamental assumptions of gender and society.

Latin American feminists, like postcolonial feminists elsewhere, struggle to defend, on the one hand, the validity and authenticity of their gender grievances in their own societies and, on the other, the specificity of their cause within the overall global feminist scene. In their home countries, they need to refute the standard accusation that feminism is a foreign importation; and on the external front, they need to protect the right to have a feminism of their own that corresponds to their cultural and postcolonial contexts. Here again a balance is sought between a universal understanding of feminism and a particular set of local priorities. For instance, Schutte believes that Latin American feminists see a communitarian rather than an individualistic approach to social issues as more appropriate given the types of solidarity structures needed in their societies.[79]

Because of the range of problems these societies face, from the cultural to the socioeconomic and political, Latin American feminists find themselves struggling on more than one front and are ultimately called upon not only to fight patriarchy, but to rethink the entire nation's fundamental assumptions regarding identity, modernity, and progress. Chilean feminist Raquel Olea says that what is to be discussed is not only women's "own room," but the whole "living room" of the common house. In this sense, the Latin American feminist struggle, in her opinion, is a struggle for an alternative civilizational project:

> Contemporary feminist discourse proposes a project of cultural change that can no longer be contained in an autonomous "women's" space. Nor can women continue to insist that we speak only from a position of oppression and victimization, which we attribute to an inequality that seems to be without remedy. It is our own discourses and practices that, in dialogue with other critical proposals and with the system of dominant representations, legitimize us in our identity or identities. In this sense, feminism does not seek a "room of its own" in which to institutionalise its utopia; rather, it installs itself in the place historically denied to women, the space of the public sphere, of discursive competence and the pacts of power: the space in which the discourses and projects of civilization and society legitimize themselves in a process of dialogue between equals, at the same time open and cyclical and permanently in flux, which produces the new forms of thought and social life.[80]

The revolt against colonialism and neocolonialism and the quest for a thought of one's own have found a powerful expression in Latin American liberation theology. This theology came to fruition in the 1960s through the efforts of Latin American priests and theologians, both Protestant and Catholic, as a response to the plight of their compatriots and based on their Christian faith. In successive ecumenical meetings in different Latin American cities, they reflected on the practical, theoretical, and spiritual responses to this plight.[81]

Two sets of factors led to the emergence of this religious and theological movement. First, the economic policies of several populist governments in the 1950s and 1960s, such as Peron's in Argentina, Vargas's in Brazil, and Cárdenas's in Mexico, benefited the middle classes and some of the urban working classes but alienated the rest of the population, especially the peasantry. These supposedly nationalist policies were in reality a local dependent capitalism that served the interests of the industrialized centers. They led to strong popular movements that demanded policy changes, but reaction to these protest movements came in the form of military dictatorships that aimed at repressing them and defending the established policies. The growing socioeconomic problems led to reconsideration of a development theory that had assumed that aligning peripheral economies to central ones would benefit the former and lead to development. Concrete applications on the ground had shown that such alignments instead aggravated socioeconomic divides in the periphery and increased overall underdevelopment in it. The link was made between the growing wealth of the First World and the growing poverty in the Third World. And second, new orientations were at the same time emerging in the churches. In 1962, the Second Vatican Council adopted some progressive theological ideas that could be taken as a framework for new forms of practical engagement with the modern world. Not everyone welcomed this theology. The political establishment disliked its criticisms and tried to repress it, sometimes violently; and some members of the Catholic Church establishment did not approve of its political involvement and were suspicious of its Marxist components.

One of liberation theology's most eloquent spokesmen is the Peruvian priest and theologian Gustavo Guttierrez. His 1971 seminal book *Teología de la liberatión* (*A Theology of Liberation*) became the movement's landmark reference.[82] For Guttierrez, liberation theology proclaims the life of Christ in the midst of poverty and the many forms of death that poverty entails. It involves living Christian faith and sharing it with people oppressed by injustice and despair. This challenge is for him the meaning of being a believer under concrete historical circumstances. It calls for a new theology that is a response to a particular situation and at the same time part of the universal understanding of Christianity. This theology cannot but have its own accent while remaining in touch with the universal through its human depth.

In line with a Latin American cultural tradition, he says, Latin American theology has hitherto echoed European theology, which has always considered itself to be "the" universal Christian theology, with no accent of its own, unaware of its own particularities. The former's emergence with a particular set of themes and priorities, distinct from those of Europe, is a coming of age. This liberation theology, Gutierrez adds, should not be mistaken for the local branch of European progressive theology. The latter developed as a reaction to the Enlightenment, to a modernity and secularism specific to European history, whereas liberation theology emerged as a reaction to the challenge of the poor. Although the two are not to be confused, they ought to be in a dialogue based on the recognition of their differences. Such a dialogue would produce genuine universality and not the uniformity imposed by the powerful party. The goal, he says, is not uniformity, but profound communion. Finally, for Guttierrez, preaching the universal love of God in Latin America means not only the articulation of a specific theology, but also the commitment to a spiritual life of prayer and the dedication to an active struggle against all form of injustice and oppression.

This quick survey of twentieth-century Latin American debates on culture shows an amazing similarity in themes and preoccupations to those we encountered in the Arab debates: the quest for authenticity, intellectual decolonization, and cultural self-affirmation; the disillusionment with formal independence; the link between cultural imitation and economic dependence; the disappointment with failed liberation movements; the complaints about socioeconomic injustice and political oppression; the uncertainty of national and regional identity; the concern regarding the absence of national cohesion; the sense of alienation; and the sense of inferiority. However, in the Latin American case, the present sense of inferiority is not associated with the memory of a past superiority, as it is in the Arab case. Nor is the quest for empowerment an attempt at recovering a past might that will replace the present Western might (Europe and the United States). Moreover, in Latin America, Europeanization seems to be on a much wider scale, with no local heritage left to fall back onto in the search for a sense of self. Finally, given the much longer and systematic colonization of the region, issues of genocide and slavery, associated with colonialism and modernity, have a prominence that is absent in the Arab debates.

The African Debates

If imitativeness has been the major concern of Latin American cultural critics, primitiveness has been that of the African thinkers. As in Latin America and the United States, the question "Is there a distinct local philosophy (in this case, African)?" has been raised in twentieth-century African debates. "Africanness" has been at the center of these debates: What is it? How is it to be defined? On what basis? Is it definable at all? Should it be defined? If yes, by whom? For what purpose? More central in the African sphere, however, has been the question of the very existence of philosophy as a mode of rigorous, systematic, and abstract thinking. This question originated in the claims that Western scholars and missionaries made about the primitiveness of the African mind, meaning its inherent inability to produce theoretical thought and "high" culture. French anthropologist Lucien Lévy-Bruhl (1857–1939), for instance, asserted in the early decades of the twentieth century that the African mind was primitive, that it lacked the normative logical features of the Western mind—namely, the principle of identity, the notion of causality, and the conception of time; in other words, he claimed that the African mind was prelogical and subconceptual.[83] Around midcentury, Belgian missionary Placide Tempels (1906–1977) countered this claim to a certain extent by stating that the African was capable of consistent thinking, but that this thinking had a logic of its own.[84] He believed that it was important to explore and understand this logic if one wanted to address Africans successfully and convert them to Christianity.

Much of the African intellectual effort since the mid–twentieth century has been devoted to disproving these claims about the African mind and to discussing Africans' intellectual and cultural capabilities. In the first wave of responses, the tendency was to "prove" Africans' mental abilities and the distinct achievements of African culture(s). The gaze later became self-reflective, like in Latin America and the Arab world, and a number of African critics undertook a critical examination of the earlier responses. The early reactions to the colonial essentialist typification of the African mind as primitive or "other" consisted in adopting this typification and turning it into a source of pride and distinct identity, producing nativist schools of thought known as "Africanism." The three most prominent schools were négritude, Egyptianism, and ethnophilosophy. [85]

The négritude school was developed by three writers of African origin: Léon Damas (1912–1978) of French Guyana, Aimé Césaire (1913–2008) of Martinique, and Léopold Sédar Senghor (1906–2001) of Senegal. It emphasized the physiological, epistemological, emotional, social, and artistic traits that characterized Africans and distinguished them in a radical way from white Europeans. Senghor, a renowned writer, thinker, and statesman, celebrates the distinct mode of being that these traits bestowed on Africans: one of communion with nature and others that allows them to have a fuller and more direct form of experience and knowledge:

> *"I think, therefore I am," wrote Descartes, who was the European* par excellence. *The African Negro could say, "I feel, I dance the Other, I am."* . . . *He has no need to think, but to live the Other by dancing it. In dark Africa, people always dance because they feel, and they always dance someone or something. Now to dance is to discover and to re-create, to identify oneself with the forces of life, to lead a fuller life, and in short, to be. It is, at any rate, the highest form of knowledge. And thus, the knowledge of the African Negro is, at the same time, discovery and creation—re-creation.*[86]

Senghor contests the misinterpretation made of his statements and asserts that his claim is not that the Africans cannot think, but that there are different forms of thought, shaped by the psychological and physiological makeup of each race. The white European type of reason is one based on visualization, analytic through utilization, whereas Africans' type of reason is embracing, sensuous, emotional, and intuitive through participation. Moreover, Senghor believes that Europeans themselves are starting to appreciate this other, African mode of knowledge and discovering its superior quality. Objectivity is on the retreat in Europe, he says. Phenomenology, existentialism, and Teilhardism in philosophy, as well as relativity, wave mechanics, quantum mechanics, and non-Euclidean geometry are examples of this new orientation: "The light of knowledge is no longer that unchanging clarity which would light on the object without touching it and being touched by it; it is a troubled flame sparked by their *embrace*, a lightning produced by *contact*, a *participation*, a *communion*. Modern philosophy wants to be experience, a living *identity* of knowledge and the known, of life and thought, of life and reality." For Senghor, *négritude* is the set of values that constitute this emotive attitude that Africans have toward the world: "It is in fact the *emotive attitude* towards the world which explains all the cultural values of the African Negro: religion, social structures, art and literature, and above all, the genius of their languages."[87]

According to Senghor, these sharp distinctions between African and European modes of experiencing and thinking do not exclude the possibility of a universal civilization and a pan-humanism, but he challenges Europe's claim to being this universal civilization—a claim based on its colonial conquests rather than on the contents of its civilization. A truly universal civilization would have to include all the distinct civilizations of the world. He believes in justice and thinks that socialism is the right path to achieve it, but in his opinion Africans need to appropriate European socialism critically according to their own needs and modes of thinking. In addressing their realities, he calls on Africans to move from the attitude of victimhood to that of an engaged agency.[88]

Interestingly, in a speech delivered on the occasion of his receiving an *honoris causa* doctoral degree from the University of Cairo in February 1967 in the presence of President Gamal Abdel Nasser and high Egyptian officials, Senghor spoke about the importance of uniting efforts between North and sub-Saharan Africa for the building of a prosperous future for the continent. This future, he thought, could not be built solely on the anticolonial struggle. The common destiny should be strengthened by the continent's diverse cultural spheres. He pointed out two of those spheres, the "Arabo Berber" and the "Negro African"—the first one characterized by Logos, referring to the work of luminaries such as St. Augustine, Averroes, and Ibn Khaldun, and the second one characterized by rhythm, love, faith, and image symbolism. If each sphere can learn from the other while remaining itself, a united Africa might come into being in the form of a balanced humanism.[89]

Senghor's fellow Senegalese thinker Cheikh Anta Diop (1923–1986) also addresses the racist claims about blacks' inherent inaptitude for culture, referring to the works of ancient Greeks, such as Galen, and of modern Europeans, such as Gobineau. In his opinion, such claims needed to be refuted with scientific arguments, but not the biased arguments of white science. The *négritude* school of thought could not, according to him, provide such refutations:

> The "Negritude" poets did not, at that time, have the scientific means
> to refute or to question these types of errors. Scientific truth had been
> White for such a long time that, with the help and writings of Lucien
> Lévy-Bruhl, all these affirmations made under the scientific banner
> had to be accepted as such by our submissive peoples. Therefore the
> "Negritude" movement accepted this so-called inferiority and boldly

assumed it in full view of the world. Aimé Césaire shouted: "Those who explored neither the seas nor the sky," and Leopold S. Senghor: "Emotion is Negro and reason is Greek."[90]

For Diop, the constituents of African specificity are to be found in history, language, and, to a lesser extent, psychology, and they need to be studied scientifically. Psychological traits change with time and circumstances. He believes that a collective African personality is rooted in the Egyptians' great civilization. The Egypto-Nubian civilization is and should be for Africa what the Greco-Latin civilization is for Europe. As for the multiple languages of Africa, their common roots have to be recognized, as such common roots have been recognized for the numerous Indo-European languages.

Ethnophilosophy was another way of asserting African intellectual aptitudes and accomplishments. It consisted in claiming that African oral traditions, including languages, proverbs, and stories, contained a wisdom and a thought that were equivalent to Europe's philosophical traditions. It too was based on the colonial characterization of the African mind, not the one denying its theoretical capabilities, but the one Tempels described, which attributed to it specific intellectual characteristics. Among the first prominent figures of this school of thinking was Alexis Kagamé (1912–1981), who developed an ontology of Rwanda based on the grammatical and semantic structures of its language, Kinyarwanda. Language, he held, prescribed a certain set of concepts and fashioned a certain conception of the world. His 1955 book *La philosophie Bantu-rwandaise de l'être* (The Bantu-Rwandan Philosophy of Being)[91] was based on Tempels's work. This book, together with Tempels's *Bantu Philosophy*, became the references for a whole set of works devoted to the description of the theoretical features of African oral traditions, both in francophone and anglophone Africa. In the 1970s, these works came under the attack of critics who denounced the serious flaws of this school of thought. Proponents and opponents of ethnophilosophy engaged in heated debates about the merits of its tenets. The first group saw ethnophilosophy along the lines of ancient Greek philosophy as it defined itself with respect to the traditional body of myths and articulated rational approaches to complex sociocultural questions of a society in crisis. The second group, however, coming from a growing academic philosophical background, wanted to demarcate philosophy from ideological worldviews and cultural nationalism, including *négritude* and Egyptianism, which they considered to be still captive of the colonial legacy.

Instead of focusing on questions of identity and colonialism, these latter critics started to shift attention to the social problems of postcolonial African states. The defenders of ethnophilosophy found this critique elitist, pro-Western, and dismissive of native traditions. In French-speaking Africa, the first critiques of ethnophilosophy came from Marcien Towa of Cameroon and Paulin Hountondji of Benin; and in English-speaking Africa, they came from Henry Odera Oruka (1944–1995) of Kenya, Kwasi Wiredu of Ghana, and Kwame Anthony Appiah of Ghana.[92]

Marcien Towa warned against the disabling effects of cultural nativism and the traps of cultural loyalty. In two books published in 1971, *Essai sur la problématique philosophique dans l'Afrique actuelle* (Essay on the Philosophical Problematic in Present Africa) and *Léopold Sédar Senghor, négritude ou servitude?* (Leopold Sedar Senghor, Negritude or Servitude), he attacks ethnophilosophy and *négritude* respectively. In his 1979 book *Idée d'une philosophie négro-africaine* (The Idea of a Negro-African Philosophy), he reiterates his critique, insisting on several points.[93] Difference and particularity with respect to others, and identity and tradition with respect to oneself cannot be regarded as absolute values as such. It is important that the obsession with originality and difference be exorcized, not by rejecting tradition completely, but by discerning its merits and shortcomings after close examination. In any case, wanting to immobilize cultural identity and tradition is futile in a universe of perpetual and increasingly rapid change. What is crucial, for him, is the awareness of the final ends, which can only be envisioned rationally through rigorous philosophical thinking and on the basis of historical givens.[94] This view implies a double function for philosophy: rational discernment and political radical action. In this view, he disagreed with his Beninese colleague Paulin Hountondji, who wanted to separate philosophy from political ideologies. Towa accused him of "theoreticism."[95] Finally, Towa believes that the West is to be reproached not for its cult of thought, but for its treason of it. The West is not guilty of the universal spread of reason, but of its criminal limitation by keeping it to itself and depriving Third World peoples of it in order to exploit them and oppress them. The only way to oppose this injustice is to transform and empower Africa with rational and philosophical thinking.[96]

Paulin Hountondji published his critique of ethnophilosophy first in 1977 in *Sur la philosophie africaine: Critique de l'ethnophilosophie* (On African Philosophy: Critique of Ethnophilosophy).[97] Twenty years later, in the preface to the second edition, he reflects on the heated debate his book provoked. He notes that the issues surrounding ethnophilosophy were not only theoretical, but also ideological and political—hence, the intensity of the discussions.[98] Moreover, they revealed for him a certain thought pattern and a "permanent temptation of the Africanist discourse" that needs to be addressed.[99] The problem with this thought pattern, he explains, is that it assumes the existence of a collective, immutable, monolithic, and "unanimist" African view of things that reduces the continent in an essentialist way to a set of fixed characteristics. For him, it was and still is important to demythologize this concept of Africa in order to recognize its complex realities: "My purpose was to demythologise the concept of Africa by bringing it back to its primary meaning, to the minimal significance that had been, for years, overloaded by gluttonous ideological speculation. . . . Today the concept of Africa is overdetermined. It needs to be reduced—relieved of all those adventitious connotations that confuse it—and restored to its primal simplicity in order to reveal, by contrast, the extreme complexity of the intellectual, cultural, political, economic, and social life of the continent."[100] It is only after freeing the continent from this overdetermination that Africans can gain the freedom to think critically about their various issues and problems and liberate themselves from the cultural self-imprisonment to which ethnophilosophy confines them. In this preface, Hountondji warns, as he did twenty years earlier, against wrong self-discovery efforts that are directed solely at the Western public and are thus caught in an "extroverted," alienated discourse geared toward the Other. However, he admits that he now appreciates more readily the need for a sense of self, for self-discovery, and sees the importance of the field of African studies, which has developed since the mid-1970s. The question now, he says, is to translate these studies into concrete policies for the continent's benefit.

But these studies, African thought in general, and African philosophy in particular have to abide by the universal principles of critique, based on the distinction between *episteme* and *doxa*. This choice in no way means an intellectual and scientific dependency on the West or a deprecation of African culture and traditions, but the need to appropriate both sets of thought, with their diverse schools and currents, with a critical eye and after rigorous rational examination. Self-affirmation should not lead to a dogmatic adherence to orality and the renunciation of writing. The latter, for him, is essential for the development of elaborate discursive critique. Oral traditions need not be discarded, but in order for them to yield their philosophical potential, they should be transcribed into written texts and made into the object of critical examination. That thought is necessarily embedded in language and culture has to be recognized, but such a recognition should not reduce thought to the constraints of language and culture. In the 1996 preface, Hountondji acknowledges the contributions of his English-speaking colleagues to this debate by referring to Oruka's sagacity philosophy, Appiah's deconstruction of identity, and Wiredu's linking of thought and language. With regard to Appiah, he raises the questions of thought and identity:

> [W]hat is it to be African? Is it belonging to a race, in this case the black race, if we decide to restrict ourselves to black Africa? Should one, to be an African, share in a common culture and adhere to the value system or systems conveyed by this culture? Must one profess a given religious or political credo?
>
> ... One had to free the horizon, reject any definition of an African that would, by implication, restrict, or confine him or her in a conceptual, ideological, religious, or political stranglehold and reinforce the illusory belief that some inexorable fate weighs him or her down.[101]

Referring to Wiredu's work on thought and language, Hountondji emphasizes the importance of the universal:

> I compared A. Kagamé's linguistic relativism, which he unduly modeled on Aristotle's doctrine of categories, with Kwasi Wiredu's warning against "tongue-relative" metaphysical problems as opposed to "tongue-neutral" ones, and his appeal to African philosophers to think in their own languages. There is room, I concluded, for a systematic exploration of the unthought thoughts, the unconscious assumptions imposed on our conceptual procedures by the languages we speak, but instead of boasting about these constraints and proudly presenting them as our philosophy, we must treat them as our counter-philosophy, an inner obstacle that must be permanently fought against, in order to free our thinking, as far as possible, from all kinds of bias, and thereby to come as close as possible to the universal.[102]

Finally, he shows appreciation for critical work on African traditional sages, in particular that of his Kenyan colleague Henry Odera Oruka.

In the 1987 essay "African Philosophy: A Brief Personal History and Current Debate," Oruka presents his project on African sages in the following way:

> My real purpose in this project was to help substantiate or invalidate the claim that traditional African peoples were innocent of logical and critical thinking. Was traditional Africa a place where no persons had the room or mind to think independently and at times even critically of the communal consensus?

> If this claim were true, then it must follow that it is not possible to discover individuals in traditional Africa who can demonstrate their ability and practice in critical thinking. And whoever is considered a thinking or a wise man must simply be, at best, a good narrator of traditionally imposed wisdom and myths. Would it be possible to identify persons of traditional African culture, capable of the critical, second-order type of thinking about the various problems of human life and nature; persons, that is, who subject beliefs that are traditionally taken for granted to independent rational re-examination and who are inclined to accept or reject such beliefs on the authority of reason rather than on the basis of a communal or religious consensus?[103]

Oruka carried out the project with a number of collaborators and presented their findings in Sage Philosophy: Indigenous Thinkers and Modern Debate on African Philosophy.[104] It shows the existence of an independent, critical thinking that the collaborators call "sagacity philosophy." The book covers how they selected the sample of sages to be interviewed and devised a methodology for identifying those discourses that might qualify as being philosophical. For Oruka, what distinguishes this "sage philosophy" from ethnophilosophy is that, unlike the latter, it does not posit a unique, perennial African thought, but instead explores elements of a critical, philosophical thinking in native, traditional African discourses.

Oruka recognizes three currents in the debates around African philosophy:

1. The ethnographical school views the African mind as being communal and strongly religious, identified with ancestral wisdom, not theoretical or deductive, but intuitive and closely related to the body. Accordingly, African philosophy is closely associated with religion and understood

to be different from other philosophies, especially the Western. Oruka objects to this ethnocentric view of philosophy and insists on the universality of reason and critique.

2.   The rationalist school holds that philosophy and systematic rationality are practiced in elite circles, both in Europe and in Africa, whereas the masses think more in mythical and nonphilosophical ways. The difference between the two continents is that whereas in Europe the elite succeeded in imposing itself on the masses, in Africa it has not yet done so. In response to this school of thought, Oruka thinks that Africa should not be denied reason in the name of particularism based on this difference. Elite and mass cultures should be recognized in both regions and reason promoted in both as a universal good. For him, as for most participants in these debates, these issues inevitably raise metaphilosophical questions about the nature of philosophy and the meaning of African philosophy.

3.   Finally, the historical school focuses on collecting texts, narratives, and discourses, and it devotes special attention to language.

Ghanaian philosopher Kwasi Wiredu, currently professor emeritus of philosophy at the University of South Florida, is among those who emphasize the significance of culture and language for thought and warn against a wrong comparison of European and African philosophies. He develops his arguments in his 1980 book *Philosophy and an African Culture.*[105] He examines the ways in which African culture may impart particular characteristics to African philosophy. He critically discusses the "universalist" and "nationalist" approaches to the question and states his sympathy with the latter, but with important reservations. First, he argues that "nationalist" philosophy cannot be equated with what is taken to be "traditional philosophy," for the latter, like the elder's stock of wisdom, cannot be considered to be genuine philosophy. True philosophy requires scientific principles— namely, habits of exactness, rigor in thinking, the pursuit of systematic coherence, and an experimental approach to things. These principles, according to Wiredu, are indispensable virtues both for the production of real philosophy and for modernization. Second, traditional ways of life do not exist in Africa any longer since the introduction of modernization, as is the case elsewhere; hence, it would be anachronistic to abide by premodern thoughts and discourses. However, he adds, African culture can and should have an impact on African philosophy in two ways: in setting philosophical preoccupations drawn from the contemporary African experience and in unveiling the role of language in philosophical elaborations.[106]

For Wiredu, two phenomena have affected philosophy in contemporary Africa: modernization under colonial-anticolonial conditions and postcolonial statehood. Therefore, he sees philosophy's role to lie in two domains: the sociopolitical and the cultural. In the first domain, philosophy's basic function is to counter ideological thinking—that is, the uncritical adoption of ready-made, dogmatic, and authoritarian ideas. Philosophy is to make an important contribution in critiquing the assumptions made by ideology about truth, difference, and moral preference. This critique can lead to the cautious formulation of societal visions that may constitute constructive projects for the community's future. In the cultural domain, where extremes of cultural self-deprecation and self-glorification are prevalent in reaction to cultural colonialism, philosophy is called on to strike a balance between enthusiasm for cultural revivalism and forward-looking self-criticism.

Moreover, Wiredu warns against comparisons between Western and African thoughts that equate the West with modernity and truth, on the one hand, and Africa with traditional thinking and superstition, on the other. African thought, he says, should not be reduced to African traditional thought. The latter should be appropriately compared to Western folk thought. And authenticity should not be reduced to traditional African culture. He thinks that contemporary African philosophers should work with Western philosophy because they do not have a philosophical legacy in their inherited cultures. Finally, he shows the close connection between language and philosophical problems, using a number of concrete examples. Decolonization, he adds, cannot be achieved by rejecting all things foreign, but by recognizing and appreciating the linguistic component of philosophical problems. Such a recognition would offer a wider and richer understanding of concepts in general.[107]

Philosopher Kwame Gyekye, also from Ghana, criticizes Wiredu and Hountondji for overvaluing the place of Western philosophy in the making of modern African philosophy and for belittling the value of traditional African philosophical thought found in proverbs, myths, and oral literature. He thinks that Wiredu's distinction between traditional and modern African societies is too strong. Philosophy, he says, is not made in the abstract, but is embedded in a living and continuing culture. For African philosophy to be genuinely African and for it to have any real relevance to contemporary Africa, it should be inspired by the traditional values, ideas, and notions that still permeate African life. In order for this cultural legacy to be inspiring, it needs to be closely studied and critically evaluated instead of being taken for granted or quickly discarded. Only when rooted in this legacy can philosophy address the pressing issues of postcolonial Africa, especially its serious moral, economic, and political problems. This view does not make African philosophy totally incommensurable with other philosophies, but gives it some special characteristics in addition to universal traits. European philosophy itself, he adds, belongs to a specific culture and is molded by its different languages.[108]

Gyekye discusses the arguments made by cultural revivalists and anti-revivalists.[109] The former believe that reviving the cultural legacy of the past would help to affirm and appreciate cultural identity and to overcome the sense of inferiority created by colonialism, would integrate the traditional with the modern, and would offer a common ground of national belonging to the different groups assembled in the new African states. The antirevivalists, in contrast, think that priority should be given to promoting ideas of science and modernity in order to allow Africans to catch up with the modern world rather than to resuscitating old cultures unable to resist the onslaught of colonialism. Instead of these two extreme positions, Gyekye advocates a cautious middle course. Traditional modes of life have, according to him, advantages that are worth preserving, such as the sense of community and the commitment of individuals to the common good, forms of humanism, and certain moral and religious values. However, communal life can also lead to nepotism, corruption, and conflictual partisanship. Tradition and modernity, he adds, are not to be seen in total opposition. Tradition is defined at every time according to the needs and priorities of the present, and modernity is never a total break from tradition. This has been the case in European modernity, and he sees no reason why it should be different in Africa.

Peter Amato writes as a non-African about the ways in which conceptions of modernity have been employed to facilitate colonization. The way in which the West has culturally and politically defined the modernity/tradition binary has prevented intercultural understanding and has thereby prevented Western modernity from properly understanding and completing itself. In this binary, modernity has been essentially associated with the West and tradition with all the rest. Only an intercultural dialogue, he thinks, can reveal to Western modernity its own traditions and myths, and by so doing contribute to its enlightenment and modernization.[110]

The significance of language for African thought and cultural decolonization has also been an issue in African literature. Major writers such as Ngugi Wa Thiong'o of Kenya and Chinua Achebe of Nigeria have expressed divergent points of view on the matter. Ngugi has strongly argued for African literature in African languages on cultural and political grounds: first to affirm and enrich African cultures and second to resist Western intellectual and political imperialism. Expressing oneself in one's mother tongue, he believes, is both a human need and a human right that colonialism has perverted. Moreover, it is in the vernacular that writers can reach out to the peasants and the masses and engage them in the struggle for freedom and democracy. In *Decolonising the Mind: The Politics of Language in African Literature*, he writes:

> *Wherever I have gone, particularly in Europe, I have been confronted with the question: why are you now writing in Gikuyu? Why do you now write in an African language? In some academic quarters I have been confronted with the rebuke, "Why have you abandoned us?" It was almost as if, in choosing to write in Gikuyu, I was doing something abnormal. But Gikuyu is my mother tongue! The very fact that what common sense dictates in the literary practice of other cultures is being questioned in an African writer is a measure of how far imperialism has distorted the view of African realities. It has turned reality upside down: the abnormal is viewed as normal and the normal is viewed as abnormal. Africa actually enriches Europe: but Africa is made to believe that it needs Europe to rescue it from poverty. Africa's natural and human resources continue to develop Europe and America: but Africa is made to feel grateful for aid from the same quarters that still sit on the back of the continent. Africa even produces intellectuals who now rationalise this upside-down way of looking at Africa.*

> *I believe that my writing in Gikuyu language, a Kenyan language, an African language, is part and parcel of the anti-imperialist struggles of Kenyan and African peoples. In schools and universities our Kenyan language—that is the languages of the many nationalities which make up Kenya—were associated with negative qualities of backwardness, underdevelopment, humiliation and punishment. We who went through that school system were meant to graduate with a hatred of the people and the culture and the values of the language of our daily humiliation and punishment. I do not want to see Kenyan children growing up in that imperialist-imposed tradition of contempt for the tools of communication developed by their communities and their history. I want them to transcend colonial alienation.[111]*

Achebe, in contrast, thinks that given the realities of postcolonial Africa—that is, the domination of English and French as well as the existence of a great variety of African languages—it is no longer realistic to write in one African language and still hope to reach people outside a specific linguistic sphere. He thinks that the choice of language should be left to individual writers and that decolonization can also take place in the language of the colonizer.[112]

In his 1992 book *In My Father's House: Africa in the Philosophy of Culture*,[113] Kwame Anthony Appiah, presently professor of philosophy at Princeton University, revisits the thirty-year-old debate on African philosophy and discusses the ideas of Césaire, Senghor, Diop, Hountondji, and Wiredu. He critically examines some of the assumptions made in the issue of ethnophilosophy—for instance, the mistaken assumption about the unity of Western philosophy and the unity of African philosophy; the inflated status attributed to philosophy, especially in Western culture; and the anxious efforts African thinkers deploy to emulate Western philosophy in the hope of gaining respect for their own cultures. Appiah calls for the demystification of philosophy in general and of Western philosophy in particular, without, however, belittling its critical value. He invites African thinkers to work with Western philosophy, but not to project Western expectations and Western priorities onto their own concerns and traditions. He believes that African philosophy should be rooted in African realities but also abide by the rigor of universal critique. He also warns against certain assumptions made about identity. All human identities, he states, are constructions, but serious and sometimes dangerous constructions. Those based on race, common history, and shared metaphysics can easily become sectarian and disabling. It is important to acknowledge that human identities are complex, multiple, and changing and that the value of identities is in the cause they serve. Without denying the virtue of African solidarity, Appiah reminds his readers of rallying causes, such as class, ecology, and gender: "If an African identity is to empower us, so it seems to me, what is required is not so much that we throw out falsehood but that we acknowledge first of all that race and history and metaphysics do not enforce an identity: that we can choose, within broad limits set by ecological, political, and economic realities what it will mean to be African in the coming years."[114]

Feminists have been active participants in the African debates on culture. As in Latin America and in the Arab world, they have underlined the connections between the various forms of oppression in their societies, tried to dismantle the fixed binaries of tradition and modernity, authenticity and alienation, and demanded the right to develop their own feminist discourses and agendas independently from those of the West. Like Latin American feminists, they have faced the challenge of struggling on two fronts: the home front of sexual and other forms of discrimination and the outer front of external imperialism and hegemony. Many of them have deplored and emphasized the need to address the disastrous consequences that the structural adjustment programs have had on African society in general and on women in particular.

Filomina Chioma Steady, social anthropologist from Sierra Leone, argues for a humanistic, inclusive African feminism inspired by the cultural and traditional gender activities of African societies and characterized more by complementarity, cooperation, and communalism than by individualism, competition, and dichotomy. She insists on the close interrelation between sexism, racism, and global economic exploitation, especially in the African case through slavery, colonialism, and neocolonialism. In order to be truly emancipatory, African feminism, in her view, needs to address these multiple forms of oppression in their interrelatedness.[115] Nigerian scholar and activist Molara Ogundipe-Leslie underlines the importance for Africans, African women in particular, to voice their needs and their visions of themselves beyond the prevailing binaries—the rural versus the urban, the traditional versus the modern, the elite versus the people, ethnicity versus the nation, and ethnic culture versus the state—which, according to her, have been imposed by the West. She also calls upon Africans and African women to go beyond the narratives of victimhood and to seek empowering visions of themselves that cannot but be different from those of Euro-American feminists who work with different givens. She advocates an African "womanist" feminism inspired by Alice Walker, a feminism that defends both the rights of women and the rights of their communities.[116] For instance, Ghanaian writer (and minister of education between 1982 and 1983) Ama Ata Aidoo thinks that the right to work is not an issue in Africa, where women have always worked very hard.[117] Some draw attention to the priority that African women in general and the feminists among them in particular give to the urgency of building bridges between groups and communities in a region torn apart by conflicts and wars. Some women have developed strategies of organizational inclusiveness for peacemaking and survival purposes. For example, the Uganda Council of Women has sought and to some extent succeeded in reaching a peaceful resolution of communal tensions. In such a context, the celebration of difference so valued in the West is not deemed appropriate.[118]

Ghanaian philosopher Safro Kwame examines the claim that the universality of the oppression of women is refuted by African matrilineal societies such as the Akan. He thinks this claim is a myth, built on a romanticized if not false view of these societies, which, he says, show a very clear discrimination against women, whether in their members' behavior or in their traditional gender views—found, for instance, in their proverbs. Sexism can prevail, he says, even when women are needed, when they work and occasionally rule, participate in decision making, and own property. The modalities of discrimination may not be the same as those of Western or non-African societies. He urges African philosophers to pay more attention to such societal issues than to metaphilosophical questions related to African philosophy.[119] One way to counter prevailing sexist views is to propagate feminist versions of popular tales, as in the gender-sensitization work that Kenyan activist and writer Wanjira Muthoni has undertaken, as have her colleagues in the Women and Memory Forum in Egypt.[120]

In the preface to an anthology of black poetry edited by Senghor in 1948, Jean-Paul Sartre celebrated the *négritude* movement and praised the power and mature eloquence with which black poets of the time talked back to whites and returned their gaze.[121] Toward the end of his approximately sixty-page-long text, however, Sartre questioned the durability of the *négritude* stance as an antiracist racism. Much as he understood, appreciated, and admired the black movement, he thought that this stance could not be the movement's final destination. After having brilliantly articulated the counterposition of black affirmation, the movement needed to surpass itself and reach an inclusive, universal humanism. Formulating his thought in a Hegelian dialectic, Sartre wrote:

> *Negritude appears as the weak stage of a dialectical progression: the theoretical and practical affirmation of white supremacy is the thesis; the position of Negritude as antithetical value is the moment of negativity. But this negative moment is not sufficient in itself and the blacks who employ it well know it; they know that it serves to prepare the way for the synthesis or the realization of the human society without racism. Thus Negritude is dedicated to its own destruction, it is passage and not objective, means and not the ultimate goal. At the moment the black Orpheus most directly embraces this Eurydice, he feels her vanish from between his arms.[122]*

Frantz Fanon (1925–1961) perceived this Sartrean proposition as treason against the black cause. He could not understand how Sartre could call for what he himself saw as an abandonment of black affirmation. Referring to the passage from which this quotation is taken, Fanon stated: "When I read that page, I felt that I had been robbed of my last chance. I said to my friends, 'The generation of the younger black poets has just suffered a blow that can never be forgiven.'" He added further:

> *What is certain is that, at the very moment when I was trying to grasp my own being, Sartre, who remained The Other, gave me a name and thus shattered my last illusion. . . . [W]hile I was shouting that, in the paroxysm of my being and my fury, he was reminding me that my blackness was only a minor term. In all truth, in all truth I tell you, my shoulders slipped out of the framework of the world, my feet could no longer feel the touch of the ground. Without a Negro past, without a Negro future, it was impossible for me to live my Negrohood. Not yet white, no longer wholly black, I was damned. Jean-Paul Sartre had forgotten that the Negro suffers in his body quite differently from the white man. Between the white man and me the connection was irrevocably one of transcendence.[123]*

Against Sartre's call for transcending *négritude*, Fanon asserted his holding on to the moment of Negro consciousness as an unsurpassable absolute:

> *But the constancy of my love had been forgotten. I defined myself as an absolute intensity of beginning. So I took up my negritude, and with tears in my eyes I put its machinery together again. What had been broken to pieces was rebuilt, reconstructed by the intuitive lianas of my hands.*
>
> *My cry grew more violent: I am a Negro, I am a Negro, I am a Negro.[124]*

In this reaction, Fanon expresses the traumatic experience not only of blacks, but also of Latin Americans, Arabs, and all those who have been gazed at and defined with denigration by a powerful Other as bad, worthless, and hopeless. He demonstrates the difficulty of surpassing the reactive moment of self-affirmation.

By comparing the journey of self-recuperation to that of Orpheus trying to bring back his beloved Eurydice from the world of the dead, Sartre illustrates the paradoxes of postcolonial self-affirmation: it is a journey fraught with dangers and doomed in a sense to failure, for the self is not there to be recovered, but awaits to be constantly made anew. In the same sense, Narcissus's triumph is at the same time his suicide. Moreover, in this preface, Sartre formulates some of the most crucial issues of self-recuperation: liberty and necessity, morality and natural determinism. In other words, he asks whether the identity to be affirmed is a ready given to be asserted and embraced or a project to be conceived and pursued with liberty, agency, and morality. As demonstrated in the discussion of the Arab debates and in the quick survey of Latin American and African discourses, the thinkers from all these areas raise these same questions at a certain stage of their long and painful decolonization process, when the self-critical moment sets in to discern the very meaning of self-recovery: Is the self a determined fact of history, race, nationalism, language, religion, ethnicity, geography, and metaphysics? Or is it a perpetual composition made within the givens of historical realities and on the basis of moral choices and preferences for which people can be held responsible and accountable? Sartre summarizes these issues at the end of the preface by raising the following questions about *négritude*: "Is it necessity or liberty? Is it that, for the authentic Negro, his directions flow from his essence as consequences flow from a principle; or rather, is one a Negro as the faithful of a religion is a believer, that is, in fear and trembling, in anguish, in perpetual remorse never to be enough that which one wishes to be? Is it a conquest by reflection? Or does reflection poison it? Is it authentic only when it is unreflected and immediate?"[125]

In my analysis of the three regional debates, I noted the shift of attention from the reactive identity affirmations of the earlier phases to the concern for humanistic, moral, and political aspects of cultural decolonization. The recent "Imagine Africa" manifesto, written by acclaimed South African writer and artist Breyten Breytenbach for the Conference on Vitalizing African Cultural Assets, held on Gorée Island, Senegal, in March 2007, expresses this concern most eloquently:

What values did independence and liberation bring? What happened to those values? Have we been living in borrowed clothes? Is there a peculiarly African way of articulating and administering power, let alone sharing it? Do we have effective checks against abuses of privilege? What is the weight or the influence or even the sustainability and mandate of our civil society structures? . . . More precisely, what is the impact of our creators and observers, those whose very purpose of being is transformation, our community of artists?

In other words—what has African imagination contributed to our understanding of what we are doing to one another and to the world?

... I take it as common cause that part of the human condition, maybe the essential flame, is the process of imagining ourselves to be.[126]

The imagination Breytenbach calls for is the moral and aesthetic faculty to create the self.

Space permitting, this comparative survey could have been expanded to include similar debates in India, the Caribbean, the South Pacific, and African America. For instance, Du Bois offers powerful insights on double consciousness from an African American perspective in *The Souls of Black Folk*; Ashis Nandy gives an interesting analyses of the postcolonial consciousness from an Indian perspective in *The Intimate Enemy: Loss and Recovery of Self Under Colonialism*; Derek Walcott relates compelling thoughts on the phenomenon of cultural imitation from a West Indian perspective in *What the Twilight Says*; Jamaica Kincaid offers gripping descriptions of postcolonial anger and corruption from Antigua in *A Small Place*; and Linda Tuhiwai Smith and Haunani-Kay Trask speak daring critiques of the politics of knowledge in postcolonial New Zealand and Hawai'i in *Decolonizing Methodologies: Research and Indigenous Peoples* and *From a Native Daughter: Colonialism and Sovereignty in Hawai'i*, respectively.[127] Widening the comparative perspective and examining individual issues more closely have to be left for future projects. For now, it is time to make some comparative remarks about the debates analyzed here.

Common Leitmotivs and Arab Specificities

The Leitmotivs of Postcolonial Debates on Culture
This brief survey of the Latin American and African debates reveals a number of interesting commonalities with the Arab debates. Among the most salient ones are the concerns with intellectual independence, universalism, capitalism, culturalism, tradition, modernization, and feminism.

INTELLECTUAL-PHILOSOPHICAL IDENTITY
AND CULTURAL IDENTITY

The search for a thought of one's own or a philosophy of one's own or both is regarded in these debates as a central aspect of the quest for intellectual independence. Concerns about the existence, identity, and role of such a systematic thought or philosophy in cultural decolonization are omnipresent. The question about the existence of such thought or philosophy involves an assumption about the important value attached to it in a culture. Some regard this assumption to be a projection of Western criteria of evaluation onto other cultures, but many see the importance of philosophy for achieving critical awareness in one's thought and action. The latter position raises in turn a number of questions about the meaning of specificity in philosophy and ultimately about the very definition of philosophy: If this "home" philosophy is to be distinct from Western philosophy, where is the distinction to be located? In the method? The style? The themes? How different can it become without ceasing to be philosophy? But, then, what is philosophy in any case? What are its universal features? What is its characteristic approach to issues? Many participants in the debates recall that these questions often lack clear answers even in Western philosophy itself, given the various schools, epochs, and regions in which it has developed.

The question about a philosophy of one's own leads not only to questions about the very nature of philosophy, but also to questions about cultural identity: What would it mean for a philosophy to be African or Latin American or Arab? Is there such a thing as an African or Latin American or Arab identity? What does it mean to be African, Latin American, or Arab? Who defines it and on what basis? Is this identity to be thought of as fixed, ahistorical, metaphysical, or biological? Or are there other ways of conceiving identity? What are the advantages and shortcomings of each way? In any case, what would it mean for philosophy to be African or Latin American or Arab in particular? In these thinkers' discourses, the issues of philosophical and cultural identity are closely interrelated.

UNIVERSALISM, EUROCENTRISM, CAPITALISM,
AND PARTICULARISM

This contextual approach to thought and philosophy brings to the fore the contextual nature of Western philosophy itself. The thinkers of the three postcolonial societies unveil the particularity of Western thought and underline the importance of locating it in its particular history and intellectual traditions. Western philosophy's claim to universality is called into question. The very notion of "universal reason" in the absolute sense is no longer taken for granted. Attention is drawn to the historical, cultural, and linguistic embeddedness of human reason, in most cases without, however, relinquishing the belief in the universality of logic and, most important, in all humans' universal capacity to reason and think for themselves. The Western bigoted attitudes toward non-Westerners in this respect is strongly denounced. Much of the "universality" of Western modes of thinking is recognized as being in reality the expression of conquest and hegemony. However, between this critique of Western universalism and the search for a particular culture and thought of one's own a balance is sought between narrow particularism and hegemonic universalism. A concern is shown for not losing the humanistic-universal dimension of particular philosophies. Calls are made to avoid chauvinistic particularism as well as shallow and fake abstract universalism.

The Western hegemonic universalism, shown to be a manifestation of Eurocentrism, is closely linked to Western capitalist expansion. Many thinkers of the regions I examined regard Eurocentrism as the ideology accompanying Western economic exploitation of these regions. In fact, some of them see at the bottom of the cultural dependency problem the more basic problem of economic dependency. They caution against reducing the whole dependency problem to a cultural and culturalist one. In all three regions, Marxist readings of the postcolonial situation abound, but in all three the demand is also made to appropriate Marx's theories critically and to adapt them to each region's realities.

CULTURALISM

Culturalist reductionism is found in both regional chauvinistic forms of nationalism and Western forms of othering, whether in xenophelia, xenophobia, or cult of difference. In all of these cases, a society is reduced to its culture, and the latter is conceived as a monolithic, deterministic, and fixed essence. The colonized societies often adopt Western philosophies of otherness and transform them into philosophies of identity in reverse: racism into *négritude*, Islam into religious fundamentalism, and the "Latin" into the Latin difference. Essentialist difference is maintained but transformed into a source of pride. More and more postcolonial thinkers warn, however, against deadlocked essentialist views of the self and the other. They point out the reductionist and deterministic shortcomings of such views as well as the ideology of absolute difference that these views imply. They see that these views leave no room for agency, change, and critique—all elements that are increasingly deemed to be necessary elements of empowerment.

WESTERNIZATION, MODERNIZATION, AND TRADITION

Cultural decolonization and the search for authenticity are associated with the need to synchronize ideas with reality: the need to connect views and theories with the concrete realities at hand. Critical thinkers in the three postcolonial regions repeatedly complain that the prevalent ideas and philosophies are imported from elsewhere, usually the West but also from distant pasts, and are thus alien to reality. This alienation is perceived especially among intellectuals and the social elite, who seem to be disconnected from the majority of the people. Disalienation is often expressed in the form of anti-Westernism and in the rejection of openness; for many, however, true disalienation needs to be initiated by an empirical exploration of the realities at hand and by an honest introspection of the self, freed from the tendency toward either self-glorification or total victimhood.

In contrast, the acute awareness of retardation and of the urgent need to catch up with advanced countries make modernization a pressing necessity. But the dilemma between modernization and westernization then emerges: How to modernize without imitating the West and losing one's soul? How to modernize without sinking deeper into dependency? How to modernize without resorting to the science and rationality possessed and led by the West? Self-preservation and development seem to be in an irresolvable tension under conditions of post- and neocolonialism. Can native traditions offer indigenous and alternative principles of development? Is "salvation" to be sought in one's culture, religion, tradition, or language? To what extent is there a live, cognitive, and pragmatic relatedness to native traditions after the colonial severance from them? Are these traditions known to their living heirs? Do they contain all the answers to the ills of the present day? How are local traditions to be defined: in terms of their oral components or religion or language or customs, or perhaps in terms of the collective memory they carry? Who is to decide and on what basis? And are local traditions "good" in their totality? Critique of tradition is often regarded as betrayal, creating thus another form of dependency, this time vis-à-vis tradition. More and more postcolonial thinkers see their situation as requiring a double dependency awareness and a double critique. They consistently emphasize the need to historicize and contextualize both the Western and the native traditions in order to make their critical appropriation possible and in order to unveil their complexities and mutations. As they see things, only such an appropriation can empower their societies to find the means of a liberating development. They regard education, the use of native languages, as well as openness to and demystification of both local traditions and the West as necessary for this empowerment.

FEMINISM AND THE CULTURAL SENSE OF SELF

Postcolonial feminism in all three regions finds itself caught up in the trap of cultural authenticity. It is accused of being a foreign importation and an internal betrayal to the unity and goodness of native cultures. The awareness of the double oppression—that of gender on the one hand, found in most, if not all traditions, and that of foreign hegemony on the other— gives rise to the struggle for a double liberation. Postcolonial feminists also experience this hegemony in the discursive context of globalization. They consistently feel the need to resist the homogenization discourse of Western feminists and to speak for themselves in order to voice the specificities of their struggle in a post- and neocolonial context. More than any other social group, postcolonial women find themselves facing the challenges of this double dependency and double hegemony. Their rethinking of cultural identity, authenticity, community, nation, tradition, modernity, and liberation stems from this predicament and leads to a number of analyses. Among them is the analysis of the colonial and postcolonial woman as the site of cultural contestation with the colonial power, as the showcase of modernization or traditionalization, as the bearer of the nation. Feminists have also made important contributions in the historicization of traditions and shown the gender, class, and other group interests that have shaped them, putting in question their alleged objectivity and neutrality. They have strongly denounced the binaries that have dominated cultural debates since the beginning of the anticolonial struggle—namely, modernity and tradition, the Western and the local. They have offered deconstructive analyses of the mystified conceptions of both modernity and traditions. Finally, they have pointed out the pervasiveness of patriarchy and authoritarianism in postcolonial thought across the ideological spectrum, from the secular left to the religious right. More than negotiating a "room of one's own," these feminists are busy renegotiating the whole "living room," as Latin American feminist Raquel Olea puts it. In fact, postcolonial feminism shares with postcolonial philosophy of culture a number of features: the critique of essentialism, the rejection of false "universal reason," the importance of historicization and contextualization, the necessity of critique, the struggle for "talking back," and the quest for empowerment.

Arab Specificities

The different colonial histories and the different types of cultural legacy in the three regions have led to different concerns and different points of emphasis in cultural decolonization. Compared to the cases of Latin America and Africa, the Arab world has fared relatively well in terms of its physical and cultural integrity: its population has been less violated by genocide, slavery, and colonial settlement than the Latin American and African populations, which is probably why modernity in Arab discourses is not strongly associated with these phenomena as it is in the other two regions. Moreover, it has been able to preserve its language, its religion, and its extensive written cultural legacy. Arabs have indeed a distinct awareness of the existence of this literate, centuries-old corpus—though their awareness is often mystified and not always well informed. In contrast to Africa and Latin America, the Arab world forcefully challenged Europe in the past and imposed itself as a leading civilizational power. How do these differences affect the Arab approach to postcolonial cultural malaise, though? They appear in the relation to heritage in general and to religious heritage in particular, in the relation to systematic thought in heritage, in the sense of rivalry with the West and the pronounced claim to power, and in a mobilization of religion geared toward power more than toward ethical empowerment.

FORMS OF CULTURAL LEGACY

It is interesting to note that the question "Is there an Arab philosophy?" does not arise in the Arab debates. A number of reasons can be given for the absence of this question. On the one hand, there prevails among Arabs a clear awareness of the existence of a solid philosophical tradition led by major figures such as al-Ghazali, Averroes, Avicenna, and others—although, as we saw, some purist Islamists such as Sayyid Qutb regard the work of these philosophers as not authentically Islamic, but an alienated work produced under "foreign" influences, mainly Greek. On the whole, however, there seems to be no need to "prove" that Arab civilization had and could produce important and original works in systematic thought and philosophy. Even the colonial West, in its own way and for its own purposes, has recognized this philosophical history, as Arab thinkers have often pointed out. The problem rather is how to reconnect with this past philosophical heritage, how to reappropriate it, for the concerns of the present age. It is to be noted that this philosophical legacy has experienced less of a revival compared to that of the literary and religious legacies. Moreover, its revival, according to numerous Arab thinkers, has not been as thorough and as serious as it should be. It still tends to be apologetic, superficial, and ideologically geared—as we saw, for instance, in the Averroes revival.

On the other hand, the question is not asked because few intellectuals of the early-modern Arab debates came from a strictly philosophical background. Most came from the clerical circles, which had access to education, and in the later phase the majority came from the humanities and the social sciences. Another reason why the question is not asked is the limited penetration of Western philosophy in the cultural and academic realms of the Arab world. However, there is considerable reflection on Arab reason and on assumptions made about reason, as we saw in the debates on Islam and modernity. Many critics have underlined the failure in modern and contemporary Arab thought to recognize the modern conception of reason and its difference from the medieval and Aristotelian conceptions, especially in the debate on the viability of the conciliatory strategy. Others have criticized the ahistorical understanding of reason in comparing epochs and proposing past intellectual models represented by major thinkers such as Ibn Khaldun and Averroes.

In the African case, the debate centers on the philosophical aspect of the oral folk tradition in the absence of a written legacy and in response to the colonial claim that Africans did not contribute to human civilization in general or to systematic and philosophical thought in particular. The question for Africans is whether the wisdom of the elders in the form of proverbs, myths, and oral debates can be considered to be philosophy. This is the debate around ethnophilosophy. The search is being conducted for a philosophy of one's own drawn from the traditional, local wisdom and at the same time complying with the requirements of the universal (Western?) academic criteria. More generally, the place of native languages and religions that have survived the colonial impact in the efforts of cultural self-recovery is a major preoccupation. In Latin America, even less of these native cultural elements have survived, and the colonial influence has been much more pervasive: thus the concern with imitation and authenticity, and the attempt at figuring out what a nonimitative culture and a nonimitative philosophical tradition that is non-European and non–U.S. American can be.

Islam as faith, theology, and jurisprudence has had a central place in the Arab discourses on decolonization, even when it is contested and rejected, as in the secularist positions. It is this part of the heritage that thinkers more readily identify with in general. Its imposing character, due to its recognized value and its association with the emergence of Islam, offers a secure source of pride and a solid pillar of identification. For the same reasons, however, it imposes itself as a formidable weight of inertia and conservatism, especially in defensive circumstances. It serves as a convenient compensatory reference in the face of present failures and as a suitable claim to a perennially existing and successful self, unaffected by the vicissitudes of history. The dominating religious understanding of heritage has given to tradition a sacral character and turned any break from it into an act of blasphemy.

All these escapist uses of the written heritage have not been helpful in nurturing critical thinking; they have transformed the heritage into a burdensome liability. Moroccan writer Abdelkebir al-Khatibi summarizes the problem in the following way: "Ibn Khaldun: a vestige! Yes, but what is a vestige? Is it the remains of a thought or the capability to continue to think?"[128] The use of the Arab literate heritage for power affirmation has not been empowering in reality because of the strong pressures toward defensiveness and the ensuing tendencies toward ideologization and hence the impoverishment of scholarly explorations.

RELIGION, LIBERATION, AND POWER

The Arab imperial past has been used in a way similar to the literate heritage. Associated with a righteous religion, a leading "world" civilization, and a military, political, economic, cultural, and scientific might, this past has a strong presence in the Arab awareness. Accordingly, the relation to the West is pronouncedly rivalrous. With time, the West acquired a comparative advantage that has put it in a dominating power position today. The perception of this past Arab power, which does not exist in a comparable scope in the African and Latin American cases, plays a double role. It inspires confidence and offers a positive image of the self, at least of the past self, but it also exacerbates the present frustration and anger. More important, it allows an escape into fantasies of power from states of pain, humiliation, desolation, weakness, and defeat, and into a wishful anticipation of that power's certain return in the future. These fantasies are an evasion of a humiliating reality, but also of a humbling and thus more constructive confrontation with reality and human vulnerability. The historical past feeds into a revenge mentality and produces a fixation on power rivalry. This attitude in turn prevents the present from becoming an opportunity for an honest dealing with reality, especially in times of such great desolation as in the past decades. The quest for power becomes a fantasy for world domination instead of a search for universal justice. It is to a great extent this quest for power that is sought in the mobilization of Islam and of all other ideologies, whether Arab or other regional nationalisms. The colonial, postcolonial, and neocolonial experiences have wounded and humiliated Arabs, but they have not in general humbled them enough to seek empowerment in a *pensée autre*, a different thought, as suggested by al-Khatibi. The painful experiences have so far failed to turn the Arab cross into a thought and a theology of liberation nurtured rather than only diminished by an existence at the margin of power and outside the lethal might of totalizing certainties.

In the Arab world, Latin America, and Africa, people have mobilized religion, Islam and Christianity, for liberation purposes and for intellectual decolonization. To my knowledge, no comparative study has yet been undertaken to explore the similarities and differences in these two phenomena. It is surely a task worth undertaking. In Latin America and Africa, Christian beliefs and values, in defiant league with the established clerical institution, have been called upon to vindicate social, economic, and political justice, leading in some cases to military action against those who pursue this justice. In some parts of Africa, Islam has been called upon to support such humanist struggles—for instance, in the work of Farid Esack in South Africa. In the Arab world, Islamic movements have mobilized religious beliefs for similar goals. The "movement of the oppressed," especially among the Shiʿis, whether in Iran or in Lebanon, has been to some extent such a phenomenon. But Islam has been mobilized primarily as a vehicle for might, facilitated by the close association many Arab Muslims make between the political, economic, and military might of past Islamic states and Islam as a religious ideology. The association also stems from the protracted confrontation between a "Christian" West and a "Muslim" Arab East, defined as such by both parties since the times of the Crusades, later during the Ottoman Empire, and more recently in the colonial era. This form of mobilization has hindered the development of a humanistic Islamic theology of liberation that aims at the ethical and spiritual empowerment of people and that leads to a robust quest for universal justice and human dignity. But it has not prevented such attempts completely: the work of Mohammad Arkoun, for instance, bears witness to the resistant vitality of this minority trend. The Palestinian theology of the cross is another significant witness.

Shifting Priorities

In addition to these common leitmotivs and Arab specificities, a comparative reading of postcolonial debates on culture reveals a certain trend toward shifting priorities. In many of these debates, including the Arab ones, there seems to have come a time in the last decades of the twentieth century when past experiences of political, social, economic, and cultural decolonization were reassessed. Conceptions of liberation, authenticity, and self-affirmation were revisited, and the hitherto applied tools of thinking were reexamined. Several notable changes can be observed in the approach to thinking the cultural self: shifts of focus from identity to democracy, from essentialism to agency, and from ideology to critical thinking.

From Identity to Democracy

Whereas the early reactions against colonialism centered around identity and self-definition, late postcolonial concerns have focused more on socioeconomic and political issues. The early strivings toward self-definition were carried out in terms of the colonizing Other (the West) and in reaction to its definitions of the colonized self. Much effort was deployed to emulate and assimilate the culture of this advanced and powerful Other in order to strengthen the self. This Other inspired both admiration and resentment. Contrary efforts were also deployed in affirming the total difference of the self from the Other. Self-glorification came in response to colonial denigration. Apology and polemics around "Us versus Them" proliferated, producing various nativist identity ideologies.

With the establishment of the postcolonial states and the disillusionment with an independence that in reality often turned out to be internally corrupt and externally dominated by neocolonial pressures, attention shifted to growing socioeconomic problems. Thinkers saw the need to turn the critical gaze inward and to radicalize internal critique, particularly in regard to the earlier reactions to colonialism. In fact, the success of the colonial hegemony raised questions about the self. It was often asked: What was wrong in us, in our culture, that made the foreign hegemony possible? Our "race"? Our religion? Our national character? Critical views of the self were presented to explain the state of weakness and defeat. But now there was an urgent need to radicalize the internal critique, and this time not to counter the Other's definitions of the self, but to address increasingly urgent problems at hand. In fact, the twentieth century was quite a disastrous one for the three regions in question: civil wars, interstate wars, growing poverty, economic dependence, disease, famine, dictatorships, and various forms of repression plagued the lives of their peoples—as they continue to do so today. The priority for critical thinkers in these regions is no longer to develop identity ideologies, but to confront these life-threatening, momentous problems from which the Other is not absent. More and more postcolonial thinkers realize that these problems cannot be addressed without freedom of thought and freedom of expression, without the free exchange of ideas and the possibility of holding rulers accountable for their actions. Democracy and individual liberties have become immanently vital for the very preservation and promotion of life, rather than being a question of imitation, whether one is like or not like the West, as was the predominant concern in the first half of the twentieth century. Democracy and freedom have become essential for the revitalization of culture and the empowerment of people in facing their predicaments. Intellectuals have undertaken a new, more radical cultural critique, with a clearer focus on civil and political rights, accompanied by various social movements in civil society mobilized for the defense of basic human rights, the monitoring of elections, and the struggle for democracy.

From Essentialism to Agency

This shift in focus does not eliminate the concern with identity, but it does indicate a new approach to it. The repressive implications of an essentialistic, deterministic, and monolithic conception of identity that leaves no room for agency, responsibility, and change are more and more exposed. Many a dictatorship was and is justified with such a view of identity associated with an ideology of authenticity. More and more critical postcolonial thinkers are presenting identity as something in the making, a construction that is open for discussion, choice, and hence agency and responsibility. Taken-for-granted descriptions of tradition, romanticized forms of nativism, and cults of difference are strongly criticized and abandoned for a more critical appropriation of values and ideas, whether native or not. However, this shift is far from being conclusive, especially under these postcolonial societies' highly volatile conditions and the enormous difficulties of the task at hand.

From Ideology to Critical Thinking

Perhaps the most general of these shifts is the move away from ideological thinking. *Ideology* is taken here to mean a set of ready-made ideas that one adopts dogmatically and is ready to impose on others, even by force. With its seducing absolutes and certainties, ideological thinking is particularly tempting in polarized situations of struggle. But its limitations on agency in various forms of repression become increasingly stifling in times of acute societal crisis, like the one currently facing these three regions. However, the mounting despair and anger that accompany such crises feed into the desperate search for absolutes and certainties, and make critical thinking a most trying challenge. Indeed, growing despair has provoked the radicalization of both ideology and critique, ideology in sometimes violent forms (such as violent militant Islamism) and critique in vulnerable but determined forms. In fact, what we witness at present is a "critical" race between critique and increasingly extremist ideologies. On the critical side, authentic thinking has been proposed instead of a "thought of authenticity."[129]

Conclusion
The New Nahda Impulses, Reclaiming the Right to Freedom and Life

In the first half of 2006 and in early 2007, the Arab daily *al-Hayat* ran a series of interviews with some twenty four Arab thinkers about their societies' current intellectual and cultural state.[1] It invited them to respond to the following questions: What place does the Arab region have on the world scene today? What are the causes of its present predicament? To what extent have Arab societies, rather than Arab regimes, been the obstacle to change? What shapes Arab mentalities nowadays? What role and responsibility have intellectuals had and what role can they have today in developing Arab societies in one direction or another? Has modernity been the cause of Arab misery? What effective legacy of the first Nahda, if any, can one still find today? What about the post-1967 second Nahda? Did it have any real impact on Arab realities and attitudes? In concluding my examination of Arab cultural critique in the second half of the twentieth century, I discuss some of the interviewees' responses as they assess an extremely tense fin de siècle and a most dramatic beginning of the new millennium. The consistent themes are the deplorable poverty in the various cognitive fields, the pressing need for rigorous critical thinking, the various forms of escapism notably toward traditionalism, the rise of religious extremism, the failures of the postcolonial state, the growing demand for democracy, and the yearning for life-affirming options.

Tunisian sociologist al-Taher Labib, founder of the Arab Sociological Association and presently head of the Arab Organization for Translation based in Beirut,[2] believes that the second Nahda produced two kinds of thinkers: the epic thinker who offered alternative visions and utopias, whether of the socialist variety or other, and the tragic thinker, who, although adhering to those visions and projects, was aware of the impossibility of their implementation in reality. Both types ended up disappointed. For Labib, it is important to distinguish the serious thinker from the so-called intellectual who is busy showing off and playing the public-relations figure, quickly metamorphosing into an "expert" whenever needed. The real thinker, according to him, has the capacity and the duty to produce meanings. Unfortunately, neither power nor society nor even the media are ready to make room for thoughtful meanings. Moreover, connecting society to thought is not a voluntaristic matter. It is more a matter of objective societal conditions. The only thinkers who were able to establish an osmosis with society were the reactionary-conservative and extremist and intolerant thinkers, and now society is paying the price for the culture of fear that dominates it and renders it receptive of such thinkers, finding itself caught between oppressive rulers and fundamentalist oppositions. Critical thought should offer a third option, the possibility of going beyond these two given options. In order to do that, Arab thought still needs to overcome a number of sterile debates over modernity versus tradition and contemporaneity versus authenticity in which references, epochs, and concepts are confused. In these either/or formulations of issues, no possibilities for resolution are left open.

Modernization in Arab societies has so far taken place without modernity—that is, without a real break from certain ways of thinking and acting. The 1960s declared such a break, but did not really carry it out, and the little that was accomplished did not grow into a solid basis. And hiding behind Arab specificities won't help, Labib declares. All nations and societies have their own specificities. What is needed is a deepening of both critical thinking and awareness in the various cognitive, cultural, social, and political fields. Otherwise, he adds, we will continue to have ideas without thought, society without people, and human rights without humans. Unless we work toward enlightening society with a critical thinking anchored in this very society, we will remain a people with a virtual and anonymous culture, with no memory, incapable of accumulating experience, ever jumping from one ideology to another. Finally, Labib, argues, what critical thought needs to develop is a plural and complex perception of the Other, the West, which requires the elaboration of institutions to study it as well as a plural and complex understanding of ourselves. Translations can make a useful contribution to this project, but the quantity and quality of what has been produced so far, in his opinion, are very poor and insufficient.

Lebanese philosopher and independent scholar Ali Harb also insists on a rigorous understanding of the actual activity of a "thinker," who is a worker of ideas within a clear discipline. Thinkers, according to him, ought to present themselves according to their precise field of professional work rather than as "intellectuals" with ideological, religious, or national affiliations. Harb understands his job as a worker in the networks of understanding, the maps of knowledge, the rules of intellectual exchange, and the modes of reason, trying to make sense of the contemporary human being in an increasingly interrelated world. His field, he says, is that of intellectual facts as they relate to truth, knowledge, language, reason, identity, and culture in the general planetary perspective and not in the limited perspective of specificities that will at the end of the day let others think for him. He regards his task as being that of constructing concepts in order to diagnose crises and articulate problematics. His project purports to move from the critique of reason to the critique of texts with the use of a new strategy of reading. According to him, Arab thinkers have confused ideological militancy with rigorous intellectual work and allowed the former to obstruct the latter. The crisis in our day and age, he says, is no longer only Arab, but worldwide. It is compounded in the Arab world by the fact that it is not addressed or analyzed properly. Some believe Arab culture to have resisted this crisis, but in reality this very culture, with its symbols, values, and institutions, needs to be seriously critiqued. Arab culture is the black box that needs to be investigated. This culture, he adds, is frozen, monolithic, narcissistic, utopian, aggressive, and lazy; it excludes the Other and produces poverty, impotence, and backwardness. Tradition is used for self-glorification instead of as symbolic capital; and modernity is generally viewed in its reactionary version, almost as a religion. Hence, he concludes, we live in the modern world, but are marginalized and dependent, incapable of producing ideas ourselves, incapable of practicing our specificity in a creative way. We uphold ideas fanatically and transform them into obstacles and tools of destruction. Arab intellectuals have been imitators, not producers of ideas. They have been ignorant of their own societies and as a result they have lost all credibility. Instead of pretending to possess the truth and patronizing people, they should listen to people and humbly do their intellectual work in their respective fields.

Kuwaiti political sociologist Muhammad al-Rumaihi, editor of the journal *Hiwar al-ʿArab* (Dialogue of the Arabs) of the Institute of Arab Thought, deplores the dearth of knowledge production in the Arab world, especially of knowledge about the Arab world itself.[3] He considers the failure of education in Arab countries to be the cultural scandal of the postindependence era, a failure that breeds fanaticism in an environment of unemployment and sociopolitical injustice.[4] The biggest "cultural" institution that grew and developed after 1967, he says, is that of censorship.[5] The main purpose of Arab rulers, who have been either military personnel or conservatives, has been to remain in power. Intellectuals could not have put their ideas to work in such an environment, even when they came into the circles of power. Committed and principled intellectuals were either thrown in jail or intimidated and silenced by fundamentalists. Others have turned from Marxism to Islamism, manifesting in the process a precariousness and a superficiality in the upholding of doctrines and positions. The reactions to the 1967 defeat did not really change any of these tendencies. The Arab world remains in need of reflective and constructive critique, which in turn necessitates intellectual and political courage. The most important question, he adds, is that of freedom. As to the cultural unity of the Arab world, he thinks it is superficial. There is very little acquaintance among countries, and people are becoming increasingly globalized and at the same time increasingly isolated from one another.

For Lebanese historian Wajih Kawtharani, the Arab world is definitely in a phase of decline. The ideas of the Nahda could not produce large intellectual and social movements because of the absence of educated masses due to the failure of education, especially in the second half of the twentieth century. If some liberal Nahda impulses were perceptible in the first half of that century, they were annihilated by the military coups and the ongoing Palestine catastrophe, producing victimhood, escapism, and a generalized sense of impotence. The post-1967 critique was in his opinion valuable and serious, but it remained in closed circles because of the absence of a large public opinion composed of a public of readers in the Kantian sense and due to a huge illiteracy rate. Political repression and a severe educational deficit in the midst of turmoil and conflict have thwarted a real cultural renewal.

Paris-based Syrian thinker Georges Tarabichi identifies himself as belonging to the generation that wanted to make a revolution in the name of Western ideologies, primarily Marxism, in order to fight Western neocolonialism and overthrow conservative and reactionary regimes. This generation's failure, epitomized in the defeat of 1967 and its disillusionment in the wake of the military coups that seized power in the name of revolution or socialism, was a severe trauma that destroyed the capacity to see reality as it is and left intellectuals with a feeling of guilt vis-à-vis their own native traditions. These traditions were now to show the way to real salvation,[6] but nothing more was produced than mediocre revivals of tradition and no genuine critique. His generation, he says, believed it did not need critique because it was already revolutionary. The Nahda's critical impulses were not robust enough, and their proponents retreated from their innovative positions under societal pressure—except for a very few, such as Ali Abdel Raziq, who stood their ground. His generation, Tarabichi says, fought Western colonialism but appreciated Western culture, unlike the present generation. But on the whole, he adds, encountering cultural modernity together with colonialism has made constructive discernment extremely difficult. Moreover, if the Napoleonic invasion was a salutary shock that gave rise to a momentum of innovation, the trauma of 1967 in contrast provoked a collective neurosis that produced extremism and obscurantism. Many intellectuals were drawn to these tendencies, and others were co-opted by power or money. Still others found themselves caught between repressive regimes and a society inclined toward extremism. Universities today are filled with either ruling-party members or seekers of strict technology. Mosques are the only gathering places outside the hegemony of rulers. Tarabichi thinks that intellectuals should go where people gather, including mosques, and address the people of goodwill. Their work should consist of raising awareness on a very long-term basis.

Saudi literary critic Abdallah al-Ghadhdhami takes the Arab intellectual elite to task for not being self-reflective enough and for not making a clear and courageous choice between conservatism and modernity. Self-critique, he says, is still perceived as a mode of self-flagellation, and the temptation to seek salvation in strong leadership still prevails today. The fragility of that elite's position is due to its unwillingness to choose honestly a clear stand for or against modernity, for or against conservatism. This unwillingness comes from a number of cultural patterns in conceiving cultural identity and cultural unity. Such patterns do not make room for difference and do not offer mechanisms for expressing and arbitrating cultural, religious, ethnic, economic, and regional political differences. Unity has been predominantly thought in a way that cancels plurality. As to the cultural self, the tendency has been to conceive it in a narcissistic, macho way (*fuhuli*) that has prevented Arabs from admitting that their past and their tradition cannot serve them today without critical reappropriation and a genuine break. Moreover, most intellectuals, he says, remain captive of their ideological doctrines, whereas people at large think and act dynamically on the basis of their vital interests related to their homes, lands, children, and future. Intellectuals have a great deal to learn from them. The second Nahda, according to al-Ghadhdhami, remained an "academic" exercise and failed in exhorting moral values such as tolerance.

Bahraini thinker Muhammad Jaber al-Ansari also blames intellectuals (as we saw in chapter 5) for not making clear and honest choices regarding modernity and rationality. In fact, he sees in this ambiguity and undecidedness the very reasons for the failure of both Nahda movements. The reform of reason, he thinks, is an existential cause. Either the Arab world will modernize itself by means of a thorough reform of its modes of thinking and systems of education and move toward democratic transformations, or it will remain outside history in backwardness and helplessness. For these reforms and transformations to be successful, they need to include religion, not to antagonize it. A religious reform is necessary for any civilizational renewal in the Arab world. The continuous aggressions against the Arab world have destroyed the ability to think. Suicide bombings indicate this defeat and are the symptoms of a growing culture of death. They are outbursts of frustration that do not produce anything constructive. The Japanese, in contrast, did not waste time in pouring anger against the West: they resisted its hegemony by adopting Western science and know-how. Arabs and Muslims, he says, have the illusion of being different from everybody else and thus cultivate a dangerous exceptionalism. They should know that the same universal laws apply to them as well. They need to develop a culture of comparison (*thaqafat al-muqarana*). They still seek refuge in mediocre revivals of *turath* (al-Jabiri) or think that anything revolutionary and rejectionist is automatically progressive (Adonis). Intellectuals everywhere in the world, al-Ansari adds, are but a small force of change, and one should not expect too much from them. Change is to come from everyone, and intellectuals should connect to people; otherwise their ideas will never become effective. For this connection to happen, they should address and reform religious ideas that remain important for people in general. No real change can be obtained by ignoring or antagonizing their religious sensitivities, especially at a time when mentalities are being shaped by defeats and anxieties. Short of connecting to people, intellectuals merely fall into a weird talkativeness that becomes a sort of noise phenomenon (*dhahira sawtiyya*). Finally, he thinks that Arab unity is basically founded on the unity of language.

Burhan Ghalyun, Syrian professor of Islamic studies at the Sorbonne, has a more positive assessment of the contemporary Arab intellectual scene. The post-1967 era witnessed the birth of Arab critique. The first Nahda was an initial foray into the translation and adoption of the language, concepts, and ideas of modernity that are now put into use to analyze real, specific, and concrete problems under the pressure of growing crises and threatening challenges. Although the battle for critical, independent, and free thinking has not yet been won, it has surely started: look at what is being written today in the major Arab newspapers compared to what was being written in the 1950s and 1960s. The latter works were much more ideological and imitative of imported doctrines, whereas the former are rather critical and anchored in reality. Modernization, he says, is not primarily a matter of intellectual understanding, but rather a historical struggle between groups and influences. The fragility of the Arab elites, including the intellectual elite until very recently, has been due to their distance from the people in general as a result of the colonial and postcolonial social stratification. Problems of modernity are to be analyzed in terms of geopolitical and social factors rather than in terms of cultural incompatibility. Modernity has been everywhere an ongoing deconstruction and reconstruction of meanings, even in the West, and it has inevitably caused chaos and anxiety. These responses were and continue to be particularly acute in the Arab geopolitical context. The compounded difficulties and the impossibility of reconstruction have led to violence and barbarism, understood here as a chaos of meaning. They have caused despair on the individual and collective levels here more than anywhere else in the world. They have led to emigration, conflict, and intolerance. The Arab world, he observes, has been in a state of painful labor. Intellectuals have a role to play in raising awareness, dismantling illusions, and liberating the mind from its various chains, although not the way party vanguards understood their role in the past. They claimed to teach people freedom and to lead

them to victory and progress, but in reality they simply justified dictatorship, discredited emancipatory values, and ultimately led to sterility and
violence.

Renowned Egyptian sociologist Saad Eddin Ibrahim shares this cautious optimism. He thinks that the year 2005 was a turning point in recent
Arab history, which witnessed the *kifaya* (enough) movement in Egypt, the
Cedar Revolution in Lebanon, and the elections in Iraq and Palestine: all
of them liberation movements led by "normal" people, not by imposing
central leadership figures or pontificating and ideologically indoctrinated
intellectuals. The masses who made these movements broke the barriers
of fear, defending their lives and their liberties in a nonviolent manner.
Although populist ideologies divided people, raised groups against each
other, and undermined trust among them, these movements united people
in a pacific demand for change. Intellectuals in these movements certainly
played a role in organizing and articulating certain basic concepts, but not
as "celebrities." The first Nahda impulses, Ibrahim says, were suppressed
by the military coups, and it is against the sociopolitical legacy of these
coups that the present generation is revolting, even in the Islamist camp.
He believes Islamists should have an acknowledged place in this significant
revolt. The sad irony is that a year after Ibrahim gave the interview, Iraq,
Palestine, and Lebanon found themselves at different levels of civil war.

Nawal el-Saadawi, renowned Egyptian feminist and the only woman to
be interviewed, thinks that the so-called liberal age of the first Nahda is
idealized and that much is still to be done in terms of critical thinking and
connecting the sociopolitical, economic, religious, and gender aspects of
the Arab predicament.

Ali Umlil, Moroccan historian, diplomat, and presently ambassador in
Lebanon, shares Ghalyun and Ibrahim's optimistic inclinations. He thinks
that after 1967, the real struggle for the Arab future began with the concomitant emergence of the Islamist and democratic movements. Democracy, in his opinion, is central morally, politically, and intellectually as the
condition for the possibility of thought. Moreover, without an independent
public opinion, no intellectual can influence politics on his or her own—
hence, the importance of educational reforms. Modernity needs not only a
reform of ideas, he says, but a societal basis as well. This basis is still fragile
in Arab societies: their economic conditions are not healthy, their democratic institutions are weak, the quality of their universities is poor overall,
and their associative organizations are young and precarious. Like many of
his interviewed colleagues, Umlil believes that the critical thinkers of the

first Nahda were not critical in a sufficiently consistent way and that the second Nahda was started but could not be completed. Like others, he thinks that a critique of reason is essential to liberate Arab minds from the oppression of the dead (the dead tradition) and from the mentality that accommodates despotism. Finally, in spite of the many channels of communication, the Arab world, according to Umlil, remains fragmented.

For Abdel Mon'im Said, head of the Ahram Center for Political and Strategic Studies and member of the High Committee for Policies in the National Democratic Party in Egypt, the two most influential phenomena of the post-1967 era are the bureaucratic state and the theocratic resistance to it. The bureaucratic state was built after independence in the postcolonial effort to establish a civil, military, and security apparatus in each Arab country. The institutions of this apparatus quickly replaced society and market, however, instead of serving society's goals and regulating market interests. They became a formidable force of repression. From the very beginning, the bureaucratic state ruled with the force of weapons and secret services, justifying itself with authoritarian ideologies. The military coups of the 1950s and 1960s reinforced these state administrations. They repressed the Nahda thinkers and unraveled the achievements of the liberal age, purging universities and institutions of free thinkers and the court system of independent judges. Because of the failing education system, these thinkers were unable to create a social movement. In contrast to Japan, which eradicated illiteracy by 1906, says Said, Egypt still has a 30 percent illiteracy rate. The bureaucratic state succeeded in destroying quality teaching and sterilizing thought. Not a single Arab university figures in the world's best five hundred universities. Among African universities, the American University of Cairo rates fourteenth. In the face of this catastrophic performance of the postindependence bureaucratic state, the theocratic resistance stands as the only well-organized oppositional force. Around these two systems, however, grows a vulnerable democratic movement, nourished by global influences and by the remnants of the Arab liberal age.

Said notes that the second Nahda has not completely died. Its thinkers defend and transmit the idea of democracy as a viable idea and as an indigenous demand. Both the bureaucratic state and the theocratic forces are using the democratic discourse in the media to defend their projects. Democrats, according to Said, need to be vigilant and cautious. They should double their efforts in raising awareness and advocating their cause through whatever media is available to them. It is true that people are tempted by fascistic and extremist calls, but they also long for change and a hopeful life. Many of them realize that the bureaucratic state can only propose immobility and that what theocracy has to offer is a morbid perspective on life. People are yearning for life-affirming views that open them up to others; they are tired of doctrines that lock them up against presumed absolute enemies. People wish to hold on to their faith without having to antagonize others. In this sense, democracy is for them a life-affirming and life-sustaining idea, but this idea has not yet become a comprehensive political position and movement. According to Said, it is the task of intellectuals to continue to disseminate and simplify liberal ideas without falling into the trap of liberal extremism. It is important to keep the dialogue open to all, including the Islamists.

Syrian philosopher Muta' al-Safadi offers an interesting analysis of the postcolonial Arab state that can also apply to other Third World regions. In a series of articles published in the London-based Arab daily al-Quds al-Arabi around the same time as the al-Hayat interviews,[7] he describes the predicament of the Arab state. The nation-state preserved the structures of the colonial state and related to society in the same way that the latter did—namely, in a relation of imposition. In the ideal state, power should be governed by the people, by the constitution agreed upon by the people, and by the institutions set by the constitution. In the postcolonial state, however, the institutions had to be created or reappropriated first by the rulers, who invariably ended up gearing them toward their own interests. The state lost not only its regulating mechanisms, but its public character as well. The first generation of leaders felt that in return for their patriotic anticolonial struggle, they were entitled to own and dispose of power without checks. The military coups that followed and replaced these rulers established a pattern for seizing power by force. Whether monarchical or republican or tribal, all Arab governments, says al-Safadi, became oligarchies. Those who came through the military coups in the aftermath of the 1948 catastrophe with the aim of redressing the defeats and reactionary policies were soon faced with their own limitations and their own failures. In the absence of a regional and international political settlement of the growing conflicts, they used state institutions to maintain power, with militarization becoming an end in itself and politics becoming an addendum to it. Corruption was structurally bound to spread, with no possible remedy to it short of changing the state's entire system. The nonjuridical, unconstitutional, and undemocratic emergence of the postcolonial state prevented a real *nahda* from developing and produced on the contrary a despotism that ultimately brought back colonial intervention. Not only did this state make a *nahda* impossible, but it also destroyed society by paralyzing it and making it incapable of forming a freely consented unity based on a genuine political contract. Impotence, concludes al-Safadi, became the central reality of Arab postcolonial life. With renewed repression exerted as a result of the so-called war on terrorism, Arab states have pushed people to despair, making them afraid to undertake the slightest change and use any of their available means to rise against the oppression. These states have thus incapacitated the second Nahda in a most radical manner. Religion perhaps has the only stock of values left that might bring back some morality to political life. In the first Nahda, religion was among the first fields to open up to the reform impulses. But obviously, al-Safadi observes, the theocratic tendencies are much too strong for any *nahda*-type reform to be possible under the present conditions.[8]

This panorama of self-reflective assessment of the advances and setbacks of Arab thought in the past four decades reveals the persistence of certain preoccupations and the growth of some renewal impulses. As is obvious in most of the interviews, the need to strengthen and deepen critique is ubiquitous. Most of these Arab intellectuals deem the radicalization of critique that began in the aftermath of 1967 insufficient. Moreover, it has remained in closed academic circles and not reached the larger public. The elitism of many intellectuals and the failure of education have alienated people from this critical effort. Complaints persist about the sterility of ideological thinking, about the difficulty of breaking from the past and ceasing to refer to it, and about the confusion between the West's imperial hegemony and Western humanistic modernity. The perception of the state and its Islamist oppositions as the two main internal sociopolitical, economic, and cultural forces to be reckoned with in any intellectual or political move has become sharper.

The question of freedom has grown more central than ever. Time and again the scope of devastation caused by state repression on all levels is deplored. The ever-recurring term used to describe the situation is *incapacitation* or *impotence* (*'ajz*) resulting from this devastation—a sort of endemic bankruptcy, collective despair, and pervasive depression, hence the attractiveness of fascist promises, salvational doctrines, and charismatic leaders. The dismantlement and fragmentation of society are particularly alarming. The subjugation of society by state terror and the never-ending states of emergency have made it impossible for society's constituting communities to forge an empowered body politic that is eager to engage in public matters and capable of doing so. Yet, despite these repressive factors, instead of the Jacobinist understanding of national and pan-Arab unity, plural conceptions of unity are being advocated that recognize the diversity of the national communities and the right of ethnic and religious minorities (Berber, Kurd, Copt, and so on) to exist and partake fully in the national political life. For most of the *al-Hayat* interviewees, no promise of hope can be found outside the empowerment and participation of people—hence, the encouragement inspired by the popular movements in a number of Arab countries and the insistence on the importance of bringing people back to center stage. Have we come full circle back to Wannous? Have people started to demand their eyes and tongues and ears after they were erased? Have they started to break the barriers of fear and silence? What chances do these popular movements have in the midst of the prevailing geopolitical turmoil? Finally, the interviewees also note the people's longing for life-affirming options, their yearning for life and joy in the midst of an increasingly morbid and violent environment.

Samir Kassir (1960–2005), the late Lebanese historian and journalist, takes up most of these issues in the 2004 booklet *Considérations sur le malheur arabe* (Thoughts on Arab Wretchedness).[9] In the preface, he positions himself as an individual Arab intellectual, secular and westernized, writing both about and to Arabs, believing that the same discourse can be held about Arabs and to Arabs. Indeed, the book, with its French Enlightenment–style title, appeared in Paris simultaneously with the Arabic translation in Beirut. It succinctly presents seven theses on Arabs' *malheur*—their misery, wretchedness, unhappiness:

1. *Arabs are the unhappiest beings in the world, even when they don't realize it,* not only because of the objective realities in their countries, such as the high illiteracy rate, the gap between rich and poor, the overpopulated cities and deserted rural areas, but also because of their perception of the situation. The bitter awareness of helplessness in not being in control of their own destiny, the sense of being diminished, and the unresolved mourning over a past greatness are all painful aspects of this perception. The sense of helplessness is aggravated by the long-standing and deteriorating conflicts in the region, where the international community seems consistently to deny Arab rights in favor of Israel. These conflicts have solicited over the years various forms of protest and resistance. But these forms of resistance, be they the intifada or guerrilla warfare, are in danger of becoming ends in themselves in the absence of a foreseeable solution, an

outcome supported by neighboring Arab "spectators" who find in them a compensation for their own governments' defeats and humiliations, and by the jihadists, who use them to feed their ideology of apocalyptic violence. In this predicament, the gaze of the Other that mocks one's impotence and confronts one's anxieties with the certainties of hopelessness is particularly harsh. The gaze onto the Other, not only the Western, but even the Third World and the Asian in particular, accentuates the gap between Arabs and the rest of the world.

2.   *Unhappiness is the best-distributed thing in the Arab world.* Kassir goes briefly through the complex problems of individual Arab countries to demonstrate the pervasiveness of the failures. According to him, these failures are not to be understood in culturist terms, but to be looked at as the manifestations of the crisis of the state: institutional fragility, absence of institutional discontinuity, unhealthy economies, unsuccessful foreign policies, a citizenry crippled by long-lasting emergency laws (for example, in Syria since 1963 and in Egypt since 1967), societies divided due to repression and hence vulnerable to external hegemony, both in the economy and in politics. Political Islam as a force of change, says Kassir, amounts to accepting the deficit in democracy as a perennial given; it is a symptom of the misery rather than a way out of it. Unlike Bassam Tibi, he thinks that political Islam is a reaction to the state rather than a reaction to cultural modernity.

3.   *This unhappiness is but a moment in history, greater today than it was yesterday.* The typical periodization of Arab history into the golden age of Islam (seventh to twelfth centuries), the decadence (twelfth to nineteenth centuries), and the Nahda (nineteenth to twentieth centuries) offers a view of history that is composed largely of an unending decline, especially with the growing conviction that the Nahda itself was yet another of Arab culture's failures. Yet, for Kassir, the so-called period of decadence had its own achievements, such as the Mamluk and Ottoman architecture and the writings of Ibn Khaldun, among others. Islamic civilization continued to thrive, and all kinds of human philosophical tendencies developed in it, from the rational to the mystical. Arab culture became a world culture and expressed the universality of human reason. The successful achievements of Arab history cannot be limited to the three or four centuries of the "golden age" and certainly not to the first forty years of Islam, as Muslim Salafists claim. The decline of the Ottoman Empire in the eighteenth century coincided with the great industrial transformations of Europe, but soon enough in the course of the nineteenth century borrowings

started to take place both in politics and culture through the Tanzimat reforms and in technology through the importation of electricity, the steam engine, the railroad, the telegraph, and so on—momentous transformations that are often forgotten today.

4. *Modernity was not the moment of misfortune.* The reduction of the Nahda to the nationalist movement leaves out many of its important dimensions. It territorializes the Nahda by limiting it to the Arab region, isolating the latter from its wider Ottoman reform context. It retains from the Nahda only the national liberation aspect, whereas in reality the Nahda carried ideals of individual liberties as well. Moreover, it neglects the Nahda's humanist enlightenment impulse. During the Nahda, says Kassir, Arab culture reconstructed itself through the discovery of the European Other, which inevitably created tensions and ambiguities. However, it did not prevent Arabs from borrowing extensively from European culture in fashion, literary genres (theater, novel, autobiography), educational reform, the press, secret societies, ideologies (feminism, socialism, Darwinism)—in contrast to Japan, which limited its borrowings to the technological—and hence manifesting a greater Arab openness to cultural modernity. The history of these important transformations is now often ignored.

5. *The unhappiness is not due to modernity, but to its lack of completion.* The modernizing impulses lasted longer than is thought today, and they affected larger circles of the population than is thought, not just a small elite. Beyond the nationalist and literary movements, they influenced the popular arts, such as singing, painting, and cinema. It is the fading of these impulses and not their activation that announces the epoch of misery. Arab modernity was certainly not an idyllic time, says Kassir, but it was dynamic and hopeful, with a sense of an open and promising future. Arabs had an active presence in the world through Abdel Nasser's Nonalignment Movement, the Algerian Revolution, and the development of modern laws in Tunisia. Where did all this go? How was this living culture traded for a culture of death and misfortune?

6. *The Arabs' misfortune is in their geography rather than in their history.* According to Kassir, no one will ever be able to fathom the impediment to modernity and development that European colonialism and the foundation of the state of Israel created in the Arab world. To this is added the oil factor, the imperialist interests that it fomented, and the oil rentier economies that subjugated their citizens through wealth. Moreover, in the colonial world Arabs are the only ones to have confronted Europe in the precolonial era and to have dominated that encounter. For them, the mem-

ory of this former position of power makes the present weakness all the more bitter because it affects the European gaze on them.

7. *Arabs' biggest misfortune is their unwillingness to get out of misfortune; if not happiness, then at least some equilibrium should be envisaged.* The retreat into particularism and essentialist justifications are not helpful. What is needed is a recentering of the universal. Intellectuals should contribute to the dissemination of the belief in the universal, in democracy, and rekindle against all odds the hope for a renaissance that will be plural. The expanding media and the networks of cultural globalization may help promote such an orientation. Some form of cohesive Arabhood has developed despite everything. Resistance should not be confounded with terrorism and vice versa. The culture of death should be overcome. Rather than a characteristic of Islam or Arabism, violence has grown in the midst of unresolved conflicts and never-ending bloodshed. Despair and cruelty have led to the cult of martyrdom. The misfortune has grown too big for Arabs' to ask for immediate happiness, Kassir adds, but what they can hope for is the abandonment of the fantasy of an unmatchable past and then a reintegration of history so that they can discover its more promising episodes and realize that helplessness and defeatism were not always their mode of being in this world.

For me, the question is, Can Arabs abandon this attachment to a glorious past when no tangible compensation seems at hand, when the sense of self seems so wounded and damaged, and when capacities seem so crippled? It would indeed take quite a leap of faith to imagine again the possible, revisit history, recall its more promising episodes, and reaffirm life. In his last interviews, Kassir kept emphasizing that what the Lebanese and the Arabs wanted most was to live. That desire for life was given yet another heavy blow with his assassination on June 2, 2005.

The desire to live and the radical rethinking of the political are the main themes of present Arab critical thought. It is a thought that emerges from the pains of wars, dictatorships, and political prisons. It has the determination and the vulnerability of life itself and the maturity and depth of prolonged existential suffering. The political understanding of civilizational anguish reconnects this thought with the first Nahda's earliest reflections in the works of Rifaʿa al-Tahtawi and Khaireddin al-Tunisi, who unambiguously saw political justice in the sense of constitutional rule as the basis of progress and prosperity. It also reconnects this thought with Abdel Rahman al-Kawakibi's sharp critique of oppression at the turn of

the twentieth century and with his insightful description of its mechanisms and manifestations. This political line of civilizational analysis joins
the critique of repression articulated by Saadallah Wannous and Abdel
Rahman Munif in the beginning of the second Nahda after 1967. Now it
spreads into the growing prison literature of Syria, Iraq, Jordan, Palestine,
Egypt, Morocco, and Tunisia. The writings by these regimes' former prisoners offer a most perspicacious analysis of their countries' ills and draw
attention to the radical causes of the malaise: arbitrary rule, abuse of state
institutions, forbidden public debate, thwarted political life, destruction of
society, and the disabling of people's agency. They aim at analyzing the
effects of this destruction and at reclaiming the political as the necessary
grounding for reconstruction and renewal—a literature worth following
closely.

This focus on the political is a shift from the emphasis on the cultural
that prevailed in the 1930s and 1940s, when a cultural vision was sought for
the newly emerging Arab countries, as well as in the 1970s and 1980s, when
tradition was presented as the solution to the defeats and the malaise. Indeed, the malaise is increasingly understood in political terms, and the
central demand is no longer for a culturalist self-examination, but for a
humanist democracy that springs from the desire to live—that is, to be free
and to exist as an able human being. This challenge, however, is tremendous in a region so severely damaged by the geopolitical disasters not only
of the past century, but even more so of the very present moment. The
struggle for life and for democracy under these conditions requires a formidable leap of faith that they can be achieved. Moreover, the emphasis on
the political has not only regained importance, but become more immanent in the sense that the issue no longer concerns imitating the West,
translating Montesquieu, or indigenizing Western liberal democratic notions, but rather preventing police-state terror, ensuring basic security and
freedom, and protecting oneself from endless forms of abuse—all of which
are painful lived realities and not just intellectual problems.

The dominating question of the first Nahda was, Why have Muslims
lagged behind while others have progressed? Its central concern was progress, and its orientation was hopeful reform. The question of the second
Nahda was, Why did the Nahda fail to come to fruition? The second Nahda
arose at a time of anguished self-reflection, so much of its focus was on the
quest for authenticity. The prevailing question today is, Why are we in a
deadlock? A recent book reflecting on the current Arab malaise has the
following telling title: *Al-Insidad al-Tarikhi: Limadha Fashila Mashru'*

al-Tanwir fi al-ʿAlam al-ʿArabi? (The Historical Deadlock: Why Did the Enlightenment Project Fail in the Arab World?).[10] Irrespective of the answer the book offers, the title alone expresses a state of despair and resignation as well as a deep sense of impotence. Have all lights gone out in the Arab world? Will violence, despotism, and despair engulf the remaining resistant intellectual and popular vital impulses?

Notes

Introduction

1. Among the rare but good studies of this growing critical trend are Issa J. Boullata, *Trends and Issues in Contemporary Arab Thought* (Albany: State University of New York Press, 1990); Hisham Sharabi, "The Scholarly Point of View: Politics, Perspectives, Paradigm," in Hisham Sharabi, ed., *Theory, Politics, and the Arab World: Critical Responses*, 1–51 (New York: Routledge, 1990); and more recently, Ibrahim Abu-Rabi, *Contemporary Arab Thought: Studies in Post-1967 Arab Intellectual History* (London: Pluto Press, 2004). Saree Makdisi looks at the post-1967 critique issues in Arabic literature in "'Postcolonial' Literature in a Neocolonial World: Modern Arabic Culture and the End of Modernity," *Boundary 2* 22, no. 1 (1995): 85–115. Palestinian literary critic Faysal Darraj has recently published a study of the Nahda and modern issues in twentieth-century Arab fiction: *Al-Dhakira al-Qawmiyya fi al-Riwaya al-'Arabiyya* (The National Memory in the Arab Novel) (Beirut: Markaz Dirasat al-Wihda al-'Arabiyya, 2007). Valuable information about contemporary Arab thinkers and activists can be found in Kevin Dwyer, *Arab Voices: The Human Rights Debate in the Middle East* (Berkeley and Los Angeles: University of California Press, 1991). A biographical index of modern and contemporary Arab thinkers can be found at the end of Samir Bouzid, *Mythes, utopie et messianisme dans le discours politique arabe moderne et contemporain* (Myth, Utopia, and Messianism in Modern and Contemporary Arabic Political Discourse) (Paris: L'Harmattan, 1997). Joseph A. Massad presents an intellectual history focused on the issues of gender and sexual desire in *Desiring Arabs* (Chicago: University of Chicago Press, 2007).

2. For an analysis of major twentieth-century discourses on Europe held by European philosophers such as Lévinas, Husserl, Derrida, and Foucault, see Elizabeth Suzanne Kassab, "Is Europe an Essence? Lévinas, Husserl, and Derrida on Cultural Identity and Ethics," *International Studies in Philosophy* 34, no. 4 (2002): 55–75; for an analysis of the intricate descriptive and prescriptive components of Western philosophies of

culture, see Elizabeth Suzanne Kassab, "Phenomenologies of Culture and Ethics: Ernst Cassirer, Alfred Schutz, and the Tasks of a Philosophy of Culture," *Human Studies* 25 (2002): 55–88; and for a similar analysis in the work of the Arab thinker Qustantin Zurayq, see Elizabeth Suzanne Kassab, "An Arab Neo-Kantian Philosophy of Culture: Constantine Zurayk on Culture, Reason, and Ethics," *Philosophy East & West* 49, no. 4 (1999): 494–512.

3. Ella Shohat, "Notes on the 'Post-colonial,'" *Social Text*, nos. 31–32 (1992): 99–113.

4. Ibid., 108. Also relevant in this connection is Anne McClintock's essay "The angel of progress: Pitfalls of the term 'Post-Colonialism,'" *Social Text*, nos. 31–32 (1992): 84–98. A mapping of such a post-colonial approach to modern Arab literature was undertaken by Magda al-Nowaihi in "'The Middle East'? Or . . . Arabic Literature and the Postcolonial Predicament," in Henry Schwarz and Sangeeta Ray, eds., *A Companion to Postcolonial Studies*, 282–303 (Malden, Mass.: Blackwell, 2000). Very sadly, Magda passed away in 2002 at age forty-four before she could realize the many promising projects she was able to envision with great clarity and erudition.

5. I look at these debates in chapter 6.

6. Albert Memmi, *Portrait du colonisé, précédé du portrait du colonisateur* (Paris: Correa, 1957); I quote from the English translation by Howard Greenfield, *The Colonizer and the Colonized*, with an introduction by Jean-Paul Sartre (Boston: Beacon, 1967), 139–40.

7. Ibid., 137.

8. Albert Memmi, *Portrait du décolonisé Arabo-musulman et de quelques autres* (Paris: Gallimard, 2004); I quote from the English translation by Robert Bononno, *Decolonization and the Decolonized* (Minneapolis: University of Minnesota Press, 2006), xiii.

1. The First Modern Arab Cultural Renaissance

1. For a brief and informative overview of these reforms, see Erik J. Zürcher, *Turkey: A Modern History* (London: I. B. Tauris, 1993). For an intellectual history of the Ottoman reformers, see Şerif Mardin, *Genesis of Young Ottoman Thought: A Study in the Modernization of Turkish Political Ideas* (Princeton, N.J.: Princeton University Press, 1962). For a study of the impact of the Young Turks revolution in the Arab regions in the last decade of the Ottoman Empire, see Hasan Kayali, *Arabs and Young Turks: Ottomanism, Arabism, and Islamism in the Ottoman Empire, 1908–1918* (Berkeley and Los Angeles: University of California Press, 1997).

2. Al-Jabarti's chronicle of the Napoleonic occupation of Egypt lays bare the different forces and characteristics of these players. See Robert L. Tignor, ed., *Napoleon in*

Egypt: Al-Jabarti's Chronicle of the French Occupation, 1798 (New York: Markus Wiener, 1993).

3. On the second centennial of Muhammad Ali Pasha, the English-language Egyptian weekly magazine *al-Ahram Weekly* produced a file on the Egyptian governor entitled *Muhammad Ali (1805–2005)*. The file can be found in its online edition at http://weekly .ahram.org.eg/2005/mhmdali.htm. See also Afaf Lutfi al-Sayyid Marsot, *Egypt in the Reign of Muhammad Ali* (Cambridge, U.K.: Cambridge University Press, 1984), and *Women and Men in Late Eighteenth Century Egypt* (Austin: University of Texas Press, 1995). For a study of the Egyptian Renaissance and the reigns of Muhammad Ali and Gamal Abdel Nasser, see Shukry Ghali's dissertation, written under the direction of Jacques Berque in Paris, "Renaissance et déclin de la pensée arabe moderne: Etude critique du régime de Mohammed Ali et celui de Nasser," published in Arabic as *Al-Nahda Wa al-Suqut fi al-Fikr al-Misri al-Hadith* (Rise and Fall in Modern Egyptian Thought) (Beirut: Dar al-Tali'a, 1978). For a critical revisiting of the Muhammad Ali era in Egypt, see Khaled Fahmy, *All the Pasha's Men: Mehmed Ali, His Army, and the Making of Modern Egypt* (Cambridge, U.K.: Cambridge University Press, 1997; reprints, Cairo: American University of Cairo Press, 2002, 2004); and Khaled Fahmy, "The Era of Muhammad 'Ali Pasha, 1805–1848," in M. W. Daly, ed., *The Cambridge History of Egypt*, vol. 2: *Modern Egypt, from 1517 to the End of the Twentieth Century*, 139–79 (New York: Cambridge University Press, 1998). Further light is shed on the period by Timothy Mitchell's critical work on the Western colonial impact on Egypt, *Colonising Egypt* (Cambridge, U.K.: Cambridge University Press, 1988; reprint, Berkeley and Los Angeles: University of California Press, 1991).

4. For studies on nationalism, political and social reform, the role of religion in society, and relations with the West drawn from the press of the time, see the collected articles in Marwan R. Buheiry, ed., *Intellectual Life in the Arab East, 1890–1939* (Beirut: Center for Arab and Middle East Studies, American University of Beirut, 1981).

5. Albert Hourani, *Arabic Thought in the Liberal Age, 1798–1939* (London: Oxford University Press, 1962), translated into Arabic by Karim 'Azqul as *Al-Fikr al-'Arabi fi 'Asr al-Nahda, 1798–1939* (Beirut: Dar an-Nahar, 1968); new edition of the translation revised by Adib al-Qintar (Beirut: Mu'assassat Naufal, 1997). See also Hisham Sharabi, *Arab Intellectuals and the West: The Formative Years, 1875–1914* (Baltimore: Johns Hopkins University Press, 1970). For a reception of the ideas of the French Revolution in the Arab East around the turn of the twentieth century, see Ra'if Khuri, *Al-Fikr al-'Arabi al-Hadith: Athar al-Thawrah al-Faransiyya fi Tawjihihi al-Siyasi wa al-Ijtima'i* (Modern Arab Thought: The Impact of the French Revolution in Its Political and Social Orientations) (Beirut: Dar al-Makshuf, 1973; Damascus: Manshurat Wizarat al-Thaqafah, 1993) , translated into English by Ihsan Abbas as *Modern Arab Thought: Channels of the French Revolution to the Arab East*, revised and edited by Charles Issawi

(Princeton, N.J.: Kingston Press, 1983); see also Sadeq Jalal al-Azm, Mustafa al-Tawati, and Muhammad bin Ahmuda, *Athar al-Thawra al-Faransiyya fi Fikr al-Nahda* (The Impact of the French Revolution on the Nahda Thought) (Tunis: al-ʿArabiyya, 1991). For Arab studies of the Nahda thinkers, see Ahmad Amin, *Zuʿama' al-Islah fi al-ʿAsr al-Hadith* (The Leaders of Reform in Modern Times) (Cairo: Maktabat al-Nahda al-Misriyya, 1948); Issam Mahfuz, *Hiwar maʿ Ruwwad al-Nahda al-ʿArabiyya* (Dialogue with the Pioneers of the Arab Renaissance) (London: Riad el-Rayyes, 1988); Majid Fakhry, *Al-Haraka al-Fikriyya wa Ruwwaduha al-Lubnaniyyun fi ʿAsr al-Nahda, 1800–1922* (The Intellectual Movement and Its Lebanese Pioneers, 1800–1922) (Beirut: Dar al-Nahar, 1992); and Ghaleb Halassa, *Al-Haribun min al-Huriyya* (The Fugitives of Freedom) (Damascus: Dar al-Mada, 2001). Finally, a sample of more recent works on the Nahda thought, issues, and thinkers includes Muhammad Jaber al-Ansari, *Tajdid al-Nahda bi Iktishaf al-Dhat wa Naqdiha* (Renewing the Nahda by Discovering the Self and Critiquing It), 2d ed. (Beirut: Al-Muʾassassa al-ʿArabiyya li al-Dirasat wa al-Nashr, 1998); Kamal Abd al-Latif, *Asʾilat al-Nahda al-ʿArabiyya: Al-Tarikh, al-Hadatha, al-Tawasul* (Questions of the Arab Nahda: History, Modernity, Continuity) (Beirut: Markaz Dirasat al-Wihda al-ʿArabiyya, 2003); Ahmad Jedi, *Mihnat al-Nahda wa Lughz al-Tarikh fi al-Fikr al-ʿArabi al-Hadith wa al-Muʿassir* (The Crisis of the Nahda and the Enigma of History in Modern and Contemporary Thought) (Beirut: Markaz Dirasat al-Wihda al-ʿArabiyya, 2005); the collected work *Qiraʾat fi al-Fikr al-ʿArabi* (Readings in Arab Thought) (Beirut: Markaz Dirasat al-Wihda al-ʿArabiyya, 2003); Maher al-Charif, *Rihanat al-Nahda fi al-Fikr al-ʿArabi* (The Stakes of the Nahda in Arab Thought) (Damascus: Dar al-Mada, 2000); Ridwan Ziadeh, *Idiyologiyya al-Nahda fi al-Khitab al-ʿArabi al-Muʿassir* (The Ideology of the Nahda in Contemporary Arab Discourse) (Beirut: Dar al-Taliʿa, 2004). The Beirut-based journal *Al-Tariq*, owned by the Lebanese Communist Party, devoted several issues to revisiting the Nahda in connection with religious reform and political Islam (56, no. 1 [1997]), with Marxism (57, no. 6 [1998]), and writing in general (61, no. 1 [2002]); it also had issues on Marxism, Islamic reform, and the thought of al-Tahtawi (62, nos. 5–6 [2003]). Founded by Antoine Tabet in 1941, this journal has since 2005 unfortunately ceased to appear. It was among the best Arab intellectual periodicals.

6. Rifaʿa Rafiʿ al-Tahtawi, *Takhlis al-Ibriz fi Talkhis Bariz* (The Extraction of Pure Gold in the Abridgment of Paris) (Beirut: Dar Ibn-Khaldun, 2003).

7. The oldest school of Islamic learning, founded in Cairo in 975 and still the center of Sunni religious authority.

8. Rifaʿa Rafiʿ al-Tahtawi, *Al-Murshid al-Amin li al-Banat wa al-Banin* (loosely rendered: Guiding Truths for Girls and Youths) (Cairo: Matbaʿat al-Madaris al-Malakiyya, 1872–1873). Another important figure in the Nahda of Egyptian education was Ali Mubarak (1824–1893), twenty-three years al-Tahtawi's junior. He was called "the

Father of Education" (Abu'l-Ta'lim). After studying in Paris, he was to become a prominent organizer, administrator, manager, teacher, and writer. He became Egyptian minister of education and was responsible for the organization of governmental and nongovernmental schools and for the creation of the first national library. He was also to become minister of public works and to be in charge of the modernization of Cairo.

9. Rifaʿa Rafiʿ al-Tahtawi, *An Imam in Paris: Tahtawi's Visit to France (1826–1831)*, introduced and translated by Daniel L. Newman (London: Saqi Books, 2004). Newman's introduction is very informative. The journal *al-Tariq* (nos. 5–6 [2003]: 116–59) presents a special dossier on al-Tahtawi's Nahda project.

10. Al-Tahtawi's travel memoirs were not the only specimen of their kind in the Nahda period. Ahmed Faris al-Shidyaq, who undertook a prolonged trip to Europe (Malta, Great Britain, and France) in 1834, produced three such memoirs with the same view of reporting about the different aspects of European life and emphasizing the constitutive elements of European progress: *Al-Wasita fi Maʿrifat Ahwal Malta* (The Way to Know About Malta) (Beirut: Muʾassassat Nasir li al-Thaqafa, Dar al-Wihda, 1978); *Al-Saq ʿAla al-Saq fi ma Huwa al-Faryaq* (Leg on Leg About Faryaq and His Travel Observations) (Beirut: Dar Maktabat al-Hayah, 1966); and *Kashf al-Mukhabbaʾ ʿAn Funun Urubba* (Discovering the Hidden in Europe's Arts) (Constantinople: n.p., 1881–82). These books contain reports about the English government in Malta, the British Parliament, sources of law, monarchy, social classes, and press, as well as the history of journalism and printing in Europe, Oxford and Cambridge universities, the churches in Great Britain and France, the postal service, the telegraph, currency, and modern Western music and theater. Faris emphasized the importance of industry, science, and freedom in the making of modern European civilization and the social values that made them possible, such as work ethic, respect for law, tolerance, and personal liberties. The Arabic newspaper he launched in Constantinople in 1860 lasted until 1883. In addition to disseminating this knowledge about modern Europe, he contributed to modernizing Arabic and worked in translation, including the new translation of the New Testament into Arabic. His alliance with the Protestant missionaries created tensions with his own Lebanese Maronite Church, which were exacerbated by the church's jailing of his brother Asʿad for his conversion to Protestantism and especially after his death in jail. In protest, Faris converted to Islam and added "Ahmad" to his name. For a study of Arab travelers in the West in the periods between 1826 and 1880, 1880 and 1918, and 1918 and 1945, see Nazik Saba Yared, *Al-Rahhalun al-ʿArab wa Hadarat al-Gharb fi al-Nahda al-ʿArabiyya al-Haditha* (Beirut: Naufal Press, 1992), translated into English by Summayya Damluji Shahbandar, and revised and edited by Tony P. Naufal and Jana Gough as *Arab Travellers and Western Civilization* (London: Saqi Books, 1996).

11. Al-Tahtawi, *An Imam in Paris*, 194.

12. See, for instance, Sabry Hafez's review article "Torture, Imprisonment, and Political Assassination in the Arab Novel," *al Jadid* 8, no. 38 (2002): no page numbers. The satellite channel *al-Jazeera* ran a series of interviews with former prisoners, primarily authors of Arab prison literature, called *Adab al-Sujun*. The transcriptions of these interviews in Arabic can be accessed at http://www.aljazeera.net/NR/exeres/3717385DBB00–4635 -B29F-4E8D11124C1D.htm. English translations by Shareah Taleghani of the poetry of two Syrian former prisoners, Faraj Bayrakdar and Hasiba Abd al-Rahman, can be found online in *Words Without Borders—The Online Magazine for International Literature* (http://www.wordswithoutborders.org). Taleghani is a member of the New York Translation Collective, which aims at offering a new approach to the translation of Arab texts. The renowned Iraqi architect Rifaat al-Jaderji, imprisoned under Saddam Hussein, emphasizes in his prison memoirs, written conjointly with his wife, Balqis Sharara, the importance of constituting a reservoir of political memory, drawn from all the lived experiences of the past decades, including the experiences of oppression and injustice. Such a stock of experience, he believes, accumulated gradually and analyzed honestly and deeply, can develop a political consciousness and conscience and become the hope of a better future, free from oppression and obscurantism. See his introduction to Rifaat al-Jaderji and Balqis Sharara, *Jidar Bayna Dhulmatayn* (A Wall Between Two Obscurities) (Beirut: Dar al-Saqi, 2003). The most insightful political writings of former prisoners, such as Syrian Yassin al-Haj Saleh, are among the sharpest expressions of this critique; see Saleh's weekly opinion pieces in the Arab daily *al-Hayat*, for instance. For a study of women's prison memoirs, see Marilyn Booth, "Prison, Gender, Praxis: Women's Prison Memoirs in Egypt and Elsewhere," *MERIP* 149 (November–December 1987): 35–41.

13. Published in 1867–1868, Khaireddin Al-Tunisi's *Aqwam al-Masalik fi Ma'rifat Ahwal al-Mamalik* (reprint, Tunis: Al-Majma' al-Tunisi li al-'Ulum wa al-Adab wa al-Funun, Bayt al-Hikma, 2000) was translated the same year into French and published in Paris as *Réformes nécessaires aux états musulmans* (Paris: Dupont, 1868). The English translation was done by Leon Carl Brown and published as *The Surest Path: The Political Treatise of a Nineteenth-Century Muslim Statesman* (Cambridge, Mass.: Harvard University Press, 1967).

14. A collection of al-Afghani's writings, translated into English and edited, can be found in Jamal al-Din al-Afghani, *An Islamic Response to Imperialism: Political and Religious Writings of Sayyid Jamal al-Din al-Afghani*, edited by Nikki R. Keddie (Berkeley and Los Angeles: University of California Press, 1968). This book includes an informative introduction by the editor, "The Life and Thought of Sayyid Jamal al-Din."

15. Al-Afghani's answer can be found in "Answer to Jamal al-Din to Renan" in al-Afghani, *An Islamic Response to Imperialism*, 181–87.

16. Relevant here are Muhammad Abduh's books *Al-Islam wa al-Nasraniyya Bayna al-'Ilm wa al-Madaniyya* (Islam and Christianity Between Science and Civilization) (Beirut: Dar al-Hadatha, 1983) and *Risalat al-Tawhid* (Cairo: Matba'at al-Manar, 1908 or 1909, 1942–1943), available in English as *The Theology of Unity*, translated by Ishaq Musa'ad and Kenneth Cragg (London: Allen and Unwin, 1966).

17. Quoted in Hourani, *Arabic Thought in the Liberal Age*, 141. The quotation is translated by Hourani and taken from Abduh's biography, written by his disciple Muhammad Rashid Rida, *Tarikh al-Ustadh al-Imam al-Shaykh Muhammad Abduh* (History of the Professor and Iman Sheikh Muhammad Abduh), vol. 1 (Cairo: Matba'at al-Manar, 1931), 11.

18. For critical studies of Abduh and Rida's reform efforts, see Malcom Kerr, *Islamic Reform: The Political and Legal Theories of Muhammad Abduh and Rashid Rida* (Berkeley and Los Angeles: University of California Press, 1966); and Ahmad Dallal, "Appropriating the Past: Twentieth-Century Reconstruction of Pre-modern Islamic Thought," *Islamic Law and Society* 7, no. 3 (2000): 325–58. For recent studies on Muhammad Abduh, see the contributions in French and Arabic to the conference organized by the French Institute of the Near East in Aleppo in November 2005 on the centennial of Abduh's death: Maher el-Charif and Sabrina Mervin, eds., *Modernités islamiques* (Islamic Modernities) (Damas, Syria: Institut Français du Proche Orient, 2006); see also Abdel Raziq Eid, *Muhammad Abduh: Imam al-Hadatha wa al-Dustur* (Muhammad Abduh: The Imam of Modernity and the Consitution) (Baghdad: Ma'had al-Dirasat al-Stratijiyya, 2006) and Muhammad al-Haddad, *Muhammad Abduh: Qira'a Jadida fi Khitab al-Islah al-Dini* (Muhammad Abduh: A New Reading in the Discourse of Religious Reform) (Beirut: Dar al-Tali'a, 2003).

19. On nationalist and Islamic Indonesians' reception of Arab Islamic modernists' ideas, see Azyumardi Azra, "The Transmission of al-Manar's Reformism to the Malay-Indonesian World: The Case of al-Imam and al-Munir," in S. A. Dudoignon, K. Hisao, and K. Yasushi, eds., *Intellectuals in the Modern Islamic World: Transmission, Transformation, Communication*, 143–58 (London: Routledge, 2006).

20. Shakib Arslan, *Limadha Ta'akhkhara al-Muslimun wa Limadha Taqaddama Ghayruhum* (Why Did Muslims Lag Behind and Why Did Others Progress?) (Beirut: Al-Hayat, 1975), translated as *Our Decline and its Causes* by M.A. Shakoor (Lahore, Pakistan: Sh. Muhammad Ashraf, 1944; reprint, 1962), and more recently as *Our Decline: Its Causes and Remedies,* translated by Ssekamanya Siraje Abdullah (Kuala Lumpur, Malaysia: Islamic Book Trust, 2004). For a historical analysis of Arslan's ideas, see Mahmud Haddad, "The Ideas of Amir Shakib Arslan: Before and After the Collapse of the Ottoman Empire," in Neguin Yavari, Lawrence G. Potter, and Jean-Marc Ran Oppenheim, eds., *Views from the Edge: Essays in Honor of Richard W. Bulliet*, 101–15 (New York: Columbia University Press, 2004).

21. Arslan, *The Causes of Our Decline*, 113.

22. For a socioreligious analysis of the Nahda intellectuals, see Sharabi, *Arab Intellectuals and the West*; and for a comparative analysis of secularism between Christian and Muslim thinkers of the period, see Nazik Saba Yared, *Secularism and the Arab World, 1850–1939* (London: Saqi Books, 2002).

23. Butrus al-Bustani et al., eds., *Da'irat al-Ma'arif* (The Circle of Knowledge), 11 vols. (Beirut: n.p., 1876–1900).

24. Antun's views were articulated in his work on Ibn Rushd. This work was recently reedited together with the texts of Antun's exchange with Muhammad Abduh: Farah Antun, *Ibn Rush wa Falsafatuhu* (Averroes and His Philosophy) (Beirut: Dar al-Farabi, 2007). For an analysis of the Antun-Abduh debate, see Alexander Flores, "Reform, Islam, Secularism: Farah Antûn and Muhammad Abduh," in Alain Roussillon, ed., *Entre réforme sociale et mouvement national* (Between Social Reform and National Movement), 565–76 (Cairo: Cedej, 1995). For a description of the circumstances of the debate, see D. M. Reid, *The Odyssey of Farah Antun: A Syrian Christian's Quest for Secularism* (Minneapolis: Bibliotheca Islamica, 1975).

25. Although Ahmad Lutfi al-Sayyid was among the liberal Egyptian nationalists associated with Abduh, he did not come under attack, perhaps because his ideas were spread through press articles rather than through major monographs. For many years, he was the editor of *al-Jarida* and a founding member of the People's Party. He was director of the national library, then professor of philosophy and rector of the Egyptian University. He saw in despotism the main cause of Egyptian misery because he felt it had bred among Egyptians a distorted relation to political authority, characterized by passivity, lack of trust, and alienation. He advocated political freedom as the key to all other forms of freedom.

26. An English translation of the two books can be found in Qasim Amin, *The Liberation of Women—The New Woman: Two Documents in the History of Egyptian Feminism*, translated by Samiha Sidhom Peterson (Cairo: American University of Cairo Press, 1992).

27. For socioeconomic readings of the controversy, see Juan Ricardo Cole, "Feminism, Class, and Islam in Turn-of-the-Century Egypt," *International Journal of Middle East Studies* 13 (1981): 387–407, and Margot Badran, "Dual Liberation: Feminism and Nationalism in Egypt, 1870s–1925," *Feminist Issues* 8, no. 1 (1988): 15–34; see also the 1978 issue of *Al-Raida*, the magazine of the Institute for Women's Studies in the Arab World in Beirut, devoted to Qasim Amin. For a selection of Arab women's writings since this Nahda period, see Margot Badran and Miriam Cooke, eds., *Opening the Gates: A Century of Arab Feminist Writing* (London: Virago, 1990); and for a study of women's writings in the Egyptian press, see Beth Baron, *The Women's Awakening in Egypt: Culture, Society, and the Press* (New Haven, Conn.: Yale University Press, 1994).

28. Reference should be made here to two other protofeminist books published by men: Egyptian Murqus Fahmi's *Al-Mar'a fi al-Sharq* (The Woman in the East) in 1894 and

Tunisian Tahir al-Haddad's *Imra'atuna fi al-Shari'a wa al-Mujtama'* (Our Woman in Islamic Law and Society) in 1929. Both argued that Arab society was backward because women were backward due to social constraints such as veiling and seclusion, especially in the upper and middle classes, and due to lack of education, which was not sanctioned by religion.

29. Qasim Amin, *Les Egyptiens: Réponse à M. Le Duc d'Harcourt* (Cairo: Jules Barbier, 1894). I look at an analysis of this shift of position by the Syrian thinker Georges Tarabichi in the section on the gendering of critique in chapter 2.

30. One wonders, Does Amin mean modern science here? Medieval Islamic civilization did witness significant scientific productions and breakthroughs.

31. For information concerning the publication and European sources of these books, see the two articles by Sylvia Haim: "Blunt and al-Kawakibi," *Oriente Moderno* 35 (1955): 133–43, and "G. Alfieri and al-Kawakibi," *Oriente Moderno* 34 (1954): 321–34. For a study of the political reform ideas of al-Tahtawi, al-Tunisi, and al-Kawakibi, see Khaldun S. al-Husry, *Three Reformers: A Study of Modern Arab Political Thought* (Beirut: Khayats, 1966). For a recent bilingual (French–Arabic) collection of essays on Islamic reformism written for a conference held in June 2002 in Aleppo on the centenary of al-Kawakibi's death see Maher al-Charif and Salam Kawakibi, eds., *Le courant réformiste musulman et sa réception dans les sociétés arabes* (The Reformist Islamic Current and Its Reception in Arab Societies) (Damascus: Institut Français du Proche Orient, 2003).

32. Among the participants in this discussion about the Arab caliphate was Muhammad Abduh's student Rashid Rida. For a historical analysis of Rida's thoughts on the subject, see Mahmud Haddad, "Arab Religious Nationalism in the Era of Colonialism: Rereading Rashid Rida's Ideas on the Caliphate," *Journal of the American Oriental Society* 117, no. 2 (1997): 253–77.

33. For a discussion of the circumstances and factors behind the rise of Arab nationalism, see Rashid Khalidi, Lisa Anderson, Muhammad Muslih, and Reeva Simon, eds., *The Origins of Arab Nationalism* (New York: Columbia University Press, 1991).

34. On January 2, 2006, the Lebanese daily *al-Nahar* produced a special issue of its literary supplement (no. 721) called *Sana'i' al-Istibdad* (The Makings of Despotism) in tribute to two prominent members of its team: its famous editorialist Samir Kassir and its then director Jubran Tueni, both assassinated in Beirut for their critique of the Syrian regime. The issue's title is obviously an echo of Kawakibi's "Tabai' al-Istibdad" (Characteristics of Despotism). The introductory editorial refers to Kawakibi's critique of despotism and connects its articles to his early Nahda critique. The contributors to the supplement are important figures of contemporary Arab critique from Syria, Irak, Egypt, Lebanon, Morocco, and Bahrein.

35. See, for instance, the writings of Yassin al-Haj Saleh in *al-Hayat* (in the section called "Tayyarat" published every Sunday), *al-Nahar*, and elsewhere.

36. Ali Abdel Raziq, *Al-Islam wa Usul al-Hukm* (Islam and the Principles of Governing) Cairo: Matbaʿat Misr, 1925); quotation taken from Ali Abdel Raziq [Abd al-Raziq], "The Caliphate and the Bases of Power," in John J. Donohue and John L. Esposito, eds., *Islam in Transition: Muslim Perspectives* (New York: Oxford University Press, 1982; 2d ed., 2006), 37.

37. Abdel Raziq, "The Caliphate and the Bases of Power," 36.

38. Muhammad Rashid Rida, *Al-Khilafa wa al-Imama al-ʿUzma* (The Caliphate and the Great Imamate) (Cairo: Matbaʿat al-Manar, 1923). See also Haddad, "Arab Religious Nationalism in the Colonial Era."

39. Taha Husayn, *Fi al-Shiʿr al-Jahili* (On Jahili Poetry) (Cairo: Dar al-Nahr li al-Nashr wa al-Tawziʿ, 1996).

40. *Fi al-Shiʿr al-Jahili* was published in the Egyptian journal *al-Qahira* 149 (April 1995). It appeared together with the court document that condemned it in 1927 and a number of articles commenting on the court verdict and Taha Husayn's work, pp. 21–118. Shakib Arslan was among the fierce critics of Husayn's views of Jahili poetry: see his introduction "Al-Shiʿr al-Jahili, a Manhul am Sahih al-Nisba?" (Jahili Poetry: Fake or Original?), in Muhammad Ahmad al-Ghamrawi, *Al-Naqd al-Tahlili li Kitab "Fi al-Adab al-Jahili"* (The Analytic Critique of the Book *On Jahili Literature*) (Cairo: Al-Matbaʿa al-Salafiyya, 1929). Arslan argues that Husayn was simply repeating Western Orientalist views.

41. Taha Husayn, *Mustaqbal al-Thaqafa fi Misr* (Cairo: Matbaʿat al-Thaqafa fi Misr, 1944), translated into English by Sidney Glazer as *The Future of Culture in Egypt* (Washington, D.C.: American Council of Learned Societies, 1954).

42. Husayn, *The Future of Culture in Egypt*, 15.

43. Ibid., 3, 9. It is interesting to note that another Egyptian figure of the Nahda posed the same question and answered with even greater firmness in 1928: Salameh Musa (1887–1958), in his book *Al-Yawm wa al-Ghad* (Today and Tomorrow), published by his own publishing house based in Cairo (Salameh Musa li al-Nashr wa al-Tawziʿ), rejected emphatically all claims about the Arab, Asian, or Oriental character of Egypt. He argued that the time had come for Egyptians to take a clear stand and acknowledge their European identity after 130 years of hesitation. In his view, Napoleon, Muhammad Ali, the British, and the successive governors of Egypt introduced European institutions and ideas and liberated the Egyptians from the nightmare of the Orient. However, Egyptians had not yet fully accepted Europe as their natural sphere of belonging. He regarded Kamal Atatürk's Turkey to be an enviable model to be followed. As he saw things, those who still identified themselves with the Orient did it out of hatred for Europe, and they had to realize that there was nothing to be gained from associating themselves or Egypt with the Orient, whereas Europe had everything noble to offer: high philosophy, sophisticated literature, refined arts (unlike the ugly and vulgar Oriental forms of music and dance), and scientific achievements. He considered the Euro-

pean to be the noblest human being to have appeared on earth to date and European culture the most developed among existing cultures. He felt that Arab culture and Arab literature should at best be studied archeologically, like Babylonian or Phoenician cultures, and saw old Arab literature as foreign to contemporary Egyptians, who needed a language and a literature that expressed their modern world. He encouraged Egyptians to europeanize themselves, even through miscegenation.

44. Al-Banna's teachings were collected and published in Arabic as *Majmu'at Rasa'il al-Imam al-Shahid Hasan al-Banna* (Beirut: Dar a-Andalus, 1965). An English translation of a selection of these texts can be found in *Five Tracts of Hasan al-Banna (1906–1949)*, selected and translated by Charles Wendell (Berkeley and Los Angeles: University of California Press, 1978).

45. Books by Qutb translated into English include *Al-'Adala al-Ijtima'iyya fi al-Islam* (Social Justice in Islam) (Cairo: Misr: Maktabat Misr, 1949), as *Social Justice in Islam* by John B. Hardie and revised by Hamid Algar (Oneonta, N.Y.: Islamic Publications International, 2000); *Ma'alim fi al-Tariq* (Signs on the Way) (Cairo: Dar al-Shuruq, [1970s]), as *Milestones* (New Delhi: Islamic Book Service, 2001); and *Muqawwimat al-Tasawwur al-Islami* (Cairo: Dar al-Shuruq, 1986), as *Basic Principles of the Islamic Worldview*, translated by Rami David (North Haledon, N.J.: Islamic Publications International, 2006).

46. Qutb, *Social Justice in Islam*, 284–86.

2. Critique After the 1967 Defeat

1. Wannous's works were recently published in a three-volume collection, *Al-A'mal al-Kamila* (The Complete Works) (Beirut: Dar al-Adab, 2004). All quotations come from this collection, and the translations are my own. The third volume contains a detailed biography of Wannous as well as a bibliography of his writings, including information about the translation and performances of his individual plays. English translations of some of his plays can be found in Salma Khadra Jayyusi, ed., *Short Arabic Plays* (New York: Interlink Books, 2003), 412–451; and Salma Khadra Jayyusi and Roger Allen, eds., *Modern Arabic Drama* (Bloomington: Indiana University Press, 1995), 77–120. Some of his essays and some articles in English about his work can be found in the journal *al-Jadid* (1996, 1997, and 2001 issues), available online at http://www.aljadid .com. On Arab theater, including Wannous's, see Mas'ud Hamdan, *Poetics, Politics, and Protest in Arab Theatre: The Bitter Cup and the Holy Rain* (Brighton, U.K.: Sussex Academic Press, 2006).

2. See Wannous, *Haflat Samar min Ajl Khamseh Huzairan*, in *Al-A'mal al-Kamilah*, 1:123–229, for quotations from the play.

3. "Bayanat li Masrah ʿArabi Jadid" (Manifestos for a New Arab Theater), in *Al-Aʿmal al-Kamilah*, 3:5–239.

4. "Al-Hulm Yatadaʿa" (The Dream Collapses), in *Al-Aʿmal al-Kamilah*, 3:235–239.

5. Because of this peace agreement signed between Egypt and Israel, Israel withdrew from the Sinai, and Egypt left the Arab strategic unity, went its separate way, and established diplomatic relations with Israel.

6. Wannous, "Ana al-Janaza wa al-Mushayyiʿun" (I Am the Deceased and the Mourner), in *Al Aʿmal al-Kamila*, 3:440–42.

7. This interview is *Wa Hunak Ashiaʾ Kathira Kana Yumkin an Yatahaddath al-Marʾ ʿAnha* (There Are Still So Many Things One Could Talk About) (1997).

8. The 1986 interview is "Hawl al-Samt . . . wa Masʾuliyyat al-Muthaqqafin" (On Silence . . . and the Responsibility of the Intellectuals), in Wannous, *Al-ʿAmal al-Kamila*, 3:447–60.

9. "Al-Juʿ ila al-Hiwar" (The Hunger for Dialogue), in Wannous, *Al Aʿmal al-Kamila*, 1:39–44.

10. Faysal Al-Darraj is a Palestinian literary critic, and Gaber Asfour an Egyptian literary critic. Abdel Rahman Munif (1933–2004) was a Saudi-Iraqi novelist and critical thinker who had to flee both of his countries (Saudi Arabia and then Iraq) because of his ideas. He was himself a prominent critic of Arab culture and politics. In his five-volume novel *Mudun al-Milh* (Beirut: Al-Muʾassassa al-ʿArabiyya li al-Dirasat wa al-Nashr, 1986–1989; the first volume is available in English as *Cities of Salt*, translated by Peter Theroux [New York: Vintage, 1987]), he depicts the social and political transformations of the Persian Gulf cities since the beginning of the oil boom, accompanied by Western interventions and local power struggles. In addition to his historical novels on Iraq and other regions of the Arab world, he published in 1975 a landmark novel in prison literature, *Sharq al-Mutawassit* (East of the Mediterranean) (Beirut: Dar al-Taliʿa, 1975). The book became a cry of revolt against political imprisonment and torture in the Arab world. Sixteen years later, in 1991, he revisited the genre and wrote a more elaborate novel, *Al-An . . . Huna aw Sharq al-Mutawassit Marratan Ukhra* (Now . . . Here, or East of the Mediterranean Another Time) (Beirut: Al-Muʾassassa al-ʿArabiyya li al-Dirasat wa al-Nashr, 1992). Syrian Louay Hussein, however, in the book drawn from his own prison and torture experience, *Al-Faqd: Hikayat min Dhakira Mutakhayyala li Sajin Haqiqi* (The Loss: Stories from an Imaginary Memory of a Real Prisoner) (Damascus: Dar Petra, 2006), criticizes Munif's 1991 book for offering a somewhat romantic view of political incarceration as a painful sacrifice for the cause of the country. For Hussein, the prison experience ought not be presented as belonging to a culture of sacrifice because it is in reality the manifestation of a culture of death and suicide. What is left in a country, he asks, in which its youth are sacrificed to the benefit of despotic oppressors? A full dossier on Munif, including a biography and a bibliography as well as critical essays, can be found in Sonja Mejcher-

Atassi, ed., *Writing—a "Tool for Change": 'Abd al-Rahman Munif Remembered*, special issue of *MIT Electronic Journal of Middle East Studies (EJMES)* 7 (spring 2007), available at http://web.mit.edu/CIS/www/mitejmes/intro.htm.

11. It is interesting that this inner/outer dichotomy is found in many postcolonial settings: the inner seen as the realm of the authentic, the traditional, and the feminine, and the outer associated with Western technology, imitation, and the masculine. See Partha Chatterjee, "The Nationalist Resolution of the Women's Question," in Kumkum Sangari and Sudesh Vaid, eds., *Recasting Women: Essays in Indian Colonial History*, 233–53 (New Brunswick, N.J.: Rutgers University Press, 1990).

12. For a reconsideration of the trend of free adaptation in the Egyptian literature of the Nahda, see Samah Selim, "The Nahda, Popular Fiction, and the Politics of Translation," in Joseph Massad, Samia Mehrez, and Maha Yahya, eds., *Magda al-Nowaihi (1958–2004): In Memory*, a special issue of *MIT Electronic Journal of Middle East Studies* 4 (Fall 2004): 71–89.

13. Yassin Hafez, *Al-Hazimah wa al-Idiolojiyya al-Mahzumah* (The Defeat and the Defeated Ideology), written between 1967 and 1977, published in 1978, then reedited in Damascus by Dar Al-Hassad in 1997, and finally reprinted in Hafez's collected works, *Al-A'mal al-Kamila li Yassin al-Hafez*, in 2005, published in Beirut by Markaz Dirasat al-Wihda al-'Arabiyya.

14. For a biography of Zurayq, see Aziz al-Azmeh, *Qustantin Zurayq, 'Arabi li al-Qarn al-'Ishrin* (Qustantin Zurayq, an Arab for the Twentieth Century) (Beirut: Institute for Palestinian Studies, 2003). In 1999, shortly before his death, UNESCO honored Zurayq at a conference devoted to his work held in Beirut.

15. The Institute for Palestinian Studies was founded in Beirut in 1963 as an independent research, documentation, and publication center on Palestinian affairs and on the Arab-Israeli conflict. It can be accessed online at http://palestine-studies.org.

16. Qustantin Zurayq, *Al-A'mal al-Kamilah* (The Complete Works) (Beirut: Markaz Dirasat al-Wihda al-'Arabiyya, 1994). I discuss the Center for Arab Unity Studies more fully in chapter 3.

17. Also available in English: Qustantin Zurayq, *The Meaning of the Disaster*, translated by B. Winder (Beirut: Khayat's College Book Cooperative, 1956). For studies in honor of Zurayq in English, French, and Arabic, see Hisham Nashabe, ed., *Studia Palaestina: Studies in Honour of Constantine K. Zurayk* (Beirut: Institute for Palestine Studies, 1988); see also George N. Atiyeh and Ibrahim M. Oweiss, eds., *Arab Civilization: Challenges and Responses. Studies in Honor of Constantine K. Zurayk* (Albany: State University of New York Press, 1988).

18. See Qustantin Zurayq, *Ma'na al-Nakba* (The Meaning of the Disaster), in *Al-A'mal al-Kamilah*, 195–260, for the first, and *Ma'na al-Nakba Mujaddadan* (The Meaning of the Disaster Renewed), in *Al-A'mal al-Kamilah*, 989–1035, for the second.

19. Qustantin Zurayq, *Fi Maʿrakat al-Hadara*, in *Al-Aʿmal al-Kamilah*, 834. All translations from Zurayq are mine.

20. It is interesting to note here that Egyptian existentialist philosopher Abdel Rahman
Badawi (1917–2002) wrote a book praising Oswald Spengler in Arabic in 1941, *Spengler*
(Beirut: Dar al Qalam; Kuwait: Wakalat al-Matbuʿat, 1982). The same author translated with equal praise the work of Albert Schweitzer on the philosophy of civilization, *Kulturphilosophie* (Munich: C. H. Beck, 1925–1926), as *Falsafat al-Hadara* (Beirut: Dar al-Andalus, 1997). For information on Badawi and his work, see Mona Anis's
review of his two-volume autobiography *Sirat Hayati* (The Story of My Life) (Beirut:
Al-Muʾassassa al-ʿArabiyya li al-Dirasat wa al-Nashr, 2000) in *al-Ahram Weekly*,
no. 477 (April 2000): 13–19, accessible online at http://weekly.ahram.org.eg/2000/477/
bk1_477.htm.

21. Zurayq is aware of the nuances of these terms in the Western debates, particularly the
German ones: *civilization*, referring more to the material aspects, and *culture*, referring to the moral and spiritual aspects. He explicitly chooses to use them interchange-
ably. Zurayq, *Fi Maʿrakat al-Hadara*, 32.

22. See Elizabeth Suzanne Kassab, "An Arab Neo-Kantian Philosophy of Culture: Constantine Zurayk on Culture, Reason, and Ethics," *Philosophy East & West* 49, no. 4
(1999): 494–512; and Elizabeth Suzanne Kassab, "Phenomenologies of Culture and
Ethics: Ernst Cassirer, Alfred Schutz, and the Tasks of a Philosophy of Culture,"
Human Studies 25 (2002): 55–88.

23. Zurayq, *Fi Maʿrakat al-Hadara*, 981–82.

24. Qustantin Zurayq, *Nahnu wa al-Tarikh*, in *Al-Aʿmal al-Kamilah*, 547.

25. I discuss this postmodern critique of the Enlightenment in postcolonial contexts more
fully in chapter 5.

26. Anouar Abdel-Malek, *La pensée arabe contemporaine* (Paris: Seuil, 1970); the quotation comes from *Contemporary Arab Political Thought*, translated by Michael Pallis
(London: Zed, 1983), 21.

27. Sadik Al-Azm, "An Interview with Sadik al-Azm," *Arab Studies Quarterly* 19, no. 3
(1997), 116, 119.

28. Sadeq Jalal al-Azm, *Al-Naqd al-Dhati baʿd al-Hazima* (Self-Criticism After the Defeat)
(Beirut: Dar al-Taliʿa, 1969; new ed., Damascus: Dar Mamduh ʿAdwan, 2007).

29. Al-Azm, "An Interview with Sadik al-Azm," 114–15. The book referred to is al-Azm,
Al-Naqd al-Dhati baʿd al-Hazima.

30. Sadeq Jalal al-Azm, *Naqd al-Fikr al-Dini* (Critique of Religious Thought) (Beirut: Dar
al-Taliʿa, 1982; originally published in 1970). For his critique of the Palestinian resistance movement of the 1970s, see his two books *Dirasat Naqdiyya li Fikr al-Muqawama
al-Filistiniyya* (A Critical Study of the Thought of the Palestinian Resistance) (Beirut:
Dar al-ʿAwda, 1973) and *Dirasat Yasariyya Hawl al-Qadiyya al-Filistiniyya* (Leftist

Studies on the Palestinian Cause) (Beirut: Dar al-Taliʿa, 1970). For a later critique, see his article "Palestinian Zionism," *Die Welt des Islams* 28 (1988): 90–98.

31. Al-Azm, "An Interview with Sadik al-Azm," 116.

32. Al-Azm, *Al-Naqd al-Dhati baʿd al-Hazimah* (1969 ed.), 70.

33. Al-Azm, *Al-Naqd al-Dhati Baʿd al-Hazimah* (2007 ed.).

34. Faysal al-Darraj, *"Al-Naqd al-Dhati Baʿd al-Hazimah* fi Tabʿa Jadida: Jalal Sadeq al-Azm: Rahiniyyat al-Kitab al-Naqdi wa Rahin al-Hazima" (*Self-Criticism After the Defeat* in a New Printing: Jalal Sadeq al-Azm: The Contemporaneity of the Critical Book and the Contemporaneity of the Defeat), *al-Quds al-ʿArabi*, June 21, 2007.

35. Yassin al-Haj Saleh, "Al-Khamis min Huzayran 1967 fi Arbaʿiniha" (The 5th of June 1967 in Its Fortieth), *al-Hayat*, June 3, 2007.

36. In chapter 5, I examine the critique of this idea of the "middle" nation and of the conciliatory strategy behind it.

37. Al-Azm, "An Interview with Sadik al-Azm," 117.

38. Such debates between science, "materialism" (Marxism), and religion were also present in Catholic Church circles in the 1970s in Europe.

39. Sadeq Al-Azm, "The Importance of Being Earnest About Salman Rushdie," *Die Welt des Islams* 31 (1991), 2.

40. Ibid., 39.

41. Ibid., 35, 48, 49 (capitals in original). See *Pour Rushdie: Cent intellectuels Arabes et Musulmans pour la liberté d'expression* (Paris: La Découverte, Carrefour des Littératures, Colibri, 1993), translated into English as *For Rushdie: Essays by Arab and Muslim Writers in Defense of Free Speech* (New York: Braziller, 1994).

42. Abdallah Laroui, *L'idéologie arabe contemporaine: Essai critique* (Contemporary Arab Ideology: A Critical Essay) (Paris: François Maspero, 1967), translated into Arabic as *Al-Idiyolojiyya al-ʿArabiyya al-Muʿassira*, 2d ed. (Beirut: Al-Markaz al-Thaqafi al-ʿArabi, 1999); and *La crise des intellectuals arabes: Traditionalisme ou historicisme?* (Paris: François Maspero, 1974), translated into English as *The Crisis of the Arab Intellectual: Traditionalism or Historicism?* by Diarmid Cammell (Berkeley and Los Angeles: University of California Press, 1976), and into Arabic as *Al-ʿArab wa al-Fikr al-Tarikhi*, 4th ed. (The Arabs and Historical Thought) (Beirut: Al-Markaz al-Thaqafi al-ʿArabi, 1998).

43. Laroui, *The Crisis of the Arab Intellectual*, 84, 100, 88, 89, 129.

44. Ibid., viii.

45. Ibid., 154.

46. Ibid., 89–90.

47. Ibid., 10, 28.

48. Ibid., 44–80, and Laroui, *L'idéologie arabe contemporaine*, 117–23. This work was written almost a decade before Edward Said's *Orientalism* (New York: Pantheon Books, 1978), in which Said refers to Laroui's 1967 analysis of von Grunebaum's Orientalist

approach. Other precursors of Said are Anouar Abdel-Malek and A. L.Tibawi. For a good collection of their texts, see Alexander Lyon Macfie, ed., *Orientalism: A Reader* (New York: New York University Press, 2000).

49. Laroui, *The Crisis of Arab Intellectual*, 70.

50. Laroui, *L'idéologie arabe contemporaine*, 6, 51–52.

51. Ibid., 73. The translations from *L'idéologie arabe contemporaine* are mine.

52. Ibid., 74.

53. Ibid. 93.

54. Ibid., 90–91, 102.

55. Ibid., 113–14.

56. Laroui, *The Crisis of the Arab Intellectual*, 154.

57. Ibid., 128.

58. Ibid., 83.

59. Laroui, *L'idéologie arabe contemporaine*, 15.

60. Laroui, *The Crisis of the Arab Intellectual*, 169.

61. Ibid., 156–57.

62. Ibid., 147–48, 156.

63. Ibid., 176–77.

64. Ibid., 28.

65. Laroui, *L'idéologie arabe contemporaine*, 57.

66. Ibid., 61.

67. In this respect, I disagree with Ibrahim Abu-Rabiʿ regarding Laroui's intellectual development. Abu-Rabiʿ thinks that Laroui has moved away from his critical and, in particular, his Marxist stands and has become to some extent a defender of the Moroccan state monarchy, which he sees as a guarantee for the intellectual liberties of the elite. I think this judgment is too harsh. Whatever his connection with the Moroccan state institutions, Laroui, at least in his lectures and writings, has remained consistent in his basic critical positions. For a collection of his recent talks and essays, see his books *Islamisme, modernisme, liberalisme* (Casablanca: Centre Culturel Arabe, 1997) and *Islam et histoire* (Paris: Flammarion, 1999). See also Ibrahim Abu-Rabiʿ, the chapter "Abdallah Laroui: From Objective Marxism to Liberal Etatism" in his book *Contemporary Arab Thought: Studies in Post-1967 Arab Intellectual History*, 344–69 (London: Pluto Press, 2004). For an overview of Moroccan philosophy, see Kamal Abdel Latif, *As'ilat al-Fikr al-Falsafi fi al-Maghreb* (Questions of Philosophical Thought in the Maghreb) (Beirut: Al-Markaz al-Thaqafi al-ʿArabi, 2003). See also Laroui's three-volume memoirs, *Khawater al-Sabah* (Morning Thoughts) (Beirut: Al-Markaz al-Thaqafi al-ʿArabi, 2001; reprinted in 2003 and 2005).

68. Abdallah Laroui, *Mafhum al-Dawla* (The Concept of the State) (Beirut: Al-Markaz al-Thaqafi al-ʿArabi, 1981; 2d ed., 2001).

69. Abdallah Laroui, *Mafhum al-ʿAql* (The Concept of Reason) (Beirut: Al-Markaz al-Thaqafi al-ʿArabi, 1996; 2d ed., 2001).

70. Ibn Khaldun (1332–1406), the famous Maghrebi thinker, is considered to be one of the main precursors of the sociohistorical sciences, famous for his classical theoretical introduction to a universal history of peoples and nations, *The Muqaddimah: An Introduction to History*, translated from the Arabic by Franz Rosenthal and abridged and edited by N. J. Dawood (Princeton, N.J.: Princeton University Press, 1967; reprinted in 1969 and then in 1989 in the Bollingen series).

71. Abdel-Malek, *Contemporary Arab Political Thought*, 16.

72. Laroui, *The Crisis of the Arab Intellectual*, 43.

73. Nawal el-Saadawi relates her prison experience in *Mudhakkarati fi Sijn al-Nisa'* (My Memoirs in the Women's Prison) (Cairo: Dar al-Mustaqbal al-ʿArabi, 1983; Beirut: Dar al-Adab, 2000, 2d ed., 2005), which Marilyn Booth has translated as *Memoirs from the Women's Prison* (London: Women's Press, 1986).

74. *Al-Marʾa wa al-Jins* (Woman and Sex, 1972); *Al-Untha Hiya al-Asl* (The Feminine Is the Original) (1974); *Al-Rajul wa al-Jins* (Man and Sex, 1976); *Al-Marʾa wa al-Siraʿ al-Nafsi* (Woman and the Psychological Conflict, 1976); and *Al-Wajh al-ʿAri li al-Marʾa al-ʿArabiyya* (The Naked Face of the Arab Woman, 1977) all reprinted in Nawal el-Saadawi, *Dirasat al-Marʾa wa al-Rajul fi al-Mujtamaʿ al-ʿArabi* (Studies of Woman and Man in Arab Society), 2d ed. (Beirut: Al-Muʾassassa al-ʿArabiyya li al-Dirasat wa al-Nashr, 1990).

75. Nawal el-Saadawi, *The Nawal el Saadawi Reader* (London: Zed Books, 1997), 2. See also her introduction to her book *The Hidden Face of Eve: Women in the Arab World*, translated and edited by Sherif Hetata (Boston: Beacon Press, 1982).

76. The selections in *The Nawal el Saadawi Reader* offer a good overview of these leitmotivs.

77. El Saadawi, *The Nawal el Saadawi Reader*, 97–98.

78. Amal Amireh, "Framing Nawal el Saadawi: Arab Feminism in a Transnational World," *Sign: Journal of Women in Culture and Society* 26, no. 1 (2000): 215–49. See also Mohja Kahf, "Packaging 'Huda': Shaarawi's Memoirs in the United States Reception Environment," in Amal Amireh and Suheir Majaj, eds., *Going Global: The Transnational Reception of Third World Women Writers*, 148–72 (New York: Garland, 2000).

79. Georges Tarabichi, *Untha Didd al-Unutha: Dirasa fi Adab Nawal al-Saadawi ʿala Dawʾ al-Tahlil al-Nafsi* (Beirut: Dar al-Taliʿa, 1984), translated into English as *Woman Against Her Sex: A Critique of Nawal el-Saadawi, with a Reply by Nawal el-Saadawi* by Basil Hatim and Elizabeth Orsini (London: Saqi Books, 1988).

80. Amireh also notes the differences in the British and American editions: the first in London by Zed Books in 1980 and the second in Boston by Beacon in 1982.

81. *Al-Raida* is available online in English and Arabic at http://www.lau.edu.lb/centers
-institutes/iwsaw/raida.html. Of American origin but based in Beirut, Rosemary
Sayigh is a veteran independent scholar of Arab issues, in particular Palestinian and
women's issues. See, for instance, her books *Palestinians: From Peasants to Revolutionaries: A People's History* (London: Zed Books, 1979) and *Too Many Enemies: The Palestinian Experience in Lebanon* (London: Zed Books, 1993); and her articles "Roles and
Functions of Arab Women: A Reappraisal," *Arab Studies Quarterly* 3, no. 3 (1981): 258–
74; "Women's Nakba Stories: Between Being and Knowing," in Ahmad H. Sa'di and
Lila Abu-Lughod, eds., *Nakba: Palestine, 1948, and the Claims of Memory*, 135–58 (New
York: Columbia University Press, 2007).

82. Tajammu' al-Bahithat al-Lubnaniyyat (Lebanese Association of Women Researchers),
Al-Nisa' al-'Arabiyyat fi al-'Ishrinat: Huduran wa Huwwiyya (Arab Women in the
Twenties: Presence and Identity) (Beirut: Al-Bahithat, n.d.).

83. See the studies presented by Afaf Lutfi Sayyid Marsot, Amira Sonbol, and Leila Hud-
son in ibid. See also Amira Sonbol, ed., *Beyond the Exotic: Women's Histories in Islamic
Societies* (Syracuse, N.Y.: Syracuse University Press, 2005); Amira Sonbol, ed., *Women,
the Family, and Divorce Laws in Islamic History* (Syracuse, N.Y.: Syracuse University
Press, 1996); and Amira Sonbol, *Creation of a Medical Profession in Egypt, 1800–1922*
(Syracuse, N.Y.: Syracuse University Press, 1991).

84. Fatima al-Zahra' Qashshi's contribution on Algeria.

85. For instance, Malak Hafni Nassif and May Ziadeh, as discussed in Mervat Hatem's
contribution.

86. Information about the Women and Memory Forum can be found on its Web site at
http://www.wmf.org.eg.

87. Uma Narayan, *Dislocating Cultures: Identities, Traditions, and Third-World Feminism*
(New York: Routledge, 1997), 9–10, emphasis in the original. On issues of culture, feminism, and the global scene, see Uma Narayan and Sandra Harding, eds., *Decentering
the Center: Philosophy for a Multicultural, Postcolonial, and Feminist World* (Bloomington: Indiana University Press, 2000).

88. On Arab feminists' biographies of the modern era, see Cynthia Nelson, "Biography and
Women's History: On Interpreting Doria Shafik," in Nikki R. Keddie and Beth Baron,
eds., *Women in Middle Eastern History: Shifting Boundaries in Sex and Gender*, 310–33
(New Haven, Conn.: Yale University Press, 1991), and Cynthia Nelson, *Doria Shafik,
Egyptian Feminist: A Woman Apart* (Gainesville: University of Florida Press, 1996); see
also Huda Shaarawi, *Harem Years: The Memoirs of an Egyptian Feminist*, translated
and introduced by Margot Badran (New York: Feminist Press, 1986).

89. For the story of Elsadda's involvement in the Women and Memory Forum, see the interview with her in Arabic, "Al-Mar'a wa al-Dhakira: Hoda Elsadda Muqabala"
(Women and Memory: An Interview with Hoda Elsadda), in *Gender and Knowledge:*

Contribution of Gender Perspectives to Intellectual Formations, special issue of *Alif: Journal of Comparative Poetics* 19 (1999): 210–30. For a brief presentation of the story-telling project, see Hoda Elsadda, "Revisiting Popular Memory and the Constitution of Gendered Identity: The Story of a Project," *Middle East Women's Studies Review* 17, nos. 1–2 (2003): 1–2. See also Malak Hifni Nassif, *Al-Nisa'iyyat* (On Women's Issues), edited by Hoda Elsadda (Cairo: Women and Memory Forum, 1998); Hoda Elsadda, ed., *Min Ra'idat al-Qarn al-'Ishrin: Shakhsiyyat wa Qadaya* (From the Pioneers of the Twentieth Century: Personalities and Causes) (Cairo: Women and Memory Forum, 2001); Hoda Elsadda, Sumayya Ramadan, and Umayma Abu Bakr, eds., *Zaman al-Nisa' wa al-Dhakira al-Badila* (The Time of Women and the Alternative Memory) (Cairo: Women and Memory Forum, 1998); Hoda Elsadda and Emad Abu-Ghazi, *Maseerat al-Mar'a al-Misriyya: "'Alamat wa Mawaqif"* (The Journey of the Egyptian Woman: "Signs and Stands") (Cairo: National Council for Women, 2001), translated into English by Hala Kamal as *Significant Moments in Egyptian Women's History*, 2 vols. (Cairo: National Council for Women, 2001; reprinted in 2003).

90. Hoda Elsadda, "Al-Mar'a: Mantiqat Muharramat: Qira'a fi A'mal Qasim Amin" (The Woman: Taboo Realm. A Reading in the Works of Qasim Amin), in *Hagar: Kitab al-Mar'a* (Hagar: The Book of the Woman), 1:144–59 (Cairo: Sina li al-Nashr, 1993).

91. Ibid., 158, my own translation.

92. Hoda Elsadda, "Malak Hifni Nassif: Halaqa Mafquda min Ta'rikh al-Nahda" (Malak Hifni Nassif: A Missing Chain in the Historiography of the Nahda), in Hoda Elsadda and Salwa Bakr, *Hagar: Kitab al-Mar'a* (Hagar: The Book of the Woman), 2:109–19 (Cairo: Sina li al-Nashr, 1994).

93. Malak Hifni Nassif, as Bahithat al-Badiya, "A Lecture in the Club of the Umma Party," published in 1910 in the volume of her collected essays and lectures, *Al-Nisa'iyyat*. The lecture is translated in Margot Badran and Miriam Cooke, eds., *Opening the Gates: A Century of Arab Feminist Writing*, 228–38 (London: Virago, 1990), quote from p. 234. This book contains excerpts from the early women's writings of the Nahda. On the women's press of the time, see Beth Baron, *The Women's Awakening in Egypt: Culture, Society, and the Press* (New Haven, Conn.: Yale University Press, 1994).

94. See Elsadda's review of the conference, "Al-su'al al-'an: Mata Yataharrar al-Jami' . . . Rijalan wa Nisa'?!" (The Question Now: When Will All Be Liberated, Men and Women?!), *Wujuhat Nadhar* 21 (December 1999): 19–21. See also a more general review of the conference by Malek Abisaab and Rula Jurdi Abisaab, "A Century After Qasim Amin: Fictive Kinship and Historical Uses of 'Tahrir al-Mar'a," *Al Jadid* 6, no. 32 (2000): no page numbers.

95. Georges Tarabachi, "'Asr al-Nahda wa al-Jurh al-Narjissi: Nasawiyyat Qasim Amin wa Aliyyat al-Tamahi ma' al-Mu'tadi" (The Nahda Epoch and the Narcissist Wound: The Feminism of Qasim Amin and the Mechanism of Identification with the Aggressor),

in Georges Tarabachi, *Min al-Nahda ila al-Radda: Tamazzuqat al-Thaqafa al-ʿArabiyya fi ʿAsr al-ʿAwlama* (From Renaissance to Regression: The Tensions of Arab Culture in the Age of Globalization), 9–38 (Beirut: Dar al Saqi, 2000).

96. Ibid., 38, my translation.

97. Leila Ahmed, *Women and Gender in Islam* (New Haven, Conn.: Yale University Press, 1992), 161, 163.

98. Ibid., 153.

99. Ibid., 151.

100. For Ahmed's views on the phenomenon of reveiling, see her essay "Arab Women: 1995," in Hisham Sharabi, ed., *The Next Arab Decade: Alternative Futures*, 208–20 (Boulder, Colo.: Westview Press, 1988); and for an insightful description of her own intellectual journey of decolonization and feminization, see her autobiographical memoirs, *A Border Passage* (New York: Penguin, 1999), especially 206–307.

101. Marnia Lazreg, *The Eloquence of Silence: Algerian Women in Question* (New York: Routledge, 1994), 135–36, emphasis in the original.

102. Ibid., 137, italics in the original.

103. Marnia Lazreg, "Feminism and Difference: The Perils of Writing as a Woman on Women in Algeria," *Feminist Studies* 14, no. 1 (1988): 81–107.

104. Lazreg, *The Eloquence of Silence*, 141, emphasis in the original.

105. Joseph Massad, *Desiring Arabs* (Chicago: University of Chicago Press, 2007), 37, 53.

106. Ibid., 158, emphasis in the original.

107. Ibid., 233.

108. Janet Abu-Lughod, "Decolonizing the Women of Islam," *Gazelle Review* 7 (1980): 51–59.

109. Sayigh, "Roles and Functions of Arab Women."

110. See also Lila Abu-Lughod, "Orientalism and Middle East Feminist Studies," *Feminist Studies* 27, no. 1 (2001): 101–13.

111. Cynthia Nelson, "Old Wine, New Bottles: Reflections and Projections Concerning Research on Women in Middle Eastern Studies," in Earl L. Sullivan and Jacqueline S. Ismael, eds., *The Contemporary Study of the Arab World*, 127–52 (Edmonton: University of Alberta Press, 1991); see also Deniz Kandiyoti, "Contemporary Feminist Scholarship and Middle East Studies," in Deniz Kandiyoti, ed., *Gendering the Middle East: Emerging Perspectives*, 1–27 (Syracuse, N.Y.: Syracuse University Press, 1996).

112. Lazreg, "Feminism and Difference," 95, emphasis in the original. See also Lazreg's essay "The Triumphant Discourse of Global Feminism: Should Other Women Be Known?" in Amireh and Majaj, eds., *Going Global*, 29–38; see also Amal Amireh, "Writing the Difference: Feminists' Invention of the 'Arab Woman,'" in Bishnupriya Ghosh and Brinda Bose, eds., *Interventions: Feminist Dialogues on Third World Women's Literature and Film*, 185–212 (New York: Garland, 1997).

113. Especially relevant to the question of decolonizing feminist scholarship is Chandra Talpade Mohanty's famous and seminal essay "Under Western Eyes: Feminist Scholarship and Colonial Discourses," in Chandra Talpade Mohanty, Ann Russo, and Lourdes Torres, eds., *Third World and the Politics of Feminism*, 51–80 (Bloomington: Indiana University Press, 1991), and reprinted in Mohanty's book *Feminism Without Borders: Decolonizng Theory, Practicing Solidarity*, 17–42 (Durham, N.C.: Duke University Press, 2003). An inspiring work dealing with similar questions in the South Pacific is Linda Tuhiwai Smith's *Decolonizing Methodologies: Research and Indigenous Peoples* (London: Zed Books, 1999).

114. See Mervat Hatem, "Egyptian Discourses on Gender and Political Liberalization: Do Secularist and Islamist Views Differ?" *Middle East Journal* 48, no. 4 (1994): 661–76; and Marnia Lazreg, "From Nation to Gender: The Reproduction of Sexual Inequality in Algeria," in Tuomo Melasuo, ed., *National Movements and World Peace*, 123–40 (Aldershot, U.K.: Averbury, 1990).

115. See, for instance, Mervat Hatem, "Economic and Political Liberalization in Egypt and the Demise of State Feminism," *International Journal of Middle East Studies* 24 (1992): 231–51.

116. Mervat Hatem, "Toward the Development of Post-Islamist and Post-nationalist Feminist Discourses in the Middle East," in Judith Tucker, ed., *Arab Women: Old Boundaries, New Frontiers*, 29–48 (Bloomington: Indiana University Press, 1993).

117. Ibid., 45.

118. I am following here Shohat's own definition of herself in Ella Shohat, "Dislocated Identities: Reflections of an Arab-Jew," *Movement Research: Performance Journal* 5 (1992): 7–8; see also Evelyn Alsultany, "Dislocations, Arab Jews, and Multicultural Feminism: An Interview with Ella Shohat," *MIT Electronic Journal of Middle East Studies* 5 (2005): 50–56, and Ella Shohat, "Mizrahi Feminism: The Politics of Gender, Race, and Multiculturalism," *News from Within* 12, no. 4 (1996): 17–26. On identity and memory issues for migrants in the United States, see Ella Shohat, "Coming to America: Reflections on Hair and Memory Loss," in Amireh and Majaj, eds., *Going Global*, 284–300.

119. Ella Shohat, "Taboo Memories and Diasporic Visions: Columbus, Palestine, and Arab-Jews," in May Joseph and Jennifer Natalya Fink, eds., *Performing Hybridity* (Minneapolis: University of Minnesota Press, 1999), 149, 150; reprinted in Shohat's recent collection of essays, *Taboo Memories and Diasporic Voices*, 201–32 (Durham, N.C.: Duke University Press, 2006). See also Ella Shohat, "Sephardim in Israel: Zionism from the Standpoint of Its Jewish Victims," *Social Text* 19–20 (1988): 1–35, which was written, as she says, in dialogue with Edward Said's "Zionism from the Standpoint of Its Victims," *Social Text* 1 (1979): 7–58. See also her interview in the documentary film *Forget Baghdad* (2002), directed by Samir on four Jewish Arab Iraqi communists who moved to Israel: Shimon Ballas, Moshe Houri, Sami Michael, and Samir Naqqash.

120. Shohat, "Taboo Memories and Diasporic Visions," 149.

121. Ibid., 153.

122. As valuable samples of such contributions, see Lila Abu-Lughod, ed., *Remaking Women: Feminism in the Middle East* (Princeton, N.J.: Princeton University Press, 1998), in which the editor's introduction summarizes these issues cogently and clearly; and Deniz Kandiyoti, ed., *Women, Islam, and the State* (Houndmills, U.K.: Macmillan, 1991). See also Mervat Hatem, "Toward a Critique of Modernization: Narrative in Middle East Women Studies," *Arab Studies Quarterly* 15, no. 2 (1993): 117–22; and Margot Badran, *Feminists, Islam, and Nation: Gender and the Making of Modern Egypt* (Princeton, N.J.: Princeton University Press, 1995). For similar issues in Iran, see Afsaneh Najmabadi, "Veiled Discourse—Unveiled Bodies," *Feminist Studies* 19, no. 3 (1993): 487–518; and in Turkey, Nilüfer Göle, *The Forbidden Modern: Civilization and Veiling* (Ann Arbor: University of Michigan Press, 1996).

3. Marxist, Epistemological, and Psychological Readings of Major Conferences

1. Lebanese scholar Suheil Idriss (1925–2008) founded *al-Adab* in 1953 in Beirut to promote writers and critics who were committed to their societies and at the same time open to the world at large. It aimed at introducing Arab readers to the modern literary activity of their world and at allowing foreigners to have an adequate knowledge of this activity. See the editorial statement in the first issue of the first volume of *al-Adab*, 1953. It attracted the pens of many of the leading Arab literary figures of the time. It also offered translations of numerous works of world literature. The journal is now edited by Samah Idriss, the son of the founding editor.

2. *Al-Adab* 19, no. 11 (1971), 82–85.

3. *Al-Adab* 19, no. 11 (1971), 2–27.

4. It is interesting to note that such shifts continue to occur. Some current advocates of Islamic fundamentalism were previously in the leftist camp.

5. Shukry Ayad, "Mafhum al-Asala wa al-Tajdid wa al-Thaqafa al-Muʿassira" (The Concept of Authenticity and Renewal and Contemporary Arab Culture), *al-Adab* 19, no. 11 (1971): 2–5.

6. Mohammad Mazali, "Al-Asala wa al-Tafattuh" (Authenticity and Opening Up), *al-Adab* 19, no. 11 (1971): 13–17.

7. Zaki Naguib Mahmud, "Mawqif al-Thaqafa al-ʿArabiyya al-Haditha fi Muwajahat al-ʿAsr" (The Position of Modern Arab Culture in the Face of the Present Age), *al-Adab* 19, no. 11 (1971): 6–12.

8. Zaki Naguib Mahmud, *Tajdid al-Fikr al-ʿArabi* (The Renewal of Arab Thought) (Beirut: Dar al-Shuruq, 1971). In English, see Zaki Naguib Mahmud, "Rational Aspects of

the Classical Arabic Culture" and "The Intellectual Life in Contemporary Egypt," in George N. Atiyeh, ed., *Arab and American Cultures*, 87–92 and 201–8 (Washington, D.C.: American Enterprise Institute for Public Policy Research, 1977).

9. *Al-Ma'rifah* is a monthly cultural journal issued by the Syrian Ministry of Culture. Some of the 1974 conference papers are included in volume 148 (1974); some of the other papers are in *al-Adab* 22, no. 5 (1974).

10. Mahdi Amil, *Azamat al-Hadara al-'Arabiyya am Azamat al-Burjwaziyya al-'Arabiyya?* (The Crisis of Arab Civilization or the Crisis of Arab Bourgeoisie?) (Beirut: Dar al-Farabi, 1974).

11. *Retardation* is indeed a very awkward term in our context, with psychopathological and often pejorative connotations, but I use it for lack of a better translation of the Arabic term *takhalluf*, which means "running late, lagging behind, lacking progress, backwardness, underdevelopment."

12. Zaki Naguib Mahmud, "Al-Hadara wa Qadiyyat al-Taqaddum wa al-Takhalluf" (Civilization and the Issue of Progress and Retardation), *al-Adab* 22, no. 5 (1974): 6–9.

13. Shaker Mustafa, "Al-Ab'ad al-Tarikhiyya li Azamat al-Tatawwur al-Hadari al-'Arabi" (The Historical Dimensions of the Development Crisis of Arab Civilization), *al-Ma'rifa* 148 (1974): 7–52.

14. Ibrahim Abu-Lughod, "Al-Isti'mar wa Azamat al-Tatawwur fi al-Watan al-'Arabi" (Colonialism and the Crisis of Development in the Arab Homeland), *al-Ma'rifa* 148 (1974): 239–51.

15. There is indeed a dearth of information about the socioeconomic and cultural movements in the three centuries preceding the Napoleonic invasion of Egypt in 1798. Valuable in this respect is the work of Ahmad Dallal, which will appear in a forthcoming book called *Islam Before Europe*.

16. Fouad Zakariyya, "Al-Takhalluf al-Fikri wa Ab'aduhu al-Hadariyya" (Intellectual Retardation and Its Civilizational Dimensions), *al-Ma'rifa* 148 (1974): 60–82.

17. Adonis, "Khawatir Hawl Madhahir al-Takhalluf al-Fikri al-'Arabi" (Some Thoughts on the Manifestations of Intellectual Retardation in Arab Society), *al-Adab* 22, no. 5 (1974): 27–29.

18. Adonis, *Fatiha li Nihayat al-Qarn* (Overture to the Century's Endings) (Beirut: Dar al-Nahar, 1998, originally published in 1980), 11. The translation from this work is mine. ("Al-Fatiha" also refers to the Islamic prayer for the dead. Might Adonis have meant his collected texts to be such a prayer for the ending of the twentieth century?)

19. On the occasion of the fiftieth anniversary of the first issue of *al-Shi'r* in 1957, the Lebanese daily *al-Nahar* devoted a special issue of its literary supplement to those who consider themselves the heirs of *al-Shi'r* today. See *al-Mulhaq* 779 (February 11, 2007).

20. For a thorough study of el-Khal's life and work in Arabic, see Jacques Amateis SDB, *Yusuf al-Khal wa Majallatuhu Shi'r* (Yusuf al-Khal and His Journal *Shi'r*) (Beirut: Dar

al-Nahar and Orient Institut der Deutschen Morgenländische Gesellschaft, Band 94, 2004).

21. Adonis, *Al-Thabit wa al-Mutahawwil: Bahth fi al-Ibda' wa al-Itiba' 'Inda al-'Arab* (The Constant and the Changing: A Study in Creativity and Imitation Among Arabs), 4 vols., 7th ed. (Beirut: Dar al-Saqi, 1994; originally published in 1973), 1:34.

22. "Al-Istishraq wa al-Istishraq al-Ma'kus" (Orientalism and Orientalism in Reverse) was first published in Arabic in 1981 in a journal and then in a collection of essays by al-Azm, *Dhahniyyat al-Tahrim: Salman Rushdi wa Haqiqat al-Adab* (The Mental Taboo: Salman Rushie and the Truth Within Literature) (Beirut: Riad el-Rayyes, 1992); it appeared in English in 1981 in the journal *Khamsin* and was then included in A. L. Macfie, ed., *Orientalism: A Reader*, 217–38 (New York: New York University Press, 2000). I quote from the text as given in Macfie's collection.

23. Al-Azm, "Orientalism and Orientalism in Reverse," 219, 221.

24. Ibid., 234.

25. Anouar Abdel-Malek, "Al-Khususiyya wa al-Asala" (Specificity and Authenticity), *al-Adab* 22, no. 5 (1974): 41–43.

26. Anouar Abdel-Malek, *Rih al-Sharq* (The East Wind) (Cairo: Dar al-Mustaqbal, 1983). Abdel-Malek further developed his enthusiasm for the Far East in a more recent book on Japan, *Al-'Arab wa al-Yaban: Hiwar 'Arabi Yabani Hawla al-Hadara wa al-Qiyam wa al-Thaqafa fi al-Yaban wa al-Watan al-'Arabi* (The Arabs and Japan: Arab-Japanese Dialogue on Civilization, Values, and Culture in Japan and in the Arab Homeland) (Amman, Jordan: Muntada al-Fikr al-'Arabi, 1992).

27. Anouar Abdel-Malek, *Egypte société militaire* (Paris: Seuil, 1962), translated into English by Charles Lam Markmann as *Egypt: Military Society, the Army Regime, the Left, and Social Change Under Nasser* (New York: Random House, 1968), and into Arabic as *Al-Mujtama' al-Misri wa al-Jaysh: 1952–1967* (Cairo: Markaz al-Mahrusah li al-Buhuth wa al-Tadrib wa al-Nashr, 1998).

28. *Al-Adab* 22, no. 5 (1974), 51, my translation.

29. Muhammad Nuwaihi, "Nahwa al-Thawra fi al-Fikr al-Dini" (Toward a Revolution in Religious Thought), *al-Adab* 18, no. 5 (1970): 25–31 and 98–107.

30. The paper was developed into a book with the same title published in Beirut by Dar al-Adab in 1983. The quotation is taken from the excerpt translated in John J. Donohue and John L. Esposito, eds., *Islam in Transition: Muslim Perspectives* (New York: Oxford University Press, 1982; 2d ed., 2006), 160.

31. It is important to note that this poverty is in line with a long-standing critique of the ulemas since the early Nahda period, as discussed in chapter 1.

32. Muhammad Nuwaihi, "Al-Din wa Azamat al-Tatawwur fi al-Watan al-'Arabi" (Religion and the Crisis of Development in the Arab Homeland), *al-Ma'rifa* 148 (1974): 204–26.

33. Mohammad Arkoun and Nasr Hamid Abu Zayd advocated a literary, and historical approach to sacred text, which provoked rejection, even outrage, as described in chapter 4 on theological critique.

34. "Al-Bayan al-Khitami" (Final Declaration), *al-Ma'rifa* 148 (1974): 292–302.

35. François Bassili, "Ihtifa' bi al-Mu'tamar al-Hadari: Thalath Nadharat Naqdiyya" (Celebrating the Civilization Conference: Three Critical Views), *al-Adab* 22, no. 6 (1974): 71–73.

36. Amil, *Azamat al-Hadara al-'Arabiyya*.

37. A sample of studies in English on Marxism in the Arab world includes Maxime Rodinson, *Marxisme et monde musulman* (Paris: Edition du Seuil, 1966), with an abridged English translation by Jean Matthews, *Marxism and the Muslim World* (New York: Penguin, 1974; reprint, New York: Monthly Review Press, 1981); Hanna Batatu, *The Old Social Classes and the Revolutionary Movements of Iraq* (Princeton, N.J.: Princeton University Press, 1978; reprint, London: Saqi Books, 2004); and Tareq Y. Ismael, *The Communist Movement in the Arab World* (London: Routledge and Curzon, 2005).

38. Here I draw on Samir Amin, *L'eurocentrisme: Critique d'une idéologie* (Paris: Antropos-Economica, 1988), translated into English by Russell Moore as *Eurocentrism* (New York: Monthly Review Press, 1989). Of particular relevance is chapter 2 of part II, "The Construction of Eurocentric Culture." For an overview of Amin's thought, see his memoirs, *A Life Looking Forward: Memoirs of an Independent Marxist* (London: Zed Books, 2007), and his retrospective assessment of the second half of the twentieth century, *Itinéraire intellectuel: Regards sur le demi-siècle 1945–90* (Paris: L'Harmattan, 1993), translated into English as *Re-reading the Postwar Period: An Intellectual Itinerary*, translated by Michael Wolfers (New York: Monthly Review Press, 1994).

39. Amin elaborates on this idea in *Déconnexion, pour sortir du système mondial* (Paris: La Découverte, 1986), translated into English as *Delinking: Towards a Polycentric World*, translated by Michael Wolfers (London: Zed Books, 1990).

40. The center's name in Arabic is Markaz Dirasat al-Wihda al-'Arabiyya. For a publication of the conference proceedings, see *Al-Turath wa Tahaddiyyat al-'Asr fi al-Watan al-'Arabi: Al-Asala wa al-Mu'asara* (Heritage and the Challenges of the Age in the Arab Homeland: Authenticity and Contemporaneity) (Beirut: Markaz Dirasat al-Wihda al-'Arabiyya, 1985).

41. In 2008, the center launched a quarterly periodical in English called *Contemporary Arab Affairs*, edited by the center's director, Khair el-Din Haseeb, and published by Routledge.

42. Berrada's comments followed the paper by Abdallah Abdelda'im, "Al-Mas'ala al-Thaqafiyya Bayn al-Asala wa al-Mu'assara" (The Cultural Question Between Authenticity and Contemporaneity), in *Al-Turath wa Tahaddiyyat al-'Asr fi al-Watan al-'Arabi*, 687–714, and are on pp. 734–38.

43. Al-Khatibi's comments followed the paper by Ahmad Sidqi al-Dajjani, "Al-Fikr al-Gharbi wa al-Thaghyir fi al-Mujtama' al-'Arabi" (Western Thought and Change in Arab Society), in *Al-Turath wa Tahaddiyyat al-'Asr fi al-Watan al-'Arabi*, 303–30, and are on pp. 334–50, especially 343.

44. Lebanese historian Mas'ud Daher has made important contributions in this respect, first with a comparative study of the Arab and Japanese renaissances, *Al-Nahda al-'Arabiyya wa al-Nahda al-Yabaniyya: Tashabuh al-Muqaddamat wa Ikhtilaf al-Nata'ij* (The Arab Renaissance and the Japanese Renaissance: Similarity in the Beginnings and Difference in the Results) (Kuwait: Al-Majlis al-Watani li al-Thaqafa wa al-Adab, 1999), and second with a historical study of the Arab perception of Japan since the nineteenth century, *Al-Yaban bi 'Uyun 'Arabiyya, 1904–2004* (Japan in Arab Eyes, 1904–2004) (Beirut: Markaz Dirasat al-Wihda al-'Arabiyya, 2005). See also Mona Abaza, "Japan as Imagined by Arabs," *IIAS Newsletter* 27 (2002): 19. It is interesting to note that renowned Egyptian theologian Nasr Hamid Abu Zayd (whose work I discuss in chapter 4) lived in Japan from 1985 to 1989, translated Nitobe Inazo's (1862–1933) *Bushido*, and wrote a lengthy introduction to it: "Al-Bushido, al-Mukawwinat al-Taqlidiyya li al-Thaqafa al-Yabaniyya" (Bushido: The Traditional Constituents of Japanese Culture), 9–56 (Kuwait: dar Su'ad al-Sabbah, 1993). Egyptian historian Ra'uf Abbas also visited Japan as a scholar in the early 1970s and then again in the late 1980s. He wrote a comparative study of two Renaissance figures, Fukuzawa Yukishi (1835–1901) in Japan and Rifa'a Tahtawi (1801–1874) in Egypt, *Al-Tanwir al-Yabani wa al-Tanwir al-Arabi* (The Japanese and Egyptian Enlightenment) (Cairo: Mirit li al-Nashr wa al-Ma'lumat, 2001). See also Abdel-Malek, *Al-'Arab wa al-Yaban*. Some studies on the relation of the Arab world with the African and the Latin American continents have also come out recently. See, for instance, the papers in *Al-'Arab wa al-Da'ira al-Ifriqiyya* (The Arabs and the African Circle) (Beirut: Markaz Dirasat al-Wihda al-'Arabiyya, 2005) and in *El mundo arabe y América Latina* (Paris: UNESCO, 1997), translated into Arabic as *Al-Watan al-'Arabi wa Amirka al-Latiniyya* (The Arab Homeland and Latin America) (Beirut: Markaz Dirasat al-Wihda al-'Arabiyya, 2005).

45. Muhammad Abed al-Jabiri, "Ishkaliyyat al-Asala wa al-Mu'asara fi al-Fikr al-'Arabi al-Hadith wa al-Mu'asir: Sira' Tabaqi am Mushkil Thaqafi?" (The Problematic of Authenticity and Contemporaneity in Contemporary and Modern Arab Thought: A Class Conflict or a Cultural Problem?), in *Al-Turath wa Tahaddiyyat al-'Asr fi al-Watan al-'Arabi*, 29–58. Excerpts of al-Jabiri's work are available in English in the small volume *Arab-Islamic Philosophy: A Contemporary Critique* (Austin: University of Texas Press, 1999) (for this volume, the author's name is spelled "al-Jabri," but I continue to use the spelling "al-Jabiri" for consistency in my own presentation). These excerpts were selected and translated into English from a French translation of his work, *Introduction*

à la critique de la raison arabe (Introduction to the Critique of Arab Reason) (Paris: Editions la Découverte, Institut du Monde Arabe, 1994).

46. Al-Jabiri, *Arab-Islamic Philosophy*, 2–3, 130.

47. Ibid., 9–14.

48. Ibid., 6–7.

49. Ibid., 28.

50. Ibid., 21–22.

51. Al-Jabiri's most relevant writings in this connection are: *Al-Khitab al-ʿArabi al-Muʿassir* (The Contemporary Arab Discourse) (Beirut: Markaz Dirasat al-Wihda al-ʿArabiyya, 1982); *Takween al-ʿAql al-ʿArabi* (The Constitution of Arab Reason) (Beirut: Dar al-Taliʿa, 1984); *Bunyat al-ʿAql al-ʿArabi* (The Structure of Arab Reason) (Beirut: Dar al-Taliʿa, 1986); *Al-ʿAql al-Siyassi al-ʿArabi* (Political Arab Reason) (Beirut: Markaz Dirasat al-Wihda al-ʿArabiyya, 1990). A fourth volume in this series on the critique of Arab reason appeared just recently: *Al-ʿAql al-Akhlaqi al-ʿArabi: Dirasa Tahliliyya Naqdiyya li Nudhum al-Qiyam fi al-Thaqafa al-ʿArabiyya* (Moral Arab Reason: An Analytic Critical Study of the Value Systems in Arab Culture) (Beirut: Markaz Dirasat al-Wihda al-ʿArabiyya, 2006).

52. Al-Jabiri, *Arab-Islamic Philosophy*, 36.

53. The Moroccan government recently recognized Amazigh, the language of the Berbers of North Africa, as a legitimate national language. On the issue of the Amazigh minority within the context of a revisited Arab nationality, see the special issues of *al-Adab* 53, nos. 1–2 and 3–4 (2005); and for a similar discussion concerning the Kurdish community, see *al-Adab* 52, nos. 3–4 (2004). The *al-Jazeera* network also has an informative file on the Amazigh in North Africa, accessible at http://www.aljazeera.net/NR/exeres/AFAFF60F-D439-47A0-AA3B-D9CFB8B0E70D.htm.

54. See Abu Hamid Muhammad al-Ghazali, *Al-Munqidh min al-Dalal, wa al-Mufsih ʿan al-Ahwal* (Damascus: Dar al-Hikma, 1994), translated into English as *Deliverance from Error and Mystical Union with the Almighty*, translated and with an introduction by Muhmmad Abulaylah, and with an introduction and notes by George F. McLean (Washington, D.C.: Council for Research in Values and Philosophy, 2001). See also Averroes, *Fasl al-Maqal fi ma Bayna al-Hikma wa al-Shariʿa min al-Ittisal* (Cairo: Dar al Maʿarif, 1972), translated into English by George Hourani as *On the Harmony of Religion and Philosophy* (London: Luzac, 1961).

55. The first volume of this new edition of *Fasl el-Maqal* appeared in 1997, edited by al-Jabiri. For the same eight hundredth anniversary occasion, the Afro-Asian Philosophy Association held a meeting in Cairo in 1994, "Ibn Rushd and the Enlightenment." This meeting was declared the First Special International Afro-Asian Philosophy Conference. The proceedings of this meeting were published as Mourad Wahba and Mona

Abousenna, eds., *Averroes and the Enlightenment* (Amherst, N.Y.: Prometheus Books, 1996).

56. Georges Tarabichi, *Naqd Naqd al-'Aql al-'Arabi: Nadhariat al-'Aql* (Critique of the Critique of Reason: The Theory of Reason) (Beirut: Dar al-Saqi, 1996).

57. Parts of the newspaper exchange were translated into English and published in the U.S.-based English-language quarterly *aljadid* 17 (April 1997).

58. Since his early controversy with al-Jabiri, Tarabichi has published a series of books on the topic: *Ishkaliyyat al-'Aql al-'Arabi* (The Issues of Arab Reason, 2002); *Wihdat al-'Aql al-'Arabi* (The Unity of Arab Reason, 2002); *Al-'Aql al-Mustaqil fi al-Islam?* (The Resigned Reason in Islam? 2004), all published by Dar al-Saqi (Saqi Books) in Beirut and London.

59. See Mahmoud Amin al-Alim's review of al-Jabiri's book on political Arab reason, "Naqd al-Jabiri li al-'Aql al-Siyasi al-'Arabi" (Al-Jabiri's Critique of Arab Political Reason), in Mahmud Amin al-Alim, *Mawaqif Naqdiyya min al-Turath* (Critical Positions Regarding Tradition), 77–92 (Cairo: Dar Qadaya Fikriyya, 1997; reprint, Beirut: Dar al-Farabi, 2007).

60. For a critique of Renan's Orientalism, see Edward Said, *Orientalism* (New York: Pantheon Books, 1978).

61. Anke von Kügelgen, *Averroes und die arabische Moderne: Ansätze zu einer Neubegründung des Rationalismus im Islam* (Averroes and Arabic Modernity: Attempts at a New Foundation of Rationalism in Islam), Islamic Philosophy, Theology, and Science, vol. 19 (Leiden: Brill, 1994). Von Kügelgen presents a brief summary of this detailed study in " 'Averroisten' im 20. Jahrhundert—Zu Ibn-Rušd-Rezeption in der arabischen Welt" (Averroists in the Twentieth Century: On the Reception of Ibn Rush in the Arab World), in Friedrich Niewöhner and Loris Sturlese, eds., *Averroismus im Mittelalter und in der Renaissance* (Averroes in the Middle Ages and in the Renaissance), 351–71 (Zürich: Spur, 1994). For a summary of her findings in English, see Anke von Kügelgen, "A Call for Rationalism: 'Arab Averroists' in the Twentieth Century," in *Averroes and the Rational Legacy in the East and the West*, special issue of *Alif: Journal of Comparative Poetics* 16 (1996): 97–132.

62. Saadallah Wannous, "Al-Thaqafa al-Wataniyya wa al-Wa'y al-Tarikhi" (On National Culture and Historical Awareness), *Qadaya wa Shahadat* 4 (1991): 5–39.

63. See Yassin Hafez, *Al-Hazima wa al-Idiolojia al-Mahzuma* (The Defeat and the Defeated Ideology) (Damascus: Dar Al-Hassad, 1997; originally published in 1978), also reprinted in Yassin Hafez, *Al-A'mal al-Kamila li Yassin al-Hafez* (The Collected Works of Yassin Hafez) (Beirut: Markaz Dirasat al-Wihda al-'Arabiyya, 2005).

64. Georges Tarabichi, *Al-Muthaqqafun al-'Arab wa al-Turath: Al-Tahlil al-Nafsi li 'Isab Jama'i* (Arab Intellectuals and Tradition: A Psychological Analysis of a Collective Neurosis) (Riad: El Rayyes Books, 1991).

65. Hence, the title of one of Tarabachi's books expands on this idea: *Min al-Nahda ila al-Radda: Tamazzuqat al-Thaqafa al-'Arabiyya fi 'Asr al-'Awlama* (From Renaissance to Regression: Tensions of Arab Culture in the Age of Globalization) (Beirut: Dar al-Saqi, 2000).

66. Hisham Djaït, *L'Europe et l'Islam* (Paris: Editions du Seuil, 1978); quotation taken from the English translation by Peter Heinegg, *Europe and Islam* (Berkeley and Los Angeles: University of California Press, 1985), 107.

67. Hassan Hanafi, *Muqaddima fi 'Ilm al-Istighrab* (Introduction to the Science of Occidentalism) (Beirut: Al-Mu'assassa al-Jami'iyya li al-Dirasat wa al-Nashrwa al-Tawzi', 1992).

68. In 2005, Tarabichi reprinted large sections of this book devoted to the analysis of Hanafi in a new volume, *Izdiwajiyyat al-'Aql: Dirasa Tahliliyya Nafsiyya li Kitabat Hassan Hanafi* (The Duality of Reason: An Analytical-Psychological Study of the Writings of Hassan Hanafi) (Damascus: Dar Petra, 2005). Some fifteen years earlier, in 1989, the Paris-based journal *al-Yom al-Sabi'* (The Seventh Day) had run a series of dialogues between Hassan Hanafi and Muhammad Abed al-Jabiri on various issues pertaining to secularism, liberalism, Nassirism, Arab unity, the Palestinian cause, the French Revolution, modernity, and tradition. Then the journal invited intellectuals to comment on the exchanges and gave Hanafi and al-Jabiri the opportunity to reply at the end. In 1990, the whole was edited by Jalloul Faysal under the title *Hiwar al-Mashreq wa al-Maghreb* (Dialogue of the Mashreq and the Maghreb) and published in Cairo by Madbuli Bookshop. Among the commentators was Georges Tarabichi, who strongly attacked both men in a piece called "Al-Intelligentsia al-'Arabiyya wa al-Idrab 'an al-Tafkir" (The Arab Intelligentsia and the Strike on Thinking), 136–46.

69. The Mu'tazilites were theologians of the ninth century who advocated a rationalist interpretation of the sacred text and theological issues.

70. Mahmud Amin al-Alim, "Mashru' Hassan Hanafi al-Hadari" (Hassan Hanafi's Civilizational Project), in al-Alim, *Mawaqif Naqdiyya min al-Turath*, 15–64.

4. Critique in Islamic Theology

1. Mohammed Arkoun, *Rethinking Islam Today*, Occasional Paper Series (Washington, D.C.: Center for Contemporary Arab Studies, Georgetown University, 1987), and Mohammed Arkoun, *The Unthought in Contemporary Islamic Thought* (London: Saqi Books in association with the Institute of Ismaili Studies, 2002). The latter contains a bibliography of Arkoun's books in English, French, and Arabic.

2. Arkoun, *The Unthought in Contemporary Islamic Thought*, 32–33, emphasis in the original.

3. Arkoun, *Rethinking Islam Today*, 17, emphasis in the original.

4. Arkoun, *The Unthought in Contemporary Islamic Thought*, 25.

5. Arkoun, *Rethinking Islam Today*, 3–4.

6. Ibid., 9, emphasis in the original.

7. Ibid., 13. *Mushaf* refers to the compiled text of the Qur'an.

8. Arkoun, *The Unthought in Contemporary Islamic Thought*, 12.

9. He also calls it "emergent reason" (ibid., 22).

10. Mohammed Arkoun, *Pour une critique de la raison islamique* (Toward a Critique of Islamic Reason) (Paris: Maisonneuve et Larose, 1984).

11. Gustav E. von Grunebaum, *Modern Islam: The Search for Cultural Identity* (Berkeley and Los Angeles: University of California Press, 1962); Arkoun's critical article is "L'Islam moderne vu par le Professeur G. E. von Grunebaum" (Modern Islam Seen by Professor G. E. von Grunebaum), *Arabica* 11 (1964): 113–26. The writings of von Grunebaum have been the object of more than one critical analysis. See, for instance, Abdallah Laroui, "The Arabs and Cultural Anthropology: Notes on the Method of Gustav von Grunebaum," in Abdallah Laroui, *The Crisis of the Arab Intellectual: Traditionalism or Historicism?* translated by Diarmid Cammell, 44–80 (Berkeley and Los Angeles: University of California Press, 1976).

12. Von Grunebaum, *Modern Islam*, 40, quoted in Arkoun, "L'Islam moderne vu par le Professeur G. E. von Grunebaum," 114.

13. Arkoun, *Rethinking Islam Today*, 24.

14. Mohammed Arkoun, *La pensée arabe* (Arab Thought) (Paris: Presses Universitaires de France, 1975; 5th ed., 1995), translated into Arabic, English, Spanish, Swedish, and Italian.

15. Arkoun, *The Unthought in Contemporary Islamic Thought*, 34, emphasis in the original.

16. For instance, see Hamid Nasr Abu Zayd, *Al-Tafkir fi Zaman al-Takfir: Didd al-Jahl wa al-Zayf wa al-Khurafa* (Thinking in the Time of Anathema: Against Ignorance and Falsehood and Myth) (Cairo: Dar Sina li al-Nashr, 1995), 226–30.

17. In Arabic, the institute's name is al-Mu'assassa al-'Arabiyya li al-Tahdith al-Fikri.

18. *Al-Hadatha wa al-Hadatha al-'Arabiyya* (Modernity and Arab Modernity) (Beirut: Al-Mu'assassa al-'Arabiyya li al-Tahdith al-Fikri and Dar Petra, 2005). The volume was dedicated to Edward Said.

19. The thesis was soon published: Muhammad Ahmad Khalafallah, *Al-Fann al-Qasasi fi al-Qur'an al-Karim* (The Art of Narration in the Qur'an) (Cairo: Maktabat al-Nahda al-Misriyya, 1958).

20. Nasr Hamid Abu Zayd, *Mafhum al-Nass: Dirasah fi 'Ulum al-Qur'an* (The Concept of the Text: A Study in the Sciences of the Qur'an) (Cairo: Al-Hay'a al-Misriyya al-'Amma li al-Kitab, 1990).

21. Nasr Hamid Abu Zayd, *Naqd al-Khitab al-Dini* (The Critique of Religious Discourse) (Cairo: Dar Sina li al-Nashr, 1992; 2d ed., 1994).

22. For a concise and informative presentation of his case, see "The Case of Abu Zaid," *Index on Censorship* 25, no. 4 (1996): 30–39, and Elliot Colla and Ayman Bakr, "'Silencing Is at the Heart of My Case': Nasr Abu Zayd, Interview," in Joel Beinin and Joe Stork, eds., *Political Islam: Essays from Middle East Report*, 327–34 (Berkeley and Los Angeles: University of California Press, 1997). See also two articles about his case and work: George N. Sfeir, "Basic Freedoms in a Fractured Legal Culture: Egypt and the Case of Nasr Hamid Abu Zayd," *Middle East Journal* 52, no. 3 (1998): 402–14, and Charles Hirschkind, "Heresy or Hermeneutics: The Case of Nasr Hamid Abu Zayd," *American Journal of Islamic Social Sciences* 12, no. 4 (1995): 464–77. For a personal and intellectual biography, see Esther R. Nelson and Nasr Hamid Abu Zaid, *Voice of an Exile: Reflections on Islam* (Westport, Conn.: Praeger, 2004). Of the rare writings by Abu Zayd in English, see *Reformation of Islamic Thought: A Critical Historical Analysis* (Amsterdam: Amsterdam University Press, 2006), which was commissioned by the Netherlands Scientific Council for Government Policy. For a cogent and informative review of a recent lecture by Abu Zayd presenting the main points of his project developed in *Reformation of Islamic Thought*, see Hala Halim, "Of Hermeneutics and Reform," *al-Ahram Weekly* 15–21 (November 2007), available at http://weekly.ahram.org.eg/2007/871/cu4.htm. Another piece by Abu Zayd can be found online, "The Qur'anic Concept of Justice," *Journal for Intercultural Philosophy, Polylog* 3 (2001), available at http://them.polylog.org/3/fan-en.htm. Finally, see his article "The Dilemma of the Literary Approach to the Qur'an," *Alif: Journal of Comparative Poetics* 23 (2003): 8–47.

23. I refer to the 1994 edition of *Naqd al-Khitab al-Dini*.

24. For the writings of some of the prominent Islamists in English translation, see, for instance, Muhammad al-Ghazzali, *Our Beginning in Wisdom*, translated by Ismail R. el Faruqi (New York: Octagon Books, 1975), and Yusuf al Qaradawi, *Islamic Awakening Between Rejection and Extremism* (Herndon, Va.: American Trust Publication and the International Institute of Islamic Thought, 1991). See also the latest edition of John Donohue and John L. Esposito, eds., *Islam in Transition: Muslim Perspectives* (New York: Oxford University Press, 1982; 2d ed., 2006).

25. See, for instance, Fadwa el Guindi, "Veiling Infitah with Muslim Ethic: Egypt's Contemporary Islamic Movement," *Social Problems* 28, no. 4 (1981): 465–85.

26. For a good description of this Islamization of Egyptian public life by the militant Islamist groups, on the one hand, and the state, on the other, see Salwa Ismail, "Confronting the Other: Identity, Culture, Politics, and Conservative Islamism in Egypt," *International Journal for Middle Eastern Studies* 30 (1998): 199–225; also Salwa Ismail, *Rethinking Islamist Politics: Culture, the State, and Islamism* (London: I. B. Tauris, 2003).

27. Abu Zayd, *Naqd al-Khitab al-Dini*, 1994 ed., 119, 126. All translations of quotes from Abu Zayd's work are mine.

28. The literature on Islamist militant groups and Islamic revivalism in general is huge and growing. Here is a small sample of suggested readings: *Islam and Politics*, special issue of *Arab Studies Quarterly* 4, nos. 1–2 (1982); *Islam and Politics*, special issue of *Third World Quarterly* 10, no. 2 (1988); Saad Eddin Ibrahim, *Egypt, Islam, and Democracy: Critical Essays* (Cairo: American University of Cairo Press, 2002); Bassam Tibi, *The Challenge of Fundamentalism: Political Islam and the New World Disorder* (Berkeley and Los Angeles: University of California Press, 1998); Beinin and Stork, eds., *Political Islam*; Azmi Bishara, "Islam and Politics in the Middle East," in Jochen Hippler and Andrea Lueg, eds., *The Next Threat: Western Perceptions of Islam*, 82–115 (London and Boulder, Colo.: Pluto in association with the Transnational Institute, 1995); Philip Khoury, "Islamic Revival and the Crisis of the Secular State in the Arab World: A Historical Reappraisal," in Ibrahim Ibrahim, ed., *Arab Resources: The Transformation of a Society*, 213–36 (London and Washington, D.C.: Croom Helm and Center for Contemporary Arab Studies, Georgetown University, 1983); Yvonne Haddad, John Obert Voll, and John L. Esposito, eds., *The Contemporary Islamic Revival: A Critical Survey and Bibliography* (New York: Greenwood Press, 1991); John Esposito, *The Islamic Threat: Myth or Reality?* (New York: Oxford University Press, 1992); Barbara Freyer Stowasser, *The Islamic Impulse* (London and Washington, D.C.: Croom Helm and Center for Contemporary Arab Studies, Georgetown University, 1987).

29. In Colla and Bakr, " 'Silencing Is at the Heart of My Case': Nasr Abu Zayd, Interview," 330–31.

30. Nasr Hamid Abu Zayd, *Dawa'ir al-Khawf: Qira'a fi Khitab al-Mar'a* (The Circles of Fear: A Reading in the Discourse on Women) (Beirut: Al Markaz al-Thaqafi al-ʿArabi, 2000). The chapter "Khitab al-Nahda wa al-Khitab al-Ta'ifi," was translated and introduced by Mona Mikhail as "The Sectarian and the Renaissance Discourse," *Alif: Journal of Comparative Poetics* 19 (1999): 203–22.

31. Mohammad Arkoun, *Lectures du Coran* (Readings of the Qu'ran) (Paris: Maisonneuve et Larose, 1982). The article is Nasr Hamid Abu Zayd, "Al-Urthudhuksiyya al-Muʿammama: ʿIndama Yudmaj al-Tarikh al-Ijtimaʿi bi al-Muqaddas" (The Generalized Orthodoxy: When Social History is Conflated with the Sacred), *al-Naqid* 74 (1994): 26–34.

32. Abu Zayd, *Dawa'ir al-Khawf*, 6.

33. Both books were edited by Buthaina Shaaban and published in 1998 in Damascus by Dar al-Mada li al-Thaqafa wa al-Nashr. Short excerpts from both books translated into English are found in Margot Badran and Miriam Cooke, eds., *Opening the Gates: A Century of Arab Feminist Writing*, 270–78 (London: Virago, 1990), and in Aziza al-Hibri, ed., *Women and Islam*, special issue of *Women's Studies International Forum*

(Oxford, U.K.: Pergamon Press, 1982), 221–26. For a presentation of Zain al-Din's thought, see Nazik Saba Yared, "Nazira Zain al-Din (1980–1976): Bayna al-Tahaddi wa al-Iltizam" (Nazira Zain al-Din [1908–1976]: Between Defiance and Commitment), in Tajammu' Bahithat al-Lubnaniyaat, ed., *Al-Nisa' al-'Arabiyat fi al-'Ishriniyyat Huduran wa Huwiyya* (Arab Women in the Twenties: Presence and Identity), 243–61 (Beirut: Bahithat, n.d.).

34. Quoted by Fawwaz Traboulsi in "An Intelligent Man's Guide to Modern Arab Feminism," *al-Raida* 20, no. 100 (Winter 2003): 15–19.

35. Fatima Mernissi, *Le harem politique* (Paris: Albin Michel, 1987), translated by Mary Jo Lakeland as *The Veil and the Male Elite: A Feminist Interpretation of Women's Rights in Islam* (Reading, Mass.: Addison-Wesley, 1991). The book was banned in Morocco by a theological decree. I quote from the English translation.

36. Mernissi, *The Veil and the Male Elite*, 10, 11.

37. Ibid., 44–45.

38. *Qibla* is the orientation of Mecca toward which a Muslim should turn while praying.

39. The year 622 AD, when the Prophet fled Mecca to Medina. This date is also taken to be the year zero in Islamic historiography.

40. For an interesting study on the ideal typification of the Prophet's wives and their use as models of inspiration and justification, see Ghassan Ascha, "The 'Mothers of the Believers': Stereotypes of the Prophet Muhammad's Wives," in Ria Kloppenborg and Wouter J. Hanegraaff, eds., *Stereotypes in Religious Traditions*, 89–107 (Leiden: Brill, 1995).

41. Mernissi, *The Veil and the Male Elite*, 148.

42. See Mahmoud Mohamed Taha, *The Second Message of Islam* (Syracuse, N.Y.: Syracuse University Press, 1987). It is translated and introduced by his student Abdullahi Ahmed An-Na'im. The introduction presents an informative background to Taha's life and work. An-Na'im, a lawyer, has been working toward the implementation of Taha's ideas in Islamic legislation. See, for instance, An-Na'im's book *Toward an Islamic Reformation: Civil Liberties, Human Rights, and International Law* (Syracuse, N.Y.: Syracuse University Press, 1990) and the volume he edited, *Human Rights in Cross-Cultural Perspectives: A Quest for Consensus* (Philadelphia: University of Pennsylvania Press, 1992).

43. Leila Ahmed, *Women and Gender in Islam: Historical Roots of a Modern Debate* (New Haven, Conn.: Yale University Press, 1992). See also her essay "Early Islam and the Position of Women: The Problem of Interpretation," in Nikki R. Keddie and Beth Baron, eds., *Women in Middle Eastern History: Shifting Boundaries in Sex and Gender*, 58–73 (New Haven, Conn.: Yale University Press, 1991).

44. Ahmed, *Women and Gender in Islam*, 91.

45. Ibid.

46. Ibid., 95. For more on the issue of gender and Qur'anic interpretation, see Barbara Freyer Stowasser, *Women in the Qur'an, Traditions, and Interpretation* (New York: Oxford University Press, 1994); and for shorter pieces by Stowasser, see "Gender Issues and Contemporary Quran Interpretation," in Yvonne Yazbeck Haddad and John L. Esposito, eds., *Islam, Gender, and Social Change*, 30–44 (New York: Oxford University Press, 1998), and "Women's Issues in Modern Islamic Thought," in Judith E. Tucker, ed., *Arab Women: Old Boundaries, New Frontiers*, 3–28 (Bloomington: Indiana University Press, 1993). See also al-Hibri, ed., *Women and Islam*.

47. Hassan Hanafi, *Al-Din wa al-Thawra fi Misr (1952–1981)* (Religion and Revolution in Egypt [1952–1981]), 8 vols. (Cairo: Maktabat Madbuli, 1988–1989).

48. I quote from the first sixty pages of the first issue of *The Islamic Left* translated by Toufic Ben Amor for the coursepack of Professor George Saliba's course "Contemporary Islamic Civilization" at the Department of Middle East and Asian Languages and Cultures at Columbia University. In these pages, Hanafi explains the objectives and rationale of the movement and the periodical. Before being included in *The Islamic Left*, this translation was published in Hanafi, *Al-Din wa al-Thawra fi Misr (1952–1981)*, vol. 8: *Al-Yasar al-Islami wa al-Wihda al-Wataniyya* (The Islamic Left and National Unity), 1–59. Two of Hanafi's articles available in English are: "The Relevance of the Islamic Alternative in Egypt," *Arab Studies Quarterly* 4, nos. 1–2 (1980): 54–74, and "From Decolonization to Cultural Liberation," in Tuomo Melasuo, ed., *National Movements and World Peace*, 159–68 (Aldershot, U.K.: Avebury, 1990); see also his two-volume work in English *Cultures and Civilizations: Conflict or Dialogue?* (Cairo: Book Center for Publishing, 2007).

49. In fact, this book is the first volume of Hanafi's two-volume work *Qadaya Mu'assira* (Contemporary Issues) (Cairo: Dar al-Fikr al-'Arabi, 1976–77; new ed., Beirut: Dar al-Tanwir, 1981): *Fi Fikrina al-Mu'assir* (On Our Contemporary Thought) is devoted, as Hanafi says in the introduction, to the articles he wrote on the impact of the dramatic events of the late 1960s on contemporary Arab thought; and *Fi al-Fikr al-Gharbi al-Mu'assir* (On Contemporary Western Thought) is devoted to contemporary Western thought but considered and analyzed from a non-Western point of view. The article in question is on pages 297–334 of the 1981 edition of *Fikrina al-Mu'assir*.

50. More serious work in this regard has been produced in South Asian scholarship. See, for instance, Dipesh Chakrabarty, *Provincializing Europe: Postcolonial Thought and Historical Difference* (Princeton, N.J.: Princeton University Press, 2000).

51. Hassan Hanafi, *Al-Turath wa al-Tajdid: Mawqifuna min al-Turath* (Heritage and Renewal: Our Position Regarding Tradition) (Cairo: Al-Markaz al-'Arabi li al-Bahth wa al-Nashr, 1980); Hassan Hanafi, *Min al-'Aqida ila al-Thawra: Muhawala fi I'adat Bina' 'Ilm Usul al-Din* (From Doctrine to Revolution: An Attempt at Rebuilding Fundamental Theology),

5 vols. (Cairo: Maktabat Madbuli, 1988). Another attempt at searching for revolutionary elements in tradition is the work of the Syrian Marxist philosopher Tayyib Tizini. His study of tradition aims at finding in it ideas regarding materialism and atheism that will help revolutionize Arab culture and connect it with universal culture. See Tayyib Tizini, *Min al-Turath ila al-Thawra* (From Tradition to Revolution) (Beirut: Dar Ibn Khaldun, 1976). As we will see, however, not all secularists base their arguments on tradition.

52. See Anke von Kügelgen, *Averroes und die arabische Moderne: Ansätze zu einer Neubegründung des Rationalismus im Islam* (Averroes and Arabic Modernity: Attempts at a New Foundation of Rationalism in Islam), 204–37, Islamic Philosophy, Theology, and Sciences, vol. 19 (Leiden: Brill 1994); and Nasr Hamid Abu Zayd, "Al-Turath bayn al-Ta'wil wa al-Talwin: Qira'a fi Mashruʿ al-Yasar al-Islami" (Turath Between Interpretation and Coloring: A Reading in the Project of the Islamic Left), in Abu Zayd, *Naqd al-Khitab al-Dini* (1994 ed.), 137–93.

53. Mahmud Amin al-Alim, "Mashruʿ Hassan Hanafi al-Hadari" (Hassan Hanafi's Civilizational Project), in Mahmud Amin al-Alim, *Mawaqif Naqdiyya min al-Turath* (Critical Positions Regarding Tradition), 15–64 (Cairo: Dar Qadaya Fikriyya, 1997; reprint, Beirut: Dar al-Farabi, 2007).

54. Fouad Zakariyya, *Al-Haqiqa wa al-Khayal fi al-Haraka al-Islamiyya al-Muʿassira* (Cairo: Dar Sina li al-Nashr, 1988), English translation: *Myth and Reality in the Contemporary Islamist Movement*, translated and with an introduction and bibliography by Ibrahim M. Abu-Rabiʿ (London: Pluto Press, 2005).

55. For Ateek, I refer to *Justice and Only Justice: A Palestinian Theology of Liberation* (New York: Orbis Books, 1989). For Mitri Raheb, I refer to *I Am a Palestinian Christian* (Minneapolis: Fortress Press, 1995). See also Mitri Raheb, *Bethlehem Besieged: Stories of Hope in Times of Trouble* (Minneapolis: Fortress Press, 2004). See also Ateek's latest book, *A Palestinian Christian Cry for Reconciliation* (New York: Orbis Books, 2009). In this connection, one cannot but mention the famous ministry and witness of Father Elias Chacour, presented in his books *Blood Brothers* (Grand Rapids, Mich.: Chosen Books, 1984; reprint, 2003) and *We Belong to the Land: The Story of a Palestinian Israeli Who Lives for Peace and Reconciliation* (San Francisco: Harper and Row, 1990). Father Chacour was nominated twice for the Nobel Peace Prize.

56. I thank my partner Harry Hagopian for drawing my attention to their work.

57. See "The Shattering of Stereotypes—Who Am I? A Christian, a Palestinian, an Arab, an Israeli," in Ateek, *Justice and Only Justice*, 7–17, and "My Identity as a Christian Palestinian," in Raheb, *I Am a Palestinian Christian*, 3–14.

58. See "On Being a Minority," in Raheb, *I Am a Palestinian Christian*, 15–25.

59. See "An Arena for Strife: The Political-Historical Background" and "Being Palestinian and Christian in Israel," in Ateek, *Justice and Only Justice*, 18–73.

60. Both Ateek and Raheb refer to the Kairos document published in September 1985 as "an attempt by concerned Christians in South Africa to reflect on the situation of death in [their] country." South African theologians and church leaders had gathered to search for ways of undertaking a course of action against apartheid and the state of emergency. They insisted on the importance of understanding the ills of the society in which Christians were called to witness for their faith. See Kairos Theologians, *The Kairos Document: Challenge to the Church* (Stonypoint, N.Y.: Theology Global Context, 1985).

61. Raheb, *I Am a Palestinian Christian*, 56. At the end of this passage, he quotes Martin Luther from his introduction to the first Wittenberg edition of his writings in 1539. See Raheb's footnote on page 154.

62. Ateek, *Justice and Only Justice*, 77, 78.

63. Marc Ellis, *Toward a Jewish Theology of Liberation* (Maryknoll, N.Y.: Orbis, 1987; 2d ed., 1989; 3rd ed., 2004). See, in particular, chapter 6, "Liberation Struggles and the Jewish Community," 145–202. For references to Ellis's work in Ateek, see *Justice and Only Justice*, 69–71, and in Raheb, see *I Am a Palestinian Christian*, 58, 154.

64. Ateek, *Justice and Only Justice*, 161.

65. Raheb, *I Am a Palestinian Christian*, 10.

66. Ibid., 103.

67. Ateek, *Justice and Only Justice*, 164.

68. Interesting forays into such a Muslim liberation theology can be found in South Africa in the work of Farid Esack: *Qur'an, Liberation, and Pluralism: An Islamic Perspective of Interreligious Solidarity Against Oppression* (Oxford, U.K.: Oneworld, 1997), and his more personal book *On Being a Muslim: Finding a Religious Path in the World Today* (Oxford, U.K.: Oneworld, 1999). Interesting works on the topic are also coming out in the United States; for example, see Omid Safi, ed., *Progressive Muslims: On Justice, Gender, and Pluralism* (Oxford, U.K.: Oneworld, 2003), and Khaled Abou El Fadl, *The Place of Tolerance in Islam*, edited by Joshua Cohen and Ian Lague (Boston: Beacon Press, 2002).

69. Ahmed, *Women and Gender in Islam*, 201.

70. Quoted and translated in Talal Asad, "The Limits of Religious Criticism in the Middle East: Notes on Islamic Public Argument," in Talal Asad, *Genealogies of Religion: Discipline and Reasons of Power in Christianity and Islam* (Baltimore: Johns Hopkins University Press, 1993), 223–24.

71. Here Asad refers to Alasdair MacIntyre, *Whose Justice? Whose Rationality?* (Notre Dame, Ind.: University of Notre Dame Press, 1988). One might also refer to the Habermas-Taylor debate on the moral neutrality of liberal democracy, especially in connection with the issues of the politics of recognition; see Amy Gutmann, ed., *Mul-*

ticulturalism: Examining the Politics of Recognition (Princeton, N.J.: Princeton University Press, 1994).

72. Asad, "The Limits of Religious Criticism in the Middle East," 236.

5. Secular Critique

1. For a detailed presentation of the debate around this period, see Nazik Saba Yared, *Secularism and the Arab World, 1850–1939* (London: Saqi Books, 2002); see also Albert Hourani, *Arabic Thought in the Liberal Age, 1798–1939* (London: Oxford University Press, 1962); for a Christian-Muslim comparison between histories of secularization processes, see Talal Asad, *Formations of the Secular: Christianity, Islam, Modernity* (Stanford, Calif.: Stanford University Press, 2003).

2. Farag Fouda, *Nakun aw la Nakun* (To Be or Not to Be) (Cairo: Dar al-Hay'a al-Misriyya al-ʿAmma li al-Kitab, 1992).

3. For more on Farag Fouda and his case, see the 1992 issues of *Index on Censorship*; for a transcription of his interrogation, see vol. 2 (1992), 23–24.

4. Farag Fouda, *Al-Haqiqa al-Gha'iba* (The Absent Truth) (Cairo: Dar al-Fikr, 1986; 3rd ed., 1988); I quote from the third edition.

5. Abd al-Salam Faraj, *Al-Farida al-Gha'iba* (The Absent Duty) (Cairo: Dar al Hurriya, 1988), translated into English by Johannes Jansen as *The Neglected Duty* (New York: Macmillan, 1986).

6. Lebanese cleric Cheikh Muhammad al-Amin also holds this position, calling for secularism and the liberation of religion from the state. See his collection of essays *Al-Ijtimaʿ al-ʿArabi al-Islami: Murajaʿat fi al-Taʿaddudiya wa al-Nahda wa al-Tanwir* (The Arab-Islamic Society: Studies in Pluralism, Renaissance, and Enlightenment) (Beirut: Dar al-Hadi, 2003).

7. Fouda, *Al-Haqiqa al-Gha'iba*, 38, my own translation.

8. Fouad Zakariyya, *Al-Haqiqa wa al-Wahm fi al-Haraka al-Islamiyya al-Muʿassira* (The Truth and Illusion About the Contemporary Islamic Movement) (Cairo: Dar al-Fikr, 1986); *Al-Sahwa al-Islamiyya fi Mizan al-ʿAql* (The Islamic Awakening in the Balance of Reason) (Cairo: Dar al-Fikr al-Muʿassir, 1987).

9. On secularism before the 1967 defeat, see Ibrahim Abu-Lughod, "Retreat from the Secular Path? Islamic Dilemmas of Arab Politics," *Review of Politics* 28 (1966): 447–76.

10. For a good study of the overall islamicization of the public sphere in Arab countries as a result of this competition for Islamic legitimacy between the state and the Islamist currents, see Salwa Ismail, *Rethinking Islamist Politics: Culture, the State, and Islamism* (London: I. B. Tauris, 2003), which includes case studies in Egypt, Algeria, and Tunisia.

11. Zakariyya, *Al-Haqiqa wa al-Wahm*, 240, my own translation.

12. See Fouad Zakariyya, "Human Rights in the Arab World: The Islamic Context," in *Philosophical Foundations of Human Rights*, with contributions by Alwin Diemer and others, 227–41 (Paris: UNESCO, 1986).

13. See Nasr Hamid Abu Zayd, "The Concept of Human Rights, the Process of Modernization, and the Politics of Western Domination," *Internationale Politik und Gesellschaft / International Politics and Society* 4 (1998): 434–37.

14. Aziz al-Azmeh, *Al-'Ilmaniyya min Manzour Mukhtalif* (Secularism from a Different Perspective) (Beirut: Markaz Dirasat al-Wihda al-'Arabiyya, 1992; reprint, 1998); Aziz al-Azmeh, *Dunia al-Din fi Hader al-'Arab* (The World of Religion in the Arabs' Present) (Beirut: Dar al-Tali'a, 1996; modified 2d. ed., 2002); Aziz al-Azmeh, *Islams and Modernities* (London: Verso, 1993; new ed., 1996); I quote from the 1996 edition *Islams and Modernities*.

15. Erich Zürcher, *Turkey: A Modern History* (London: I. B. Tauris: 1993), 64.

16. The International Monetary Fund and the World Bank implemented these policy changes in order to reduce the fiscal imbalances, in particular those of developing countries. The changes aimed at promoting economic growth, generating income, and paying off the debt these countries had accumulated. They included the reduction of trade barriers, privatization, deregulation, and reduction of social expenditures, but these measures had a negative impact on the more vulnerable sectors of society that benefited from state public expenditures, such as women, civil society organizations, and the poor.

17. Al-Azmeh, *Islams and Modernities*, 82–83, see also p. 25.

18. Particularly interesting in this respect are Frederick Beiser's works : *The Fate of Reason: German Philosophy from Kant to Fichte* (Cambridge, Mass.: Harvard University Press, 1987), and *Enlightenment, Revolution, and Romanticism: The Genesis of Modern German Political Thought 1790–1800* (Cambridge, Mass.: Harvard University Press, 1992). Also to be noted is the recent revived interest in Herder's thought: see, for instance, Kurt Mueller-Vollmer, ed., *Herder Today* (Berlin: Walter de Gruyter, 1990); Fred Dallmayr, "Truth and Diversity: Some Lessens from Herder," *Journal of Speculative Philosophy* 11 (1997): 101–24; Vicky Spencer, "Towards an Ontology of Holistic Individualism: Herder's Theory of Identity, Culture, and Community," *History of European Ideas* 22 (1996): 245–60; Brian J. Whitton, "Herder's Critique of the Enlightenment: Cultural Community Versus Cosmopolitan Rationalism," *History and Theory* 27 (1988): 146–68; and Benjamin W. Redekop, "Language, Literature, and Publikum: Herder's Quest for Organic Enlightenment," *History of European Ideas* 14 (1992): 235–53. For relevant texts by Herder, see the translated excerpts in Johann Gottfried Herder, *J. G. Herder on Social and Political Culture*, translated, edited, and with introduction by F. M. Barnard (London: Cambridge University Press, 1969), and Johann Gottfried Herder, *Against Pure Reason: Writings on Religion,*

Language, and History, translated, edited, and with an introduction by Marcia Bunge (Minneapolis: Fortress Press, 1993). And for discussions of Herder's use of vitalistic and organic notions, see F. M. Barnard, "Natural Growth and Purposive Development: Vico and Herder," *History and Theory* 18 (1979): 16–36, and Elias Palti, "The 'Metaphor of Life': Herder's Philosophy of History and Uneven Developments in Late Eighteenth-Century Natural Sciences," *History and Theory* 38 (1999): 322–47.

19. The collected works of Sati' al-Husri on nationalism were published in Beirut in the mid-1980s in a seventeen-volume series by Markaz Dirasat al-Wihda al-'Arabiyya.

20. See Tibi's excellent study of the development of Arab nationalism and of the influence of late German romanticism on it: Bassam Tibi, *Arab Nationalism Between Islam and the Nation-State*, 3rd ed. (New York: St. Martin's Press, 1997); this edition was the expanded and revised version of the first English translation, *Arab Nationalism: A Critical Enquiry*, edited and translated by Marion Farouk-Sluglett and Peter Sluglett (London: MacMillan, 1981). The German original was initially published in Frankfurt as *Nationalismus in der Dritten Welt am arabischen Beispiel* (Frankfurt am Main: Europäische Verlagsanst, 1971) and then in a modified version as *Vom Gottesreich zum Nationalstaat: Islam und panarabischer Nationalismus* (Frankfurt am Main: Surhkamp, 1987). Tibi acknowledges Herder's critical allegiance to the Enlightenment (*Arab Nationalism*, 128). However, Herder must be exonerated from the charge of populist nationalism, although his explicitly nonpolitical definition of "the people" contains potential elements of politicization that could be and were utilized, especially by German nationalists after 1806. Nevertheless, Herder's notion of "the people" is qualitatively different from that of the populist nationalists of the nineteenth century, especially in that it forms a central feature of his humanism, which owes much to the ideas of the Enlightenment. It must also not be overlooked that in spite of his polemics against the Enlightenment, especially his "anti-Enlightenment" broadsheet with the ironic title *Also a Philosophy of History for the Education of Mankind*, Herder stands firmly within the tradition of the Enlightenment, in contradistinction to the populist nationalists. His philosophy of history contains elements that may be considered part of the Enlightenment as well as elements with which populist nationalists could identify.

21. Al-Azmeh, *Islams and Modernities*, 18.

22. Ibid., 19–20.

23. Hisham Sharabi, *Neopatriarchy: Theory of Distorted Change in Arab Society* (New York: Oxford University Press, 1988), x.

24. Marnia Lazreg, "Feminism and Difference: The Perils of Writing as a Woman on Women in Algeria," *Feminist Studies* 14, no. 1 (1988), 99, 100, emphasis in the original.

25. Al-Azmeh, *Islams and Modernities*, 22, 28.

26. Ibid., 29.

27. Wajih Kawtharani's books include: *Al-Ittijahat al-Ijtima'iyya wa al-Siyasiyya fi Jabal Lubnan wa al-Mashreq al-'Arabi, 1860–1920* (The Social and Political Orientations in Mount Lebanon and the Arab East) (Beirut: Ma'had al-Inma' al-'Arabi, 1978), and *Al-Sulta wa al-Mujtama' wa al-'Amal al-Siyasi: Min Tarikh al-Wilaya al-'Othmniya fi Bilad al-Sham* (Power, Society, and Political Work: From the History of the Ottoman Province in the Sham Area) (Beirut: Markaz Dirasat al-Wihda al-'Arabiyya, 1988).

28. Among Ridwan al-Sayyid's writings are: *Siyasat al-Islam al-Mu'assir* (The Policies of Contemporary Islam) (Beirut: Dar al-Kitab al-'Arabi, 1997) and *Al-sira' 'Ala al-Islam: Al-Usuliyya wa al-Islah wa al-Siyasat al-Dawliyya* (The Conflict over Islam: Fundamentalist Reform and International Politics) (Beirut: Dar al-Kitab al-'Arabi, 2004).

29. Bassam Tibi, *The Crisis of Modern Islam: A Pre-industrial Culture in the Scientific-Technological Age* (Salt Lake City: University of Utah Press, 1988); *The Challenge of Fundamentalism: Political Islam and the New World Disorder* (Berkeley and Los Angeles: University of California Press, 1997; updated ed., 2002); *Islam Between Culture and Politics* (New York and Cambridge, Mass.: Palgrave in association with the Weatherhead Center for International Affairs, Harvard University, 2001).

30. Bassam Tibi, "Culture and Knowledge: The Politics of Islamicization of Knowledge as a Postmodern Project? The Fundamentalist Claim to De-Westernization," *Theory, Culture, & Society* 12 (1995): 1–24.

31. Ibid., 1–2.

32. Tibi, *Islam Between Culture and Politics*, 142–43; see also p. 121.

33. Tibi, "Culture and Knowledge," 7.

34. Tibi, *Islam Between Culture and Politics*, 92.

35. Tibi, *The Challenge of Fundamentalism*, 80.

36. Ibid., 80–81.

37. Ibid., 80.

38. Tibi, *Islam Between Culture and Politics*, 137.

39. Tibi, "Culture and Knowledge," 10.

40. Tibi, *Islam Between Culture and Politics*, 107.

41. Ibid., 132.

42. Tibi, "Culture and Knowledge," 17.

43. Soheir Morsy, Cynthia Nelson, Reem Saad, and Hania Sholkamy, "Anthropology and the Call for Indigenization of Social Science in the Arab World," in Earl L. Sullivan and Jacqueline S. Ismael, eds., *The Contemporary Study of the Arab World*, 81–111 (Edmonton: University of Alberta Press, 1991).

44. Soraya Altorki, a Saudi anthropologist based in Egypt at the American University of Cairo, insists on this importance. She writes on the advantages and inconveniences of doing "indigenous" anthropological work in the literal sense of the word—that is, studying one's own community, or in her case Saudi women of a certain social class. She

explains this approach in the beginning of "The Anthropologist in the Field: A Case of 'Indigenous Anthropology' from Saudi Arabia," in Hussein Fahim, ed., *Indigenous Anthropology in Non-Western Countries*, 167–75 (Durham: University of North Carolina Press, 1982), and reprinted in Saad Eddin Ibrahim and Nicholas S. Hopkins, eds., *Arab Society: Social Science Perspectives*, 76–83 (Cairo: American University of Cairo Press, 1985). She states:

> There appears to be an odd assumption underlying the concept of indigenous anthropology, an assumption that questions the universality of its epistemology. But is anthropology not that field of knowledge in which scholarship, perhaps more than in any other discipline, has always aspired to extricate itself from the observer's own culture-bound perceptions of social reality? If the goal of ethnographic research is to analyze patterns of action and modes of thought in their unique cultural contexts or, as it is often said, from the "natives' point of view," all anthropology is indigenous in a very real sense. Furthermore, the erosion of ethnocentric conceptual schemes that characterized the early phase of anthropological theory has derived from a continuous process of critical review within rather than outside the discipline. Our current concerns with the historical role of anthropology during the colonial period of European imperialism and with its place in the contemporary world are a recent product of this process.

> These remarks imply neither a eulogy nor an apology for anthropology: I merely want to distance myself from the facile and unreflective attacks, often heard from social scientists in Third World countries, which indict the discipline as a hand maiden of colonialism and indict the whole profession by the sins of a few of its members. Consequently, if for the purpose of this paper I retain the term *indigenous anthropology*, I do not impute to it any special or separate epistemological status; instead I use this expression to denote nothing more or less than the work of an anthropologist in and on his/her own society. (76 in *Arab Society*)

The volume edited by Hussein Fahim, an Egyptian anthropologist, contains the proceedings of an interesting symposium organized in 1978 on the issue of indigenous anthropology, including contributions from Indian, Egyptian, Saudi Arabian, African, Brazilian, Mexican, Japanese, South Pacific, European, and U.S. anthropologists. It demonstrates that developing a knowledge of one's own in postcolonial countries is a similar concern across cultures, religions, and languages, and it offers a useful comparative perspective. See also Hussein Fahim, "Foreign and Indigenous Anthropology: The Perspectives of an Egyptian Anthropologist," *Human Organization* 36, no. 1 (1977): 80–86.

45. Morsy et al., "Anthropology and the Call for Indigenization of Social Science in the Arab World," 97.

46. Tahar Ben Jelloun, "Décolonisation de la sociologie au Maghreb: Utilité et risques d'une fonction critique," *Le Monde Diplomatique*, August 1974, 28, translated by Nicholas S. Hopkins as "Decolonizing Sociology in the Maghreb: Usefulness and Risks of a Critical Function," in Saad Eddin Ibrahim and Nicholas S. Hopkins, eds., *Arab Society: Social Science Perspectives*, 70–75 (Cairo: American University of Cairo Press, 1977).

47. Ben Jelloun, "Decolonizing Sociology in the Maghreb," 75, emphasis in the original.

48. Abdelkader Zghal and Hachmi Karoui, "Decolonization and Social Science Research: The Case of Tunisia," *Middle East Studies Association Bulletin* 7, no. 3 (October 1973): 11–27. For an interesting presentation of the modernization and retraditionalization phenomena in postcolonial Tunisia, see Abdelkader Zghal, "The Reactivation of Tradition in a Post-traditional Society," *Daedalus* 102, no. 1 (1973): 225–37.

49. Zghal and Karoui, "Decolonization and Social Science Research," 17.

50. Abdelkebir Khatibi, "Double Criticism: The Decolonization of Arab Sociology," in Halim Barakat, ed., *Contemporary North Africa: Issues of Development and Integration*, 9–19 (Washington, D.C.: Center for Contemporary Arab Studies, Georgetown University, 1985). The French articles are included in his book *Maghreb pluriel* (Plural Maghreb) (Paris: Denoël, 1983).

51. Khatibi, *Maghreb pluriel*, 28.

52. According to Khatibi, Abdallah Laroui too remains captive of this metaphysics. See ibid., 31–35.

53. Ibid., 24, 13.

54. Mohammad Bennis, "The Plurality of the One," in Barakat, ed., *Contemporary North Africa*, 250.

55. Khatibi, *Maghreb pluriel*, 17–18.

56. Ibid., 39.

57. For a cogent presentation of Khatibi's thought, see Mustapha Hamil, "Interrogating Identity: Abdelkebir Khatibi and the Postcolonial Prerogative," *Alif: Journal of Comparative Poetics* 22 (2002): 72–88; and for essays on thought and literature in the Maghreb, see Mildred Mortimer, ed., *Maghrebian Mosaic: A Literature in Transition* (Boulder, Colo.: Lynne Rienner, 2000).

58. I refer to three particular texts by Hisham Sharabi: *Neopatriarchy*; "Introduction: Patriarchy and Dependency and the Future of Arab Society," in Hisham Sharabi, ed., *The Next Arab Decade: Alternative Futures*, 1–8 (Boulder, Colo.: Westview Press, 1988); and "The Scholarly Point of View: Politics, Perspective, Paradigm," in Hisham Sharabi, ed., *Theory, Politics, and the Arab World: Critical Responses*, 1–51 (New York: Routledge, 1990). In the volume *The Next Arab Decade*, other essays of particular relevance to our topic are John Waterbury, "Social Science Research and Arab Studies in

the Coming Decade," 293–302, and El Sayed Yassin, "In Search of a New Identity of the Social Sciences in the Arab World: Discourse, Paradigm, and Strategy," 303–11.

59. Sharabi, *Neopatriarchy*, 123.

60. Sharabi, "The Scholarly Point of View," 2, emphasis in the original.

61. Sharabi, "Introduction," 7.

62. Sharabi, *Neopatriarchy*," 21.

63. Ibid., 23.

64. Sharabi, "Introduction," 2–3, emphasis in the original.

65. Sharabi, *Neopatriarchy*, 12–13, 18, 150. For a critique of Sharabi's ideas, see Stephen Sheehi, "Failure, Modernity, and the Works of Hisham Sharabi: Towards a Post-colonial Critique of Arab Subjectivity," *Critique: Journal of Critical Studies of Iran and the Middle East* 10 (1997): 39–54.

66. Sharabi, *Neopatriarchy*, 11.

67. Muhammad Jaber al-Ansari, *Al-Fikr al-ʿArabi wa Siraʿ al-Addad: Kayfa Ihtawat al-Tawfiqiyya al-Siraʿ al-Mahzur Bayn al-Usuliyya wa al-ʿIlmaniyya wa al-Hasm al-Mʾuajjal Bayn al-Islam wa al-Gharb. Tashkhis Hala li al-la Hasm fi al-Hayat al-ʿArabiyya wa al-Ihtiwa al-Tawfiqi li al-Jadaliyyat al-Mahzura* (Arab Thought and the Struggle of Opposites: How Conciliatory Thought Contained the Forbidden Struggle Between Fundamentalism and Secularism and the Postponed Settlement Between Islam and the West. Diagnosis of the No-Settlement Situation in Arab Life and the Conciliatory Containment of Forbidden Dialectics) (Beirut: Al-Muʾassassa al-ʿArabiyya li al-Dirasat wa al-Nashr, 1999).

68. Rémy Brague offers a different take on the selective borrowing from the Greek heritage in *Europe: La voie romaine* (Europe: The Roman Way) (Paris: Criterion, 1992), which argues that the Arabs had no interest in the humanistic side of the Greek heritage.

69. Abu Hamid Muhammad al-Ghazali, *Al-Munqidh mi al-Dalal wa al-Mufsih ʿan al-Ahwal* (Damascus: Dar al-Hikma, 1994), English translation: *Deliverance from Error and Mystical Union with the Almighty*, translated and introduced by Muhammad Abu-laylah, with an introduction and notes by George F. McLean (Washington, D.C.: Council for Research in Values and Philosophy, 2001).

70. The Batinis emphasize the importance of seeking the inner (*batini*) meaning of the sacred text in addition to its apparent (*zahiri*) meaning. The question then is about the persons or institutions that can authorize such a reading and the criteria in terms of which it should be conducted. This question has opened the way to controversial and sometimes tendentiously occult interpretations.

71. Hourani, *Arabic Thought in the Liberal Age*, 139.

72. Al-Ansari mentions, among other names, Yaʿqub Sarruf (1852–1927), Shibly Shumayyil (1860–1916), Farah Antun (1871–1922), Suleiman Bustani (1856–1925), and Salameh Mussa (1887–1958).

73. For a comparison between the Christian and the Muslim approach to the issues of reform in the nineteenth and early twentieth centuries, see Hourani, *Arabic Thought in the Liberal Age*, as well as Hisham Sharabi, *Arab Intellectuals and the West: The Formative Years 1875–1914* (Baltimore: Johns Hopkins University Press, 1970); Saba Yared, *Secularism and the Arab World*; and Nazik Saba Yared, *Arab Travellers and Western Civilization* (London: Saqi Books, 1996).

74. Taha Husayn, *'Ala Hamish al-Sira* (On the Margin of the Biography of the Prophet) (Cairo: Lajnat al-Ta'lif wa al-Tarjama wa al-Nashr, 1935). In June 1936, the Egyptian literary historian and critic Ahmad Amin wrote an article in the weekly Egyptian literary periodical *al-Risala*, "Al-Naqd Aydan" (Critique Again) (152 [June 1, 1936]: 881–83), in which he deplored the state of literature and literary critique in his country and its deterioration compared to what it was twenty years earlier. His criticism focused on three problems: the lack of courage, the interference of politics, and the lack of specialization. Writers and critics nowadays, he said, have abandoned their courageous and frank positions and adopted a more complacent and populist strategy for the sake of safety. They have seen how the preceding generation was attacked, intimidated, and punished for its daring ideas and how it was left without effective support from others in times of dangers. So they have drawn their lessons and adopted a more conformist attitude. Moreover, literary works are evaluated under political pressure to please those in power, whether in the literary sphere or in government. Lastly, critics allow themselves to move from one field of writing to another, without serious knowledge of those fields. All these factors, said Amin, have harmed the quality of writing, but even more so that of literary critique. He contrasts this state of affairs with that of developed countries, in which threatened critics are protected by effective supporters and in which critique is conducted with serious regulations. A week later, Taha Husayn wrote a rebuttal entitled "Fi al-Naqd: Ila Sadiqi Ahmad Amin" (On Critique: To My Friend Ahmad Amin) (*al-Risala* 153 [June 8, 1936]: 921–22 and 957–58). In it, he took Amin's statements personally and defended his generation of writers against Amin's accusations of complacency, affirming that they have stood in the face of power and public opinion and paid the price for it in different ways. Amin answered him in the same issue of the journal with the article "Fi al-Naqd al-Adabi Aydan" (On Literary Critique Again) (*al-Risala* 153 [June 8, 1936]: 963–65), regretting that Husayn should take his remarks personally and clarifying his ideas further, deploring again the diminishing margins of freedom. Egyptians writers Tawfiq al-Hakim, and Ismail Mazhar also joined the debate with articles in the same journal issue, "Fi al-Naqd: Ila al-Ustadh Ahmad Amin" (On Critique: To Professor Ahmad Amin), *al-Risala* 153 (June 8, 1936): 1003, and "Fi al-Naqd al-Adabi" (On Literary Critique), *al-Risala* 153 (June 8, 1936): 1252–53, respectively. Mazhar agreed with Amin and noted that the weaknesses of critique were not only limited to

the literary domain, but also plagued science and philosophy as well, and that they were due to the absence of rigorous rational principles and foundations. Critique, he said, was conducted as a subjective estimation (*taqdir*) rather than as a rigorous evaluation (*taqrir*). Taha Husayn and Ahmad Amin's autobiographies offer an informative background to the intellectual debates and concerns of the time. See Taha Husayn, *Al-Ayyam* (Cairo: Dar al-Maʿarif, 1974), translated by E. H. Paxton, Hilary Wayment, and Kenneth Cragg as *The Days: Taha Hassein, His Autobiography in Three Parts* (Cairo: American University of Cairo Press, 1997); and Ahmad Amin, *Hayati* (Cairo: Maktabat al-Nahda al-Misriyya, 1958), translated and introduced by Issa J. Boullata as *My Life: The Autobriography of an Egyptian Scholar, Writer, and Cultural Leader* (Leiden: Brill, 1978).

75. See Aziz al-Azmeh, "Tawatturat al-Siyassa wa Intikassat fikr al-Hadatha" (Political Tensions and the Defeat of Modern Thought), in *ʿAsr al-Nahda: Muqaddimat Liberaliyya li al Hadatha* (The Age of Nahda: Liberal Beginnings for Modernity), 75–95 (Beirut: Al-Markaz al-Thaqafi al-ʿArabi, 2000).

76. Muhammad Hussein Haykal, *Fi Manzil al-Wahi* (In the House of Revelation) (Cairo: Matbaʿat Dar al-Kutub al-Misriyya, 1936).

77. Abbas Mahmud al-Aqqad, *ʿAbqariyyat Muhammad* (The Genius of Muhammad) (Cairo: Dar al-Islam, 1943; 2d ed., 1972).

78. On a sarcastic note, in *Baba Sartre* (Daddy Sartre) (Beirut: Riad el-Rayyes Books, 2001), Iraqi novelist Ali Badr depicts a caricature of the Arab existentialists of the 1970s and 1980s who followed existentialism as yet another fashion.

79. Aʾisha Abdel Rahman, *Maqal fi al-Insan: Dirasa Qurʾaniyya* (Essay on the Human: A Qurʾanic Study) (Cairo: Dar al-Maʿarif, 1969).

80. Naimy was on al-Ansari's dissertation committee.

81. Nadeem Naimy, "Ishkaliyyat al-Fikr al-Islami fi ʿAsr al-Nahda" (The Problematic of Islamic Thought in the Age of the Nahda), in *ʿAsr al-Nahda*, 51–74.

82. See Muhammad Abduh, *Risalat al-Tawhid* (The Monotheistic Mission) (Cairo: Matbaʿat al-Manar, 1908 or 1909), translated as *The Theology of Unity* by Ishaq Musaʿad and Kenneth Cragg (London: Allen and Unwin, 1966); and Muhammad Abduh, *Al-Islam wa al-Nasraniyya Bayna al-ʿIlm wa al-Madaniyya* (Islam and Christianity Between Science and Civilization) (Beirut: Dar al-Hadatha, 1983).

83. Nadeem Naimy, "Iʿadat Tashkil al-Siyasa al-Thaqafiyya: Tashjiʿ al-Ibdaʿ wa al-Musharaka fi al-Hayat al-Thaqafiyya" (Reshaping Cultural Policy: Encouraging Creativity and Participation in Cultural Life), in *Nahwa Siyasa Thaqafiyya ʿArabiyya li al-Tanmiya* (Toward an Arab Cultural Politics for Development), 18–33 (N.p.: Matbaʿat al-Munazzama al-ʿArabiyya li al-Tarbiya wa al-Thaqafa wa al-ʿUlum, ALECSO, 2001).

84. Nadeem Naimy, "Al-ʿArab wa Siraʿ al-Hadarat" (The Arabs and the Conflict of Civilizations), unpublished manuscript in author's files.

85. See, for instance, Mohammad 'Abed al-Jabiri, *Al-Khitab al-'Arabi al-Mu'assir* (The Contemporary Arab Discourse) (Beirut: Markaz Dirasat al-Wihda al-'Arabiyya, 1982).

86. Burhan Ghalyun has written extensively on the question of democracy in the Arab world. His books include *Bayan min Ajl al-Dimuqratiyya* (Manifesto for Democracy) (Beirut: Al-Markaz al-Thaqafi al-'Arabi, n.d.; 5th ed., 2006); *Al-Ikhtiyar al-Dimuqrati fi Suriya* (The Democratic Choice in Syria) (Damascus: Dar Petra, 2003); and *Al-Mihna al-'Arabiyya: Al-Dawla Didd al-Umma* (The Arab Crisis: The State Against the Nation) (Beirut: Markaz Dirasat al-Wihda al-'Arabiyya, 1993). See Ghalyun's exchange with Samir Amin on the issues of state and religion in Burhan Ghalyun and Samir Amin, *Hiwar al-Dawla wa al-Din* (The Dialogue on the State and Religion) (Beirut: Al-Markaz al-Thaqafi al-'Arabi, 1996).

87. According to the head of the Center for Arab Unity Studies, Kheireddin Hasib, none of the Arab countries approached agreed to host the conference, so the decision was taken to hold it in Cyprus. This outcome, he thought, was in itself telling about the state of democracy in the Arab world. It showed him the importance of devoting serious attention to the topic, for the Arab unity that the center aspired to was that of free Arabs, not of oppressed Arabs. See Kheireddin Hasib, "Kalimat al-Iftitah" (Opening Word), in *Azamat al-Dimuqratiyya fi al-Watan al-'Arabi* (The Crisis of Democracy in the Arab Homeland), 29–32 (Beirut: Markaz Dirasat al-Wihda al-'Arabiyya, 1984; reprint, 1987). The Center for Arab Unity Studies published a number of edited volumes on the subject, for instance: *Hawl al-Khayar al-Dimuqrati: Dirasat Naqdiyya* (On the Democratic Choice: Critical Studies) (1994); *Huquq al-Insan al-Arabi* (The Rights of the Arab Human Being) (1999, reprinted in 2004); *Huquq al-Insan: Al-Ru'a al-'Alamiyya wa al-Islamiyya wa al-'Arabiyya* (Human Rights: The World, Islamic, and Arab Visions) (2005); and *Al-Khalij al-'Arabi wa al-Dimuqratiyya: Nahwa Ru'ya Mustaqbaliyya li Ta'ziz al-Masa'i al-Dimuqratiyya* (The Arab Gulf and Democracy: Toward a Future Vision for the Reinforcement of the Democratic Efforts) (2002).

88. The Ibn Khaldun Center for Development Studies (Markaz Ibn Khaldun li al-Dirasat al-Inma'iyya) focuses its research and its publications on issues of civil society and democratization, sects, ethnic and minority groups, and gender and human development. See http://www.eicds.org. In 2000, the center, its staff, and its founder, now chair of its directing board, Saad Eddin Ibrahim, professor of sociology at the American University of Cairo, were the object of legal charges by the Egyptian government. The latter accused the center and its staff of receiving foreign funds without permission, forging official documents, and tarnishing Egypt's image abroad. Ibrahim spent fourteen months in jail in spite of U.S., European, and some local support. According to him, the government was in reality displeased by the center's efforts at monitoring elections and denouncing discrimination against the Coptic minority and women. It was a political trial that aimed at intimidating and silencing the center. A defense of

his case can be found in Saad Eddin Ibrahim, "A Reply to My Accusers," *Journal of Democracy* 11, no. 4 (2000): 58–63.

89. Saad Eddin Ibrahim, "Muqaddima" (Introduction), in *Azamat al-Dimuqratiyya fi al-Watan al-ʿArabi*, 11–28. On democracy in the Arab world, see Saad Eddin Ibrahim, *Egypt, Islam, and Democracy: Critical Essays* (Cairo: American University of Cairo Press, 2002).

90. Ghassan Salamé, "Introduction: Where Are the Democrats?" in Ghassan Salamé, ed., *Democracy Without Democrats? The Renewal of Politics in the Muslim World* (London: I. B. Tauris, 1994), 13–14. See also Salamé's related writings in Arabic: *Al-Mujtamaʿ wa al-Dawla fi al-Mashreq al-ʿArabi* (Society and State in the Arab East) (Beirut: Markaz Dirasat al-Wihda al-ʿArabiyya, 1986), and *Nahwa ʿAqd Ijtimaʿi ʿArabi Jadid* (Toward a New Arab Social Contract) (Beirut: Markaz Dirasat al-Wihda al-ʿArabiyya, 1988).

91. Salamé, "Introduction," 14.

92. See, for instance, Ghassan Salamé, ed., *The Foundations of the Arab State* (London: Croom Helm, 1987); Giacomo Luciani, ed., *The Arab State* (Berkeley and Los Angeles: University of California Press, 1990); Nazih Ayyubi, *Over-stating the Arab State: Politics and Society in the Middle East* (London: I. B. Tauris, 1995). Again here the insights of political activists in the democratic opposition are valuable. See, for instance, the writings of Moncef Marzouki, a Tunisian medical doctor who has been a leading figure of the Human Rights League in Tunisia and ran for the presidency in the mid-1990s, challenging the dictatorial police state of his country. He was intimidated and thrown in jail several times and eventually forced into exile in Paris. Among his books in Arabic are *Al-istiqlal al-Thani: Min Ajl al-Dawla al-ʿArabiyya al-Dimuqratiyya al-Haditha* (The Second Independence: For the Modern Democratic Arab State) (Beirut: Dar al-Kunuz al-Adabiyya, 1996); *ʿAn Ayyat Dimuqratiyya Yatahaddathun?* (About Which Democracy Do They Speak?) (Damascus and Paris: Dar al-Ahali Arab Commission for Human Rights, 2005); in French, *Le mal arabe: Entre dictatures et intégrismes: La démocratie interdite* (The Arab Trouble: Between Dictatorships and Fundamentalisms: The Forbidden Democracy) (Paris: L'Harmattan, 2004).

93. Ghassan Salamé, "Sur la causalité d'un manque: Pourquoi le monde arabe n'est-il donc pas démocratique?" (On the Causality of a Lack: Why Is the Arab World Not Democratic?), *Revue Française de Science Politique* 41, no. 3 (1991): 307–40.

94. The culturalist explanation is today largely discredited, but not out of use. For a discussion of its flaws and of its virtues when cautiously used, see Michael C. Hudson, "The Political Culture Approach to Arab Democratization: The Case for Bringing It Back in, Carefully," and Lisa Anderson, "Democracy in the Arab World: A Critique of the Political Culture Approach," both in Rex Brynen, Bahgat Korany, and Paul Noble, eds., *Political Liberalization and Democratization in the Arab World*, vol. 1: *Theoretical Perspectives*, 61–75 and 77–92 (Boulder, Colo.: Lynne Rienner, 1995).

95. Aziz al-Azmeh, "Populism Contra Democracy: Recent Democratist Discourse in the Arab World," in Salamé, ed., *Democracy Without Democrats?*114. For an examination of the place of democracy in the debate about the second Nahda, see Salwa Ismail, "Democracy in Contemporary Arab Intellectual Discourse," in Brynen, Korany, and Noble, eds., *Political Liberalization and Democratization in the Arab World*, 93–111.

96. Ibid., 121.

97. Ibid., 128.

98. Lisa Anderson, "Arab Democracy: Dismal Prospects," *World Policy Journal* 18, no. 3 (2001): no page numbers.

99. Ibid., no page number.

100. Ibid.

101. Azmi Bishara, *Fi al-Mas'ala al-'Arabiyya: Muqaddima li Bayan Dimuqrati 'Arabi* (On the Arab Question: Prolegomena to an Arab Democratic Manifesto) (Beirut: Markaz Dirasat al-Wihda al-'Arabiyya, 2007).

102. For a discussion of Middle Eastern exceptionalism, see the special issue of *Arab Studies Journal* 6, no. 1 (1998).

103. Iliya Harik, *Al-Dimuqratiyya wa Tahaddiyat al-Hadatha Bayn al-Sharq wa al-Gharb* (Democracy and the Challenges of Modernity Between East and West) (Beirut: Dar al-Saqi, 2001).

104. Brief translated excerpts from the writings of al-Ghannushi and al-Awa can be found in John J. Donohue and John L. Esposito, eds., *Islam in Transition: Muslim Perspectives* (New York: Oxford University Press, 1982; 2d ed., 2006).

6. Breaking the Postcolonial Solitude

1. For a panorama of the issues of the time, see the presentation of one of the main contributors to the early-twentieth-century debate, Georg Simmel, in his two-part essay "Tendencies of German Life and Thought Since 1870," *International Monthly* (1902): 93–111 and 166–84. See also Thomas E. Willey, *Back to Kant: The Revival of Kantianism in German Social and Historical Thought, 1860–1914* (Detroit: Wayne State University Press, 1978), and Fritz K. Ringer, *The Decline of the German Mandarins: The German Academic Community, 1890–1933* (Cambridge, Mass.: Harvard University Press, 1969). For an anthology of some of the important texts of the philosophy and sciences of culture of the times, see John Rundell and Stephen Mennell, ed., *Classical Readings in Culture and Civilization* (London: Routledge, 1998), and Ralf Konersmann, ed., *Kulturphilosophie* (Philosophy of Culture) (Leipzig: Reclam, 1996). For an examination of the artistic representation of some of these cultural themes, see Mathias Eberle, *World*

War I and the Weimar Artists: Dix, Grosz, Beckmann, Schlemmer (New Haven, Conn.: Yale University Press, 1985). For recent studies on the philosophy and sciences of culture of the times, see the two volumes edited by Gangolf Hübinger, Rüdiger vom Bruch, and Friedrich Wilhelm Graf, *Kultur und Kulturwissenschaften um 1900* (Culture and the Sciences of Culture Around 1900), vol. 1: *Krise der Moderne und Glaube an die Wissenschaft* (The Crisis of Modernity and the Faith in Science), and vol. 2: *Idealismus und Positivismus* (Idealism and Positivism) (Stuttgart: Steiner, 1989, 1997). For an older but still valuable account, see Wilhelm Perpeet, "Kulturphilosophie" (Philosophy of Culture), *Archiv für Begriffsgeschichte* 20 (1976): 42–99.

2. See, on this topic, Modris Eksteins, *Rites of Spring: The Great War and the Birth of the Modern Age* (Boston: Houghton Mifflin, 1989).

3. Friedrich Nietzsche, *The Use and Abuse of History*, translated by Adrian Collins (New York: Macmillan, 1985), 23–24, 69. It is interesting to note that many of these themes were elaborated by Søren Kierkegaard half a century earlier, for instance in his essay *The Present Age*, translated by Alexander Dru (New York: Harper and Row, 1962), in which he writes: "Thus our own age is essentially one of understanding, and on the average, perhaps, more knowledgeable than any former generation, but it is without passion. Every one knows a great deal, we all know which way we ought to go and all the different ways we can go, but nobody is willing to move" (77).

4. Nietzsche, *The Use and Abuse of History*, 8, 45.

5. The lecture is in Wilhelm Dilthey, *Wilhelm Dilthey: Selected Writings*, edited by H. P. Rickman (Cambridge, U.K.: Cambridge University Press, 1976), 112. For other writings by Dilthey, see also William Kluback and Martin Weinbaum, eds., *Dilthey's Philosophy of Existence: Introduction to Weltanschauugslehre* (London: Vision, 1957). For a useful introduction to Dilthey's work, see M. A. Hodges, *The Philosophy of Wilhelm Dilthey* (London: Routledge, 1952).

6. Dilthey, *Wilhelm Dilthey*, 121. See in this connection Edmund Husserl's 1910–11 elaboration on these same themes, partly in response to Dilthey, in "Philosophy as Rigorous Science," translated by Quentin Lauer, in Edmund Husserl, *Phenomenology and the Crisis of Philosophy: Philosophy as Rigorous Science, and Philosophy and the Crisis of European Man* (New York: Harper and Row, 1965).

7. Dilthey's major works in this respect are *Einleitung in die Geisteswissenschaften* (Introduction to the Human Sciences) (Leipzig: Duncker and Humbolt, 1883) and *Der Aufbau der geschichtlichen Welt in den Geisteswissenschaften* (The Construction of the Historical World in the Human Sciences) (Berlin: Verlag der Königlichen Akademie der Wissenschaften, 1910).

8. This essay, together with a number of other ones, such as "The Conflict of Modern Culture," "The Meaning of Culture," "The Future of Our Culture," "The Crisis of Culture," and "The Idea of Europe," can be found in George Simmel, *Georg Simmel: Sociologist*

and European, translated and edited by Peter A. Lawrence, 193–272 (New York: Barnes & Noble, 1976), with an introduction by Lawrence. Simmel's famous essay "On the Concept and Tragedy of Culture" can be found in Georg Simmel, *The Conflict in Modern Culture and Other Essays,* translated and edited by Peter Etzkorn, 27–46 (New York: Teachers College Press, 1968). See also Rudolph H. Weingartner, *Experience and Culture: The Philosophy of Georg Simmel* (Middletown, Conn.: Wesleyan University Press, 1962); Lewis Coser, "Georg Simmel," in Lewis Coser, *Masters of Sociological Thought: Ideas in Historical and Social Context,* 177–215 (New York: Hartcourt Brace Jovanovich, 1971); Guy Oakes, "Introduction," in Georg Simmel, *Essays on Interpretation in Social Science,* translated and edited by Guy Oakes, 3–94 (Totowa, N.J.: Rowman and Littlefield, 1980); and a special issue on Georg Simmel for *Theory, Culture, and Society* 8, no. 3 (1991).

9. Simmel, *Georg Simmel: Sociologist and European,* 197.

10. From the wide range of Cassirer's writings, the most important essays of direct relevance for us here are collected in Ernst Cassirer, *The Logic of the Humanities,* translated by Clarence Howe Smith (New Haven, Conn.: Yale University Press, 1961), and Ernst Cassirer, *Symbol, Myth, and Culture: Essays and Lectures of Ernst Cassirer, 1935–1945,* edited by Donald Phillip Verene (New Haven, Conn.: Yale University Press, 1979). For an overall presentation of Cassirer's life and work, see Verene's introduction to *Symbol, Myth, and Culture,* 1–45, and John Michael Krois, *Cassirer: Symbolic Forms and History* (New Haven, Conn.: Yale University Press, 1987).

11. Cassirer, *The Logic of the Humanities,* 189, 192.

12. This classification is not to be taken in an absolute sense. For links between the philosophy of life and neo-Kantian elements in Dilthey's thought, see Hodges, *The Philosophy of Wilhelm Dilthey.*

13. Heinrich Rickert, *The Limits of Concept Formation in Natural Science: A Logical Introduction to the Historical Sciences,* translated and edited by Guy Oakes (Cambridge, U.K.: Cambridge University Press, 1986). For a good introduction to the history and arguments of this search for a foundation of the human sciences, see Oakes's introduction to the book, vii–xxx.

14. Ernst Cassirer, *The Philosophy of Symbolic Forms,* 4 vols. (New Haven, Conn.: Yale University Press, 1955, 1957, and 1996).

15. In Cassirer, *Symbol, Myth, and Culture,* 81.

16. In Cassirer, *The Logic of the Humanities,* 37. For a critical examination of the ethical component of philosophies and phenomenologies of culture, see Elizabeth Suzanne Kassab, "Phenomenologies of Culture and Ethics: Ernst Cassirer, Alfred Schutz, and the Tasks of a Philosophy of Culture," *Human Studies* 25 (2002): 55–88.

17. Found in Edmund Husserl, *The Crisis of European Sciences and Transcendental Phenomenology* (Evanston, Ill.: Northwestern University Press, 1970), 269–99 and 3–18.

18. Found in Emmanuel Lévinas, *Les imprévus de l'histoire* (The Unforeseen of History) (Paris: Fata Morgana, 1994), 27–41. For a critical discussion of these crisis essays on Europe, see Elizabeth Suzanne Kassab, "Is Europe an Essence? Lévinas, Husserl, and Derrida on Cultural Identity and Ethics," *International Studies in Philosophy* 34, no. 4 (2002): 55–75.

19. Oswald Spengler, *Der Untergang des Abendlandes*, 2 vols., vol. 1: *Welthistorische Perspektiven* (World Historical Perspectives), and vol. 2: *Gestalt und Wirklichkeit* (Form and Reality) (Munich: C. H. Beck'sche Verlagsbuchhandlung, 1918 and 1922); English translation: *The Decline of the West*, abridged edition by Helmut Werner from the translation by Charles Francis Atkinson (New York: Oxford University Press, 1991).

20. Max Weber, *Die protestantische Ethik und der Geist des Kapitalismus*, first published in *Archiv für Sozialwissenschaft und Sozialpolitik* 20–21 (1904–1905), then reprinted in Weber's *Gesammelte Aufsätze zur Religionssoziologie* (Collected Articles on the Sociology of Religion) (Tübingen, Germany: J. C. B. Mohr [Paul Siebeck], 1920); translated by Talcott Parsons in 1930 as *Protestant Ethic and the Spirit of Capitalism* (London: Routledge, 1992). For a comparative study of Husserl's and Weber's understanding of Europe's particular adoption of rationality, see Elizabeth Suzanne Kassab, "L'image de l'Europe chez Husserl et Weber: Le processus de rationalité chez Weber et l'appel à la raison chez Husserl" (The Image of Europe in Husserl and Weber: The Rational Process in Weber and the Call to Reason in Husserl), in Pierre Million, ed., *Max Weber et le destin des sociétés modernes* (Max Weber and the Destiny of Modern Societies), 181–93 (Grenoble, France: Recherches sur la Philosophie et le Langage, 1995).

21. Paul Valéry, "La crise de l'esprit," in Paul Valéry, *Oeuvres* (Works), 1:988–1014 (Paris: Gallimard, Bibliothèque de la Pléiade, 1957–60); English translation, "The Crisis of the Mind," in Paul Valéry, *History and Politics*, translated by Denis Folliot and Jackson Mathews, (New York: Pantheon Books, 1962), 5:23. He added: "Tout ne s'est pas perdu, mais tout s'est senti périr. Un frisson extraordinaire a couru la moelle de l'Europe."

22. Albert Schweitzer, *Kulturphilosophie* (Munich: C. H. Beck, 1925–1926), translated by C. T. Campion as *The Philosophy of Civilization* (New York: Macmillan, 1959).

23. Schweitzer, *The Philosophy of Civilization*, 18–19.

24. Ibid., 53.

25. Kulturbund invited Husserl to give his famous talk "Crisis of the European Sciences" in Vienna in 1935.

26. I owe my knowledge of this journal to my late friend Rüdiger Kramme, who passed away prematurely in the summer of 2004. See his "'Kulturphilosophie' und 'Internationalität' des 'Logos' im Spiegel seiner Selbstbeschreibung" ("Philosophy of Culture" and "Internationality" of the "Logos" in the Mirror of Its Own Self-Description), in Hübinger, vom Bruch, and Graf, *Idealismus und Positivismus*, 122–34, and "Philosophische Kultur als Programm: Die Konstituierungsphase des Logos" (Philosophical

Culture as Program: The Constitution Phase of Logos), in Hubert Treiber and Karol Sauerland, eds., *Heidelberg im Schnittpunkt intellectueller Kreise* (Heidelberg at the Intersection of Intellectual Circles), 119–49 (Opladen, Germany: Westdeutscher, 1995).

27. Richard Kroner, Nikolai von Bubnoff, Georg Mehlis, Sergius Hessen, and Fedor Stepun, *Vom Messias: Kulturphilosophische Essays* (On the Messiah: Essays in the Philosophy of Culture) (Leipzig: Verlag von Wilhelm Engelmann, 1909), 5–9, my own translation.

28. See Jacques Derrida, *L'autre cap* (Paris: Editions de Minuit, 1991), translated by Pascale-Anne Brault and Michael B. Naas as *The Other Heading: Reflections on Today's Europe* (Bloomington: Indiana University Press, 1995); and Joseph Fontana, *Europa ante el espejo* (Barcelona: Crítica, 1994), translated by Colin Smith as *The Distorted Past: A Reinterpretation of Europe* (Cambridge, Mass.: Blackwell, 1995); French and Italian translations of these books also appeared in 1995.

29. See Johann Friedrich Herder, *Ideas for a Philosophy of the History of Mankind, 1784–1791*, excerpted in Johann Gottfried Herder, *J. G. Herder on Social and Political Culture*, translated, edited, and with an introduction by F. M. Barnard, 282–87 (London: Cambridge University Press, 1969); and Jean-Paul Sartre, *Colonialism and Neocolonialism*, translated by Azzedine Haddour, Steve Brewer, and Terry McWilliams (New York: Routledge, 2001).

30. Mathew Arnold, "Sweetness and Light" (1867–69), in Mathew Arnold, *Culture and Anarchy and Other Writings*, 58–80 (Cambridge, U.K.: Cambridge University Press, 2001). From this epoch, see also T. W. Higginson, "A Plea for Culture," *Atlantic Monthly* 19 (1867): 29–37, and C. D. Warner, "What Is Your Culture to Me?" *Scribners Monthly* 4 (1872): 470–78.

31. See, for instance, John Dewey, "The House Divided Against Itself" (1929), "American— by Formula" (1930), and "The Crisis in Culture," in John Dewey, *Individualism Old and New*, 5–9, 10–17, and 59–70 (Amherst, N.Y.: Prometheus, 1929).

32. Ralph Waldo Emerson, "The American Scholar," in Ralph Waldo Emerson, *Selected Essays*, 83–105 (New York: Penguin Books, 1982).

33. George Santayana, "The Genteel Tradition in American Philosophy" (1911), in George Santayana, *The Genteel Tradition*, 38–64 (Lincoln: University of Nebraska Press, 1998).

34. Among Waldo Frank's works, the following books are relevant here: *Our America* (New York: Boni and Liveright, 1919); *The Re-discovery of America: An Introduction to a Philosophy of American Life* (New York: Scribner's, 1929); and *Chart for Rough Waters: Our Role in a New World* (New York: Doubleday, Doran, 1940).

35. Reinhold Niebuhr, "The Innocent Nation in an Innocent World" (1949), in Reinhold Niebuhr, *The Irony of American History*, 17–42 (New York: Scribner Library, 1962).

36. Randolph Bourne, "Trans-national America," *Atlantic Monthly* 118 (1916): 86–97, reprinted in Randolph Bourne, *The Radical Will: Selected Writings 1911–1918*, edited by Olaf Hansen, 248–64 (Berkeley and Los Angeles: University of California Press, 1992).

37. For this generation of cultural critics, see Casey Nelson Blake, *Beloved Community: The Cultural Criticism of Randolph Bourne, Van Wyck Brooks, Waldo Frank, and Lewis Mumford* (Chapel Hill: University of North Carolina Press, 1990).

38. For a critical analysis of the more recent debates, see David A. Hollinger, *Postethnic America: Beyond Multiculturalism* (New York: Basic, 1995).

39. See W. E. B. Du Bois, *The Souls of Black Folk* (New York: Oxford University Press, 2007; originally published in 1903); and Vine Deloria Jr., *Custer Died for Your Sins: An Indian Manifesto* (New York: Macmillan, 1969).

40. The participants' contributions were published in *Partisan Review* 19, nos. 3, 4, and 5 (1952) and a year later in Arvin Newton and others, contributors, *America and the Intellectuals: A Symposium* (New York: Partisan Review, 1953). Citations are taken from the journal, here 19, no. 3, 284. The participants' names as they appear in the journal are: Arvin Newton, James Burnham, Allan Dowling, Leslie A. Fiedler, Norman Mailer, Reinhold Niebuhr, Philip Rahv, David Riesman, Mark Shorer, Lionel Trilling, William Barrett, Jacques Barzun, Joseph Frank, Horace Gregory, Louis Kronenberger, C. Wright Mills, Louise Bogan, Richard Chase, Sidney Hook, Irving Howe, Max Lerner, William Phillips, Arthur Schlesinger Jr., and Delmore Schwartz.

One of the journal editors, Philip Rahv, a few years earlier, in 1947, had edited a set of essays written by major American writers on their experiences of Europe, *Discovery of Europe: The Story of American Experience in the Old World* (Boston: Houghton Mifflin, 1947). Of direct relevance to our topic is his introduction (xi–xix). A selection of literature about the journal and its intellectual context includes: William Phillips, *A Partisan View: Five Decades of the Literary Life* (New York: Stein and Day, 1983); Warren Susman, ed., *Culture and Commitment 1929–1945* (New York: George Braziller, 1973); Warren Susman, *Culture as History: The Transformation of American Society in the Twentieth Century* (New York: Pantheon Books, 1984); Richard Hofstadter, *Anti-intellectualism in American Life* (New York: Knopf, 1970), especially the conclusion; Russell Jacoby, *The Last Intellectuals: American Culture in the Age of Academe* (New York: Basic, 1987), especially chapter 4; Thomas Bender, *New York Intellect: A History of Intellectual Life in New York City, from 1750 to the Beginnings of Our Own Time* (Baltimore: Johns Hopkins University Press, 1987); also relevant to the themes of the symposium is Horace M. Kallen, *Culture and Democracy in the United Sates* (Piscataway, N.J.: Transaction, 1998).

41. *Partisan Review* 19, no. 3, 286.

42. The proceedings for this 1944 conference were published in *Travaux du Congrès International de Philosophie consacré aux problèmes de la connaissance* (Proceedings of the Inter-American Congress of Philosophy Meeting Devoted to the Problems of Knowledge) (Port-au-Prince, Haiti: Imprimerie de l'État, 1947).

43. The proceedings for the 1947 conference were published in the journal *Philosophy and Phenomenological Research (PPR)* 9 (1949).

44. Ibid., 512–13.

45. For his philosophy of culture, see F. S. C. Northrop, *The Meeting of East and West* (New York: Macmillan, 1946).

46. *PPR* 9, 361, emphasis in the original. For more on the American mind by Ralph Barton Perry, see his book *Characteristically American* (New York: Alfred A. Knopf, 1949) and the chapter "World Culture and National Culture" in his book *One World in the Making*, 170–203 (New York: Current Books, 1945).

47. W. E. B. Du Bois, *The World and Africa* (New York: Viking Press, 1947), 26, 23, 1.

48. *PPR* 9 (1949), 351.

49. Ibid., 542, 543. See also Leopoldo Zea, "Philosophy as an Instrument of Interamerican Understanding," *Social Epistemology* 1 (1987): 123–30.

50. The protests were published in the *American Philosophical Association Proceedings and Addresses (APA)* of 1986 (vol. 59) and 1987 (vol. 60): Richard Rorty, "From Logic to Language to Play: A Plenary Address to the InterAmerican Congress," *APA* 59 (1986): 747–53; Thomas Auxter, "The Debate over Cultural Imperialism," *APA* 59 (1986): 753–57; Ofelia Schutte, "Notes on the Issue of Cultural Imperialism," *APA* 59 (1986): 757–59; letters to the editor from Leopolodo Zea and Virginia Black, *APA* 60 (1987): 516–19 and 519–22. For a more detailed examination of these two midcentury U.S. debates, see Elizabeth Suzanne Kassab, "Cultural Affirmation, Power, and Dissent: Two Mid-century U.S. Debates," in Linda Alcoff and Mariana Ortega, eds., *United "America"? A Race and Nationalism Reader* (Albany: State University of New York Press, forthcoming).

51. On the issue of multiculturalism, see Allan Bloom, *The Closing of the America Mind* (New York: Simon and Schuster, 1987); William Bennett, *The De-Valuing of America* (New York: Touchstone Books, 1992); John Arthur and Amy Shapiro, eds., *Campus Wars: Multiculturalism and the Politics of Difference* (Boulder, Colo.: Westview Press, 1995).

52. The lecture is included in Octavio Paz, *The Labyrinth of Solitude: Life and Thought in Mexico*, translated by Lysander Kemp (New York: Grove Press, 1985), 220, emphasis in the original.

53. Within this comparative perspective, an interesting field of investigation is the late-twentieth-century Western and non-Western debates on authenticity. Indeed, intense Western debates have centered around societal issues of late capitalism, communitarianism, and identity politics, as well as around issues of individual identity in connection with the notion of authenticity. Unfortunately, it is not possible to delve

into these debates in this already long book. It will have to be undertaken in a later study where I will examine the late-twentieth-century Western and non-Western discussions of authenticity, autonomy, and critique, and revisit the legacies of the enlightenment and romanticism.

54. Samuel Ramos, *Profile of Man and Culture in Mexico*, translated by Peter G. Earle (Austin: University of Texas Press, 1962).

55. Ibid., 34.

56. Ibid., 103–4.

57. Ibid., 102.

58. Ibid., 108, emphasis in the original.

59. Paz, *The Labyrinth of Solitude*, 171. For another interesting sketch of Mexican characteristics, see Alfonso Reyes, *Mexico in a Nutshell and Other Essays*, translated by Charles Ramsdell (Berkeley and Los Angeles: University of California Press, 1964).

60. Paz, *The Labyrinth of Solitude*, 168–69.

61. Ibid., 169, 216, emphasis in the original.

62. For Leopoldo Zea, see "The Actual Function of Philosophy in Latin America," in Jorge J. E. Gracia, ed., *Latin American Philosophy in the Twentieth Century: Man, Values, and the Search for Philosophical Identity*, 219–30 (Buffalo, N.Y.: Prometheus, 1986); and *The Latin American Mind*, translated by James H. Abbott and Lowell Dunam (Norman: University of Oklahoma Press, 1963). For a recent study of Zea's thoughts on culture and philosophy, see Mario Saenz, *The Identity of Liberation in Latin American Thought: Latin American Historicism and the Phenomenology of Leopoldo Zea* (Lanham, Md.: Lexington Books, 1999). For an affirmative construction of Latin American identity, see José Marti, *José Marti Reader: Writings on the Americas*, edited by Deborah Shnookal and Mirta Muñiz (Melbourne: Ocean Press, 1999), and Roberto Fernandez Retamar, "Our America and the West," *Social Text* 5, no. 3 (1986): 1–25.

63. Zea, "The Actual Function of Philosophy in Latin America," 222, emphasis in the original.

64. Ibid.

65. Ibid., 224.

66. Ibid., 225.

67. Augusto Salazar Bondy, "The Meaning and Problems of Hispanic American Thought," in Gracia, ed., *Latin American Philosophy in the Twentieth Century*, 241–42.

68. Ibid., 243.

69. See José Carlos Mariategui, *Seven Interpretive Essays on Peruvian Reality*, translated by Marjory Urquidi (Austin: University of Texas Press, 1971).

70. Bondy quoted by Ofelia Schutte in "Philosophy and the Problem of Cultural Identity: From Ramos to Salazar Bondy," in her book *Cultural Identity and Social Liberation in Latin American Thought* (Albany: State University of New York Press, 1993), 103.

71. For recent work on the question "Is there a Latin American philosophy?" see Oscar R. Marti, "Is There a Latin American Philosophy?" *Metaphilosophy* 14, no. 1 (1983): 46–52; Jorge J. E. Gracia, "Introduction: Latin American Philosophy Today," *Philosophical Forum* 20, nos. 1–2 (1988–89): 4–32, and "Ethnic Labels and Philosophy: The Case of Latin American Philosophy," *Philosophy Today* 43 (1999): 42–49; Eduardo Mendieta, "Is There a Latin American Philosophy?" *Philosophy Today* 43 (1999): 50–61; and Vicente Medina, "The Possibility of an Indigenous Philosophy: A Latin American Perspective," *American Philosophical Quarterly* 29, no. 4 (1992): 373–80.

72. Roberto Schwarz, "National by Imitation," in John Beverly, Michael Aronna, and José Oviedo, eds., *The Postmodernism Debate in Latin America*, 264–81 (Durham, N.C.: Duke University Press, 1995); the collected volume was originally published as a special issue of *Boundary 2* 20, no. 3 (1992). See also Roberto Schwarz, *Misplaced Ideas: Essays on Brazilian Culture*, edited and with an introduction by John Gledson (London: Verso, 1992).

73. Amos Nascimento, "Colonialism, Modernism, and Postmodernism in Brazil," in Eduardo Mendieta, ed., *Latin American Philosophy: Currents, Issues, Debates*, 124–49 (Bloomington: Indiana University Press, 2003). See also Amos Nascimento, ed., *A Matter of Discourse: Community and Communication in Contemporary Philosophies* (Aldershot, U.K.: Ashgate, 1998).

74. Enrique Dussel, "Eurocentrism and Modernity," in Beverly, Aronna, and Oviedo, eds., *The Postmodernism Debate in Latin America*, 65–76.

75. Enrique Dussel, *Philosophy of Liberation*, translated from the Spanish by Aquilina Martinez and Christine Morkovsky (Maryknoll, N.Y.: Orbis, 1985), 8. For general analyses of Latin American philosophy of liberation, see Horacio Cerutti-Guldberg, "Actual Situation and Perspectives on Latin American Philosophy of Liberation," *Philosophical Forum* 20 (1988–89): 43–61; and Mario Saenz, "Philosophies of Liberation and Modernity: The Case of Latin America," *Philosophy Today* 38 (1994): 115–34.

76. Ofelia Schutte, "Origins and Tendencies of the Philosophy of Liberation in Latin American Thought: A Critique of Dussel's Ethics," *Philosophical Forum* 22 (1991): 270–95.

77. Elina Vuola, "Thinking Otherwise: Dussel, Liberation Theology, and Feminism," in Linda Martin Alcoff and Eduardo Mendieta, eds., *Thinking from the Underside of History: Enrique Dussel's Philosophy of Liberation*, 149–80 (Lanham, Md.: Rowman and Littlefield, 2000). See in the same volume Lynda Lange, "Burnt Offerings to Rationality: A Feminist Reading of the Construction of Indigenous Peoples in Dussel's Theory of Modernity," 135–47.

78. For an overview of feminist activists and theoreticians across Latin America, see Nancy Saporta Sternbach, Marysa Navarro-Aranguren, Patricia Chuchryk, and Sonia E. Alvarez, "Feminisms in Latin America: From Bogota to San Bernardo," *Signs* 17, no. 2 (1992): 393–434.

79. For an overview of Latin American feminism and issues of cultural identity, see Ofelia Schutte, "Philosophy and Feminism in Latin America: Perspectives on Gender Identity and Culture," *Philosophical Forum* 20 (1988–1989): 62–84.

80. Raquel Olea, "Feminism: Modern or Postmodern?" in Beverly, Aronna, and Oviedo, eds., *The Postmodernism Debate in Latin America*, 199.

81. For an informative history of liberation theology, see Leonardo Boff and Clodovis Boff, *Introducing Liberation Theology*, translated by Paul Burns (Maryknoll, N.Y.: Orbis Books, 1987).

82. Gustavo Guttierrez, *Teología de la liberatión* (Lima: CEP, 1971), translated and edited by Sister Caridad Inda and John Eagleton as *A Theology of Liberation: History, Politics, and Salvation* (Maryknoll, N.Y.: Orbis, 1973).

83. See, for instance, Lucien Lévy-Bruhl, *Les fonctions mentales dans les sociétés inférieures* (The Mental Functions of Inferior Societies) (Paris: F. Alcan, 1910), translated by Lilian A. Clare as *How Natives Think* (New York: Knopf, 1925); and Lucien Lévy-Bruhl, *Mentalité primitive* (Paris: F. Alcan, 1922), translated by Lilian A. Clare as *Primitive Mentality* (London: Allen and Unwin, 1923).

84. Placide Tempels, *Bantoe-filosofie: Oorspronkelijke tekst* (Antwerp: De Sikkel, 1946); most African thinkers used A. Rubbens's French translation of the book from the Dutch: *La philosophie bantoue* (Paris: Présence Africaine, 1949), which was translated into English by Colin King as *Bantu Philosophy*, with a foreword by Margaret Read (Paris: Présence Africaine, 1959).

85. A good selection of texts representing these three schools can be found in Albert Mosley, ed., *African Philosophy: Selected Readings* (Englewood Cliffs, N.J.: Prentice Hall, 1995). Given this focus in African cultural debates on Africans' ability to think theoretically (and the constraints of space here), I do not cover the African discussions of theology in general or African liberation theology in particular, hoping to be able to do so in a future study.

86. Léopold Sédar Senghor, "Negrohood: Psychology of the African Negro," in Mosley, ed., *African Philosophy*, 120, emphasis in the original. Among Senghor's writings on the topic in the original French, see *Négritude et humanisme* (Negrohood and Humanism) (Paris: Editions du Seuil, 1964), *Négritude et civilisation de l'universel* (Negrohood and the Civilization of the Universal) (Paris: Seuil, 1977), and *Ce que je crois: Négritude, francité et civilisation de l'universel* (What I Believe: Negrohood, Frenchness, and the Civilization of the Universal) (Paris: Grasset, 1988).

87. Senghor, "Negrohood," 122, 127, emphasis in the original.

88. See Léopold Sédar Senghor, *Nation et voie africaine du socialisme* (Paris: Présence Africaine, 1961), translated into English by Mercer Cook as *On African Socialism* (New York: Praeger, 1964).

89. The speech is given in Léopold Sédar Senghor, *Fondements de l'africanité; ou, Négritude et arabité* (Paris: Présence Africaine, [1967?]), translated by Mercer Cook as *Foundations of "Africanité," or "Négritude" and "Arabité"* (Paris: Présence Africaine, 1971).

90. Cheikh Anta Diop, *Civilisation ou barbarie: Anthropologie sans complaisance* (Paris: Présence Africaine, 1981); I quote from the translation *Civilization or Barbarism: An Authentic Anthropology* by Yaa-Lengi Meema Ngemi and edited by Harold J. Salemson and Marjolijn de Jager, with an informative introduction by John Henrik Clarke (New York: Lawrence Hill, 1991), 217. See also Cheikh Anta Diop, *The African Origin of Civilization: Myth or Reality*, translated by Mercer Cook (New York: Lawrence Hill, 1974), based on excerpts from two of his original books in French, *Nations nègres et culture* (Negro Nations and Culture) (Paris: Editions africaines, 1955) and *Antériorité des civilisations nègres: Mythe ou vérité* (Priority of Negro Civilization: Myth or Truth) (Paris: Présence Africaine, 1967). On Egyptianism and Afrocentrism, see Stephen Howe, *Afrocentrism: Mythical Pasts and Imagined Homes* (London: Verso, 1998), which has an extensive bibliography.

91. Alexis Kagamé, *La philosophie Bantu-rwandaise de l'être* (The Bantu-Rwandan Philosophy of Being) (Brussels: Académie des Sciences Coloniales, 1955).

92. For an overview of this debate, see Abiola Irele's introduction in Paulin Hountondji, *African Philosophy: Myth and Reality*, translated by Henry Evans with Jonathan Rée, 7–30 (Bloomington: Indiana University Press, 1996). See also Abiola Irele, *The African Experience in Literature and Ideology* (London: Heinemann, 1981; reprint, Bloomington: Indiana University Press, 1990). Further overviews can be found in Ivan Karp and D. A. Masolo, "Introduction: African Philosophy as Cultural Inquiry," in Ivan Karp and D. A. Masolo, eds., *African Philosophy as Cultural Inquiry*, 1–18 (Bloomington: Indiana University Press, 2000), and Robert E. Birt, "Feature Review: Identity and the Question of African Philosophy," *Philosophy East & West* 41, no. 1 (1991): 95–109.

93. See the following works by Marcien Towa: *Essai sur la problématique philosophique dans l'Afrique actuelle* (Essay on the Philosophical Problematic in Present Africa) (Yaoundé, Cameroun: CLE, 1971); *Léopold Sédar Senghor, négritude ou servitude?* (Leopold Sedar Senghor, Negritude or Servitude) (Yaoundé, Cameroon: CLE, 1971); *Idée d'une philosophie négro-africaine* (The Idea of a Negro-African Philosophy) (Yaoundé, Cameroon: CLE, 1979); and "Conditions for the Affirmation of a Modern African Philosophical Thought," in Tsenay Serequeberhan, ed., *African Philosophy: The Essential Readings*, 187–200 (New York: Paragon House, 1991).

94. Towa, *Idee d'une philosophie négro-africaine*, 65, 66, 67.

95. Ibid., 103. The end of the book includes an exchange between the author and his critics, 71–114.

96. Ibid., 62.

97. Paulin Hountondji, *Sur la philosophie africaine: Critique de l'ethnophilosophie* (Paris: François Maspero, 1977); see note 92 for the translation of this work, *African Philosophy: Myth and Reality*. In English, see also Paulin Hountondji, *Struggle for Meaning: Reflections on Philosophy, Culture, and Democracy in Africa*, translated by John Conteh-Morgan, with a foreword by Kwame Anthony Appiah (Athens: Ohio University Center for International Studies, 2002).

98. It is interesting to note here that after studying philosophy in Paris, Hountondji became a professor of philosophy at the National University of Benin. He was involved in Benin's return to democracy in 1992 and became minister of education and minister for culture and communication in the Beninese government between 1992 and 1994.

99. Hountondji, *African Philosophy*, viii.

100. Ibid., xi.

101. Ibid., x.

102. Ibid., xxiii.

103. Henry Odera Oruka, "African Philosophy: A Brief Personal History and Current Debate," in Guttorm Floistad, ed., *Contemporary Philosophy: A New Survey*, vol. 5: *African Philosophy* (The Hague: Martinus Nijhoff, 1987), 51–52. This volume contains other essays on the topic, including Lucius Outlaw, "'African Philosophy': Deconstructive and Reconstructive Challenges," 9–44, and Lansana Keita, "African Philosophy in Context: A Reply to Hountondji's 'Que peut la philosophie,'" 79–98. Additional essays on the topic can be found in Richard A. Wright, ed., *African Philosophy: An Introduction* (Lanham, Md.: University Press of America, 1984), in particular P. O. Bodunrin, "The Question of African Philosophy," 1–24; Henri Maurier, "Do We Have an African Philosophy?" 25–40; Richard Wright, "Investigating African Philosophy," 41–56; and Benjamin E. Oguah, "African Western Philosophy: A Comparative Study," 213–26. See also Emmanuel Chukwudi Eze, "What Is African Philosophy?" in Emmanuel Chukwudi Eze, ed., *African Philosophy: An Anthology*, 1–56 (Cambridge, Mass.: Blackwell, 1998); Ernest Wamba-dia-Wamba, "Philosophy and African Intellectuals: Mimesis of Western Classicism, Ethnophilosophical Romanticism, or African Self-Mastery?" *Quest* 5, no. 1 (1991): 4–17; and Innocent Onyewuenyi, "Is There an African Philosophy?" *Journal of African Studies* 3 (1976): 513–28.

104. Henry Odera Oruka, ed., *Sage Philosophy: Indigenous Thinkers and Modern Debate on African Philosophy* (Leiden: Brill, 1990). From Oruka, see also, "Sagacity in African Philosophy," *International Philosophical Quarterly* 23, no. 4 (1983): 383–93, reprinted in Tsenay Serequeberhan, ed., *African Philosophy: The Essential Readings*, 47–62 (New York: Paragon House, 1991); "Cultural Fundamentals in Philosophy: Obstacles in Philosophical Dialogues," *Quest* 4, no. 2 (1990): 20–37; and "On Philosophy and Humanism

in Africa," *Philosophy and Social Action* 5, nos. 1–2 (1979): 7–13. For a discussion of this "sagacity" school, see Gail Presbey, "Who Counts as a Sage? Problems in the Future Implementation of Sage Philosophy," *Quest* 11, no. 2 (1997): 53–68; and the essays in Parker English and Kibujjo M. Kalumba, eds., *African Philosophy: A Classical Approach* (Upper Saddle River, N.J.: Prentice Hall, 1996).

105. Kwasi Wiredu, *Philosophy and an African Culture* (Cambridge, U.K.: Cambridge University Press, 1980). See also Kwasi Wiredu, "Formulating Modern Thought in African Languages: Some Theoretical Considerations," in V. Y. Mudimbe, ed., *The Surreptitious Speech: Presence Africaine and the Politics of Otherness, 1947–1987*, 201–24 (Chicago: University of Chicago Press, 1992).

106. Kwasi Wiredu, *Cultural Universals and Particulars: An African Perspective* (Bloomington: Indiana University Press, 1996).

107. Kwasi Wiredu, *Conceptual Decolonization in African Philosophy* (Ibadan, Nigeria: Hope, 1995); and Kwasi Wiredu, "The Need for Conceptual Decolonisation in African Philosophy," in Heinz Kimmerle and Franz Wimmer, eds., *Philosophy and Democracy in Intercultural Perspective*, 11–22 (Amsterdam: Rodopi, 1997). On the significance of language for African philosophy, see also Samuel Oluoch Imbo, "What Should the Language(s) of African Philosophy Be?" in his book *An Introduction to African Philosophy*, 97–122 (Lanham, Md.: Rowman and Littlefield, 1998). On decolonization in general, see Chinweizu, *Decolonising the African Mind* (Lagos, Nigeria: Pero Press, 1987).

108. Kwame Gyekye, *An Essay on African Philosophical Thought: The Akan Conceptual Scheme* (Philadelphia: Temple University Press, 1995).

109. Kwame Gyekye, *Tradition and Modernity: Philosophical Reflections on the African Experience* (New York: Oxford University Press, 1997). See also Jean-Marie Makang, "Of the Good Use of Tradition: Keeping the Critical Perspective in African Philosophy," in Emmanuel Chukwudi Eze, ed., *Postcolonial African Philosophy: A Critical Reader*, 324–38 (Cambridge, Mass.: Blackwell, 1997).

110. Peter Amato, "African Philosophy and Modernity," in Eze, ed., *Postcolonial African Philosophy*, 71–99.

111. Ngugi wa Thiong'o, *Decolonising the Mind: The Politics of Language in African Literature* (Nairobi, Kenya: Heinemann, 1986), 27–28.

112. See, for instance, Achebe's 1980 interview with Rosemary Colmer, "The Critical Generation," in Bernth Lindfors, ed., *Conversations with Chinua Achebe*, 57–63 (Jackson: University Press of Mississippi, 1997). See also Biodun Jeyifo, ed., *Conversations with Wole Soyinka* (Jackson: University Press of Mississippi, 2001).

113. Kwame Anthony Appiah, *In My Father's House: Africa in the Philosophy of Culture* (New York: Oxford University Press, 1992).

114. Ibid., 176.

115. Filomina Chioma Steady, "African Feminism: A Worldwide Perspective," in Rosalyn Terborg-Penn, Sharon Harley, and Andrea Benton Rushing, eds., *Women in Africa and the African Diaspora*, 3–24 (Washington, D.C.: Howard University Press, 1987).

116. Molara Ogundipe-Leslie, "Introduction: Moving the Mountains, Making the Links," in Molara Ogundipe-Leslie, *Re-creating Ourselves: African Women and Critical Transformations*, 1–18 (Trenton, N.J.: Africa World Press, 1994). Nigerian literary critic Chikwenye Ogunyemi advocates the same kind of "womanism." See the interview with her in Susan Arndt, "African Gender Trouble and African Womanism: An Interview with Chikwenye Ogunyemi and Wanjira Muthoni," *Signs* 25, no. 3 (2000): 709–26.

117. Ama Ata Aidoo, "The African Woman Today," in Obioma Naemeka, ed., *Sisterhood, Feminisms, and Power: From Africa to the Diaspora*, 39–50 (Trenton, N.J.: Africa World Press, 1998).

118. See Aili Mari Tripp, "Rethinking Difference: Comparative Perspectives from Africa," *Signs* 25, no. 3 (2000): 649–75.

119. Safro Kwame, "Feminism and African Philosophy," in Safro Kwame, ed., *Readings in African Philosophy: An Akan Collection*, 253–68 (Lanham, Md.: University Press of America, 1995).

120. Arndt, "African Gender Trouble and African Womanism."

121. Jean-Paul Sartre, "Orphée noir," in Léopold Sédar Senghor, ed., *Anthologie de la nouvelle poésie nègre et malgache de langue française* (Anthology of the New Negro and Madagascan Poetry in the French Language), ix–xliv (Paris: Presses Universitaires de France, 1948), translated by S. W. Allen as *Black Orpheus* (Paris: Présence Africaine, 1976). For Sartre's writings on colonialism, see his collected essays in *Colonialism and Neocolonialism*.

122. Sartre, *Black Orpheus*, 59–60.

123. Frantz Fanon, "The Fact of Blackness," in Franz Fanon, *Black Skin, White Masks* (New York: Grove Press, 1967), 133, 138.

124. Ibid., 138. In the 1963 "Appendix: From Toussaint L'Ouverture to Fidel Castro" to his 1938 book *The Black Jacobins: Toussaint L'Ouverture and the San Domingo Revolution* (2d rev. ed., New York: Random House, 1963) C. L. R. James expresses a similar disapproval of Sartre's stand on *négritude*. He says: "Jean-Paul Sartre has done the finest of critical appreciations of *Cahier* [*d'un retour au pays natal* of Aimé Césaire] as poetry, but his explanation of what he conceives Negritude to mean is a disaster," 401. This criticism is surprising because what James seems to emphasize in Césaire's thought is precisely the move from *négritude* to a common humanity that Sartre advocates in *Black Orpheus*. I think that the difference between the two positions resides in the mode of linking *négritude* to the universal: for Senghor and James, it is an affirmed and fixed *négritude* contributing to and becoming part of the universal, whereas for Sartre it is an overcome *négritude* that is to transcend itself toward a universal humanity.

125. Sartre, *Black Orpheus*, 58.

126. From the conference Web site at http://www.imagineafrica.org/idea.

127. Du Bois, *The Souls of Black Folk*; Ashis Nandy, *The Intimate Enemy: Loss and Recovery of Self Under Colonialism* (Delhi: Oxford University Press, 1983); Derek Walcott, *What the Twilight Says: Essays* (New York: Farrar, Straus and Giroux, 1998), and "The Caribbean: Culture or Mimicry?" *Journal of Interamerican Studies and World Affairs* 16, no. 1 (1974): 3–13; Jamaica Kincaid, *A Small Place* (New York: Farrar, Straus and Giroux, 1988); Linda Tuhiwai Smith, *Decolonizing Methodologies: Research and Indigenous Peoples* (London: Zed Books, 1999); and Haunani-Kay Trask, *From a Native Daughter: Colonialism and Sovereignty in Hawai'i* (Honolulu: University of Hawai'i Press, 1999).

128. Abdelkebir al-Khatibi, "Double Criticism: The Decolonization of Arab Sociology," in Halim Barakat, ed., *Contemporary North Africa: Issues of Development and Integration* (Washington, D.C.: Center for Contemporary Arab Studies, Georgetown University, 1985), 14.

129. Among the most eloquent expressions of this journey from ideology to humanistic critical thought—and the most beautiful at that—is Mahmud Darwish's (1941–2008) poetic odyssey from narrow nationalism to deep humanistic, existential meditation. Celebrated by critics and the general Arab public alike as the greatest contemporary Arab poet, Darwish often expressed his difficulty getting heard by his readers and hearers (his poetry readings were attended by thousands and sometimes by tens of thousands when held in sport stadiums) outside the immediate politiconationalist register. Himself actively involved in the political struggles of his Palestinian homeland, he demanded the right to be liberated from the constraints of the tragic historical circumstances in order to express the wider concerns of the human condition and the right not to be confined to identity affirmation in order to explore the wider humanistic poetic levels. Indeed, his later poetry became increasingly meditative on issues of love and death, without, however, disconnecting from the ever-present experiences of occupation and injustice. Among the numerous interviews in which he articulated this frustration, see, for instance, the series of five interviews he did with Lebanese writer and critic Abdo Wazen in *al-Hayat* in 2005 (December 10, 11, 12, 13, and 14). On this theme, see also an article by one of Darwish's companions, Lebanese communist thinker Muhammad Dakrub, "Maqala fi Tamhid wa Faslayn wa ma Yushbih al-Khatima" (An Article with an Introduction, Two Chapters, and What Resembles a Conclusion), in *Mulhaq al-Nahar* (858 [August 17, 2008]: 6–8, the cultural supplement of the Lebanese daily *al-Nahar*), which was dedicated to Darwish on the occasion of his passing away on August 9, 2008.

Conclusion

1. Here is a list of the interviews, although it might not be exhaustive: Samir Amin (January 23, 2006), Georges Tarabichi (January 30, 2006), Taher Labib (February 6, 2006), Burhan Ghalyun (February 13, 2006), Ali Umlil (February 20, 2006), Wajih Kawtharani (February 27, 2006), Muhammad al-Rumaihi (March 6, 2006), Abdel Mon'im Said (March 13, 2006), Ibrahim al-Bahili (March 27, 2006), Saad Eddin Ibrahim (April 3, 2006), Abdallah al-Ghadhdhami (April 10, 2006), Tayyeb Tizini (April 17, 2006), Turki Hamad (April 24, 2006), Mahmud Abdel Fadil (May 1, 2006), Ali Harb (May 8, 2006), Muhammad Jamal Barut (May 15, 2006), Saad el-Bazi'i (May 22, 2006), Al-Haytham al-Ayyubi (June 5, 2006), Muhammad Jaber al-Ansari (June 12, 2006), Nawal el-Saadawi (June 19, 2006), Fakhri Karim (July 3, 2006), Ismail Siraj al-Din (January 1, 2007), Moncef Marzouki (February 2, 2006), Nassif Hitti (February 12, 2007).

2. The Abu Dhabi Council for Culture and Heritage has recently launched a new translation project called Kalima (Word). It will produce a hundred translations a year with special attention paid to quality and diversity, covering a wide range of works from world literature, the social and natural sciences, and the humanities at large. It would be interesting to compare at a future point this upcoming translation movement with the one that Rifa'a Tahtawi initiated in the nineteenth century. As a matter of fact, the whole set of projects launched by the United Arab Emirates and other Persian Gulf countries devoted to the establishment of educational and cultural institutions will certainly be interesting to monitor. This region manifests in this sense a vitality that is quite unique in the Arab world, albeit one that is initiated and organized by the rulers and often geared toward cultural consumption—that is, toward the importation of cultural goods and institutions, such as prestigious museums and universities from the West, without involving the local populations in their creation and planning. The repercussions of this movement in the Persian Gulf region and in the rest of the Arab world are still to be observed. Together with the democratic movements in Morocco, they represent the rare foci of promising dynamics in the Arab region.

3. Franck Mermier, currently head of the Institut Français du Proche Orient in Beirut, offers an informative overview of the publishing activity in the Arab world in his book *Le livre et la ville: Beyrouth et l'édition arabe* (The Book and the City: Beirut and the Arab Edition) (Paris: Actes Sud, Sindbad, 2005), recently translated into Arabic as *Al-Kitab wa al-Madina: Bayrut wa al-Nashr al-'Arabi* (Beirut: Mukhtarat, 2006).

4. According to the latest report of the Arab League Educational, Cultural, and Scientific Organization (ALECSO, founded in 1970 and based in Tunis) released in January 2008, one-third of the Arab population, roughly 100 million Arabs (out of 335 million), is illiterate, with 75 million of them between the ages of fifteen and forty-five. The rate

reaches 46.5 percent among the female population, despite the 1976 ALECSO program for eradicating illiteracy in the Arab world and the 1980 fund for adult literacy program.

5. See the issues of the journal *al-Adab* devoted to censorship in the Arab world: vol. 49, nos. 3–4 and 5–6 (2001); vol. 50, nos. 7–8 (2002). See also Mona A. Nsouli and Lokman I. Meho, *Censorship in the Arab World: An Annotated Bibliography* (Lanham, Md.: Scarecrow Press, 2006).

6. See Fahmy Jedaane, *Fi al-Khalass al-Niha'i: Maqal fi wu'ud al-Islamiyyin wa al-'Ilmaniyyin wa al-Liberaliyyin* (On Final Salvation: Essay on the Promises of the Islamists, the Secularists, and the Liberals) (Amman, Jordan: Dar al-Shuruq, 2007).

7. Muta' al-Safadi, "Al-Nahda wa Ishkaliyyat al-Tashir al-Siyasi: Ihbat Dawlat al-Istiqlal Tamhidan li Tafkik al-Mujtama'"(The Nahda and the Desertification of Politics: Collapse of the Independence State as a Prelude to the Dismantling of Society,) July 3, 2006; "Safinat al-Mashru' al-Nahdawi ila Ayn . . . Tasyiss al-Din aw Tadyin al-Siyasa?" (The Boat of the Nahda Project: Where To? The Politicization of Religion and the Sacralization of Politics), April 10, 2006; and "Akher Idyolojia 'Arabiyya: Tarsikh Thaqafat al-'Ajz ka 'Aqida Intisariyya" (Latest Arab Ideology: Anchoring the Culture of Impotence as a Doctrine of Victory), May 8, 2006.

8. On issues of Arab state formation and development, see Giacomo Luciani, ed., *The Arab State* (Berkeley and Los Angeles: University of California Press, 1990); see also Ghassan Salamé, ed., *The Foundations of the Arab State* (London: Croom Helm, 1987), and Nazih Ayyubi, *Over-stating the Arab State: Politics and Society in the Middle East* (London: I. B. Tauris, 1995).

9. Samir Kassir, *Considérations sur le malheur arabe* (Thoughts on Arab Wretchedness) (Paris: Actes Sud, 2004), simultaneously translated into Arabic by Jean Hachem as *Ta'ammulat fi al-Shaqa' al-'Arabi*, revised by Haytham al-Amin and with an introduction by Elias Khoury (Beirut: Dar al-Nahar, 2005), and a year later into English by Will Hobson as *Being Arab* (London: Verso, 2006). Kassir was born in Beirut of an originally Palestinian father and a Syrian mother, a background that informed much of his intellectual and political endeavor. He studied history at the Sorbonne, and his dissertation on the first half of the Lebanese Civil War was published as *La Guerre du Liban: De la dissension national au conflit régional (1975–1982)* (The Lebanese War: From National Dissension to Regional Conflict [1976–1982]) (Paris: Karthala and Cermoc, 1994). Together with the Paris-based Syrian dissident Farouk Mardam-Bey, head of the Arab series in Actes Sud, he published a two-volume study of the French foreign policy in the Israeli-Palestinian conflict, *Itinéraires de Paris à Jérusalem: La France et le conflit israélo-arabe* (Itineraries from Paris to Jerusalem: France and the Arab-Israeli Conflict), vol. 1: *1917–1958*, and vol. 2: *1958–1991* (Paris: Livres de la Revue d'Etudes Palestiniennes, 1992 and 1993). His last major work was a big volume on the

history of Beirut, *Histoire de Beyrouth* (Paris: Fayard, 2003). Beginning in his early twenties, he wrote for the French periodical *Le Monde Diplomatique*, and in the early 1990s he edited the Lebanese French periodical *L'Orient-Express* for a number of years. It quickly became a distinguished publication through its innovative layout and original, non-Orientalist, but also atypically Arab nationalist approach to cultural and political issues of the Arab world. Later on he became professor of history at the Université Saint-Joseph of Beirut and renowned editor at the Lebanese daily *an-Nahar*. This daily supported the short-lived democratic Syrian movement that started after the death of Hafez al-Asad in 2000 and came to be known as the Damascus Spring. (For the Damascus Spring, see Alan George, *Syria: Neither Bread nor Freedom* [London: Zed, 2003], and *Un printemps syrien* (Syrian Spring), a special issue of the journal *Confluences Mediterranee* 44 [2002–2003]). It opened its pages to a number of Syrian dissidents. The director of *an-Nahar*, Jubran Tuéni, son of its owner Ghassan Tuéni, was assassinated by means of a massive car bomb as he was heading to his office in 2005. Kassir's eloquent editorials became famous for their courageous and visionary outlook during the harshest period of repression in Lebanon at the turn of the twenty-first century under the Syrian hegemony. He was intimidated and threatened. In recent years, he had become actively involved in the founding of the Democratic Left Party and played an important role in shaping the popular uprising that followed the assassination of Lebanese prime minister Rafiq al-Hariri in February 14, 2005. The uprising came to be known as the Cedar Revolution, directed against the Syrian-Lebanese repressive apparatus. Kassir was assassinated by means of a car bomb as he went out of his Beirut home on June 2, 2005. He was barely forty-five years old.

10. Hisham Saleh, *Al-Insidad al-Tarikhi: Limadha Fashila Mashru' al-Tanwir fi al-'Alam al-'Arabi?* (The Historical Deadlock: Why Did the Enlightenment Project Fail in the Arab World?) (Beirut: Dar al-Saqi, 2007). I disagree with the author's culturalist answer, but find the theme significant and emblematic of the present Arab debates.

Bibliography

The bibliography is divided into six sections covering Arabic, Latin American, African, European, U.S. American, and other works.

Arabic

Abaza, Mona. "Japan as Imagined by Arabs." *IIAS Newsletter* 27 (2002): 19.

Abbas, Ra'uf. *Al-Tanwir al-Yabani wa al-Tanwir al-Arabi* (The Japanese and Egyptian Enlightenment). Cairo: Mirit li al-Nashr wa al-Maʿlumat, 2001. English translation: *Japanese and Egyptian Enlightenment: Comparative Study of Fukuzawa Yukichi and Rifaʿa al-Tahtawi,* no translator given. Tokyo: Institute for the Study of Languages and Cultures of Asia and Africa, 1990.

Abd al-Latif, Kamal. *Asʾilat al-Nahda al-ʿArabiyya: Al-Tarikh, al-Hadatha, al-Tawasul* (Questions of the Arab Nahda: History, Modernity, Continuity). Beirut: Markaz Dirasat al-Wihda al-ʿArabiyya, 2003.

Abdel Latif, Kamal. *Asʾilat al-Fikr al-Falsafi fi al-Maghreb* (Questions of Philosophical Thought in the Maghreb). Beirut: Al-Markaz al-Thaqafi al-ʿArabi, 2003.

Abdel-Malek, Anouar. *Al-ʿArab wa al-Yaban: Hiwar ʿArabi Yabani Hawla al-Hadara wa al-Qiyam wa al-Thaqafa fi al-Yaban wa al-Watan al-ʿArabi* (The Arabs and Japan: Arab-Japanese Dialogue on Civilization, Values, and Culture in Japan and in the Arab Homeland). Amman, Jordan: Muntada al-Fikr al-ʿArabi, 1992.

——. *Egypte société militaire.* Paris: Seuil, 1962. English translation: *Egypt: Military Society, the Army Regime, the Left, and Social Change Under Nasser.* Translated by Charles Lam Markmann. New York: Random House, 1968. Arabic translation: *Al-Mujtamaʿ al-Misri wa al-Jaysh: 1952–1967.* Cairo: Markaz al-Mahrusah li al-Buhuth wa al-Tadrib wa al-Nashr, 1998.

——. "Al-Khususiyya wa al-Asala" (Specificity and Authenticity). *Al-Adab* 22, no. 5 (1974): 41–43.

———. *La pensée arabe contemporaine*. Paris: Seuil, 1970. English translation: *Contemporary Arab Political Thought*, translated by Michael Pallis. London: Zed, 1983.

———. *Rih al-Sharq* (The East Wind). Cairo: Dar al-Mustaqbal, 1983.

Abdel Rahman, A'isha. *Maqal fi al-Insan: Dirasa Qur'aniyya* (Essay on the Human: A Qur'anic Study). Cairo: Dar al-Ma'arif, 1969.

Abdel Raziq [Abd al-Raziq], Ali. "The Caliphate and the Bases of Power." In John J. Donohue and John L. Esposito, eds., *Islam in Transition: Muslim Perspectives* 29–37. New York: Oxford University Press, 1982; 2d ed., 2006.

———. *Al-Islam wa Usul al-Hukm* (Islam and the Principles of Governing). Cairo: Matba'at Misr, 1925.

Abduh, Muhammad. *Al-Islam wa al-Nasraniyya Bayna al-'Ilm wa al-Madaniyya* (Islam and Christianity Between Science and Civilization). Beirut: Dar al-Hadatha, 1983.

———. *Risalat al-Tawhid* (The Monotheistic Mission). Cairo: Matba'at al-Manar, 1908 or 1909, 1942–1943. English translation: *The Theology of Unity*. Translated by Ishaq Masa'ad and Kenneth Cragg. London: Allen and Unwin, 1966.

Abisaab, Malek and Rula Jurdi Abisaab. "A Century After Qasim Amin: Fictive Kinship and Historical Uses of 'Tahrir al-Mar'a." *Al Jadid* 6, no. 32 (2000): n.p.

Abou El Fadl, Khaled. *The Place of Tolerance in Islam*. Edited by Joshua Cohen and Ian Lague. Boston: Beacon Press, 2002.

Abu-Lughod, Ibrahim. "Al-Isti'mar wa Azamat al-Tatawwur fi al-Watan al-'Arabi" (Colonialism and the Crisis of Development in the Arab Homeland). *Al-Ma'rifa* 148 (1974): 239–51.

———. "Retreat from the Secular Path? Islamic Dilemmas of Arab Politics." *Review of Politics* 28 (1966): 447–76.

Abu-Lughod, Janet. "Decolonizing the Women of Islam." *Gazelle Review* 7 (1980): 51–59.

Abu-Lughod, Lila. "Orientalism and Middle East Feminist Studies." *Feminist Studies* 27, no. 1 (2001): 101–13.

———, ed. *Remaking Women: Feminism in the Middle East*. Princeton, N.J.: Princeton University Press, 1998.

Abu-Rabi', Ibrahim. *Contemporary Arab Thought: Studies in Post-1967 Arab Intellectual History*. London: Pluto Press, 2004.

Abu Zayd, Nasr Hamid. "Al-Bushido, al-Mukawwinat al-Taqlidiyya li al-Thaqafa al-Yabaniyya" (Bushido: The Traditional Constituents of Japanese Culture). In Nitobe Inazo, *Al-Bushido*, translated by Nasr Hamid Abu Zayd, 9–56. Kuwait: Dar Su'ad al-Sabbah, 1993.

———. "The Concept of Human Rights, the Process of Modernization, and the Politics of Western Domination." *Internationale Politik und Gesellschaft / International Politics and Society* 4 (1998): 434–37.

———. *Dawa'ir al-Khawf: Qira'a fi Khitab al-Mar'a* (The Circles of Fear: A Reading in the Discourse on Women). Beirut: Al-Markaz al-Thaqafi al-'Arabi, 2000.

——. "The Dilemma of the Literary Approach to the Qur'an." *Alif: Journal of Comparative Poetics* 23 (2003): 8–47.

——. *Mafhum al-Nass: Dirasah fi 'Ulum al-Qur'an* (The Concept of the Text: A Study in the Sciences of the Qur'an). Cairo: Al-Hay'a al-Misriyya al-'Amma li al-Kitab, 1990.

——. *Naqd al-Khitab al-Dini* (The Critique of Religious Discourse). Cairo: Dar Sina li al-Nashr, 1992; 2d ed., 1994.

——. "The Qur'anic Concept of Justice." *Journal for Intercultural Philosophy, Polylog* 3 (2001). Available at http://them.polylog.org/3/fan-en.htm.

——. *Reformation of Islamic Thought: A Critical Historical Analysis*. Amsterdam: Amsterdam University Press, 2006.

——. "The Sectarian and the Renaissance Discourse." Translated and with an introduction by Mona Mikhail. *Alif: Journal of Comparative Poetics* 19 (1999): 203–22.

——. *Al-Tafkir fi Zaman al-Takfir: Didd al-Jahl wa al-Zayf wa al-Khurafa* (Thinking in the Time of Anathema: Against Ignorance and Falsehood and Myth). Cairo: Dar Sina li al-Nashr, 1995.

——. "Al-Urthudhuksiyya al-Mu'ammama: 'Indama Yudmaj al-Tarikh al-Ijtima'i bi al-Muqaddas" (The Generalized Orthodoxy: When Social History Is Conflated with the Sacred). *Al-Naqid* 74 (1994): 26–34.

Adonis. *Fatiha li Nihayat al-Qarn* (Overture to the Century's Endings). Beirut: Dar al-Nahar, 1998; originally published in 1980.

——. "Khawatir Hawl Madhahir al-Takhalluf al-Fikri al-'Arabi" (Some Thoughts on the Manifestations of Arab Intellectual Retardation in Arab Society). *Al-Adab* 22, no. 5 (1974): 27–29.

——. *Al-Thabit wa al-Mutahawwil: Bahth fi al-Ibda' wa al-Itiba' 'Inda al-'Arab* (The Constant and the Changing: A Study in Creativity and Imitation Among Arabs). 4 vols. 7th ed. Beirut: Dar al-Saqi, 1994.

Al-Afghani, Jamal al-Din. *An Islamic Response to Imperialism: Political and Religious Writings of Sayyid Jamal al-Din al-Afghani*. Edited by Nikki R. Keddie. Berkeley and Los Angeles: University of California Press, 1968.

Ahmed, Leila. "Arab Women: 1995." In Hisham Sharabi, ed., *The Next Arab Decade: Alternative Futures*, 208–20. Boulder, Colo.: Westview Press, 1988.

——. *A Border Passage*. New York: Penguin, 1999.

——. "Early Islam and the Position of Women: The Problem of Interpretation." In Nikki R. Keddie and Beth Baron, eds., *Women in Middle Eastern History: Shifting Boundaries in Sex and Gender*, 58–73. New Haven, Conn.: Yale University Press, 1991.

——. *Women and Gender in Islam: Historical Roots of a Modern Debate*. New Haven, Conn.: Yale University Press, 1992.

Al-Alim, Mahmud Amin. *Mawaqif Naqdiyya min al-Turath* (Critical Positions Regarding Tradition). Cairo: Dar al-Qadaya Fikriyya, 1997; reprint, Beirut: Dar al-Farabi, 2007.

Alsultany, Evelyn. "Dislocations, Arab Jews, and Multicultural Feminism: An Interview with Ella Shohat." *MIT Electronic Journal of Middle East Studies* 5 (2005): 50–56.

Altorki, Soraya. "The Anthropologist in the Field: A Case of 'Indigenous Anthropology' from Saudi Arabia." In Hussein Fahim, ed., *Indigenous Anthropology in Non-Western Countries*, 167–75. Durham: University of North Carolina Press, 1982. Reprinted in Saad Eddin Ibrahim and Nicholas S. Hopkins, eds., *Arab Society: Social Science Perspectives*, 76–83. Cairo: American University of Cairo Press, 1985.

Amateis, Jacques, SDB. *Yusuf al-Khal wa Majallatuhu Shiʿr* (Yusuf al-Khal and His Journal *Shiʿr*). Beirut: Dar al-Nahar and Orient Institut der Deutschen Morgenländische Gesellschaft, Band 94, 2004.

Amil, Mahdi. *Azamat al-Hadara al-ʿArabiyya am Azamat al-Burjwaziyya al-ʿArabiyya?* (The Crisis of Arab Civilization or the Crisis of Arab Bourgeoisie?). Beirut: Dar al-Farabi, 1974.

Amin, Ahmad. "Fi al-Naqd al-Adabi Aydan" (On Literary Critique). *Al-Risala* 153 (June 8, 1936): 963–65.

——. *Hayati.* Cairo: Maktabat al-Nahda al-Misriyya, 1958. English translation: *My Life: The Autobiography of an Egyptian Scholar, Writer, and Cultural Leader.* Translated and introduced by Issa J. Boullata. Leiden: Brill, 1978.

——. "Al-Naqd Aydan" (Critique Again). *Al-Risala* 152 (June 1, 1936): 881–83.

——. *Zuʿamaʾ al-Islah fi al-ʿAsr al-Hadith* (The Leaders of Reform in Modern Times). Cairo: Maktabat al-Nahda al-Misriyya, 1948.

Al-Amin, Muhammad. *Al-Ijtimaʿ al-ʿArabi al-Islami: Murajaʿat fi al-Taʿaddudiya wa al-Nahda wa al-Tanwir* (The Arab Islamic Society: Studies in Pluralism, Renaissance, and Enlightenment). Beirut: Dar al-Hadi, 2003.

Amin, Qasim. *Les Egyptiens: Réponse à M. Le Duc d'Harcourt* (Egyptians: A Response to the Duc d'Harcourt). Cairo: Jules Barbier, 1894.

——. *The Liberation of Women—The New Woman: Two Documents in the History of Egyptian Feminism.* Translated by Samiha Sidhom Peterson. Cairo: American University of Cairo Press, 1992.

——. *Al-Marʾa al-Jadida* (The New Woman). Cairo: Al-Majlis al-Aʿla li al-Thaqafa, 1999.

——. *Tahrir al-Marʾa.* Cairo: Maktabat Dar al-Kutub wa al-Wathaʾiq al-Qawmiyya bi al-Qahira, 2008.

Amin, Samir. *Déconnexion, pour sortir du système mondial.* Paris: La Découverte, 1986. English translation: *Delinking: Towards a Polycentric World.* Translated by Michael Wolfers. London: Zed Books, 1990.

——. *L'eurocentrisme: Critique d'une idéologie.* Paris: Antropos-Economica, 1988. English translation: *Eurocentrism.* Translated by Russell Moore. New York: Monthly Review Press, 1989.

———. *Itinéraire intellectuel: Regards sur le demi-siècle 1945–90.* Paris: L'Harmattan, 1993. English translation: *Re-reading the Postwar Period: An Intellectual Itinerary.* Translated by Michael Wolfers. New York: Monthly Review Press, 1994.

———. *A Life Looking Forward: Memoirs of an Independent Marxist.* London: Zed Books, 2007.

Amireh, Amal. "Framing Nawal el Saadawi: Arab Feminism in a Transnational World." *Sign: Journal of Women in Culture and Society* 26, no. 1 (2000): 215–49.

———. "Writing the Difference: Feminists' Invention of the 'Arab Woman.'" In Bishnupriya Ghosh and Brinda Bose, eds., *Interventions: Feminist Dialogues on Third World Women's Literature and Film,* 185–212. New York: Garland, 1997.

Amireh, Amal and Suheir Majaj, eds. *Going Global: The Transnational Reception of Third World Women Writers.* New York: Garland, 2000.

Anderson, Lisa. "Arab Democracy: Dismal Prospects." *World Policy Journal* 18, no. 3 (2001): no page numbers.

———. "Democracy in the Arab World: A Critique of the Political Culture Approach." In Rex Brynen, Bahgat Korany, and Paul Noble, eds., *Political Liberalization and Democratization in the Arab World,* vol. 1: *Theoretical Perspectives,* 77–92. Boulder, Colo.: Lynne Rienner, 1995.

Anis, Mona. Review of Abdel Rahman Badawi's two-volume autobiography, *Sirat Hayati* (The Story of My Life). *Al-Ahram Weekly* 477 (April 2000): 13–19. Available at http://weekly.ahram.org.eg/2000/477/bk1_477.htm.

Al-Ansari, Muhammad Jaber. *Al-Fikr al-ʿArabi wa Siraʿ al-Addad: Kayfa Ihtawat al-Tawfiqiyya al-Siraʿ al-Mahzur Bayn al-Usuliyya wa al-ʿIlmaniyya wa al-Hasm al-Mʿuajjal Bayn al-Islam wa al-Gharb: Tashkhis Hala li al-la Hasm fi al-Hayat al-ʿArabiyya wa al-Ihtiwaʾ al-Tawfiqi li al-Jadaliyyat al-Mahzura* (Arab Thought and the Struggle of Opposites: How Conciliatory Thought Contained the Forbidden Struggle Between Fundamentalism and Secularism and the Postponed Settlement Between Islam and the West: Diagnosis of the No-Settlement Situation in Arab Life and the Conciliatory Containment of Forbidden Dialectics). Beirut: Al-Muʾassassa al-ʿArabiyya li al-Dirasat wa al-Nashr, 1999.

———. *Tajdid al-Nahda bi Iktishaf al-Dhat wa Naqdiha* (Renewing the Nahda by Discovering the Self and Critiquing It). 2d ed. Beirut: Al-Muʾassassa al-ʿArabiyya li al-Dirasat wa al-Nashr, 1998.

Antun, Farah. *Ibn Rush wa Falsafatuhu* (Averroes and His Philosophy). Beirut: Dar al-Farabi, 2007.

Al-Aqqad, Abbas Mahmud. *ʿAbqariyyat Muhammad* (The Genius of Muhammad). Cairo: Dar al-Islam, 1943; 2d ed., 1972.

Al-ʿArab wa al-Daʾira al-Ifriqiyya (The Arabs and the African Circle). Beirut: Markaz Dirasat al-Wihda al-ʿArabiyya, 2005.

Arkoun, Mohammed. "L'Islam moderne vu par le Professeur G. E. von Grunebaum" (Modern Islam Seen by Professor G. E. von Grunebaum). *Arabica* 11 (1964): 113–26.

——. *Lectures du Coran* (Readings of the Qur'an). Paris: Maisonneuve et Larose, 1982.

——. *La pensée arabe* (Arab Thought). Paris: Presses Universitaires de France, 1975; 5th ed., 1995.

——. *Pour une critique de la raison islamique* (Toward a Critique of Islamic Reason). Paris: Maisonneuve et Larose, 1984.

——. *Rethinking Islam Today*. Occasional Paper series. Washington, D.C.: Center for Contemporary Arab Studies, Georgetown University, 1987.

——. *The Unthought in Contemporary Islamic Thought*. London: Saqi Books in association with the Institute of Ismaili Studies, 2002.

Arslan, Shakib. "Introduction: Al-Shiʿr al-Jahili, a Manhul am Sahih al-Nisba?" (Jahili Poetry: Fake or Original?). In Muhammad Ahmad al-Ghamrawi, *Al-Naqd al-Tahlili li Kitab "Fi al-Adab al-Jahili"* (The Analytic Critique of the Book *On Jahili Literature*), first 53 pages (Arabic pagination). Cairo: Al-Matbaʿa al-Salafiyya, 1929.

——. *Limadha Taʾakhkhara al-Muslimun wa Limadha Taqaddama Ghayruhum* (Why Did Muslims Lag Behind, and Why Did Others Progress?). Beirut: Al-Hayat, 1975. English translation: *Our Decline and Its Causes*. Translated by M. A. Shakoor. Lahore, Pakistan: Sh. Muhammad Ashraf, 1944; reprint, 1962. New translation: *Our Decline: Its Causes and Remedies*. Translated by Ssekamanya Siraje Abdullah. Kuala Lumpur, Malaysia: Islamic Book Trust, 2004.

Asad, Talal. *Formations of the Secular: Christianity, Islam, Modernity*. Stanford, Calif.: Stanford University Press, 2003.

——. "The Limits of Religious Criticism in the Middle East: Notes on Islamic Public Argument." In Talal Asad, *Genealogies of Religion: Discipline and Reasons of Power in Christianity and Islam*, 200–236. Baltimore: Johns Hopkins University Press, 1993.

Ascha, Ghassan. "The 'Mothers of the Believers': Stereotypes of the Prophet Muhammad's Wives." In Ria Kloppenborg and Wouter J. Hanegraaff, eds., *Stereotypes in Religious Traditions*, 89–107. Leiden: Brill, 1995.

ʿAsr al-Nahda: Muqaddimat Liberaliyya li al Hadatha (The Age of Nahda: Liberal Beginnings for Modernity). Beirut: Al-Markaz al-Thaqafi al-ʿArabi, 2000.

Ateek, Naim. *Justice and Only Justice: A Palestinian Theology of Liberation*. New York: Orbis Books, 1989.

Ateek, Naim. *A Palestinian Christian Cry for Reconciliation*. New York: Orbis Books, 2009.

Atiyeh, George N. and Ibrahim M. Oweiss, eds. *Arab Civilization: Challenges and Responses. Studies in Honor of Constantine K. Zurayk*. Albany: State University of New York Press, 1988.

Averroes. *Fasl al-Maqal fi ma Bayna al-Hikma wa al-Shariʿa min al-Ittisal*. Cairo: Dar al-Maʿarif, 1972. English translation: *On the Harmony of Religion and Philosophy*. Translated by George Hourani. London: Luzac, 1961.

Ayad, Shukry. "Mafhum al-Asala wa al-Tajdid wa al-Thaqafa al-Mu'assira" (The Concept of Authenticity and Renewal and Contemporary Arab Culture). *Al-Adab* 19, no. 11 (1971): 2–5.

Ayyubi, Nazih. *Over-stating the Arab State: Politics and Society in the Middle East.* London: I. B. Tauris, 1995.

Azamat al-Dimuqratiyya fi al-Watan al-'Arabi (The Crisis of Democracy in the Arab Homeland). Beirut: Markaz Dirasat al-Wihda al-'Arabiyya, 1984; reprint, 1987.

al-Azm, Sadeq Jalal. *Dhahniyyat al-Tahrim: Salman Rushdi wa Haqiqat al-Adab* (The Mental Taboo: Salman Rushie and the Truth Within Literature). Beirut: Riad el-Rayyes, 1992.

——. *Dirasat Naqdiyya li Fikr al-Muqawama al-Filistiniyya* (A Critical Study of the Thought of the Palestinian Resistance). Beirut: Dar al-'Awda, 1973.

——. *Dirasat Yasariyya Hawl al-Qadiyya al-Filistiniyya* (Leftist Studies on the Palestinian Cause). Beirut: Dar al-Tali'a, 1970.

——. "The Importance of Being Earnest About Salman Rushdie." *Die Welt des Islams* 31 (1991): 1–49.

——. "An Interview with Sadik al-Azm." *Arab Studies Quarterly* 19, no. 3 (1997): 113–26.

——. *Al-Naqd al-Dhati ba'd al-Hazima* (Self-Criticism After the Defeat). Beirut: Dar al-Tali'a, 1969; new edition, Damascus: Dar Mamduh 'Adwan, 2007.

——. *Naqd al-Fikr al-Dini* (Critique of Religious Thought). Beirut: Dar al-Tali'a, 1982; originally published in 1970.

——. "Orientalism and Orientalism in Reverse." In Alexander Lyon Macfie, ed., *Orientalism: A Reader*, 217–38. New York: New York University Press, 2000.

——. "Palestinian Zionism." *Die Welt des Islams* 28 (1988): 90–98.

al-Azm, Sadeq Jalal, Mustafa al-Tawati, and Muhammad bin Ahmuda. *Athar al-Thawra al-Faransiyya fi Fikr al-Nahda* (The Impact of the French Revolution on the Nahda Thought). Tunis: Al-'Arabiyya, 1991.

al-Azmeh, Aziz. *Dunia al-Din fi Hader al-'Arab* (The World of Religion in the Arabs' Present). Beirut: Dar al-Tali'a, 1996; modified 2d ed., 2002.

——. *Al-'Ilmaniyya min Manzour Mukhtalif* (Secularism from a Different Perspective). Beirut: Markaz Dirasat al-Wihda al-'Arabiyya, 1992; reprint, 1998.

——. *Islams and Modernities.* London: Verso, 1993; new ed., 1996.

——. "Populism Contra Democracy: Recent Democratist Discourse in the Arab World." In G. Salamé, ed., *Democracy Without Democrats? The Renewal of Politics in the Muslim World*, 112–29. London: I. B. Tauris, 1994

——. *Qustantin Zurayq, 'Arabi li al-Qarn al-'Ishrin* (Qustantin Zurayq, an Arab for the Twentieth Century). Beirut: Institute for Palestinian Studies, 2003.

——. "Tawatturat al-Siyassa wa Intikassat Fikr al-Hadatha" (Political Tensions and the Defeat of Modern Thought). In *'Asr al-Nahda: Muqaddimat Liberaliyya li al Hadatha* (The

Age of Nahda: Liberal Beginnings for Modernity), 75–95. Beirut: Al-Markaz al-Thaqafi al-ʿArabi, 2000.

Azra, Azyumardi. "The Transmission of al-Manar's Reformism to the Malay-Indonesian World: The Case of al-Imam and al-Munir." In S. A. Dudoignon, K. Hisao, and K. Yasushi, eds., *Intellectuals in the Modern Islamic World: Transmission, Transformation, Communication*, 143–58. London: Routledge, 2006.

Badawi, Abdel Rahman. *Sirat Hayati* (The Story of My Life). Beirut: Al-Muʾassassa al-ʿArabiyya li al-Dirasat wa al-Nashr, 2000.

——. *Spengler*. Beirut and Kuwait: Dar al Qalam and Wakalat al-Matbuʿat, 1982; first published in 1941.

Badr, Ali. *Baba Sartre* (Daddy Sartre). Beirut: Riad el-Rayyes Books, 2001.

Badran, Margot. "Dual Liberation: Feminism and Nationalism in Egypt, 1870s–1925." *Feminist Issues* 8, no. 1 (1988): 15–34.

——. *Feminists, Islam, and Nation: Gender and the Making of Modern Egypt*. Princeton, N.J.: Princeton University Press, 1995.

Badran, Margot and Miriam Cooke, eds. *Opening the Gates: A Century of Arab Feminist Writing*. London: Virago, 1990.

Al-Banna, Hasan. *Five Tracts of Hasan al-Banna (1906–1949)*. Selected and translated by Charles Wendell. Berkeley and Los Angeles: University of California Press, 1978.

——. *Majmuʿat Rasaʾil al-Imam al-Shahid Hasan al-Banna* (The Collection of the Letters of the Imam and Martyr Hasan al-Banna). Beirut: Dar a-Andalus, 1965.

Barakat, Halim, ed. *Contemporary North Africa: Issues of Development and Integration*. Washington, D.C.: Center for Contemporary Arab Studies, Georgetown University, 1985.

Baron, Beth. *The Women's Awakening in Egypt: Culture, Society, and the Press*. New Haven, Conn.: Yale University Press, 1994.

Bassili, François. "Ihtifaʾ bi al-Muʾtamar al-Hadari: Thalath Nadharat Naqdiyya" (Celebrating the Civilization Conference: Three Critical Views). *Al-Adab* 22, no. 6 (1974): 71–73.

Batatu, Hanna. *The Old Social Classes and the Revolutionary Movements of Iraq*. Princeton, N.J.: Princeton University Press, 1978; reprint, London: Saqi Books, 2004.

"Al-Bayan al-Khitami" (Final Declaration). *Al-Maʿrifa* 148 (1974): 292–302.

Beinin, Joel and Joe Stork, eds. *Political Islam: Essays from Middle East Report*. Berkeley and Los Angeles: University of California Press, 1997.

Ben Jelloun, Tahar. "Décolonisation de la sociologie au Maghreb: Utilité et risques d'une fonction critique." *Le Monde Diplomatique,* August, 1974. English translation: "Decolonizing Sociology in the Maghreb: Usefulness and Risks of a Critical Function." Translated by Nicholas S. Hopkins in Saad Eddin Ibrahim and Nicholas S. Hopkins, eds., *Arab Society: Social Science Perspectives*, 70–75. Cairo: American University of Cairo Press, 1977.

Bennis, Mohammad. "The Plurality of the One." In Halim Barakat, ed., *Contemporary North Africa: Issues of Development and Integration*, 250–63. Washington, D.C.: Center for Contemporary Arab Studies, Georgetown University, 1985.

Bishara, Azmi. *Fi al-Mas'ala al-'Arabiyya: Muqaddima li Bayan Dimuqrati 'Arabi* (On the Arab Question: Prolegomena to an Arab Democratic Manifesto). Beirut: Markaz Dirasat al-Wihda al-'Arabiyya, 2007.

——. "Islam and Politics in the Middle East." In Jochen Hippler and Andrea Lueg, eds., *The Next Threat: Western Perceptions of Islam*, 82–115. London and Boulder, Colo.: Pluto in association with the Transnational Institute, 1995.

Booth, Marilyn. "Prison, Gender, Praxis: Women's Prison Memoirs in Egypt and Elsewhere." *MERIP* 149 (November–December 1987): 35–41.

Boullata, Issa J. *Trends and Issues in Contemporary Arab Thought*. Albany: State University of New York Press, 1990.

Bouzid, Samir. *Mythes, utopie et messianisme dans le discours politique arabe moderne et contemporain* (Myth, Utopia, and Messianism in Modern and Contemporary Arabic Political Discourse). Paris: L'Harmattan, 1997.

Brynen, Rex, Bahgat Korany, and Paul Noble, eds. *Political Liberalization and Democratization in the Arab World*. Vol. 1: *Theoretical Perspectives*. Boulder, Colo.: Lynne Rienner, 1995.

Buheiry, Marwan R., ed. *Intellectual Life in the Arab East, 1890–1939*. Beirut: Center for Arab and Middle East Studies, American University of Beirut, 1981.

Al-Bustani, Butrus, et al., eds. *Da'irat al-Ma'arif* (The Circle of Knowledge). 11 vols. Beirut: n.p., 1876–1900.

"The Case of Abu Zaid." *Index on Censorship* 25, no. 4 (1996): 30–39.

Chacour, Elias. *Blood Brothers*. Grand Rapids, Mich.: Chosen Books, 1984; reprint, 2003.

——. *We Belong to the Land: The Story of a Palestinian Israeli Who Lives for Peace and Reconciliation*. San Francisco: Harper and Row, 1990.

Al-Charif, Maher. *Rihanat al-Nahda fi al-Fikr al-'Arabi* (The Stakes of the Nahda in Arab Thought). Damascus: Dar al-Mada, 2000.

Al-Charif, Maher and Kawakibi, Salam, eds. *Le courant réformiste musulman et sa réception dans les sociétés arabes* (The Reformist Islamic Current and Its Reception in Arab Societies). Damascus: Institut Français du Proche Orient, 2003.

Al-Charif, Maher and Sabrina Mervin, eds. *Modernités islamiques* (Islamic Modernities). Damascus, Syria: Institut Français du Proche Orient, 2006.

Cole, Juan Ricardo. "Feminism, Class, and Islam in Turn-of-the-Century Egypt." *International Journal of Middle East Studies* 13 (1981): 387–407.

Colla, Elliot and Ayman Bakr. "'Silencing Is at the Heart of My Case': Nasr Abu Zayd, Interview." In Joel Beinin and Joe Stork, eds., *Political Islam: Essays from Middle East Report*, 327–34. Berkeley and Los Angeles: University of California Press, 1997.

Daher, Mas'ud. *Al-Nahda al-'Arabiyya wa al-Nahda al-Yabaniyya: Tashabuh al-Muqaddamat wa Ikhtilaf al-Nata'ij* (The Arab Renaissance and the Japanese Renaissance: Similarity in the Beginnings and Difference in the Results). Kuwait: Al-Majlis al-Watani li al-Thaqafa wa al-Adab, 1999.

——. *Al-Yaban bi 'Uyun 'Arabiyya, 1904-2004* (Japan in Arab Eyes, 1904-2004). Beirut: Markaz Dirasat al-Wihda al-'Arabiyya, 2005.

Dakrub, Muhammad. "Maqala fi Tamhid wa Faslayn wa ma Yushbih al-Khatima" (An Article with an Introduction, Two Chapters, and What Resembles a Conclusion). *Mulhaq al-Nahar* 858 (August 17, 2008): 6-8.

Dallal, Ahmad. "Appropriating the Past: Twentieth-Century Reconstruction of Pre-modern Islamic Thought." *Islamic Law and Society* 7, no. 3 (2000): 325-58.

Darraj, Faysal. *Al-Dhakira al-Qawmiyya fi al-Riwaya al-'Arabiyya* (The National Memory in the Arab Novel). Beirut: Markaz Dirasat al-Wihda al-'Arabiyya, 2007.

——. "*Al-Naqd al-Dhati Ba'd al-Hazimah* fi Tab'a Jadida, Jalal Sadeq al-Azm: Rahiniyyat al-Kitab al-Naqdi wa Rahin al-Hazima" (*Self-Criticism After the Defeat* in a New Printing: Jalal Sadeq al-Azm: The Contemporaneity of the Critical Book and the Contemporaneity of the Defeat), *Al-Quds al-'Arabi*, June 21, 2007.

Djaît, Hisham. *L'Europe et l'Islam*. Paris: Editions du Seuil, 1978. English translation: *Europe and Islam*. Translated by Peter Heinegg. Berkeley and Los Angeles: University of California Press, 1985.

Donohue, John J. and John L. Esposito, eds. *Islam in Transition: Muslim Perspectives*. New York: Oxford University Press, 1982; 2d ed., 2006.

Dwyer, Kevin. *Arab Voices: The Human Rights Debate in the Middle East*. Berkeley and Los Angeles: University of California Press, 1991.

Eid, Abdel Raziq. *Muhammad Abduh: Imam al-Hadatha wa al-Dustur* (Muhammad Abduh: The Imam of Modernity and the Constitution). Baghdad: Ma'had al-Dirasat al-Istratijiyya, 2006.

Elsadda, Hoda. "Malak Hifni Nassif: Halaqa Mafquda min Ta'rikh al-Nahda" (Malak Hifni Nassif: A Missing Chain in the Historiography of the Nahda). In Hoda Elsadda and Salwa Bakr, eds., *Hagar: Kitab al-Mar'a* (Hagar: The Book of the Woman), 2:109-19. Cairo: Sina li al-Nashr, 1994.

——. "Al-Mar'a: Mantiqat Muharramat: Qira'a fi A'mal Qasim Amin" (The Woman: Taboo Realm. A Reading in the Works of Qasim Amin). In Hoda Elsadda and Salwa Bakr, eds., *Hagar: Kitab al-Mar'a* (Hagar: The Book of the Woman), 1:144-59. Cairo: Sina li al-Nashr, 1993.

——. "Al-Mar'a wa al-Dhakira: Hoda Elsadda, Muqabala" (Women and Memory: An Interview with Hoda Elsadda). In *Gender and Knowledge: Contribution of Gender Perspectives to Intellectual Formations*, special issue of *Alif: Journal of Comparative Poetics* 19 (1999): 210-30.

——, ed. *Min Ra'idat al-Qarn al-'Ishrin: Shakhsiyyat wa Qadaya* (From the Pioneers of the Twentieth Century: Personalities and Causes). Cairo: Women and Memory Forum, 2001.

——. "Revisiting Popular Memory and the Constitution of Gendered Identity: The Story of a Project." *Middle East Women's Studies Review* 17, nos. 1–2 (2003): 1–2.

——. "Al-Su'al al-'An: Mata Yataharrar al-Jami' . . . Rijalan wa Nisa'?!" (The Question Now: When Will All Be Liberated, Men and Women?!). *Wujuhat Nadhar* 21 (December 1999): 19–21.

Elsadda, Hoda and Emad Abu-Ghazi. *Maseerat al-Mar'a al-Misriyya: "'Alamat wa Mawaqif"* (The Journey of the Egyptian Woman: "Signs and Stands"). Cairo: National Council for Women, 2001. English translation: *Significant Moments in Egyptian Women's History*. 2 vols. Translated by Hala Kamal. Cairo: National Council for Women, 2001; reprint, 2003.

Elsadda, Hoda, Sumayya Ramadan, and Umayma Abu Bakr. *Zaman al-Nisa' wa al-Dhakira al-Badila* (The Time of Women and the Alternative Memory). Cairo: Women and Memory Forum, 1998.

Esposito, John. *The Islamic Threat: Myth or Reality?* New York: Oxford University Press, 1992.

Fahim, Hussein. "Foreign and Indigenous Anthropology: The Perspectives of an Egyptian Anthropologist." *Human Organization* 36, no. 1 (1977): 80–86.

——, ed. *Indigenous Anthropology in Non-Western Countries*. Durham: University of North Carolina Press, 1982.

Fahmi, Murqus. *Al-Mar'a fi al-Sharq* (The Woman in the East). Cairo: 1894.

Fahmy, Khaled. *All the Pasha's Men: Mehmed Ali, His Army, and the Making of Modern Egypt*. Cambridge, U.K.: Cambridge University Press, 1997; reprints, Cairo: American University of Cairo Press, 2002, 2004.

——. "The Era of Muhammad 'Ali Pasha, 1805–1848." In M. W. Daly, ed., *The Cambridge History of Egypt*, vol. 2: *Modern Egypt, from 1517 to the End of the Twentieth Century*, 139–79. New York: Cambridge University Press, 1998.

Fakhry, Majid. *Al-Haraka al-Fikriyya wa Ruwwaduha al-Lubnaniyyun fi 'Asr al-Nahda, 1800–1922* (The Intellectual Movement and Its Lebanese Pioneers, 1800–1922). Beirut: Dar al-Nahar, 1992.

Faraj, Abd al-Salam. *Al-Farida al-Gha'iba* (The Absent Duty). Cairo: Dar al Hurriya, 1988. English translation: *The Neglected Duty*. Translated by Johannes Jansen. New York: Macmillan, 1986.

Faysal, Jalloul, ed. *Hiwar al-Mashreq wa al-Maghreb* (Dialogue of the Mashreq and the Maghreb). Cairo: Maktabat al-Madbuli, 1990.

Flores, Alexander. "Reform, Islam, Secularism: Farah Antûn and Muhammad Abduh." In Alain Roussillon, ed., *Entre réforme sociale et mouvement national* (Between Social Reform and National Movement), 565–76. Cairo: Cedej, 1995.

Fouda, Farag. *Al-Haqiqa al-Gha'iba* (The Absent Truth). Cairo: Dar al-Fikr, 1986; 3rd ed., 1988.

——. *Nakun aw la Nakun* (To Be or Not to Be). Cairo: Dar al-Hay'a al-Misriyya al-'Amma li al-Kitab, 1992.

George, Alan. *Syria: Neither Bread nor Freedom*. London: Zed, 2003.

Ghali, Shukry. *Al-Nahda wa al-Suqut fi al-Fikr al-Misri al-Hadith* (Rise and Fall in Modern Egyptian Thought). Beirut: Dar al-Tali'a, 1978.

Ghalyun, Burhan. *Bayan min Ajl al-Dimuqratiyya* (Manifesto for Democracy). 5th ed. Beirut: Al-Markaz al-Thaqafi al-'Arabi, 2006.

——. *Al-Ikhtiyar al-Dimuqrati fi Suriya* (The Democratic Choice in Syria). Damascus: Dar Petra, 2003.

——. *Al-Mihna al-'Arabiyya: Al-Dawla Didd al-Umma* (The Arab Crisis: The State Against the Nation). Beirut: Markaz Dirasat al-Wihda al-'Arabiyya, 1993.

Ghalyun, Burhan and Samir Amin. *Hiwar al-Dawla wa al-Din* (The Dialogue on the State and Religion). Beirut: Al-Markaz al-Thaqafi al-'Arabi, 1996.

Al-Ghazali, Abu Hamid Muhammad. *Al-Munqidh min al-Dalal, wa al-Mufsih 'an al-Ahwal*. Damascus: Dar al-Hikma, 1994. English translation: *Deliverance from Error and Mystical Union with the Almighty*. Translated and introduced by Muhammad Abulaylah. With an introduction and notes by George F. McLean. Washington, D.C.: Council for Research in Values and Philosophy, 2001.

Al-Ghazzali, Muhammad. *Our Beginning in Wisdom*. Translated by Ismail R. el Faruqi. New York: Octagon Books, 1975.

El Guindi, Fadwa. "Veiling Infitah with Muslim Ethic: Egypt's Contemporary Islamic Movement." *Social Problems* 28, no. 4 (1981): 465–85.

Al-Hadatha wa al-Hadatha al-'Arabiyya (Modernity and Arab Modernity). Beirut: Al-Mu'assassa al-'Arabiyya li al-Tahdith al-Fikri and Dar Petra, 2005.

Al-Haddad, Mahmud. *Muhammad Abduh: Qira'a Jadida fi Khitab al-Islah al-Dini* (Muhammad Abduh: A New Reading in the Discourse of Religious Reform). Beirut: Dar al-Tali'a, 2003.

Haddad, Mahmud. "Arab Religious Nationalism in the Era of Colonialism: Rereading Rashid Rida's Ideas on the Caliphate." *Journal of the American Oriental Society* 117, no. 2 (1997): 253–77.

——. "The Ideas of Amir Shakib Arslan: Before and After the Collapse of the Ottoman Empire." In Neguin Yavari, Lawrence G. Potter, and Jean-Marc Ran Oppenheim, eds., *Views from the Edge: Essays in Honor of Richard W. Bulliet*, 101–15. New York: Columbia University Press, 2004.

Al-Haddad, Tahir. *Imra'atuna fi al-Shari'a wa al-Mujtama'* (Our Woman in Islamic Law and Society). Tunis: n.p., 1929.

Haddad, Yvonne Yazbeck and John L. Esposito, eds. *Islam, Gender, and Social Change.* New York: Oxford University Press, 1998.

Haddad, Yvonne, John Obert Voll, and John L. Esposito. eds. *The Contemporary Islamic Revival: A Critical Survey and Bibliography.* New York: Greenwood Press, 1991.

Hafez, Sabry. "Torture, Imprisonment, and Political Assassination in the Arab Novel." *Al Jadid* 8, no. 32 (2002): no page numbers.

Hafez, Yassin. *Al-Hazima wa al-Idiolojia al-Mahzuma* (The Defeat and the Defeated Ideology). Damascus: Dar Al-Hassad, 1978; reprint, 1997. Also reprinted in Yassin Hafez, *Al-A'mal al-Kamila li Yassin al-Hafez* (The Collected Works of Yassin Hafez). Beirut: Markaz Dirasat al-Wihda al-'Arabiyya, 2005.

Haim, Sylvia. "Blunt and al-Kawakibi." *Oriente Moderno* 35 (1955): 133–43.

———. "G. Alfieri and al-Kawakibi." *Oriente Moderno* 34 (1954): 321–34.

al-Haj Saleh, Yassin. "Al-Khamis min Huzayran 1967 fi Arba'iniha" (The 5th of June 1967 in its Fortieth), *Al-Hayat* (June 3, 2007).

Al-Hakim, Tawfiq. "Fi al-Naqd: Ila al-Ustadh Ahmad Amin" (On Critique: To Professor Ahmad Amin). *Al-Risala* 153 (June 8, 1936): 1003.

Halassa, Ghaleb. *Al-Haribun min al-Huriyya* (The Fugitives of Freedom). Damascus: Dar al-Mada, 2001.

Halim, Hala. "Of Hermeneutics and Reform." *Al-Ahram Weekly* 15–21 (November 2007). Available at http://weekly.ahram.org.eg/2007/871/cu4.htm.

Hamdan, Mas'ud. *Poetics, Politics, and Protest in Arab Theatre: The Bitter Cup and the Holy Rain.* Brighton, U.K.: Sussex Academic Press, 2006.

Hamil, Mustapha. "Interrogating Identity: Abdelkebir Khatibi and the Postcolonial Prerogative." *Alif: Journal of Comparative Poetics* 22 (2002): 72–88.

Hanafi, Hassan. *Cultures and Civilizations: Conflict or Dialogue?* Vol. 1: *The Meridian Thought.* Vol. 2: *Cultural Creativity and Religious Dialogue.* Cairo: Book Center for Publishing, 2007.

———. *Al-Din wa al-Thawra fi Misr (1952–1981)* (Religion and Revolution in Egypt [1952–1981]). 8 vols. Cairo: Maktabat Madbuli, 1988–1989.

———. "From Decolonization to Cultural Liberation." In Tuomo Melasuo, ed., *National Movements and World Peace*, 159–68. Aldershot, U.K.: Avebury, 1990.

———. *Min al-'Aqida ila al-Thawra: Muhawala fi I'adat Bina' 'Ilm Usul al-Din* (From Doctrine to Revolution: An Attempt at Rebuilding Fundamental Theology). 5 vols. Cairo: Maktabat Madbuli, 1988.

———. *Muqaddima fi 'Ilm al-Istighrab* (Introduction to the Science of Occidentalism). Beirut: Al-Mu'assassa al-Jami'iyya li al-Dirasat wa al-Nashrwa al-Tawzi', 1992.

———. *Qadaya Mu'assira* (Contemporary Issues). Vol. 1: *Fi Fikrina al-Mu'assir* (On Our Contemporary Thought). Vol. 2: *Fi al-Fikr al-Gharbi al-Mu'assir* (On Western Contemporary Thought). Cairo: Dar al-Fikr al-'Arabi, 1976–1977; new ed., Beirut: Dar al-Tanwir, 1981.

——. "The Relevance of the Islamic Alternative in Egypt." *Arab Studies Quarterly* 4, nos. 1–2 (1980): 54–74.

——. *Al-Turath wa al-Tajdid: Mawqifuna min al-Turath* (Heritage and Renewal: Our Position Regarding Tradition). Cairo: Al-Markaz al-ʿArabi li al-Bahth wa al-Nashr, 1980.

Harik, Iliya. *Al-Dimuqratiyya wa Tahaddiyat al-Hadatha Bayn al-Sharq wa al-Gharb* (Democracy and the Challenges of Modernity Between East and West). Beirut: Dar al-Saqi, 2001.

Hasib, Kheireddin. "Kalimat al-Iftitah" (Opening Word). In *Azamat al-Dimuqratiyya fi al-Watan al-ʿArabi* (The Crisis of Democracy in the Arab Homeland), 29–32. Beirut: Markaz Dirasat al-Wihda al-ʿArabiyya, 1984; reprint, 1987.

Hatem, Mervat. "Economic and Political Liberalization in Egypt and the Demise of State Feminism." *International Journal of Middle East Studies* 24 (1992): 231–51.

——. "Egyptian Discourses on Gender and Political Liberalization: Do Secularist and Islamist Views Differ?" *Middle East Journal* 48, no. 4 (1994): 661–76.

——. "Toward a Critique of Modernization: Narrative in Middle East Women Studies." *Arab Studies Quarterly* 15, no. 2 (1993): 117–22.

——. "Toward the Development of Post-Islamist and Post-nationalist Feminist Discourses in the Middle East." In Judith Tucker, ed., *Arab Women: Old Boundaries, New Frontiers*, 29–48. Bloomington: Indiana University Press, 1993.

Hawl al-Khayar al-Dimuqrati: Dirasat Naqdiyya (On the Democratic Choice: Critical Studies). Beirut: Markaz Dirasat al-Wihda al-ʿArabiyya, 1994.

Haykal, Muhammad Hussein. *Fi Manzil al-Wahi* (In the House of Revelation). Cairo: Matbaʿat Dar al-Kutub al-Misriyya, 1936.

Al-Hibri, Aziza, ed. *Women and Islam.* Special monograph issue of *Journal of Women's Studies International Forum.* Oxford, U.K.: Pergamon Press, 1982.

Hirschkind, Charles. "Heresy or Hermeneutics: The Case of Nasr Hamid Abu Zayd." *American Journal of Islamic Social Sciences* 12, no. 4 (1995): 464–77.

Hourani, Albert. *Arabic Thought in the Liberal Age, 1798–1939.* London: Oxford University Press, 1962. Arabic translation: *Al-Fikr al-ʿArabi fi ʿAsr al-Nahda, 1798–1939.* Translated by Karim ʿAzqul. Beirut: An-Nahar, 1968. New edition of the translation revised by Adib al-Qintar. Beirut: Muʾassassat Naufal, 1997.

Hudson, Michael C. "The Political Culture Approach to Arab Democratisation: The Case for Bringing It Back in, Carefully." In Rex Brynen, Bahgat Korany, and Paul Noble, eds., *Political Liberalization and Democratization in the Arab World*, vol. 1: *Theoretical Perspectives*, 61–75. Boulder, Colo.: Lynne Rienner, 1995.

Huquq al-Insan al-ʿArabi (The Rights of the Arab Human Being). Beirut: Markaz Dirasat al-Wihda al-ʿArabiyya, 1999; reprint, 2004.

Huquq al-Insan: Al-Ruʾa al-ʿAlamiyya wa al-Islamiyya wa al-ʿArabiyya (Human Rights: The World, Islamic, and Arab Visions). Beirut: Markaz Dirasat al-Wihda al-ʿArabiyya, 2005.

Husayn, Taha. 'Ala Hamish al-Sira (On the Margin of the Biography of the Prophet). Cairo: Lajnat al-Ta'lif wa al-Tarjama wa al-Nashr, 1935.

——. Al-Ayyam. Cairo: Dar al-Ma'arif, 1974. English translation: The Days: Taha Hussein, His Autobiography in Three Parts. Translated by E. H. Paxton, Hilary Wayment, and Kenneth Cragg. Cairo: American University of Cairo Press, 1997.

——. "Fi al-Naqd: Ila Sadiqi Ahmad Amin" (On Critique: To My Friend Ahmad Amin). Al-Risala 153 (June 8, 1936): 921–22 and 957–58.

——. Fi al-Shi'r al-Jahili (On Jahili Poetry). Cairo: Dar al-Nahr li al-Nashr wa al-Tawzi', 1996.

——. Mustaqbal al-Thaqafa fi Misr. Cairo: Matba'at al-Thaqafa fi Misr, 1944. English translation: The Future of Culture in Egypt. Translated by Sidney Glazer. Washington, D.C.: American Council of Learned Societies, 1954.

Hussein, Louay. Al-Faqd: Hikayat min Dhakira Mutakhayyala li Sajin Haqiqi (The Loss: A Story from an Imaginary Memory of a Real Prisoner). Damascus: Dar Petra, 2006.

Al-Husry, Khaldun S. Three Reformers: A Study of Modern Arab Political Thought. Beirut: Khayats, 1966.

Ibn Khaldun. The Muqaddimah: An Introduction to History. Translated from the Arabic by Franz Rosenthal. Abridged and edited by N. J. Dawood. Princeton, N.J.: Princeton University Press, 1967; reprinted in 1969 and then in 1989 in the Bollingen series.

Ibrahim, Ibrahim, ed. Arab Resources: The Transformation of a Society. London and Washington, D.C.: Croom Helm and Center for Contemporary Arab Studies, Georgetown University, 1983.

Ibrahim, Saad Eddin. Egypt, Islam, and Democracy: Critical Essays. Cairo: American University of Cairo Press, 2002.

——. "Muqaddima" (Introduction). In Azamat al-Dimuqratiyya fi al-Watan al-'Arabi (The Crisis of Democracy in the Arab Homeland), 11–28. Beirut: Markaz Dirasat al-Wihda al-'Arabiyya, 1984; reprint, 1987.

——. "A Reply to My Accusers." Journal of Democracy 11, no. 4 (2000): 58–63.

Ibrahim, Saad Eddin and Nicholas S. Hopkins, eds. Arab Society: Social Science Perspectives. Cairo: American University of Cairo Press, 1985.

Islam and Politics. Special issue of Arab Studies Quarterly 4, nos. 1–2 (1982).

Islam and Politics. Special issue of Third World Quarterly 10, no. 2 (1988).

Ismael, Tareq Y. The Communist Movement in the Arab World. London: Routledge and Curzon, 2005.

Ismail, Salwa. "Confronting the Other: Identity, Culture, Politics, and Conservative Islamism in Egypt." International Journal for Middle Eastern Studies 30 (1998): 199–225.

——. "Democracy in Contemporary Arab Intellectual Discourse." In Rex Brynen, Bahgat Korany, and Paul Noble, eds., Political Liberalization and Democratization in the Arab World, 93–111. Boulder, Colo.: Lynne Rienner, 1995.

——. *Rethinking Islamist Politics: Culture, the State, and Islamism.* London: I. B. Tauris, 2003.

Al-Jabiri, Muhammad Abed. *Al-ʿAql al-Akhlaqi al-ʿArabi: Dirasa Tahliliyya Naqdiyya li Nudhum al-Qiyam fi al-Thaqafa al-ʿArabiyya* (Moral Arab Reason: An Analytic Critical Study of the Value Systems in Arab Culture). Beirut: Markaz Dirasat al-Wihda al-ʿArabiyya, 2006.

——. *Al-ʿAql al-Siyassi al-ʿArabi* (Political Arab Reason). Beirut: Markaz Dirasat al-Wihda al-ʿArabiyya, 1990.

—— [Al-Jabri, Muhammad Abed]. *Arab-Islamic Philosophy: A Contemporary Critique.* Austin: University of Texas Press, 1999.

——. *Bunyat al-ʿAql al-ʿArabi* (The Structure of Arab Reason). Beirut: Dar al-Taliʿa, 1986.

——. *Introduction à la critique de la raison arabe* (Introduction to the Critique of Arab Reason). Paris: Editions la Découverte and Institut du Monde Arabe, 1994.

——. "Ishkaliyyat al-Asala wa al-Muʿasara fi al-Fikr al-ʿArabi al-Hadith wa al-Muʿasir: Siraʿ Tabaqi am Mushkil Thaqafi?" (The Problematic of Authenticity and Contemporaneity in Contemporary and Modern Arab Thought: A Class Conflict or a Cultural Problem?). In *Al-Turath wa Tahaddiyyat al-ʿAsr fi al-Watan al-ʿArabi: Al-Asala wa al-Muʿassara* (Heritage and the Challenges of the Age in the Arab Homeland: Authenticity and Contemporaneity), 29–58. Beirut: Markaz Dirasat al-Wihda al-ʿArabiyya, 1985.

——. *Al-Khitab al-ʿArabi al-Muʿassir* (The Contemporary Arab Discourse). Beirut: Markaz Dirasat al-Wihda al-ʿArabiyya, 1982.

——. *Takween al-ʿAql al-ʿArabi* (The Constitution of Arab Reason). Beirut: Dar al-Taliʿa, 1984.

Al-Jaderji, Rifaat and Balqis Sharara. *Jidar Bayna Dhulmatayn* (A Wall Between Two Obscurities). Beirut: Dar al-Saqi, 2003.

Jayyusi, Salma Khadra, ed. *Short Arabic Plays.* New York: Interlink Books, 2003.

Jayyusi, Salma Khadra and Roger Allen, eds. *Modern Arabic Drama.* Bloomington: Indiana University Press, 1995.

Jedaane, Fahmy. *Fi al-Khalass al-Nihaʾi: Maqal fi Wuʿud al-Islamiyyin wa al-ʿIlmaniyyin wa al-Liberaliyyin* (On Final Salvation: Essay on the Promises of the Islamists, the Secularists, and the Liberals). Amman, Jordan: Dar al-Shuruq, 2007.

Jedi, Ahmad. *Mihnat al-Nahda wa Lughz al-Tarikh fi al-Fikr al-ʿArabi al-Hadith wa al-Muʿassir* (The Crisis of the Nahda and the Enigma of History in Modern and Contemporary Thought). Beirut: Markaz Dirasat al-Wihda al-ʿArabiyya, 2005.

Kahf, Mohja. "Packaging 'Huda': Shaarawi's Memoirs in the United States Reception Environment." In Amal Amireh and Suheir Majaj, eds., *Going Global: The Transnational Reception of Third World Women Writers,* 148–72. New York: Garland, 2000.

Kandiyoti, Deniz. "Contemporary Feminist Scholarship and Middle East Studies." In Deniz Kandiyoti, ed., *Gendering the Middle East: Emerging Perspectives,* 1–27. New York: Syracuse University Press, 1996.

——, ed. *Women, Islam, and the State*. Houndmills, U.K.: Macmillan, 1991.

Kassab, Elizabeth Suzanne. "An Arab Neo-Kantian Philosophy of Culture: Constantine Zurayk on Culture, Reason, and Ethics." *Philosophy East & West* 49, no. 4 (1999): 494–512.

Kassir, Samir. *Considérations sur le malheur arabe* (Thoughts on Arab Wretchedness). Paris: Actes Sud, 2004. Arabic translation: *Ta'ammulat fi al-Shaqa' al-'Arabi*. Translated by Jean Hachem. Revised by Haytham al-Amin and with an introduction by Elias Khoury. Beirut: Dar al-Nahar, 2005. English translation: *Being Arab*. Translated by Will Hobson. London: Verso, 2006.

——. *La Guerre du Liban: De la dissension nationale au conflit régional (1975–1982)* (The Lebanese War: From National Dissension to Regional Conflict [1976–1982]). Paris: Karthala and Cermoc, 1994.

——. *Histoire de Beyrouth* (History of Beirut). Paris: Fayard, 2003.

Kassir, Samir and Farouk Mardam-Bey. *Itinéraires de Paris à Jérusalem: La France et le conflit israélo-arabe* (Itineraries from Paris to Jerusalem: France and the Arab-Israeli Conflict). Vol. 1: *1917–1958*. Vol. 2: *1958–1991*. Paris: Livres de la Revue d'Etudes Palestiniennes, 1992, 1993.

Kawtharani, Wajih. *Al-Ittijahat al-Ijtima'iyya wa al-Siyasiyya fi Jabal Lubnan wa al-Mashreq al-'Arabi, 1860–1920* (The Social and Political Orientations in Mount Lebanon and the Arab East). Beirut: Ma'had al-Inma' al-'Arabi, 1978.

——. *Al-Sulta wa al-Mujtama' wa al-'Amal al-Siyasi: Min Tarikh al-Wilaya al-'Othmaniya fi Bilad al-Sham* (Power, Society, and Political Work: From the History of the Ottoman Province in the Sham Area). Beirut: Markaz Dirasat al-Wihda al-'Arabiyya, 1988.

Kayali, Hasan. *Arabs and Young Turks: Ottomanism, Arabism, and Islamism in the Ottoman Empire, 1908–1918*. Berkeley and Los Angeles: University of California Press, 1997.

Keddie, Nikki R. and Beth Baron, eds. *Women in Middle Eastern History: Shifting Boundaries in Sex and Gender*. New Haven, Conn.: Yale University Press, 1991.

Kerr, Malcolm. *Islamic Reform: The Political and Legal Theories of Muhammad Abduh and Rashid Rida*. Berkeley and Los Angeles: University of California Press, 1966.

Khalafallah, Muhammad Ahmad. *Al-Fann al-Qasasi fi al-Qur'an al-Karim* (The Art of Narration in the Qur'an). Cairo: Maktabat al-Nahda al-Misriyya, 1958.

Khalidi, Rashid, Lisa Anderson, Muhammad Muslih, and Reeva Simon, eds. *The Origins of Arab Nationalism*. New York: Columbia University Press, 1991.

Al-Khalij al-'Arabi wa al-Dimuqratiyya: Nahwa Ru'ya Mustaqbaliyya li Ta'ziz al-Masa'i al-Dimuqratiyya (The Arab Gulf and Democracy: Toward a Future Vision for the Reinforcement of the Democratic Efforts). Beirut: Markaz Dirasat al-Wihda al-'Arabiyya, 2002.

Al-Khatibi, Abdelkebir. "Double Criticism: The Decolonization of Arab Sociology." In Halim Barakat, ed., *Contemporary North Africa: Issues of Development and Integration*, 9–19. Washington, D.C.: Center for Contemporary Arab Studies, Georgetown University, 1985.

——. *Maghreb pluriel* (Plural Maghreb). Paris: Denoël, 1983.

Khoury, Philip. "Islamic Revival and the Crisis of the Secular State in the Arab World: A Historical Reappraisal." In Ibrahim Ibrahim, ed., *Arab Resources: The Transformation of a Society*, 213–36. London and Washington, D.C.: Croom Helm and Center for Contemporary Arab Studies, Georgetown University, 1983.

Khuri, Ra'if. *Al-Fikr al-ʿArabi al-Hadith: Athar al-Thawrah al-Faransiyya fi Tawjihihi al-Siyasi wa al-Ijtimaʿi* (Modern Arab Thought: The Impact of the French Revolution in Its Political and Social Orientations). Beirut: Dar al-Makshuf, 1973; Damascus: Manshurat Wizarat al-Thaqafah, 1993. English translation: *Modern Arab Thought: Channels of the French Revolution to the Arab East*. Translated by Ihsan Abbas. Revised and edited by Charles Issawi. Princeton, N.J.: Kingston Press, 1983.

Laroui, Abdallah. *La crise des intellectuals arabes: Traditionalisme ou historicisme?* Paris: François Maspero, 1974. English translation: *The Crisis of the Arab Intellectual: Traditionalism or Historicism?* Translated by Diarmid Cammell. Berkeley and Los Angeles: University of California Press, 1976. Arabic translation : *Al-ʿArab wa al-Fikr al-Tarikhi*. 4th ed. Beirut: Al-Markaz al-Thaqafi al-ʿArabi, 1998.

——. *L'idéologie arabe contemporaine: Essai critique* (Contemporary Arab Ideology: A Critical Essay). Paris: François Maspero, 1967. Arabic translation: *Al-Idiyolojiyya al-ʿArabiyya al-Muʿassira*. 2d ed. Beirut: Al-Markaz al-Thaqafi al-ʿArabi, 1999.

——. *Islam et histoire* (Islam and History). Paris: Flammarion, 1999.

——. *Islamisme, modernisme, liberalisme* (Islamism, Modernism, Liberalism). Casablanca: Centre Culturel Arabe, 1997.

——. *Khawater al-Sabah* (Morning Thoughts). 3 vols. Beirut: Al-Markaz al-Thaqafi al-ʿArabi, 2001; reprints, 2003, 2005.

——. *Mafhum al-ʿAql* (The Concept of Reason). Beirut: Al-Markaz al-Thaqafi al-ʿArabi, 1996; 2d ed., 2001.

——. *Mafhum al-Dawla* (The Concept of the State). Beirut: Al-Markaz al-Thaqafi al-ʿArabi, 1981; 2d ed., 2001.

Lazreg, Marnia. *The Eloquence of Silence: Algerian Women in Question*. New York: Routledge, 1994.

——. "Feminism and Difference: The Perils of Writing as a Woman on Women in Algeria." *Feminist Studies* 14, no. 1 (1988): 81–107.

——. "From Nation to Gender: The Reproduction of Sexual Inequality in Algeria." In Tuomo Melasuo, ed., *National Movements and World Peace*, 123–40. Aldershot, U.K.: Avebury, 1990.

——. "The Triumphant Discourse of Global Feminism: Should Other Women Be Known?" In Amal Amireh and Lisa Suhair Majaj, eds., *Going Global: The Transnational Reception of Third World Women Writers*, 29–38. New York: Garland, 2000.

Luciani, Giacomo, ed. *The Arab State*. Berkeley and Los Angeles: University of California Press, 1990.

Macfie, Alexander Lyon, ed. *Orientalism: A Reader*. New York: New York University Press, 2000.

Mahfuz, Issam. *Hiwar maʿ Ruwwad al-Nahda al-ʿArabiyya* (Dialogue with the Pioneers of the Arab Renaissance). London: Riad el-Rayyes, 1988.

Mahmud, Zaki Naguib. "Al-Hadara wa Qadiyyat al-Taqaddum wa al-Takhalluf" (Civilization and the Issue of Progress and Retardation). *Al-Adab* 22, no. 5 (1974): 6–9.

——. "The Intellectual Life in Contemporary Egypt." In George N. Atiyeh, ed., *Arab and American Cultures*, 201–8. Washington, D.C.: American Enterprise Institute for Public Policy Research, 1977.

——. "Rational Aspects of the Classical Arabic Culture." In George N. Atiyeh, ed., *Arab and American Cultures*, 87–92. Washington, D.C.: American Enterprise Institute for Public Policy Research, 1977.

——. "Mawqif al-Thaqafa al-ʿArabiyya al-Haditha fi Muwajahat al-ʿAsr" (The Position of Modern Arab Culture in the Face of the Present Age). *Al-Adab* 19, no. 11 (1971): 6–12.

——. *Tajdid al-Fikr al-ʿArabi* (The Renewal of Arab Thought). Beirut: Dar al-Shuruq, 1971.

Makdisi, Saree. "'Postcolonial' Literature in a Neocolonial World: Modern Arabic Culture and the End of Modernity." *Boundary 2* 22, no. 1 (1995): 85–115.

Mardin, Şerif. *Genesis of Young Ottoman Thought: A Study in the Modernization of Turkish Political Ideas*. Princeton, N.J.: Princeton University Press, 1962.

Marzouki, Moncef. *ʿAn Ayyat Dimuqratiyya Yatahaddathun?* (About Which Democracy Do They Speak?). Damascus and Paris: Dar al-Ahali and Arab Commission for Human Rights, 2005.

——. *Al-Istiqlal al-Thani: Min Ajl al-Dawla al-ʿArabiyya al-Dimuqratiyya al-Haditha* (The Second Independence: For a Modern Democratic Arab State). Beirut: Dar al-Kunuz al-Adabiyya, 1996.

——. *Le mal arabe: Entre dictatures et intégrismes: La démocratie interdite* (The Arab Trouble: Between Dictatorships and Fundamentalisms: The Forbidden Democracy). Paris: L'Harmattan, 2004.

Massad, Joseph A. *Desiring Arabs*. Chicago: University of Chicago Press, 2007.

Mazali, Mohammad. "Al-Asala wa al-Tafattuh" (Authenticity and Openness). *Al-Adab* 19, no. 11 (1971): 13–17.

Mazhar, Ismail. "Fi al-Naqd al-Adabi" (On Literary Critique). *Al-Risala* 153 (June 8, 1936): 1252–53.

Mejcher-Atassi, Sonja, ed. *Writing: A "Tool for Change." 'Abd al-Rahman Munif Remembered*. Special issue of *MIT Electronic Journal of Middle East Studies* 7 (Spring 2007). Available at http://web.mit.edu/CIS/www/mitejmes/intro.htm.

Memmi, Albert. *Portrait du colonisé Arabo-musulman et de quelques autres*. Paris: Gallimard, 2004. English translation: *Decolonization and the Decolonized*. Translated by Robert Bononno. Minneapolis: University of Minnesota Press, 2006.

Mermier, Franck. *Le livre et la ville: Beyrouth et l'édition arabe* (The Book and the City: Beirut and the Arab Edition). Paris: Actes Sud, Sindbad, 2005. Arabic translation: *Al-Kitab wa al-Madina: Bayrut wa al-Nashr al-'Arabi*. Beirut: Mukhtarat, 2006.

Mernissi, Fatima. *Le harem politique*. Paris: Albin Michel, 1987. English translation: *The Veil and the Male Elite: A Feminist Interpretation of Women's Rights in Islam*. Translated by Mary Jo Lakeland. Reading, Mass.: Addison-Wesley, 1991.

Mitchell, Timothy. *Colonising Egypt*. Cambridge, U.K.: Cambridge University Press, 1988; reprint, Berkeley and Los Angeles: University of California Press, 1991.

Morsy, Soheir, Cynthia Nelson, Reem Saad, and Hania Sholkamy. "Anthropology and the Call for Indigenization of Social Science in the Arab World." In Earl L. Sullivan and Jacqueline S. Ismael, eds., *The Contemporary Study of the Arab World*, 81–111. Edmonton: University of Alberta Press, 1991.

Mortimer, Mildred, ed. *Maghrebian Mosaic: A Literature in Transition*. Boulder, Colo.: Lynne Rienner, 2000.

El mundo arabe y América Latina (The Arab World and Latin America). Paris: UNESCO, 1997. Arabic translation: *Al-Watan al-'Arabi wa Amirka al-Latiniyya* (The Arab Homeland and Latin America). Translated and and with an introduction by Abdel Wahid Akmir. Beirut: Markaz Dirasat al-Wihda al-'Arabiyya, 2005.

Munif, Abdel Rahman. *Al-An . . . Huna aw Sharq al-Mutawassit Marratan Ukhra* (Now . . . Here, or East of the Mediterranean Once Again). Beirut: Al-Mu'assassa al-'Arabiyya li al-Dirasat wa al-Nashr, 1992.

———. *Mudun al-Milh* (Cities of Salt). 5 vols. Beirut: Al-Mu'assassa al-'Arabiyya li al-Dirasat wa al-Nashr, 1986–1989. English translation of the first volume: *Cities of Salt*. Translated by Peter Theroux. New York: Vintage, 1987.

———. *Sharq al-Mutawassit* (East of the Mediterranean). Beirut: Dar al-Tali'a, 1975.

Musa, Salameh. *Al-Yawm wa al-Ghad* (Today and Tomorrow). Cairo: Salameh Musa li al-Nashr wa al-Tawzi', 1928.

Mustafa, Shaker. "Al-Ab'ad al-Tarikhiyya li Azamat al-Tatawwur al-Hadari al-'Arabi" (The Historical Dimensions of the Development Crisis of Arab Civilization). *Al-Ma'rifa* 148 (1974): 7–52.

Na'im, Abdullahi Ahmed, ed. *Human Rights in Cross-Cultural Perspectives: A Quest for Consensus*. Philadelphia: University of Pennsylvania Press, 1992.

——. *Toward an Islamic Reformation: Civil Liberties, Human Rights, and International Law.* Syracuse, N.Y.: Syracuse University Press, 1990.

Naimy, Nadeem. "Iʿadat Tashkil al-Siyasa al-Thaqafiyya: Tashjiʿ al-Ibdaʿ wa al-Musharaka fi al-Hayat al-Thaqafiyya" (Reshaping Cultural Policy: Encouraging Creativity and Participation in Cultural Life). In *Nahwa Siyasa Thaqafiyya ʿArabiyya li al-Tanmiya* (Toward an Arab Cultural Politics for Development), 18–33. N.p.: Matbaʿat al-Munazzama al-ʿArabiyya li al-Tarbiya wa al-Thaqafa wa al-ʿUlum, ALECSO, 2001.

——. "Ishkaliyyat al-Fikr al-Islami fi ʿAsr al-Nahda" (The Problematic of Islamic Thought in the Age of the Nahda). In *ʿAsr al-Nahda: Muqaddimat Liberaliyya li al-Hadatha* (The Age of the Nahda: Liberal Beginnings of Modernity), 51–74. Beirut: Al-Markaz al-Thaqafi al-ʿArabi, 2000.

Nashabe, Hisham, ed. *Studia Palaestina: Studies in Honour of Constantine K. Zurayk.* Beirut: Institute for Palestine Studies, 1988.

Nassif, Malak Hifni. *Al-Nisaʾiyyat* (On Women's Issues). Edited by Hoda Elsadda. Cairo: Women and Memory Forum, 1998.

Nelson, Cynthia. "Biography and Women's History: On Interpreting Doria Shafik." In Nikki R. Keddie and Beth Baron, eds., *Women in Middle Eastern History: Shifting Boundaries in Sex and Gender,* 310–33. New Haven, Conn.: Yale University Press, 1991.

——. *Doria Shafik, Egyptian Feminist: A Woman Apart.* Gainesville: University of Florida Press, 1996.

——. "Old Wine, New Bottles: Reflections and Projections Concerning Research on Women in Middle Eastern Studies." In Earl L. Sullivan and Jacqueline S. Ismael, eds., *The Contemporary Study of the Arab World,* 127–52. Edmonton: University of Alberta Press, 1991.

Nelson, Esther R. and Nasr Hamid Abu Zaid. *Voice of an Exile: Reflections on Islam.* Westport, Conn.: Praeger, 2004.

Al-Nowaihi, Magda. "'The Middle East'? Or . . . Arabic Literature and the Postcolonial Predicament." In Henry Schwarz and Sangeeta Ray, eds., *A Companion to Postcolonial Studies,* 282–303. Malden, Mass.: Blackwell, 2000.

Nsouli, Mona A. and Lokman I. Meho. *Censorship in the Arab World: An Annotated Bibliography.* Lanham, Md.: Scarecrow Press, 2006.

Nuwaihi, Muhammad. "Al-Din wa Azamat al-Tatawwur fi al-Watan al-ʿArabi" (Religion and the Crisis of Development in the Arab Homeland). *Al-Maʿrifa* 148 (1974): 204–26.

——. "Nahwa al-Thawra fi al-Fikr al-Dini" (Toward a Revolution in Religious Thought). *Al-Adab* 18, no. 5 (1970): 25–31 and 98–107.

——. *Nahwa al-Thawra fi al-Fikr al-Dini* (Toward Revolution in Religious Thought). Beirut: Dar al-Adab, 1983.

Pour Rushdie: Cent intellectuels Arabes et Musulmans pour la liberté d'expression. Paris: La Découverte, Carrefour des Littératures, and Colibri, 1993. English translation: *For*

Rushdie: Essays by Arab and Muslim Writers in Defense of Free Speech. New York: Braziller, 1994.

Un printemps syrien (Syrian Spring). Special issue of *Confluences méditerranée* 44 (2002–2003).

Al-Qaradawi, Yusuf. *Islamic Awakening Between Rejection and Extremism.* Herndon, Va.: American Trust Publication and the International Institute of Islamic Thought, 1991.

Qira'at fi al-Fikr al-'Arabi (Readings in Arab Thought). Beirut: Markaz Dirasat al-Wihda al-'Arabiyya, 2003.

Qutb, Sayyid. *Al-'Adala al-Ijtima'iyya fi al-Islam.* Cairo: Dar Misr li al-Tiba'a, 1949. English translation: *Social Justice in Islam.* Translated by John B. Hardie. Revised by Hamid Algar. Oneonta, N.Y.: Islamic Publications International, 2000.

——. *Ma'alim fi al-Tariq* (Signs on the Way). Cairo: Dar al-Shuruq, [c. 1970s]. English translation: *Milestones.* New Delhi: Islamic Book Service, 2001.

——. *Muqawwimat al-Tasawwur al-Islami.* Cairo: Dar al-Shuruq, 1986. English translation: *Basic Principles of the Islamic Worldview.* Translated by Rami David. North Haledon, N.J.: Islamic Publications International, 2006.

Raheb, Mitri. *Bethlehem Besieged: Stories of Hope in Times of Trouble.* Minneapolis: Fortress Press, 2004.

——. *I Am a Palestinian Christian.* Minneapolis: Fortress Press, 1995.

Reid, D. M. *The Odyssey of Farah Antun: A Syrian Christian's Quest for Secularism.* Minneapolis: Bibliotheca Islamica, 1975.

Rida, Muhammad Rashid. *Al-Khilafa wa al-Imama al-'Uzma* (The Caliphate and the Great Imamate). Cairo: Matba'at al-Manar, 1923.

——. *Tarikh al-Ustadh al-Imam al-Shaykh Muhammad Abduh* (History of the Professor and Iman Sheikh Muhammad Abduh). Vol. 1. Cairo: Matba'at al-Manar, 1931.

Rodinson, Maxime. *Marxisme et monde musulman.* Paris: Edition du Seuil, 1966. Abridged English translation: *Marxism and the Muslim World.* Translated by Jean Matthews. New York: Penguin, 1974; reprint, New York: Monthly Review Press, 1981.

El-Saadawi, Nawal. *Dirasat al-Mar'a wa al-Rajul fi al-Mujtama' al-'Arabi* (Studies of Woman and Man in Arab Society). 2d ed. Beirut: Al-Mu'assassa al-'Arabiyya li al-Dirasat wa al-Nashr, 1990.

——. *The Hidden Face of Eve: Women in the Arab World.* Translated and edited by Sherif Hetata. Boston: Beacon Press, 1982.

——. *Mudhakkarati fi Sijn al-Nisa'* (My Memoirs in the Women's Prison). Cairo: Dar al-Mustaqbal al-'Arabi, 1983; Beirut: Dar al-Adab, 2000, 2d ed., 2005. English translation: *Memoirs from the Women's Prison.* Translated by Marilyn Booth. London: Women's Press, 1986.

——. *The Nawal el Saadawi Reader.* London: Zed Books, 1997.

al-Safadi, Muta'. "Akher Idiyolojia 'Arabiyya: Tarsikh Thaqafat al-'Ajz ka 'Aqida Intisariyya" (Latest Arab Ideology: Anchoring the Culture of Impotence as a Doctrine of Victory). *Al-Quds al-Arabi*, May 8, 2006.

——. "Al-Nahda wa Ishkaliyyat al-Tashir al-Siyasi: Ihbat Dawlat al-Istiqlal Tamhidan li Tafkik al-Mujtama'" (The Nahda and the Desertification of Politics: Collapse of the Independence State as a Prelude to the Dismantling of Society." *Al-Quds al-Arabi*, July 3, 2006.

——. "Safinat al-Mashru' al-Nahdawi ila Ayn . . . Tasyiss al-Din aw Tadyin al-Siyasa?" (The Boat of the Nahda Project: Where To? The Politicization of Religion and the Sacralization of Politics). *Al-Quds al-Arabi*, April 10, 2006.

Safi, Omid, ed. *Progressive Muslims: On Justice, Gender, and Pluralism*. Oxford, U.K.: Oneworld, 2003.

Said, Edward. *Orientalism*. New York: Pantheon Books, 1978.

——. "Zionism from the Standpoint of Its Victims." *Social Text* 1 (1979): 7–58.

Salamé, Ghassan, ed. *The Foundations of the Arab State*. London: Croom Helm, 1987.

——. "Introduction: Where Are the Democrats?" In Ghassan Salamé, ed., *Democracy Without Democrats? The Renewal of Politics in the Muslim World*, 13–14. London: I. B. Tauris, 1994.

——. *Al-Mujtama' wa al-Dawla fi al-Mashreq al-'Arabi* (Society and State in the Arab East). Beirut: Markaz Dirasat al-Wihda al-'Arabiyya, 1986.

——. *Nahwa 'Aqd Ijtima'i 'Arabi Jadid* (Toward a New Arab Social Contract). Beirut: Markaz Dirasat al-Wihda al-'Arabiyya, 1988.

——. "Sur la causalité d'un manque: Pourquoi le monde arabe n'est-il donc pas démocratique?" (On the Causality of a Lack: Why Is the Arab World Not Democratic?). *Revue Française de Science Politique* 41, no. 3 (1991): 307–40.

Saleh, Hashim. *Al-Insidad al-Tarikhi: Limadha Fashila Mashru' al-Tanwir fi al-'Alam al-'Arabi?* (The Historical Deadlock: Why Did the Enlightenment Project Fail in the Arab World?). Beirut: Dar al-Saqi, 2007.

Sayigh, Rosemary. *Palestinians: From Peasants to Revolutionaries: A People's History*. London: Zed Press, 1979.

——. "Roles and Functions of Arab Women: A Reappraisal." *Arab Studies Quarterly* 3, no. 3 (1981): 258–74.

——. *Too Many Enemies: The Palestinian Experience in Lebanon*. London: Zed Books, 1993.

——. "Women's Nakba Stories: Between Being and Knowing." In Ahmad H. Sa'di and Lila Abu-Lughod, eds., *Nakba: Palestine, 1948, and the Claims of Memory*, 135–58. New York: Columbia University Press, 2007.

Al-Sayyid, Ridwan. *Al-sira' 'Ala al-Islam: Al-Usuliyya wa al-Islah wa al-Siyasat al-Dawliyya* (The Conflict over Islam: Fundamentalist Reform and International Politics). Beirut: Dar al-Kitab al-'Arabi, 2004.

——. *Siyasat al-Islam al-Mu'assir* (The Policies of Contemporary Islam). Beirut: Dar al-Kitab al-'Arabi, 1997.

Al-Sayyid Marsot, Afaf Lutfi. *Egypt in the Reign of Muhammad Ali.* Cambridge, U.K.: Cambridge University Press, 1984.

——. *Women and Men in Late Eighteenth Century Egypt.* Austin: University of Texas Press, 1995.

Selim, Samah. "The Nahda, Popular Fiction, and the Politics of Translation." In Joseph Massad, Samia Mehrez, and Maha Yahya, eds., *Magda al-Nowaihi (1958–2004): In Memory,* special issue of *MIT Electronic Journal of Middle East Studies* 4 (Fall 2004): 71–89.

Sfeir, George N. "Basic Freedoms in a Fractured Legal Culture: Egypt and the Case of Nasr Hamid Abu Zayd." *Middle East Journal* 52, no. 3 (1998): 402–14.

Shaarawi, Huda. *Harem Years: The Memoirs of an Egyptian Feminist.* Translated and with an introduction by Margot Badran. New York: Feminist Press, 1986.

Sharabi, Hisham. *Arab Intellectuals and the West: The Formative Years, 1875–1914.* Baltimore: Johns Hopkins University Press, 1970.

——. "Introduction: Patriarchy and Dependency and the Future of Arab Society." In Hisham Sharabi, ed., *The Next Arab Decade: Alternative Futures,* 1–8. Boulder, Colo.: Westview Press, 1988.

——. *Neopatriarchy: A Theory of Distorted Change in Arab Society.* New York: Oxford University Press, 1988.

——, ed. *The Next Arab Decade: Alternative Futures.* Boulder, Colo.: Westview Press, 1988.

——. "The Scholarly Point of View: Politics, Perspectives, Paradigm." In Hisham Sharabi, ed., *Theory, Politics, and the Arab World: Critical Responses,* 1–51. New York: Routledge, 1990.

——, ed. *Theory, Politics, and the Arab World: Critical Responses.* New York: Routledge, 1990.

Sheehi, Stephen. "Failure, Modernity, and the Works of Hisham Sharabi: Towards a Postcolonial Critique of Arab Subjectivity." *Critique: Journal of Critical Studies of Iran and the Middle East* 10 (1997): 39–54.

Al-Shidyaq, Ahmed Faris. *Kashf al-Mukhabba' 'An Funun Urubba* (Discovering the Hidden in Europe's Arts). Constantinople: n.p., 1881–82.

——. *Al-Saq 'Ala al-Saq fi ma Huwa al-Faryaq* (Leg on Leg About Faryaq and His Travel Observations). Beirut: Dar Maktabat al-Hayah, 1966.

——. *Al-Wasita fi Ma'rifat Ahwal Malta* (The Way to Know About Malta). Beirut: Mu'assassat Nasir li al-Thaqafa and Dar al-Wihda, 1978.

Shohat, Ella. "Coming to America: Reflections on Hair and Memory Loss." In Amal Amireh and Lisa Suhair Majaj, eds., *Going Global: The Transnational Reception of Third World Women Writers,* 284–300. New York: Garland, 2000.

——. "Dislocated Identities: Reflections of an Arab-Jew." *Movement Research: Performance Journal* 5 (1992): 7–8.

——. "Mizrahi Feminism: The Politics of Gender, Race, and Multi-culturalism." *News from Within* 12, no. 4 (1996): 17–26.

——. "Notes on the 'Post-colonial.'" *Social Text,* nos. 31–32 (1992): 99–113.

——. "Sephardim in Israel: Zionism from the Standpoint of Its Jewish Victims." *Social Text* 19–20 (1988): 1–35.

——. "Taboo Memories and Diasporic Visions: Columbus, Palestine, and Arab-Jews." In May Joseph and Jennifer Natalya Fink, eds., *Performing Hybridity,* 131–56. Minneapolis: University of Minnesota Press, 1999. Reprinted in Ella Shohat, *Taboo Memories and Diasporic Voices,* 201–32. Durham, N.C.: Duke University Press, 2006.

Sonbol, Amira, ed. *Beyond the Exotic: Women's Histories in Islamic Societies.* Syracuse, N.Y.: Syracuse University Press, 2005.

——. *Creation of a Medical Profession in Egypt, 1800–1922.* Syracuse, N.Y.: Syracuse University Press, 1991.

——, ed. *Women, the Family, and Divorce Laws in Islamic History.* Syracuse, N.Y.: Syracuse University Press, 1996.

Stowasser, Barbara Freyer. "Gender Issues and Contemporary Quran Interpretation." In Yvonne Yazbeck Haddad and John L. Esposito, eds., *Islam, Gender, and Social Change,* 30–44. New York: Oxford University Press, 1998.

——. *The Islamic Impulse.* London and Washington, D.C.: Croom Helm and the Center for Contemporary Arab Studies, Georgetown University, 1987.

——. *Women in the Qur'an, Traditions, and Interpretation.* New York: Oxford University Press, 1994.

——. "Women's Issues in Modern Islamic Thought." In Judith E. Tucker, ed., *Arab Women: Old Boundaries, New Frontiers,* 3–28. Bloomington: Indiana University Press, 1993.

Sullivan, Earl L. and Jacqueline S. Ismael, eds. *The Contemporary Study of the Arab World.* Edmonton: University of Alberta Press, 1991.

Taha, Mahmoud Mohamed. *The Second Message of Islam.* Translated and introduced by Abdullahi Ahmed An-Na'im. Syracuse, N.Y.: Syracuse University Press, 1987.

Al-Tahtawi, Rifaʿa Rafiʿ.

——. *Al-Murshid al-Amin li al-Banat wa al-Banin* (loosely rendered: Guiding Truths for Girls and Youths). Cairo: Matbaʿat al-Madaris al-Malakiyya, 1872–1873.

——. *Takhlis al-Ibriz fi Talkhis Bariz* (The Extraction of Pure Gold in the Abridgment of Paris). Beirut: Dar Ibn-Khaldun, 2003. *An Imam in Paris: Tahtawi's Visit to France (1826–1831).* Translated and with an introduction by Daniel L. Newman. London: Saqi Books, 2004.

Tajammuʿ al-Bahithat al-Lubnaniyyat (Lebanese Association of Women Researchers), ed. *Al-Nisaʾ al-ʿArabiyyat fi al-ʿIshrinat: Huduran wa Huwwiyya* (Arab Women in the Twenties: Presence and Identity). Beirut: Al-Bahithat, n.d.

Tarabichi, Georges. *Al-'Aql al-Mustaqil fi al-Islam?* (The Resigned Reason in Islam?). Beirut: Dar al-Saqi, 2004.

——. "'Asr al-Nahda wa al-Jurh al-Narjissi: Nasawiyyat Qasim Amin wa 'Aqliyyat al-Tamahi ma' al-Mu'tadi" (The Nahda Epoch and the Narcissist Wound: The Feminism of Qasim Amin and the Mechanism of Identification with the Aggressor). In Georges Tarabichi, *Min al-Nahda ila al-Radda: Tamazzuqat al-Thaqafa al-'Arabiyya fi 'Asr al-'Awlama* (From Renaissance to Regression: The Tensions of Arab Culture in the Age of Globalization), 9–38. Beirut: Dar al-Saqi, 2000.

——. *Ishkaliyyat al-'Aql al-'Arabi* (The Issues of Arab Reason). London: Saqi Books, 2002.

——. *Izdiwajiyyat al-'Aql: Dirasa Tahliliyya Nafsiyya li Kitabat Hassan Hanafi* (The Duality of Reason: An Analytical-Psychological Study of the Writings of Hassan Hanafi). Damascus: Dar Petra, 2005.

——. *Min al-Nahda ila al-Radda: Tamazzuqat al-Thaqafa al-'Arabiyya fi 'Asr al-'Awlama* (From Renaissance to Regression: Tensions of Arab Culture in the Age of Globalization). Beirut: Dar al-Saqi, 2000.

——. *Al-Muthaqqafun al-'Arab wa al-Turath: Al-Tahlil al-Nafsi li 'Isab Jama'i* (Arab Intellectuals and Tradition: A Psychological Analysis of a Collective Neurosis). Riyadh, Saudi Arabia: El Rayyes Books, 1991.

——. *Naqd Naqd al-'Aql al-'Arabi: Nadhariat al-'Aql* (Critique of the Critique of Reason: The Theory of Reason). Beirut: Dar al-Saqi, 1996.

——. *Untha Didd al-Unutha: Dirasa fi Adab Nawal al-Saadawi 'ala Daw' al-Tahlil al-Nafsi.* Beirut: Dar al-Tali'a, 1984. English translation: *Woman Against Her Sex: A Critique of Nawal el-Saadawi, with a Reply by Nawal el-Saadawi.* Translated by Basil Hatim and Elizabeth Orsini. London: Saqi Books, 1988.

——. *Wihdat al-'Aql al-'Arabi* (The Unity of Arab Reason). Beirut: Dar al-Saqi, 2002.

Tibi, Bassam. *The Challenge of Fundamentalism: Political Islam and the New World Disorder.* Berkeley and Los Angeles: University of California Press, 1997; updated ed., 2002.

——. *The Crisis of Modern Islam: A Pre-industrial Culture in the Scientific-Technological Age.* Salt Lake City: University of Utah Press, 1988.

——. "Culture and Knowledge: The Politics of Islamicization of Knowledge as a Postmodern Project? The Fundamentalist Claim to De-westernization." *Theory, Culture, and Society* 12 (1995): 1–24.

——. *Islam Between Culture and Politics.* New York and Cambridge, Mass.: Palgrave in association with the Weatherhead Center for International Affairs, Harvard University, 2001.

——. *Nationalismus in der Dritten Welt am arabischen Beispiel.* Frankfurt am Main: Europäische Verlagsanst, 1971. English translation: *Arab Nationalism: A Critical Enquiry.* Edited and translated by Marion Farouk-Sluglett and Peter Sluglett. London: Mac-

Millan, 1981. Expanded and revised edition: *Arab Nationalism Between Islam and the Nation-State*. New York: St. Martin's Press, 1997.

——. *Vom Gottesreich zum Nationalstaat: Islam und panarabischer Nationalismus* (From God's Empire to Nation-State: Islam and Pan-Arab Nationalism). Frankfurt am Main: Suhrkamp, 1987.

Tignor, Robert L., ed. *Napoleon in Egypt: Al-Jabarti's Chronicle of the French Occupation, 1798*. New York: Markus Wiener, 1993.

Tizini, Tayyeb. *Min al-Turath ila al-Thawra* (From Tradition to Revolution). Beirut: Dar Ibn Khaldun, 1976.

Traboulsi, Fawwaz. "An Intelligent Man's Guide to Modern Arab Feminism." *Al-Raida* 20, no. 100 (Winter 2003): 15–19.

Tucker, Judith E., ed. *Arab Women: Old Boundaries, New Frontiers*. Bloomington: Indiana University Press, 1993.

Al-Tunisi, Khaireddin. *Aqwam al-Masalik fi Ma'rifat Ahwal al-Mamalik* (The Straightest Path in Knowing the States of Kingdoms). Tunis: Al-Majma' al-Tunisi li al-'Ulum wa al-Adab wa al-Funun, Bayt al-Hikma, 2000; originally published in 1867–68. French translation: *Réformes nécessaires aux états musulmans*. Paris: Dupont, 1868. English translation: *The Surest Path: The Political Treatise of a Nineteenth-Century Muslim Statesman*. Translated by Leon Carl Brown. Cambridge, Mass.: Harvard University Press, 1967.

Al-Turath wa Tahaddiyyat al-'Asr fi al-Watan al-'Arabi: Al-Asala wa al-Mu'assara (Heritage and the Challenges of the Age in the Arab Homeland: Authenticity and Contemporaneity). Beirut: Markaz Dirasat al-Wihda al-'Arabiyya, 1985.

Von Grunebaum, Gustav E. *Modern Islam: The Search for Cultural Identity*. Berkeley and Los Angeles: University of California Press, 1962.

Von Kügelgen, Anke. *Averroes und die arabische Moderne: Ansätze zu einer Neubegründung des Rationalismus im Islam* (Averroes and Arabic Modernity: Attempts at a New Foundation of Rationalism in Islam). Islamic Philosophy, Theology, and Science, vol. 19. Leiden: Brill, 1994.

——. "'Averroisten' im 20. Jahrhundert—Zu Ibn-Rušd-Rezeption in der arabischen Welt" (Averroists in the Twentieth Century: On the Reception of Ibn Rush in the Arab World). In Friedrich Niewöhner and Loris Sturlese, eds., *Averroismus im Mittelalter und in der Renaissance* (Averroes in the Middle Ages and the Renaissance), 351–71. Zürich: Spur, 1994.

——. "A Call for Rationalism: 'Arab Averroists' in the Twentieth Century." *Alif: Journal of Comparative Poetics* 16 (1996): 97–132.

Wahba, Mourad and Mona Abousenna, eds. *Averroes and the Enlightenment*. Amherst, N.Y.: Prometheus Books, 1996.

Wannous, Saadallah. *Al-A'mal al-Kamila* (The Complete Works). Beirut: Dar al-Adab, 2004.

——. "Al-Thaqafa al-Wataniyya wa al-Wa'y al-Tarikhi" (National Culture and Historical Awareness). *Qadaya wa Shahadat* 4 (1991): 5–39.

Waterbury, John. "Social Science Research and Arab Studies in the Coming Decade." In Hisham Sharabi, ed., *The Next Arab Decade: Alternative Futures*, 293–302. Boulder, Colo.: Westview Press, 1988.

Wazen, Abdo. Series of five interviews with Mahmud Darwish. *Al-Hayat*, December 10, 11, 12, 13, 14, 2005.

Yared, Nazik Saba. "Nazira Zain al-Din (1980–1976): Bayna al-Tahaddi wa al-Iltizam" (Nazira Zain al-Din [1908–1976]: Between Defiance and Commitment). In Tajammu' al-Bahithat al-Lubnaniyyat (Lebanese Association of Women Researchers), ed., *Al-Nisa' al-'Arabiyat fi al-'Ishriniyyat Huduran wa Huwiyya* (Arab Women in the Twenties: Presence and Identity), 243–61. Beirut: Bahithat, n.d.

——. *Al-Rahhalun al-'Arab wa Hadarat al-Gharb fi al-Nahda al-'Arabiyya al-Haditha* (Arab Travelers and Western Civilization in the Modern Arab Renaissance). Beirut: Naufal Press, 1992. English translation: *Arab Travellers and Western Civilization*. Translated by by Summayya Damluji Shahbandar. Revised and edited by Tony P. Naufal and Jana Gough. London: Saqi Books, 1996.

——. *Secularism and the Arab World, 1850–1939*. London: Saqi Books, 2002.

Yassin, El Sayed. "In Search of a New Identity of the Social Sciences in the Arab World: Discourse, Paradigm, and Strategy." In Hisham Sharabi, ed., *The Next Arab Decade: Alternative Futures*, 303–11. Boulder, Colo.: Westview Press, 1988.

Zain al-Din, Nazira. *Al-Fatat wa al-Shuyukh* (The Girl and the Sheikhs). Edited by Buthaina Shaaban. Damascus: Dar al-Mada li al-Thaqafa wa al-Nashr, 1998; originally published around 1929.

——. *Al Sufur wa al-Hijab* (Unveiling and Veiling). Edited by Buthaina Shaaban. Damascus: Dar al-Mada li al-Thaqafa wa al-Nashr, 1998; originally published in 1928.

Zakariyya, Fouad. *Al-Haqiqa wa al-Khayal fi al-Haraka al-Islamiyya al-Mu'assira*. Cairo: Dar Sina li al-Nashr, 1988. English translation: *Myth and Reality in the Contemporary Islamist Movement*. Translated and with an introduction and bibliography by Ibrahim M. Abu-Rabi'. London: Pluto Press, 2005.

——. *Al-Haqiqa wa al-Wahm fi al-Haraka al-Islamiyya al-Mu'assira* (The Truth and Illusion About the Contemporary Islamic Movement). Cairo: Dar al-Fikr, 1986.

——. "Human Rights in the Arab World: The Islamic Context." In *Philosophical Foundations of Human Rights*, with contributions by Alwin Diemer and others, 227–41. Paris: UNESCO, 1986.

——. *Al-Sahwa al-Islamiyya fi Mizan al-'Aql* (The Islamic Awakening in the Balance of Reason). Cairo: Dar al-Fikr al-Mu'assir, 1987.

——. "Al-Takhalluf al-Fikri wa Ab'aduhu al-Hadariyya" (Intellectual Retardation and Its Civilizational Dimensions). *Al-Ma'rifa* 148 (1974): 60–82.

Zghal, Abdelkader. "The Reactivation of Tradition in a Post-traditional Society." *Daedalus* 102, no. 1 (1973): 225–37.

Zghal, Abdelkader and Hachmi Karoui. "Decolonization and Social Science Research: The Case of Tunisia." *Middle East Studies Association Bulletin* 7, no. 3 (October 1973): 11–27.

Ziadeh, Ridwan. *Idiyologiyya al-Nahda fi al-Khitab al-ʿArabi al-Muʿassir* (The Ideology of the Nahda in Contemporary Arab Discourse). Beirut: Dar al-Taliʿa, 2004.

Zurayq, Qustantin. *Al-Aʿmal al-Kamilah* (The Complete Works). Beirut: Markaz Dirasat al-Wihda al-ʿArabiyya, 1994.

——. *The Meaning of the Disaster.* Translated by B. Winder. Beirut: Khayat's College Book Cooperative, 1956.

Zürcher, Erik J. *Turkey: A Modern History.* London: I. B. Tauris: 1993.

Latin American

Alcoff, Linda Martin and Eduardo Mendieta, eds. *Thinking from the Underside of History: Enrique Dussel's Philosophy of Liberation.* Lanham, Md.: Rowman and Littlefield, 2000.

Black, Virginia. Letter to the editor. *American Philosophical Association Proceedings and Addresses* 60 (1987): 519–22.

Boff, Leonardo and Clodovis Boff. *Introducing Liberation Theology.* Translated by Paul Burns. Maryknoll, N.Y.: Orbis Books, 1987.

Bondy, Augusto Salazar. "The Meaning and Problem of Hispanic American Thought." In Jorge J. E. Gracia, ed., *Latin American Philosophy in the Twentieth Century*, 233–44. Buffalo, N.Y.: Prometheus, 1986.

Cerutti-Guldberg, Horacio. "Actual Situation and Perspectives on Latin American Philosophy of Liberation." *Philosophical Forum* 20 (1988–89): 43–61.

Dussel, Enrique. "Eurocentrism and Modernity." In John Beverly, Michael Aronna, and José Oviedo, eds., *The Postmodernism Debate in Latin America*, 65–76. Durham, N.C.: Duke University Press, 1995. The collected volume was originally published as a special issue of *Boundary 2* 20, no. 3 (1992).

——. *Philosophy of Liberation.* Translated from the Spanish by Aquilina Martinez and Christine Morkovsky. Maryknoll, N.Y.: Orbis, 1985.

Gracia, Jorge J. E. "Ethnic Labels and Philosophy: The Case of Latin American Philosophy." *Philosophy Today* 43 (1999): 42–49.

——. "Introduction: Latin American Philosophy Today." *Philosophical Forum* 20, nos. 1–2 (1988–89): 4–32.

——, ed. *Latin American Philosophy in the Twentieth Century.* Buffalo, N.Y.: Prometheus, 1986.

Guttierrez, Gustavo. *Teología de la liberatión.* Lima: CEP, 1971. English translation: *A Theology of Liberation: History, Politics, and Salvation.* Translated and edited by Sister Caridad Inda and John Eagleton. Maryknoll, N.Y.: Orbis, 1973.

Lange, Lynda. "Burnt Offerings to Rationality: A Feminist Reading of the Construction of Indigenous Peoples in Dussel's Theory of Modernity." In Linda Martin Alcoff and Eduardo Mendieta, eds., *Thinking from the Underside of History: Enrique Dussel's Philosophy of Liberation*, 135–47. Lanham, Md.: Rowman and Littlefield, 2000.

Mariategui, José Carlos. *Seven Interpretive Essays on Peruvian Reality*. Translated by Marjory Urquidi. Austin: University of Texas Press, 1971.

Marti, José. *José Marti Reader: Writings on the Americas*. Edited by Deborah Shnookal and Mirta Muñiz. Melbourne: Ocean Press, 1999.

Marti, Oscar R. "Is There a Latin American Philosophy?" *Metaphilosophy* 14, no. 1 (1983): 46–52.

Medina, Vicente. "The Possibility of an Indigenous Philosophy: A Latin American Perspective." *American Philosophical Quarterly* 29, no. 4 (1992): 373–80.

Mendieta, Eduardo. "Is There a Latin American Philosophy?" *Philosophy Today* 43 (1999): 50–61.

Nascimento, Amos. "Colonialism, Modernism, and Postmodernism in Brazil." In Eduardo Mendieta, ed., *Latin American Philosophy: Currents, Issues, Debates*, 124–49. Bloomington: Indiana University Press, 2003.

——, ed. *A Matter of Discourse: Community and Communication in Contemporary Philosophies*. Aldershot, U.K.: Ashgate, 1998.

Olea, Raquel. "Feminism: Modern or Postmodern?" In John Beverly, Michael Aronna, and José Oviedo, eds., *The Postmodernism Debate in Latin America*, 192–200. Durham, N.C.: Duke University Press, 1995.

Paz, Octavio. *The Labyrinth of Solitude: Life and Thought in Mexico*. Translated by Lysander Kemp. New York: Grove Press, 1985.

Ramos, Samuel. *Profile of Man and Culture in Mexico*. Translated by Peter G. Earle. Austin: University of Texas Press, 1962.

Retamar, Roberto Fernandez. "Our America and the West." *Social Text* 5, no. 3 (1986): 1–25.

Reyes, Alfonso. *Mexico in a Nutshell and Other Essays*. Translated by Charles Ramsdell. Berkeley and Los Angeles: University of California Press, 1964.

Rorty, Richard. "From Logic to Language to Play: A Plenary Address to the Inter-American Congress." *American Philosophical Association Proceedings and Addresses* 59 (1986): 747–53.

Saenz, Mario. *The Identity of Liberation in Latin American Thought: Latin American Historicism and the Phenomenology of Leopoldo Zea*. Lanham, Md.: Lexington Books, 1999.

——. "Philosophies of Liberation and Modernity: The Case of Latin America." *Philosophy Today* 38 (1994): 115–34.

Saporta Sternbach, Nancy, Marysa Navarro-Aranguren, Patricia Chuchryk, and Sonia E. Alvarez. "Feminisms in Latin America: From Bogota to San Bernardo." *Signs* 17, no. 2 (1992): 393–434.

Schutte, Ofelia. *Cultural Identity and Social Liberation in Latin American Thought*. Albany: State University of New York Press, 1993.

——. "Notes on the Issue of Cultural Imperialism." *American Philosophical Association Proceedings and Addresses* 59 (1986): 757–59.

——. "Origins and Tendencies of the Philosophy of Liberation in Latin American Thought: A Critique of Dussel's Ethics." *Philosophical Forum* 22 (1991): 270–95.

——. "Philosophy and Feminism in Latin America: Perspectives on Gender Identity and Culture." *Philosophical Forum* 20 (1988–1989): 62–84.

Schwarz, Roberto. *Misplaced Ideas: Essays on Brazilian Culture*. Edited and with an introduction by John Gledson. London: Verso, 1992.

——. "National by Imitation." In John Beverly, Michael Aronna, and José Oviedo, eds., *The Postmodernism Debate in Latin America*, 264–81. Durham, N.C.: Duke University Press, 1995. The collected volume was originally published as a special volume of *Boundary 2* 20, no. 3 (1992)

Travaux du Congrès International de Philosophie consacré aux problèmes de la connaissance (Proceedings of the Inter-American Congress of Philosophy Meeting Devoted to the Problems of Knowledge). Port-au-Prince, Haiti: Imprimerie de l'État, 1947.

Vuola, Elina. "Thinking Otherwise: Dussel, Liberation Theology, and Feminism." In Linda Martin Alcoff and Eduardo Mendieta, eds., *Thinking from the Underside of History: Enrique Dussel's Philosophy of Liberation*, 149–180. Lanham, Md.: Rowman and Littlefield, 2000.

Zea, Leopoldo. "The Actual Function of Philosophy in Latin America." In Jorge J. E. Gracia, ed., *Latin American Philosophy in the Twentieth Century: Man, Values, and the Search for Philosophical Identity*, 219–30. Buffalo, N.Y.: Prometheus, 1986.

——. *The Latin American Mind*. Translated by James H. Abbott and Lowell Dunam. Norman: University of Oklahoma Press, 1963.

——. Letter to the editor. *American Philosophical Association Proceedings and Addresses* 60 (1987): 516–19.

——. "Philosophy as an Instrument of Interamerican Understanding." *Social Epistemology* 1 (1987): 123–30.

African

Aidoo, Ama Ata. "The African Woman Today." In Obioma Naemeka, ed., *Sisterhood, Feminisms, and Power: From Africa to the Diaspora*, 39–50. Trenton, N.J.: Africa World Press, 1998.

Amato, Peter. "African Philosophy and Modernity." In Emmanuel Chukwudi Eze, ed., *Postcolonial African Philosophy: A Critical Reader*, 71–99. Cambridge, Mass.: Blackwell, 1997.

Appiah, Kwame Anthony. *In My Father's House: Africa in the Philosophy of Culture.* New York: Oxford University Press, 1992.

Arndt, Susan. "African Gender Trouble and African Womanism: An Interview with Chikwenye Ogunyemi and Wanjira Muthoni." *Signs* 25, no. 3 (2000): 709–26.

Birt, Robert E. "Feature Review: Identity and the Question of African Philosophy." *Philosophy East & West* 41, no. 1 (1991): 95–109.

Bodunrin, P. O. "The Question of African Philosophy." In Richard A. Wright, ed., *African Philosophy: An Introduction,* 1–24. Lanham, Md.: University Press of America, 1984.

Chinweizu. *Decolonising the African Mind.* Lagos, Nigeria: Pero Press, 1987.

Diop, Cheikh Anta. *The African Origin of Civilization: Myth or Reality.* Translated by Mercer Cook. New York: Lawrence Hill, 1974. Based on excerpts from two of Diop's original books in French: *Nations nègres et culture* (Negro Nations and Culture). Paris: Editions Africaines, 1955; and *Antériorité des civilisations nègres: Mythe ou vérité* (Priority of Negro Civilization: Myth or Truth). Paris: Présence Africaine, 1967.

——. *Civilisation ou barbarie: Anthropologie sans complaisance.* Paris: Présence Africaine, 1981. English translation: *Civilization or Barbarism: An Authentic Anthropology.* Translated by Yaa-Lengi Meema Ngemi. Edited by Harold J. Salemson and Marjolijn de Jager. With an introduction by John Henrik Clarke. New York: Lawrence Hill, 1991.

English, Parker and Kibujjo M. Kalumba, eds. *African Philosophy: A Classical Approach.* Upper Saddle River, N.J.: Prentice Hall, 1996.

Esack, Farid. *On Being a Muslim: Finding a Religious Path in the World Today.* Oxford, U.K.: Oneworld, 1999.

——. *Qur'an, Liberation, and Pluralism: An Islamic Perspective of Interreligious Solidarity Against Oppression.* Oxford, U.K.: Oneworld, 1997.

Eze, Emmanuel Chukwudi. "What Is African Philosophy?" In Emmanuel Chukwudi Eze, ed., *African Philosophy: An Anthology,* 1–56. Cambridge, Mass.: Blackwell, 1998.

Fanon, Frantz. *Black Skin, White Masks.* New York: Grove Press, 1967.

Gyekye, Kwame. *An Essay on African Philosophical Thought: The Akan Conceptual Scheme.* Philadelphia: Temple University Press, 1995.

——. *Tradition and Modernity: Philosophical Reflections on the African Experience.* New York: Oxford University Press, 1997.

Hountondji, Paulin. *Struggle for Meaning: Reflections on Philosophy, Culture, and Democracy in Africa.* Translated by John Conteh-Morgan. With a foreword by Kwame Anthony Appiah. Athens: Ohio University Center for International Studies, 2002.

——. *Sur la philosophie africaine: Critique de l'ethnophilosophie.* Paris: François Maspero, 1977. English translation: *African Philosophy: Myth and Reality.* Translated by Henry Evans with Jonathan Rée. Introduction by Abiola Irele. Bloomington: Indiana University Press, 1996.

Howe, Stephen. *Afrocentrism: Mythical Pasts and Imagined Homes.* London: Verso, 1998.

Imbo, Samuel Oluoch. *An Introduction to African Philosophy*. Lanham, Md.: Rowman and Littlefield, 1998.

Irele, Abiola. *The African Experience in Literature and Ideology*. London: Heinemann, 1981; reprint, Bloomington: Indiana University Press, 1990.

James, C. L. R. *The Black Jacobins: Toussaint L'Ouverture and the San Domingo Revolution*. 2d rev. ed. New York: Random House, 1963; originally published in 1938.

Jeyifo, Biodun, ed. *Conversations with Wole Soyinka*. Jackson: University Press of Mississippi, 2001.

Kagamé, Alexis. *La philosophie Bantu-rwandaise de l'être* (The Bantu-Rwandan Philosophy of Being). Brussels: Académie des Sciences Coloniales, 1955.

Kairos Theologians. *The Kairos Document: Challenge to the Church*. Stonypoint, N.Y.: Theology Global Context, 1985.

Karp, Ivan and D. A. Masolo, eds. *African Philosophy as Cultural Inquiry*. Bloomington: Indiana University Press, 2000.

Keita, Lansana. "African Philosophy in Context: A Reply to Hountondji's 'Que peut la philosophie.'" In Guttorm Floistad, ed., *Contemporary Philosophy: A New Survey*, vol. 5: *African Philosophy*, 79–98. The Hague: Martinus Nijhoff, 1987.

Kwame, Safro. "Feminism and African Philosophy." In Safro Kwame, ed., *Readings in African Philosophy: An Akan Collection*, 253–68. Lanham, Md.: University Press of America, 1995.

Lévy-Bruhl, Lucien. *Les fonctions mentales dans les sociétés inférieures* (The Mental Functions of Inferior Societies). Paris: F. Alcan, 1910. English translation: *How Natives Think*. Translated by Lilian A. Clare. New York: Knopf, 1925.

——. *Mentalité primitive*. Paris: F. Alcan, 1922. English translation: *Primitive Mentality*. Translated by Lilian A. Clare. London: Allen and Unwin, 1923.

Lindfors, Bernth, ed. *Conversations with Chinua Achebe*. Jackson: University Press of Mississippi, 1997.

Makang, Jean-Marie. "Of the Good Use of Tradition: Keeping the Critical Perspective in African Philosophy." In Emmanuel Chukwudi Eze, ed., *Postcolonial African Philosophy: A Critical Reader*, 324–38. Cambridge, Mass.: Blackwell, 1997.

Maurier, Henri. "Do We Have an African Philosophy?" In Richard A. Wright, ed., *African Philosophy: An Introduction*, 25–40. Lanham, Md.: University Press of America, 1984.

Mosley, Albert, ed. *African Philosophy: Selected Readings*. Englewood Cliffs, N.J.: Prentice Hall, 1995.

Ngugi wa Thiong'o. *Decolonising the Mind: The Politics of Language in African Literature*. Nairobi, Kenya: Heinemann, 1986.

Oguah, Benjamin E. "African Western Philosophy: A Comparative Study." In Richard A. Wright, *African Philosophy: An Introduction*, 213–26. Lanham, Md.: University Press of America, 1984.

Ogundipe-Leslie, Molara. "Introduction: Moving the Mountains, Making the Link." In Molara Ogundipe-Leslie, *Re-creating Ourselves: African Women and Critical Transformations*, 1–18. Trenton, N.J.: Africa World Press, 1994.

Onyewuenyi, Innocent. "Is There an African Philosophy?" *Journal of African Studies* 3 (1976): 513–28.

Oruka, Henry Odera. "African Philosophy: A Brief Personal History and Current Debate." In Guttorm Floistad, ed., *Contemporary Philosophy: A New Survey*, vol. 5: *African Philosophy*, 45–77. The Hague: Martinus Nijhoff, 1987.

———. "Cultural Fundamentals in Philosophy: Obstacles in Philosophical Dialogues." *Quest* 4, no. 2 (1990): 20–37.

———. "On Philosophy and Humanism in Africa." *Philosophy and Social Action* 5, nos. 1–2 (1979): 7–13.

———. "Sagacity in African Philosophy." *International Philosophical Quarterly* 23, no. 4 (1983): 383–93. Reprinted in Tsenay Serequeberhan, ed., *African Philosophy: The Essential Readings*, 47–62. New York: Paragon House, 1991.

———, ed. *Sage Philosophy: Indigenous Thinkers and Modern Debate on African Philosophy.* Leiden: Brill, 1990.

Outlaw, Lucius. "'African Philosophy': Deconstructive and Reconstructive Challenges." In Guttorm Floistad, ed., *Contemporary Philosophy: A New Survey*, vol. 5: *African Philosophy*, 9–44. The Hague: Martinus Nijhoff, 1987.

Presbey, Gail. "Who Counts as a Sage? Problems in the Future Implementation of Sage Philosophy." *Quest* 11, no. 2 (1997): 53–68.

Sartre, Jean-Paul. "Orphée noir." In Léopold Sédar Senghor, ed., *Anthologie de la nouvelle poésie nègre et malgache de langue française* (Anthology of the New Negro and Madagascan Poetry in the French Language), ix–xliv. Paris: Presses Universitaires de France, 1948. English translation: *Black Orpheus.* Translated by S. W. Allen. Paris: Présence africaine, 1976.

Senghor, Léopold Sédar, ed. *Anthologie de la nouvelle poésie nègre et malgache de langue française* (Anthology of the New Negro and Madagascan Poetry in French Language). Paris: Presses Universitaires de France, 1948.

———. *Fondements de l'africanité; ou, Négritude et arabité.* Paris: Présence africaine, [1967?]. English translation: *Foundations of "Africanité," or "Négritude" and "Arabité."* Translated by Mercer Cook. Paris: Présence Africaine, 1971.

———. *Nation et voie africaine du socialisme.* Paris: Présence Africaine, 1961. English translation: *On African Socialism.* Translated by Mercer Cook. New York: Praeger, 1964.

———. *Négritude et civilisation de l'universel* (Negrohood and the Civilization of the Universal). Paris: Seuil, 1977.

———. *Négritude et humanisme* (Negrohood and Humanism). Paris: Editions du Seuil, 1964.

———. "Negrohood: Psychology of the African Negro." In Albert Mosley, ed., *African Philosophy: Selected Readings*, 116–27. Englewood Cliffs, N.J.: Prentice Hall, 1995.

———. *Ce que je crois: Négritude, francité et civilisation de l'universel* (What I Believe: Negro-hood, Frenchness, and the Civilization of the Universal). Paris: Grasset, 1988.

Steady, Filomina Chioma. "African Feminism: A Worldwide Perspective." In Rosalyn Terborg-Penn, Sharon Harley, and Andrea Benton Rushing, eds., *Women in Africa and the African Diaspora*, 3–24. Washington, D.C.: Howard University Press, 1987.

Tempels, Placide. *Bantoe-filosofie: Oorspronkelijke tekst.* Antwerpen: De Sikkel, 1946. French translation from the Dutch: *La philosophie bantoue.* Translated by A. Rubbens. Paris: Présence Africaine, 1949. English translation: *Bantu Philosophy.* Translated from the French by Colin King. With a foreword by Margaret Read. Paris: Présence Africaine, 1959.

Towa, Marcien. "Conditions for the Affirmation of a Modern African Philosophical Thought." Translated by Aster Gashaw in Tsenay Serequeberhan, ed., *African Philosophy: The Essential Readings*, 187–200. New York: Paragon House, 1991.

———. *Essai sur la problématique philosophique dans l'Afrique actuelle* (Essay on the Philosophical Problematic in Present Africa). Yaoundé, Cameroon: CLE, 1971.

———. *Idée d'une philosophie négro-africaine* (The Idea of a Negro-African Philosophy). Yaoundé, Cameroon: CLE, 1979.

———. *Léopold Sédar Senghor, négritude ou servitude?* (Léopold Sédar Senghor, Negritude or Servitude?). Yaoundé, Cameroon: CLE, 1971.

Tripp, Aili Mari. "Rethinking Difference: Comparative Perspectives from Africa." *Signs* 25, no. 3 (2000): 649–75.

Wamba-dia-Wamba, Ernest. "Philosophy and African Intellectuals: Mimesis of Western Classicism, Ethnophilosophical Romanticism, or African Self-Mastery?" *Quest* 5, no. 1 (1991): 4–17.

Wiredu, Kwasi. *Conceptual Decolonization in African Philosophy.* Ibadan, Nigeria: Hope, 1995.

———. *Cultural Universals and Particulars: An African Perspective.* Bloomington: Indiana University Press, 1996.

———. "Formulating Modern Thought in African Languages: Some Theoretical Considerations." In V. Y. Mudimbe, ed., *The Surreptitious Speech: Presence Africaine and the Politics of Otherness, 1947–1987*, 201–24. Chicago: University of Chicago Press, 1992.

———. "The Need for Conceptual Decolonisation in African Philosophy." In Heinz Kimmerle and Franz Wimmer, eds., *Philosophy and Democracy in Intercultural Perspective*, 11–22. Amsterdam: Rodopi, 1997.

———. *Philosophy and an African Culture.* Cambridge, U.K.: Cambridge University Press, 1980.

Wright, Richard A., ed. *African Philosophy: An Introduction.* Lanham, Md.: University Press of America, 1984.

———. "Investigating African Philosophy." In Richard A. Wright, ed., *African Philosophy: An Introduction*, 41–56. Lanham, Md.: University Press of America, 1984.

European

Barnard, F. M. "Natural Growth and Purposive Development: Vico and Herder." *History and Theory* 18 (1979): 16–36.

Beiser, Frederick. *Enlightenment, Revolution, and Romanticism: The Genesis of Modern German Political Thought 1790–1800*. Cambridge, Mass.: Harvard University Press, 1992.

——. *The Fate of Reason: German Philosophy from Kant to Fichte*. Cambridge, Mass.: Harvard University Press, 1987.

Brague, Rémy. *Europe: La voie romaine* (Europe: The Roman Path). Paris: Criterion, 1992.

Cassirer, Ernst. *The Logic of the Humanities*. Translated by Clarence Smith Howe. New Haven, Conn.: Yale University Press, 1961.

——. *The Philosophy of Symbolic Forms*. 4 vols. New Haven, Conn.: Yale University Press, 1955, 1957, and 1996.

——. *Symbol, Myth, and Culture: Essays and Lectures of Ernst Cassirer, 1935–1945*. Edited by Donald Phillip Verene. New Haven, Conn.: Yale University Press, 1979.

Coser, Lewis. *Masters of Sociological Thought: Ideas in Historical and Social Context*. New York: Hartcourt Brace Jovanovich, 1971.

Dallmayr, Fred. "Truth and Diversity: Some Lessens from Herder." *Journal of Speculative Philosophy* 11 (1997): 101–24.

Derrida, Jacques. *L'autre cap*. Paris: Editions de Minuit, 1991. English translation: *The Other Heading: Reflections on Today's Europe*. Translated by Pascale-Anne Brault and Michael B. Naas. Bloomington: Indiana University Press, 1995.

Dilthey, Wilhelm. *Der Aufbau der geschichtlichen Welt in den Geisteswissenschaften* (The Construction of the Historical World in the Human Sciences). Berlin: Verlag der Königlichen Akademie der Wissenschaften, 1910.

——. *Einleitung in die Geisteswissenschaften* (Introduction to the Human Sciences). Leipzig: Duncker and Humbolt, 1883.

——. *Wilhelm Dilthey: Selected Writings*. Edited by H. P. Rickman. Cambridge, U.K.: Cambridge University Press, 1976.

Eberle, Mathias. *World War I and the Weimar Artists: Dix, Grosz, Beckmann, Schlemmer*. New Haven, Conn.: Yale University Press, 1985.

Eksteins, Modris. *Rites of Spring: The Great War and the Birth of the Modern Age*. Boston: Houghton Mifflin, 1989.

Fontana, Joseph. *Europa ante el espejo*. Barcelona: Crítica, 1994. English translation: *The Distorted Past: A Reinterpretation of Europe*. Translated by by Colin Smith. Cambridge, Mass.: Blackwell, 1995.

Herder, Johann Gottfried. *Against Pure Reason: Writings on Religion, Language, and History*. Translated, edited, and with an introduction by Marcia Bunge. Minneapolis: Fortress Press, 1993.

———. *Auch eine Philosophie der Geschichte zur Bildung der Menschheit* (Also a Philosophy of History for the Education of Humankind). Riga, Latvia: Hartknoch, 1774.

———. *J. G. Herder on Social and Political Culture*. Translated, edited, and with an introduction by F. M. Barnard. London: Cambridge University Press, 1969.

Hodges, M. A. *The Philosophy of Wilhelm Dilthey*. London: Routledge, 1952.

Hübinger, Gangolf, Rüdiger vom Bruch, and Friedrich Wilhelm Graf, eds. *Kultur und Kulturwissenschaften um 1900* (Culture and the Sciences of Culture Around 1900). Vol. 1: *Krise der Moderne und Glaube an die Wissenschaft* (The Crisis of Modernity and the Faith in Science). Vol. 2: *Idealismus und Positivismus* (Idealism and Positivism). Stuttgart: Steiner, 1989, 1997.

Husserl, Edmund. *The Crisis of European Sciences and Transcendental Phenomenology*. Evanston, Ill.: Northwestern University Press, 1970.

———. *Philosophie als strenge*. Frankfurt am Main: Klostermann, 1965. English translation: "Philosophy as Rigorous Science." Translated and with an introduction by Quentin Lauer in Edmund Husserl, *Phenomenology and the Crisis of Philosophy: Philosophy as Rigorous Science, and Philosophy and the Crisis of European Man*, New York: Harper and Row, 1965.

Kassab, Elizabeth Suzanne. "L'image de l'Europe chez Husserl et Weber: Le processus de rationalité chez Weber et l'appel à la raison chez Husserl" (The Image of Europe in Husserl and Weber: The Rational Process in Weber and the Call to Reason in Husserl). In Pierre Million, ed., *Max Weber et le destin des sociétés modernes* (Max Weber and the Destiny of Modern Societies), 181–93. Grenoble, France: Recherches sur la Philosophie et le Langage, 1995.

———. "Is Europe an Essence? Lévinas, Husserl, and Derrida on Cultural Identity and Ethics." *International Studies in Philosophy* 34, no. 4 (2002): 55–75.

———. "Phenomenologies of Culture and Ethics: Ernst Cassirer, Alfred Schutz, and the Tasks of a Philosophy of Culture." *Human Studies* 25 (2002): 55–88.

Kierkegaard, Søren. *The Present Age*. Translated by Alexander Dru. New York: Harper and Row, 1962.

Kluback, William and Martin Weinbaum, eds. *Dilthey's Philosophy of Existence: Introduction to Weltanschauugslehre*. London: Vision, 1957.

Konersmann, Ralf, ed. *Kulturphilosophie* (Philosophy of Culture). Leipzig: Reclam, 1996.

Kramme, Rüdiger. "'Kulturphilosophie' und 'Internationalität' des 'Logos' im Spiegel seiner Selbstbeschreibungen" ("Philosophy of Culture" and "Internationality" of the "Logos" in the Mirror of Its Own Self-Description). In Gangolf Hübinger, Rüdiger vom Bruch, and Friedrich Wilhelm Graf, eds., *Kultur und Kulturwissenschaften um 1900* (Culture and the Sciences of Culture Around 1900), vol. 2: *Idealismus und Positivismus* (Idealism and Positivism), 122–34 (Stuttgart: Steiner, 1997).

———. "Philosophische Kultur als Programm: Die Konstituierungsphase des Logos" (Philosophical Culture as Program: The Constitution Phase of Logos). In Hubert Treiber and

Karol Sauerland, eds., *Heidelberg im Schnittpunkt intellectueller Kreise* (Heidelberg at the Intersection of Intellectual Circles), 119–49. Opladen, Germany: Westdeutscher, 1995.

Krois, John Michael. *Cassirer: Symbolic Forms and History.* New Haven, Conn.: Yale University Press, 1987.

Kroner, Richard, Nikolai von Bubnoff, Georg Mehlis, Sergius Hessen, and Fedor Stepun. *Vom Messias: Kulturphilosophische Essays* (On the Messiah: Essays in the Philosophy of Culture). Leipzig: Verlag von Wilhelm Engelmann, 1909.

Lévinas, Emmanuel. *Les imprévus de l'histoire* (The Unforeseen of History). Paris: Fata Morgana, 1994.

Mueller-Vollmer, Kurt, ed. *Herder Today.* Berlin: Walter de Gruyter, 1990.

Nietzsche, Friedrich. *The Use and Abuse of History.* Translated by Adrian Collins. New York: Macmillan, 1985.

Oakes, Guy. "Introduction." In Georg Simmel, *Essays on Interpretation in Social Science,* translated and edited by Guy Oakes, 3–94. Totowa, N.J.: Rowman and Littlefield, 1980.

Palti, Elias. "The 'Metaphor of Life': Herder's Philosophy of History and Uneven Developments in Late Eighteenth-Century Natural Sciences." *History and Theory* 38 (1999): 322–47.

Perpeet, Wilhelm. "Kulturphilosophie" (Philosophy of Culture). *Archiv für Begriffsgeschichte* 20 (1976): 42–99.

Redekop, Benjamin W. "Language, Literature, and Publikum: Herder's Quest for Organic Enlightenment." *History of European Ideas* 14 (1992): 235–53.

Rickert, Heinrich. *The Limits of Concept Formation in Natural Science: A Logical Introduction to the Historical Sciences.* Translated and edited by Guy Oakes. Cambridge, U.K.: Cambridge University Press, 1986.

Ringer, Fritz K. *The Decline of the German Mandarins: The German Academic Community, 1890–1933.* Cambridge, Mass.: Harvard University Press, 1969.

Rundell, John and Stephen Mennell, eds. *Classical Readings in Culture and Civilization.* London: Routledge, 1998.

Schweitzer, Albert. *Kulturphilosophie* (Philosophy of Culture). Munich: C. H. Beck, 1925–1926. English translation: *The Philosophy of Civilization.* Translated by C. T. Campion. New York: Macmillan, 1949; later edition, New York: Prometheus, 1987. Arabic translation: *Falsafat al-Hadara.* Translated by Abdel Rahman Badawi. Beirut: Dar al-Andalus, 1997.

Simmel, Georg. *The Conflict in Modern Culture and Other Essays.* Translated and edited by Peter Etzkorn. New York: Teachers College Press, 1968.

——. *Essays on Interpretation in Social Science.* Translated and edited by Guy Oakes. Totowa, N.J.: Rowman and Littlefield, 1980.

——. *Georg Simmel: Sociologist and European.* Translated and edited by P. A. Lawrence. New York: Barnes & Noble, 1976.

——. "Tendencies of German Life and Thought Since 1870." *International Monthly* (1902): 93–111, 166–84.

Spencer, Vicky. "Towards an Ontology of Holistic Individualism: Herder's Theory of Identity, Culture, and Community." *History of European Ideas* 22 (1996): 245–60.

Spengler, Oswald. *Der Untergang des Abendlandes.* Vol. 1: *Welthistorische Perspektiven* (World Historical Perspectives). Vol. 2: *Gestalt und Wirklichkeit* (Form and Reality). Munich: C. H. Beck'sche, 1918 and 1922. English translation: *The Decline of the West.* Abridged edition by Helmut Werner from the translation by Charles Francis Atkinson. New York: Oxford University Press, 1991.

Treiber, Hubert and Karol Saucrland, eds. *Heidelberg im Schnittpunkt intellectueller Kreise* (Heidelberg at the Intersection of Intellectual Circles). Opladen, Germany: Westdeutscher, 1995.

Valéry, Paul. "La crise de l'esprit." In Paul Valéry, *Oeuvres* (Works), 1:988–1014. Paris: Gallimard, Bibliothèque de la Pléiade, 1957–60. English translation: "The Crisis of the Mind." In Paul Valéry, *History and Politics,* translated by Denis Folliot and Jackson Mathews, 5:23–36. New York: Pantheon Books, 1962.

Weber, Max. *Die protestantische Ethik und der Geist des Kapitalismus. Archiv für Sozialwissenschaft und Sozialpolitik* 20–21 (1904–1905). Reprinted in Max Weber, *Gesammelte Aufsätze zur Religionssoziologie* (Collected Articles on the Sociology of Religion). Tübingen, Germany: J. C. B. Mohr (Paul Siebeck), 1920. English translation: *Protestant Ethic and the Spirit of Capitalism.* Translated by Talcott Parsons in 1930. London: Routledge, 1992.

Weingartner, Rudolph H. *Experience and Culture: The Philosophy of Georg Simmel.* Middletown, Conn.: Wesleyan University Press, 1962.

Whitton, Brian J. "Herder's Critique of the Enlightenment: Cultural Community Versus Cosmopolitan Rationalism." *History and Theory* 27 (1988): 146–68.

Willey, Thomas E. *Back to Kant: The Revival of Kantianism in German Social and Historical Thought, 1860–1914.* Detroit: Wayne State University Press, 1978.

U.S. American

Arnold, Mathew. *Culture and Anarchy and Other Writings.* Cambridge, U.K.: Cambridge University Press, 2001.

Arthur, John and Amy Shapiro, eds. *Campus Wars: Multiculturalism and the Politics of Difference.* Boulder, Colo.: Westview Press, 1995.

Auxter, Thomas. "The Debate over Cultural Imperialism." *American Philosophical Association Proceedings and Addresses* 59 (1986): 753–57.

Bender, Thomas. *New York Intellect: A History of Intellectual Life in New York City, from 1750 to the Beginnings of Our Own Time.* Baltimore: Johns Hopkins University Press, 1987.

Bennett, William. *The De-valuing of America*. New York: Touchstone Books, 1992.

Blake, Casey Nelson. *Beloved Community: The Cultural Criticism of Randolph Bourne, Van Wyck Brooks, Waldo Frank, and Lewis Mumford*. Chapel Hill: University of North Carolina Press, 1990.

Bloom, Allan. *The Closing of the America Mind*. New York: Simon and Schuster, 1987.

Bourne, Randolph. *The Radical Will: Selected Writings 1911–1918*. Edited by Olaf Hansen. Berkeley and Los Angeles: University of California Press, 1992.

Deloria, Jr., Vine. *Custer Died for Your Sins: An Indian Manifesto*. New York: Macmillan, 1969.

Dewey, John. *Individualism Old and New*. Amherst, N.Y.: Prometheus, 1929.

Du Bois, W. E. B. *The Souls of Black Folk*. New York: Oxford University Press, 2007; originally published in 1903.

——. *The World and Africa*. New York: Viking Press, 1947.

Emerson, Ralph Waldo. *Selected Essays*. New York: Penguin Books, 1982.

Frank, Waldo. *Chart for Rough Waters: Our Role in a New World*. New York: Doubleday, Doran, 1940.

——. *Our America*. New York: Boni and Liveright, 1919.

——. *The Re-discovery of America: An Introduction to a Philosophy of American Life*. New York: Scribner's, 1929.

Gutmann, Amy, ed. *Multiculturalism: Examining the Politics of Recognition*. Princeton, N.J.: Princeton University Press, 1994.

Higginson, T. W. "A Plea for Culture." *Atlantic Monthly* 19 (1867): 29–37.

Hofstadter, Richard. *Anti-intellectualism in American Life*. New York: Knopf, 1970.

Hollinger, David A. *Postethnic America: Beyond Multiculturalism*. New York: Basic, 1995.

Jacoby, Russell. *The Last Intellectuals: American Culture in the Age of Academe*. New York: Basic, 1987.

Kallen, Horace M. *Culture and Democracy in the United Sates*. Piscataway, N.J.: Transaction, 1998.

Kassab, Elizabeth Suzanne. "Cultural Affirmation, Power, and Dissent: Two Mid-century U.S. Debates." In Linda Alcoff and Mariana Ortega, eds., *United "America"? A Race and Nationalism Reader*. Albany: State University of New York Press, forthcoming.

MacIntyre, Alasdair. *Whose Justice? Whose Rationality?* Notre Dame, Ind.: University of Notre Dame Press, 1988.

Niebuhr, Reinhold. *The Irony of American History*. New York: Scribner Library, 1962.

Northrop, F. S. C. *The Meeting of East and West*. New York: Macmillan, 1946.

Partisan Review 19, nos. 3–5 (1952). Collected and printed as *America and the Intellectuals: A Symposium*. New York: Partisan Review, 1953.

Perry, Ralph Barton. *Characteristically American*. New York: Alfred A. Knopf, 1949.

——. *One World in the Making*. New York: Current Books, 1945.

Phillips, William. *A Partisan View: Five Decades of the Literary Life*. New York: Stein and Day, 1983.

Rahv, Philip. *Discovery of Europe: The Story of American Experience in the Old World*. Boston: Houghton Mifflin, 1947.

Santayana, George. *The Genteel Tradition*. Lincoln: University of Nebraska Press, 1998.

Susman, Warren, ed. *Culture and Commitment 1929–1945*. New York: George Braziller, 1973.

——. *Culture as History: The Transformation of American Society in the Twentieth Century*. New York: Pantheon Books, 1984.

Warner, C. D. "What Is Your Culture to Me?" *Scribners Monthly* 4 (1872): 470–78.

Other

Chakrabarty, Dipesh. *Provincializing Europe: Postcolonial Thought and Historical Difference*. Princeton, N.J.: Princeton University Press, 2000.

Chatterjee, Partha. "The Nationalist Resolution of the Women's Question." In Kumkum Sangari and Sudesh Vaid, eds., *Recasting Women: Essays in Indian Colonial History*, 233–53. New Brunswick, N.J.: Rutgers University Press, 1990.

Diemer, Alwin and others, contributors. *Philosophical Foundations of Human Rights*. Paris: UNESCO, 1986.

Ellis, Marc. *Toward a Jewish Theology of Liberation*. Maryknoll, N.Y.: Orbis, 1987; 2d ed., 1989; 3rd ed., 2004.

Göle, Nilüfer. *The Forbidden Modern: Civilization and Veiling*. Ann Arbor: University of Michigan Press, 1996.

Kincaid, Jamaica. *A Small Place*. New York: Farrar, Straus and Giroux, 1988.

McClintock, Anne. "The Angel of Progress: Pitfalls of the Term 'Post-colonialism.'" *Social Text*, nos. 31–32 (1992): 84–98.

Melasuo, Tuomo, ed. *National Movements and World Peace*. Aldershot, U.K.: Avebury, 1990.

Memmi, Albert. *Portrait du colonisé Arabo-musulman et de quelques autres*. Paris: Gallimard, 2004. English translation: *Decolonization and the Decolonized*. Translated by Robert Bononno. Minneapolis: University of Minnesota Press, 2006.

——. *Portrait du colonisé, précédé du portrait du colonisateur*. Paris: Correa, 1957. English translation: *The Colonizer and the Colonized*. Translated by Howard Greenfeld. With an introduction by Jean-Paul Sartre. Boston: Beacon Press, 1967.

Mohanty, Chandra Talpade. "Under Western Eyes: Feminist Scholarship and Colonial Discourses." In Chandra Talpade Mohanty, Ann Russo, and Lourdes Torres, eds., *Third World and the Politics of Feminism*, 51–80. Bloomington: Indiana University Press, 1991. Reprinted in Chandra Talpade Mohanty, *Feminism Without Borders: Decolonizing Theory, Practicing Solidarity*, 17–42. Durham, N.C.: Duke University Press, 2003.

Najmabadi, Afsaneh. "Veiled Discourse—Unveiled Bodies." *Feminist Studies* 19, no. 3 (1993): 487–518.

Nandy, Ashis. *The Intimate Enemy: Loss and Recovery of Self Under Colonialism*. Delhi: Oxford University Press, 1983.

Narayan, Uma. *Dislocating Cultures: Identities, Traditions, and Third-World Feminism*. New York: Routledge, 1997.

Narayan, Uma and Sandra Harding, eds. *Decentering the Center: Philosophy for a Multicultural, Postcolonial, and Feminist World*. Bloomington: Indiana University Press, 2000.

Sartre, Jean-Paul. *Colonialism and Neocolonialism*. Translated by Azzedine Haddour, Steve Brewer, and Terry McWilliams. London: Routledge, 2001.

Smith, Linda Tuhiwai. *Decolonizing Methodologies: Research and Indigenous Peoples*. London: Zed Books, 1999.

Trask, Haunani-Kay. *From a Native Daughter: Colonialism and Sovereignty in Hawai'i*. Honolulu: University of Hawai'i Press, 1999.

Walcott, Derek. "The Caribbean: Culture or Mimicry?" *Journal of Interamerican Studies and World Affairs* 16, no. 1 (1974): 3–13.

——. *What the Twilight Says: Essays*. New York: Farrar, Straus and Giroux, 1998.

Index